Strategic Cooperation and Partnerships Between Australia and South Asia:

Economic Development, Trade, and Investment Opportunities Post COVID-19

Anita Medhekar
Central Queensland University, Australia

Sreeparna Saha
Central Queensland University, Australia

Farooq Haq
Canadian University Dubai, UAE

IGI Global
PUBLISHER of TIMELY KNOWLEDGE

A volume in the Advances in Finance, Accounting, and Economics (AFAE) Book Series

Published in the United States of America by
IGI Global
Business Science Reference (an imprint of IGI Global)
701 E. Chocolate Avenue
Hershey PA, USA 17033
Tel: 717-533-8845
Fax: 717-533-8661
E-mail: cust@igi-global.com
Web site: http://www.igi-global.com

Library of Congress Cataloging-in-Publication Data

Names: Medhekar, Anita, 1962- editor. | Saha, Sreeparna, 1983- editor. | Haq, Farooq Muhammad, 1971- editor.
Title: Strategic cooperation and partnerships between Australia and South Asia : economic development, trade, and investment opportunities post-covid-19 / Anita Medhekar, Sreeparna Saha, and Farooq Muhammad Haq, editors.
Description: Hershey, PA : Information Science Reference, [2022] | Includes bibliographical references and index. | Summary: "The overall objectivesof this book is to provide an overview of the Australian trade and investment relationship with South Asian Countries and identify the trends and developments of bilateral trade relationship of Australia with South Asian countries in strategic areas of trade, tourism, investment, education, prior and post Covid-19"-- Provided by publisher.

Identifiers: LCCN 2021047648 (print) | LCCN 2021047649 (ebook) | ISBN 9781799886570 (hardcover) | ISBN 9781799886587 (paperback) | ISBN 9781799886594 (ebook)
Subjects: LCSH: Australia--Commerce--South Asia. | South Asia--Commerce--Australia. | Australia--Foreign relations--South Asia. | South Asia--Foreign relations--Australia. | Investments, Foreign--Australia. | Investments, Foreign--South Asia.
Classification: LCC HF3948.A8 S87 2022 (print) | LCC HF3948.A8 (ebook) | DDC 382.0994059--dc23/eng/20211013
LC record available at https://lccn.loc.gov/2021047648
LC ebook record available at https://lccn.loc.gov/2021047649

This book is published in the IGI Global book series Advances in Finance, Accounting, and Economics (AFAE) (ISSN: 2327-5677; eISSN: 2327-5685)

British Cataloguing in Publication Data
A Cataloguing in Publication record for this book is available from the British Library.

Advances in Finance, Accounting, and Economics (AFAE) Book Series

Ahmed Driouchi
Al Akhawayn University, Morocco

ISSN:2327-5677
EISSN:2327-5685

Mission

In our changing economic and business environment, it is important to consider the financial changes occurring internationally as well as within individual organizations and business environments. Understanding these changes as well as the factors that influence them is crucial in preparing for our financial future and ensuring economic sustainability and growth.

The **Advances in Finance, Accounting, and Economics (AFAE)** book series aims to publish comprehensive and informative titles in all areas of economics and economic theory, finance, and accounting to assist in advancing the available knowledge and providing for further research development in these dynamic fields.

Coverage

- Banking
- Comparative Accounting Systems
- Economic Downturn
- E-finance
- Wages and Employment
- E-Accounting
- Finance and Accounting in SMEs
- Microfinance
- Accounting Standards
- Bankruptcy

IGI Global is currently accepting manuscripts for publication within this series. To submit a proposal for a volume in this series, please contact our Acquisition Editors at Acquisitions@igi-global.com or visit: http://www.igi-global.com/publish/.

The Advances in Finance, Accounting, and Economics (AFAE) Book Series (ISSN 2327-5677) is published by IGI Global, 701 E. Chocolate Avenue, Hershey, PA 17033-1240, USA, www.igi-global.com. This series is composed of titles available for purchase individually; each title is edited to be contextually exclusive from any other title within the series. For pricing and ordering information please visit http://www.igi-global.com/book-series/advances-finance-accounting-economics/73685. Postmaster: Send all address changes to above address.

Titles in this Series

For a list of additional titles in this series, please visit: www.igi-global.com/book-series/advances-finance-accounting-economics/73685

Transitioning From Globalized to Localized and Self-Reliant Economies
Ruchika Gupta (Amity University, India) Priyank Srivastava (Amity University, India) Shiv Ranjan (Amity University, India) and M. Affan Badar (Indiana State University, USA)
Business Science Reference • © 2022 • 256pp • H/C (ISBN: 9781799887058) • US $195.00

COVID-19 Pandemic Impact on New Economy Development and Societal Change
Cristina Raluca Gh. Popescu (University of Bucharest, Romania & The Bucharest University of Economic Studies, Romania & The National Institute for Research and Development in Environmental Protection (INCDPM), Romania & National Research and Development Institute for Gas Turbines (COMOTI), Romania)
Business Science Reference • © 2022 • 425pp • H/C (ISBN: 9781668433744) • US $195.00

Microfinance and Sustainable Development in Africa
Yahaya Alhassan (University of Sunderland in London, UK) and Uzoechi Nwagbara (University of the West of Scotland, UK & Cardiff Metropolitan University, UK)
Business Science Reference • © 2022 • 368pp • H/C (ISBN: 9781799874997) • US $195.00

Redefining Global Economic Thinking for the Welfare of Society
Md Mashiur Rahman (Bank Asia Ltd., Bangladesh) Richa Goel (Amity University, Noida, India) Anthony P. Gomes (TeamPeople, USA) and Md Almas Uzzaman (Independent Researcher, Australia)
Business Science Reference • © 2022 • 268pp • H/C (ISBN: 9781799882589) • US $225.00

FinTech Development for Financial Inclusiveness
Muhammad Anshari (Universiti Brunei Darussalam, Brunei) Mohamad Nabil Almunawar (Universiti Brunei Darussalam, Brunei) and Masairol Masri (Universiti Brunei Darussalam, Brunei)
Business Science Reference • © 2022 • 269pp • H/C (ISBN: 9781799884477) • US $225.00

Evaluating Trade and Economic Relations Between India and Southeast Asia
Anita Medhekar (Central Queensland University, Australia) and Harpreet Kaur (Central Queensland University, Australia)
Business Science Reference • © 2022 • 347pp • H/C (ISBN: 9781799857747) • US $195.00

Handbook of Research on Global Aspects of Sustainable Finance in Times of Crises
Ibrahim Yasar Gok (Süleyman Demirel University, Turkey & Freie Universität Berlin, Germany)
Business Science Reference • © 2022 • 442pp • H/C (ISBN: 9781799885016) • US $285.00

IGI Global
PUBLISHER of TIMELY KNOWLEDGE

701 East Chocolate Avenue, Hershey, PA 17033, USA
Tel: 717-533-8845 x100 • Fax: 717-533-8661
E-Mail: cust@igi-global.com • www.igi-global.com

We dedicate this book to our parents for all their love, support, and encouragement:

Mrs. Shaila Chitnis-Medhekar and Mr. Sharad Medhekar

Mrs. Reeta Saha and Mr. Dipak Saha

Mrs. Asghari Haq and Mr. Ata-ul-Haq

Table of Contents

Foreword *by Kirti Dharwardkar* xvii

Foreword *by Mahesh Gandhi* xix

Preface xxi

Acknowledgment xxx

Chapter 1
Australia's Bilateral and Multilateral Health Sector Partnership With South Asian Nations: Opportunities and Challenges 1
Anita Medhekar, Central Queensland University, Australia

Chapter 2
Australia's Bilateral and Multilateral Partnership With South Asian Nations: Opportunities and Challenges in the Transitioning Energy Sector 23
Sreeparna Saha, Central Queensland University, Australia

Chapter 3
Review of Opportunities in Collaboration Between Australia and Pakistan for the Education of Marketing Post COVID-19 57
Farooq Haq, Canadian University Dubai, UAE

Chapter 4
Digital Strategic Partnership for Australian and South Asian Enterprises 76
Kamaljeet Sandhu, University of New England, Australia

Chapter 5
Australia as an Enabler to Sustainable Indian Ocean Island Economies 95
Ikhlaas Gurrib, Canadian University Dubai, UAE

Chapter 6
Bilateral Cooperation Between Australia and Bangladesh in Diverse Areas: An Analysis to Cope With the COVID-19 Aftermath 117
Muhammad Mahboob Ali, Dhaka School of Economics, University of Dhaka, Bangladesh

Chapter 7
India and Australia's New Education Policy: Lessons for SAARC Nations....................................... 146
Manisha Goswami, Agra University, Mathura, India

Chapter 8
Strategic Partnership of Bangladesh With Australia to Protect From Possible Debt Trap and Diseconomies of Scale of One-Belt One-Road: Lessons for SAARC Nations.................................... 166
S. Jobayear Ahmed, Bangladesh Rural Advancement Committee (BRAC), Bangladesh

Chapter 9
Medical, Pharmaceutical, and Healthcare Trade Relationships Between Australia and South Asian Nations 199
Ahmad A. Okasha, Canadian University Dubai, UAE
Eman Zabalawi, Amity University, Dubai, UAE

Chapter 10
The Recycling of Australian Offshore Structures in Bangladesh: Challenges and Opportunities...... 219
Mohammad Zulfikar Ali, Curtin University, Australia
Nahid Islam, Curtin University, Australia

Chapter 11
Review of Post-COVID-19 Tourism Marketing Partnership Opportunities Between Australia and Pakistan 243
Farooq Haq, Canadian University Dubai, UAE
Anam Syed Maheen, Canadian University Dubai, UAE

Chapter 12
Post-COVID-19 Australian and Indian Collaboration for Enhanced Effectiveness in the Resource Sector for Renewable Energy 259
Gayatri Gopidas Nair, Canadian University Dubai, UAE
Rahul Vinit Mehta, Canadian University Dubai, UAE

Chapter 13
New Trade Frontiers Between India and Australia: Challenges and Opportunities Post COVID-19. 280
Risha Khandelwal, JECRC University, India
Princi Gupta, JECRC University, India

Chapter 14
Australia's Trade and Investment Strategy in the Post-COVID-19 Era: Prospects for Australia-Bangladesh Partnership... 301
Mamta B Chowdhury, Western Sydney University, Australia
Ataus Samad, Western Sydney University, Australia
Md Sayfullah, Bangladesh High Commission, Canberra, Australia

Chapter 15
Exploring Partnerships Between Australia and South Asia for Crowdfunding Social Enterprises: A Post-COVID-19 Strategy 327
Chureerat Haq, Charles Darwin University, Australia
Susan E. Bandias, Charles Darwin University, Australia
Faiz Shah, Asian Institute of Technology, Thailand
Rajeev Sharma, Charles Darwin University, Australia

Compilation of References 349

About the Contributors 394

Index 400

Detailed Table of Contents

Foreword *by Kirti Dharwardkar* xvii

Foreword *by Mahesh Gandhi* xix

Preface xxi

Acknowledgment xxx

Chapter 1
Australia's Bilateral and Multilateral Health Sector Partnership With South Asian Nations: Opportunities and Challenges 1
Anita Medhekar, Central Queensland University, Australia

Pandemic-related public health crises are important challenges of the 21st century. The COVID-19 pandemic healthcare crisis has resulted in international border closures; healthcare supply value-chain disruptions; increased infections, deaths, and coronavirus vaccine production and rollout issues; vaccine inequity and gaps between supply and demand for healthcare goods and services. This chapter aims to focus on the opportunities and challenges for bilateral and multilateral partnerships between Australia and the eight South Asian nations post pandemic to establish mutually beneficial bilateral and multilateral collaboration and partnerships for production of vaccine, research, and education into the healthcare sector. Australia can share its health expertise related to digital health, medicare, medical technologies, production of life-saving vaccines, and access to affordable and accredited quality of healthcare for combined 2 billion people living in South Asia and Australia, which is the key to meeting UNSDGs of good health, well-being for all, economic progress, and prosperity of South Asian nations.

Chapter 2
Australia's Bilateral and Multilateral Partnership With South Asian Nations: Opportunities and Challenges in the Transitioning Energy Sector 23
Sreeparna Saha, Central Queensland University, Australia

This chapter aims to investigate the potential cooperation between Australia and the SAARC nations to facilitate generation and distribution of energy to better manage this sector and fulfil their commitments towards climate change conditions. As carbon emissions from non-renewables severely threatened the climate conditions, an effective transition to renewable resources is essential. In the Paris Agreement, Australia and SAARC nations committed to reduce their individual carbon emissions. But the SAARC lag in their commitments as they fail to unleash renewables and rely on fossil fuel. Australia leads in renewables, and SAARC provides a large market for it to relate services and technologies and improve energy efficiency and competitiveness. This chapter investigates the opportunities for strategic collaboration between these nations; challenges of energy trading, energy security, inefficient institutions, volatile prices and investment flows, collaborative capacity generation and distribution; and analyses comparative advantages for the countries to have mutually beneficial agreements to meet UNSDGs of affordable clean energy and climate action.

Chapter 3
Review of Opportunities in Collaboration Between Australia and Pakistan for the Education of Marketing Post COVID-19 57
Farooq Haq, Canadian University Dubai, UAE

This chapter presents opportunity for collaboration between Australian and Pakistani tertiary education for advanced teaching of marketing. The research presents a study suggesting innovating marketing education post COVID-19 based on class interviews with examples from the world of politics. University students studying marketing were interviewed in this qualitative study by conducting in-class focus groups. Respondents were inquired about their opinion on using various teaching strategies with politics as a case to explain elements of the marketing mix. Recommendations to use class discussions, role-play, and cold-call engagement are contributions of this chapter, presenting learning by applying politics as a marketing challenge to explain the marketing theory. Politics as a marketing example can be used by academic and industrial marketing trainers and educators, leading towards a strategic opportunity for collaboration between Australian and Pakistani education planners and institutions for stablishing strong institutions for peace and justice.

Chapter 4
Digital Strategic Partnership for Australian and South Asian Enterprises 76
Kamaljeet Sandhu, University of New England, Australia

This study aims to identify the important roles in digital strategic partnership for Australian-Asian enterprises. Research has shown that the world's two biggest economies in the coming years will be in Asia, and they are China and India. Australia's strategic location and close geographic proximity to Asia and its engagement in economic, business, education, health, cultural, and technological cooperation have led to opportunities in digital strategic partnership for Australian-Asian enterprises. A case study approach is used to analyse the strategic investment opportunities in digital and telecommunication technologies with Australia and Asian trading partners to develop a digital strategy. Over many years, Australia has demonstrated leadership for exchange of strategic information, ideas, and closer participation with Asia, which has led to building a strong relationship in terms of government-to-government, people-to-people, and business-to-business, which can be transformed for innovative digital strategic partnership in the South Asian region.

Chapter 5
Australia as an Enabler to Sustainable Indian Ocean Island Economies 95
Ikhlaas Gurrib, Canadian University Dubai, UAE

The purpose of this study is to provide a deeper understanding of how Australia and Indian Ocean island economies of Mauritius, Maldives, and Sri Lanka can mutually benefit from each other to promote sustainability and economic output. Specifically, this study investigates what makes the three island economies attractive to promote regional and international trade and how Australia can help achieve a sustainable blue economy. The author initially provides some background of the current state in the island economies and Australia, post-COVID-19 crisis impact, the different financial and regulatory policies, bilateral trade agreements, and ministerial level organisations promoting trade partnerships. Key recommendations aligned with various Sustainable Development Goals (SDGs), especially SDG 14, are provided. Active involvement from experienced nations like Australia to Small Island Developing States (SIDS) is required, including some incentivized alliance between the private and public sector to achieve a sustainable ocean or blue economy, post COVID-19 crisis.

Chapter 6
Bilateral Cooperation Between Australia and Bangladesh in Diverse Areas: An Analysis to Cope With the COVID-19 Aftermath 117
Muhammad Mahboob Ali, Dhaka School of Economics, University of Dhaka, Bangladesh

This chapter discussed the multi- sectoral bilateral cooperation between Australia and Bangladesh during and post-COVID-19-related to interregional trade, foreign investment, ready-made-garments export, education, blue economy, microfinance, tourism, renewable energy, and finally, fulfillment of targets of SDGs. How do diverse areas of bilateral cooperation between Bangladesh and Australia become more efficient and effective in resource utilization and bring socio-economic benefits? Advancement in economic cooperation in both the countries may be improved from trade and investment, enhancement of education using Australian model, improvement and enhancement in energy, blue economy, education, health, and RMG sector. Australian partnership will be helpful for government agencies, policy makers, and associated stakeholders of Bangladesh for future improvements and development interventions in diverse multisector areas. Emphasis needs to be given to ecofriendly sustainability as suggested by the author to meet the climate change and sustainability goals.

Chapter 7
India and Australia's New Education Policy: Lessons for SAARC Nations.. 146
Manisha Goswami, Agra University, Mathura, India

Nepal, Bangladesh, and Indian education sectors suffer from limited foreign collaborations; less research orientation; redundant and obsolete curricula; and less relevance of courses with job opportunities available. Especially in the case of India, few initiatives were taken to improve quality of education. India adopted new education policy that opened the doors to strategic collaboration with international universities, as India has begun to concentrate on vocational education and training for the first time. This research examines the scope and restrictions of institutional partnerships between India, other SAARC nations, and Australian higher education institutions. This study is based on the analysis of data presented in the different case studies like Rajasthan Royals and Deakin Australian Universities, IIT Bombay and Monash Australian, Indian Academy of Science and Innovation Research (AcSIR) and RMIT Australian University.

Chapter 8
Strategic Partnership of Bangladesh With Australia to Protect From Possible Debt Trap and Diseconomies of Scale of One-Belt One-Road: Lessons for SAARC Nations.................................... 166
S. Jobayear Ahmed, Bangladesh Rural Advancement Committee (BRAC), Bangladesh

Bangladesh is a developing nation that is about to complete its Golden Jubilee partnership by 2022 with

Australia, a country that has been supporting Bangladesh through aid, assistance, grant, loan, trade, scholarship, etc. Recently, the regional and global superpower China has increased its influence in the Indian Ocean region both through its military and through the OBOR or BRI where it has also shown interest to work with Bangladesh in both fronts. Bangladesh is a very small country but strategically very important, with access to the Indian Ocean. Therefore, it is important to check whether the OBOR initiatives put any negative impact on the neighboring SAARC nations and partner states. The study therefore attempted to identify the potential diseconomies of scale and the solutions Australia-Bangladesh relations might offer.

Chapter 9
Medical, Pharmaceutical, and Healthcare Trade Relationships Between Australia and South Asian Nations 199
Ahmad A. Okasha, Canadian University Dubai, UAE
Eman Zabalawi, Amity University, Dubai, UAE

The global coronavirus (COVID-19) pandemic shocked the whole world. It had a disastrous impact on the economies and the healthcare systems of South Asian countries. Australia was able to minimize the COVID-19 impact by imposing a strict lockdown. The healthcare system and the healthcare industry in Australia are advanced and provide high quality pharmaceutical products and healthcare services. Australia has a lot to offer to South Asian countries in public health programs, quality of healthcare, complementary medicine products, clinical data management and development, and drug developments. Healthcare systems in South Asian countries vary significantly. Australia can play a significant role in developing the healthcare systems of South Asia. For instance, Australia can provide the traditional medicine sectors in South Asian countries with scientifically effective complementary medicines. Improving healthcare bilateral investment and the trade relationship between South Asia countries and Australia is a win/win partnership for SAARC nations post pandemic.

Chapter 10
The Recycling of Australian Offshore Structures in Bangladesh: Challenges and Opportunities...... 219
Mohammad Zulfikar Ali, Curtin University, Australia
Nahid Islam, Curtin University, Australia

The circular economy has emerged as a policy goal with respect to the trade relationships between developed and developing countries. The aim of the circular economy is to take responsibility for the costs involved in recycling by going away from the linear economic model, which is briefly stated as 'take-recycle-dispose' with unused materials in at one end and externalised the wastes at the other. Recycling numerous unused structures is a persisting problem for Australia that can be resolved following this circular economy approach. To that end, an underlying aim of this chapter is to propose a bilateral agreement between Bangladesh and Australia that aims at recycling offshore structures of Australian companies in Bangladesh's ship recycling industry (hereinafter referred to as recycling industry). This chapter also sheds light on the challenges for Bangladesh in recycling the offshore structures in a sustainable way but disputes that those offshore structures will only increase the waste burden for Bangladesh.

Chapter 11
Review of Post-COVID-19 Tourism Marketing Partnership Opportunities Between Australia and Pakistan 243
Farooq Haq, Canadian University Dubai, UAE
Anam Syed Maheen, Canadian University Dubai, UAE

This chapter presents a deliberation on an opportunity for tourism marketing partnership between Australian and South Asia, with a focus on Pakistan. Tourism being the star performing industry across the globe has faced unprecedented crash due to COVID-19. Post-COVID-19 market opening relies heavily on the fundamental option of partnerships between governments and private players. The tourism demand has triggered partnerships between government and private agencies across various countries that have convergence in areas of culture, politics, and economy. Australia and Pakistan are among the countries who do not have geographical proximity, but they enjoy congruence in agriculture-based economy and sports-based entertainment. Moreover, both countries have diverse tourism resources serving travelers in hedonistic, mountain, snow, spiritual, sports, and events. This chapter highlights the types of tourism marketing that could be facilitated in a post-COVID-19 environment between Australia and Pakistan and phases involved in the partnership essential for meeting United Nations SDGs.

Chapter 12
Post-COVID-19 Australian and Indian Collaboration for Enhanced Effectiveness in the Resource Sector for Renewable Energy 259
Gayatri Gopidas Nair, Canadian University Dubai, UAE
Rahul Vinit Mehta, Canadian University Dubai, UAE

India and Australia have a diverse range of ties, spanning from geostrategic collaboration and trade to global influence. An initial period of warmth followed by decades of coldness characterizes the relationship between Australia and India. This chapter makes a case for improving resource sector related bilateral relations between New Delhi and Canberra to aim for a sustainable future through strategic collaboration in climate change and the renewable energy sector. Trade and investment possibilities exist between the two countries, and over the years, the engagements between countries have been neglected. The worldwide focus on renewable energy adoption through technological innovation and collaboration is thriving. This research focuses on understanding if there has been a change in the relationship between the two since the pandemic. Through the analysis and observation of qualitative data, suggestions with the current scenario and the future scope of both countries, particularly in the resources and energy sector, have been discussed in this chapter.

Chapter 13
New Trade Frontiers Between India and Australia: Challenges and Opportunities Post COVID-19. 280
Risha Khandelwal, JECRC University, India
Princi Gupta, JECRC University, India

The rising geopolitical tensions between China and Australia can develop new trade frontiers between India, Australia, and the South Asian region as a whole. With this view, the chapter aims to study the present state of bilateral trade relations between India-Australia, identify obstacles that hindered the growth of trade relations between India-Australia in the past, understand the impact of comprehensive economic cooperation for free trade agreement between the two countries. The chapter further discusses the challenges that COVID-19 has posed for trade between Australia and China as well as the future opportunities for bilateral trade between India and Australia. The 2020-21 Australia-India Joint Statement on Comprehensive Strategic Partnership and Comprehensive Economic Cooperation agreement is a step forward in a positive direction in meeting many of the UN SDGs. This chapter is essential for understanding the complexities of "trade creation" between (India and Australia) and "trade diversion" between (China and Australia).

Chapter 14
Australia's Trade and Investment Strategy in the Post-COVID-19 Era: Prospects for Australia-Bangladesh Partnership.. 301
Mamta B Chowdhury, Western Sydney University, Australia
Ataus Samad, Western Sydney University, Australia
Md Sayfullah, Bangladesh High Commission, Canberra, Australia

This chapter examines how the trade and investment relationship between Australia and the Asia-Pacific nations has been evolving over the past decades. The chapter also reflects on the gradual shift of trade and diplomatic relationships in this region since the outbreak of the COVID-19 pandemic. The ongoing global pandemic has not only been disrupting the global economic and geopolitical environment but also reshaping the trade relationship in the region. The chapter explores the greater trade and investment opportunities between Australia and South Asia with a special emphasis on the increased potential bilateral trade partnership with Bangladesh. Following the neoclassical comparative advantage theories, this study suggests that long-run economic benefits and synergies can be enhanced by utilising the ample trade opportunities created by the COVID-19 pandemic to achieve numerous UNSDGs. Therefore, strengthening further trade and diplomatic alliances between Australia and Bangladesh will be mutually beneficial and generate positive growth and development effects for both countries.

Chapter 15
Exploring Partnerships Between Australia and South Asia for Crowdfunding Social Enterprises: A Post-COVID-19 Strategy 327
Chureerat Haq, Charles Darwin University, Australia
Susan E. Bandias, Charles Darwin University, Australia
Faiz Shah, Asian Institute of Technology, Thailand
Rajeev Sharma, Charles Darwin University, Australia

Social enterprises have proven to be an effective mechanism for addressing economic, social, and environment problems in a number of countries. While conventional businesses have, in general, encountered difficult times during the COVID-19 pandemic, online businesses have tended to register success as a direct result of mobility constraints imposed on multinational or regional value-chains during this time. Social enterprises have continued to demonstrate their value as reservoirs of social and economic resilience during this unprecedented global crisis. Thought leaders like Muhammad Yunus see micro-economies, comprising locally focused social businesses linked digitally into distant value chains, as a viable strategy for economic growth in difficult times to achieve the SDGs. This chapter examines the potential of strategic business collaborations between social enterprises in Australia and South Asia that can leverage crowdfunding as a tool for mutual advantage and explores opportunities and challenges for Australian interests entering the financial services sector in South Asia.

Compilation of References 349

About the Contributors 394

Index 400

Foreword

The coronavirus (COVID-19) pandemic disrupted both supply and demand sides of an interconnected world economy during 2020 and still the aftermath is hurting the growth figures of economies of many countries of the world. South Asian and Pacific nations are not an exception to it.

The strategic partnership is key to overcome the challenges and explore the new opportunities among the countries. The book on *Strategic Cooperation and Partnerships Between Australia and South Asia: Economic Development, Trade, and Investment Opportunities Post COVID-19* has researched and compiled in the 15 chapters numerous avenues for Australia and South Asian countries to collaborate and enhance this strategic partnership post-pandemic.

The pandemic has put the health sector of many developed countries on test and opened many fault lines of the operations across the world. But the brighter side is that it has opened many new partnership opportunities in various sectors of the economy. The authors of the book shown the concern over lockdown leads to closure of border and widespread infections deaths has hampered the health services supply chain. Many underdeveloped countries saw the shortage of vaccines and medicines. The countries like Australia having advance healthcare system can strategically partner with South Asian countries to fight the COVID-19 impact and save many valuable lives. There is a huge potential in the sector of pharmaceutical and healthcare related trade between Australia and South Asian nations.

The stipulated growth of many countries may cost the climate change and imbalance in the earth's environment. The growing temperature of earth is an issue of rising concern for the world. This demands the immediate attention of all developed countries along with smaller countries to act to protect the environment. There is an urgent need to have mutual consensus to minimise the environmental damage and explore the sustainable energy sources. Post- COVID-19 era there is an urgent need to bring more technological innovation and collaboration between Australia, India, and the rest of South Asia to tap the possible opportunities in the renewable energy sector.

The education opportunities across the world are becoming attractive for many bright students. The India's New Education Policy is trying to bring significant reforms in this sector. The book offers a classic example to many SAARC countries a pathway on how India and Australia are building the institutional collaboration on new educational policy. The authors have also tried to explore the opportunities in education sectors of other countries such as Pakistan.

The COVID-19 has witnessed the immense supply chain disruptions in world economic activity and gradual shift in geopolitical equations. This had led to reshaping the new trade relationships between Australia and South Asia (Special focus on Bangladesh).

In the current pandemic scenario, we witness the global tension in Indo-Pacific region and saw the rising influence of China in the region. The book has presented how the strategic partnership among the nations of the region may help to save them from falling prey in the debt trap of One-Belt One-Road program of China. The book under its 15 chapters covered few interesting segments such as Recycling Crisis of Australian Offshore Structures in Bangladesh, which has a hidden fear of increasing the waste burden on Bangladesh. COVID-19 has pushed the role of Digital reforms across the world, the strategic alliance of SAARC nation and Australian enterprises may boost the South Asian Enterprises to reap the fruits of modern business strategies at an affordable price.

The various bilateral and multilateral cooperation for advancement in the field of education, information technology, tourism, resources and renewable energy sector, investments and many more areas may benefit the SAARC countries to push their economy towards higher growth which has slowed down due to pandemic disruption. The Australia shares many strong common bonds with the eight (8) SAARC nations as a common thread of sports, large cultural exchange, tourism, and education destination. The changing equation of China with Australia and countries in South China Sea may divert the outflow of investments to emerging SAARC economies as a hot destination. The bitter experience of some of the SAARC countries of debt trap of OBOR can be a lesson for others to join hands with each other and grow their nations by establishing bilateral and multilateral relations under the SAARC with Australia.

Knowing the few authors of the book and their previous writings, I am extremely positive that this new book on *Strategic Cooperation and Partnerships Between Australia and South Asia: Economic Development, Trade, and Investment Opportunities Post COVID-19* will be a great platter of reading to the researchers, diplomates, and trade commissioners where they can read the available opportunities of collaborations and investments in various sectors in each other's country. Nothing less, it will be a great reading experience in total for business enterprises and investors in SAARC region who look forward to enhancing their bilateral and multilateral trade and investment relations with each other and with Australia.

I appreciate the efforts of all the contributing authors for offering in depth overview on various possible aspect to the reader, which help them to clearly visualize the scenario before taking any decisions.

Kirti Dharwardkar
S.B. Pati Institute of Management, India & Pune University, India

Foreword

Strategic cooperation and partnerships among South Asian countries have vital importance. It becomes all the more significant as COVID-19 have temporarily brought the region to a near halt. Governments of the region proactively stabilized activity through monetary easing, providing fiscal stimulus, and supportive financial regulation, but the situation is fragile amidst policy challenges. The informal economy in South Asia has been severely affected. Many unorganized workers, self-employed people, and microenterprises have experienced a large drop in earnings as the service sectors that were affected most by the lockdowns are dominated by informality. The economic context had changed very soon in South Asia, which until a few years was one of the fastest-growing regions of the world. South Asia needs strategic-integration and closer economic- cooperation. Most South Asian countries generate low tax revenue and also run large fiscal deficits, often accompanied by economic shocks which limit their scope to out manoeuvre economic uncertainties.

For boosting the economy and investments, the liberalization of trade in goods and services, strengthening of supply chain management in all sectors, transportation and banking cooperation are needed to be effective for converting the region into a land bridge between Europe, Central Asia and South-East Asia and strategic cooperation and partnership with Australia for economic development, trade, and investment opportunities post-pandemic. The main theme of such a common agenda revolves around strategic integration so that the South Asian countries take advantage of each other's facilities and capabilities, with strategic trade relations with Australia. Such strategic integration is expected to maximise and develop inter-country and intra-regional trade and commerce and also ensure participation of the region with one voice globally.

The fact cannot be ignored that in International Diplomacy, size matters. The bigger and more powerful a country is, the greater its clout. Simultaneously, much depends on how a small country projects itself and interacts with other countries. This book attempts to cover a vast canvas. There is a strong historical, cultural and trade bonding among the nations of this region and it became all the more important after India's trade policy to promote economic relations with whole of South Asia and Australia. The distinguished authors have attempted to cover all burning topics under fifteen chapters including food security, tourism opportunities, healthcare sector, trading blocs, climate change, alternative energy etc. The importance of trade between India, South Asian countries and Australia, have been intelligently described and explained through this book. The subject matter is presented in a lucid style so that it could be easily understood even by those who do not have any academic background of Economics.

The international trade plays a very important role in the economic development and achieving the sustainable development goals in this region. The potential markets are not confined to the national frontiers, resulting in; the overseas markets have become the primary markets. While going through the contents of the book, *Strategic Cooperation and Partnerships Between Australia and South Asia: Economic Development, Trade, and Investment Opportunities Post COVID-19,* I can confidently say that the readers, researchers, and business people will be benefited in understanding the various challenges and opportunities before the nations of the South Asian region. I wish the authors all the best for their sincere efforts and valuable contribution.

Mahesh Gandhi
Independent Researcher, India

Preface

The book *Strategic Cooperation and Partnerships Between Australia and South Asia: Economic Development, Trade, and Investment Opportunities Post COVID-19* sheds light on the cooperation and strategic partnership required between Australia and the South Asian Association for Regional Cooperation (SAARC), for trade in goods and services, and investment opportunities and challenges in various sectors of the economy- in the present and post-COVID-19, into the future. Owing to a strong cultural and historical connections between the SAARC nations, including the common linkage with Australia in context of being member of commonwealth, cricket diplomacy, and English as a widely spoken common language in South Asia, numerous Australian university alumni connections, and the South Asian diaspora have, and are contributing to the Australian economy with skilled workforce in every sector: education, health, tourism, energy, and information technology. Given this background, strategic cooperation and trading partnership of Australia with South Asian nations is the need of the future for building sustainable economic and trade relationships with trusted partners for mutual economic development, trade, and investment opportunities. Therefore, strategic cooperation and partnership are even more crucial in post-pandemic scenario, as the pandemic had been devastating for the highly populated developing SAARC economies, but its intensity was much less on the Australian economy with its sound resource sector, health, technology and infrastructure sectors, and prompt policy actions.

Despite there being political and sometimes ideological differences between Australia and the SAARC countries, most of them share democratic values and uphold the rule of law. Given the economic potential of the SAARC nations, history shows that bilateral and multilateral trade and investment relationships and potential between the SAARC countries and with Australia is yet to be fully exploited. Australia can find a huge market in the eight (8) South Asian countries of approximately 1.8 billion population, which is a critical source of supply of skilled labour such as doctors, engineers, technology professionals, trading sector, international students, and export of agricultural goods like wheat, pulses and lentils and tourism for Australia. Moreover, SAARC nations also need Australian resources, agri-foods, grains, coal, iron-ore, direct foreign investment and Australian expertise in health, education, mining, information technology, cybersecurity, maritime security, scientific innovation, alternative energy sector and climate change to meet its sustainable development goals.

The objective of this book and authors is to enhance trade, tourism, investment, technical and economic cooperation at bilateral and multilateral level between Australia and the South Asian nations. Australian government with famous South Asian Australian diaspora from various field of business, education, agriculture, medical, scientists, engineers, artists and sport personalities could be invited at every SAARC meeting, as a trusted partner post-COVID-19 into the future, because the South Asian diaspora plays an important role in contributing to the economic development and growth of the Australian economy. Further, "The Indian Economic Strategy 2035" released by the Australian Department of Foreign Affairs and Trade focusing on the ten sectors of the economy, with opportunities and recommendations and Australia -India comprehensive economic cooperation agreement, is also very relevant to all the SAARC nations.

Recent Quadrilateral (QUAD) meetings in 2020 and 2021 of the foreign ministers and leaders from the four democratic countries of Australia, India, Japan, and the USA, with shared values has highlighted the importance of partnership between Australia and the SAARC nations, as people who value all-inclusive economic development, growth, progress, prosperity and peace in the South Asian region, cannot just think of India without the SAARC countries who share a common history, heritage, culture, members of commonwealth and other family and trade ties. It is important for the SAARC nations and Australia to work together as a team to strengthen their economic ties and cooperation at bilateral level, and at a greater multilateral level with SAARC trading block group as a whole, to not only make SAARC functional and working for mutual economic development, peace, progress and prosperity of the future generations, but also build reliable value supply chains for production, distribution, access, availability and transport of goods between the SAARC nations and also for Australian goods to have strategic ports along the "Indian Ocean-Bay of Bengal-Arabian Sea" with road-rail links for transporting its goods within the South Asian countries.

Further, there is rising tensions between China-Australia relations, since Australia supported a call for a global enquiry into COVID-19 public health concerns. China has imposed a trade-ban, with high tariff on Australian exports in 2020 and 2021 on resources and grains such as barley, beef, cotton, coal, iron-ore, timber, lobsters, wheat, wine and also impacting tourism and education exports. Furthermore, security tensions in the South China Seas and the Indo-Pacific region, and the COVID-19 related trade and travel restrictions to minimise the spread of the coronavirus and its recessionary impact on the nations during the pandemic period is tragic. Australia, therefore, has to at Track-1 and Track-2 diplomatic levels, seek trusted partners and markets for its export of goods to group of eight SAARC countries, who also have a large need for Australian resources, food grains and expertise for their economic development and growth.

This book is a valuable contribution given the changing geo-political environment pre- and post-pandemic. The 15 chapters unravel and explore the importance of economic relations between Australia and the eight South Asian nations for building cooperation and partnerships in strategic sectors of the economy for trade and investment opportunities post-COVID-19. It is time that the SAARC countries come together to reap the benefits from bilateral and multilateral trade, investment, travel and tourism opportunities and make the dysfunctional SAARC operational at Track-1and Track-2 diplomatic levels, with Australia as its key partner in economic development and growth related to the various sectors of the economy, such as trade in goods and services, investment in information technology, resources sector, infrastructure- road, rail, seaports, and airports, health, education, climate change, and helping to meet not only the United Nations Sustainable Development Goals, but also to meet future development challenges to produce pharmaceutical medicines, COVID-19 vaccine, shared scientific research, cyber and maritime security concerns for free and open strategy in the "Indian Ocean- Bay of Bengal- Arabian Sea" region, to promote peace, stability, maritime security and sustainable development with trusted partners.

Australia and the South Asian economies, need to evaluate their strategic situation since the COVID-19 and work towards strengthening trade relations and political stability and security in the Indian Ocean region, as well as cooperating in facing common enemies across international boundaries for border security, cyber security, and maritime security. Some of the topics covered in this book with strong theoretical background, include healthcare and pharmaceutical sector collaboration, climate change and alternative renewable energy sector, education sector, tourism opportunities, trading blocs, sustainability of Indian ocean island/blue economies, digital economy, one-belt and one-road debt trap, recycling of Australia's off-shore structures like cruise ships, exploring partnerships between Australia and South Asia for crowd funding social enterprises, new foreign trade and investment opportunities for Australia and SAARC nations to improve overall economic relations between Australia and South Asian countries to meet the United Nations Sustainable Development Goals.

The journey for developing this book has been a long one, where international authors have made a valuable contribution to the body of knowledge, highlighted challenges, opportunities and brought forward innovative recommendations and solutions to enhance strategic bilateral trade and investment partnership between Australia and the South Asian region. Few authors also faced personal loss due to COVD-19 and still persevered to contribute their chapters for the book and we are grateful to them. This book provides relevant theoretical framework and cases in the challenges and opportunities for establishing bilateral and multilateral trade relationships between Australia and the SAARC group of eight countries, to enhance strategic trade and investment in the post-pandemic years, to solve common problems, shares issues, values and meet the United Nations 17 Sustainable Development Goals. This book is a valuable reference tool for economists, government officials, policymakers, diplomats, trade analysts, practitioners, researchers, academicians, and students interested in evaluating economic, trade and investment, opportunities between Australia and the SAARC group of eight South Asian nations.

ORGANISATION OF THE BOOK

The following is the brief description of the 15 chapters organised in this book.

Chapter 1, titled "Australia's Bilateral and Multilateral Health Sector Partnership With South Asian Nations: Opportunities and Challenges," introduces the significance of improving bilateral and multilateral relations and opportunities between Australia and the South Asian nations in the healthcare sector. Pandemic related public health crisis is an important challenge of the 21st century. Global COVID-19 pandemic healthcare crisis has resulted in international border closures, healthcare supply value chain disruptions, increased infections and deaths, and coronavirus vaccine production and rollout issues, vaccine inequity and gaps between supply and demand for healthcare goods and services. The author provides various opportunities and challenges faced for bilateral and multilateral partnerships between Australia and the eight (8) South Asian nations post-pandemic to establish mutually beneficial bilateral and multilateral collaboration and partnerships for production of vaccine, distribution, access and affordability, research and education into health sector. It then provides a detailed literature review and discussing the importance of enhancing trade cooperation and partnership to cope with pandemic like emergency, for the mutual benefit of Australia and the South Asian Association for Reginal Cooperation (SAARC) nations. Various trade agreements are discussed, and macroeconomic overview of Australia and the SAARC countries is provided included pandemic related data for the period of 2000-2021. Chapter recommends that Australia can share its health expertise related to digital-health, medicare, medical technologies, production of life-saving vaccines, and access to affordable and accredited quality of healthcare for combined 2 billion people living in South Asia and Australia, which is the key to good health, well-being for all, meeting United Nations SDGs for industry and innovation in the hearth sector, reducing inequality, promoting peace, justice and strong institutions and partnerships to achieve these goals, along with economic progress, and prosperity of the South Asian nations.

Chapter 2, titled "Australia's Bilateral and Multilateral Partnership With South Asian Nations: Opportunities and Challenges in the Transitioning Energy Sector," aims to investigate potential cooperation between Australia and the SAARC nations to facilitate generation and distribution of energy to better manage this sector and fulfil their commitments towards climate change conditions. As carbon emissions from non-renewables severely threatened the climate conditions, an effective transition to renewable resources is essential. Australia and SAARC nations committed to reduce their individual carbon emissions in Paris Agreement. However, the SAARC nations have continued to rely on fossil fuels and meet their emission reduction targets. The distribution of carbon-emission by various economic sectors is discussed, against the backdrop of increasing demand by South Asian population's average electricity usage, and per-capita consumption of the SAARC nations. Australia leads in renewables, such as solar and wind energy and SAARC nations provide a large market for Australia to provide technological services to improve energy efficiency and competitiveness and move to renewable energy such as solar. Author also provides a detail investigation into demand and supply disparities in the energy sector in each of the SAARC nations, to understand the scope of bilateral and multilateral trade practices. Finally, this chapter investigates the opportunities for strategic collaboration between the SAARC nations, challenges of energy trading, energy security, inefficient institutions, volatile prices and investment flows, collaborative capacity generation and distribution; and analyses comparative advantages for the countries to have mutually beneficial agreements. This will further lead to meeting the United Nations SDGs related to goal number 7= affordable and clean energy, 13= climate action and 17=partnerships to achieve these goals.

Chapter 3, titled "Review of Opportunities in Collaboration Between Australia and Pakistan for Education of Marketing: An Analysis," reviews and presents opportunity for collaboration between Australian and Pakistani tertiary education for advanced teaching of marketing. The research presents a study suggesting innovating marketing education post Covid-19; based on class interviews with examples from the world of politics. University students studying marketing were interviewed in this qualitative study by conducting in-class focus groups. Respondents were inquired about their opinion on using various teaching strategies with politics as a case to explain elements of the marketing mix. Recommendations to use class discussions, role-play and cold-call engagement are contributions of this chapter, presenting learning by applying politics as a marketing challenge to explain the marketing theory, and how it influences policy making. Politics as a marketing example can be used by academic and industrial marketing trainers and educators, leading towards a strategic opportunity for future collaboration and partnership between Australian and Pakistani education planners and institutions, as a strategy for meeting United Nations SDGs 4 and 16 through education and strong institutions for peace and justice to enhance bilateral relationship.

Chapter 4, titled "Digital Strategic Partnership for Australian and South Asian Enterprises," aims to identify the important roles in Digital Strategic Partnership for Australian-Asian Enterprises. Research has shown that the world's two biggest economies in the coming years will be in Asia, and they are China and India. Australia's strategic location and close geographic proximity to Asia and its engagement in economic, business, education, health, cultural, and technological cooperation have led to opportunities in digital strategic partnership for Australian-Asian Enterprises. Over many years Australia have demonstrated leadership for exchange of strategic information, ideas, and closer participation with Asia. A case study approach is used to analyse the strategic investment opportunities in digital and telecommunication technologies with Australia and Asian trading partners to develop a digital strategy. New digital startup companies such as FinTech and RegTech and strategic partnership can benefit consumers, businesses, and governments. This has led to building a strong relationship in terms of government to government, people to people, and business to business which can be transformed for innovative Digital Strategic Partnership in the South Asian region and meeting United Nations SDG- eight related to Industry, Innovation, and Infrastructure to enhance social and financial inclusion with positive learning and healthcare outcomes.

Chapter 5, titled "Australia as an Enabler to Sustainable Indian Ocean Island Economies," explores Australia's role as an island continent, to assist the small island blue economies of the Indian ocean region to have a sustainable existence and survive the climate change and global warming impacts on its people and the economy. These island economies share common history of British colonization The author provides a deeper understanding on how Australia and Indian ocean island economies of Mauritius, Maldives, and Sri Lanka can mutually benefit from each other, to promote sustainability and have positive economic impact on the island economies. The author of this chapter critically investigates what makes the three island economies attractive to promote regional and international trade, and how Australia can help achieve a sustainable blue economy. The author initially provides some background of the current state in the island economies and Australia, post COVID-19 crisis impact, the different financial and regulatory policies, bilateral trade agreements, and ministerial level organisations promoting trade partnerships. Key recommendations aligned with various Sustainable Development Goals (SDGs), especially SDG 14, are provided. Active involvement in terms of foreign direct investment and sharing expertise, from experienced nations like Australia to Small Island Developing States (SIDS) is required as Indian ocean island economies are the key corridors for Australia's cargo to Africa and the Middle Eastern countries, in order to have sustainable blue economies, post the COVID-19 crisis.

Chapter 6, titled "Bilateral Cooperation Between Australia and Bangladesh in Diverse Areas: An Analysis to Cope With the COVID-19 Aftermath." In this chapter the author discusses the bilateral cooperation between Australia and Bangladesh during and post-Covid-19 related to interregional trade, foreign investment, Ready-Made-Garments export, education, blue economy, microfinance, tourism, renewable energy and finally fulfillment of targets of SDGs. Main discussion focusses on how does diverse areas of bilateral cooperation between Bangladesh and Australia become more efficient and effective in resources utilization and bring socio-economic benefits? Advancement in economic cooperation in both the countries may be improved from trade and investment, enhancement of education using Australian model, improvement and enhancement in energy, blue economy, education, health and ready-made-garment sector. Australian partnership will be helpful for government agencies, policy makers and associated stakeholders of Bangladesh for future improvements and development interventions in diverse multisector areas. Emphasis needs to be given to ecofriendly sustainability as suggested by the author to meet the climate change and sustainability goals.

Chapter 7, titled "India and Australia's New Education Policy and Institutional Collaboration: Lessons for SAARC Nations," focusses on Nepal, Bangladesh, and the Indian education sector which suffers from limited foreign collaborations, less research orientation, redundant, obsolete curriculum, and fewer relevancies of courses with available job opportunities. Various projects are undertaken by the governments of South Asian countries for improving quality education and partnerships with Australian institutions in faculty and student exchange, joint research collaboration, joint PhD supervision, university-industry partnerships, and joint offering of degrees. Especially in case of India few initiatives were taken to improve quality of education related to United Nations SDG- four. India adopted 'New Education Policy' that opened the doors to strategic collaboration with international universities, as India has begun to seriously concentrate on vocational education and training for the first time. This research examines the scope and restrictions of institutional partnerships between India, other SAARC nations and Australian higher education institutions. This study is based on the analysis of data presented in the different case studies like Rajasthan Royals and Deakin Australian Universities, IIT Bombay and Monash Australian, Indian Academy of Science and Innovation Research (AcSIR) and RMIT Australian University.

Chapter 8 is titled "Strategic Partnership of Bangladesh With Australia to Avoid One-Belt One-Road Debt Trap: Lessons for SAARC Nations." The Australia and Bangladesh Relationship dates to 1972 and is about to step into Golden Jubilee by 2022. Australia is among the first few developed states which recognized Bangladesh immediately after the 1971 war of liberation. The country Bangladesh achieved versatile growth in the last 50 years wherein the contribution of Australia was remarkable. At present with the onset of COVID 19, the global tension in the Indo-Pacific and the influence of the rising China it is important to look for alternative choices to forge a sustainable partnership agreement for the future, for bilateral trade, investment opportunities for economic development and growth in order to meet United Nations SDGs. Therefore, it is likely that the relations will proceed further if the interests like Strategic partnership of Australia and Bangladesh can be nurtured to curb the Maritime Power, One-Belt One-Road and Debt Trap of the rising China with lessons for SAARC nations.

Chapter 9 is titled "Medical, Pharmaceutical, and Healthcare Trade Relationships Between Australia and South Asian Nations." The global coronavirus (COVID-19) pandemic shocked the whole world. It had a disastrous impact on the economies and the healthcare systems of South Asian countries. Australia was able to minimize the COVID-19 impact by imposing a strict lockdown. The healthcare system and the healthcare industry in Australia are advanced and provide high quality pharmaceutical products and healthcare services. Australia has a lot to offer to South Asian Countries in public health programs, quality of healthcare, complementary medicine products, clinical data management and development, and drug developments. Healthcare systems in South Asian countries vary significantly. Australia can play a significant role in developing the healthcare systems of South Asia. For instance, Australia can provide the traditional medicine sectors in South Asian countries with scientifically effective complementary medicines. Improving healthcare bilateral investment and trade relationship between South Asia countries and Australia is a win/win partnerships for SAARC nations post-pandemic.

Chapter 10 is titled "The Recycling Crisis of Australian offshore Structures in Bangladesh: Challenges and Opportunities." The circular economy has emerged as a policy goal with respect to the trade relationships between developed and developing countries. The aim of the circular economy is to take responsibility for the costs involved in recycling by going away from the linear economic model, which is briefly stated as 'take-recycle-dispose' with unused materials in at one end and externalised the wastes at the other. Recycling numerous unused structures is a persisting problem for Australia that can be resolved following this circular economy approach. To that end, an underlying aim of this Chapter is to propose a bilateral agreement between Bangladesh and Australia that aims at recycling offshore structures of Australian companies in Bangladesh's ship recycling industry (hereinafter referred to as recycling industry). This Chapter also sheds light on the challenges for Bangladesh in recycling the offshore structures in a sustainable way creating job opportunities, but also disputes those offshore structures will only increase the waste burden for Bangladesh.

Chapter 11 is titled "Review of Post-COVID-19 Tourism Marketing Partnership Opportunities Between Australia and Pakistan." Authors in this chapter presents a deliberation on an opportunity for tourism marketing partnership between Australian and South Asian nations, with a focus on Pakistan. Tourism being the star performing industry across the globe has faced unprecedented crash due to COVID-19.

Post COVID-19, market opening relies heavily on the fundamental option of partnerships between governments and private players. The tourism demand has triggered partnerships between government and private agencies across various countries that have convergence in areas of culture, politics, and economy. Authors point out that the two countries may not have geographical proximity, but they have strong agriculture-based economy and sports-based entertainment. Moreover, both countries have diverse tourism resources serving travelers in hedonistic, mountain, snow, spiritual, sports and events tourism. This chapter highlights the types of tourism marketing that could be facilitated in a Post COVID-19 environment between Australia and Pakistan in particular and South Asia in general, and presents phases involved in the bilateral or multilateral partnership agreements essential for meeting United Nations sustainable development goals.

Chapter 12 is titled "Post-COVID-19 Australian and Indian Collaboration for Enhanced Effectiveness in the Resource Sector for Renewable Energy." India and Australia have a diverse range of ties, spanning from geostrategic collaboration and trade to global influence. An initial period of warmth followed by decades of coldness characterizes the relationship between Australia and India. In this chapter authors make a case for improving resource sector related bilateral relations between New Delhi and Canberra, with the aim for a sustainable future through strategic collaboration in climate change and the renewable energy sector. Trade and investment possibilities exist between the two countries, and over the years, the engagements between countries have been neglected. However, since the pandemic there is a renewed energy between Australia and India to collaborate and form bilateral partnerships and free trade agreements in strategic areas of trade, technology, pharmaceuticals, investment in resources sector, and renewable energy to combat climate change. The worldwide focus on renewable energy adoption through technological innovation and collaboration is thriving. This research focuses on understanding if there has been a change in the relationship between the two since the pandemic. Through the analysis and observation of qualitative data, suggestions with the current scenario and the future scope of both countries, particularly in the resources and energy sector have been discussed in this chapter.

Chapter 13 is titled "New Trade Frontiers between India and Australia: Challenges and Opportunities Post COVID-19." The authors in this chapter discuss that the rising geopolitical tensions between China and Australia, can develop new trade frontiers between India, Australia, and South Asian region as a whole. With this view the chapter aims to study the present state of bilateral trade relations between India-Australia, identify obstacles that hindered the growth of trade relations between India-Australia in the past, understand the impact of current comprehensive economic cooperation for free trade agreement between the two countries. Authors further, discuss the challenges that COVID-19 has imposed for Australian trade in goods, with China imposing trade ban and tariffs on Australian goods such as coal, iron ore, cotton, red-meet, lobsters, barley, wine, and timber. Authors suggest that Australia can find new trusted trade partners in the SAARC countries and provide future opportunities for bilateral trade between India and Australia. The 2020-21 Australia-India Joint Statement on Comprehensive Strategic Partnership and Comprehensive Economic Cooperation agreement is a step forward in a positive direction in meeting many of the SDGs. This chapter is essential for understanding the complexities of "trade creation" between (India and Australia) and "trade diversion" between (China and Australia).

Chapter 14 is titled "Australia's Trade and Investment Strategy in the Post-COVID-19 Era: Prospects for Australia-Bangladesh Partnership." In this chapter the authors examine how the trade and investment relationship between Australia and the Asia-Pacific nations have evolved and changed over the past decades with focus on Bangladesh in particular. The chapter also reflects on the gradual shift of trade and diplomatic relationships in this region since the outbreak of the Covid-19 pandemic towards the

South Asian nations. The ongoing global pandemic has not only been disrupting the global economic and geopolitical environment but also reshaping the trade relationship in the region. The chapter explores the greater trade and investment opportunities between Australia and South Asia with a special emphasis on the increased potential bilateral trade partnership with Bangladesh. Following the neoclassical comparative advantage theories, the authors suggest that long-run economic benefits for South Asia in general and Bangladesh in particular can be enhanced by utilising the trade opportunities with Australia created by the COVID-19 pandemic to achieve numerous United Nations SDGs for Bangladesh. Therefore, strengthening further trade and diplomatic alliances between Australia and Bangladesh will be mutually beneficial in areas of ready-made-garment exports, cotton, agri-business, jute, leather goods, pharmaceuticals, information and communication technologies, tourism, and higher education to generate positive economic growth and development impact for both countries.

Chapter 15 is titled "Exploring Partnerships Between Australia and South Asia for Crowd Funding Social Enterprises: A Post-COVID-19 Strategy." In this chapter the authors discuss that social enterprises have proven to be an effective mechanism for addressing economic, social, and environment problems in a number of countries. Authors state that conventional businesses have, suffered during the Covid-19 pandemic. However, online businesses have grown and been successful as a direct result of mobility constraints imposed on multinational or regional value-chains during this time. Authors emphasize that social enterprises have continued to demonstrate their value as reservoirs of social and economic resilience during this unprecedented global crisis. But the challenge is of establishing trust, regulating crowd funding and financial viability of social enterprises. The founder of micro-lending Nobel Laureate Muhammad Yunus see micro-economies, comprising locally focused social businesses linked digitally into distant value chains, as a viable strategy for economic growth in difficult times to achieve the United Nations SDGs. This chapter examines the potential of strategic business collaborations between social enterprises in Australia and South Asia that can leverage crowdfunding as a tool for mutual advantage and explores opportunities and challenges for Australian interests entering the financial services sector in South Asia.

There is a challenge of making the SAARC regional grouping functional at all levels - social, cultural, and economic relationships with appropriate economic strategies for implementing policies for the mutual benefit of Australia and the SAARC nations amidst the changing geo-political environment since COVID-19 and build trusted long-term trading relationship with each other. In the last decade the world has experienced natural disasters and the global financial crisis. In the March 2000 World Health Organized announced, the Global COVID-19 crisis as a pandemic health emergency, and we are still suffering from the impact of various versions of the coronavirus, lockdown and its economic impact on various sectors of the economy, business, trade and investment activities. With COVID-19 driven recessionary impact due to social distancing, travel, and trade restrictions, closing of national and international borders, the economies of the countries have experienced high unemployment rate, negative Gross Domestic Product growth rate and global supply chain disruptions of goods and services. The book is timely and aims to be a leading source of information for having bilateral and multilateral cooperation between Australia and the SAARC nations in South Asia need to come together to face the future global challenges and cultivate the economic opportunities to find solutions to the shared problems of health crisis due to COVID-19, food security, cyber security, education, climate change, unemployment, infrastructure development, technological innovation, and border and maritime security concerns.

We acknowledge the valuable contributions made by all the authors; without their support and contributions the book would not have been completed. Finally, we would like to thank the blind reviewers,

Editorial Advisory Board, Katelyn McLoughlin - Assistant Book Development Editor and Coordinator, and the IGI Global Development Team for their regular help and support during the various stages of editorial process and development stage of the book.

Anita Medhekar
Central Queensland University, Australia

Sreeparna Saha
Central Queensland University, Australia

Farooq Haq
Canadian University Dubai, UAE

Acknowledgment

We appreciate and acknowledge the efforts of everyone towards the development of this book. We wish to sincerely thank all- Authors, Reviewers, Editorial Advisory Board and IGI Global Development team for their invaluable contributions.

We are deeply grateful to all the 'Authors' for their responses to the call for chapter proposals, revisions involved, and final chapter submissions for this book on *Strategic Cooperation and Partnerships Between Australia and South Asia: Economic Development, Trade, and Investment Opportunities Post COVID-19.* Without their valuable contributions and cooperation we would not have been able to complete this book successfully.

We are also thankful to the blind reviewers of the chapters, who made their contribution by providing invaluable suggestions and feedback, which were implemented by the authors. We are also grateful to the numerous reviewers who wanted to be anonymous for their valuable contribution in the review process.

Particularly, we show our gratitude to all the chapter authors who contributed their valuable time and expertise to this book. The authors made numerous revisions to the chapters for presenting their research, and improvements in the process of chapter development. The work progressed in highly coordinated manner despite the authors belonging to different parts of the world, in this global pandemic situation.

This work carries, behind it, the encouragement, support and good wishes of family, many friends and colleagues, though it is difficult to mention their names individually.

We would also like to thank and also acknowledge members of the IGI-Global Publishers' team, Jan Travers Director of Intellectual Property and Contracts and Katelyn McLoughlin, IGI Global Editorial Book Development Coordinator, for their continuing guidance, giving the authors additional time, co-ordination, suggestions, and support during the development stage of this book.

We are also grateful to Book Development Editorial and Publishing Team of IGI Global for their valuable assistance during the final stage of the editing process of this book.

Finally, we would like to thank IGI Global publishers for their commitment to quality international research, ethics, peer review, and publishing on current topics impacting the changing geopolitical environment, international trade, investment, and economic relations and partnerships during and post-COVID-19 period.

Acknowledgment

Anita Medhekar
Central Queensland University, Australia

Sreeparna Saha
Central Queensland University, Australia

Farooq Haq
Canadian University Dubai, UAE

Chapter 1
Australia's Bilateral and Multilateral Health Sector Partnership With South Asian Nations:
Opportunities and Challenges

Anita Medhekar
https://orcid.org/0000-0002-6791-4056
Central Queensland University, Australia

ABSTRACT

Pandemic-related public health crises are important challenges of the 21st century. The COVID-19 pandemic healthcare crisis has resulted in international border closures; healthcare supply value-chain disruptions; increased infections, deaths, and coronavirus vaccine production and rollout issues; vaccine inequity and gaps between supply and demand for healthcare goods and services. This chapter aims to focus on the opportunities and challenges for bilateral and multilateral partnerships between Australia and the eight South Asian nations post pandemic to establish mutually beneficial bilateral and multilateral collaboration and partnerships for production of vaccine, research, and education into the healthcare sector. Australia can share its health expertise related to digital health, medicare, medical technologies, production of life-saving vaccines, and access to affordable and accredited quality of healthcare for combined 2 billion people living in South Asia and Australia, which is the key to meeting UNSDGs of good health, well-being for all, economic progress, and prosperity of South Asian nations.

INTRODUCTION

This chapter aims to focus on the opportunities and challenges for health sector bilateral and multilateral partnerships between Australia and the eight (8) South Asian nations which are all members of South Asian Association of Regional Cooperation (SAARC) Afghanistan, Bangladesh, Bhutan, India, Maldives,

DOI: 10.4018/978-1-7998-8657-0.ch001

Nepal, Pakistan, and Sri Lanka. COVID-19 Pandemic related global public health emergency has forced nations to lockdown, essential shopping, social distancing, and closing borders along with restrictions on trade and travel for business and higher education, tourism, and demand supply gaps, resulting in supply chains bottlenecks in all sectors of the economy including health. Nations of the world and the medical scientific community and pharmaceutical companies have put their resources together to discover a vaccine for coronavirus, within a year.

It is now essential to explore how Australia can find new markets for trade, investment, tourism, international education, and business opportunities for its resources, services, manufacturing, and technology sectors in South Asian countries and vice versa. Increasing number of people from South Asian countries and India are choosing Australia for permanent migration, business, education, and tourism (Bhosale, 2018). This has become very apparent since COVID-19 which has impacted negatively on Australian higher education sector, tourism, small and medium businesses and with nearly nine thousand Indians and other South Asian population of Australian citizens, now stranded in South Asian countries due to border closures. Australia benefits from medical human resources like doctors, nurses, specialists physicians, surgeons, and allied healthcare professionals from South Asian countries. Therefore, Australia must engage in a sustainable manner with all South Asian countries and vice-versa to find investment opportunities in health sector related education, employment, innovation and entrepreneurship opportunities in the production and transfer of technology of health-related goods and services. For example, production and supply of life-saving medicines, health technology, medical equipment, digital e-health platforms, public hygiene, including training of medical and allied health human resources, generate health related employment opportunities for the mutual economic benefit, development, and growth in the post-pandemic future, under the SAARC umbrella, which is the key to health, well-being, economic progress, and prosperity of nations.

Australia has been working on strengthening its bilateral relationship with India since it signed negotiations for a Comprehensive Economic Cooperation Agreement (CECA) in May 2011.Both the countries have had nine rounds of negotiations, the last one being in September 2015 (Hall, 2015). In April 2017, Mr Turnbull Prime Minister of Australia, visited India to strengthen the two-way strategic cooperation between the two countries for economic growth and knowledge sharing in ten strategic areas (Thakur & Sharma, 2018). This was followed by Australia-India Joint Statement on a Comprehensive Strategic Partnership Agreement (AI-JS-CSPA) in June 2020 on thirteen (13) key strategic areas with 49 points. This was a virtual meeting between the prime ministers of the two countries and their cabinet (DFAT, 2020).

The inaugural QUAD ministerial meeting was held in September 2019, followed by historic QUAD video-linked online summit on the 12-March-2021, between, the four heads of democratic nations of Australia, India, USA, and Japan, with the aim to form a strategic cooperation, partnership and coronavirus vaccination alliance for investment, production, and distribution to keep the nations safe, stable, and secure (Sharma, 2021). USA President Biden, expressed it as "practical solutions and concrete results" to global problems, including COVID-19, climate change and cyber security, to have a "free and open Indo-Pacific" region as mentioned by the Japanese prime minister Yoshihide Suga (Ngaibiakching & Pande, 2020; Panda, 2017). Further, with increasing maritime power of China and boundary disputes in the South China sea, East China Sea, Taiwan Strait, Indo-Pacific region and The Bay of Bengal, India is to join a joint navy meeting and exercise between USA, Japan, Australia, and France which was held in April-May 2021, demonstrating multilateral defence and security partnership at sea and commitment to free and open Indo-pacific region (Deccan Herald, 1-April-2021).

Australia India Economic Strategy 2020-2035 (Varghese, 2018) covers ten economic sectors such as investment, trade, education, mining technology, Agri-business, tourism, energy, health, infrastructure, financial services, sports, science, and innovation defence, can be extended to rest of South Asian countries. This paper is going to focus on the health sector related cooperation and partnerships for investment, trade, health research, education, to fill the demand needs and supply gaps between Australia and SAARC member nations. The first step being to jointly use its capacities to produce one (1) billion doses by 2022, and distribute coronavirus vaccine, for the benefit of other Asian and Pacific Island economies. This will be funded by USA, manufactured by Johnson & Johnson India and distribution logistics of "Last mile" to South-East Asian nations by Australia. "Last mile" activities generally include the steps needed to get shots in arms, from health workforce training to awareness campaigns and helping procure the disposable medical items needed to administer injections" (Greg, 2021). It is important that not only coronavirus vaccine is made available to the SAARC nations, after being produced in India, but also export of health care expertise, goods and services; Australia and the SAARC countries can help each other to meet the United Nations Sustainable Development Goals which are linked to health; (3) Good Health and Wellbeing, (9) Industry, Innovation and Infrastructure, (10), Reducing Inequality (16) Peace, Justice, and Strong Institutions, (17) Partnerships for the Goals (UN, 2020).

Australia thereby needs an alternative strategic bilateral and multilateral coalition with a combined population of nearly 2 billion with SAARC nations, to find new opportunities for trade, investment, innovation in the health sector which will be mutually beneficial to meet the United Nations Sustainable Development Goals (SDGs) for the future. This review chapter aliens with the theme of the book related to the healthcare services. This chapter is structured as follows. First section provides an overview of the Australian, India and other SAARC nations trade and investment strategic partnership and cooperation; section two provides background literature review on bilateral and multilateral trade and strategic partnerships of Australia with SAARC nations in general and related to health sector in particular; thirdly the chapter will review and identify future opportunities and challenges for cooperation and partnership in health sector post COVID-19 investment, education and trade in health related goods and services, and healthcare supply chain cooperation mutually beneficial to Australia and South Asian nations. Last section provides discussion, future research directions and conclusions.

BACKGROUND LITERATURE

Bilateral and Multilateral Trade Cooperation and Partnerships

Adam Smith in his book "The Wealth of Nations" proposed that free trade in the absence of tariff, quotas, and other non-tariff government barriers between nations, improved overall welfare of all nations. It therefore allows each country to specialise in the production of goods cheaply and efficiently at lower opportunity costs than other countries (Smith, 1776). Bilateral trade partnership takes please between two nations, agreeing to free flow of goods and granting most favoured nation status. Whereas multilateral trade partnerships take place between more than three nations, where the nations agree to reduce and dismantle their tariff and non-tariff barriers (Krugman, Obstfeld, & Melitzm, 2018; Medhekar, 2021).

India has signed various multi-lateral agreements to improve economic relations with the East-Asian neighbours. For example, (i) 'South Asian Free Trade Agreement' (SAFTA) with neighbouring countries of Bhutan, Bangladesh, Maldives, Nepal, Pakistan and SriLanka. (ii) In 2009, India' signed a 'Long Term

Cooperative Partnership for Peace and Prosperity' with ASEAN countries. (iii) In 2010 India -ASEAN Asian Free Trade Agreement (AI-FTA) for partnership in economic, political, and socio-cultural initiative for mutual benefit. This was followed by (iv) 'Bay of Bengal Initiatives Multi-Sectoral Technical and Economic Cooperation' (BIMSTEC) headquarters in Bangladesh with seven member countries India, Nepal, Bhutan, SriLanka, Myanmar, and Thailand, with 23 percent of global population. Its aim is to cooperate for economic and social development and growth in various sectors - trade, transport, technology, energy, tourism, fisheries, agri-business, poverty alleviation climate change, environment, counter terrorism, public health, and people-to-people-contact (Medhekar, 2021).

In 2014 partnership with ASEAN was graduated to being 'Strategic Partnership', given the maritime security concerns and geo-political situation in the Indo-Pacific Ocean region and the South China Sea (Das & Thomas, 2016; Haokip, 2015; Hussain, 2017). In 2014, Modi governments Act-East foreign policy extends beyond ASEAN to Australia, New Zealand, and Japan with no territorial motives, but for multilateral strategic cooperation, national border and maritime security, trade, investment, and economic development partnerships (Medhekar & Kaur, 2021; Ngaibiakching & Pande, 2020; Ranjan, 2016; Sajjanhar, 2016; Tandon, 2016; Yhome, 2015; Wojczewski, 2019). According to Rana (2018), who critically comments that "In order to continue its impressive economic growth, India requires a peaceful and stable environment in its neighbourhood. India cannot emerge as a global power if it is unable to attain primacy in its own region" (p. 566), which is to establish cooperation and partnership between and within the SAARC region, before looking beyond South Asian region.

Further with the supply chain disruptions due to COVID-19, increasingly the countries realised how much they depended on China for import and export of finished goods and raw commodities. The significance of QUAD (Sharma, 2021), where in July 2020, Australia, India, USA and Japan signed the Supply Chain Resilience Initiative (SCRI) between the countries, given that COVID-19 pandemic and trade disruptions have revealed critical medical supplies and other goods supply chains vulnerabilities in the region, mainly to as per the joint statement made by the three countries Ministers "The SCRI aims to create a virtuous cycle of enhancing supply chain resilience with a view to eventually attaining strong, sustainable, balanced and inclusive growth in the region". Australian Minister for Trade, Tourism and Investment Dan Tehan said, "Australia's supply chains have generally proven resilient, but the pandemic has highlighted the need for greater international cooperation to strengthen supply chains" (Bloomberg Economics, 2021, April 28).

Australia and SAARC Member Countries Related Agreements

Australia since May 2011 has been working on strengthening its bilateral strategic partnership with India when the two countries jointly signed a Comprehensive Economic Cooperation Agreement (CECA), followed by nine rounds of negotiations, the last one being in September 2015. On the 4th of June 2020, the Honourable Prime Ministers of the two countries Scott Morrison and Narendra Modi had an online meeting and signed a "Joint Statement on a Comprehensive Strategic Partnership (AI-JS-CSP) on twelve (12) key strategic areas with 49 points, which also included globally coordinated response to COVID-19 and a commitment to build an open, prosperous and a stable post-COVID world (DFAT, 2020). This was a virtual meeting between the prime ministers cabinets of the two countries.

The key areas of *Australia and India* 2020 *CSP* were based on common interests, mutual understanding, trust, shared values of democracy, rule of law and an increasing engagement and a common vision of open, free and rule of law for the Indo-pacific region. The twelve key areas for commitment to cooperation and partnership for security, economic development, peace, and prosperity can be extended to all the SAARC nations:

1. *Enhancing Science, Technology, and Research Cooperation* for managing COVID-19 economic impact, medical research, diversify supply chains for critical health technology, and cyber security and mining.
2. *Maritime Cooperation* for a shared vision for an open and inclusive Indo-Pacific including Association of South East Asian Nations (ASEAN) to support sustainability of water resources, oceans, and maritime related issues.
3. *Defence Cooperation* for border and maritime security challenges through military engagement, and collaborating on military science and technology, shared joint exercises through mutual logistic support agreement.
4. R*egional and Multilateral Cooperation* for an open, inclusive and rule of law-based Indo-Pacific and South -Pacific regions, for maritime peace, prosperity, security, and stability with ASEAN at the centre. Both countries also agreed to cooperate on bilateral cooperation for nuclear energy for visual purposes.
5. *Combating Terrorism* in fall forms for peace, stability, and prosperity of the region. A comprehensive approach to be adapted according to the 2015 United Nations G-20 statement on 'Fight Against Terrorism' including cyber-security of virtual financial assets and technology used for hacking and money laundering to finance terrorism.
6. *Economic Cooperation f*or a prosperous shared future through trade and investment between the two countries, including a rules-based multilateral trading system to promote open markets, trade liberalisation, economic development, growth, and prosperity. Cooperation to ensure that Australian businesses are aware of opportunities to trade and investment in India's 'Smart Cities' initiatives and 'Make in India' programs, and Indian business of opportunities to invest in Australia.
7. *Innovation and Entrepreneurship* for fostering and collaborating for start-up initiatives and incubation centres, develop innovative products. Australia and India committed to diversity bilateral-trade by integrating micro, small, and medium enterprises of both countries with major industries supply chains.
8. *Agriculture Cooperation and Water Resource Management* partnership for jointly sharing agriculture expertise which are mutually beneficial to face challenges of climate change, besides collaborating in agricultural education, research, development, capacity building, grain management, reduce post-harvest loss to ensure farmers income is not affected by supply chain disruptions.
9. *Education, Culture, Tourism, and people-to-people ties for exchange and cooperation* for education research and skills development, tourism, and people-to-people connection and contribution of India-Australian diaspora for bilateral relationship.
10. *Support in United Nations and International Bodies* for permanent membership of United Nations Security Council for 2021-22 and international energy agency.
11. *Public Administration Cooperation* between the two countries for reforms in public administration and Governance.
12. *Implementation of Comprehensive Strategic Partnership* with regular prime ministerial level annual Australia-India Joint Ministerial Commission to enhance trade and investment relations, energy dialogue, Australia-India education council, between the two countries.

Table 1. Overview of the Australian and South Asian Economies 9 May 2021

Country	% GDP Annual Growth 2020	% GDP Annual Growth 2019	Inflation Last 2020 or 2021	Unemployment Jan 2021 or Last %	Unemployment % Oct 2020 or Last	Interest Rate % April 2021	Current Account % GDP 2019	% Govt Debt to GDP 2020	% Govt. Budget Deficit 2020
Australia	-1.1	3.7	0.1	5.6	7	0.9	2.5	24.8	-4.3
Afghanistan	4.03	1.58	4.4	11.2	11.1	15	-21.2	7.8	-0.9
Bangladesh	5.20	8.20	5.47	5.3	4.20	4.75	-1.5	31.7	-5.35
Bhutan	5.50	3.1	7.72	2.7	3.40	6.86	-12.2	122	-6.2
India	0.40	-7.3	5.52	6.5	7.0	4	-0.9	69.62	-9.5
Maldives	-51.60	-5.0	-1	6.4	6.1	7	-29.2	24.7	-27.5
Nepal	2.30	7.00	3.02	4.44	2.85	5	-7.6	30.2	-5.4
Pakistan	-0.38	1.91	9.05	4.40	4.10	7	-1.1	87	-8.1
Sri Lanka	1.3	1.5	4.1	5.2	5.8	4.5	-2.2	86.8	-6.8

Source Trading Economics

The recent example of a multilateral strategic partnership historic QUAD leadership video-linked online summit on the 12-March-2021, between, the four maritime heads of democratic nations of Australia, India, USA, and Japan was held with the aim to form a strategic cooperation, partnership, and coronavirus vaccination alliance to keep the nations safe, stable, and secure from coronavirus, and to be a stabilising QUAD force with increasing economic and military Chinese aggression in the Indo-Pacific region (Sharma, 2021).

RERearch METHOD

Secondary source of information from various refereed articles, organisations home page such as SAARC and BIMSTEC, current news and statistical data bases were examined to collect the data for this qualitative descriptive review (Creswell, 2014).

OPPORTUNITIES AND CHALLENGES FOR THE HEALTH SECTOR DURING AND POST -PANDAMIC: AUSTRALIA AND SOUTH ASIAN COUNTRIES

Pandemic is defined as a simultaneous worldwide transmission of influenza like an epidemic occurring worldwide. This influenza pandemics can vary in terms of severity of the disease based on number of infections and deaths and the ease of transmissibility between large number of people across country and international borders (Heath, 2011). The Australia-India Economic Strategy 2035 provides an overview of the importance of the health sector for economic development, and bilateral opportunities for investment, trade in health care goods and services, employment creation, driver of innovation and entrepreneurship, and integrate healthcare value chains with Australia strengths and competitive advantage in the health sector (Varghese, 2018). Further, how Australia can meet India's demand for healthcare and objectives

Figure 1. Map of South Asia with capital cities (Eight SAARC nations)
Source: Google image

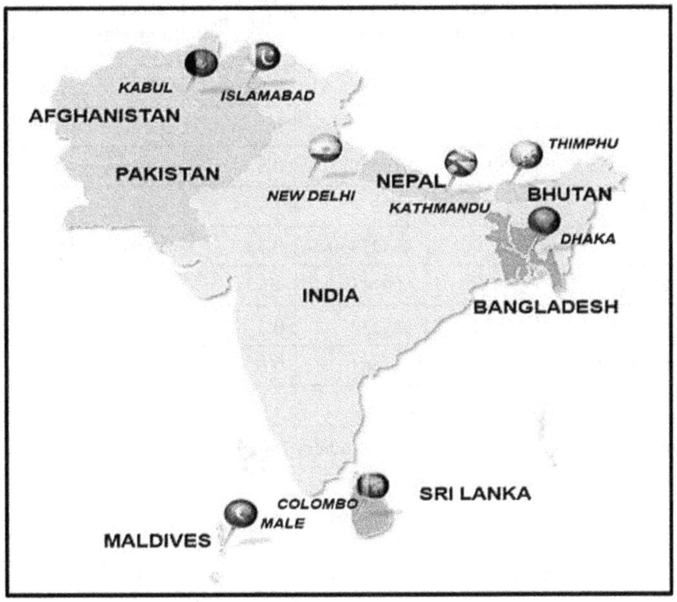

of India's national health mission. These opportunities of strategic partnerships in the health sector with Australia can be extended to whole of the South Asian Nations, in the post-COVD-19 future.

Opportunities

India comprises of one fifth of the global population and combined with other seven SAARC nations (Figure-1) and with Australia it is equal to nearly two billion. Global pandemic has made the countries realise the supply chain disruptions in healthcare goods, services and essential commodities, burden imposed by infectious/ communicable and non-communicable life-style related diseases such as heart and diabetes, shortage of medical equipment, life-saving drugs, personal protective equipment (PPE), hospital beds, and low doctor nurse patient ratio per 1000 people. Australia has 55.89 hospitals per thousand population (Trading Economics, 2021). However, no reliable data is available for number of hospitals per thousand population for South Asian nations.

Healthcare is privatised in India and other South Asian countries. According to The Lancet (2016), in India private sector provides 78% of healthcare in urban areas and 71% in rural areas. India's public expenditure on health is 1.4% of GDP (Golechha, 2015) and private sector (3.65 of GDP) health expenditure is combined 4% of GDP, compared to global average of 9% of GDP. The Modi government has promised to increase this to 2.5% of GDP, by 2025 (The Economic Times, 2018). Similar is the situation in all SAARC nations with increasing burden falling on the private sector with no health insurance schemes. Private healthcare in SAARC nations is out-of-pocket expenditure and is accessible by those who can afford to pay and for overseas medical tourists (Medhekar, 2013, 2019; Medhekar et al., 2019).

Table 2 shows the current corona virus related information for Australia and the eight (8) South Asian countries. Note that many cases of infections and deaths go unreported in South Asian countries.

Table 2. Australia and South Asia: Coronavirus Information

Country	Populat -ion in Millions	Coronavirus Cases	Deaths Persons	Recovered Persons	Hospital Beds per 1000	Doctors Per 1000	Nurses per 1000	Vaccine Doses per 100	Health Expen % GDP
Australia	24	20, 7982	1994	25486	3.84	4.01	13.41	152	9.28
Afghanistan	33.20	157218	7308	69205	0.4	0.29	0.2	12.84	9.40
Bangladesh	166.50	157, 6011	27981	816250	0.8	0.47	0.4	57.55	2.34
Bhutan	0.76	2640	3	1773	1.7	0.38	1.9	148	3.06
India	1347.12	34580832	468790	29427330	0.53	0.76	1.7	88.16	1.28
Maldives	0.56	91464	248	69974	4.3	3.61	6.4	141	9.41
Nepal	28.61	821121	11524	596132	0.3	0.6	3.1	57.95	5.54
Pakistan	212.30	1284189	28709	903484	0.6	0.98	0.7	54.63	3.20
Sri Lanka	24.41	562520	14305	225952	4.2	0.88	2.2	138	3.76

Source: data collected from various sources: Trading Economics Country Data; WHO, World Bank (Notes: vaccination rate as single dose) Data current as on 1 Dec 2021.

Bhutan has the lowest death, which is positively related to high vaccination rate of 148 per 100 persons, in comparison with India, which is facing a tragic health crisis in the second wave of coronavirus with increasing positive cases, shortage of medications, PPE, ventilators, oxygen, beds, medical doctors and nurses, ambulances, increasing deaths, and shortage of firewood at the crematoriums and spaces in the burial grounds.

Figure -2 shows that until April the 15th, the number of deaths per one million population in South Asian group of eight SAARC countries. SriLanka and Bangladesh has the second and third lowest death rates. India with 1.3 billion population is still struggle with increased cases and deaths per-millions of populations, whereas Maldives with a population of 550 thousand, has second highest death rate (Dhaka Tribune, 2021). Since then, the number of deaths has increased as seen from current data in Table-2.

Overall demand for health care related goods and services, corona-vaccine and personal protective equipment, facemasks, oxygen, ventilators, hospital beds, and life-saving outpaced the supply in South Asian countries during the March-May 2021, given the unprecedented rise in positive coronavirus cases

Figure 2. Deaths per one-million population in SAARC countries
Source: Dhaka Tribune (April 15, 2021)

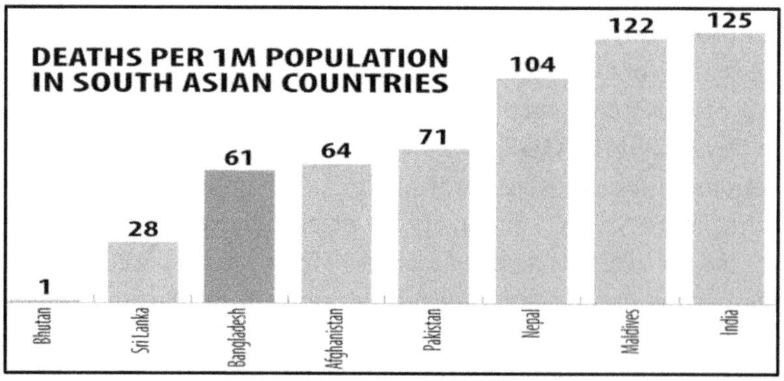

and deaths in the second wave. Public health expenditure per-capita is low compared to Australia: Maldives US $930; SriLanka US $160; Bhutan US $1025; India US $75; Nepal US $65; Afghanistan US $65, Pakistan US $45, and Bangladesh US $40 (Changoiwala, 2020). Further, total number of hospitals in Australia, are 55.89 per-millions of population. Data for total number of hospitals for the eight South Asian SAARC countries is not available to make a comparison.

The following opportunities can be explored in the health sector between Australia and SAARC nations:

1. *Production and supply of domestically produced medicines and vaccines (CoviShield):* It is essential that Australia and South Asian countries can share their expertise in medical and pharmaceutical research, Bio-technology, scientific knowledge and produce essential life-saving medicines, which can be produced at an affordable price to meet increasing demand of its combined population of approximately two billion. For example, CoviShield vaccine developed by Serum Institute of India, Cyrus Poonawalla Group in Pune India, with oxford (The Economics Times, 2021). The agreement with World Health organisation (WHO) should have been for IIS -India to supply to the whole of South Asian region (SAARC group of developing countries), for equitable distribution, including Australia.
2. *Production and supply of domestically produced medical technology*: Australia can share its expertise in production of medical equipment, personal protective equipment, technology, diagnostic machinery, and devices, to build state-of-the art medical infrastructure facilities and diagnostic clinics for the public hospitals. Similarly, in case of future health emergencies as well as in normal situations, Australia with the group of SAARC nations can share its expertise in joint research and development, investment and production of medicines, vaccines, medical equipment, and other medical goods, thus ensuring supplies for 2 billion populations at an affordable cost.
3. *Production and supply of Oxygen and lifesaving drugs:* Second wave of corona-virus in India has been a tragic incidence with shortage of oxygen, hospital beds, and essential life-saving drugs and vaccines. With hundred thousand of positive cases there is shortage of oxygen and hospitals are at full capacity. Australia can help India and South Asian countries to prepare for future health emergencies and have sufficient stock of supply, to meet the increasing demand supply in case of pandemic like health emergency.
4. *Share expertise in Universal Public Health System*: Australia has world leading public sector funded universal healthcare system. Australia can help at a bilateral level the SAARC nations to set up equitable access to medicare system and determining factors on how to allocate funds and resources by giving priority to the health sector and access to affordable and universal health-care to all the population (Australian Government Medicare, 2021).
5. Share expertise in *e-Health and My Health Records system:* Australia can help at a bilateral level the SAARC nations to set up technology enabled healthcare management solutions, e-health, digital health technologies, patients 'My Health Record' information technology system for better management of healthcare resources, for positive healthcare outcomes and health-records cybersecurity and privacy (Australian Digital Health Agency, 2019). Global Patient Portal (GPP) a free online health resource, was launched in India in 2015, for servicing low and middle-income populations in India. It allows Indian patients to use and maintain their own electronic health records for information flow between the individuals and healthcare professionals, which is not adopted widely by the population.

6. *Flying doctor healthcare services to remote areas:* Australia is renowned in providing flying doctors healthcare services to population in remote and regional areas. Australia can provide expert training and setting up flying doctor clinical and ambulance services, healthcare clinics to South Asian nations in servicing remote areas, so that universal healthcare can be easily accessible and available to populations living in remote mountains, desert areas and villages in normal and in emergency situations.
7. *Export and import opportunities:* Australia and India can establish export and import opportunities for pharmaceuticals, alternative Ayurvedic medicines and other medical equipment and diagnostic devices. Production plants can be set up in South Asian nations with Australian expertise, which will not only provide employment opportunities, but also produce certified quality of affordable medical goods for a combined population of two billion. This will also benefit other South Asian nations through bilateral and multilateral trade agreements under the SAARC umbrella, manufacturing of medicines, vaccines, and medical equipment, ensuring essential medical supplies and healthcare supply chains.
8. *South Asian Nations Source of skilled labour:* Australia population is approximately 24 million as per last census. However, there is always shortage of skilled labour in various sectors of the economy, including the health sector. Given the skill shortage of medical professionals, Australia relies on migrant doctors, specialists, allied healthcare professionals, and nurses from South Asian countries. There are large number of medical professionals working in remote regional areas and capital cities from South Asia, specially, India, Pakistan, Bangladesh, SriLanka and Nepal. It is tragic that South-Asian counties have lost their medical staff to coronavirus due to treating corona -positive patients and shortage of protective equipment.
9. *Health Education:* Australia including India and other south Asian nations have some world class top medica schools. Australia and SAARC nations can have exchange programs of scholars and students from medical schools, internship programs, for advancing the best practices in teaching, learning and knowledge in the field of medical education, nursing, and allied healthcare programs.
10. *Bio-Security:* There is risk related to transmission of viruses such as SARS, Corona from the animals and environment to humans, resulting in new versions of contagious diseases (Basray et al., 2021). In the 21st century world experienced five global health emergencies such as SARS-2003, Swine Flu or H1N1 -2009, Polio- 2013, Congo-Ebola-2014 and 2019 and COVID-19 (WHO 2021), even though some of them were confined to Asian and African regions. However, COVID-19, was declared by the World Health Organisation as a global health emergency (WHO, 2020). With globalisation and ease of travel there is increasing international travel for business, tourism, work, and medical purposes, along with international trade between countries, which has given rise to easy human-to-human transmission through contact and outbreaks of pandemic like infectious viruses, threatening human bio-security on the planet. Australia and SAARC countries can work together to manage infection prevention, control, and have a biosecurity related risk management and public health awareness education and plan to prevent such epidemic and pandemic like biosecurity health crisis.

Challenges

There are various challenges related to forming sustainable bilateral and multilateral cooperation and partnerships between Australia and the SAARC group of nations. It is important firstly for the SAARC nations particularly for India and Pakistan to cooperate and solves all border disputes and make SAARC functional. COVID-19 pandemic related regional and global supply chain disruptions in goods and services and trade disputes have made us released that all countries must cooperate and form partnerships to help each other to build future resilient healthcare supply chains production and distribution, which are sustainable during all times including natural disasters and pandemic like situations. Further, the QUAD summit held in March 2021 between the four democratic nations USA, Japan, Australia, and India, is a quadrilateral security framework for strategic cooperation with a shared vision to not only counterbalance the power of China in the Indo-Pacific region, but a joint statement focussing on vaccination alliance for solving the economic and health impact of the coronavirus global pandemic, and ensure global health security for providing affordable, equitable access, and effective vaccine production in India funded by the 3 developed QUAD countries, and distribution for economic recovery (Bhattacharya, 2021; D'Ambrogio, 2021). Furthermore, India has shown 'Vaccine Diplomacy' soft-power towards SAARC member countries and 72 developing nations, by donating Coronavirus Vaccines, which is due to collaboration with the West, to produce at the world's largest pharmaceutical industry, Serum Institute of India -Pune (Dhume, 2021).

1. *Doing business with South Asian countries:* Australians must understand the South Asian culture in the emerging markets, to learn how to do business in these countries by building long term sustainable commitment and relationships. The central and state governments of SAARC nations can develop contacts via Australian Department of Foreign Affairs and Trade, hold workshops and seminars organised by country based High Commissions to help to overcome these challenges (DFAT, 2020).
2. *Health Policy:* All the SAARC nations have their 'National Health Policy' agenda. However, the health expenditure as a percentage of Gross Domestic Product (GDP) is less than 2% in the most populated country -India. Australia can help the SAARC nations by showing Australian example as to how they have implemented a universal health policy successfully for all Australians such as medicare system (Dixit & Sambasivan, 2018).
3. *Remote and Rural areas healthcare services:* It is a challenge in SAARC nations to provide affordable quality of clinical healthcare and diagnostic services to rural and remote population. There is a shortage of primary and secondary healthcare clinics and medical professionals and beds per 1000 people as shown in Table-2. People travel to capital cities for seeing a specialist consultant, for diagnostic tests and surgery (Medhekar, 2019). These countries can learn from Australia in terms of medical service provision to remote regional areas and incentives for doctors and allied medical staff to encourage them to work in rural medical centers and diagnostic clinics.
4. *Public health education and literacy:* It is a challenge in South Asian countries, given the large percentage of illiteracy, that governments at all levels must provide public health education and literacy of the general population in villages, urban and rural slum, and at educational institutions, which is very essential during normal times and in any health emergency like situation and post-COVID-19. They must provide tips on how to follow hygiene and other social distancing measures in pandemic like health emergencies and emergencies related to any natural disasters such as cyclone and floods.
5. *Digital health records cyber security and privacy:* COVID-19 has made countries realise about the Cyber-Security and privacy of patients medical records. Indian software industry is much advanced and South Asian countries could focus on digitising and adopting My-Health Record (MHR) style of

system like Australia (Australian Digital Health Agency. 2019) to track individual health specially in global and national health emergency like situation, whether they are COVID-19 positive or negative or have taken the vaccine or not, as it helps in tracking populations public health (Offner et al., 2020; Pavithra & Chandrasekaran, 2021; Wirth, 2020).

6. *Aged-care facilities and services:* In India, even though there is no issue of ageing population, there are many old parents now staying alone due to increase in rise of children moving away from home to other states for jobs, going overseas for education, work or migrating to other countries. Parents are therefore left alone, and they need aged-care and home help. Many private entrepreneurs have realised and taken the business opportunity to start aged-care facilities for the last 15 years in major capital and metro cities for senior citizens of India. All aged-care facilities are privately owned and managed by business entrepreneurs, and a small number by non-government organisations (NGOs) and religious denominations registered as NGOs, providing, aged care needs to the Indian senior citizens as per their income levels. In counties like Thailand and India, due to provision of state-of-the-art medical facilities to medical tourists, in private corporate hospitals, there has also been an increase in retirement tourism from western senior citizens in the last two decades, who do not have private health insurance and for better affordable lifestyle in retirement with house help and state-of-the-art private medical facilities (Medhekar et al., 2019; Scuzzarello, 2020).
7. *Tele-medicine:* In global health pandemic, due to COVID-19 regulations of social distancing mask wearing, and lockdowns, doctors have also switched to provide tele-medicine or ehealth consulting using technology such as phone, skype, or zoom, unless required to see the patients in person. Therefore, South Asian countries can get Australian expertise in cybersecurity of patients personal health data, as to how they have adopted tele-medicine in a global health emergency situation where social distancing is a must to stop the spread of coronavirus (Burke et al., 2019; Pavithra & Chandrasekaran, 2021)
8. *Production of healthcare goods, and medical equipment:* Global health pandemic has not only imposed regulations such as social distancing and lockdowns but also closing borders and grounded airlines and road transport to stop the spread of coronavirus infections (WHO, 2021). This has made countries realise to be self-sufficient, due to the healthcare supply-chain disruptions and shortage of healthcare goods and medical equipment, such as personal protective equipment for frontline staff, gloves, ventilators, oxygen cylinders, beds, and other lifesaving equipment, vaccine test kits, cold storage of medicine, cold-transport, and diagnostic medical machines, where countries have relied on imports from other countries (Bhattacharya, Hossain, & Singh, 2020; Ferrer & Medhekar, 2012; Sharma, Gupta & Jha, 2020).
9. *Production of essential medicines and lifesaving vaccines:* Since March 2021, coronavirus infections and death have risen exponentially in India, and India's public and private healthcare systems are operating at full capacity, with shortages and failure to not being able to cope with the national healthcare disaster and increase the production capacity to meet the demand for vaccines, ventilators, and oxygen cylinders. Even though Serum Institute of India in Pune, is the largest producer of vaccines in the world, it is struggling to produce sufficient vaccines and meet the global and domestic demand for corona-vaccines as India depends on imports of raw materials from USA to make CoviShield vaccine, under licence from AstraZeneca (Menon, 2021). There are supply chain shortages of vaccine, essential life-saving medicines, oxygen cylinders, and ventilators (Aldrighetti et al., 2019; Iyenger et al., 2020; Lee et al, 2013).

10. *Human resources for health:* The importance of having more healthcare professionals per 1000 population has come to the forefront, during the pandemic. In developing countries of South Asia and Africa, there is a severe shortage of doctors, nurses, emergency-care and other allied healthcare staff in the hospitals, clinics of urban, regional, and rural areas. There is now an increasing demand for healthcare professionals and workers at all levels in all developed and developing countries including South Asian economies. Therefore, investment in healthcare workforce post-COVID-19 is essential, as it "not only strengthens the health system, but also generates employment and contributes to economic growth" (Karan et al., 2021, p.1).
11. *Vaccine roll-out strategy:* Australia must depend on other countries like India to import the vaccines. Australia's COVID-19 National vaccine rolls out strategy is in five phases, to the most vulnerable Australians, followed by all the states of Australia. Vaccine is not mandatory, but will be free for all citizens, permanent residents, and all visa-holders. In February 2021, corona- vaccine was given to the quarantine and border workers, frontline healthcare workers, aged-care and disability staff and aged-care residents (Australian Government, 2021). In case of India, even though it is the largest producer of corona-vaccines in the world, there is a large demand and supply gap, resulting in severe shortage of vaccines. By the end of 2021, with 2.2 million doses produced per day, India can vaccinate only 30% of its eligible population (Kanitkar, 2021). Other South Asian countries are also depending on import of vaccine from India and other countries. With a combined South Asian population of nearly 1.8 billion it seems impossible to cover all the population by two doses by the end of 2021. In hindsight, Indian government could have focussed on lockdowns, following strict COVID-19 regulations, vaccinated its frontline healthcare staff, building healthcare capacity in hospitals beds, healthcare human resources, essential healthcare supplies of medical goods, equipment, COVId-19 hospitals, and vaccine production, distribution, and roll-out of the coronavirus vaccine first to the South Asian SAARC countries, which have high density of population, to stop the spread of coronavirus infections, and prevented the tragic second wave of coronavirus, shortages of oxygen, medical equipment ventilators, and resulting disaster and deaths witnessed by the world.

RECOMMENDATIONS AND FUTURE RESEACH DIRECTIONS

World Health Organisation has rightly mentioned, that ensuring affordable and equitable access to vaccines across the word is important, as "With a fast-moving pandemic, no one is safe, unless everyone is safe" (WHO, 2020). Further, as the COVID-19 pandemic's second wave tragedy has unfolded since March 2021, India and South Asian countries cannot be complacent. India is faced with healthcare goods supply chain shortages in critical lifesaving medicines, hospitals with full capacity, shortage of vaccines, oxygen, PPE, surgical masks, hospital beds, ventilators, ambulances, and other medical goods and equipment, that the countries healthcare system is not coping with this increased pressure. Australian Prime Minister Scott Morrison, announced on 17th April 2021 to donate up to 3000 non-invasive ventilators, PPEs for healthcare workers, one million surgical masks, 500,000 P2/N95 masks, 1000 surgical gowns, 100,000 medical goggles, 100,000 pairs of gloves, and 20,000 face shields, tanks, other consumable medical goods, and 1000 oxygen concentrators (Sibel, 2021). Similarly, SAARC member country Pakistan's Prime Minister Imran Khan has also offered medical relief help to cooperate and demonstrate solidarity with the people of India to fight the challenges faced by the pandemic and supply ventilators, digital x-ray machines, Bi-PAPPPEs, and a fleet of 50 ambulances by Edhi Foundation (The Tribune, 2021, April 29). T

It has never been more so important for Australia and the SAARC nations to collaborate in all sectors of the economy and form partnerships for mutual benefit across priority areas such as health, stem cell, vaccine production, digital health, education, science, bio-medical technology and devices, food and water security, information and communication technology, and cybersecurity (Department of Industry, Science, Energy & Resources, 2020). Given the common goal of the world is to keep everyone safe, to produce the vaccine and stop the spread of coronavirus, medical scientists and pharmacists have collaborated in an unprecedented scale to produce the vaccine in shortest possible time in history and save humanity from the pandemic in the 21st century. Coronavirus vaccine invention and innovation must be accompanied with an efficient, effective, and equitable healthcare systems in all countries. South Asian countries need to be ready for any health emergency, develop, produce, acquire, build healthcare and hospital capacity with sustained investment. Countries need to provide equitable access to COVID-19 test, treatment, and corona-vaccine and effectively roll-out the vaccines in an equitable manner to vulnerable population, frontline workers, and nearly two billion people.

Future research should look at how to make healthcare supply chains resilient by taking necessary initiatives cooperatively between Australia and the SAARC region. What lessons can be learnt from COVID-19 supply chain disruptions and vulnerabilities revealed for critical medical supplies, lifesaving drugs, vaccines, PPEs, and regional and international trade in goods and services including travel. Qualitative studies based on stakeholders interviews can be taken, to determine the factors or to build and enhance supply chain resilience with a view to eventually attaining sustainable, inclusive economic development and growth in Australia and the SAARC region. Interviews with healthcare and medical supply chain stakeholders: such as Pharmaceutical sector, medical education sector, to increase supply of medical professionals, doctors, nurses, allied healthcare workers, medical equipment, diagnostic clinical and surgical equipment, oxygen cylinder producers, PPE manufacturers, producers and suppliers of all essential healthcare goods, ambulances, government officials and cold transport owners (road, air, or sea) for lifesaving drugs and vaccines in the region. Similarly general population and medical professionals/healthcare workers and providers can be interviewed or surveyed to find out their experiences during the pandemic related to supply chain shortages and disruptions, hospitals full capacity, shortages of essential lifesaving drugs, oxygen, and vaccines during the peak of the corona crisis in Australia and the SAARC countries.

CONCLUSION

During the pandemic South Asian countries manufacturing sector, exports, and the logistic supply chain took a hard hit due to pandemic related lockdown measures for coronavirus infection control and prevention. The post-pandemic economic recovery is going be difficult, unless proper public health policy actions are taken for preventing the spread of coronavirus, vaccinating the population, and other supportive measures for attracting foreign direct investment in health, pharmaceuticals, medical devises, manufacturing, and healthcare service sectors for economic recovery.

This chapter aims to focus on the opportunities and challenges for health sector bilateral and multilateral partnerships between Australia and the eight (8) South Asian nations which are all member of South Asian Association of Regional Cooperation (SAARC) Afghanistan, Bangladesh, Bhutan, India, Maldives,

Nepal, Pakistan, and Sri Lanka). COVID-19 Pandemic related global public health emergency has forced nations to lockdown, essential shopping, social distancing, and closing borders along with restrictions on trade and travel for business and higher education, tourism, and demand supply gaps, resulting in supply chains bottlenecks in all sectors of the economy including health. Nations of the world and the medical scientific community and pharmaceutical companies put their resources together to discover a vaccine for coronavirus, within a year. Australia thereby needs an alternative strategic bilateral and multilateral coalition with a population of nearly 2 billion of SAARC nations, to find new opportunities for export, trade, investment, innovation in the health sector which will be mutually beneficial to meet the United Nations Sustainable Development Goals (SDGs).

This chapter provides an overview of Australia, India, and other SAARC nations trade and investment strategic cooperation related to health sector. The chapter identified future opportunities and challenges for cooperation and partnership post-COVID-19 investment in medical resources, healthcare human resources, health education and trade in health-related goods and services, and healthcare supply chain cooperation, which will be mutually beneficial to Australia and South Asian nations, with future research directions, and conclusions.

It is important that all the eighth group of the SAARC nations, post COVID-19 commit to meet in a sustainable manner the United Nations Sustainable Development Goals, which are linked to health; (3) Good health and Wellbeing, (9) Industry, Innovation, and Infrastructure, (10), Reducing Inequality, (16) Peace, Justice, and Strong Institutions, and (17) form Partnerships for the Goals under the SAARC umbrella. Finally, India's handling of COVID-19 and being so relaxed during the first wave in June 2020, the beginning of second wave since March 2021, exposed the healthcare systems weakness in terms of being pandemic ready, preparedness, and demonstrates that no country can be complacent regarding global pandemic now and in the future. Developing countries in the SAARC region must cooperate and collaborate in a transparent and accountable manner with developed counties like Australia or Japan, to invest in healthcare in a sustainable manner to build and strengthen their healthcare capacity in medical research and development, healthcare human resources, doctors and nurses, health education, increase the number of diagnostic clinics, oxygen production plants, hospital, beds, doctors, and nurses per 1000 population. Further, given the scarce resources, SAARC nations must increase the percentage of GDP resources investment in education, health, infrastructure, medical research, and medical technology. Post-COVID-19, all eight (8) South Asian nations should have a renewed joint commitment and a common goal under the SAARC umbrella, to not only help each other and share expertise, be self-sufficient in terms of producing pharmaceutical goods for the SAARC region and Australia, and also to have a universally affordable, equally accessible delivery of primary to tertiary healthcare, diagnostic tests, medicine, and vaccinations, for an efficient and effective healthcare system to face any future pandemic like national and global health emergency.

REFERENCES

Aldrighetti, R., Zenmaro, I., Fianco, S., & Battini, D. (2019). Healthcare Supply Chain Simulation with Disruption Considerations: A Case Study from Northern Italy. *Global Journal of Flexible Systems Managment*, *20*(1), S81–S102. doi:10.100740171-019-00223-8

Asialink. (2019). *Where we Live*. Address to Asialink PM Scott Morrison. Retrieved from https://asialink.unimelb.edu.au/stories/australia-and-the-indo-pacific-an-address-by-prime-minister-scott-morrison

Australian Digital Health Agency (ADHA). (2019). *My Health Record.* Retrieved from https://www.myhealthrecord.gov.au/for-you-your-family/what-is-my-health-record

Australian Government. (2021). *COVID-19 Corona Vaccine rollout strategy*. Retrieved from https://www.australia.gov.au/covid19vaccines

Australian Government Medicare. (2021). *Medicare Services in Australia*. Retrieved from https://www.health.gov.au/health-topics/medicare

Basray, R., Malik, A., Waqar, W., Chaudhry, A., Malik, M. W., Kham, M. A., Ansari, J. A., & Ikram, A. (2021). Impact of environmental factors on COVID-19 cases and mortalities in major cities of Pakistan. *Journal of Biosafety and Biosecurity*, *3*(1), 10–16. doi:10.1016/j.jobb.2021.02.001 PMID:33786420

Bhatacharya, S., Hossain, M. M., & Singh, A. (2020). Addressing the shortage of personal protective equipment during the COVID-19 pandemic in India-A public health perspective. *AIMS Public Health*, *7*(2), 223–227. doi:10.3934/publichealth.2020019 PMID:32617351

Bhattacharya, N. (2021, May 18). *China's warning to Bangladesh on the Quad*. Retrieved from https://thediplomat.com/2021/05/chinas-warning-to-bangladesh-on-the-quad/

Bhosale, S. (2018). Why India is Emerging as Australia's Natural Ally. *The Sydney Moring Herald.* Retrieved from https://www.smh.com.au/world/asia/why-india-is-emerging-as-australia-s-natural-ally-20180905-p501yp.html

Bloomberg Economics. (2021, April 28). Australia, Japan, and India form Supply Chain initiative to counter China. *Bloomberg.*

Burke, W., Oseni, T., Jolfraei, A., & Gongal, I. (2019). Cybersecurity Indexes for eHealth. *Proceedings of the Australasian Computer Science Week Multiconference*, 1-18. 10.1145/3290688.3290721

Changoiwala, P. (2020, June 23). *Why South Asia's COVID-19 Numbers Are So Low (For Now).* Retrieved from https://www.quantamagazine.org/why-south-asias-covid-19-numbers-are-so-low-for-now-20200623/

Creswell, J. W. (2014). *Qualitative Inquiry and Research Design: Choosing Among Five Approaches* (3rd ed.). SAGE.

D'Ambrogio, E. (2021). The Quad: An emerging multilateral security framework of democracies in the Indo-Pacific region. *European Parliament Research Services.* Available at https://www.europarl.europa.eu/RegData/etudes/BRIE/2021/690513/EPRS_BRI(2021)690513_EN.pdf

Deccan Herald. (2021, April 1). *India to Counter China's foray in Bay of Bengal with BIMSTEC meet, 5 nation navy drill.* https://www.deccanherald.com/national/india-to-counter-chinas-foray-in-bay-of-bengal-with-bimstec-meet-5-nation-navy-drill-968854.html

Department of Industry, Science, Energy & Resources. (2019). *Collaborating with India on Science and Research*. Retrieved from www.industry.gov.au/funding-and-incentives/science-and-research/collaborating-with-india-on-science-and-research

DFAT. (2020). *Joint Statement on a Comprehensive Strategic Partnership between Republic of India and Australia*. Retrieved from https://www.dfat.gov.au/geo/india/Pages/joint-statement-comprehensive-strategic-partnership-between-republic-india-and-australia

Dhaka Tribune. (2021, April 15). *COVID-19 deaths per million: Bangladesh's rate is third lowest in South Asia*. Retrieved from www.dhakatribune.com/bangladesh/2021/04/15/covid-deaths-per-million-bangladesh-6th-in-s-asia

Dhume, S. (2021, March 8). *India Beats China at Vaccine Diplomacy*. Retrieved from https://www.wsj.com/articles/india-beats-china-at-vaccine-diplomacy-11616086729

Dixit, S. K., & Sambasivan, M. (2018). A review of the Australian healthcare system: A policy perspective. *SAGE Open Medicine*, *6*, 1–14. doi:10.1177/2050312118769211 PMID:29686869

Duckett, S. (2018). Expanding the breadth of Medicare: Learning from Australia. *Health Economics, Policy, and Law*, *13*(3-4).

Ferrer, M. V., & Medhekar, A. (2012). The Factors Impacting on the Management of Global Medical Tourism Service Supply Chain. *Journal of Global Business Review*, *2*(2), 206–211. doi:10.5176/2251-3426_THoR1212

Golechha, M. (2015). Healthcare agenda for the Indian government. *The Indian Journal of Medical Research*, *141*(2), 151–153. doi:10.4103/0971-5916.155541 PMID:25900948

Greg, J. (2021). *Australia joins US, India, and Japan in 'unprecedented' deal for coronavirus vaccines after historic QUAD meeting*. Retrieved from https://www.abc.net.au/news/2021-03-13/QUAD-australia-us-india-japan-in-massive-covid-vaccine-deal/13245198

Hall, I. (2015). Is a 'Modi doctrine' emerging in India's foreign policy? *Australian Journal of International Affairs*, *69*(3), 247–252. doi:10.1080/10357718.2014.1000263

Heath, K. (2011). The classical definition of a pandemic is not elusive. *Bulletin of the World Health Organization*, *89*(7), 540–541. doi:10.2471/BLT.11.088815 PMID:21734771

Iyenger, K. P., Vaishya, R., Bahl, S., & Vaish, A. (2020). Impact of the coronavirus pandemic on the supply chain in healthcare. *British Journal of Healthcare Management*, *26*(6), 1–4. Advance online publication. doi:10.12968/bjhc.2020.0047

Kanitkar, T. (2021, April 25). *COVID-19 vaccine day analysis*. Retrieved from www.firstpost.com/india/covid-19-vaccine-data-analysis-at-current-rate-of-2-2mn-doses-per-day-india-can-only-cover-30-population-by-end-2021-9562811.html

Karan, A., Negandhi, H., Hussain, S., Zapata, T., Mairembam, D., ... Zodpe, S. (2021). Size, composition, and distribution of health workforce in India: Why and where to invest? *Human Resources for Health*, *19*(39), 1–14. doi:10.118612960-021-00575-2 PMID:33752675

Krugman, P. R., Obstfeld, M., & Melitz, M. J. (2020). *International Trade Theory and Policy* (11th ed.). Pearson Education.

Lee, E. V., Ferdinand, P., Benecke, B., Mason, J., & Burel, G. (2013). Advancing Public Health and Medical Preparedness with Operations Research. *Journal on Applied Analytics*, *43*(1), 79–98. Advance online publication. doi:10.1287/inte.2013.0676

Medhekar, A. (2019). Emerging Trends of Wellness and Medical Tourism in India. In S. Paul & S.K. Kulshreshtha (Eds.), Global Developments in Healthcare and Medical Tourism. IGI Global. doi:091218-104208

Medhekar, A. (2021). Australia-India: Bilateral Trade Opportunities and Challenges. In *Emerging Business and Trade Opportunities between Oceania and Asia*. IGI Global Publishing. doi:10.4018/978-1-7998-4126-5.ch004

Medhekar, A., & Kaur, H. (2022). Look-East Act-East Policy: India and South East Asian Economic Cooperation. In A. Medhekar & H. Kaur (Eds.), *Evaluating Trade and Economic Relations Between India and Southeast Asia* (pp. 1–22). IGI Global Publishing., doi:10.4018/978-1-7998-5774-7.ch001

Medhekar, A., Wong, H. Y., & Hall, J. E. (2019). Factors influencing inbound medical travel to India. *Journal of Health Organization and Management*, *33*(2), 155–172. doi:10.1108/JHOM-08-2018-0234 PMID:30950309

Menon, S. (2021, April 29). *India Coronavirus: can it make enough vaccines to meet demand?* Retrieved from https://www.bbc.com/news/world-asia-india-55571793

Ngaibiakching & Pande, A. (2020). India's Act East Policy and ASEAN: Building a Regional Order Through Partnership in the Indo-Pacific. *International Studies, 57*(1), 67-78.

Offner, K. L., Sitnikova, E., Joiner, K., & MacIntyre, C. R. (2020). Towards understanding cybersecurity capability in Australian healthcare organisations: A systematic review of recent trends, threats, and mitigation. *Intelligence and National Security*, *35*(4), 556–585. doi:10.1080/02684527.2020.1752459

Panda, A. (2017, Nov. 13). US, Japan, India, and Australia hold working-level Quadrilateral meeting on regional cooperation: The 'QUAD' is back. *The Diplomat*. Retrieved from https://thediplomat.com/2017/11/us-japan-india-and-australia-hold-working-level-QUADrilateral-meeting-on-regional-cooperation/

Pavithra, V., & Chandrasekaran, J. (2021). Developing Security Solutions for Telemedicine Applications: Medical Image Encryption and Watermarking. In *Research Anthology on Telemedicine Efficacy, Adoption, and Impact on Healthcare Delivery* (pp. 612-631). Retrieved from www.igi-global.com/chapter/developing-security-solutions-for-telemedicineapplications/

Rana, M. (2018). Transformation of Indo-Bangladesh Relations: From Insecurity to Cooperation in Northeast India. *Strategic Analysis*, *42*(6), 559–577. doi:10.1080/09700161.2018.1559976

Ranjan, V. (2016). Australia and India in Asia: When 'Look West' Meets Act East. *Strategic Analysis*, *40*(5), 425–439. doi:10.1080/09700161.2016.1209906

Sajjanhar, A. (2016, May). Taking Stock of India's 'Act East Policy'. *Observer Research Foundation*, (142), 1–6.

Scuzzarello, S. (2020). Practising privilege. How settling in Thailand enables older Western migrants to enact privilege over local people. *Journal of Ethnic and Migration Studies*, *46*(8), 1606–1628. doi:10.1080/1369183X.2020.1711570

Sharma, A. (2021). *The first summit QUAD meeting Reaffirms a free, open, and secure Indo pacific.* Retrieved from https://www.internationalaffairs.org.au/australianoutlook/the-first-summit-QUAD-meeting-reaffirms-a-free-open-and-secure-indo-pacific/

Sharma, A., Gupta, P., & Jha, R. (2020). COVID-19: Impact on Health Supply Chain and Lessons to be Learnt. *Journal of Health Management*, *22*(20), 248–261. doi:10.1177/0972063420935653

Shringla, H. V. (2018). India–Bangladesh Relations: An Indian Perspective. *Strategic Analysis*, *42*(5), 524–528. doi:10.1080/09700161.2018.1523080

Sibal, S. (2021, April 27). Retrieved from https://www.dnaindia.com/world/report-covid-19-crisis-australia-announces-support-pm-scott-calls-situation-heartbreaking-2888102

Smith, A. (1776). *An Inquiry into the nature and causes of the Wealth of Nations.* Retrieved from https://www.econlib.org/library/Smith/smWN.html

Tandon, A. (2016). India's Foreign Policy Priorities and the Emergence of a Modi Doctrine. *Strategic Analysis*, *40*(5), 349–356. doi:10.1080/09700161.2016.1209909

Thakur, R., & Sharma, A. (2018). India in Australia's strategic framing in the Indo-Pacific. *Strategic Analysis*, *42*(2), 69–83. doi:10.1080/09700161.2018.1439328

The Economic Times. (2018). India to increase public health spending. Retrieved from India to increase public health spending to 2.5% of GDP: PM Modi. *The Economic Times.*

The Economic Times. (2021). *Covax says India's serum Institute bound to supply virus vaccines.* Retrieved from https://health.economictimes.indiatimes.com/news/industry/covax-says-indias-serum-institute-bound-to-supply-virus-vaccines/81985191

The World Bank. (2021a). Retrieved from https://data.worldbank.org/indicator/SH.MED.NUMW.P3

The World Bank. (2021b). Retrieved from https://data.worldbank.org/indicator/SH.MED.BEDS.ZS

The World Bank. (2021c). *South Asia.* Retrieved from https://www.worldbank.org/en/region/sar

The World Bank. (2021d). *Current Health Expenditure (% of GDP).* Retrieved from https://data.worldbank.org/indicator/SH.XPD.CHEX.GD.ZS

Trading Economics. (2021a). *Australia Economic Indicators.* Retrieved from https://tradingeconomics.com/australia/gdp

Trading Economics. (2021b). *Afghanistan Economic Indicators.* Retrieved from https://tradingeconomics.com/afghanistan/gdp

Trading Economics. (2021c). *Bangladesh Economic Indicators.* Retrieved from https://tradingeconomics.com/bangladesh/indicators

Trading Economics. (2021d). *Bhutan Economic Indicators*. Retrieved from https://tradingeconomics.com/bhutan/indicators

Trading Economics. (2021e). *India Economic Indicators*. Retrieved from https://tradingeconomics.com/india/indicators

Trading Economics. (2021f). *Maldives Economic Indicators*. Retrieved from https://tradingeconomics.com/maldives/gdp

Trading Economics. (2021g). *Nepal Economic Indicators*. Retrieved from https://tradingeconomics.com/nepal/gdp

Trading Economics. (2021h). *Pakistan Economic Indicators*. Retrieved from https://tradingeconomics.com/pakistan/indicators

Trading Economics. (2021i). *SriLanka Economic Indicators*. Retrieved from https://tradingeconomics.com/sri-lanka/indicators

Tyushka, A. (2019). *Strategic partnerships, international politics, and IR theory*. doi:10.4337/9781788972284.00010

United Nations. (2021e). *Sustainable Development Goals. 17 Goals to transform our world*. Retrieved from https://www.un.org/sustainabledevelopment/ https://sdgs.un.org/goals

Varghese, P. (2018). *Indian Economic Strategy 2035*. Department of Foreign Affairs and Trade. Retrieved from https://dfat.gov.au/geo/india/ies/index.html

WHO. (2020b). *Working for global equitable access to COVID-19 vaccines*. Retrieved from https://www.who.int/initiatives/act-accelerator/covax

WHO. (2021). *Infection prevention and control guidance for long-term care facilities in the context of COVId-19 update*. Retrieved from https://www.who.int/publications/i/item/WHO-2019-nCoV-IPC_long_term_care-2021.1

WHO. (2020a, Jan. 31). *Coronavirus declared global health emergency by WHO*. Retrieved from https://www.bbc.com/news/world-51318246 https://www.who.int/countries/bgd/

Wirth, A. (2020). Cyberinsights: COVID-19 and What It Means for Cybersecurity. *Biomedical Instrumentation & Technology*, *54*(3), 216–219. Advance online publication. doi:10.2345/0899-8205-54.3.216 PMID:32442003

Wojczewski, T. (2019). Identity and world order in India's post-Cold War foreign policy discourse. *Third World Quarterly*, *40*(1), 180–198. doi:10.1080/01436597.2018.1552079

Yhome, K. (2015). From "Look East" to "Act East": What it Means for India's Northeast? *Eastern Quarterly*, *11*(1-2), 18–29.

ADDITIONAL READING

Australia-India Council. (2019). Australia-India Council. Retrieved from dfat.gov.au/people-to-people/foundations-councils-institutes/australia-india-council/governance/Pages/australia-india-council-strategic-plan-2017-2020.aspx

BIMSTEC. (2021). Bay of Bengal Initiatives Multi-Sectoral Technical and Economic Cooperation. Retrieved from https://bimstec.org/

Hall, I. (2015). Is a 'Modi doctrine' emerging in Indian foreign policy? *Australian Journal of International Affairs*, *69*(3), 247–252. doi:10.1080/10357718.2014.1000263

Ollapally, D. M. (2018). How Does India's Look East Policy Look after 25 Years? *Asia Policy*, *13*(2), 146–149. doi:10.1353/asp.2018.0031

Palit, A. (2016). India's Act east Policy and Implications for Southeast Asia. Southeast Asian Affairs, 81-92.

Sarma, A., & Choudhury, S. (Eds.). (2017). *Mainstreaming the Northeast in India's Look and Act East Policy*. Springer. https://link.springer.com/book/10.1007/978-981-10-5320-7

Shani, V. (2009). India's foreign policy: Key drivers. *South African Journal of International Affairs*, *14*(2), 21–35. doi:10.1080/10220460709545493

Sikri, R. (2009). India's "Look East" Policy. *Asia-Pacific Review*, *16*(1), 131–145. doi:10.1080/13439000902957624

Singh, R. (2016, June 21). India's Act East Policy Role of Defence Diplomacy. *South Asia Defence and Strategic Review*, *10*(2), 54.

Ziipao, R. R. (2018). Look/Act East Policy, Roads and Market Infrastructure in North-East India. *Strategic Analysis*, *42*(5), 476–489. doi:10.1080/09700161.2018.1523082

KEY TERMS AND DEFINITIONS

Bilateral Trade Agreement: Bilateral trade agreement is between two countries when they decide to mutually reduce trade barriers, which leads to specialisation and increases allocative and productive efficiency and consumers income. Bilateral trade agreement can also be between two unions such as European Union (EU) and OECD; EU and Balkan Countries; EU and Gulf Cooperation council countries (GCCC) Bahrain, Kuwait, Oman, Qatar, Saudi Arabia, and the United Arab Emirates.

Cybersecurity Risk: Measures taken by an organsiation such as banks, hospitals, universities, schools, businesses, governments, and individuals to protect their own computer or computer systems in an organsiation as a whole from internet hackers, malwares, or cyber-attacks.

Digital Health Technology: Digital health technology also known as e-health technology is convergence of digital technologies and internet with healthcare records and reports, mobile-phones, apps, tablets, and computer vis the internet to improve people's health and maximise impact. Digital health helps to enhance efficiency in healthcare service delivery for effective and positive healthcare outcomes, providing personalized and precise healthcare plan.

Global Health Crisis: Global health crisis is defined as a health emergency crisis such as an epidemic or a pandemic occurring across international borders, where transmission takes place simultaneously worldwide, affecting many people such as SARS virus, Ebola, and Coronavirus.

Multilateral Trade Agreement: Multilateral trade agreement is between many countries or group of countries, who see opportunities to export their goods within the member countries in the group, moving towards liberalising world trade, where countries gain from free trade.

Strategic Partnerships: Strategic partnerships defined as a long-term collaboration between two countries based on either political, economic, health, education, defence, security, trade, and investment factors. For example, India has signed comprehensive strategic partnership with Australia and other 30 countries.

Sustainable Development: Sustainable development is defined as a development activity that uses the scarce economic resources in a sustainable manner to meet the needs of the present people to achieve the United Nations 17- SDGs, without compromising the ability of the future generations to meet their needs. That is building an inclusive, sustainable, and resilient future for the people on Earth. The Sustainable Development concept was introduced in 1987 by United Nations and is defined as any economic development programs which is capable to manage and utilise scare resources presently to maintain social, economic, and environmental sustainably to meet the needs of the future generations.

Chapter 2
Australia's Bilateral and Multilateral Partnership With South Asian Nations:
Opportunities and Challenges in the Transitioning Energy Sector

Sreeparna Saha
Central Queensland University, Australia

ABSTRACT

This chapter aims to investigate the potential cooperation between Australia and the SAARC nations to facilitate generation and distribution of energy to better manage this sector and fulfil their commitments towards climate change conditions. As carbon emissions from non-renewables severely threatened the climate conditions, an effective transition to renewable resources is essential. In the Paris Agreement, Australia and SAARC nations committed to reduce their individual carbon emissions. But the SAARC lag in their commitments as they fail to unleash renewables and rely on fossil fuel. Australia leads in renewables, and SAARC provides a large market for it to relate services and technologies and improve energy efficiency and competitiveness. This chapter investigates the opportunities for strategic collaboration between these nations; challenges of energy trading, energy security, inefficient institutions, volatile prices and investment flows, collaborative capacity generation and distribution; and analyses comparative advantages for the countries to have mutually beneficial agreements to meet UNSDGs of affordable clean energy and climate action.

INTRODUCTION

Traditional fossil fuels such as coal, natural gas, and oil have geared the path of economic growth, so much for so long that the overutilization of these non-renewable energy resources led to excessive carbon emissions bringing climate challenges to the forefront of sustainable development agenda. The challenge

DOI: 10.4018/978-1-7998-8657-0.ch002

now is to prevent the global temperature from reaching an alarming height due to the greenhouse effect, in which heat gets trapped close to the earth's surface by the greenhouse gases (GHG that includes carbon dioxide, methane, and nitrous oxides). This has been significantly changing the world's climate, heavily disrupting environmental, societal, and economic sustainability, and propelling research towards an improved understanding of the problem and plausible policy solutions. Following the Paris Agreement (2016) and the United Nations Climate Change Conference (2021), countries all over the world have been impelled into collaborations and techniques to manage in reducing GHG to attain their commitment towards a low emission future. This chapter aims to focus on the opportunities and challenges of bilateral and multilateral partnerships between Australia and the eight (8) South-Asian nations which are all members of the South-Asian Association of Regional Cooperation (SAARC), namely Afghanistan, Bangladesh, Bhutan, India, Maldives, Nepal, Pakistan, and Sri Lanka, to mutually help in transitioning energy sector for a sustainable future.

According to the US National Aeronautics and Space Administration (NASA), nineteen of the warmest years have occurred since 2000, with 2020 being recorded as the warmest year since the beginning of record-keeping in 1880. The National Centres for Environmental Information (NCEI, 2021) reported that the global surface temperature for the January-June 2021 period was the eighth highest on the 142-year record, with global surface temperature in June 2021 alone recorded to be 0.88°C warmer than that of the 20th-century average. The occurrence of continuous warming and climate conditions are leading to frequent and intense natural disasters globally and putting the risk of extinction on the 3 billion world population living in areas that are too hot for humans by 2070 (Regan, 2020). Immediate and appropriate action is now an essential cornerstone of the sustainable development framework, which calls for international collaborations in investment, technology, services, and education to tackle these growing concerns.

Among the four fundamental economic sectors (energy; agriculture, forestry, and land use; industry; and waste) that contribute the most to GHG productions, energy tops the list (contribution from electricity, heat, industry, and transportation) and drives primary attention in finding an effective transition for its sources. Figure 1 below captures the distribution of GHG emissions by economic sectors. This chapter aims to investigate the scopes for strategic partnerships in the alternative energy sector between the developed economy of Australia and the developing economies of SAARC nations. Australia, with a land area of 7,682,300 km^2, population density of 3.3 persons per km^2 and an abundance of renewable to fossil fuel resources, has been witnessing an impressive reduction in sectoral energy consumption in recent years owing to its rapid progress in technologies. Australia also has an impressive electricity interconnection system as it operates and manages its national electricity market, the longest interconnected power system in the world. However, while its abundant renewable energy resources such as solar, wind, and tidal are still underutilised, coal and natural gas remain its major export earners. The South-Asian economies are undergoing economic expansion, and are struggling with their high population density, increasing energy consumption, shortage of energy resources and lagging energy exploration capability. Australia benefits from Indian and South-Asian human and manufacturing resources adding value to its energy sector from mines to energy regulations. It also attracts investments for Australian mining and mineral processing and earns from exporting mining products to these nations. It is thus essential to explore how Australia can find new markets for trade, investment, international education and business opportunities for its resources, services, manufacturing, and technology sectors in South Asian countries and vice versa.

Figure 1. Distribution of GHG emission by economic sectors
Source: Our World in Data

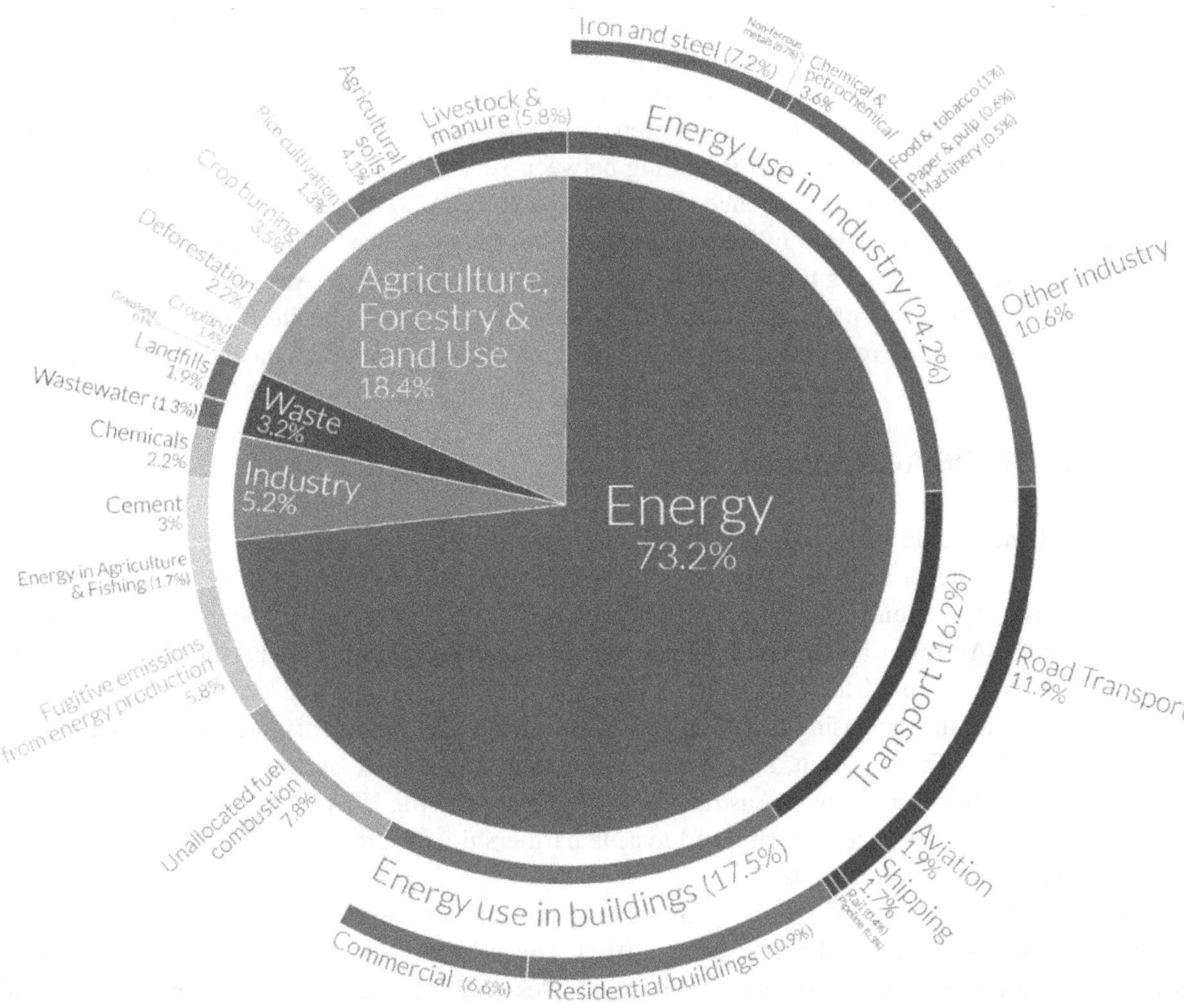

The energy sector aims to lower GHG emissions to prevent the increase of global average temperature to well below 2^{0}C above the pre-industrial levels. It would significantly shrink the risks of further climate degradations where countries need adjustability to the already changed climates by fostering climate resilience, developing low-cost, low-emission technologies of modern energy - essential to reach the United Nations Sustainable Development Goal (SDG) 7. But this needs heavy investments in technologies and research. The COVID-19 pandemic has slowed down the economic growth of nations and diverted the focus from climate resilience strategies to the recovery from the health crisis. The pandemic made it even harder for South-Asian developing economies to surge the necessary flow of investments as the region's GDP shrank from 3.1% in 2019 to -8.6% in 2020. As contrasted to the forecasted GDP growth of 5.1% in 2019 where the region was almost at per with SDG 7, all South-Asian economies have been severely impacted by the pandemic owing to an amplified and accelerated impact of existing vulnerabilities and in challenges to restore the global value chains (GVCs) (see Jian, 2021 for details). The pandemic made

2020 tough for Australia as well with a fall in GDP of 1.1% during 2020 but its renewable energy sector's incredible progress continued to provide hope for the nations climate change target (CEC, 2020).

Countries around the world are deepening their understanding of the renewable energy sector and funding innovative technologies and projects but still struggling to pace up to their commitment to reducing greenhouse gas productions since the intermittent supply of wind, solar and water poses severe challenges for an efficient transition from non-renewables to renewables. The two broad questions are: how any bilateral and multilateral energy trading between Australia and the SAARC nations be mutually beneficial? What additional challenge such trade would bring to these nations? This chapter aims to find answers to these questions by putting light on the energy scenarios in SAARC nations and in Australia, and then by assessing the trade possibilities. It will explore how Australia can find efficient new markets for trade, investment, international knowledge sharing, and business opportunities for its energy resources, services, manufacturing, and technology sectors in South-Asia and vice versa.

RELATED TRADE AGREEMENTS

Australia and India have been progressing on strengthening bilateral partnerships and signed nine rounds of negotiations for a Comprehensive Economic Cooperation Agreement (CECA) between 2011 and 2015. This cooperation further strengthened with the Australian prime minister's visit to India in 2017, followed by Australia-India Joint Statement on a Comprehensive Strategic Partnership Agreement (AI-JS-CSPA) in 2020 on thirteen key areas including energy, technology, and knowledge partnerships (DFAT, 2020). With the increasing maritime power of China and boundary disputes in the South China Sea, East China Sea, Taiwan Strait, Indo-Pacific region and The Bay of Bengal, India is collaborating in a navy meeting and exercise with Australia, France, Japan, and the USA as held in April-May 2021, exhibiting multilateral defence, security, and marine partnership, towards a free and open Indo-pacific region (Deccan Herald, 1-April-2021).

However, India's remarkable economic growth and primacy are somewhat subject to a peaceful and stable relationship with its neighbours (Rana, 2018). Towards that, India signed various multilateral partnerships with its East-Asian neighbours which includes (a) the 'South Asian Free Trade Agreement' (SAFTA) with neighbouring Bhutan, Bangladesh, Maldives, Nepal, Pakistan and SriLanka; (b) a 'Long Term Cooperative Partnership for Peace and Prosperity' with ASEAN countries (in 2009), (c) India-ASEAN Free Trade Agreement (AI-FTA) for partnership in the economic, political, and socio-cultural initiative (in 2010), (d) 'Bay of Bengal Initiatives Multi-Sectoral Technical and Economic Cooperation' (BIMSTEC) headquarters in Bangladesh with seven member countries India, Nepal, Bhutan, SriLanka, Myanmar, and Thailand. In 2014, the Indian government's Act-East foreign policy extends beyond ASEAN to Australia, New Zealand, and Japan without territorial motives, but multilateral strategic cooperation, national border and maritime security, trade, investment, and economic developmental partnerships (see for example Ngaibiakching & Pande, 2020; Wojczewski, 2019). The 'Australia and India 2020 comprehensive strategic partnership', that focuses on twelve key areas for commitment to cooperation and partnership for security, economic development, peace, and prosperity can be extended to all the SAARC nations, towards achieving SDG 7 affordable and clean energy; SDG 9 industry, innovation, and infrastructure; SDG 10 reducing Inequality; SDG 13 climate actions; SDG 16 peace, justice and strong institutions; SDG 17 Partnerships for the Goals. Considering the current energy scenario in Australia and SAARC nations, the broad scopes for mutually beneficial energy trade following COVID-19 can be outlined as below:

1. *Mitigating the massive technology gap* - Australia shows rapid progress in modern technologies supporting the production, storage, and distribution of non-renewable resources (2253 Megawatt of capacity generation from 34 completed renewable energy projects in 2019 (CEC, 2020), yet remains hostile to the price fluctuations. The developing South-Asian nations are trying to catch up with the transitional energy markets, yet are lagging far behind, mostly due to their massive population size that led their demand for energy to outperform domestic supply, often highly inefficient policy interventions, volatile price signals resulting in lack of investment incentives (DFAT, 2018; Pyper, 2021).
2. *Exploring India's competitive advantage* - India, the world's second-largest coal-producing and consuming nation, and the third-largest emitter of GHG, showcase promising growth in low-cost solar and wind-based electricity generation (large-scale approaches that combine grid and off-grid electrification for greater energy access, microgrid and rooftop solar systems) from renewable resources (Pyper, 2021). COVID-19 has put a halt in the upswing of the renewable energy market in India but potentially it is to be the largest market for renewables, not only because of the economies of scale it offers but also for its geographically central location that shares borders with other SAARC nations, making it ideal for interconnected power systems. Pakistan, Bangladesh, Bhutan, and Sri Lanka showcase intermittent but promising progress, witnessing the South-Asian region's massive potential for the renewable industry. However, the challenges are not only in terms of non-equitable production and consumption dependence at the national and regional levels but also in the institutionalisation of the energy policies (Shukla et al., 2017).
3. *Alternative market for the Australian energy sector* - Following the recent geopolitical turmoil of China and the USA, Australia's traditional mining and energy sectors have faced the heat of reduced international demand and stringent trade policies. Australia needs alternative strategic bilateral and multilateral collaborations that provide new opportunities for trade, investment, innovation, and knowledge sharing in all sectors including the transitioning energy sector. The SAARC nations provide a large market (nestling nearly 2 billion people) for related services and technologies to improve energy efficiency and the commitment to renewables (DIIS, 2019, IEA 2020). This possibility of mutually beneficial collaborations and partnerships align with the SDGs for a sustainable future.

RESEARCH METHODOLOGY

A secondary source of information from various refereed articles, organisations home pages such as SAARC and CEC, current news and statistical databases were examined to collect the data for this qualitative descriptive review.

Table 1. Demographic distribution and share in the world's population

Rank	Member Nation	Population (2021)	Share in Total World Population (in %)
1	India	1,393,409,038	17.88
2	Pakistan	225,199,937	2.89
3	Bangladesh	166,303,498	2.13
4	Afghanistan	39,835,428	0.51
5	Nepal	29,674,920	0.38
6	Sri Lanka	21,497,310	0.28
7	Bhutan	779,898	0.01
8	Maldives	543,617	0.01

Source: Numbers adapted from World Population Review

AN OVERVIEW OF THE ENERGY SCENARIO IN THE SAARC NATIONS

The southern region of the Asian continent that comprised of sub-Himalayan countries, covers around 3% of the world's total area and contains approximately 24% of the world's total population. In 1985, the seven traditional countries, namely Bangladesh, Bhutan, India, Maldives, Nepal, Pakistan, and Sri Lanka established a regional intergovernmental platform – SAARC – to promote regional integration and economic development, in which Afghanistan joined later in 2007. Demographically, India dominates the region with a population of 1.39 billion. Table 1 summarises the demographic distribution of SAARC nations.

Apart from its demography South Asia is one of the most important regions in terms of its significantly excess energy demand owing to its limited access to refined fuels, thin grid reliability, distorted energy prices and weighty import dependence. Interestingly, the region has nations with contrasting economic profiles, energy consumption patterns and portfolios, yet commonly have low economic diversity, accelerating demand for energy projected to grow at more than double of the world over the coming decades (IEA, 2020). According to the World Development Indicators database, the region's accumulative nominal GDP share accounted for only 4% of the world's total GDP, where 14% of the region's population (225 million people) lacks electricity connection. The problem is deep-rooted with distorted utilisation of capacity, weak policy formulation and implementation which is hindering the social and economic development, costing the region 4 -7% of its GDP. However, according to SAARC Energy Outlook 2030, each country's usage varies with its availability, access, underlying geopolitics, commercial and economic viability, available technologies for the exploration of energy and the level of energy trading.

Energy is essential to all aspects of modern society and investment alone is insufficient to restore efficiency in this sector. Following, the region's power crisis is attributable to three types of distortions: (1) institutional, stemming from the uncontested government ownership, soft-budget constraints, and privileged supply, under which governments have frequently bailed out heavily indebted utilities; (2) regulatory, stemming from subsidies, cross-subsidies between consumer groups, and the mispricing of coal, gas, and electricity; and (3) social, stemming from the negative externalities of energy production and consumption (for example, impacts on health, climate change, gender inequality) and provision of heavily subsidized electricity to farmers for pumping water that incentivises water-intensive farming

Table 2. Economic cost of power sector distortions

Member Nations	Loss From Power Sector Distortions		Largest Source of Economic Cost			The Environmental Cost of Black Carbon From Kerosene Lighting	The Net Social Benefit Measured in Terms of the Opportunity Cost
	In Billion $	Share in GDP (%)	Source	Loss in Billion $	Share in GDP (%)		
Bangladesh	11.2	5.0	Under-pricing of gas	4.5	2	$ 0.6 million	$345 million
India	86.1	4.1	Environmental externality from extreme coal use	35.4	1.7	$ 6.4 billion	$35.4 billion in India
Pakistan	17.7	6.5	Unreliable access to electricity	12.9	4.8	$ 2.1 million	no data

Source: Prepared by the author with numbers adapted from World Development Indicators database and Zhang (2019)

causing the depletion of groundwater. The estimated cost of these distortions is significant to the nations. Table 2 summarises the costs to the three largest economies of SAARC, Bangladesh, India and Pakistan that accounted for 98% of the regional energy supply, between 2015-2016.

Economic distortions have resulted in smaller-than-world-average energy consumption per capita in this region. Figure 2 below shows the nation wise per capita energy consumption, where electricity consumption per capita captures the average kilowatt-hours (kWh) of electricity demanded per person in respective nations. Notably, it's lowest in Afghanistan, which suffers from severe inaccessibility of clean energy even for basic household activities such as cooking and heating.

Figure 3 captures the national share of fossil fuel in generating electricity. It shows while the Maldives are entirely dependent on exported fuel for electricity, all other nations except Bhutan (100% electricity generated by hydropower) are heavily reliant on fossil fuels for electricity generation.

This low energy consumption and generation are reflected through the low economic complexities of the nations and their well-being. Although the region showcases impressive economic growth, it's asymmetric as captured in Figure 4 where per capita GDP growth in Afghanistan and Nepal (both having

Figure 2. Per capita energy consumption of the SAARC nations
Source: Katekar et. al. 2021

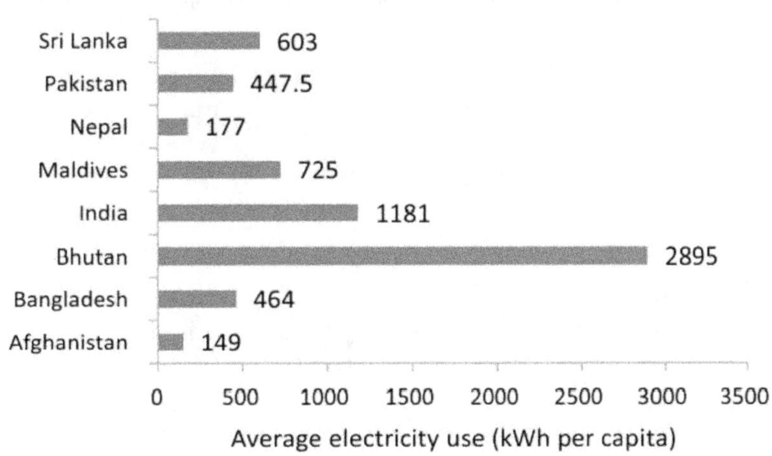

Figure 3. SAARC nations' share of fossil fuel in electricity generation
Source: Katekar et. al. 2021

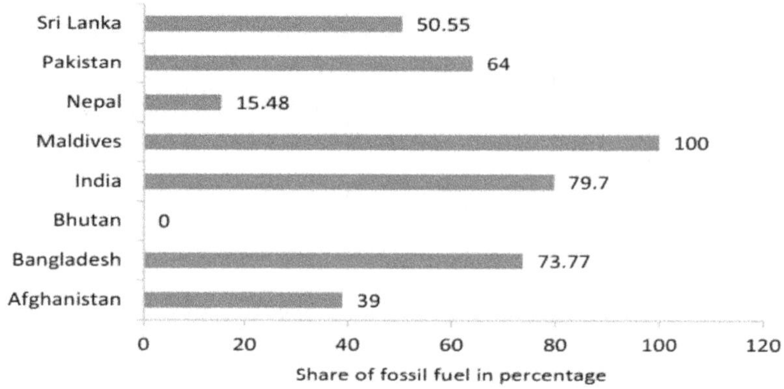

lower consumption of energy) are considerably smaller than other nations (relative to their respective population share reflected in Table 1).

The chapter now investigates the national energy demand-supply disparity by looking at each member nation's energy scenarios to understand the scopes of bilateral and multilateral trade practices:

Afghanistan

Afghanistan is one of the least developed nations in the world with the fourth-largest population among the SAARC nations. Presently, 35% of the country is electrified while only 10% of the rural households have access to electricity (SAARC Energy Centre, 2018). Household demand for energy is primarily fulfilled by firewood, charcoal, kerosene, candles, biogas, agricultural and animal wastes. The overall electricity generation is 519 MW, much lower than other member nations. In the primary energy mix, hydropower contributes the highest (49%) while thermal gas and oil contribute 39% and distributed generators add up to the rest of 12% (Ahmadzai & McKinna, 2018).

Figure 4. Growth rates of per capita real GDP for the SAARC nations
Source: Nepal-India Data (https://nepalindata.com/insight/growth-rates-of-real-gdp-by-saarc-countries/)

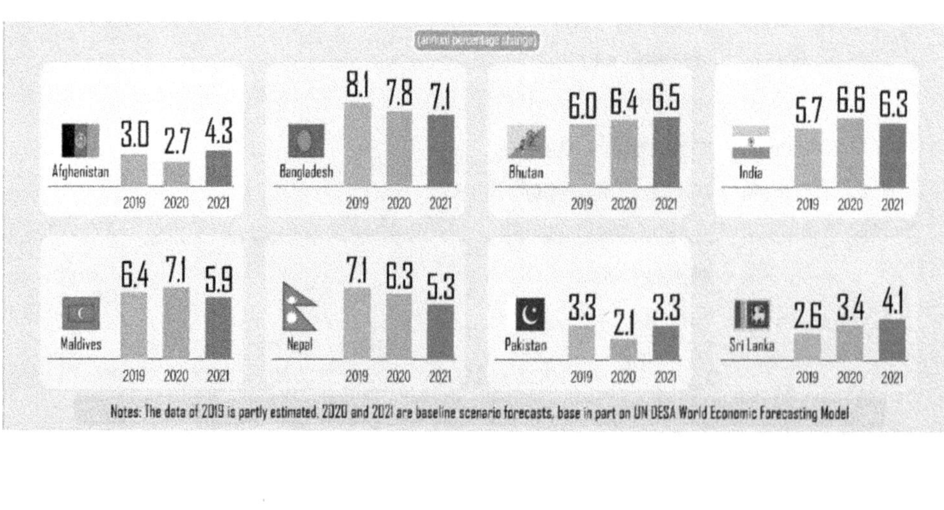

Current Demand

The current per capita electricity consumption is pitiable owing to its lack of demand from the industrial, household, transportation, and agriculture sector. Its energy demand is predominantly import-dependent with around 80% of the fossil fuels are being imported, putting an enormous burden on its economy. Reportedly, the demand for energy is estimated to rise to 3500 MW in 2032, which can certainly be fulfilled with the nation's available energy potential, if supported by organised planning (Katekar et. al., 2021).

Current Generation

The country's current potential lies in 23 GW of hydropower, 67 GW of wind power, 222 GW of solar power and 36.4 trillion of estimated natural gas resources (Katekar et. al., 2021). The government has initiated projects for shorter-term imports of energy and developed resource-based power using renewable resources (Farabi-Asl, 2019).

Bangladesh

Bangladesh has shown a ramping economic growth in the pre-COVID scenario, with a compounded annual growth rate (CAGR) of more than 6.6% from the fiscal year 2013 to 2019. Its government is ambitious to reach the status of a high-income country by 2041, which needs poverty alleviation programs, improvement in the health sector and massive infrastructure development, which certainly calls for greater energy generation and energy security. While sound and efficient policies and government intervention are required for its development, considering its current resource scarcity and GHG emissions, this demands heavy private sector investment and technological advancement.

Current Demand

The current total energy consumption in Bangladesh is around 47 MTOE per year, and the demand is rising continuously at a rate of 6% per year (Katekar et. al., 2021). While rapid urbanisation and social development increase the national demand for energy, its generation capacity is falling short, thereby making the energy sector import-dependent. Almost all major fuels namely, coal, crude oil, petroleum products, gas, and electricity, Bangladesh imports more than half of its required energy, especially for petroleum products (accounts for around 6.6 million metric tons per year) and crude oil, its import share is significantly high (see SAARC Energy Centre, 2018). The Ministry of Power, Energy and Mineral Resources reports that as of 2019, the consumption of coal and imported liquefied natural gas (LNG) is steadily increasing and expecting to almost double by 2025 as compared to their 2015 levels.

Current Generation

The total installed capacity of Bangladesh is 15,559 MW as per the fiscal year 2018 and its per capita generation of electricity is 464 kWh, where 90% of households access electricity (SAARC Energy Centre, 2018). In the primary energy mix, natural gas and biomass contribute the most – 49.2% and 34.6% respectively, petroleum contributes around 15.6% wherein coal and hydro contribute the least – only 0.4% and 0.3% respectively (Katekar et. al., 2021). Large scale renewable power generation is negligible

Figure 5. Installed capacity growth in Bangladesh
Source: SAARC Energy Centre (2018)

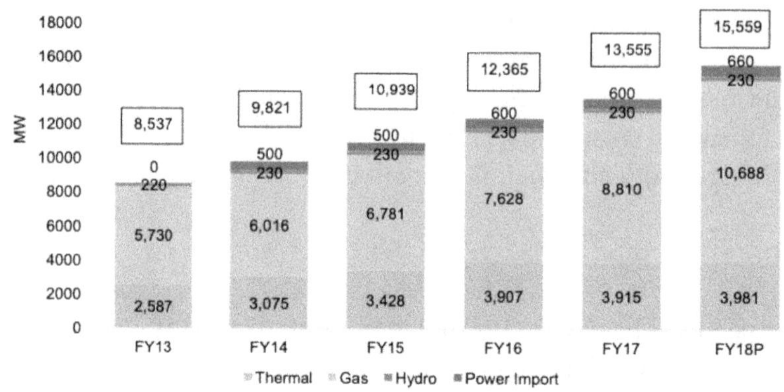

in the country. The Ministry of Power, Energy and Mineral Resources reports that as of 2019 while the domestic gas production is depleting continuously, the electricity generation from home solar systems is increasing - current contribution reached 325 MW (Adnan et. al., 2018). The government is promoting the use of clean stoves for energy-efficient cooking purposes that already gained momentum with one million installations in 2017 and expected to install another 4 million by 2022 and 30 million by 2030 (Government of the people's Republic of Bangladesh, 2012). Figure 5 below captures the growth of installed capacity:

The Government is progressing towards its target of 100% rural electrification by the end of 2022 and has taken initiatives to fulfil it. These are resulting in the generation and use of renewable energy with subsidised price and tariff schemes and includes generation of electricity by Bio-Mass Gasification methods and by utilisation of rice husks.

Bhutan

Both economy-wise and population-wise, Bhutan is one of the smallest nations in SAARC, but it is in a leading position when it comes to the progress of generation and utilisation of efficient energy resources. Currently, 99.5% of Bhutan's power generation comes from hydropower resources and the rest they import from neighbouring nations, primarily from India. Bhutan generates electricity for 100% of its households and exports the additional generation. However, Katekar et. al. (2021) reports that from 2008 onwards a disproportionate fall in the export demand is consistently raising the gap between total domestic electric generation and exports, causing losses to its economy.

Current Demand

More than the three-quarter share of Bhutan's overall power demand comes from its industrial sector only, followed by the building sector (among the residential, commercial, and institutional buildings, more than half the demand for power comes from the residential sector). While Liquified Petroleum Gas (LPG), electricity and firewood are predominantly demanded by the urban and rural households, it is expected that their demand will significantly rise by 2035 along with the demand for coal (expected to grow by

Figure 6. Installed capacity growth in Bhutan as compared to power sales
Source: SAARC Energy Centre (2018)

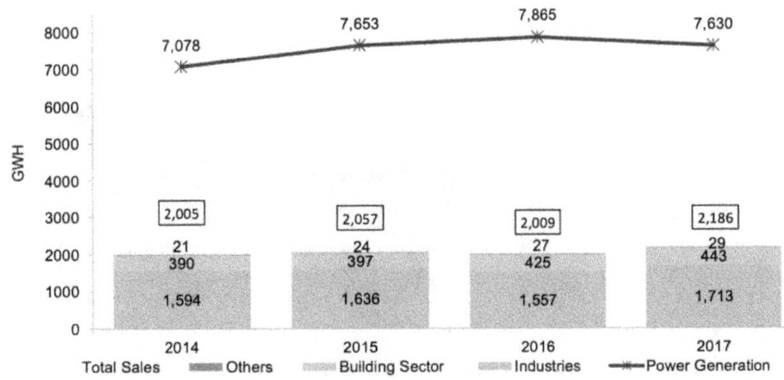

11.6% predominantly following the growth in industries, which are largest consumers) and petroleum oil (expected to grow by 9.9% following the demand rise in the transport sector) (IRENA, 2019). However, the overall growth of demand is rather sluggish. With no major fossil fuel reserves except one minor coal reservoir, for most of its fossil fuel needs - primarily from the industrial and building sectors – it is dependent on imports. India is the prime importer for Bhutan when it comes to Petroleum Oil products (Petrol, Diesel, Kerosene, LPG, Fuel Oil), where they are consumed by all economic sectors in Bhutan with no significant domestic petroleum production (SAARC Energy Centre, 2018).

Current Generation

Bhutan's power generation is almost exclusively dependent on hydropower with a present installed hydropower capacity of 1615 MW (Alam et. al., 2017). The government targets to develop an additional 20 MW of energy using renewables during the fiscal years 2020-25 (Department of Renewable Energy B, 2016). Bhutan is successfully delivering 100 units of free electricity per month to each of its rural households. Progressive programs such as the Bhutan Biogas Project (BBP) and Bhutan Sustainable Rural Biomass Energy (BSRBE) are being launched to promote biogas and improved cookstoves as clean cooking fuel in those areas (Katekar et. al. 2021).

India

In terms of economy, geographical size and population, India is the largest among the SAARC member nations, which has shown a steady growth at a compounded annual growth rate (CAGR) of more than 6.5% over the past five fiscal years. There is a steady growth in demand for energy – driven by the growing needs of both households and industries, coupled with the surge in investment flows from both domestic and foreign sources, that aided the pace of this country's growth. Although for energy generation, the primary reliance of the country is still on its traditional fossil fuels (primarily Coal), conductive government policies and significant private investments strongly indicate the country's intentions to improve its renewable energy supplies in near future. According to the SAARC Energy Outlook 2030, India's primary energy consumption will increase to 1,392 million tonnes of oil equivalent (MTOE) in fiscal 2030 from 817 MTOE in fiscal 2018, growing at a CAGR of 4.5% (SAARC Energy Centre, 2018).

Figure 7. Installed capacity growth of India
Source: SAARC Energy Outlook (2018)

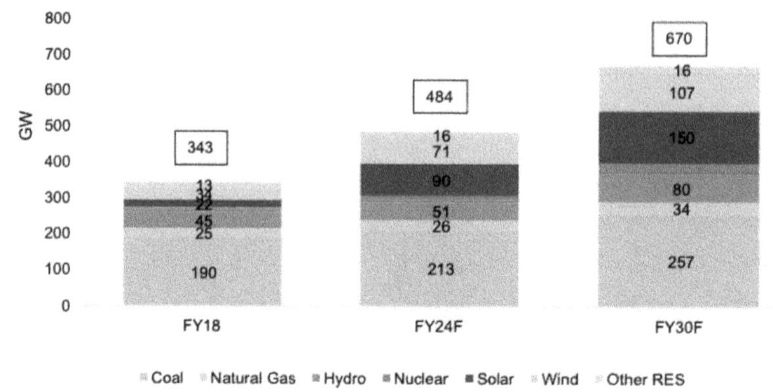

Current Demand

India showcases a below-average per capita electricity consumption as compared to the world average. Figure 2 indicates that the per capita electricity consumption in India is 1,181 kWh, well below the world average of 3,200 kWh. According to the DFAT (2018b) report, as all four major energy-consuming sectors, i.e., industry, household, transport, and agriculture will demand more energy to feed their growth, demand for electricity (constitutes 15% of final energy consumption) is forecasted to grow at a rate of 5.8% per annum. Traditionally, as India has been domestically producing the two largest sources of its energy – coal and biomass – the course has been allowing for an autarkic approach to the country's energy policy. But with India's strategic interest in sustainable energy solutions and uptake in technologies to adopt renewable energy resources, energy is becoming one of the most dynamic sectors and is attracting global interest. However, the demand is geographically asymmetric in India – while on the one hand rapid urban growth hikes the demand for transportation and household energy consumption, on the other hand, nearly 304 million population lacks access to electricity and 800 million lacks access to clean energy to perform basic household activities.

Current Generation

Power supply in India has increased by 345 BU between the fiscal years of 2013 to 2018, which reflects a growth rate of 5.6% CAGR, reducing the base energy deficit. As of 2018, the total installed capacity of the country is 342.7 Gigawatt (GW) and expected to rise 41.11% by the end of the fiscal year 2024. Figure 7 below captures the projected growth of installed capacity contributed by the primary energy mix, i.e., coal, natural gas, hydro, nuclear, solar, wind and other renewable sources.

However, demand for energy outpaced the supply to a large extent - imported crude oil and natural gas fulfil nearly 70% of its primary energy demand (see SAARC Energy Centre, 2018 and Katekar et. al., 2021). While coal continues to contribute more than half (58.1%) to the primary energy mix, nuclear contributes the least (1.2%) in it. Following India's commitment to lower emissions future in Paris agreement towards sustainable energy mix, it is progressing towards reaching its goal of electricity capacity with 65% of non-fossil fuel resources (hydro, nuclear, solar, wind and biomass) that requires 540.32 GW of installed capacity (NITI, Aayog & IEEJ, 2017). Reportedly in the shorter term, the forward strategic plan of the government and private investments are aiming to achieve 175 GW of installed capacity of renewable energy, universal electrification of all households, and a 10% decline in oil and gas imports by 2022.

Maldives

The Maldives, with the smallest population share among the SAARC members, has been witnessing a real GDP growth of above 6% CAGR over the last five years with a little sluggishness raised out of CO-VID- 19 pandemic. The energy needs are primarily driven by the nation's growth in the tourism sector, public infrastructure, and construction sector. While providing 100% electricity to all its households, the absence of traditional fossil fuel resources makes it completely dependent on imported fossil fuels to meet energy requirements.

Current Demand

The Maldives continues to have a strong demand for energy from its transportation (sea and road), infrastructure and tourism sectors, boosting the primary demand for energy. The SAARC Energy Centre (2018) forecasts that the energy consumption in this group of islands is to increase by more than 105% in 2030 as compared to its 2017 level. Maldives Customs Services (2019) report that in 2019 alone, Maldives imported 723,000 tons of refined petroleum products among which, diesel accounted for 80%, petrol accounted for 12%, aviation fuel accounted for 6%, and LPG accounted for 2% of the imports. The demand for cooking fuel across the islands is being met by a mix of kerosene, LPG, diesel and gasoline.

Current Generation

The share of imported fossil fuel in Maldives's energy mix is astronomical - about 10% of its GDP, which puts pressure on the economy's finances. Maldives Customs Service data suggests that from January to June 2021, Maldives imported petroleum products worth USD$38.29 million, which is an increase of 37.5% from January to June 2020 levels. However, sufficient private investments can lower the costs of fuel imports and electricity production by exploiting its underutilised abundant renewable energy resources, i.e., solar, wind, and ocean. A study by Asian Development Bank (2020) reports that by 2020, a total of 454 MW of diesel generators and 21.5 MW of renewable energy systems have been installed across the country. The report also suggests that the supportive programs are fuelling the country's transition to fuel efficiency and expected that it will achieve its target of 70% of maximum electricity day demand in inhabited islands to be generated from renewables, while at least 20% of maximum electricity day demand in the Greater Male' Region by 2023.

Nepal

Nepal's economy has witnessed a significant rebound from a growth rate of 0.4% in 2016 to around 6.9% in 2017, continued to maintain an impressive growth rate up until 2021, which witnessed a relatively slower growth rate owing to the economic impacts of COVID-19. The growth of its industrial and construction sectors is gearing up its demand for energy mix, whereas traditional fuel continues to dominate its total primary energy requirements.

Figure 8. Installed capacity growth in Nepal
Source: SAARC Energy Outlook (2018)

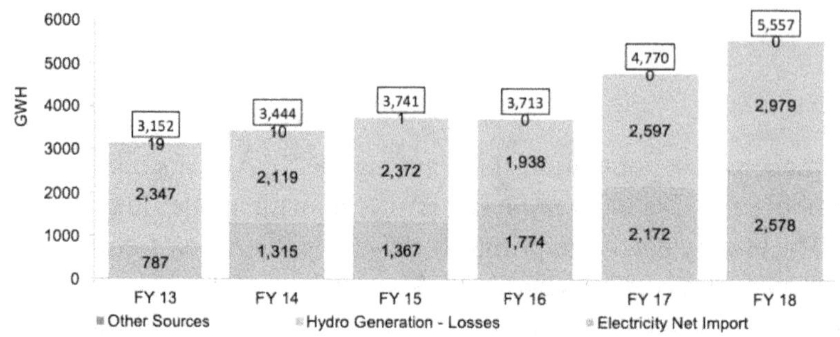

Current Demand

Nepal's energy demand consists of the demand for traditional fuels, imported coal and petroleum products (POL) such as diesel, petrol, and LPG. The demand for electricity comes from industrial and household (for lighting and heating) sectors and is mostly met by its hydropower resources, constituting about 95% of its total energy generation. For cooking and other domestic activities, traditional biomass (in rural areas), fuelwood, kerosene, LPG (mostly by high-income households) are demanded (Lam et. al., 2017). For transportation, it consumes imported petroleum products at a very large scale which puts a heavy burden on its economy.

Current Generation

The installed capacity of hydropower assets is only about 2% of its total potential of 43,000 MW which, if developed, can serve the increasing domestic energy demand, and provide electricity to 40% of the population who do not have access to it. Presently, Nepal's government has accelerated the development of this abundant potential not only to help accelerate its economic and social growth but also to endow revenue generation from exporting the excess energy to neighbouring countries (for detail, see Asian Development Bank, 2017 & Katekar et. al., 2021). Figure 8 below highlights the total power generation in Nepal where hydropower plants' system losses are subtracted from their generation.

SAARC Energy Centre (2018) reports that Nepal's installed capacity of hydropower plants, thermal power plants and grid-connected solar is 1,020 MW, 53.41 MW and 100 KW respectively which, in absence of Nepal's traditional energy reserves, results in massive electricity import from India and around 6% loss of GDP due to intermittent electricity supply.

Pakistan

Pakistan, showcases one of the strongest economic growths among the SAARC nations, owing to its rapid industrialisation and sectoral growth factors. Its population growth and socio-economic growth strategies fuelling its increasing demand for energy that currently is growing at a rate of 5% per year (SAARC Energy Centre, 2018). However, it still suffers from overdependence on imported fossil fuel that it's targeting to bring down with rapid transition to renewables' generation and consumption. SAARC

Figure 9. Installed capacity growth in Pakistan
Source: SAARC Energy Outlook (2018)

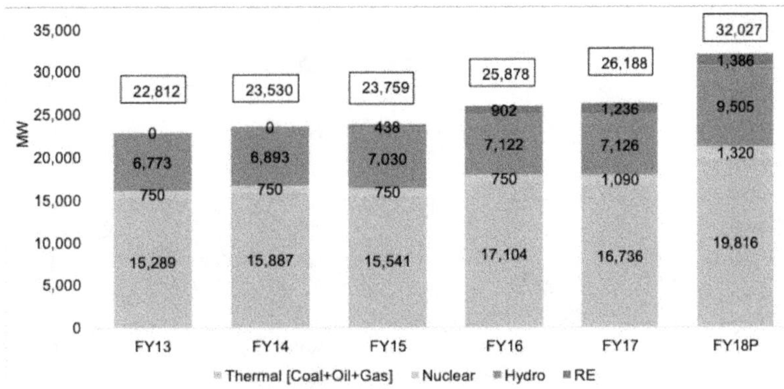

Energy Centre (2018) reports that Pakistan has an ambitious plan to reduce 20% of its current GHG emissions by 2030 by institutionalising its energy policies.

Current Demand

Pakistan's primary energy requirements are predominantly met by oil and gas, which still produces more than half of the electricity demand across the nation. While the current electrification levels are at 70% with a growing demand for electricity at a CAGR of 4.52%, current generation, transmission and distribution systems are struggling to meet this pace, resulting in frequent load-shedding situations (SAARC Energy Centre, 2018). Domestic activities in rural Pakistan (dispersed and accounted for two-thirds of the population) demand traditional fuels, whereas the urban population use LPG and electricity. To meet its GHG reduction target, the country needs effective utilisation of renewable resources, power generation and distribution systems (Naz et. al., 2017).

Current Generation

Presently, Pakistan's total installed capacity is 33 GW and in this energy mix, 64% is generated from fossil fuel, 27% from hydro, 7% from nuclear and only 2% from renewable resources (see Irfan et. al., 2020). Irfan et. al. (2020) further report that natural gas will contribute nearly 43.8% to Pakistan's energy mix by 2035 after which its domestic production will fall and the demand for imported gas will rise further. Figure 9 below summarises the country's installed capacity growth.

Pakistan's power sector growth is unsatisfactory as compared to the rest of the region owing to its low annual capacity utilisation, especially its capacity of renewable resources. Hydropower generation has been a concern owing to insufficient water availability and unreliable rainfall patterns, resulting in forced outages.

Figure 10. Installed capacity growth in Sri Lanka
Source: SAARC Energy Outlook (2018)

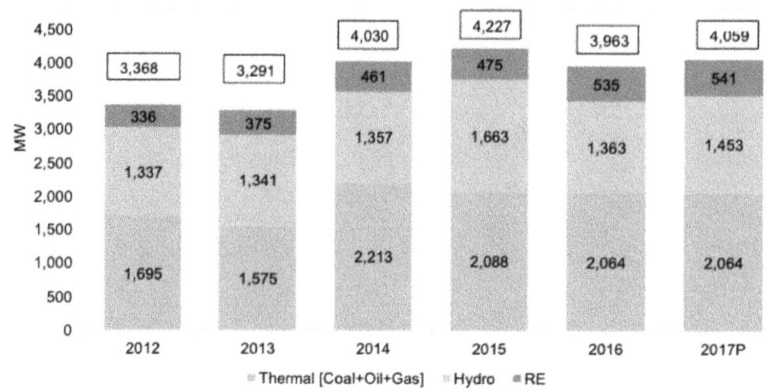

Sri Lanka

Sri Lanka, the sixth-largest populated nation among the SAARC, has been witnessing a steady growth of GDP and achieved universal electrification. In its current energy mix, petroleum products (POL) contribute the most – 43%, followed by biomass (37%), coal (11%), hydro (6%) and renewables (3%) (ADP and UNDP, 2017). The country's excess demand for energy outpaced its generation, making it dependant on imported petroleum products. Sri Lankan Government is propelling towards the generation and distribution of renewable energy, not only to achieve 100% of electricity production from renewables by 2050 but also to save the US$18-US$19 billion from fossil fuel imports by that time.

Current Demand

SAARC Energy Centre (2018) reports that as per electricity sales, domestic consumption constitutes 38%, industrial and commercial consumption respectively constitute 33% and 29% of the total sales. This also reports that the demand growth for energy is at 5.1% CAGR, which is well-matched with its GDP growth. While the country is far from progress in railway electrification and electric vehicle charging systems, its electricity transmission and distribution systems have achieved a 0% unplanned outage mark. Presently, electricity is expensive with an annual electricity demand of around 14,150 GWh, which is expected to rise by 4.9% over the next 20 years (International Trade Administration, 2021; Economy Next, 2021).

Current Generation

Sri Lankan energy sector is one of its fastest-growing, where the primary energy is generated from thermal (coal and fuel oil), hydro, and con-conventional renewable resources (solar and wind power). The current generation is 4,043 MW that is targeted to rise to 6,900 MW by 2025, where the country has already achieved 98% of grid connectivity (International Trade Administration, 2021). Figure 10 below summarises the country's installed capacity growth.

Sri Lanka's progress to lower GHG emissions is one of the best among the SAARC members. The government aims to achieve a target of generating 70% of its electricity from renewables by 2030. Economy Next (2021) reports the country's ambitious plan to be energy equivalent with present Germany, in which it aims to generate 2000 MW of energy from solar from its current levels of 500 MW by 2030, and eventually to be zero-carbon by 2050. The government is promoting, and institutionalising energy efficiency programs including mandatory energy labelling for common appliances and bringing focus to small-scale hydro and wind power projects.

Table 3 highlights SAARC member nations' long-term projected growth, based on current energy scenarios.

AN OVERVIEW OF THE AUSTRALIAN TRADE AND INVESTMENT STRATEGIC PARTNERSHIP, AND COOPERATION IN THE ENERGY SECTOR

This section begins with the current energy scenario in Australia and then focus on its trade and investment strategic partnership, and possible sectoral cooperation with the SAARC nations. The Department of Industry, Science, Energy and Resources {DISER} (2020) reports that during the pre-pandemic fiscal year 2018-19, Australian average annual GDP growth was 1.9% and population growth was 1.5% with a GDP of $1.9 trillion and a population of 25.4 million (,. Its current energy mix accounted for 94% of fossil fuel, in which crude oil, LPG and refined products dominate the energy consumption (38.8% share of total) that are demanded by the industry, transport, households and refineries (DISER, 2020).

Energy Scenario in Australia

The Australian energy sector is established and has a global mindset. Australia's competitive advantage stems from the availability of considerable conventional energy resources (LNG, Thermal coal, Uranium) and significant untapped unconventional resources (Shale gas, Coal seam gas), with the major commodity traders and energy resource fields being relatively closer to the markets in India, Bhutan, Sri Lanka, and Maldives (DFAT, 2018). The world-class research facility, expertise in energy transitions, access to high-quality renewable resources, strong regulatory and legal institutions to shield intellectual property rights has brought Australia at the forefront in transitioning towards a low-carbon future. Over the past five years, this sector witnessed an unprecedented growth towards renewable resource innovation (biomass, hydro, wind and solar), transmission and distribution, remote electrification, dispatchable renewables, smart grids and facilities, innovative finance models and technologies for renewables generation and battery storage.

Energy generation from fossil fuel still accounts for more than three-fourths share of the total generation, in which coal dominates with 56.4% share followed by gas with 20.5% share. However, over the past two years, demand for coal is slowly falling with the shift in energy generation from renewables. Presently, 20.9% of energy in Australia is generated from renewable resources, among which wind power generated the most (7.4%), closely followed by hydro (5.4%) and small-scale solar photovoltaics (4.7%) (DISER, 2020).

Transport is the largest user of energy in Australia (about 28%) followed by electricity supply (about 25%), where the latter is witnessing an incremented generation from renewables. Clean Energy Council (2021) reports that in 2020 alone, 27.7% of Australian electricity is generated from renewables, more than 3 GW of small-scale solar capacity and 2 GW of large-scale capacity (with 32 completed and 76 additional solar and wind projects that will add another 8 GW) has been added. It further reports that

Table 3a. SAARC member nations' long-term projected growth

South-Asian countries	Energy Outlook 2030
Afghanistan	• **Hydro** to remain the major contributor in power generation; its contribution expected to rise 3.4 times by fiscal 2030 • Electrification expected to reach ~52% by fiscal 2030 from 35% now, thereby improving primary energy usage • **Gas** usage to rise as ~650 MW gas-based power plants are expected to be set up • **Coal** usage to increase as additional 2,000-3,000 tonne per day (TPD) of cement capacities come on stream • End-use LPG demand and transport sector growth to result in strong **POL** growth of ~7.2% CAGR • Consumption of **biomass,** which is used extensively by households, for heating and cooking will continue to rise due to strong rural usage as power supply is intermittent
Bangladesh	• **Gas**, which accounts for about two-thirds of the primary energy consumption in fiscal 2018, to remain the mainstay going forward; depleting domestic production to be substituted through LNG imports • **Coal** usage will grow manifold to ~12 million tonne by fiscal 2030 owing to massive buildup of coal-fired thermal plants in the country (~6,000 MW) • Increased transportation activity to boost **POL** demand by a healthy 6.4% • **Renewable energy (RE)** usage to remain small; no new large-scale hydro projects planned; distributed solar and wind power projects negligible
Bhutan	• Biomass and electricity generated from hydro projects have around 60% share in the total primary energy consumption of Bhutan • Power generated from **hydro** projects, which comprised more than 99% of the total installed capacity (1,614 MW) of the country in 2017, is expected to increase to 5,272 MW by 2030 • **Biomass** demand is expected to grow at a rate of less than 1% to reach around 259 KTOE by 2030 • Overall demand for **POL products**, which are mainly consumed by the transport sector, is expected to increase 2.4 times at a CAGR of around 7% from 2017 until 2030 with growing population of conventional vehicles • **Coal**, which is mainly consumed by sectors such as heavy cement and ferro-alloy-based industries, is expected to see an increase in demand from 284 kilo tonne in 2017 to around 744 kilo tonne in 2030, growing at 7.7% CAGR

Source: Table prepared with data from SAARC Energy Centre (2018)

Table 3b. (continued)

India	• Demand for **coal,** which at present accounts for about 65% of the country's total primary energy needs, will continue to rise manifold; its usage in power is set to rise to ~1,220 million tonne by fiscal 2030 • **Gas** demand in the country is expected to reach ~217 million metric standard cubic meter per day (mmscmd) by fiscal 2024 at a CAGR of 5% and ~252 mmscmd by fiscal 2030 at a CAGR of 2.5%, driven primarily by fertilizer and city gas distribution (CGD) sectors • Robust capacity additions of ~150 GW of **solar** energy and ~70 GW of **wind** energy expected between fiscals 2018 and 2030 • Additional ~12 GW of **nuclear** plants expected to come up by fiscal 2030, increasing its contribution in the generation mix to 4.5-5.0% from the present 4.3% • **Petroleum product** consumption expected to log a subdued CAGR of 4.1% as demand gets crimped on account of rising substitution by CNG, ethanol blending, and greater focus on electric vehicles
The Maldives	• **Diesel** is expected to remain the primary fuel for meeting the country's power demand. It is estimated that in addition to 214 MW of centralized installed diesel-based power capacity in inhabited islands, tourist resorts cumulatively have 260 MW of diesel-based captive power capacity • Demand for **cooking gas** is expected to rise, with the fuel effectively replacing kerosene as the primary energy source for cooking • Only 10% of total electricity demand is estimated to be met frm RE sources by 2030.
Nepal	• **Traditional fuels,** which met around 71% of total primary energy requirement of Nepal in fiscal 2018, are expected to see their share decline to 54% by fiscal 2030 with the share of cleaner fuels rising • Power supply, which is dominated by **hydro** power plants, is expected to grow by around 4.1 times to 4,457 MW during the period, mainly driven by the addition of new hydel plants • Growth in industrial activities is expected to increase the total **coal** demand by around 2.5 times to 2,993 kilo tonne by fiscal 2030 compared with 1206 kilo tonne in fiscal 2018 • Consumption of **POL** products is expected to grow at a CAGR of 8.3% between fiscals 2018-2030 to reach ~6 million tonne, mainly driven by strong growth in the transport and industrial sectors led by a GDP growth of 4.5-5.0%

Australian battery storage sector is home to the world's largest battery with the installation of 238 MWh capacity in 2020 alone and an additional 595 MWh capacity in the pipeline. Several support programs are being institutionalised to develop Australia's renewable hydrogen industry.

Table 3c. (continued)

Pakistan	• Demand for **coal** has been growing steadily to 11.58 million tonne in fiscal 2018. With more than 10 new coal-fired power plants coming up, which would utilize produce from the Thar block, the usage of the fuel is expected to grow by 4.5 times to 60 million tonne in fiscal 2030 • **Gas** requirement (constrained) will increase marginally from 5,174 million cubic feet per day (mmcfd) in fiscal 2019 to ~5,900 mmcfd in fiscal 2030 on the back of power production, domestic and industrial use • Three new **nuclear** plants are expected to come up in the next decade, increasing power generation from 7,897 million units (MUs) in fiscal 2019 to ~27,850 MUs in fiscal 2030 • **POL** demand will grow at a healthy 5.2% CAGR driven mainly by the transportation segment and improved economic activity • An additional ~8,000 MW of **solar, wind and biomass-**based power projects are expected to come up, improving RE's share in power generation to ~9% in fiscal 2030 from 2% in fiscal 2018
Sri Lanka	• With the entire country being electrified and no significant outages, power supply is not expected to grow significantly. Most of the electricity is sourced through hydro and gas • Owing to more than 1000 MW of coal fired power plants expected to come up, **coal** usage is expected to rise to ~4.91 million tonnes in FY30 from 2.08 million tonnes in 2017 • **Natural gas** usage is expected to reach ~37.5 bcf by FY30 on the back of ~1000 MW of new gas based power plants • **Hydro power**, the main stay for Sri Lanka, accounted for ~33% of total generated power in 2017, however significant future growth is unlikely • The country is a very big consumer of **bioenergy** with ~12 million tons of bio fuel used in 2017. However, due to expected drawdowns in household and commercial use, cumulative biofuel usage will drag to ~9.7 million tonnes by FY30

Energy Trade

The majority of Australian energy production is exported - totalling 15,910.9 petajoules (PJ) during 2018-19, where black coal tops the list (70%), followed by LNG (25.7%), crude oil (3.4%), LPG and other refined products (0.9%) (DISER, 2020). While the export demand raised over the fiscal year 2018-19, its imports (predominantly refined petroleum products and crude oil) remain stable resulting in a rise in net exports – a phenomenon that Australia is witnessing persistently over the last two decades. Figure 11 below summarises Australia's energy balance (a gap between production and consumption) from the fiscal year 1978-79 to 2018-19 period.

The Australian energy sector has been impacted least by the COVID-19 pandemic, owing to its proximity to the Asian markets reinforcing its position as a major global exporter of energy. Tang (2020) from the Australian Trade and Investment Commission reports that while in the last decade Australia competed with Qatar as the world's largest exporter of LNG, in the coming decade it will lead in the

Figure 11. Energy balance in Australia
Source: DISER (2020)

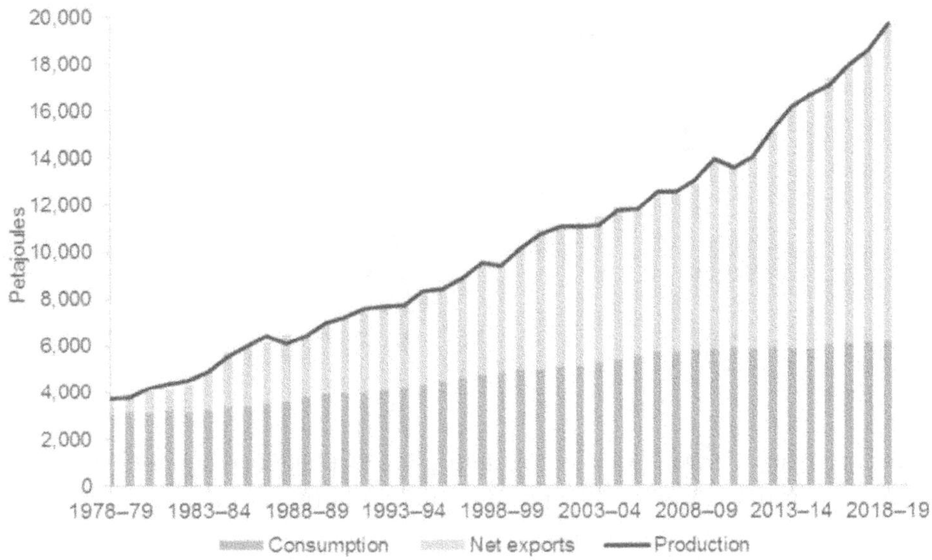

lithium industry owing to the propelled demand for lithium-ion batteries as rechargeable energy storage. Presently, Australia is the biggest exporter of lithium with a production capacity of 55% of the world, whose demand is anticipated to grow with the surge of electric vehicle sales from 2 million to 28 million by 2030 (REQ, 2020). According to DISER (2020), Australia is the third-largest producer of uranium oxide, (accounting for 12% of the world's production in 2018-19) and exports 100% of its production which is enriched overseas for nuclear power plants to use. In 2019, Australia was the world's largest thermal coal exporter (a primary source of electricity generation) with the fourth largest generation capacity and the largest exporter of natural gas, the cleanest burning fossil fuel (REQ, 2020). However, both this thermal coal and natural gas export earnings are expected to fall owing to contraction of seaborne markets and shrinking generation capacity respectively. Australia only imports natural gas produced in the Joint Petroleum Development Area which gets liquefied in Australia for export. Figure 12 below summarises the country's energy trade scenario.

Key Challenges

- Grid Management

Australian clean energy transition is achieving some massive milestones, not only with technology to generate small and large-scale capacities but also with innovative infrastructure-complementing designs of solar systems (viz., solar panels complementing the requirements of green roofs). However, the influx of renewables brings challenges for grid operation and management as it lowers the demand for electricity from main grids, causing fluctuation and voltage issues due to the intermittent generation that subjects to grid failure. While the best solution is the development of competing industries (such as electric vehicles or green-hydrogen industries to soak up the excess supply of low-cost energy) many

Figure 12. Energy trade in Australia
Source: DISER (2020)

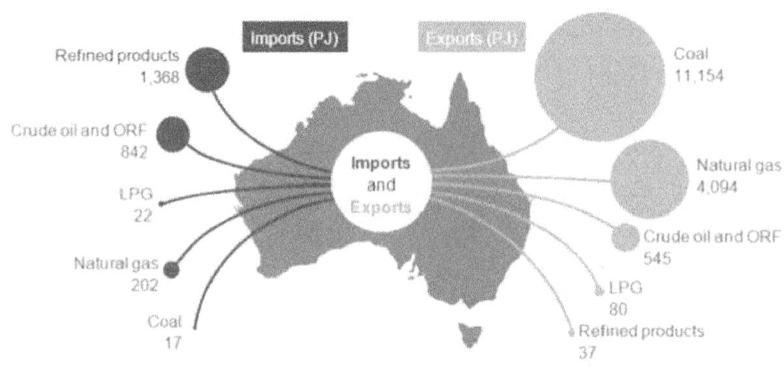

other alternatives are being actively adopted, including tariff plans and support programs promoting community batteries, virtual power plants and institutionalisation of remotely turning off individual solar systems (Clean Energy Council, 2021).

- Transmission and Distribution

This challenge arises as the newly developed renewable generators are not necessarily located favourably, in which transmission and distribution of the generated energy can be directly connected with the established main grids and towers. Mitigation strategies include installation of large grid-connected batteries, interconnected power-grid systems, community batteries, stand-alone power systems (APS), modified energy modelling, integration of distributed energy resources (DER) (viz., commercial, and residential solar photovoltaics and batteries) and development of energy zones. Technology innovation is growing rapidly but is still subject to upstream and downstream distribution challenges.

- Safe, Reliable, Sustainable, and Affordable Transition

As traditional fossil fuel remains the quintessential source of energy, transitioning to low-carbon resources entails reliability (viz., intermittency issue), safety (from the connectivity of DER to possible structural unemployment) and affordability issues (costly renewable energy supply chain), even though they are environmentally sustainable. Australian energy governing bodies are committed to ticking these all four dimensions with institutionalising energy policy and programs in the allocation of their resources, but the learning curve is far from being flat.

LITERATURE REVIEW

The literature focusing on the relationship of renewable energy (RE) consumption and economic growth, gets uninterrupted attention from environmental economists and policymakers worldwide. While seemingly the two feed into each other, literary studies aiming to establish a causality relation in RE consumption-economic growth nexus are divided into three arrays. One that establishes a unidirectional causality shows that, while for some nexus economic growth drives higher consumer demand for renewables (for example see Sadorsky, 2009 for emerging economies, Al-mulali et. al., 2013 for 108 diverse economies and Cho et al., 2015 for developed economies), for other nexuses it is just the reverse (for example see Bilgili and Ozturk, 2015a and 2015b for G7 countries and Sub-Sahara African countries, Fotourehchi, 2017, and Anwar et al., 2017 for developing countries). Second array of literature establishes a bidirectional causality between RE consumption-economic growth nexus (for example see Apergis and Payne, 2010 and 2012 for OECD and mixed economies respectively, Sebri and Ben-Salha, 2014 for BRICS, Cho et al., 2015 for less developed countries) and the third establishes no causality (for example see Chang et al., 2015 for G7 and Marques and Fuinhas, 2012 for European countries). The relationships differ between nations largely because of their differences in energy and growth curves, economic complexities and with specifications on investment potentials. However, most of the countries - developed or developing, benefit from capital and energy technologies (Apergis & Danuletiu, 2014; Kuran et al., 2018; Salim & Rafiq, 2012; Shahbaz et al., 2020).

The institutional, regulatory, and social distortions are slugging the growth of South-Asia's major energy economies. The Indian renewable energy sector is the fourth most attractive market in the world, the fourth largest global generator of wind energy and ranked at fifth position in installed renewable capacity (DFAT, 2018; Leach & Deshmukh, 2012). India's energy capacity is leading the SAARC circle, growing with several large, small, and micro-scale capacity projects (wind, solar and hydro) towards a low-emission future, supported by a series of policy initiatives (for detail see MNRE, 2020 and Sen et. al., 2015). The second is Pakistan, progressing with renewables at a much slower pace with several small and micro-scale capacities (led by hydro, wind, and biogas), supported by policy and series of investments (for detail see Ghimire, 2007, Pandey and Bajgain, 2007, and Tareen et. al., 2019). The third is Bangladesh whose renewable capacity has been dominated by small-scale projects, with the world's largest micro-generation of renewables namely, Grameen Shakti that worked towards the national grid connectivity of rural electricity and gas networks (for detail see Asif and Barua 2011, and Katekar et. al., 2021).

All the SAARC member nations suffer from energy deprivation. The dependency of each nation on a specific energy resource fetches the potential of mutual benefit from strategic bilateral and multilateral partnerships between them. However, attempt to form any such free trade agreements within the SAARC circle have suffered from an unfavourable political collaboration between the member nations. When multilateral trade agreements demand collaboration between more than three nations without discrimination between the nations involved, it is often the case that the two most privileged nations with favourable trade conditions get an incentive to exploit or avoid the others from getting a unilateral distribution of the desired benefits. Thus, bilateral trade agreements more often overshadow the multilateral trade agreements and SAARC is no different.

The region's energy cooperation began in the 1960s with the development of power interconnection systems between India-Bhutan and India-Nepal which propelled with the establishment of SAARC. Bhutan was a net importer of power till 1987 but after the commissioning of the Chukha hydropower plant, it became a power surplus country and started exporting to India, which manifolds with the commissioning of Tala hydropower plant in 2007. India is a net exporter of POL products, with major partners outside the SAARC circle (Navpreet, 2020). Table 4 summarises the power and POL products trade scenario.

Table 4. Power and POL trade scenario in SAARC in 2018

Countries	Electricity [GWH] Gross Demand	Domestic Supply	Surplus/ Deficit Position	Deficit/ Surplus %	Major importing/ exporting nations
Afghanistan	4,981	1,076	Deficit	-78%	Iran, Tajikistan, Uzbekistan, Turkmenistan
Bangladesh	65,124	58,300	Deficit	-10%	India
Bhutan	2,186	7,630	Surplus	249%	India
India	1,205,266	1,202,099	Deficit	0%	Bangladesh, Bhutan, Nepal
Maldives	1,405	1,405	Self-Sufficient	0%	-
Nepal	5,557	4,476	Deficit	-19%	India
Pakistan	120,392	118,916	Deficit	-1%	Iran
Sri Lanka	15,763	15,763	Self-Sufficient	0%	-

Countries	POL ('000 tonne) Gross Demand	Domestic Supply	Surplus/ Deficit Position	Deficit/ Surplus %	Major importing/ exporting nations
Afghanistan	2,019	0	Deficit	-100%	Iran, Russia, Turkmenistan, UAE
Bangladesh	6,384	1,166	Deficit	-82%	Singapore, UAE, Saudi Arabia
Bhutan	158	0	Deficit	-100%	India
India	204,922	252,839	Surplus	23%	EU, Singapore, Japan
Maldives	561	0	Deficit	-100%	UAE, Singapore, Malaysia
Nepal	2,307	0	Deficit	-100%	India
Pakistan	29,037	10,741	Deficit	-63%	UAE, Oman, Kuwait, Saudi Arabia
Sri Lanka	5,168	1,867	Deficit	-64%	Singapore, China, Malaysia, India

Source: SAARC Energy Centre 2018

OPPORTUNITIES

There are opportunities in the growing market for a resilient, low-carbon energy sector in terms of support services, technology and commodities in which Australia is competitive. The following three key resources carry the best opportunity for mutually beneficial cooperation:

Liquified Natural Gas (LNG, Produced by Cooling Natural Gas to -161°C)

It has been gaining increased attention as being an economically attractive and cleaner substitute for diesel-based power generations, when it comes to augmenting energy supply, diversifying fuel mix and energy security issues. It's a cleaner-burning fuel compared to coal and kerosene, produces less GHG and particles per unit of energy production. Expanding the energy mix with provisions for natural gas would reduce the POL-dependence, in which the economies to an extent would be less hostile to oil price shocks.

Reportedly an internalisation of environmental costs through an appropriate mechanism such as a clean development mechanism (CDM), would enhance natural gas's competitiveness for gas-based power generation. This opens opportunities for gas-based localised electricity generation and transmission through intra-regional power interconnections providing a viable electricity supply for the developing SAARC nations (as seen in other similar economies such as Mexico). The development of large-scale regional LNG importation and regasification terminal should be considered by larger SAARC members (India, Pakistan, and Bangladesh), suitably on their seacoasts, in which they gain the advantages of economies of scale in transport, regasification and procurement benefits (for detail see ADB, 2011). The initial investments in infrastructure for natural gas transport can suitably be extended to smaller SAARC members (Sri-Lanka, Bhutan, Afghanistan) with larger demand. The smaller nations, however, can access this low-cost bulk power generation through regional power infrastructure including cross-border power interconnections and minimise any potential risks through suitable institutionalisation.

Being the largest LNG exporter, Australia would benefit from an inflow of investments from the larger SAARC members who pursue to diversify supply for energy security and infrastructure development. DFAT (2018) and IEA (2020) reports the prospective Indian market in promoting LNG as (i) India's gas-based power generation and distribution aspires to grow to 15% by 2030, (ii) consumption to increase 218% by 2030 from its 2014 levels but corresponding gas generation to increase only around 127% for which India would need 84 billion cubic meters of imported LNG. Australia can further widen this opportunity by considering investments in large-scale regional LNG importation, regasification terminal, knowledge, and technology partnership in establishing cross-border power interconnections.

Hydrogen

Hydrogen is fast gaining attractiveness for energy storage and transportation, where Australian technology has advanced significantly. As it's expensive, efficient commercialisation of affordable conversion technologies would make them viable to the larger economies of the SAARC circle. Green-hydrogen's (produced from solar and wind) direct utilisation in fuel cells for power, transport, and fertilisers could save millions of dollars in government support programs for heavily populated SAARC nations. Given the recent surge in solar power, the Sri Lankan economy holds strong potential for this industry with possible cross border power interconnections and trade.

Australia, with its advancement in green-hydrogen generation and storage, can establish itself as a supplier of hydrogen fuel to India, as considered by the India Economic Strategy to 2035 (DFAT, 2018).

Figure 13. Relative contribution of power resources in 2017
Source: Navpreet, 2020

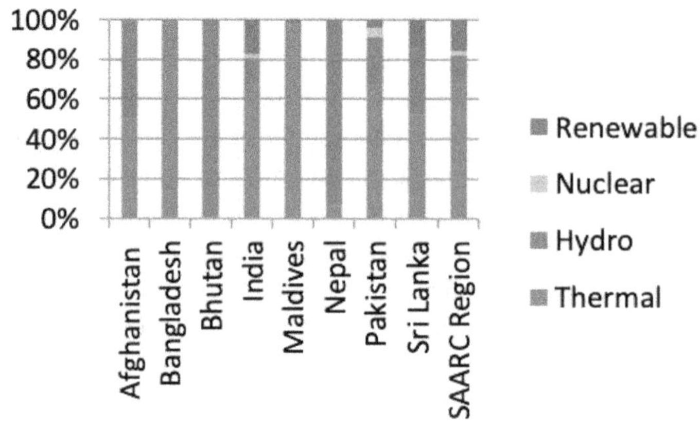

Renewable Resources

Opportunities in this sector arise given the SAARC countries' dependence on imported energy resources owing to the sectoral distortions while being endowed with untapped abundant renewables. The combined power generation from renewables accounted for only 10% of this alliance's total generation. In terms of access to safe, reliable, sustainable, and affordable energy, SAARC is far behind the world average. In the fiscal year 2018-19, the per capita power generation of the region was 903.6 KWh with the lowest contribution from Afghanistan at 32.5 KWh per capita (Navpreet, 2020). Each of the SAARC nations' power generation is dominated by a single resource (for example, Bhutan and Nepal are driven by hydro while the Maldives are driven by imported fossil fuels), but thermal fuel (gas, coal, and petroleum) dominates the combined generation capacity with 67.3% share. The region has abundant hydro potential but put together they generate only 14.9% power from hydro. Figure 13 summarises the relative contribution of resources in the power.

Australia, given its portfolio in metal and mineral inputs for renewables (including bauxite, silica, tellurium, lithium-ion, and cadmium), along with its knowledge, expertise, technology, and innovation, can broaden its energy market with strategic partnerships with the SAARC. The larger SAARC countries have a massive and increasing demand for renewables that converge with Australian capabilities and thus providing mutual scope in the following areas (for detail see DISER, 2020, SAARC Energy Centre, 2018 and DFAT, 2018):

- Residential off-grid capacity through an appropriate framework for regulatory policy and remunerative net metering policy,
- Emerging pumped hydro (specifically in India) design and management
- Low-cost solar photovoltaics that increases its competitiveness with fossil fuels
- Support services, consulting, system engineering and technology
- Residential and commercial system installation, transmission, and distribution
- Smart grid technologies and energy curve balancing strategies
- Storage technology and battery
- Delivering training on renewable energy skills

- Policy frameworks, standardising performance, and regulations
- Promoting investment opportunities that are general bottleneck given the regulatory framework

Given the persistent predominance of coal in the SAARC energy sector, these nations can offer opportunities in:

- Coal washing and next-gen coal-combustion technologies
- The support of foreign capital as needed by Australian massive resource base and technology such as Carbon capture, usage, and storage (utilising Australian expertise)
- A merger of Australian expertise and SAARC's manufacturing and service capacity to produce cost-effectively
- Economies of scale and outbound investments focusing on energy security attentions

CHALLENGES

Cross-border energy trade (CBET) is subject to time-consuming regional agreements owing to the technical, operational, commercial, and political concerns that are driven by socio-economic and political scenarios. India, the regional leader - both in terms of its market power and energy scenario, is the only country that shares borders with all other SAARC nations and thereby, would be the centre of CBET especially when it comes to developing any necessary cross-border infrastructure interconnections. The major challenges in establishing trade partnerships are briefed in four categories (for detail see DFAT, 2018; Navpreet, 2020; Paudyal, 2013):

The Policy and Regulatory Concerns

The energy policies should aim towards affordability, superior energy security, greater sustainability, and economic growth. While homogeneity in prices is an impediment for cooperation, centralised energy sectors (especially for major markets such as India where the sector is monopolised with high barriers) impedes cross-border power trades, investment stability and price competitiveness. The regulatory frameworks lack clarity, especially for oil, gas, and electricity distribution to rural and poor regions. Lack of institutional frameworks to support land acquisition and to combat corruption to produce reliable independent reports concerning environmental, power and utility issues negatively impact cooperation potentials.

Politics

The lack of political harmony has been vexing regional cooperation in the SAARC. Internal political conflicts, political transitions, and unstable governments (viz., India-Pakistan, Pakistan-Afghanistan, Sri Lanka-Bangladesh-Bhutan) have decelerated the progress of regional and cross-border cooperation. Currently, most of the power generation and transmission projects between SAARC nations are only being organised at bilateral levels instead of multilateral long-term regional levels due to this.

Technology, Skill, and Infrastructure

Impediments include poor transmission and distribution systems, unstable product life-cycle costs, complex certification processes, especially for renewables. The massive infrastructure potentials are yet to be explored. Australia's advanced technology and infrastructure are still far too expensive for most of the SAARC nations. Skill and research distribution is dispersed and lacks uniformity.

Constraints on the Australian Energy Industries

Relatively high operating cost owing to its high labour cost, limited commercialisation of research activities, regulatory burden including 'law fare' challenges in the courts and policy changes that reflects through costly export commodities. Skill shortage is a persistent problem along with a lack of affordable transmission and distribution infrastructure.

FUTURE RESEARCH DIRECTIONS

India, the largest and inevitable market in SAARC, with a diverse policy landscape, largely spread ministry with complex decisiveness across the regional, state, and federal levels showcase diverse prioritisation of energy concerns. But socio-economic complexity, public ownership of utilities and political diversity in prioritising energy policies are common for all the SAARC nations. Given these, future research should explore public-private partnership options to secure investment flows, standardisation of trade policies such as tariffs, possibilities for mutually strengthening native hydro energy and interconnected power systems towards an effective transition to renewables. The possibilities of multilateral trade partnerships need to be explored.

CONCLUSION

In the United Nations Climate Change Conference (2021), Australia and SAARC nations have committed to energy security and effective transition towards sustainability. It's now required for them to embrace collaborations to explore their relative competitive advantages to optimise the goal. The mutual divergence of energy demand, capacity, investment potential and institutional distortions demands strategic cooperation between these nations through effective trade agreements that will propel this unprecedented transition. The bilateral trade opportunities between India-Australia, India-Bhutan, India-Nepal, and India-Bangladesh have unleashed energy potential, market collaboration and political harmony. The policy and regulatory frameworks, individual energy-prioritisation and institutional impediments are some major bottlenecks at present, that need to harmonize for progressing towards power cooperation.

REFERENCES

Adnan, M., Abir, N., & Rahman, T. (2018). Energy scenario of Bangladesh and future challenges. *International Journal of Scientific and Engineering Research*, *9*(3), 1001–1005.

Ahmadzai, S., & McKinna, A. (2018). Afghanistan electrical energy and trans-boundary water systems analyses: Challenges and opportunities. *Energy Reports*, *4*, 435–469. doi:10.1016/j.egyr.2018.06.003

Al-Mulali, U., Fereidouni, H. G., Lee, J. Y., & Sab, C. N. B. C. (2013). Examining the bi-directional long run relationship between renewable energy consumption and GDP growth. *Renewable & Sustainable Energy Reviews*, *22*, 209–222. doi:10.1016/j.rser.2013.02.005

Alam F., Alam Q, Reza S, Khurshid-Ul-Alam S M, Saleque K, & Chowdhury H. (2017). Sourcing green power in Bhutan: a review. *Energy Procedia, 110*(December), 586–591. doi:10.1016/j.egypro.2017.03.189

Anwar, A., Arshed, N., & Nabeela Kousar, N. (2017). Renewable Energy Consumption and Economic Growth in Member of OIC Countries. *European Online Journal of Natural and Social Sciences*, 111–129.

Apergis, N. & Danuletiu, D. C. (2014). Renewable energy and economic growth: Evidence from the sign of panel long-run causality. *International Journal of Energy Economics and Policy,* 578-587.

Apergis, N., & Payne, J. E. (2010). Renewable energy consumption and economic growth: Evidence from a panel of OECD countries. *Energy Policy*, *38*(1), 656–660. doi:10.1016/j.enpol.2009.09.002

Apergis, N., & Payne, J. E. (2012). Renewable and non-renewable energy consumption-growth nexus: Evidence from a panel error correction model. *Energy Economics*, *34*(3), 733–738. doi:10.1016/j.eneco.2011.04.007

Asian Development Bank. (2017). *Nepal energy sector assessment, strategy, and roadmap*. doi:10.22617/TCS178936-2

Asian Development Bank. (2020). *A Brighter Future for Maldives Powered by Renewables: Road Map for the Energy Sector 2020–2030*. Retrieved from https://www.adb.org/sites/default/files/publication/654021/renewables-roadmap-energy-sector-maldives.pdf

Asian Development Bank and United Nations Development Program. (2017). *Assessment of Sri Lanka's power sector: 100% electricity generation through renewable energy by 2050*. Retrieved from https://www.adb.org/publications/electricity-generation-renewable-energy-2050-sri-lanka

Asif, M., & Barua, D. (2011). Salient features of the Grameen Shakti renewable energy program. *Renewable & Sustainable Energy Reviews*, *15*(9), 5063–5067. doi:10.1016/j.rser.2011.07.050

Australia-India Council (AIC). (2019). *Australia-India Council*. Retrieved from dfat.gov.au/people-to-people/foundations-councils-institutes/australia-india-council/governance/Pages/australia-india-council-strategic-plan-2017-2020.aspx

Bilgili, F., & Ozturk, I. (2015a). Biomass energy and economic growth nexus in G7 countries: Evidence from dynamic panel data. *Renewable & Sustainable Energy Reviews*, *49*, 132–138. doi:10.1016/j.rser.2015.04.098

Bilgili, F., & Ozturk, I. (2015b). Economic growth and biomass consumption nexus: Dynamic panel analysis for Sub-Sahara African countries. *Applied Energy*, 110–116.

Chang, T., Gupta, R., Inglesi-Lotz, R., Simo-Kengne, B., Smithers, D., & Trembling, A. (2015). Renewable energy and growth: Evidence from heterogeneous panel of G7 countries using Granger causality. *Renewable & Sustainable Energy Reviews*, *52*, 1405–1412. doi:10.1016/j.rser.2015.08.022

Cho, S., Heo, E., & Kim, J. (2015). Causal relationship between renewable energy consumption and economic growth: Comparison between developed and less-developed countries. *Geosystem Engineering,* 284-291.

Clean Energy Council (CEC). (2020). *Clean Energy Australia Report 2020.* Retrieved from https://assets.cleanenergycouncil.org.au/documents/resources/reports/clean-energy-australia/clean-energy-australia-report-2020.pdf

Deccan Herald. (2021, April 1). *India to Counter China's foray in Bay of Bengal with BIMSTEC meet, 5 nation navy drill.* Retrieved from https://www.deccanherald.com/national/india-to-counter-chinas-foray-in-bay-of-bengal-with-bimstec-meet-5-nation-navy-drill-968854.html

Department of Industry, Science, Energy and Resources. (2020). Australian Energy Update 2020: Australian Energy Statistics, September. Author.

Department of Innovation Industry & Science (DIIS). (2019). *Collaborating with India on Science and Research.* Retrieved from www.industry.gov.au/funding-and-incentives/science-and-research/collaborating-with-india-on-science-and-research

Department of Renewable Energy B. (2016). *Bhutan energy directory 2015.* Author.

DFAT. (2018). *Indian Economic Strategy 2035.* Department of Foreign Affairs and Trade. Retrieved from https://dfat.gov.au/geo/india/ies/index.html

DFAT. (2020). *Joint Statement on a Comprehensive Strategic Partnership between Republic of India and Australia.* https://www.dfat.gov.au/geo/india/Pages/joint-statement-comprehensive-strategic-partnership-between-republic-india-and-australia

Economy Next. (2021). *Sri Lanka generation plan renewable power share for 2030 equal to Germany: CEB engineers.* Retrieved from https://economynext.com/sri-lanka-generation-plan-renewable-power-share-for-2030-equal-to-germany-ceb-engineers-84506/

Farabi-Asl, H. (2019). *Energy challenges for clean cooking in Asia, the background, and possible policy solutions.* doi:10.1007/978-1-349-67278-3_116

Fotourehchi, Z. (2017). Clean Energy Consumption and Economic Growth: A Case Study for Developing Countries. *International Journal of Energy Economics and Policy,* 61-64.

Ghimire, P. C. (2007). Final report on technical study of biogas plants installed in Pakistan. *Asia/Africa biogas programme.*

Government of the People's Republic of Bangladesh. (2012). *Bangladesh country action plan for clean cook stoves.* Author.

International Energy Agency (IEA). (2020). *World Energy Outlook 2020.* IEA. Retrieved from https://www.iea.org/reports/world-energy-outlook-2020

International Trade Administration. (2021). *Country Commercial Guides – Sri Lanka: Energy*. Retrieved from https://www.trade.gov/country-commercial-guides/sri-lanka-energy

IRENA. (2019). *Renewable's readiness assessment: Kingdom of Bhutan*. Issue December.

Irfan, M., Zhao, Z. Y., Panjwani, M. K., Mangi, F. H., Li, H., Jan, A., Ahmad, M., & Rehman, A. (2020). Assessing the energy dynamics of Pakistan: Prospects of biomass energy. *Energy Reports*, *6*, 80–93. doi:10.1016/j.egyr.2019.11.161

Jian, Z. (2021). *World Economic Situation and Prospects*. United Nations. Retrieved from https://www.un.org/development/desa/dpad/wpcontent/uploads/sites/45/WESP2021_CH3_SA.pdf

Katekar, V. P., Asif, M., & Deshmukh, S. S. (2021). Energy and Environmental Scenario of South Asia. *Energy and Environmental Security in Developing Countries*, 75-103.

Kharbanda, V. K., & Panda, R. R. (2016). *Report on regional energy/electricity regulatory institutional mechanism in South Asia: South Asia forum of electricity/energy regulators*. SAFER.

Kutan, A. M., Paramati, S. R., Ummalla, M., & Zakari, A. (2018). Financing renewable energy projects in major emerging market economies: Evidence in the perspective of sustainable economic development. *Emerging Markets Finance & Trade*, *54*(8), 1761–1777. doi:10.1080/1540496X.2017.1363036

Lam, N. L., Upadhyay, B., Maharjan, S., Jagoe, K., Weyant, C. L., Thompson, R., Uprety, S., Johnson, M. A., & Bond, T. C. (2017). Seasonal fuel consumption, stoves, and end-uses in rural households of the far-western development region of Nepal. *Environmental Research Letters*, *12*(12), 125011. Advance online publication. doi:10.1088/1748-9326/aa98cc

Leach, M., & Deshmukh, S. (2012). Sustainable energy law and policy. *Environ Energy Law*, 122–138.

Maldives Customs Service. (2019). *Total Imports 2019*. Retrieved from https://www.customs.gov.mv/Media/Documents/downloads

Marques, A. C., & Fuinhas, J. A. (2012). Is renewable energy effective in promoting growth? *Energy Policy*, *46*, 434–442. doi:10.1016/j.enpol.2012.04.006

MNRE G 2019–20. (2020). *Annual report 2019–20*. Ministry of New and Renewable Energy, Government of India.

National Aeronautics and Space Administration. (2021). *Global Climate Change: Vital Signs of the Planet*. Retrieved from https://climate.nasa.gov/vital-signs/global-temperature/

National Centres for Environmental Information. (2021). *Assessing the Global Climate in June 2021*. Retrieved from https://www.ncei.noaa.gov/news/global-climate-202106

Navpreet. (2020). Potential and Prospects for Regional Power Cooperation in the SAARC Region. *Journal of Critical Reviews*, *7*(11).

Naz, S., Page, A., & Agho, K. E. (2017). Household air pollution from use of cooking fuel and under-five mortality: The role of breastfeeding status and kitchen location in Pakistan. *PLoS One*, *12*(3), 1–14. doi:10.1371/journal.pone.0173256 PMID:28278260

Ngaibiakching & Pande, A. (2020). India's Act East Policy and ASEAN: Building a Regional Order Through Partnership in the Indo-Pacific. *International Studies, 57*(1), 67-78.

NITI, Aayog, & IEEJ. (2017). *Energizing India.* A Joint Project Report of NITI Aayog and IEEJ. doi:10.1016/j.ijcard.2017.07.068

Pandey, B., & Bajgain, S. (2007). Feasibility study of domestic biogas in Pakistan. *RSPN*, (July), 1–38.

Paudyal, M. (2013). *Role of Private Sector in the Growth of Power Infrastructure in South Asia.* Investment Board, Government of Nepal.

Pyper, J. (2021). *How India's Renewable Energy Sector Survived and Thrived in a Turbulent 2020.* Published Online at GreenTech Media. Retrieved from https://www.greentechmedia.com/articles/read/india-solar-energy-transition-pandemic-2020

Rana, M. (2018). Transformation of Indo-Bangladesh Relations: From Insecurity to Cooperation in Northeast India. *Strategic Analysis, 42*(6), 559–577. doi:10.1080/09700161.2018.1559976

Regan, H. (2020, May 6). *Billions of people could live in areas too hot for humans by 2070.* CNN.

Resource and Energy Quarterly. (2020). Office of the Chief Economist.

Ritchie, H. (2020). *Sector by sector: Where do global greenhouse gas emissions come from?* OurWorldInData.org.

Ritchie, H., & Roser, M. (2020). *Environmental impacts of food production.* Retrieved from: https://ourworldindata.org/environmental-impacts-of-food

SAARC Energy Centre. (2018). *SAARC Energy Outlook 2030.* CRISIL Ltd. Retrieved from https://www.saarcenergy.org/wp-content/uploads/2019/05/SAARC-Energy-Outlook-2030-Final-Report-Draft.pdf

Sadorsky, P. (2009). Renewable energy consumption and income in emerging economies. *Energy Policy, 37*(10), 4021–4028. doi:10.1016/j.enpol.2009.05.003

Salim, R. A., & Rafiq, S. (2012). Why do some emerging economies proactively accelerate the adoption of renewable energy? *Energy Economics, 34*(4), 1051–1057. doi:10.1016/j.eneco.2011.08.015

Sebri, M., & Ben-Salha, O. (2014). On the causal dynamics between economic growth, renewable energy consumption, CO2 emissions and trade openness: Fresh evidence from BRICS countries. *Renewable & Sustainable Energy Reviews, 39*, 14–23. doi:10.1016/j.rser.2014.07.033

Sen, S., Ganguly, S., Das, A., Sen, J., & Dey, S. (2015). Renewable energy scenario in India: Opportunities and challenges. *Journal of African Earth Sciences.* Advance online publication. doi:10.1016/j.jafrearsci.2015.06.002

Shahbaz, M., Raghutla, C., Chittedi, K. R., Jiao, Z., & Vo, X. V. (2020). *The Impact of Renewable Energy Consumption on Economic Growth: Evidence form the Renewable Energy Country Attractive Index.* MPRA Paper No. 101168

Shukla, A. K., Sudhakar, K., & Baredar, P. (2017). Renewable energy resources in South Asian Countries: Challenges, policy and recommendations. *Energy Centre, Resource-efficient Technologies, 3*(3), 342–346. doi:10.1016/j.reffit.2016.12.003

Tang, E. (2020). Australia's 'Big Five': The Dynamic Industries that power trade & Investment. *Australian Trade and Investment Commission - Economic Analysis*. Retrieved from https://www.austrade.gov.au/news/economic-analysis/australias-big-five-the-dynamic-industries-that-power-trade-investment

Tareen, W. U. K., Dilbar, M. T., Farhan, M., Ali Nawaz, M., Durrani, A. W., Memon, K. A., Mekhilef, S., Seyedmahmoudian, M., Horan, B., Amir, M., & Aamir, M. (2019). Present status and potential of biomass energy in Pakistan based on existing and future renewable resources. *Sustainability, 12*(1), 249. doi:10.3390u12010249

United Nations. (2021). *Sustainable Development Goals. 17 Goals to transform our world.* Retrieved from https://www.un.org/sustainabledevelopment/

Wojczewski, T. (2019). Identity and world order in India's post-Cold War foreign policy discourse. *Third World Quarterly, 40*(1), 180–198. doi:10.1080/01436597.2018.1552079

Zhang, F. (2019). In the Dark: How Much Do Power Sector Distortions Cost South Asia? South Asia Development Forum. Washington, DC: World Bank. doi:10.1596/978-1-4648-1154-8

ADDITIONAL READING

Asialink. (2019). Where we Live. Address to Asialink PM Scott Morrison. Retrieved from https://asialink.unimelb.edu.au/stories/australia-and-the-indo-pacific-an-address-by-prime-minister-scott-morrison

Australia-India Council (AIC). (2019). Australia-India Council. Retrieved from dfat.gov.au/people-to-people/foundations-councils-institutes/australia-india-council/governance/Pages/australia-india-council-strategic-plan-2017-2020.aspx

Australian Energy Market Operator. (2020). *Quarterly Energy Dynamics, Q2*, 2020.

Bergenwall, S. (2016). Assessing India's Rise and the Road Ahead. *Strategic Analysis, 40*(5), 386–404. doi:10.1080/09700161.2016.1209905

Bhosale, S. (2018). Why India is Emerging as Australia's Natural Ally. The Sydney Moring Herald. Retrieved from https://www.smh.com.au/world/asia/why-india-is-emerging-as-australia-s-natural-ally-20180905-p501yp.html

Brewster, D. (2010). Australia and India: The Indian Ocean and the limits of strategic convergence. *Australian Journal of International Affairs, 64*(5), 549–565. doi:10.1080/10357718.2010.513369

Ganguly, S. (2017). Had Modi truly changed India's foreign Policy? *The Washington Quarterly, 40*(2), 131–143. doi:10.1080/0163660X.2017.1328929

Palit, A. (2016). India's Act east Policy and Implications for Southeast Asia. Southeast Asian Affairs, 81-92.

Sikri, R. (2009). India's "Look East" Policy. *Asia-Pacific Review*, *16*(1), 131–145. doi:10.1080/13439000902957624

Thakur, R., & Sharma, A. (2018). India in Australia's strategic framing in the Indo-Pacific. *Strategic Analysis*, *42*(2), 69–83. doi:10.1080/09700161.2018.1439328

KEY TERMS AND DEFINITIONS

Electricity Interconnection Power System: This links two or more independent power grids within a country or at cross-border or regional levels that allow for electricity exchanges leading to optimized use and sharing of different source-generated electricity. It enables the otherwise physically impossible long-distance utilisation of renewables.

Energy Consumption: It measures the amount of energy used in an economy, which is equal to the domestic production plus imports minus exports (and changes in stocks).

Paris Agreement: Often referred to as the Paris Accords, is an international treaty on climate change, covering climate change mitigation, adaptation, and finance. The Agreement is a legally binding international treaty that entered into force on 4 November 2016 to include commitments from 191 countries to reduce their GHG emissions and work together to adapt to the impacts of climate change by strengthening their commitments over timc.

Chapter 3
Review of Opportunities in Collaboration Between Australia and Pakistan for the Education of Marketing Post COVID-19

Farooq Haq
https://orcid.org/0000-0002-1620-9226
Canadian University Dubai, UAE

ABSTRACT

This chapter presents opportunity for collaboration between Australian and Pakistani tertiary education for advanced teaching of marketing. The research presents a study suggesting innovating marketing education post COVID-19 based on class interviews with examples from the world of politics. University students studying marketing were interviewed in this qualitative study by conducting in-class focus groups. Respondents were inquired about their opinion on using various teaching strategies with politics as a case to explain elements of the marketing mix. Recommendations to use class discussions, role-play, and cold-call engagement are contributions of this chapter, presenting learning by applying politics as a marketing challenge to explain the marketing theory. Politics as a marketing example can be used by academic and industrial marketing trainers and educators, leading towards a strategic opportunity for collaboration between Australian and Pakistani education planners and institutions for stablishing strong institutions for peace and justice.

INTRODUCTION

This chapter presents a unique study that suggests innovating marketing education based on in-class discussions with examples from the world of politics. This study does not imply that there is a specific need to change the approach to teach marketing, however, productive changes and innovation in teaching is a natural process that applies in education of marketing (Nix, 2021; Rayburn, Anderson & Sierra, 2020). Australian education has presented itself as a role model in international education in the last

DOI: 10.4018/978-1-7998-8657-0.ch003

three decades and has successfully applied global collaboration for productive expansion in various geographic and demographic segments (McCubbin, Hammer & Ayriss, 2021). Australia can extend its engagement and education-based relations with the South Asian nations in general and with Pakistan specifically, based on post Covid-19 developments, as illustrated in this chapter.

Marketing education in universities around the world has been based on commercial examples of cars, smartphones, shoes, bags, and sports products, where most of these products are being sold under various brand names that invest in innovative marketing and earn trillions of dollars every year (Rayburn et al., 2020). Students studying marketing; graduate with the understanding that marketing can only be applied to products, services, and brands, and hence ignoring a large area of political marketing. The rise of political marketing is based on new political leaders emerging in national and global politics due their sharp and focused marketing techniques, which can be used as cross-learning for university students, as part of their deep learning. Moreover, the Covid-19 Pandemic has broken many norms with commercial and personal daily practices. The impact of Covid-19 on Australian education has been exponential. However, some lessons could be learnt on opening doors for educational partnerships (Thatcher et al., 2020). This chapter indicates that among new emerging opportunities based on the impact of Covid-19, educational collaboration between Australia and South Asia needs to be further examined.

Since political marketing is a global case hence universities in various countries can collaborate and share the relevant knowledge and practices to enhance the marketing skills of their students. This chapter aims to suggest such a collaboration between Australian and Pakistani Universities to improve the deep learning of marketing students by cross-studying the case of success and failure in politics. The population was limited as students could be interviewed in two Australian and two Pakistani Universities. Interviews were conducted on relevant campuses, hence restricting their open thoughts. This chapter presents a qualitative study conducted on university students in both countries analysing their deep learning skills based on their application of the marketing theory to the political parties and leaders in their respective countries.

Vlosky and Wilson (2020) specified that technology has changed the way of teaching with new methods emerging regularly and claiming to be a revolution in teaching and learning. Specific studies conducted on technology used by marketing students indicated that students appreciate technological sources as being significant for business professionals, with comparatively lesser benefits for their abilities at obtaining knowledge in real world marketing (Nix, 2021; Vlosky & Wilson, 2020). The observation and structure of the interviews with university students were embedded in the education literature on surface and deep learning approaches as well as critical and imaginative thinking. The recommendations of this exercise were linked with two different labels associated with the 'performances of understanding' of students in the class (Biggs, 2003, p.36). Firstly, the SOLO (Structure of the Observed Learning Outcome) taxonomy developed by Biggs and Tang (2007); and secondly, the five teaching approaches specified by Trigwell, Prosser and Waterhouse (1999).

Biggs (2003) explains the SOLO taxonomy based on five levels of teaching: pre-structural, uni-structural, multi-structural, relational, and extended abstract. Trigwell et al. (1999) delivered five approaches or strategies to teaching: A: teacher-focused strategy where knowledge is transmitted, B: teacher-focused strategy where students acquire knowledge, C: teacher/student interaction strategy, D: student-focused strategy where students develop conceptions and E: student-focused strategy where students change their conceptions. Aronshtam, Shrot and Shmallo (2021) in their latest study supported the benefits of using SOLO by indicating that students with good earlier grades will have higher probability that their solutions would be categorized at higher taxonomic levels. The major objective of this paper is to suggest how a relational and extended abstract level from SOLO, as well as approach D and E (Trigwell et al., 1999) could be achieved by cross-teaching marketing by using politics as case studies in Australian and Pakistani Universities.

This chapter is structured as follows. The first section of the chapter introduces the growing economic and educational significance of Australia's engagement with a South Asian country such as Pakistan, for bilateral trade and development opportunities. Section 2 provides the literature review studying the theories and methods of teaching and learning and its value as an opportunity for collaboration between countries based on cases of political marketing. Section 3 outlines the methodology of exploratory qualitative research adopted for this study. This research agrees with the idea that teaching is a process of facilitating the information, some disciplines where students must follow a strict study discipline with atomistic and surface approaches; the facilitating strategy may not be applied successfully. Section 4 delivers the findings of interviews and focus groups with university students in both countries related to cross-teaching respective political marketing. The final section 5 discusses and recommends the application of the marketing mix for cases of political marketing in both countries, highlighting the opportunities of further collaboration in education and development.

BACKGROUND

Australia and Its Partnerships

Since the economic boom in Australia that peaked after the wars in 1960s, it always tried to patronise Asian countries as a socio-economic teacher. However, in late 1980s and early 1990s the situation had changed hence Australian think tanks and politicians started to see Asian nations as partners for future sustainable growth (Ravenhill, 1997). The rise of Asian Tigers, especially a small state like Singapore exceeding per capita income from Australia, and Japanese and Koreans massive foreign direct investment in Asia, rang bells for Australian think tanks. Ravenhill (1997) expressed this change triggering the shift in Australian foreign, economic, cultural, and trade policies oriented towards Asian nations. This re-orientation expanded Australian partnership in diplomacy and trade, also associated with education flow and relationship with various Asian countries. The educational relationships started with the neighbouring Indonesia, through knowledge transfer under various transnational initiatives to build collaborations between Indonesian and Australian universities (Sutrisno & Pillay, 2015).

Following the Asian engagement strategy, Australia also planned to have better trade, political and economic relations with SAARC (South Asian Association of Regional Cooperation) countries. Due to geographic non-proximity, Australia could only have observer status in SAARC like Japan, USA, and Iran (Ahmar, 2011). Bandara and Smith (2002) presented various opportunities for partnership for development between Australia and SAARC in area of economy, sports, politics, and education. The globally recognized standard education provided by the Australian higher educational institutes attracts several Asian students as considered better and closer than Europe or the US (Sutrisno & Pillay, 2015).

Large number of students originally from SAARC nations, are selecting to study in Australia in order to achieve the permanent residency (Bandara & Smith, 2002). Currently, university degrees are Australia's leading service export to India, which is worth AUD 5.5 billion, where more than 120,000 Indian, Sri Lankan and Maldivian students studied in Australian institutes (Bandara & Smith, 2002). Australia has planned to expand education collaboration in the SAARC through the New Colombo Plan, hence Australian students have been witnessed to engage in various educational events within the SAARC nations (Bandara & Smith, 2002). Furthermore, the devastating impact of Covid-19 on Australian education has identified unprecedented opportunities for Australia to seek multi-lateral educational partnerships in new regions (Thatcher et al., 2020).

Marketing Education

Marketing as a subject was recognised as a part of the MBA program in 1970s after the acceptance of the marketing mix. Borden (1964) came up with the 12Ps of marketing mix and McCarthy (1964) sharpened them into the famous 4Ps, which are: product, price, place, and promotion. Since then, there has been an argument whether marketing can be taught or is it an instinct. One polar end argued that most celebrated and successful marketers had no formal education in marketing. Other polar group stressed that by studying marketing as a subject, an individual can learn how to analyse, select, design, and implement a strategy as a marketer. This paper does not suggest any opinions for or against the argument, but reflects upon better ways of marketing education based on daily life examples. This paper adopts the 4Ps as a framework to teach marketing but with an innovative tool of politics rather than conventional products and brands. Moreover, the business examples of Pepsi and Coke have been used too often; hence this paper identifies the significance of innovation in using examples such as political parties marketing their party agenda and people (candidates) to win governments.

Literature review indicated several models providing different methods to improve the interaction of students in a classroom, which is always critical for the learning of marketing. The discussion on the surface and deep learning of students (Biggs & Tang, 2007; Marton & Saljo, 1976) leading to their critical and imaginative thinking (Dearing, 1997; Gokhale, 1995) as a productive learning approach was selected for this study. Theoretical concepts of marketing become meaningless if they are not supported or illustrated by real life examples (Zhou et al., 2021). Evans (2021) further strengthened this fact by saying that the personal work experience of students encompasses the case study method, used often in marketing education, which provides more control and hence reassures students a profound learning outcome.

Modern day marketers have illustrated various marketing concepts by using non-commercial examples such as social groups, non-profit organisations, and government bodies (Hostetter Jr, 2017). This study will elaborate on the usage of politics as an example to explain marketing theory and practice. The teaching approaches of group activities, class discussions, role plays, and cold call engagement will be used to illustrate examples of politics to explain the marketing theory. For effective teaching of marketing, students should be trained to have a deep learning and be creative and critical during their learning process for marketing as a subject.

Since the author of this chapter is a dual national from Australia and Pakistan, therefore this research paper was initiated and conducted in these two countries. Moreover, since COVID-19 the global economic, geo-political, health and social conditions are changing, this chapter offers a unique perspective into opportunities for partnership between Australia and Pakistan to enhance teaching and learning in the field of Marketing.

LITERATURE REVIEW

The Theory of Teaching and Learning

This paper suggests better ways to teach marketing in lectures at Business Schools in Australia and Pakistan. The observation and structure of the lectures were embedded in the education literature on surface and deep approaches as well as critical and imaginative thinking. The recommendations of this exercise were linked with two different labels associated with the 'performances of understanding' of students in the class (Biggs, 2003, p.36). Firstly, the SOLO (Structure of the Observed Learning Outcome) taxonomy developed by Biggs and Collins (1982), recently supported by Aronshtam et al. (2021); secondly, the five teaching approaches specified by Trigwell, Prosser and Waterhouse (1999).

Biggs (2003) explains the SOLO taxonomy based on five levels of teaching: pre-structural, uni-structural, multi-structural, relational, and extended abstract. Trigwell et al. (1999) delivered five approaches or strategies to teaching: **A: teacher-focused strategy where knowledge is transmitted, B: teacher-focused strategy where students acquire knowledge, C: teacher/student interaction strategy, D: student-focused strategy where students develop conceptions and E: student-focused strategy where students change their conceptions**. The major objective of this paper is to suggest how a relational and extended abstract level from SOLO, as well as approach D and E (Trigwell et al., 1999) could be achieved to teach marketing by using politics as an example at Australian and Pakistani Universities.

In order to achieve the above-mentioned objectives, following questions were designed to observe and evaluate the teaching of marketing (Hostetter Jr, 2017; Laurillard, 2002; Ramsden, 2008):

1. Are the students learning to be critical thinkers and analysts of the marketing knowledge rather than descriptors of knowledge?
2. Are the marketing students developing their intellectual and thinking skills?
3. Are the students being training students to be able to comprehend marketing principles or generalisations?

It is important to discuss the purposes of education, before illustrating the strategies that can be used to improve teaching and learning processes for marketing as a subject. Day (2000) stressed upon the need to re-orientate the education mechanism towards the world changing with globalisation, the rise of Asia, customer-focus of markets and various environmental changes. McRae (1995) earlier delivered a warning based on the annual report of International Labour organisation (ILO) suggesting that rising unemployment in the West would lead to an economic downturn due to changes in international markets and the structure of industrial economics shifting from production of low value-added good and services to high-technological and sophisticated service industries. This shift in the structure of industrial economics has altered the shape of the employment picture and the need for professional skills has reached unprecedented levels.

The above discussion implies that the purpose for education is driven by the needs and demands of industry and markets. Therefore, students of higher education, specifically studying marketing subjects, should be educated to build their real business knowledge and sharpen their professional skills (McCubbin, Hammer & Ayriss, 2021; Nix, 2021). This direction of student-oriented studies and pragmatism for future education was also echoed by the Bradley Report conducted by the Australian Government on higher education practices (Bradley Report, 2008). The above-mentioned ideas reflect upon the need to teach marketing by adopting a relational and extended abstract level from SOLO and approaches D and E (Trigwell et al., 1999).

Approaches for Teaching

To further elaborate on the approach to teach marketing, a teaching strategy is linked to the teaching approach adopted by a teacher (Biggs & Tang, 2007; Ramsden, 2008). The learning approaches described by Ramsden (2008) give a clear picture about this concept, he presented two overarching issues:

1. 'How', the structural aspect of teaching, based on holistic and atomistic approaches. The holistic approach focussing on the 'whole' with respect to various parts of the issue, while the atomistic approach focussing only on specific parts of the issue.
2. 'What', the meaning aspect of teaching, based on deep and surface approaches. The deep approach focussing on the depth of the tasks linked to the issue, while the surface approach focussing on obvious tasks linked to the issue.

Since marketing needs to be taught as a pragmatic, real life and dynamic subject, the holistic and deep learning methods are the obvious choice. The adoption of holistic and deep learning methods linked to relational and extended abstract levels and approaches D and E require further elaboration on various teaching strategies that is discussed below.

Strategy to Facilitate Education

This strategy suggests teaching as a process of facilitating the information delivered by the teacher, and its reception and application by students. Some disciplines where students need to follow a strict study discipline and follow the outline, the atomistic and surface approaches; there the facilitating strategy may not be applied successfully. Since in marketing students prefer to study independently, the strategy of facilitating for marketing students is effectively applicable.

Interactive Strategy

The interactive strategy is similar to relational level of SOLO and approaches C and D; it involves the open interaction between the teacher and students. This strategy suggests a dialogue in the class where the teacher and students learn and share the knowledge with each other. The interactive strategy as a part of the facilitating strategy needs class discussions, role play and cold call engagement.

Passive Learning Strategy

Passive strategy is opposite from the interactive strategy and similar to pre-structured level of SOLO and approach A and B. This strategy suggests that students shall wait for the task to be given before any participation or contribution. The passive strategy could be applicable in some areas of study where students need to follow a strict study routine and receive knowledge at the first stage and then apply it when directed. In marketing, passive teaching strategy can never be successful as it kills the dynamic and innovative nature of the discipline.

Group Activities and Case-Based Teaching Strategy

Marketing encourages teamwork; hence the group strategy can never be ignored. When adopting group teaching strategy for marketing subjects, it is strongly advisable to link the group study with case-based teaching (Evans 2021; Ments, 1999). If students are taught or assessed in groups, then topic-based teaching does not indicate the connection between objectives and outcomes. If case-based teaching is used, it promotes deep thinking among students in a particular group and highlights the objectives and outcomes of the teaching practice.

Class Discussions

Classroom discussion is the most frequently used and more often embraced active learning strategy since it is inherently democratic and offers students a greater degree of freedom in the classroom motivating them to be active and responsible for their own learning (Evans, 2000; Brookfield & Preskill, 1999). Brookfield and Preskill (1999) suggest classroom discussion help students develop critical understanding, self-awareness, appreciation for diverse perspectives, and ability to act.

The discussion method described by Ewens (2000, p. 21) as: 'the instructor and a group of students consider a topic, issue, or problem and exchange information, experiences, ideas, opinions, reactions, and conclusions with one another'. A common dilemma any instructor faces, however, is what to do about students who are less inclined to participate voluntarily. This problem is also faced by marketing lecturers and the only solution is cold calling that is discussed in subsequent sections.

Biggs and Tang (2007) explain that through discussion students practice the process to figure out solutions for their problems by following concepts, formulating arguments, and discussing their and others' ideas in a public setting that is the classroom. Brookfield and Preskill (1999) emphasise that class discussion is an effective means for helping students develop critical understanding, self-awareness, appreciation for diverse perspectives, and preparing them to act in the real world. Furthermore, instructional developers suggest that compared to the traditional lecture method, discussion elicits higher level of reflective thinking and problem solving, including application, analysis, synthesis, and evaluation, and that information learned through discussion is generally retained better than information learnt through a lecture (Evans 2021; Ewens, 2000; Laurillard, 2002).

Role Play Strategy

A role play strategy in education and training is considered as a historic practice where Romans used it in their war games (Ments, 1999). The role play is being adopted in various teaching approaches and is recognised as giving more control to the student to get involved with the teaching process. It is well understood that doing is the best way of learning, Ments (1999, p. 2) stresses upon the need for role play based on students' observation, 'I hear, and I forget, I see, and I remember, I do, and I understand'.

Role play is now understood as a specific simulation that is based on interactions among different people. Therefore, McSharry and Jones (2000) suggest that role play is a training technique that is a combination of play, games, and simulation. (Ments, 1999, p.9) defined role play as: 'the experiencing of a problem under an unfamiliar set of constraints in order that one's own ideas may emerge and one's understanding increase'. For teachers, role play gives them the opportunity to link the subject with the practical side while students can get a sense of ownership and control of their education (McSharry &

Jones, 2000). Another benefit for students is that they can use role play for more frequent and meaningful interactions with each other in certain roles that are based on scenarios and set of role descriptions (Ments, 1999).

The application of the role play strategy is based on three dimensions illustrated by Ments (1999): the role-player, situation, and learning. The first dimension indicates if the person is real or imaginary, and in or out of the learning group. The second dimension indicates if the situation is simple or complex, new, or familiar, detailed or outlined and short or long term oriented. The third dimension indicates if the learning is participative or observed and if it requires a skill or technique and concludes with sensitization or an attitude shift. The application of the three dimensions of role play to teach marketing by politics as an example is discussed ahead in this paper.

Cold Call Engagement Strategy

The instructor must decide if he or she should cold call to enhance both individual student learning and classroom discussion quality. The term cold call is used to any instance in which a teacher calls on a student whose hand is not raised; this technique is less emphasised upon in current literature. Despite the support for the use of discussion in teaching, not all students are equally likely to participate, which can limit the value of discussion, especially for students less inclined to volunteer (Brookfield & Preskill, 1999). Dallimore, Hertenstein and Platt (2006) identified significant issues linked to cold calling: student comfort, preparation, frequency of participation.

The students' diversity based on their backgrounds play a key role in adopting cold call engagement. Diversity in students learning is important as students in Australian Universities come from different backgrounds and possess various strengths and weaknesses. Kemmis, Marginson, Porter and Rizvi (2009) summarised the issues of diversity in Australian higher education, by calling it to be systematically and programmatically more diverse. Systematic diversity refers to several universities offering various educational packages, programmatic diversity refers to the variety of educational programs being offered to students around the world (Kemmis et al., 2009). It is suggested that the dynamic nature of relations and networks and their impact on global knowledge market in today's world, plus the popularity and adoption of multiculturalism, lays the foundation of diversity in Australian higher education (Kemmis et al., 2009).

How to solve issues will cold calling are analysed here. Tell the student before the class that he or she will be called on and the question you will ask; this approach is especially effective with international students who must respond in a second language (Dallimore, Hertenstein & Platt, 2006). Following measures are further suggested for effective adoption of call engagement with students (Brookfield & Preskill, 1999; Dallimore et al., 2006):

- Pose a question to the entire class and give them several seconds to reflect (possibly suggesting they write their answers) before cold calling on one student.
- After posing a question, allow students to work briefly in small groups on a response. Then cold call, asking, "What did your group conclude?" This is effective with undergraduate students or students from cultures that value consensus. Simpler questions are generally less intimidating than more difficult questions.

Political Marketing

Political marketing has recently been recognised due to the role of marketing in incredible election victories witnessed in many countries over the last few years (Lees-Marshment, 2001; Wring, 1997). Political marketing advances by engaging with new and advanced concepts of marketing and branding as a powerful tool for understanding political images (Scammell, 2015; Speed, Butler & Collins, 2015). Despite several research papers being published on political marketing recently, an integration between a theoretical framework and practical political marketing has yet to be established (Henneberg, 2008; Ormrod & Henneberg, 2010; Scammell, 2015). This lack of an accepted application of political marketing makes it an interesting subject that has an unlimited scope for research. This open debate on political marketing enhances the effectiveness of using politics as examples to teach marketing better.

This paper has a limited scope to present a better way of marketing education based on examples from the world of politics. However, some understanding of political marketing is necessary to apprehend the findings and suggestions of this study. Henneberg (2008) claims that the rise of political marketing takes the credit of the fact that today most political actors are not only performers, but they also think as marketers. The shift in marketing of politics and overall practice of politics is due to the exchange character of political marketing, qualification of the market environment social acceptance of the profession of politics and its obvious links with ethical deliberations (Henneberg & O'Shaughnessy, 2009; Speed et al., 2015).

Political marketing in Australia was primarily researched by O' Cass (1996). O' Cass (1996) studied various factors related to the marketing concept within an Australian political party. The key topics of the study were linked with the perception of marketing as a tool, related viewpoints, and impact and relevance of it within the political party. It is concluded that politicians can be referred to as consumer brands, contesting with marketing strategies in order to gain market shares, and hence election campaigns are being compared to marketing campaigns (Lees-Marshment, 2001; O' Cass, 1996; Wring, 1997). Wring (1997) also suggested that to win elections some groups seem to go so far as marketing their leader as a soap brand, which can be further mapped with the market positioning theory.

Ling (2008) presented the study on how during 2007 Australian Elections, Maxine McKew seemed to have embraced and borrowed the Adidas slogan of 'Impossible is nothing' as a Labor candidate and when in 2007 she conquered over Liberal Prime Minister John Howard, from a constituency dominated by him for 33 years. Ling (2008) argues that the defeat of Prime Minister John Howard was credited to the marketing campaign, convincing the public that change was inevitable, even if it was not needed. On similar grounds, Yousaf (2016) described the importance of political marketing in Pakistan as different parties were preparing for General Elections in 2018. It was rightly argued in the research that any political party applying political marketing and presenting its leader as the personal brand will win the elections as traditional and status-based elections were a thing of the past (Yousaf, 2016). Similarly, Shahid, Hassan and Sadaf (2021) illustrated how political brand and image marketing supported the positioning of political parties and leaders for victory in Pakistani elections.

Henneberg (2008) observed that conventional marketing strategies are now more congruent with political marketing composition. The development of political marketing is due to the importance of product and image development leading towards better positioning of candidates and their policies, coherent planning of marketing campaigns and extensive usage of political market research (Henneberg, 2008; Henneberg and O'Shaughnessy, 2009; Ormrod & Henneberg, 2010). All above mentioned developments in political marketing indicates that politics could be well adopted as a robust and real-life example to explain the theory and practice of marketing to students of business studies.

MAIN FOCUS OF THE CHAPTER

Research Issues and Problems

Australia and Pakistan have many similarities, vitally including Commonwealth membership, love for sports mainly cricket, hockey and squash, and national focus on tourism (Haq & Wong, 2013; Haider, 2020). Pakistani population residing in Australia has increased to 91,000 in 2019, with more than 15000 Pakistani students studying in Australian Universities (Haider, 2020). Since both countries share Commonwealth traditions and educational systems, most educational institutes adopt similar educational frameworks, especially at university levels. Covid-19 has damaged the international student market of Australia, dropping from four million students in 2018 to 70,000 in 2020 (Thatcher et al., 2020). Pakistan is also trying to upgrade its tourism and education industries to attract overseas travellers and students, this is where she can learn from Australia (Haider, 2020; Khan, 2021). A significant opportunity in collaboration between Australia and Pakistan lies for the untapped international university education, which includes area of e-learning, degree accreditation, curriculum development, and in class teaching methods. The research presented in this chapter highlights the last option of in class teaching methods, where university students in marketing were inquired about conceptualising and applying political marketing in Australia, and then later in Pakistan.

The collaboration between Australia and Pakistan regarding the international university education for marketing politics is unique research contributing towards the aims and objectives of this book. Furthermore, the conclusions of this study also provide a research goal to enhance marketing education in other countries. The qualitative methodology used focus group discussions with university students in Australia and Pakistan studying marketing. The examples of politics as marketing challenges in both countries have been highlighted with respect to the teaching strategies. The use of politics as marketing challenges indicates a novel partnership between Australia and Pakistan in university education that supports effective university teaching practices that could be adopted during and post COVID-19 situation across various countries.

This chapter will look at: (i) Revisiting the theories of teaching to examine the significance of strategic cooperation and partnerships between Australia and Pakistan in context of education pedagogy and bilateral development with respect to mutual growth as post-Covid-19. (ii) Evaluate the six strategies to facilitate education and development opportunities of economy and politics across Australia and Pakistan. (iii) Present the application of marketing strategies based on interviews and focus groups with students in both countries to produce successful political marketing. (iv) Provide students' assessment of using case of politics for cross-teaching marketing and offer recommendations for education-based collaboration and related future research directions.

METHODOLOGY

The major objective of this chapter was to investigate how to improve the teaching of marketing after Covid-19; by using politics as an example at Australian and Pakistani Universities. In order to achieve this research objective, following questions were crafted to observe and study the response from university students in both countries:

1. How do you see elements of marketing mix applied by political parties and leaders to win elections in your country, give examples?
2. Do you develop your intellectual and thinking skills from this discussion and focus group?
3. How do you see brand marketing of political parties and leaders in your country, give examples?

This paper adopted thematic analysis to analyse the qualitative data collected from marketing students in Australian and Pakistani Universities. The method of thematic analysis was applied as advocated by Lincoln and Guba (2003), which suggests an open review of all data collected considering the research objective and recognises the emerging and anchoring themes. These ideas are the emerging themes of this paper contributing towards the opportunities for partnership between Australian and Pakistani Universities based on teaching marketing with political examples.

FINDINGS AND RECOMMENDATIONS

The focus groups conducted with university students studying marketing in Australia and Pakistan indicated new insights for teaching and learning. Findings from the focus groups regarding political marketing and its implication for university education and international collaborations will be presented in this section.

The Marketing Education and Pedagogy

The approaches and strategies for education discussed earlier have been applied to use politics as a tool to teach marketing. Details of the applying regarding various teaching approaches with the aim to achieve deep learning, relational and extended abstract levels (Biggs & Tang, 2007; Biggs, 2003) and approaches D and E (Trigwell et al., 1999) for teaching and learning in marketing are detailed below:

Class Discussions and Group Activities

The class discussion approach provided students with more freedom of thought, promoted critical thinking and recognition of multiple perspectives of marketing in daily life (Laurillard, 2002). The product of politics can be divided into various facets: the party's overarching philosophy, the candidate, the economic, social, environmental, foreign, health and education policy.

In class discussions different topics and concepts of marketing were used to exchange ideas between students and the lecturer. The most relevant concept to highlight the example of politics was the marketing mix: product, price, place, and promotion. Three methods were used to apply marketing mix to politics as a learning practice:

Method 1: Four groups were formed in the class with 3-5 students in each group. Each group was assigned one of the Ps: product or price or place or promotion. In Australia, one common political theme was considered, for example, the Australian Labour Party (ALP), the Liberal Party, Kevin Rudd, Julia Gillard, Tony Abbott, etc. In Pakistan, political themes were Pakistan Tehreek-e-Insaaf (PTI), Muslim League, Pakistan People's Party, Imran Khan, Nawaz Sharif, and Mr Bhutto. Each group representing a 'P' had an internal discussion for 15-25 minutes regarding the theme of the day. Then each group presented their findings and suggestions with reference to the 'P' selected for their group regarding the assigned theme.

Method 2: Another similar class discussion activity was conducted by dividing the class into four groups and assigning a 'P' to each group. In Australia, the theme provided was the poor performance of Australian Labour Party (ALP) in 2010 federal elections. Each group had to present their thoughts about poor performance of ALP in elections with respect to each 'P' assigned to them. Similarly, in Pakistan, theme was the success of (PTI) in 2018 Elections based on effective use of political marketing. A summary of the groups' thoughts presented for applying each P to the poor marketing of the ALP is given below:

1. Product

The weakness of ALP linked to product strategy was the lack of transparency in their ideas and actions. The product related strategic error was the axing of Kevin Rudd as the Prime Minister and his deputy Julia Gillard taking his seat. The students thought that this move damaged the product identity and the brand of ALP in elections.

Meanwhile, Pakistan Tehreek-e-Insaaf used Imran Khan as the product and brand identity of the party (Shahid, Hassan & Sadaf, 2021; Yousaf, 2016). He had his successful sports career and remarkable philanthropic achievements to outshine all other leaders.

2. Place

The discussion about placement strategy was not very clear and students expressed their thoughts about placement related to electorates on state, city, and local levels. The researcher gave them the feedback to think of any way for ALP or PTI to get in touch with their target customers or the voters to pass on their message effectively, for example, by using modern technologies such as internet, Facebook, twitter, and other web 2.0 technologies.

3. Pricing

Pricing seemed to be a difficult strategy for political marketing since students could not assess the pricing issues. However, they came up with other cost factors perceived by the public before they could cast their votes. Hence, students in both countries talked about two key elements of *value* and *trust* that reflected the pricing for voters as they assessed the cost embedded within these elements.

4. Promotion

The Australian group thought that the basic theme of ALP, 'real Julia', which disconnected with the 'ALP" brand as a party, reflected a poor marketing judgement on behalf of the party. Moreover, the status-quo from ALP regarding the sacking of Kevin Rudd as leader damaged any promotion ideas as the public wanted clear answers. These two issues led to other mistakes such as lack of proper targeting of potential voters and a failure to present a policy-based distinction between ALP and other major political parties in Australia.

Meanwhile, Pakistan Tehreek-e-Insaaf and Imran Khan used the marketing slogan of 'Naya (new) Pakistan', which was well received by voters looking to crash the status-quo and have a new government.

Method 3: The class was divided into 3-4 groups of 3-5 students. Each group was assigned one of the political parties of Australia, such as the Labour, Liberal, or Green Party, or PTI, Muslim League, Pakistan People's Party in Pakistan. Then groups were asked to apply the 4Ps of the marketing mix for the political party and suggest how the party could improve its marketing strategies. Each group would discuss their findings and suggestions within the group and then present it in front of the class.

In all focus groups in both countries, students expressed that political parties need to be more marketing efficient by understanding needs of their voters or publics. The strength of each party must be mapped with the needs of public to highlight the difference that could be seen if the party came into power.

The mapping of the marketing mix elements with political marketing in Australasia and Pakistan along with the channels for partnership in education is illustrated in the Table 1 given below:

Table 1. Political marketing mix for Australia and Pakistan

Marketing Mix Elements	Australia	Pakistan	Educational Partnership Channels
Product	• Labor and Liberal parties • PM Scott Morrison	• Justice and People's parties • PM Imran Khan	➢ Curriculum development ➢ Research collaboration
Pricing	• Economic policies • Global relationships	• Economic policies • Anti-corruption actions	➢ Economic and trade collaboration
Place	• Social Media • Press conferences	• Social Media • Public speeches	➢ Online education ➢ Academic conferences
Promotion	• Safe and clean Australia	• Naya (new) Pakistan	➢ Social Media ➢ Students and academic exchange programs

Role Play in the Marketing Class

The strategy of role plays to teach marketing by using politics is more relevant to the class of post graduate students in both countries. One reason is the fact that students at post graduate level have more interest and a better understanding of the political environment. The other reason is that the number of students is comparatively less, which makes the communication smoother and more flexible in the class.

Formation of groups is not compulsory, and each student is asked to play the role of a self-selected politician. The three dimensions of role play strategy given by Ments (1999) are applied here. The politician is a real person and out of the learning group, situation is simple and familiar since all post graduate students are aware of the political atmosphere in Australia and Pakistan. Moreover, this exercise is participative since all mature adults take part in elections and hence are actively involved in politics. As the selected politician, the student presents the 4Ps of the marketing mix.

As an example, a student playing the role of Kevin Rudd or Imran Khan will present the marketing mix as: product is the person himself and his leadership qualities and political vision, price would be the vote that people will give to him, place would be the locations where he could pitch his ideas and where the public could cast their votes, promotion will indicate various tactics he would use to promote his qualities featured as the product. At the end, students in the class will ask questions from him as Kevin Rudd or Imran Khan, and all questions and answers should be marketing oriented.

Cold Call Engagement

Cold call engagement has been part of a debate about its benefits and shortcomings. In marketing it is necessary since marketers cannot be effective if they cannot communicate and present their ideas with aggression (Dallimore et al., 2006). Marketing students need to be vocal and to be professional marketers they must be equipped with interpersonal skills and the art of negotiations. The important rule for cold calling as suggested by Brookfield and Preskill (1999) is to warn students before the class that in the class there will be cold calling on the subject of Australian or Pakistani politics. Moreover, an assessment conducted in the class is most effective if students are trained and prepared for it by the teacher (Biggs & Tang, 2007; Box, 2005; Day, 2000).

If students are divided into groups for a group discussion, then cold calling for a group is another approach used successfully. This approach is used in connection to the Class Discussions and group activities where students already belong to a certain group representing one of the 'P' of marketing mix or a certain political party. This facilitates the cold calling while discussing various marketing concepts when a student in a group could be asked to respond to a question about his or her group belonging to politics as the tool to teach marketing.

Students' Assessment of Using Politics in Marketing

The students who attended the focus group as class discussion, role play, and cold call engagement session based on politics as a tool to teach marketing were asked to assess the sessions to evaluate its effectiveness as a teaching and learning exercise. It is considered very important to understand the perception of students regarding such sessions to improve the overall quality and delivery of teaching and learning (Gibbs & Simpson, 2004; Ramsden 2008). All students present in the class were given a survey with four open ended questions asking their opinions on various methods of teaching applied with politics as a tool to teach marketing. It was an anonymous survey where students did not have to disclose their identities and independently wrote their opinions about the session on Australian and Pakistani politics, and how it helped them in learning marketing.

The major themes that emerged from the assessment from students are described below:

1. Practical application: Most students noted that the session revealed how the marketing theory under study could be practically applied to a real-life situation.
2. Abstract products: Students expressed their excitement and good learning opportunity if an abstract product such as ALP or PTI was analysed, which they thought was never heard of, or read in any textbooks, magazines, or websites.
3. Branding issues: Brands are everywhere, but students thought that it was a revelation that ALP was also a brand. Moreover, they learnt that how poor branding, 'real Julia', could damage a substantial

brand such as the ALP. Contrarily, how 'Naya Pakistan' brand could be the winning stroke by PTI in Pakistan.

FUTURE RESEARCH DIRECTIONS

This study has presented a novel idea of teaching marketing with the product and branding of politics in Universities in Australia and Pakistan. The chapter also highlights the post Covid-19 opportunity for collaboration between Australia and SAARC nations in general, specifically Pakistan for teaching and learning techniques in business disciplines. A future study is suggested to be conducted with education providers such a university professors and lecturers, in order to receive their perspectives on teaching marketing as politics and engaging with other countries. Similarly, senior government officers working with ministry or department of education could also be engaged in research to learn about their insights into collaboration in teaching styles for different countries.

CONCLUSION

This paper talks about more collaborative ways to teach marketing to university students and how it offers partnership opportunities in education across countries. A unique example of politics is discussed, which helps students to be more participative and have a deep learning experience in their marketing lectures. Politics as a tool to teach marketing is successful when methods of class discussions, role play, and cold call engagement are applied. This paper explicitly details how the teaching and learning experience works in a lecture. The distinct teaching strategy of using politics was applied primarily in Australia and replicated in Pakistan with similar results and varying contexts. The students involved in this experience at Australian and Pakistani Universities were also inquired about their opinions. This paper reports that all students in both countries expressed positive response towards this technique.

Other than the pedagogical support; this paper presents a unique opportunity for partnership between Australia and South Asian countries in general, and Pakistan in particular. The study recommends educational partnerships between Australia and SAARC nations in order to manage the Covid-19 damage and build an education collaboration to handle any future pandemics.

REFERENCES

Ahmar, M. (2011). 'China in SAARC? To What Effect?': A Pakistani Perspective. *Strategic Analysis, 35*(3), 508–510. doi:10.1080/09700161.2011.559996

Aronshtam, L., Shrot, T., & Shmallo, R. (2021). Can we do better? A classification of algorithm run-time-complexity improvement using the SOLO taxonomy. *Education and Information Technologies, 1*(5), 1–22. doi:10.100710639-021-10532-0

Bandara, J. S., & Smith, C. (2002). Trade Policy Reforms in South Asia and Australia-South Asia Trade: Intensities and Complementarities. *South Asia Economic Journal, 3*(2), 177–199. doi:10.1177/139156140200300204

Biggs, J. (2003). *Teaching for quality learning at university: What the student does*. Society for Research into Higher Education & Open University Press.

Biggs, J., & Collins, K. F. (1982). *Evaluating the Quality of Learning: The SOLO Taxonomy*. Academic Press.

Biggs, J., & Tang, C. (2007). *Teaching for quality learning at university*. Open University Press.

Borden, N. H. (1964). The concept of the marketing mix. *Journal of Advertising Research*, *1*(1), 2–7.

Brookfield, S. D., & Preskill, S. (1999). *Discussion as a way of teaching: Tools and techniques for democratic classrooms*. Jossey-Bass.

Dallimore, E. J., Hertenstein, J. H., & Platt, M. B. (2006). Nonvoluntary Class Participation in Graduate Discussion Courses: Effects of Grading and Cold Calling. *Journal of Management Education*, *30*(2), 354–377. doi:10.1177/1052562905277031

Day, C. (2000). Teachers in the twenty-first century: time to renew the vision. *Teacher and Teaching: Theory and Practice, 6*(1), 101-115.

Dearing, R. (1997). Higher Education in the Learning Society, Report of the National Committee of Inquiry into Higher Education, London: HMSO.

Evans, C. (2021). Exploiting students' part-time work to enhance learning, teaching and assessment. *Industry and Higher Education*, *35*(1), 10–13. doi:10.1177/0950422220930182

Ewens, W. (2000). Teaching using discussion. In R. Neff & M. Weimer (Eds.), *Classroom communication: Collected readings for effective discussion and questioning* (pp. 21–26). Atwood.

Fernando, S., & Camilleri, E. (2020). *New perspective on Australia-South Asia foreign policy*. http://dspace.jgu.edu.in:8080/jspui/bitstream/10739/3365/1/New%20perspective%20on%20Australia.pdf

Gokhale, A. A. (1995). Collaborative learning enhances critical thinking. *Journal of Technology Education*, *7*(1), 22–30. doi:10.21061/jte.v7i1.a.2

HaiderT. (2020). *Pakistani Population in Australia*. Retrieved from https://www.sbs.com.au/language/english/pakistani-population-in-australia-increases-to-91-000

Haq, F., & Wong, H. Y. (2013). Branding Islamic spiritual tourism: An exploratory study in Australia and Pakistan. *European Journal of Business and Management*, *5*(11), 154–162.

Henneberg, S. C. (2008). An Epistemological Perspective on Research in Political Marketing. *Journal of Political Marketing*, *7*(2), 151–182. doi:10.1080/15377850802053158

Henneberg, S. C., & O'Shaughnessy, N. (2009). Political Relationship Marketing: Some Micro/Macro Thoughts. *Journal of Marketing Management*, *25*(1/2), 5–29. doi:10.1362/026725709X410016

Hostetter, L. R. Jr. (2017). Teaching Innovations in Marketing: A Brand-Based Student-Led Inquiry of Marketing Concepts and Practices. *Marketing Education Review*, *27*(2), 1–6. doi:10.1080/10528008.2016.1274633

Kemmis, S., Marginson, S., Porter, P., & Rizvi, F. (2009). *Enhancing Diversity in Australian higher Education*. Paper presented to the University of Western Australia by Stephen Kemmis Research & Consulting Pty ltd.

Khan, T. M. (2021). Use of social media and WhatsApp to conduct teaching activities during the COVID-19 lockdown in Pakistan. *International Journal of Pharmacy Practice*, *29*(1), 90–90. doi:10.1111/ijpp.12659 PMID:32715575

Laurillard, D. M. (2002). *Rethinking University teaching* (2nd ed.). Routledge Falmer. doi:10.4324/9780203160329

Lees-Marshment, J. (2001). The marriage of politics and marketing. *Political Studies*, *49*(4), 692–713. doi:10.1111/1467-9248.00337

Lincoln, Y. S., & Guba, E. G. (2003). Paradigmatic controversies, contradictions, and emerging confluences. In N. K. Denzin & Y. S. Lincoln (Eds.), *The Landscape of Qualitative Research: Theories and Issues* (2nd ed., pp. 253–291). Sage.

Ling, P. (2008). Political marketing in Australia. *IMC Journal*, *7*(1), 15–20.

Marton, F., & Saljo, R. (1976). On qualitative differences in learning. I - Outcome and Process. *The British Journal of Educational Psychology*, *46*(1), 4–11. doi:10.1111/j.2044-8279.1976.tb02980.x

McCarthy, E. J. (1964). *Basic Marketing: A Managerial Approach*. Richard D. Irwin, Inc.

McCubbin, A., Hammer, S., & Ayriss, P. (2021). Learning and teaching benchmarking in Australian universities: The current state of play. *Journal of Higher Education Policy and Management*, *1*, 1–18. doi:10.1080/1360080X.2021.1934244

McRae, H. (1995, Feb. 26). The privilege of unemployment, *Independent on Sunday*, p. 4. https://www.independent.co.uk/news/business/the-privilege-of-unemployment-the-economy-analysis-1574883.html

McSharry, G., & Jones, S. (2000). Role-play in science teaching and learning. *The School Science Review*, *82*(298), 73–82.

Ments, M. V. (1999). *The effective use of role play*. Kogan Page Publishers.

Nix, J. M. L. (2021). Co-teachers' perceptions of collaborative EFL teaching: A case study in Taiwan. *Asia Pacific Education Review*, *1*(4), 1–14. doi:10.100712564-021-09684-y

O'Cass, A. (1996). Political marketing and the marketing concept. *European Journal of Marketing*, *30*(10/11), 37–53. doi:10.1108/03090569610149782

Ormrod, R. P., & Henneberg, S. C. (2010). Strategic Political Postures and Political Market Orientation: Towards an Integrated Concept of Political Marketing Strategy. *Journal of Political Marketing*, *9*(1), 294–313. doi:10.1080/15377857.2010.518106

Ramsden, P. (2008). *Learning to teach in Higher Education*. Routledge Falmer.

Ravenhill, J. (1997). *From paternalism to partnership: Australia's relations with ASEAN*. Australian National University Research Publications. https://openresearch-repository.anu.edu.au/handle/1885/40378

Rayburn, S. W., Anderson, S., & Sierra, J. J. (2020). Future thinking continuity of learning in marketing: A student perspective on crisis management in higher education. *Marketing Education Review*, *1*, 1–15.

Report, B. (2008). *Review of Australian Higher Education*. Final report, 2008, Department of Education, Employment and Workplace Relations, Canberra.

Scammell, M. (2015). Politics and image: The conceptual value of branding. *Journal of Political Marketing*, *14*(1-2), 7–18. doi:10.1080/15377857.2014.990829

Shahid, M. N., Hassan, W., & Sadaf, L. (2021). Exploring the Political Co-Brand Image & Positioning from External Stakeholder's Perspective in Pakistan. *Journal of Political Marketing*, *1*(1), 1–30. doi:10.1080/15377857.2021.1930328

Speed, R., Butler, P., & Collins, N. (2015). Human branding in political marketing: Applying contemporary branding thought to political parties and their leaders. *Journal of Political Marketing*, *14*(1-2), 129–151. doi:10.1080/15377857.2014.990833

Sutrisno, A., & Pillay, H. (2015). Knowledge transfer through a transnational program partnership between Indonesian and Australian universities. *Asia Pacific Education Review*, *16*(3), 379–388. doi:10.100712564-015-9384-7

Thatcher, A., Zhang, M., Todoroski, H., Chau, A., Wang, J., & Liang, G. (2020). Predicting the impact of COVID-19 on Australian universities. *Journal of Risk and Financial Management, 13*(9), 188-208.

Trigwell, K., Prosser, M., & Waterhouse, F. (1999). Relations between teachers' approaches to teaching and students' approaches to learning. *Higher Education*, *37*(1), 57–70. doi:10.1023/A:1003548313194

Vlosky, R. P., & Wilson, D. T. (2020). Technology in the Classroom: Teaching Business Marketing in the Twenty-First Century. In Fundamentals of Business Marketing Education (pp. 159-170). Routledge.

Wring, D. (1997). Reconciling marketing with political science: Theories of political marketing. *Journal of Marketing Management*, *13*(7), 651–663. doi:10.1080/0267257X.1997.9964502

Yousaf, S. (2016). Political marketing in Pakistan: Exaggerated promises, delusive claims, marketable development projects and change advocacy. *Journal of Public Affairs*, *16*(2), 140–155. doi:10.1002/pa.1562

Zhou, Y., Jin, C. H., Huang, J. W., & Wang, R. M. (2021). Research on the impact of the Internet on the informatization teaching reform of marketing in universities. In *Computational Social Science* (pp. 576–583). CRC Press. doi:10.1201/9781003144977-87

ADDITIONAL READING

Fasslabend, W. (2015). The Silk Road: A political marketing concept for world dominance. *European View*, *14*(2), 293–302. doi:10.100712290-015-0381-3

KEY TERMS AND DEFINITIONS

Educational Collaboration: This collaboration is based on different institutions getting together to teach a specific topic and share the teaching pedagogy, goals, and outcomes.

Interactive Learning Strategy: It is like relational level of SOLO technique and is based on open interaction between the teacher and students. This strategy proposes a two-way discussion in the class where the teacher and students learn and share the information with each other.

Marketing Mix: The adoption of the 4Ps of marketing mix include products, pricing, place and promotion.

Passive Learning Strategy: This strategy requires students to patiently wait for the task to be given by teacher for any discussion or participation in the class. The passive learning strategy is useful in some areas of study where students need to adopt a given course of learning and cannot use their own ideas, for example in hard sciences.

Political Marketing: The marketing strategies and activities adopted by political parties or individuals with a sole objective of getting votes and winning elections by marketing themselves.

SOLO Taxonomy: It is based on five levels of teaching: pre-structural, uni-structural, multi-structural, relational, and extended abstract.

Chapter 4
Digital Strategic Partnership for Australian and South Asian Enterprises

Kamaljeet Sandhu
https://orcid.org/0000-0003-4624-6834
University of New England, Australia

ABSTRACT

This study aims to identify the important roles in digital strategic partnership for Australian-Asian enterprises. Research has shown that the world's two biggest economies in the coming years will be in Asia, and they are China and India. Australia's strategic location and close geographic proximity to Asia and its engagement in economic, business, education, health, cultural, and technological cooperation have led to opportunities in digital strategic partnership for Australian-Asian enterprises. A case study approach is used to analyse the strategic investment opportunities in digital and telecommunication technologies with Australia and Asian trading partners to develop a digital strategy. Over many years, Australia has demonstrated leadership for exchange of strategic information, ideas, and closer participation with Asia, which has led to building a strong relationship in terms of government-to-government, people-to-people, and business-to-business, which can be transformed for innovative digital strategic partnership in the South Asian region.

INTRODUCTION

Australia has a unique geographical location and proximity to Asia which provides opportunities that Australian businesses can benefit. For many years Australia have been exporting minerals and agricultural products to Asian countries, but in recent times another bigger opportunity has risen which are Digital in nature. Australia has one of the advanced digital infrastructures that can easily connect to the Asian digital infrastructure, through which large volumes of trade and commerce can be exchanged. The case for digital access is clear. Businesses in Asia are undergoing rapid digital transformation. Digitization boosts social and financial inclusion as well as learning and health outcomes (Drees-Gross & Zhang 2021).

DOI: 10.4018/978-1-7998-8657-0.ch004

Handforth and Tan (2021) argue that successful implementation of any kind of infrastructure requires a comprehensive and strategic approach, and even more so for digital infrastructure. Unlike other more traditional infrastructure sectors, digital enterprise infrastructure requires coordination across many moving parts, from mobile spectrum allocations – the radio frequencies that enable mobile connectivity – to balancing the rights of landowners; policy and legislation to ensure that no one (and nowhere) is left unconnected and ensuring equitable access to – and ownership of – devices.

Duan et al (2021) and Westerman et al (2014) describe digital enterprise transformation — the use of technology to radically improve performance or reach of enterprises — is a hot topic for companies across the globe. Executives in all industries are using digital advances such as analytics, mobility, social media and smart embedded devices as well as improving their use of traditional technologies such as ERP to change customer relationships, internal processes and value propositions.

Ingram (2020) suggests that digital enterprise technology is disrupting traditional means of communications, business, learning, how we function at work and at home, and even governing. It is speeding up and deepening access to information and communications, reducing the cost of technologies, driving productivity, boosting efficiency, speeding innovation, accelerating economic growth, empowering financial inclusion, building innovative and resilient solutions, and facilitating government transparency and citizen-government interaction. Therefore, digital connectedness is a glue that is holding together different sections of community, society, enterprise, and the government.

Somani (2021) reports that over the coming years, the commercial world's focus on connectivity will sharpen significantly as governments' emphasis on building digital infrastructure continues to grow. The digital character of modern data makes infrastructure a prerequisite for collecting, exchanging, storing, processing, and distributing data. Harnessing the full economic and social value of modern data services calls for digital infrastructure that is universally accessible, while also offering adequate internet speed at affordable cost (World Development Report 2021).

ASEAN (Association of Southeast Asian Nations) brings together ten Southeast Asian states – Brunei, Cambodia, Indonesia, Laos, Malaysia, Myanmar, the Philippines, Singapore, Thailand and Vietnam – into one organisation. Australia became ASEAN's first Dialogue Partner in 1974 and Australia became Strategic Partners in 2014 (DFAT, 2021). ASEAN is Australia's second largest trading partner as a bloc and is essential to Australia's economic recovery from the COVID-19 pandemic (DFAT, 2021). In 2019-20, Australia's trade with ASEAN countries was $113.7 billion, which is greater than Australia's two-way trade with Japan and the United States. Australia's two-way investment with ASEAN in 2019 was over $259 billion. Australia has strong trade links are supported by the regional and bilateral free trade agreements that act as pathways for Australian business to tap into ASEAN and the ASEAN Economic Community (DFAT, 2021).

Australia has been a popular destination for Asian students to pursue higher education at Australian universities. Austrade (2021) commissioned a report on "Growth and opportunity in Australian international education" in which it was found that Australia's onshore international education sector is forecast to grow from 650,000 enrolments today to 940,000 by 2025 (which equates to a compounding annual growth rate of 3.8 per cent). The international education sector's contribution to export earnings is expected to almost double to in excess of $33 billion by 2025. The top eight source markets for onshore international learner enrolments across all sectors in 2025 are expected to be China, India, Vietnam, Thailand, Nepal, Malaysia, Brazil and South Korea (Jain & Lamba 2021). In recent times, local and international students in Asia and Australia have connected to digital technologies for digital learning and Australian universities have been at the forefront for digital teaching.

Much of the growth in onshore learner enrolments will be driven by Asia – in particular China, India, Nepal, Vietnam and Thailand. Over the period to 2025, the fastest growing sectors in onshore international education are expected to be higher education and VET (in percentage terms). By 2025, these two sectors are expected to account for 72 per cent of all onshore international learner enrolments. China is set to remain Australia's largest source market for onshore enrolments in 2025 and is expected to occupy the largest number of higher education, schooling and ELICOS enrolments. The largest number of VET onshore enrolments in 2025 are forecast to come from India (16 per cent), Thailand (eight per cent) and South Korea (seven per cent). The argument for acceleration to digital teaching and learning cannot be underestimated.

Thu (2021) argues that Australia should bet on digital engagement with Southeast Asia, and it should adopt a comprehensive and long-term strategy that would modernize its traditional diplomacy and would effectively support the region's resilience to cyberattacks, address its immediate needs and invest in its growing potential (Sandhu, 2021). This should be a whole-of-government commitment, similar to the Pacific step-up. The pandemic has accelerated the digital transformation across the globe. But digital capability and cyber maturity across Southeast Asia is very uneven. Singapore, for example, is one of the world's most technologically advanced countries, while Laos and Myanmar lag far behind. At the same time, Southeast Asia is one of the most dynamic regions in the world when it comes to adapting to technological change.

Thu (2021) suggests that Indonesia, Vietnam and Thailand are developing e-commerce markets and homes for some of the world's most energetic innovation hubs (Saavedra et al., 2020). This should inform and shape Canberra's strategic and commercial engagement with the region, and its approach to development aid. Australia can make a significant contribution in bridging gaps between different countries' digital capabilities. Its cyber capacity and resilience are among the world's top 10, according to Harvard University's 2020 National Cyber Power Index.

But the pandemic has further exposed and deepened digital divides within individual countries. For example, when schools closed, online teaching was only an option for those with access to computers and the internet. Children in rural, poorer or less connected places missed out on education—the very means to overcome poverty and limited opportunities. If not addressed, this has the potential to create a 'Covid generation' that will have lost key educational opportunities. Similarly, occupations were disrupted to varying degrees by the pandemic. Southeast Asia has a strong informal service-based economy. The national lockdowns, and the tourism and business travel freezes, took away the livelihoods of many, particularly in the hospitality and services sectors. Australia could help to support efforts to retrain workers and teach them digital skills.

Thu (2021) claims digital, tech and science capabilities are critical for the longer-term post-Covid recovery. In helping to fund initiatives across Southeast Asia, Australia will forge durable economic ties with its partners in the region—including countries such as Indonesia, Thailand and Vietnam, which are expected to surpass Australia's GDP in a couple of decades. Australia's support should be considered an investment in future two-way development, rather than just one-way aid. The strategy should include supplying computers and hardware, improving skills, and retraining and assisting the region's workforce to adapt to the technological revolution. Some action is already underway. For example, Australia's CSIRO, in partnership with the Department of Foreign Affairs and Trade, operates in Singapore, Vietnam and Indonesia to support training in science, biosecurity, technology and the digital economy. But this work needs to be increased and should form part of an overarching policy. Figure 1 shows Digital Strategic Partnership and engagement for Australian-Asian Enterprises on three levels which includes government to government, businesses to businesses, and people to people that will cement the solid digital foundation.

Figure 1. Digital strategic partnership for Australian-Asian enterprises

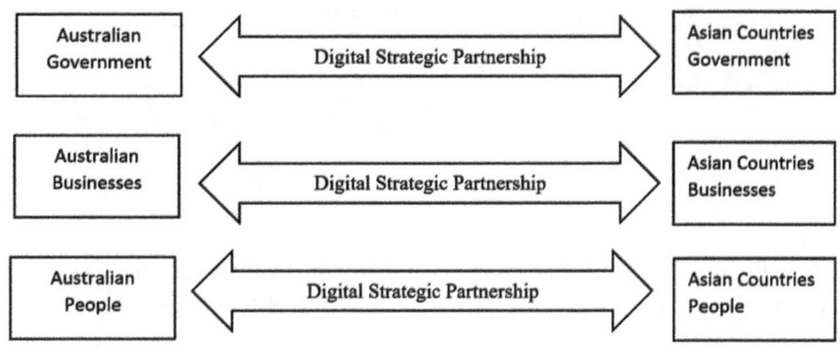

BACKGROUND

In recent year years Australia has made significant investment in digital infrastructure such as NBN and providing high speed internet connection to homes and businesses. Access to data assists businesses to stay competitive by gaining access to useful market intelligence, identifying growth opportunities, designing innovative goods and services, improving pricing, and operating more efficiently. This has also opened access to a global digital economy that functions 24 hours a day, seven days a week, and 365 days a year which creates enormous business opportunities in local and international markets.

Countries such as Australia, Singapore have shown to have strong privacy and information laws. Importantly, the Privacy Act 1988 protects personal information collected for inclusion in a record or publication and continues to apply when personal information of Australians is transferred to another country. Improved protections for source code and exchange of data provides protection to intellectual property. Access to or disclosure of software source code will not be required to be transferred to Singapore as a condition for the import, distribution, sale or use of software – this rule covers both mass-market software and bespoke/custom software (Moss & Sandhu 2020).

In a study by ITU (2021) reveals that COVID-19 pandemic has pushed consumers and businesses alike to adopt digital services and technologies, thus accelerating digital transformation in consumer behaviour and business activity by several years which is shown in the figure 2.

While China and India have the highest population in the world, they are also the largest telecommunication markets in the Asian region as shown by the data in figure 3.

Mobile Market Developments

The ITU (2021) report suggests that the Asia-Pacific mobile markets are fairly advanced, with mobile cellular subscriptions far in excess of 100 per 100 inhabitants in 22 out of the 38 countries for which data were available. In 16 countries, subscription rates are less than 100 per 100 inhabitants, with 7 countries between 70 and 95.5 subscriptions per 100 inhabitants, including Bhutan (95.5), Nauru (94.6), Vanuatu (88.4), India (84.3), Pakistan (76.4), Solomon Islands (71.4) and Tuvalu (70.4). Countries with

Figure 2. Accelerating the impact of COVID-19 on digital transformation
Source: ITU, based on insights from 2020 McKinsey consumer and enterprise surveys

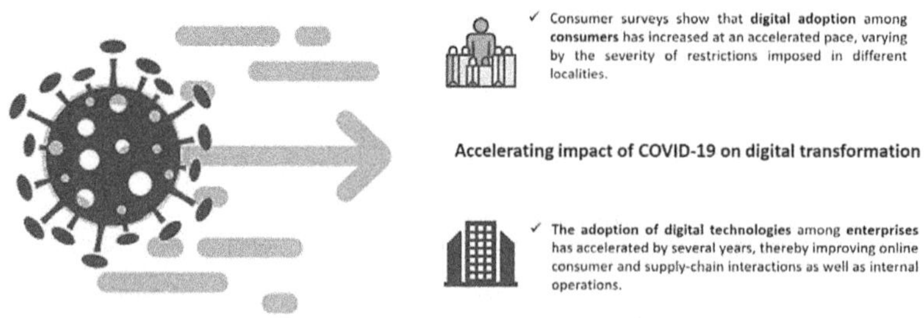

subscription rates per 100 inhabitants of between 45 and 60 include Samoa (63.6), Lao P.D.R. (60.8), Tonga (59.4), Afghanistan (59.3), Papua New Guinea (47.6) and Kiribati (46.5) shown in figure 4. Only three countries, namely the Marshall Islands, Micronesia and the Democratic People's Republic of Korea

Figure 3. Key ICT statistics, Asia-Pacific region, 2017-2019
Source: ITU WTI Database and World Bank data (for gross national income (GNI) data)

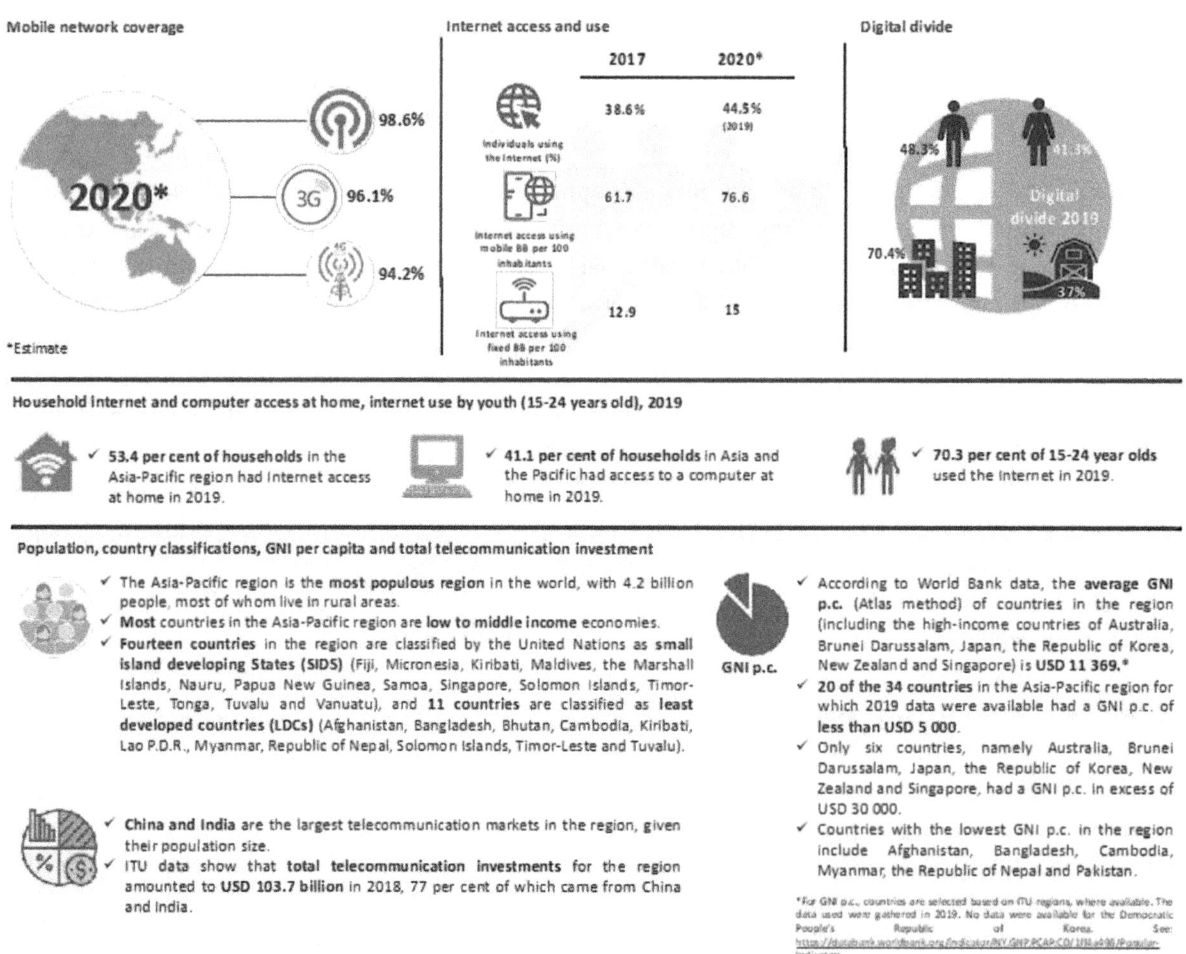

Figure 4. Mobile cellular subscriptions, 38 Asia-Pacific countries, 2019
Source: Based on the ITU WTI Database, July 2020 edition

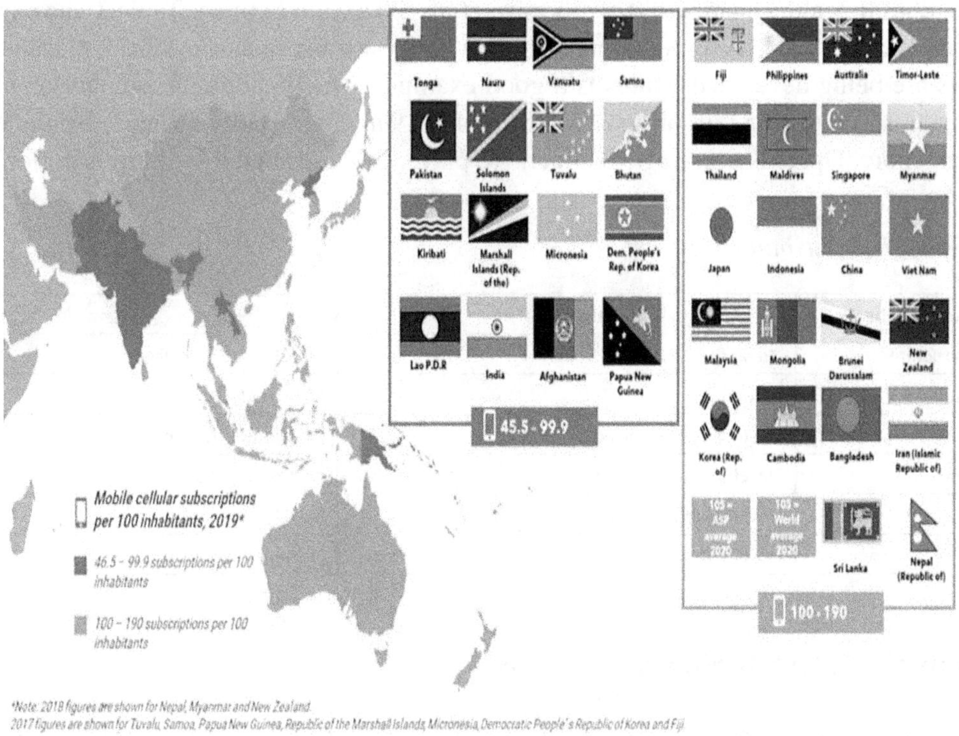

have subscription rates per 100 inhabitants of less than 30. For the Asia-Pacific region, the 2020 average subscription rate was estimated by ITU at 104.6 per 100 inhabitants, which is just short of the world average of 105 subscriptions per 100 inhabitants.

The next section identifies a case based analysis approach in which a key theme is analyzed in context with real world issues.

MAIN FOCUS OF THE CHAPTER

Case Analysis 1: Australia and Asian Trading Partners

Australia has strategic interest in the major economies of Asia including China, India, Singapore, Thailand, Indonesia, and Malaysia. The Australia-Singapore Digital Economy Agreement (DEA) upgrades the Singapore-Australia Free Trade Agreement (SAFTA) through a new Digital Economy chapter, providing modernized trade rules that assist businesses and consumers to engage with and benefit from digital trade and the digital economy (DFAT, 2021). Singapore-Australia in recent times have forged closer relationships in digital investments but deeper strategic partnership is required to transform the digital trade and digital economy of both countries. For example, Singapore has an advanced digital infrastructure that is digitally connected such as air transport, banking and finance, biotechnology, and many others that can provide Australian businesses with opportunities for digital investments. Similarly Singaporean businesses can invest in digital infrastructure such as telecommunication, broadband internet (e.g. NBN), digital health (Sandhu, 2020; Tanniru et al., 2020), and others. Table 1 shows key digital attributes between Australia and other Asian countries. Some attributes can be considered to be advanced while others are being developed. Optus is a good example, which and is the second-largest wireless carrier in Australia, with 10.5 million subscribers as of 2019 and is a wholly owned subsidiary of Singtel based in Singapore. Optus is a strategic competitive player in Australian telecommunication industry.

Table 1. Key digital attributes

Key Digital Attributes	Australia	Asia
Digital Infrastructure	Advanced	Developing/Advanced
Digital Literacy	Advanced	Developing/Advanced
Digital Business Adoption	Developing/Advanced	Developing/Advanced
Digital Markets	Developing/Advanced	Developing/Advanced
Digital Government	Developing/Advanced	Developing/Advanced
Digital Banking & Finance	Developing/Advanced	Developing/Advanced

Case Analysis 2: Strategic Partnerships

The key outcomes from the DEA (DFAT 2021) include on building a strong partnership. Australia has established major strategic partnerships with Asian countries for data management and control. Cross-border data flows and location of computing facilities such as data warehouses for storing digital data. Exchange of important data in cybersecurity can enhance both countries cybersecurity systems. Allows for the transfer of data between Australia and Singapore for business purposes, including in the financial sector. Such important digital financial systems data can provide higher levels of opportunities for businesses and governments of both countries. Businesses will not be forced to build data storage centres, or use local computing centres, as a condition of conducting business. In fact through closer cooperation and strategic partnerships more employment opportunities for highly skilled IT labor force in both countries can benefit. Australia already attracts an inflow of highly skilled IT labor immigrants, which is predicted to grow exponentially as newer digital infrastructures are built. South Korea, Singapore, Japan, Malaysia, New Zealand, and Australia has the highest proportion of households with Internet access shown in Figure 5.

Providing businesses with a stable digital platform is an important feature for digitalisation. Stronger cooperation and partnership in recognizing intellectual property rights leads to safer and stable business environment. Improves business certainty through the recognition and protection of intellectual property where the integrity and ownership of source code is crucial to a business's competitiveness in local and global markets. Extends protection to SMEs, which are significant suppliers of bespoke/custom software. Safeguarding digital property rights provides stronger investors confidence into valuable innovative new startups for safer digital businesses practices which leads to resource mobilization and capital investments in digital enterprises.

Figure 5. Proportion of households with Internet access, Asia-Pacific region, and most recent year (2017, 2018 or 2019).
Source: ITU, based on the ITU WTI Database, 2020. Data for 2019 were available for the following countries only: Bangladesh, Brunei Darussalam, Cambodia, the Republic of Korea, Malaysia, Pakistan, the Philippines, Singapore and Thailand.

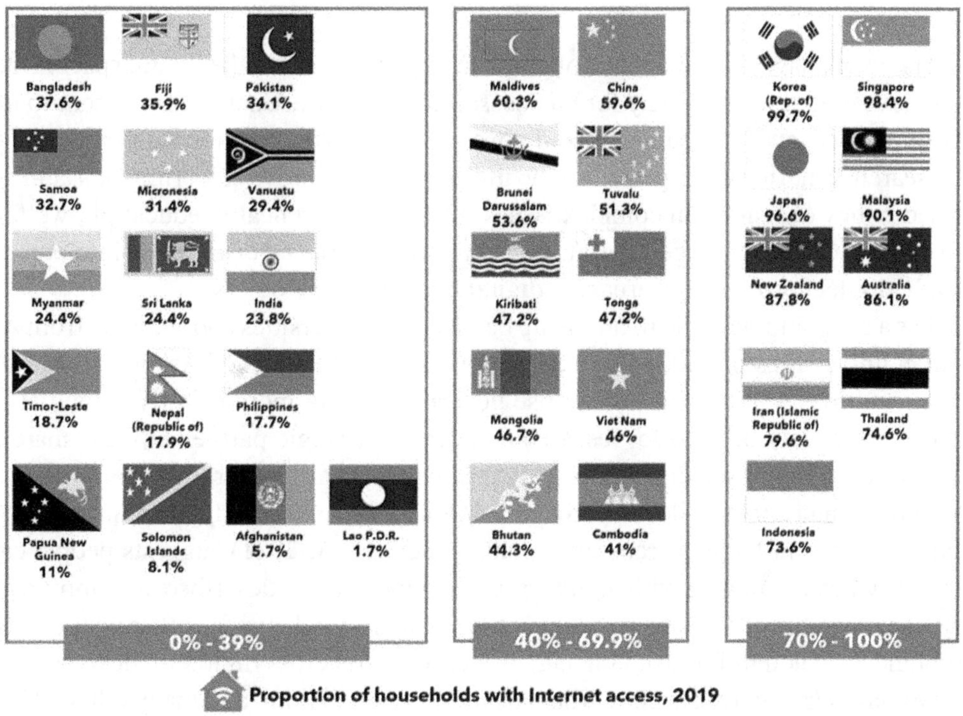

Over the next several years, digital trade is expected to grow many times. Digital trade facilitation can greatly benefit trading partner through closer and strategic relationships between government-to-government, business to business, and people to people. Digital enterprises also lead to formation of digital communities. New commitments on e-invoicing and e-payment frameworks, to ensure these are implemented in a way that is compatible and based on international frameworks. Also includes rules to enhance compatibility of electronic transactions frameworks, including recognition of e-authentication and signatures, which are standard digital business practices, to work towards a single window for paperless trading and to expedite express shipments.

Digital financial transaction in real time has opened enormous opportunities for the banking and finance sector to leverage digital tools for real-time settlement of transactions. Many banks in Australia and the Asian countries have moved to digital platforms to transact in real time. This promotes the adoption of internationally accepted standards for online payment systems for digital enterprises, which improve the digital trade experience for businesses and support cash flow and payment security for SMEs. Innovation in digital currencies (e.g., CBDC, central bank digital currency, cryptocurrencies, etc.) has provided opportunities for seamless and smooth digital transaction.

Trust is an important attribute in the digital environment. Trust between consumer and the business (C2B), trust between business-to-business (B2B), and trust between business to government (B2G) is a primary driver for digital commerce. Business and consumer trust in digital trade has been growing which has led to improved enforcement and compliance provisions on online consumer protection, personal information protection, and discouraging unsolicited commercial electronic messages (spam) and strategic partnership in cybersecurity to end cybercriminals business from conducting illegal activities (Sandhu, 2021). A new commitment to cooperate in creating and promoting a safe online environment to protect citizens, especially children and vulnerable members of the community, from harmful online experiences.

Data ownership, management, and control plays an important role in the digital space. Open government data provides digital transparency for businesses and citizens. A new commitment to improve the accessibility of publicly available, anonymized government information, for the purpose of economic, social and research benefit; sharing and analyzing data can improve government's ability to make better-informed policy decisions on complex issues, for example in health, education, welfare, and the environment. This can create stronger digital strategic partnership, and can expand into other areas such as digital heath, digital corporate governance, digital tax, and many others.

Australia has a close and strategic relationship between its universities and students from Asian countries. Australian universities provide higher education to large numbers of Asian students. Academics and research institutions will also be able to use government data more effectively and at lower cost. Digital data can effectively be used for research and deeper strategic partnership and share innovative outcomes. Across a variety of sectors, access to government data allows for the development of new and customized products and services demanded by business, government and the community.

Australian Government Digital Transformation Agency (DTA, 2021) suggests people can face numerous problems when interacting with digital systems, which can be described as common pain points. There can be language barriers as many countries have their own languages that people feel comfortable to communicate. Though English language is widely used across digital platforms, recently many other languages have also evolved such as Mandarin, Cantonese, Hindi, and many others. Google offers service in which a webpage can be translated into a local language, which has been very beneficial for the local users whose first language, is not English.

Case Analysis 3: Obstacles and Opportunities

Within the Digital Economy Agreement (DEA, 2021) there can be number of obstacles and opportunities. The study identifies common pain points describe problems people experience when accessing products and services, and identified to common pain points across multiple life events. People experience these pain points regardless of the service, level of government or sector.

The common pain points were most recently iterated in January 2021, which was generated from analysis of research across 11 life event journeys. Common pain points help us understand the systemic issues that affect how people access services. They help us identify whole-of-government opportunities to make information and services simple and easy to access.

Common pain points can be applied in different ways:

- To guide conversations on collaborative work in which people from different multicultural backgrounds work together.
- Help contextualise existing work to make it easier to understand.
- Inform new work and encourage more targeted research, which can benefit people.

Use the common pain points alongside evidence, expertise and testing specific to the context they are being applied that can transform and connect people from different countries through a common digital platform.

11 Common Pain Points for Consideration

Research suggests that there are eleven common pain points to consider which are-

1. Not aware of progress or important changes

People do not know about where digital processes are up to, why things happen or important changes. This could be because they did not receive or access information. It becomes difficult for them to plan and can put them into an avoidable negative situation. In this context digital connectivity and ease is important which can also be an opportunity for businesses to establish as profitable ventures.

2. Difficult to find information

People experience challenges finding the information they need. This could be because it is spread across multiple sources, or the amount of information is overwhelming. Digital information overload can become an obstacle for a digital worker to source large amounts of digital information.

3. Difficult to understand or use information

People can find it difficult to make sense of or use information. This can be because the language is too complex, it is not available in their preferred language, or is presented in a format they cannot access. Sometimes information can be inaccurate or out of date.

4. Not aware of available support

People are not aware of services and resources that could support them. This means that they do not look for or access support or information that could improve their situation.

5. Uncertain about entitlements and obligations

People are unsure about their entitlements and obligations when interacting with service providers. The policies, rules and processes are often complex and difficult to understand. This means that they can miss out on support or not fulfill obligations.

6. Unclear how to reach an outcome

People are uncertain about what they need to do to reach an outcome, particularly when they need to interact with multiple services or organisations. They often feel lost and frustrated and may need to ask for help.

7. Too much time and effort to complete tasks

Accessing services can be time consuming and difficult. This can include waiting in person or on the phone, putting together applications, gathering evidence, following up on mistakes or checking progress. Long times taken to receive services can cause challenges when people need immediate support.

8. Required to provide information multiple times

People find it frustrating to provide the same information multiple times. This is magnified when they have already provided the information as part of achieving the same or a similar outcome.

9. Unable to use preferred channel

People are not able to use their preferred channel to complete a task. This could be because they are pushed towards a particular channel, experience issues using a channel or need to interact with multiple channels. As a result, tasks are more difficult or impossible for them to complete without extra assistance.

10. Difficult or impossible to complete task

People face challenges using services that do not account for their needs and circumstances. Needs and circumstances can be diverse and influenced by factors such as age, gender, culture, language, ability, location, or socio-economic status. This means people may not be able to use a service, use work arounds or settle for an unsuitable interaction.

11. Not getting the right support

People feel that they are not getting the right support to help them reach an outcome. This can be for a range of reasons including the support not being enough, the staff they deal with not having the right skills, a lack of trust in the organisations they have to deal with and or a perception of poor service quality.

The Australian Digital Transformation Strategy (DTA, 2021) outlines vision to be a world leading digital government for the benefit of all Australians. The Digital Transformation Agency (DTA) has developed the Whole-of-government Digital Service Platforms Strategy (the Strategy) to help enable the Digital Transformation Strategy. The Strategy is intended to provide guidance for Commonwealth Government departments and agencies involved in digital service platforms. The Strategy applies to whole-of-government digital service platforms developed by the Commonwealth Government, but state, territory and local governments may choose to follow the Strategy if they wish.

Case Analysis 4: Developing the Digital Strategy

DTA (2021) explored the current strategic context including examples from other governments around the world, for current Australian government context and constraints, as well as other related strategies. Developing specific vision, goals and principles for digital platforms is to ensure these platforms support the broader Digital Transformation Strategy. The Strategy is supported by the Digital Platforms Operating Model, which provides the leading practice for the organisation, capabilities and processes, skills and culture, technology and data applicable to digital platforms. In addition, it outlines the governance and performance frameworks, and funding considerations required to enable whole-of-government collaboration and outcomes as shown in figure 6.

Figure 6. The digital platforms strategy framework.
Source: DTA (2021)

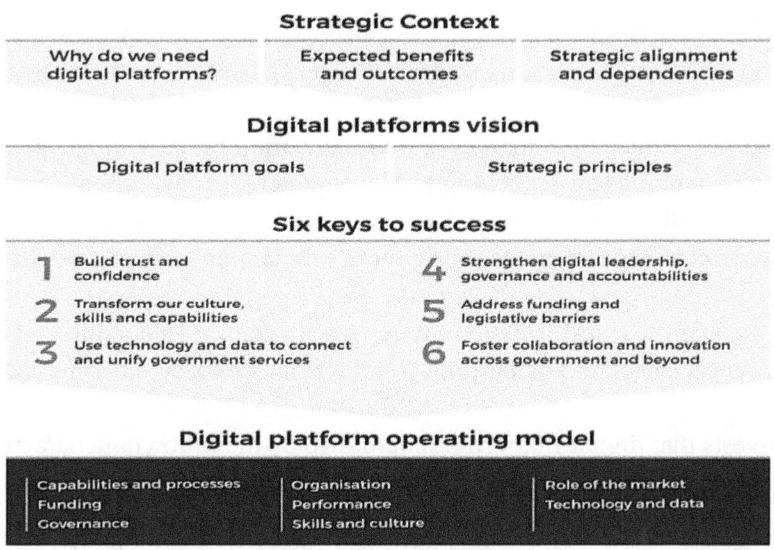

Whole-of-Government Digital Platforms

A key characteristic of Digital works is to provide key information to the user at one point. This concept has widely been used in many studies of TAM (Technology Acceptance Model, Davis 1989) in which the key attributes of usefulness and ease of use has been identified. DTA (2021) describes A whole-of-government (WofG) approach to developing government services is needed to ensure that these services are easily accessible, convenient and meet user needs. This approach will enhance the value and experience delivered to people and businesses, while improving the efficiency and effectiveness of government.

WofG digital platforms increase the integrity and consistency of government service delivery, and provide a unified and seamless user experience. Research has shown that the less effort user has to exert higher will be the use of the system and vice versa. WofG digital platforms provide capabilities that are shared across policy areas and deliver greater value through common technical foundations. They need to be simple and easy to use and provide usefulness to the users (Davis, 1989). WofG digital platforms include a range of technologies that enable departments to develop, exchange and connect services, without needing to design, test and operate the underlying systems themselves. WofG digital platforms can be adopted with minimal customisation to take full advantage of the efficiencies these platforms offer.

The benefit of digital platforms is the ability to share functionality, consolidate services and develop methods of exchanging data to deliver better value and experiences for users. The key characteristic of digital platforms is that they are reusable building blocks of simple, common, non-business specific services that are needed across government. They are accessed via simple, common government Application Programming Interfaces (APIs) which in turn provide access to the underlying infrastructure and can be easily replaced as needed shown in figure 7.

Case Analysis 5: Summarising Key Findings for a Digital Platform

DTA (2021) explains a digital platform is:

- A collection of reusable business services that can be accessed by consumers (such as departments and agencies) in delivering information, services and experiences to end users (such as people and businesses)
- Able to support government and market-driven innovation by providing open frameworks, standards and tools (where relevant) allowing producers to create new digital services
- Applicable across policy and service delivery areas and deliver value and enhanced integrity to the whole government ecosystem, enabling more efficient and effective delivery of government services
- Aligned with the Digital Transformation Strategy, with central leadership and oversight to ensure consistent user experiences and better policy and service delivery outcomes across government

DTA (2021) suggests that digital Platforms should display the following characteristics:

- Address common needs shared by a range of departments and agencies across government
- Easy and cost efficient to adopt to avoid duplication of effort and implementation of separate solutions to meet the same user need
- Interoperable by design to provide the ability to integrate and exchange information with other platforms and systems with ease through open standards and APIs
- Independent and channel agnostic to provide the ability to run independently, avoid technology 'lock-in' and provide the ability to be consumed via different channels
- Secure and compliant with adequate security measures in place to meet legislative, regulatory and other compliance requirements
- Reliable and highly scalable to give confidence that services will perform as expected, are accessible and can scale to meet user demand
- Continuously improving with the ability to monitor, measure, and analyse performance and generate useful insights to keep the platform relevant
- Meet technical and design standards such as DTA's Digital Service Standard and API Standards.

SOLUTIONS AND RECOMMENDATIONS

Digitalisation of enterprises can face major obstacles both technical (e.g. technical infrastructure such as computer hardware, software, etc.) and non-technical (e.g. cultural issues, traditions, habits of people etc.). The key to driving digital success is to understand the problem and finding the best solutions. Graham (2021) explains new research has revealed a major gap in digital skills across Australia's workforce, with 87 per cent of jobs now requiring these skills, and a need for 156,000 new technology workers to

Figure 7. Current platforms landscape
Source: DTA (2021).

Current platforms landscape

Experience	**Consistent UX / UI** - users move across government seamlessly and tasks across departments fit together neatly.	**Life event journeys** - end-to-end journeys for common events are clearly mapped out for people, for example, becoming a citizen	**Consent driven** - transparency about why, what and how data is being shared. Users have control and final say about how the complete tasks	**Authorisation** - permission for families, partners, dependants and businesses to complete selected transactions on behalf of others
	Multiple entry points - users interact with government when and where it suits them, online and offline	**Proactive notifications** - proactive and predictive transactions driven by data, event-driven architecture and AI	**AI and data** - tailoring services to individuals using AI and data holdings to predict and target what users need	**Help and support** - admin accounts and virtual assistance to ensure that users can get the help they need online, on the phone and at a shop front
Platforms to be developed	myGov dashboard	Payments in	End user services	Business registers
Platforms in development	Digital identity	Tell Us Once	Inbox	Notifications

keep pace with the rapid transformation of businesses. The findings highlight an urgent need to improve digital skills to ensure economic recovery from COVID-19 and to avoid jeopardising a $10 billion growth in the technology, media and communications industries by 2025. The new report, '*Ready, Set, Upskill - Effective Training for the Jobs of Tomorrow*' was released by RMIT Online, in collaboration with Deloitte Access Economics, following surveys of 1,000 Australian working professionals and employers.

The report also revealed that three out of four Australians want to learn about emerging technologies, such as cybersecurity and artificial intelligence, and that four in five Australian business leaders think that adopting new technologies is important to achieve business goals. RMIT Online CEO Helen Souness said responding to Australia's digital skills gap is a national imperative, and Australia's economic recovery will rely heavily on the availability of these skills to power business transformation.

The events of last year have underlined the urgency of bridging this skills gap. Australian employers across all industries need to prioritise training and upskilling to transform, survive and thrive in the post-COVID world. This includes shifting their perspective on training to consider it as a core business activity rather than a nice-to-have," she said. With four in five Australian business leaders agreeing that adopting new technologies is important to achieve business goals, the decisions we make now will be a key driver of our economic success. The managers for digital innovation and cooperation can provide leadership for implementing and steering digital projects that can be beneficial to Australia and the Asian trading partners. Deeper understanding of the cultural issues related to the technical platform will enhance the development and cooperation for digital exchange of information and ideas. There may also be several limitations such as developing advanced digital systems that may be costly and time consuming and may require specialised skills.

FUTURE RESEARCH DIRECTIONS

Digital inclusion index (DII, 2021) explains that the digital inclusion is about access to information and communications technology and the resulting social and economic benefits. It has sometimes been described in terms of the 'digital divide' – the gap between people with effective access to digital and information technologies, in particular the internet, and those with very limited or no access at all. Access and affordability can present barriers to digital inclusion, but an individual's digital engagement and confidence is also affected by digital literacy, perceptions of relevance, motivation and concerns about safety.

DII (2021) found although the digital divide is closing, in Australia there are still deep gaps evident with a large number of vulnerable individuals without basic internet access or skills, which is revealed from the following key data:

- There were 1.25 million Australian households without internet access at home in 2016-17 (14%)
- 18.4% of Australians born in non-English speaking countries, do not access internet compared to a 13.5% national average.
- 79.1% of people educated to year 12 or below use the internet, compared with 96.7% of people with a tertiary qualification.
- Only 55.2% of people aged 65 or more are internet users compared to 86.5% national average
- More than 1.3 million Australians with disability did not access the internet in the last 3 months. One quarter of these people report lack of confidence and knowledge as a reason for not accessing the internet.
- 24.7% of Indigenous Australian households do not access the internet from home compared with the national average of 14.7%. Levels of home internet access for Indigenous Australian households diminishes further with remoteness – 45.2% of such households in remote and very remote locations do not access the internet at home.
- More than two thirds of people who are homeless had difficulty paying their mobile phone bill in the last 12 months.

Asian Infrastructure Investment Bank (AIIB) research that showed digital infrastructure needs an injection of more than $1 trillion in the near future to meet demand for 5G, data centres and digital applications such as smart cities and intelligent transportation, with 50% of that attributable to Asia (Melville, 2021).

Future research needs to focus on the key attributes such as digital infrastructure, digital literacy, digital business adoption, digital markets, digital government, and digital banking & finance that will drive the digitalisation and strategic partnership between Australia and the Asian countries. While the Asia-Pacific region has seen continued growth in most areas of ICT infrastructure, access and use, many challenges persist that have been magnified by the COVID-19 pandemic (ITU, 2021). Mobile network coverage stands at 98.6 per cent, with both 3G and 4G mobile network coverage above 90 per cent. Internet use by individuals has grown from 38.6 per cent in 2017 to 44.5 per cent in 2019, 53.4 per cent of homes have access have Internet access, and 70.3 per cent of 15- to 24-year-olds are using the Internet. Future studies need to focus on wider populations and make comparisons based on geographical distribution between having internet access and not having internet access which will then provide a clear picture of the population groups not having access to digital services. Such studies need to emphasise on mobile access that have massive penetration and higher use adoptions for accessing digital services via mobile/smart phones.

CONCLUSION

Digital strategic partnership and cooperation between Australia and the Asian countries will drive digitalisation of key industries (e.g. banking and finance, health, government, travel tourism and many others) it needs to be clearly understood that there will be many obstacles on the way as technology is not a magic bullet for all solutions. People, digital enterprises, government are the primary drivers for digitalisation and as such are key stakeholders. There are enormous benefits that digitalisation can offer which includes closer cooperation and understanding between people to people, enterprise to enterprise to enterprise and government to government on a digital platform between Australia and other Asian countries.

Australia and the Asian countries have been working together in developing digital standards. Digital standards can provide enterprises with safer, stable, and more effective digital platforms. Collaboration on the development of key standards to support digital trade, which can lead to investments and finding innovative solutions. This work has already begun with a jointly commissioned study to identify priority opportunities for increased digital standardization, published in October 2020. Though there may be areas where the digital standards may differ (e.g. different taxation etc.) but more than that will be common grounds in which digital standards would effective work across different countries.

New startups specializing in Fintech and RegTech are becoming popular. For example, recently (e.g. in 2021) Afterpay a leading Australia FinTech was acquired by Square a leading international American company. Such new digital startups and strategic partnership can benefit consumers, businesses, and government. FinTech and RegTech can also benefit digital enterprises. Collaboration between FinTech and RegTech enterprises and industry bodies to explore business opportunities for Australian and Singaporean enterprises, and to develop standards for open banking. This will lead to closer digital cooperation that can benefit from digital infrastructure for enterprises that can lead to higher investments to expand the adoption of digital businesses.

Australia is surrounded by ocean and the need to connect with fiber optic cables and networks on the ocean bed is a critical infrastructure to connect the internet to Asian countries and to the pacific region countries. Submarine data cables for expanding critical digital infrastructure. Commitments to facilitate submarine cable installation, maintenance and repair, and the prevention of cable disruptions. Such digital infrastructure needs maintenance on a regular basis and a deeper strategic partnership with Asian countries that can enhance investments and maintenance of such critical digital infrastructure. These critical digital infrastructures are long-term assets and requires long-term investments.

Cooperation between Australia and Asian countries that reflects the broader digital economy agenda, including joint regional capacity building in digital trade, online copyright issues, small and medium enterprises, and cybersecurity. Strategic partnership between government to government, business to business, and people to people are important to forge a deeper relationship that can then provide new digital opportunities. However, there will be many challenges on the way, however good communication and transparency can make way for stronger digital foundation.

ACKNOWLEDGMENT

This research received no specific grant from any funding agency in the public, commercial, or not-for-profit sectors.

REFERENCES

Austrade. (2021). *Growth and opportunity in Australian international education*. Retrieved from: https://www.austrade.gov.au/australian/education/services/australian-international-education-2025/growth-and-opportunity

Davis. (1989). Technology Acceptance Model. *MIS Quarterly, 13*(3), 319-340. Retrieved from: https://www.jstor.org/stable/249008

DFAT. (2021). *Association of Southeast Asian Nations (ASEAN)*. Retrieved from: https://www.dfat.gov.au/international-relations/regional-architecture/asean

DFAT. (2021a). *Australia-Singapore Digital Economy Agreement: summary of key outcomes*. Retrieved from: https://www.dfat.gov.au/trade/services-and-digital-trade/australia-singapore-digital-economy-agreement-summary-key-outcomes

DFAT. (2021b). *Australia-Singapore Digital Economy Agreement*. Retrieved from: https://www.dfat.gov.au/trade/services-and-digital-trade/australia-and-singapore-digital-economy-agreement

DII. (2021). *Digital Inclusion Index. About Digital Inclusion in Australia*. Retrieved from: https://digitalinclusionindex.org.au/about/about-digital-inclusion/

DTA. (2021). *Common Pain Points*. Retrieved from: https://www.dta.gov.au/our-projects/govx/common-pain-points

Duan, C., Kotey, B., & Sandhu, K. (2021). Integrated Business Strategies for Transnational Digital Entrepreneurship: Case Studies for Immigrant Startups. In *Handbook of Research on Management and Strategies for Digital Enterprise Transformation*. IGI Global. Retrieved from: https://www.igi-global.com/book/handbook-research-management-strategies-digital/244649

Duan, C., Kotey, B., & Sandhu, K. (2021). Ecosystem Strategies for Transnational Digital Entrepreneurship: A Conceptual Framework of Three Ecosystems. In *Disruptive Technology and Digital Transformation for Business and Government*. IGI Global. Retrieved from: https://www.igi-global.com/book/disruptive-technology-digital-transformation-business/271732

Gibb, S. (2020). Digital Transformation in Southeast Asia. *Medium*. Retrieved from: https://medium.com/endeavourventures/digital-transformation-in-southeast-asia-4f9682c568e3

Graham, J. (2021). *New report reveals Australia's major digital skills gap*. RMIT University. Retrieved from: https://www.rmit.edu.au/news/all-news/2021/feb/digital-skills-gap-report

Handforth, C., & Tan, S. (2021). *Mapping the Waypoints in Asia's Digital Future*. UNDP Global Centre for Technology, Innovation, and Sustainable Development. Asia and the Pacific. Retrieved from: https://www.asia-pacific.undp.org/content/rbap/en/home/presscenter/articles/2021/mapping-the-waypoints-to-asias-digital-future-.html

Ingram, G. (2020). The digital world. In *Development in Southeast Asia: Opportunities for donor collaboration.* Center for Sustainable Development at Brookings. Retrieved from: https://www.brookings.edu/wp-content/uploads/2020/12/Development-Southeast-Asia-Ch2-Digital.pdf

ITU. (2021). Digital trends in Asia and the Pacific 2021. In *Information and communication technology trends and developments in the Asia-Pacific region, 2017-2020*. ITU Switzerland. Retrieved from: https://www.itu.int/dms_pub/itu-d/opb/ind/D-IND-DIG_TRENDS_ASP.01-2021-PDF-E.pdf

Jain, E., & Lamba, J. (2021). Management and Digitalization Strategy for Transforming Education Sector: An Emerging Gateway Persuaded by COVID-19. In *Emerging Challenges, Solutions, and Best Practices for Digital Enterprise Transformation*. IGI Global. Retrieved from: https://www.igi-global.com/book/emerging-challenges-solutions-best-practices/271733

Melville, A. (2021). The Global Digital Infrastructure Survey 2021. *IJ Global, Project Finance and Infrastructure Journal.* Retrieved from: https://ijglobal.com/articles/155544/the-global-digital-infrastructure-survey-2021

Moss, S., & Sandhu, K. (2020). A Study of Factors Influencing Digital Accounting Software Selection in Thailand. In *Digital Transformation and Innovative Services for Business and Learning*. IGI Global. Retrieved from: https://www.igi-global.com/book/digital-transformation-innovative-services-business/245338

Saavedra, A., Kotey, B., & Sandhu, K. (2020). The Digital Value Propositions for Virtual Business Incubators. In *Digital Innovations for Customer Engagement, Management, and Organizational Improvement*. IGI Global. Retrieved from: https://www.igi-global.com/book/digital-innovations-customer-engagement-management/245337

Sandhu, K. (2020). Advances for Artificial Intelligence in Health Data Analytics to Drive Digital Systems Innovation. In *Opportunities and Challenges in Digital Healthcare Innovation*. IGI Global. Retrieved from: https://www.igi-global.com/book/opportunities-challenges-digital-healthcare-innovation/241178

Sandhu, K. (Ed.). (2021). Advancing Cybersecurity for Digital Transformation: Opportunities and Challenges. In Handbook of Research on Advancing Cybersecurity for Digital Transformation. IGI Global. doi:10.4018/978-1-7998-6975-7

Somani, S. (2021). *Emerging infrastructure trends in Asia Pacific. A look at the future of the sector.* KPMG International entities. Retrieved from: https://home.kpmg/xx/en/blogs/home/posts/2021/05/emerging-infrastructure-trends-in-asia-pacific.html

Tanniru, M., Xi, Y., & Sandhu, K. (2020). Leadership to Advance Innovation for Digital Healthcare Transformation. In *Leadership, Management, and Adoption Techniques for Digital Service Innovation*. IGI Global. Retrieved from: https://www.igi-global.com/book/leadership-management-adoption-techniques-digital/237849

Thu, H. (2021). *Australia should bet on digital engagement with Southeast Asia*. Retrieved from: https://www.aspistrategist.org.au/australia-should-bet-on-digital-engagement-with-southeast-asia/

Westerman, G., Bonnet, D., & McAfee, A. (2014). The Nine Elements of Digital Transformation. *MIT Sloan Management Review*. Retrieved from: https://sloanreview.mit.edu/article/the-nine-elements-of-digital-transformation/

ADDITIONAL READING

Drees-Gross, F., & Zhang, P. (2021). Poor digital access is holding Latin America and the Caribbean back. Here's how to change it. World Bank Blogs. Retrieved from: https://blogs.worldbank.org/latinamerica/poor-digital-access-holding-latin-america-and-caribbean-back-heres-how-change-it

World Development Report, WDR (2021). Data infrastructure. Retrieved from: https://wdr2021.worldbank.org/stories/connecting-the-world/

KEY TERMS AND DEFINITIONS

Digital Enterprises: Include firms such as private, public, and government institution having been digitally transformed that empowers the businesses, processes, systems, technology, and people.

Digital Infrastructure: Is the hardware, software, networks, people, and modern IT solutions that drive an innovative digital platform.

Digital Strategic Partnership: Is the cooperation, collaboration, and exchange of strategic digital information to exploring innovative digital opportunities between two or more countries that includes organisations which can be private, public, or government institutions, that work together towards strategic partnership to achieve a common beneficial digital goal.

Chapter 5
Australia as an Enabler to Sustainable Indian Ocean Island Economies

Ikhlaas Gurrib
Canadian University Dubai, UAE

ABSTRACT

The purpose of this study is to provide a deeper understanding of how Australia and Indian Ocean island economies of Mauritius, Maldives, and Sri Lanka can mutually benefit from each other to promote sustainability and economic output. Specifically, this study investigates what makes the three island economies attractive to promote regional and international trade and how Australia can help achieve a sustainable blue economy. The author initially provides some background of the current state in the island economies and Australia, post-COVID-19 crisis impact, the different financial and regulatory policies, bilateral trade agreements, and ministerial level organisations promoting trade partnerships. Key recommendations aligned with various Sustainable Development Goals (SDGs), especially SDG 14, are provided. Active involvement from experienced nations like Australia to Small Island Developing States (SIDS) is required, including some incentivized alliance between the private and public sector to achieve a sustainable ocean or blue economy, post COVID-19 crisis.

INTRODUCTION

The world economy came to a standstill since early 2020 with the unprecedented COVID-19 pandemic. While various economies are trying to reach community immunization to reduce the number of COVID-19 cases, various studies already tapped into assessing the impact of the coronavirus on a global scale. For instance, Estrada *et al.* (2020) analysed several markets and warned that the actual health crisis can led to damages analogous to the 1929 Great Depression. Eichenbaum, Rebelo and Trabandt (2020) estimated that U.S. total consumption and gross domestic product (GDP) will drop by nearly 20 per cent.

This impact is also observed in various developed and developing countries with governments ordering businesses to close, except for essential activities. Shehzad *et al.* (2020) reported that uncertainty in

DOI: 10.4018/978-1-7998-8657-0.ch005

European stocks was bigger during the COVID-19 relative to the financial crisis of 2008. While Bakas and Triantafyllou (2020) studied the effect of the pandemic uncertainty on commodities, Gurrib (2021) and Gurrib *et al.* (2021) found that shocks like the number of COVID-19 cases affected stock prices in healthcare and energy sectors but were short-lasting events. Comparatively, Prabheesh, Padhan and Garg (2020) argued that COVID-19 reinforced the relationship between oil prices and Asian stock markets. The relationship between oil prices and economic activity is well established with, on one hand, proponents like Anolick *et al.* (2021) supporting oil affects economic policy, and others like Gurrib (2018a, 2018b, 2019) and Lescaroux and Mignon (2009) supporting those commodities like crude oil prices are not strong forecasters of financial market activity, as captured by movements of market indices.

The health care sector of Mauritius, Sri Lanka and the Maldives have been affected by COVID-19 differently, where Mauritius and the Maldives prioritized health care over economic activity. This involved partial and complete lockdown episodes and closure of borders during the period March 2020 to October 2021 (PWC, 2021). On October 1st of 2021, Mauritius began welcoming fully vaccinated tourists, including some quarantine provisions to cater those who are not vaccinated (BBC, 2021). While all the three nations imposed some lockdown, the period of lockdown affected the number of cases. For example, as of 14th October 2021, Mauritius had 16,472 cases with 123 deaths. Comparatively, Sri Lanka had 528,000 cases with over 13,000 deaths, and Maldives witnessing 85,838 cases with 237 deaths. Mauritius adopted a more rigorous lockdown over a lengthier period. Sri Lanka had the highest death tolls, which increased from under 1,000 in April 2021 to 13,000 by September 2021 (Worldometers, 2021). This was mainly attributed to the unrestricted reopening of Sri Lanka borders as warned by the Sri Lanka Medical Association (SLMA) (Times of India, 2021). The Maldives reopened its borders on the 15th of July 2020, and despite a surge in COVID-19 cases since then, benefited from the archipelago's islands being scattered. This allowed local authorities to naturally contain COVID-19 cases on affected islands. The reopening of borders for the islands was warranted to recover from loss of economic activity, where the tourist sector is a vital contributor.

For the purpose of this study, COVID-19 brought the world to adopt globally aligned economic policies to recover from the health crisis financially. The Reserve Bank of Australia (RBA), consistent with the European Securities and Market Authority (ESMA) policy actions to contain COVID-19 effects on global economies, dropped its cash rate by 50 basis points in March 2020 (ESMA, 2020). Australia further dropped the cash rate in November 2020 to 0.1%, a rate never seen in the last thirty years (RBA, 2021a). While Australia's GDP increased by nearly 10 per cent in 2021 and unemployment rate dropped below 5 per cent, the country has been negatively impacted by the Delta variant, resulting in restrictions on various economic activities (RBA, 2021b). Similar to various currencies, the Australian dollar (AUD) dropped significantly in value vis-à-vis the U.S. dollar (USD) during the early COVID-19 impact in March 2020, with 1 AUD = 0.58 USD. As of September 2021, the local currency has recovered and worth around 0.7 USD (XE, 2021). While this is a good sign of economic recovery, to attract further attention to the Australian economy, international partnerships are key.

A highly valid question then remains as to which sectors should partnerships give priority? The population of Australia population is concentrated near the coast, with roughly 80% of people living within 50 km of the ocean. With more than 70% per cent of Australia's territory lying beneath the ocean and a marine estate of 10 million square kilometers, the sea is convincingly a huge part of the Australian identity and contributes significantly to Australia's employment and economic growth, with a contribution of 3.7% of the nation's GDP in 2018. The blue economy sits high on the agenda of policy makers in Australia, including areas like sustainable usage, effective management of the environment and protection of marine life. As reported in the AIMS (2020) report, growth in the sustainable use of the ocean's surrounding Australia is critical to Australia's future. While too early to assess the impact of COVID-19 onto the blue economy, border restrictions, oil and natural gas price uncertainties, reduction in demand for high end seafood, and more money-cautious travelers, all point to a negative impact which needs to be addressed.

With the Indian Ocean covering all the Western Australian state, this study looks at Mauritius, Sri Lanka, and Maldives, which can potentially become key corridors for Australia to Africa. Ranked 13th globally out of 190 countries for the ease of doing business, Mauritius is ranked first among all African countries, and second in the upper middle-income category (World Bank, 2020). Likewise, Sri Lanka's tourist arrivals increased more than fivefold since the long-lasting civil conflict which finally ended in 2009 (Preiss, 2019). Despite the Maldives have more than 80% of its 1190 islands with less than 1 metres above sea level, making them highly vulnerable to rising ocean levels and climate change, the country enjoyed tourist arrivals above 1.7 million during recent pre-COVID years, and above expected tourist numbers during 2020 (Marcus, 2021). These are testaments of actions taken to progress via policy development and implementation in areas of transparency, taxes, innovative technologies, recruitment and retention of talent, economic incentives, managing the COVID-19 crisis, among others. The three islands witnessed British colonization with independence granted by Britain in 1948 for Sri Lanka, 1965 for the Maldives, and 1968 for Mauritius. This led to the islanders to live in democracy for significant number of years, with its population benefiting from English as a language of instruction in the education sector. Specifically, this study provides an eye opener to some key inter-governmental organizations in place between Australia and the three islands, which can facilitate the use of trade enhancement tools like trade agreements.

This paper is organized as follows. This study first provides an overview of the current economic status of small islands, including factors which make them attractive corridors for trade. This is supported by the different regional and international agreements in place to encourage transactions between the three islands and the outer world. The research objectives are laid out, with a decomposition of issues and challenges facing the small island economies. The study then looks at the ocean economy as a prominent sector worth exploring. Finally, some recommendations ae provided on the next steps to enhance the possibility of the Australia-Mauritius partnership in the prominent area of blue economy sustenance, resilience, and development. Some conclusive remarks close the chapter.

BACKGROUND

Current Economic Status and COVID-19

While it is outside the scope of this study to compare all socio-economic factors among island economies, it is worthwhile to provide a summary of main factors driving the countries, including Australia. This is illustrated as follows in Table 1. As observed, all the countries except for Maldives experienced a recovery in the Gross Domestic Product in the first quarter of 2021. It is important to note however, that Maldives first quarter GDP figures deteriorated to a lesser extent than observed in the last three quarters where the GDP fell between 33% and 47.4% respectively. Mauritius had the highest unemployment rate of 10.1%, explained by the lengthiest complete lockdown period. While inflation rates ranged between 0.4% and 5.7%, Australia, as the more developed nation, enjoyed lower cost of borrowing with

Table 1. Socio Economic Indicators

	Mauritius	Sri Lanka	Maldives	Australia
GDP Annual growth rate (%)	18.8	4.3	-8.5	9.6
Unemployment rate (%)	10.5	5.1	6.4	4.6
Inflation rate (%)	5.4	5.7	0.4	3.8
Interest rate (%)	1.85	5	7	0.1
Government debt to GDP (%)	73.4	101	52.6	24.8
Corporate tax rate (%)	15	24	15	30
Coronavirus vaccination rate	132	127	136	122
Ease of doing business	13	99	147	14

Source: Trading Economics (2021a)

Note: The unemployment rate is the number of people actively looking for a job relative to the labor force. The cash rate is the official interest rate in Australia and represents the overnight lending rates between financial institutions. Similarly, the repo rate is used in Mauritius, the standard deposit and lending facility rate in Sri Lanka, and reverse repo in Maldives. The Coronavirus vaccination rate represents the number of doses administered per 100 people in the population. This is counted as a single dose. The ease of doing business index ranks 190 countries on how the regulatory framework facilitates business activities, with a lower the index value being preferred.

a cash rate of 0.1%, reflecting the continuous effort from its reserve bank to boost economic activity, amidst lockdown due to COVID-19 cases in some states such as New South Wales and Victoria. To support economic activities, Mauritius provided wage assistant support schemes, which inflated the government debt significantly. Although not shown here, all the four countries witnessed an increase in the government debt to GDP ratio compared to previous years. To reduce the number of COVID-19 cases, all governments have endeavored to get their population to be vaccinated to achieve immunity. Mauritius and Maldives enjoyed the lowest corporate tax rates of 15%, making them highly attractive to attract investments in the country. Interestingly, all the 3 islands reported higher coronavirus vaccination rates than Australia. This can be attributed to more aggressive governmental campaigns from the small islands, to be perceived as "more COVID safe" and attract more tourists to the islands. The ease of doing business index ranks Mauritius and Australia, at 13th and 14th respectively, with Sri Lanka and Maldives at 99th and 147th out of 190 countries.

Mauritius, with a population around 1.3 million, is internationally known for its crystal clear, reef protected and white sandy beaches, which makes it the perfect place for tourists for swimming, snorkeling, kitesurfing, and even big game fishing (Bauso, 2021). The tropical island is centrally located in the Indian Ocean, in between the African continent and Australia. It is highly multi-cultural, with descendants originating from India, China, Africa, and Europe. Being colonized first by the French and then by the British, the Mauritian community is highly fluent in both English and French, since education right from pre-primary levels include those languages as part of the curriculum. Although small in size, the country has been impacted by COVID-19, contracting by nearly 15% in terms of output and investments, 12% in terms household consumption, accompanied with an inflation of 2.5%, caused primarily by worldwide increase in commodity prices. Affected areas include quarantine measures which affected the food security and livelihoods of small-scale fishermen, reduced demand for seafood due to reduced tourists and restaurant closures, shortage in medical supplies due to port and travel restrictions and decline in tourism due to closed borders.

Nonetheless, the country has incessantly strived to tackle various challenges, including imposing policy measures to contain the impact of COVID-19, both at economic and health levels. These include containing the unemployment rate at around 9% with interventions like wage assistance and self-employed assistance schemes. While such measures allow a significant part of the population to obtain temporary support income and provides a temporary boost to the financial resilience of small businesses, this also increases the public debt significantly, and needs to be addressed in the long run (KPMG, 2021). The government policy measures of 2021 are geared towards a more positive outlook compared to the previous one, with the availability of vaccine. According to Ritchie *et al.* (2021), as of September 2021, more than 60% of the population were fully vaccinated. While government policies in 2020 were oriented to protect jobs and health of its citizens, following its massive successful vaccination campaign, the economy is now poised for re-opening its borders fully from October 1st, 2021. Opening the economy is in line with the three strategic pillars of the current budget, to shape a new economic architecture, boost investment and restore confidence.

Regulatory and Business

Besides its resolution to counteract the negative economic and health related impacts of COVID-19, institutions are actively working to position Mauritius at the forefront of Africa, with regulatory and business strategies. Important framework has been put in place to combat financial crime and corruption. These include updating the Combatting Financing of Terrorism (CFT) and Anti-money laundering (AML) regulations to be aligned with the Financial Action Task Force (FATF) international standards to prevent illegal activities that cause harm to economies. In December 2020, Mauritius as a key member of Eastern and Southern Africa Anti-Money Laundering Group (ESAAMLG), presented its 3rd enhanced follow-up report and technical compliance re-rating (FATF, 2020). As per the report, Mauritius has made sufficient progress in addressing deficiencies in some areas and continues to work and inform ESAAMLG of any future progress made to comply with FATF recommendations to combat financial crime. This is a vital activity for the nation, especially, given that ESAAMLG members currently include 18 countries and a number of regional/international observers such as the International Monetary Fund (IMF), World Bank, United Nations, FATF and AUSTRAC (Australian Transaction Reports and Analysis Centre) which is the Australian government financial intelligence agency to monitor and identify money laundering activities. The effort pursued in this area is reflected with the international community rating Mauritius with an improved Corruption Perception Index (CPI) score of 53 in 2020 (Transparency International, 2020). This score has improved continuously since 2017, with the country currently holding the 52nd rank out of 138 countries. For comparison purposes only, India is ranked 86th, South Africa (69th), and Malaysia (57th) respectively. One of the important ongoing works of Transparency Mauritius, a representative of Transparency International, relates to the pledge of key companies to be more transparent and accountable of political financing (Transparency Mauritius, 2014). Comparatively, both Sri Lanka and Maldives do not enjoy strong views from the World Bank, when it comes to each country's ability to underwrite and implement proper regulatory changes which help to promote private sector business. Mauritius ranks in the 75th percentile in terms of regulatory quality, compared to Sri Lanka (34th percentile) and Maldives (15th percentile), where 0 represents the lowest rank and 100 is the highest rank. Australia positions itself high in the upper 90th percentile rank (Trading Economics, 2021e).

Tourism Sector

Surrounded by crystal clear waters, the tourism sector is bound to be a major revenue contributor. In fact, the services sector is the largest for Mauritius and represents about 75 percent of the country's GDP. The robust recovery for Mauritius in the second quarter of 2021 was particularly due to resumed activity in key sectors like tourism which were affected by severe lockdown episodes. Mauritius witnessed five consecutive periods of economic recession during 2020-2021, where the tourism sector severely was affected with significant drops in accommodation and food services (Trading Economics, 2021b). Similar drops were also witnessed in Sri Lanka since 2020, with tourism revenues ranging from $0.5 to $6 million over the January – July 2021 period (Trading Economics, 2021c). Similarly, tourist arrivals in Maldives, which depends heavily on tourism revenue, had arrivals which ranged from 20,000 to 100,000 during the period October 2020 - June 2021 (Trading Economics, 2021d).

Financial Services Sector

To promote the financial services sector which represents 12 percent of Mauritius' GDP (Trading Economics, 2021b), several initiatives have been proposed including the implementation of a digital centralized information exchange platform by the Financial Services Commission (FSC) where digital licensing would be possible. With much attention gained on financial markets in regard to cryptocurrencies such as Bitcoin, Ethereum and Ripple, the Financial Services Act (FSA) is also poised to amendment to include terminologies such as RegTech (regulatory technologies) and FinTech (financial technologies). Deloitte (2021) identified five key areas of regulation as more firms are using technologies. These include regulatory reporting, risk management, identity management and control, compliance, and transaction monitoring. As per the latest budget of 2021, Mauritius regulators are updating the FSA to allow the FSC to set up FinTech innovation hubs. To facilitate the acquisition of talent in these areas of interest, the Economic Development Board (EDB) is projected to partner with international firms in the recruitment process, and promote both occupational and residency permits for professionals, retirees, and investors. To make it more attractive place for investors, the property sector is also targeted, with several invest hotel schemes (IHS) benefits where for example, owners will be allowed to occupy their units for 6 months as opposed to 3 previously. On top of benefiting from a vaccinated taskforce, ongoing regulatory work in technologies and finance, and attracting/retaining professionals, retirees and investors, the tax regime in Mauritius also attracts investors. For instance, there are several incentives which encourage economic activity like private universities benefiting from a reduced tax rate of 3% compared to 15%; carry forward of unused tax credits for manufacturing firms to ten years; double tax reduction on research and development expenses targeting African markets; and tax holidays extended to ten years for various sectors including asset management. Like Mauritius, where insurance and financial services represented about 4.5% of total service exports in 2019, Sri Lanka's insurance and financial services contributed about 4.6% to the country's service exports. The Maldives insurance and financial services contribution to the nation's service exports was however insignificant, with the country focusing on more important sectors like tourism and fishing (Trading Economics, 2021f). Australia's insurance and financial services contributed a healthier 7.5% of the country's service exports in 2020.

Global Trading Partnerships

Table 2 summarizes key bilateral agreements in place between each of the islands and major trading partners, including FTA bilateral agreements. Institutions like the Mauritius Chamber of Commerce and Industry (MCCI) and the Ministry of Foreign Affairs, Regional Cooperation, and International Trade (MFA) have been working rigorously to create trading opportunities with important partners such as China, India, Africa, and Europe (MCCI, 2021). For instance, the Free Trade Agreement (FTA) with China, which is effective from January 2021, is the first one to be signed with an African country (Mauritius), where the agreement covers 4 areas, namely, trade in services, trade in goods, economic cooperation, and investment. While trade in services include commitments between both Mauritius and China in prominent sectors like financial services, construction, health services and technologies, Mauritius now access more than 7000 duty free products from the emerging market giant. A similar cooperation initiative is in place between India and Mauritius as part of the Comprehensive Economic Cooperation and Partnership Agreement (CECPA), where both countries obtain preferential market access for specific service sectors as from February 2021. Furthermore, like the Economic Partnership Agreement (EPA) signed with the European Union (EU), an EPA with the UK (activated since January 2021) provide trade preferences with no quota imposition and duty-free products on important export items such as tuna, sugar and garments. On a regional basis, MCCI is actively working to promote regional trade in the Southern African Development Community (SADC) and Common Market for Eastern and Southern Africa (COMESA). With its 21 Member States (including Mauritius), a population of over 580 million, a GDP of over $800 billion, a geographical territory representing more than 65% of Africa, a global trade in goods worth over US$ 300 billion, COMESA collectively represents a major marketplace (COMESA, 2021). Similarly, SADC, with its fifteen member states, all from Africa, helps to encourage sustainable economic growth and socio-economic development through efficient production, deep integration, good governance practices and resilient security (SADC, 2020). In line with this, the African Continental Free Trade Agreement (AFCFTA) which was activated since January 2021, provides Mauritius, as a member, preferential access on specific goods with mutual trade benefits. The only agreement in place between Mauritius and Australia is the Tax Information Exchange Agreement (TIEA) which was activated since December 2010, leaving room for many collaborations between the two nations.

Sri Lanka was not dormant either. For example, an intimal framework agreement was set up between Australia and Sri Lanka as the Trade and Investment Framework Agreement (TIFA) in November 2017, where the main objects were to encourage bilateral economic relations based on shared benefit from more investment and trade activities. This resulted in further correspondence such as the Strategic Maritime Dialogue and the Second Joint Trade and Investment Committee meetings. Another important agreement is the FTA between Sri Lanka and India in December 1998, the Indo-Sri Lanka FTA (ISFTA), which was particularly successful in promoting trade liberalization in South Asia. Although not reported here, Sri Lanka also signed a similar FTA with Pakistan in 2002. India's FTA was impactful for Sri Lanka with sectors like pearl harvesting and textile industries growing over 100% in its first two years of implementation since March 2000 (Kelegama & Karunaratne, 2013). While Sri Lanka does not have any FTA with China, several related negotiation talks have been held since 2014. China is an important trade partner with Sri Lanka, with Ceylon's imports roaming between 15-20% in the last five years, a proportion also held in terms of Sri Lanka's imports from India. An FTA could allow import tariffs to be removed, as part of trade liberalization. Further, the ISFTA have contributed only about 6% of Sri Lanka's imports from India, showcasing that the trade agreements not effectively used. While Sri

Lanka does not share any FTA with African countries, it is a non-member state of AU, and is involved with African regional institutions like IORA. Further, Sri Lanka benefits from trade relations with the European Union (EU) in terms of the Cooperation and Partnership Agreement (CPA) since 1995. One of the most recent projects strengthening the Sri Lanka- European Union bilateral relationship is the EU-Sri Lanka Innovation Partnership (EU-SLIP) which focuses on incubating/accelerating business startups in Sri Lanka (European Commission, 2021b).

The Maldives, compared with Mauritius and Sri Lanka, did not witness a smooth ride so far when it comes to bilateral agreements with key emerging markets like China. While the Maldives enjoy a long lasting FTA with India, the FTA with China however, despite being signed in December 2017, faced lots of scrutiny and parliamentary oppositions when it came to implementing the trade agreement. Mostly, arguments were raised that an FTA with China would only benefit the emerging giant, and that financial support would only result in debt traps for the smaller party. Particularly, the FTA with China does not benefit fisheries which represent the most important industry for the archipelago. To support Maldives, the European Union provides financial support to help implement its Nationally Determined Contributions (NDC) and conduct round tables such as the EU Business roundtable, to discuss how to improve trade and investment relations between Maldives and Europe. The relationship with Australia has mostly been limited with some marine based sponsored projects from the Department of Foreign Affairs and Trade (DFAT).

OBJECTIVES OF THE CHAPTER

The main objectives of this study are to

- Highlight the economic impact of COVID-19 on three island economies, namely Mauritius, Sri Lanka and the Maldives.
- Provide an overview of the efforts pursued in the areas of regulation and business, service sectors such as tourism and finance, and trade partnerships including free trade agreements.
- Look at the case example of Mauritius, and how Australia can be an enabler to allow for a sustainable blue economy.

To our knowledge, we are the first to tap into studying how small island economies can tackle a post COVID-19 era, with an emphasis on activating a sustainable and resilient blue economy.

ISSUES AND CHALLENGES

Despite the fact that COVID-19 impacted all the three island economies negatively, the extent of the impact was different. With the Mauritian government opting for longer periods of complete lockdowns than the other two as part of prioritizing health over the economy, this resulted in relatively more dire economic consequences with higher unemployment rates, higher inflation rates due to higher cost of imported goods because of a depreciated Mauritius rupee, and relatively high government debt to GDP because of the wage assistance schemes put in place to support business and income earners. While the health sector has been prioritized over other sectors, the Mauritian government is fully conscious

Table 2. Bilateral agreements with global partners

	Australia	India	China	Africa	Europe and UK
Mauritius	TIEA (December 2010)	CECPA (February 2021)	FTA (January 2021)	AFCFTA (January 2021)	EPA UK (January 2021)
				COMESA (October 2000)	EPA EU (August 2009)
				SADC (August 2008)	
Sri Lanka	TIFA (November 2017)	ISFTA (December 1998)		Nonmember state of AU	Cooperation and Partnership Agreement EU (1995)
					EU-SLIP (2021)
Maldives		FTA (1981)	FTA (December 2017)		Financing agreement EU (June 2019)

Source: COMESA (2021), SADC (2020), European Commission (2021b), (Kelegama & Karunaratne, 2013)

Note: TIEA is the Tax Information Exchange Agreement; CECPA is the Comprehensive Economic Cooperation and Partnership Agreement; FTA is the Free Trade Agreement; AFCFTA is the African Continental Free Trade Agreement; SADC is the Southern African Development Community (SADC); COMESA is the Common Market for Eastern and Southern Africa,; EPA is the Economic Partnership Agreement; TIFA is the Trade and Investment Framework Agreement; ISFTA is the Indo-Sri Lanka FTA, AU is the African Union; EU is the European Union; and EU-SLIP is the EU-Sri Lanka Innovation Partnership. Dates in brackets refer to the time when each agreement was implemented, except for China where it represents the date the FTA was signed.

that the country already faced four consecutive quarters of recession since March 2020, and this was primarily due to the borders being closed. Simply put, the economy came to a halt, with sub services sectors like tourism affected tremendously and economic activity was bound to restart before the last quarter of 2021, which is the peak season for tourism in Mauritius. To that effect, in the government budget of 2021, it was expected that the Mauritian economy would be opened fully again in October 2021 with precautionary health measures put in place to welcome tourists. Further, three strategic pillars were identified to develop a new economic architecture, boost investment and restore confidence. As mentioned earlier, while various sectors such as regulatory, tourism and financial services were areas of focus, little has been done in terms of tapping into the blue economy of Mauritius. While much work is being pursued to promote regulatory framework to encourage business, tourism, and finance sectors, with active involvement with trade agreements and partners, specific to the marine industry, the country has been more involved in dealing with aftermath consequences of marine disaster events such as the Wakashio oil spill of 2020, than trying to use and promote its blue economy.

Comparatively, in Sri Lanka, number of COVID-19 cases are high, due to a more relaxed approach than Mauritius. Nonetheless, although the fisheries sector contributed only around 1.1%, the travel and tourism sector represented about 12.6% of Sri Lanka's GDP in 2019, providing much room for the ocean economy as a valuable contributor to the country's GDP. The Ministry of Fisheries reported that the growth rate of fisheries contribution to GDP, at current market prices in 2019 was 9.9%, a figure not seen in the last 5 years. While this can partly be explained by an increase in total fish production, there was a drop in marine fish production in 2019 compared to the previous two years, with however an increase in inland and aquaculture. Precisely, both coastal and offshore (deep sea) fish production fell in 2019 relative to the previous year (Ministry of Fisheries, 2020). Investments in major assets have been dropping since 2017 in areas such as fishing fleets and fishing nets. Since 2018, there have been some investments in innovative aquaculture systems such as caged and pen culture systems, both in freshwater and brackish water), with however, poor upscaling as per the National Aquaculture Development Authority (NAQDA). This was reflected in shrimps' production which increased significantly in 2018, but then failed to gained momentum in 2019, with drops in shrimps' production under aquaculture. With less farms in 2019 compared to 2018, fish fingerlings production also dropped. The lack of marine production, caused primarily by a lack of production facilities and sustainability in innovative aquaculture systems, resulted in a lower net current account surplus of Rs14.5 million in 2019 compared to Rs15.2 million in the previous year. A depreciating Sri Lanka rupee against the US dollar helped to increase the competitiveness of Sri Lanka's exports on the global market, with however the country also importing more fish and fishery products in 2019. While EU continues to be the main importer for Sri Lanka's seafood, only 32 of the 75 medium and large-scale companies have approved EU processing plants (EDB, 2019). While Sri Lanka established a Vessel Monitoring System (VMS) to monitor deep sea fishing fleets, more regulatory work is needed to avoid sanctions like the EU fishing ban in 2015 (Kearns, 2015).

While the Maldives faces some political issues in terms of implementing free trade agreements with China vis-à-vis other existing trading partners, the tourism sector contributes about 30% of Maldives GDP. Fisheries have always played an important part of the country's output. While there have been some talks with the EU on giving duty free access to fishery products in the EU, as part of increasing state revenues, there are some more challenges faced by the fisheries when exporting their goods. For instance, the clearance process is slowed by inappropriate facilities, cargo scanners, and inefficient document submission to regulatory bodies. Although state committees such as the National Trade Facilitation Committee (NTFC) was established in 2015 and later reactivated in 2019, Maldives witnessed a deterioration in World Bank doing business ranking for Maldives (ADB, 2020). This was also reflected in the 2018 OECD trade facilitation indicators (TFI), where Maldives ranked lower than Sri Lanka and India. In line with trade facilitation processes, the Maldives has recently partnered with the Asian Development Bank to establish a single point of entry for all import and export legal requirements. This would help reduce transaction costs for both the private sector and public sector. While Maldives ratified the World Trade Organization's (WTO) Trade Facilitation Agreement (TFA) in late 2019, its full implementation is yet to be seen.

In line with the simplification, modernization and harmonization of export and import processes which is a critical part of the global trading system nowadays, on top of regulatory reforms and private/public sector partnerships, investments in technology are much needed to propel the blue economy. This would not only facilitate trade processes, but also promote necessary security and transparency. Alternatively stated, there is a need to develop and implement proper regulatory reforms to facilitate trade processes while complying with international standards, encourage local and international private/public sector sharing of expertise and financing, and invest in technologies to promote the exploitation of marine resources such as renewable ocean energies. Australia, which value its blue waters, can provide some useful, practical applications which would eventually pave the way towards sustainable island economies, which depend on a lot of tourism and the marine industries.

While Mauritius and Sri Lanka value China as an important trading partner, as mentioned earlier the Maldives government tends to perceive China as a partner where benefits are only one-sided. In fact, the China's Belt and Road Initiative (BRI) has resulted in many countries accumulating debt burden with hidden loans worth nearly $400 billion. These are primarily caused by private loans which are not fully reported under the World Bank Debtor Reporting System (DRS). The Maldives is one of the eight countries where sovereign debt exposure to China exceeded 25% of GDP (Malik *et al.*, 2021). Despite that Maldives have since then engaged with China to get some debt relief, Maldives public stakeholders are less motivated to go ahead and implement FTA with China. This is observed since the exit of the former Maldivian President Yameen, where the Maldives are more favorable of reinforcing its India First policy compared to collaboration with China. The Quadrilateral Security Dialogue (Quad) which involves Australia, India, Japan, and the US, has emerged to reduce China's growing economic influence in the Indian Ocean. Australia, as a member of the Quad, can play an important role for all the three islands, in training and development, climate change and security. While it is beyond the scope of this study to look at each of the three islands of interest, the case example of Mauritius and the blue economy, and how Australia can contribute towards enabling a sustainable blue economy is analysed.

Blue Economy – An Investment Dive Worth Exploring for Australia

The Mauritius - Australia Connection

Besides ESAAMLG which connects Mauritius and Australia through cooperative actions fighting financial crime and enhancing transparency in economic activities, the Indian Ocean Rim Association (IORA), with currently 23 members, can provide an important bridge to connect both countries further. With Australia chairing the IORA between 2013 and 2015, and the IORA secretariat based in Mauritius, the IORA can enable both countries from benefiting from a platform, with further trading opportunities between the two nations. In fact, the IORA is a vital organization for Australia as it is the only ministerial level forum which deals with the Indian Ocean territory in terms of trade partnerships. In 2015, Mauritius held the first blue economy conference for IORA, where all members recognized the value of the blue economy (IORA, 2015). Specifically, the different areas recognized were as follows:

1. Renewable ocean energy as a tool to bring down energy costs and reduce the impact of non-renewable energies on climate change.
2. Offshore hydrocarbons and seabed minerals to encourage new investment opportunities in the Indian Ocean.
3. Seaport and Shipping to motivate investment, trade and maritime networks in the Indian Ocean.
4. Fisheries and Aquaculture to guarantee food security and help to reduce poverty alleviation and promote sustainable living.

The IORA further recognized the need to promote proper management of marine resources and reinforce capacity building in Small Island Developing States (SIDS), Least Developed Countries (LDCs) and developing economies. As part of meeting achieving Sustainable Development Goals (SDGs), for example, SDG 14 which relates to "Life below water" linked to SIDS, Mauritius and some other Indian Ocean islands partnered with the EU to strengthen island capabilities for good governance of fisheries, management of coastal zones, and the management of coastal, marine and island biodiversity (SDG, 2016). Such a program endeavors to strengthen regulation and compliance with international and regional agreements such as the Nairobi Convention (UNEP, 2021), and United Nations Convention on the Law of the Sea (UNCLOS, 1982) and Illegal, Unreported, and Unregulated (IUU) fishing practices (European Commission, 2021a). IORA members, which include both Mauritius and Australia, acknowledge that priority sectors of the blue economy consist of renewable ocean energy, fisheries and aquaculture, shipping and seaports, hydrocarbons and seabed minerals, all of which should be assessed, and actions taken within a safe environment, as a means to provide societal and economic benefits to inhabitants. Indeed, several actionable items include improving networking, collaborative research among member states, while also involving richer public and private sector partnerships across involved nations.

The Sri Lanka Australia Connection

Both countries share long lasting diplomatic relations since 1947, with various poverty alleviation and development in human capital. The Australian government recognizes Sri Lanka's effort towards national reconciliation since the conflict ended on the island in 2009, and the reforms put in place to achieve deeper global integration (Ministry of Foreign Affairs, 2017). As members of the IORA, both Sri Lanka and Australia benefit from a secure and peaceful marine territory. As part of enhancing cooperation between the two nations, both countries jointly declared on partnering, through associations such as IORA and Asian Regional Forum (ARF), to support and strengthen regional norms and rule-based practices. Specific to the maritime industry, both countries showed commitment to explore training opportunities and expert aid, including continued cooperation on search and rescue missions and maritime safety through the Indian Ocean memorandum of understanding on port state control. As of 2019, twenty countries are part of this memorandum, including Australia, Mauritius, Sri Lanka, and the Maldives (IOMOU, 2020).

As part of enabling further trade opportunities between Australia and Sri Lanka, Australia is committed to continue supporting Sri Lanka with expert advice and trade facilitating processes. With Sri Lanka's energy requirements evolving, Australia's private sector in energy can provide expertise where Australia is a leader, especially when it comes to energy renewables like ocean energy. Australia also showed commitment in their 2017 joint declaration to help Sri Lanka develop sustainable tourism and mining industries. More importantly, both countries are motivated to collaborate further in the agricultural sector, by developing the dairy and fisheries industries with the Australian Centre for International Agricultural Research (ACIAR).

More recently, the International Organization for Migration (IOM) together with the Australian government (through the Australian High Commission) have funded a multi-day fishing vessel monitoring system for Sri Lanka in 2021. This is aimed at combatting illegal fishing, promoting border protection and security in the Indian Ocean, preventing drug and human trafficking, and helps to provide help to fishermen in distressed ships (Presidential Secretariat, 2021).

The Maldives Australia Connection

With diplomatic relations established in 1974, Australia and Maldives bilateral trade remained steady over the last ten years, with a total bilateral trade of $160 million in 2018, where 25% represented Australia exports. These were mostly Australian food and beverage for the tourists in Maldives. The Department of Foreign Affairs and Trade (DFAT) has sponsored nearly $2.5 million over the last 8 years to the United Nations Development Program (UNDP) integrated governance project, where the main objectives were to increase transparency of public entities, encourage a fair and equitable access to the legal system, and build stronger civic societies. More specific to our study, Australia funded 20% of the $10 million Climate Change Trust Fund of the World Bank over 2013-2018, to enhance tourism activities, employment and ecosystem preservation. Further, during 2015-2017, the Australian Maritime Safety Authority

(AMSA) funded a $2.6 million program which was targeted of enhancing maritime search capacities, through training and development in operations management and adopting better maritime systems. The Maldives, Sri Lanka and Mauritius all benefited from this program (DFAT, 2021). Australia continues to contribute about $2 million annually in the Official Development Assistance (ODA), focusing on scholarships in various educational areas such as economics, commerce, and management.

CASE OF MAURITIUS: THE VALUE OF THE BLUE ECONOMY

Despite Australia being known as one of the largest maritime jurisdictions, to explicitly define the blue economy is a challenging task. In line with Economist (2015), it is assumed that a sustainable ocean economy materializes when economic activity is aligned with the long-term capability of marine ecosystems to support this activity while remaining buoyant and healthy. While the services and industries which can be grouped under the blue economy umbrella are many, the AIMS index of the Australia marine industry helps to assess the contribution of Australia's blue economy to its country's economic bottom-line. In 2018, Australia's blue economy was estimated to be over $80 billion, representing an increase of over four hundred per cent over the last twenty years (AIMS, 2020). This is based on revenue from 14 marine industry sub-sectors, including boatbuilding and repair, water-based transport, domestic and international tourism, ship building and repair, marinas and boating infrastructure, marine equipment retailing, oil exploration and production, liquefied petroleum gas (LPG) production, natural gas production, marine-based aquaculture, commercial fishing, and recreational fishing.

Although the impact COVID-19 is yet to be fully assessed on the blue economy, since COVID-19 is still impacting the global economies, it is worth reiterating that both Australia and Mauritius, being surrounded by the sea, have adversely been affected in various import/export related industries like tourism, food, transport, with the closure of borders affecting both commercial and cargo flights, and shipping experiencing over months of delivery delays. The increased uncertainty regarding COVID-19 progression with variants such as Delta, second and third waves of COVID-19 witnessed in various countries globally, and volatile commodity prices, led to higher cost of living, especially for Mauritius which depends heavily on tourism sector revenues, and still opted to priorities protecting health over economic damage.

With an ocean policy approved since 1998, the island-continent has, since then, well progressed with its policy intention of taking the whole range of marine uses and activities across all maritime sectors in Australia into account and provide a coordinated approach to management based on Ecologically Sustainable Development (ESD) initiatives. For example, by implementing the Environment Protection and Biodiversity Conservation (EPBC) 1999 Act, the Australia policy makers can play a more vital role to monitor ecologically sustainable management of fisheries, including assessing their environmental performance. While such policies are more geared towards serving Australia's territories, a more global economic perspective is required from experienced nations like Australia, to support a gradual transition to a more sustainable, inclusive and resilient global economy. Recent research on assessing the views of energy sources recently points out that viable energy sources like solar needs to be considered (Contu, Elshareif and Gurrib, 2021). On a global scale, international bodies such as the United Nations (UN), World Health Organization (WHO) are working to tackle climate change issues. Climate change increases the risks of extreme weather conditions that can cause critical damage to the small island economies, in areas such as food security, spreading of infectious diseases and air/water pollution. Previous events were the various 2017 Atlantic hurricanes which caused severe damage to Caribbean islands, with hurricane Irma being the strongest ever recorded hurricane. Small island economies, where more than 60 million people reside, have long been recognized as especially vulnerable to the adverse effects of climate change (UNFCCC, 2018). Following the 2015 Paris Agreement and 2008 World Health Assembly, the next United National Framework Convention on Climate Change (UNFCCC) is expected to be held in October in Glasgow. It is expected that high emitting countries would participate more against climate change challenges, with more than 93% of small island developing economies (SIDS) having/ or intend to submit national climate pledges (UNFCCC, 2021).

SOLUTIONS AND RECOMMENDATIONS

Below are some key recommendations which can enable this possibility, while meeting specific SDGs related directly or indirectly to a sustainable blue economy. These can serve as important tools, post early COVID-19 crisis, to set the pace for a solid foundation for a sustainable blue economy, where future generations will benefit further than today's one. Recommendations are derived mainly from the High-level panel for a sustainable ocean economy, also known as the Ocean panel, where significant work is aimed at meeting several United Nations SDGs. To date, more than 15 blue papers and numerous special reports that been written by the Ocean Panel. Australia, as a key member among the other 13 world leaders of the panel, has a vital role to play to help neighboring small island developing states like Mauritius. Even though global fiscal support accounted for more than $10 trillion in 2020 (Zhang, 2020), as part of a global economic recovery, insignificant weight has sadly been attributed to the role that the ocean economy and its various industries can play in transitioning to a more inclusive and resilient world economy.

While Northrop *et al.* (2020) from the Ocean panel proposes five priority areas necessitating actions, this study focusses only on four factors which are relevant to the Mauritius economy. Specifically, our recommendation is in terms of (i) investing in the coastal and marine ecosystem, (ii) investing in sustainable community driven marine farming, (iii) encouraging sustainable renewable energies from the ocean, and (iv) capacity building in the health sector. Combined together, investments in these four areas will allow the Mauritian island community to benefit both from short- and long-term job opportunities, improved living standards, improved health life of coral reefs and seafood stock recovery, diversification in economic driven areas for coastal communities, opportunities for water security in areas like desalination, and lesser greenhouse gas emissions. Although these benefits would accrue over both the short and long term, it is important to further broadly define some policy actions which would allow such investments to take place. Due to the scope of this study, a focus on the research and development, regulatory, public/private sector alliance and capacity building in the health sector is made.

Research and Development

Firstly, Australia can help Mauritius sectors including tourism, marine preservation, energy, and community driven non-fed fish farming. For instance, investing in pilot projects such as developing low carbon alternative feed options for fed mariculture would provide socio, economic and environmental benefits, whilst satisfying SDGs like SDG 14 (life below water) and SDG 13 (climate action). Investments in ocean renewable energies can also be encouraged, with Australian agencies such as the Australian

Renewable Energy Agency (ARENA), under the umbrella of IORA, playing an important role in the area of wave energy projects. To date, ARENA has funded about 15 ocean-based projects, enabling prospective investors to identify sites requiring further exploration, and policymakers to better understand how ocean energy can contribute to an economy (ARENA, 2021). Further, due to its extensive experience over the Great Barrier reef protection, the Australian marine authorities can help in data collection of the Mauritian coastline, which can be particularly important to protect or restore important marine reserves in the tourism driven economy. A specific local example needing much attention is the Blue Bay marine park in the south part of the island, which although being declared a wetland site under the Ramsar Convention on Wetlands of International Importance since 2008, has suffered tremendously due to abusive tourism activities in the marine reserve.

Regulation and Incentives

Secondly, while the Mauritian government is actively working to reduce financial crimes with continuous regulatory reforms, more regulatory work is required in its blue economy. For instance, legal reforms can be implemented to encourage fisheries management by introducing subsidies to small businesses connected to the fishing industry. This can include financial support for eco-tourism business entities and artisanal fishing, which will also help to promote marine preservation. In the same spirit, some tourism or municipality/village council fees can be introduced to reinstate coastline which have been impacted by human or adverse weather conditions. A recent example is the MV Wakashio oil spill (Reliefweb, 2020) which ecologically affected important areas on the island such as Point d'Esny wetlands, Blue Bay marine park, Ile aux Aigrette's nature reserve and Mahebourg fishing reserves.

Private/Public Sector Partnerships

Thirdly, the value of the private/public partnership cannot be underestimated. For instance, the Mauritian government, through its Central Bank, can provide access to state backed loans, duty free imports of fixed assets like vessels, tax exemptions and preferential interest rates to the private sector which can include private investors from the Australian government. This can also be extended to include eco-friendly businesses funding from the public sector to investors as part of developing innovative marine entrepreneurship ventures like mariculture. In the same vein, some industry specific insurance policies can be drafted to help cater for the small businesses involved with the sea, where the tropical island has been witnessing some seriously impactful cyclones in the last three decades.

Capacity Building in Health

Mauritius, compared with the other islands under study, has been very proactive and determined to tackle the COVID-19 pandemic right from its onset. However, it has recently been facing challenges when it opened fully its borders from October 1, 2021. Daily cases have increased significantly, which while expected as in Maldives, resulted in more death casualties, particularly for those who were admitted to the Ear, Nose and Throat (ENT) hospital. While the urgent flight of the ex-prime minister because he was tested positive, to India, sounds rational, this attracted media attention in that this was perceived as a preferential treatment, due to social status (AfricLaw, 2021). While Mauritius is well equipped to meet its fully vaccinated population target, the country lacks in high-tech medical services to tackle complex health issues like COVID-19 patients with complications. Likewise, various health cases related to cancer are sent to neighboring countries. COVID-19 casualties tend to be high since the equipment are not really meant to tackle COVID-19. To this end, it is important for the government to make significantly more budgetary allocations to the health care sector. This can include both the acquisition of more sophisticated, well-proven, medical equipment, continuous training and development to local doctors from overseas specialists, and also more comprehensive funding of patients who need foreign treatment. While Mauritius has a free public health care system, the services provided need a serious boost. An assessment of the health care sector is much needed to provide longer life expectancies to its people.

Australia enjoys one of the best healthcare systems in the world, by providing quality, safe, and affordable healthcare to all, resulting in longer life expectancies. While Medicare and the public hospital system provides free or low-cost access to all Australians, private health insurance is also available, giving more choice to the Australian. The Medicare system covers all public health costs, including the Pharmaceutical Benefits Scheme (PBS) which subsidizes the cost of various medicines, and provides the list of all brand names and generic medicines, which are used in Australia, after being proven to be safe and effective. Similarly, the Medicare Benefits Schedule (MBS) provides a list of all healthcare services which the state subsidizes. A medical board of experts keeps the list updated to ensure best practices. The Australian government, on top of these schedules, subsidizes aged care services, provides funding to health and medical research through the Medical Research Future Fund, and coordinates national responses to healthcare emergencies like COVID-19. While Mauritius also works hard to coordinate national rcsponses related to COVID-19, it would further benefit the islanders to have (i) a Medicare type system which regulates and is accountable for the health care costs going to society, (ii) more private health care insurance providers which would allow the Mauritian people to feel less impacted with high medical care costs, (iii) a scheme similar to PBS where various prescription medicines are subsidized by the state, (iv) a MBS scheme which provides a full clear view of the healthcare services provided on the island, with gaps identified, and (v) a fully accountable medical board which regulates the medicines used on the island. At a later stage, some medical research fundings can be put in place, with joint collaboration with international medical experts from countries like Australia. These important health care recommendations would help in the capacity building of the health care sector in Mauritius.

FUTURE RESEARCH DIRECTIONS

This study highlights of importance of sector specific research and development initiatives guided by marine experts such as Australia, properly set and implemented marine based regulations and the value of private/public sector projects with preferential investing schemes and incentives. A future research avenue would involve aligning these value propositions with associations such as IORA to be able create the opportunity for other island economies to assess and consider these recommendations as part of enriching their blue economies' management and potential revenues.

CONCLUSION

With more than 30 small islands developing states being affected by COVID-19, it is vital to embrace the ocean economy as part of the recovery agenda. This paper looks at Mauritius, Sri Lanka, the Maldives and Australia, first giving an overview of the impact of early COVID-19 on the different nations, bilateral agreements, and existing relationships with Australia and the 3 island economies. This study emphasizes on Mauritius as a case example. Despite Mauritius being a small island in the Indian Ocean, the country has progressed significantly, since gaining independence, in various areas of economy activity, regulation, compliance with regional and international trade agreements, and active memberships in ministerial level associations to work towards meeting SDGs. Despite being ranked 13th in the world of the ease of doing business, the Mauritian government decided since early 2020 to combat COVID-19 by prioritizing health over economic consequences. The small island is set to get its population fully vaccinated by the end of 2021, which will help boost the tourism sector, the most important revenue sector. While the state continues to work actively to boost the local economy further, it is strongly supported that the ocean economy should be an area of focus, since Mauritius has an abundant exclusive economic zone of 2.3 million square kilometers, which has yet to be explored.

Australia, as a key member of various associations and organizations such as Ocean Panel and IORA, can help Mauritius to gradually transition into an inclusive, sustainable, and resilient blue economy. This can be achieved by setting a solid framework to encourage investments in the coastal and marine areas belonging to Mauritius, encouraging community driven marine farming, and starting to activate climate conscious projects related to sustainable renewable energies from the ocean. Such investments would trigger social benefits which outweigh social costs, job opportunities, enhanced livelihoods of the islanders, better health coral reef life, food security project like desalination and drinkable water, and eventually lower greenhouse gas emissions. To attract such investments, the Mauritian government needs to provide incentives in research and development projects targeting ocean and ocean energy, preferential financing treatments to foreign investors and local small businesses, and more action-based partnerships between the private and public sectors between Mauritius and Australia. The Australian government and its agencies, with tremendous exposure on ocean-based projects, can provide a support in leading island-based projects, which are targeted to meet sustainable development goals related to climate change and the blue economy. Last, but not least, the health sector in Mauritius needs serious uplifting with more budgetary allocations made into high-tech medical equipment and services, a Medicare type system to capture healthcare costs to the public, similar schemes such as PBS and MBS, more private healthcare insurance, and an active medical board with medical experts constantly reviewing the safety and quality of healthcare services provided on the island. Such recommendations can be implemented, once activated as prioritized agenda items in meetings held by bodies such as the Indian Ocean Rim Association, where both Mauritius and Australia play an active role.

REFERENCES

ADB. (2020). *Maldives: Economic Update 2019*. Asian Development Bank. Retrieved from https://www.adb.org/sites/default/files/institutional-document/544946/maldives-economic-update-2019.pdf

AfricLaw. (2021). *Is Covid-19 bringing out the inequalities in the delivery of health services in Mauritius?* AfricLaw. Retrieved from https://africlaw.com/2021/10/11/is-covid-19-bringing-out-the-inequalities-in-the-delivery-of-health-services-in-mauritius/#more-2391

AIMS. (2020). *AIMS Index of Marine Industry 2020 report*. Australian Institute of Marine Science. Retrieved from https://www.aims.gov.au/aims-index-of-marine-industry

Anolick, N., Batten, J. A., Kinateder, H., & Wagner, N. (2021). Time for gift giving: Abnormal share repurchase returns and uncertainty. *Journal of Corporate Finance*, *66*(101787), 101787. Advance online publication. doi:10.1016/j.jcorpfin.2020.101787

ARENA. (2021). *Renewable Energy*. ARENA. Retrieved from https://arena.gov.au/renewable-energy/ocean/#main

Bakas, D., & Triantafyllou, A. (2020). Commodity price volatility and the economic uncertainty of pandemics. *Economics Letters*, *193*(109283), 109283. Advance online publication. doi:10.1016/j.econlet.2020.109283

Bauso, A. O. (2021). *25 Most Beautiful Beaches in the World.* Travel + Leisure. Retrieved from https://www.travelandleisure.com/trip-ideas/beach-vacations/most-beautiful-beaches-in-the-world

BBC. (2021). *Mauritius reopens to fully vaccinated tourists.* BBC. Retrieved from https://www.bbc.com/news/topics/cdl8n2edxept/mauritius

COMESA. (2021). *Common Market for Eastern and Southern Africa*. https://www.comesa.int/members/

Contu, D., Elshareif, E. E., & Gurrib, I. (2021). Assessing Views towards Energy Sources with Social Media Data: The Case of Nuclear Energy in the UAE. *Processes (Basel, Switzerland)*, *9*(11), 1945. doi:10.3390/pr9111945

Deloitte. (2021). *RegTech Universe 2021: Take a closer look at who is orbiting in the RegTech space.* Deloitte. Retrieved from https://www2.deloitte.com/lu/en/pages/technology/articles/regtech-companies-compliance.html

DFAT. (2021). *Maldives Brief.* Department of Foreign Affairs and Trade. Retrieved from https://www.dfat.gov.au/geo/maldives/maldives-country-brief

Economist. (2015). *Ocean Prosperity Roadmap: Fisheries and Beyond.* The Economist https://www.greengrowthknowledge.org/sites/default/files/downloads/resource/1.-Ocean-Prosperity-Roadmap-Synthesis-Report-5.30.15A.pdf

EDB. (2019). *Industry Capability Report: Sri Lankan Fisheries Sector*. Export Development Board. https://www.srilankabusiness.com/ebooks/fish---fishery-products---industry-capability-report---december-2019.pdf

Eichenbaum, M., Rebelo, S., & Trabandt, M. (2020). *The Macroeconomics of Epidemics.* National Bureau of Economic Research. Working Paper 26882. doi:10.3386/w26882

ESMA. (2020). *ESMA Report on Trends, Risks and Vulnerabilities.* European Securities and Markets Authority. https://www.esma.europa.eu/sites/default/files/library/esma_50-165-1287_report_on_trends_risks_and_vulnerabilities_no.2_2020.pdf

European Commission. (2021a). *EU rules to combat IUU fishing*. European Commission. https://ec.europa.eu/oceans-and-fisheries/fisheries/rules/illegal-fishing_en

European Commission. (2021b). *The EU enhances collaboration with Sri Lanka's innovation and start-up ecosystem actors*. European Union. https://eeas.europa.eu/delegations/sri-lanka/105377/eu-enhances-collaboration-sri-lanka%E2%80%99s-innovation-and-start-ecosystem-actors_en

FATF. (2020). *Mauritius: 3rd enhanced follow-up report and technical compliance re-rating*. Financial Action Task Force. https://www.fatf-gafi.org/media/fatf/documents/reports/fur/ESAAMLG-3rd-Follow-Up-Report-Mauritius-2020.pdf

Gurrib, I. (2018a). Can an energy futures index predict US stock market index movements? *International Journal of Energy Economics and Policy*, *8*(5), 230–240. https://www.econjournals.com/index.php/ijeep/article/view/6622/3947

Gurrib, I. (2018b). The relationship between the Nasdaq Composite Index and energy futures markets. *Investment Management and Financial Innovations*, *15*(4), 1–16. doi:10.21511/imfi.15(4).2018.01

Gurrib, I. (2019). Can energy commodities affect energy blockchain based cryptos? *Studies in Economics and Finance*, *36*(4), 682–699. doi:10.1108/SEF-10-2018-0313

Gurrib, I. (2021). Early COVID-19 Policy Response on Healthcare Equity Prices. *Studies in Economics and Finance*, *38*(5), 987–1006. doi:10.1108/SEF-02-2021-0075

Gurrib, I., Kweh, Q. L., Contu, D., & Kamalov, F. (2021). COVID-19, Short-selling Ban and energy Stock Prices. *Energy Research Letters*, *1*(4). Advance online publication. doi:10.46557/001c.18562

IOMOU. (2020). *2019 Report*. Indian Ocean memorandum of understanding on port state control. https://safety4sea.com/wp-content/uploads/2020/05/Indian-Ocean-MoU-Annual-Report-2019-2020_05.pdf?__cf_chl_jschl_tk__=pmd_2tIrQZ8mF0Gp_WgWlKdV0JkYs02Ok.dUG_ZJXQumYlo-1634549871-0-gqNtZGzNAlCjcnBszQi9

IORA. (2015). *Declaration of the Indian Ocean Rim Association on enhancing Blue Economy Cooperation for Sustainable Development in the Indian Ocean Region*. Indian Ocean Rim Association. https://www.iora.int/media/8216/iora-mauritius-declaration-on-blue-economy.pdf

Kearns, M. (2015). *EU fishing ban takes its toll on Sri Lanka*. Seafood Source. https://www.seafoodsource.com/news/supply-trade/eu-fishing-ban-takes-its-toll-on-sri-lanka

Kelegama, S., & Karunaratne, C. (2013). *Experiences of Sri Lanka in the Sri Lanka – India FTA and the Sri Lanka – Pakistan FTA. United Nations Conference on Trade and Development. https:*//unctad.org/system/files/official-document/ecidc2013misc1_bp10.pdf

Kilian, L. (2009). Not all oil price shocks are alike: Disentangling demand and supply shocks in the crude oil market. *The American Economic Review*, *99*(3), 1053–1069. doi:10.1257/aer.99.3.1053

KPMG. (2021). *Mauritius Budget Highlights 2021/22*. KPMG. https://assets.kpmg/content/dam/kpmg/mu/pdf/2021/mu-Mauritius-Budget-Highlights-2021-2022.pdf.

Lescaroux, F., & Mignon, V. (2009). On the influence of oil prices on economic activity and other macroeconomic and financial variables. *OPEC Energy Review*, *32*(4), 343–380. doi:10.1111/j.1753-0237.2009.00157.x

Malik, A., Parks, B., Russell, B., Lin, J., Walsh, K., Solomon, K., Zhang, S., Elston, T., & Goodman, S. (2021). *Banking on the Belt and Road: Insights from a new global dataset of 13,427 Chinese development projects*. AidData at William & Mary.

Marcus, B. C. L. (2021). *How the Maldives became the biggest 2020 international tourism success story*. CNN. Retrieved October 14, 2021, from https://edition.cnn.com/travel/article/maldives-tourism-arrivals-coronavirus-intl-hnk/index.html

MCCI. (2021). *Mauritius Chamber of Commerce and Industry*. President Report. https://www.mcci.org/president-report-2021/

Ministry of Fisheries. (2020). *Fisheries Statistics 2020*. Ministry of Fisheries. https://www.fisheriesdept.gov.lk/web/images/Statistics/FISHERIES-STATISTICS--2020-.pdf

Ministry of Foreign Affairs. (2017). *Joint Declaration on Enhanced Cooperation between Australia and Sri Lanka*. Ministry of Foreign Affairs. https://mfa.gov.lk/jd-a-sl/

Northrop, E., Konar, M., Frost, N., & Hollaway, E. (2020). *A Sustainable and Equitable Blue Recovery to the COVID-19 Crisis: Summary for Decision Makers, Secretariat of the High-Level Panel for a Sustainable Ocean Economy*. World Resources Institute. https://oceanpanel.org/sites/default/files/2020-09/20_HLP_Report_COVID_Blue_Recovery.pdf

Prabheesh, K. P., Padhan, R., & Garg, B. (2020). COVID-19 and the oil price–stock market nexus: Evidence from net oil-importing countries. *Energy Research Letters, 1*(2), 13745. doi:10.46557/001c.13745

Preiss, R. M. (2019). Sri Lanka's Market: An Investment Gem Hidden in Too Much Pessimism. *Forbes*. Retrieved October 14, 2021, from https://www.forbes.com/sites/rainermichaelpreiss/2019/08/07/sri-lankas-market-an-investment-gem-hidden-in-too-much-pessimism/?sh=521f301d5df6

Presidential Secreteriat. (2021). *A multi-day fishing vessel monitoring system from Australia to Sri Lanka. Presidential Secretariat*. https://www.presidentsoffice.gov.lk/index.php/2021/07/16/a-multi-day-fishing-vessel-monitoring-system-from-australia-to-sri-lanka/

PWC. (2021). *National lockdown in Mauritius until 30 April 2021*. Price Waterhouse Coopers. https://www.pwc.com/mu/en/about-us/press-room/lockdown-communique.html

RBA. (2021a). *Cash Rate Target*. Reserve Bank of Australia. https://www.rba.gov.au/statistics/cash-rate/

RBA. (2021b). *Statement by Philip Lowe, Governor: Monetary Policy Decision*. https://www.rba.gov.au/media-releases/2021/mr-21-19.html

Reliefweb. (2020). *Mauritius: MV Wakashio Oil Spill - Aug 2020*. Reliefweb. https://reliefweb.int/disaster/ac-2020-000180-mus

Ritchie, H., Mathieu, E., Rodés-Guirao, L., Appel, C., Giattino, C., Ortiz-Ospina, E., Hasell, J., Macdonald, B., Beltekian, D., & Roser, M. (2020). *Coronavirus Pandemic (COVID-19)*. Our World in Data. https://ourworldindata.org/coronavirus

Ruiz Estrada, M. A., Koutronas, E., & Lee, M. (2020). Stagpression: The Economic and Financial Impact of COVID-19 Pandemic. SSRN *Electronic Journal*. doi:10.2139/ssrn.3593144

SADC. (2020). *SADC Facts and Figures.* Southern African Development Community. https://www.sadc.int/about-sadc/overview/sadc-facts-figures/

SDG. (2016). *Partnerships for SDGs - 2016 special report.* United Nations Department of Economic and Social Affairs. https://sustainabledevelopment.un.org/content/documents/2329Partnership%20Report%202016%20web.pdf

Shehzad, K., Xiaoxing, L., & Kazouz, H. (2020). COVID-19's disasters are perilous than Global Financial Crisis: A rumor or fact? *Finance Research Letters, 101669*, 101669. Advance online publication. doi:10.1016/j.frl.2020.101669 PMID:32837374

TimesofIndia. (2021). Sri Lanka to end Covid-19 lockdown on October 1. *Times of India.* https://timesofindia.indiatimes.com/world/south-asia/sri-lanka-to-end-covid-19-lockdown-on-october-1/articleshow/86615691.cms

Trading Economics. (2021a). *Mauritius Coronavirus COVID-19 Vaccination Rate.* Trading Economics. https://tradingeconomics.com/

Trading Economics. (2021b). *Mauritius Economy Remains in Recession.* Trading Economics. https://tradingeconomics.com/mauritius/gdp-growth-annual

Trading Economics. (2021c). *Tourism Revenues in Sri Lanka.* Trading Economics. https://tradingeconomics.com/sri-lanka/tourism-revenues

Trading Economics. (2021d). *Tourist Arrivals in Maldives.* Trading Economics. https://tradingeconomics.com/maldives/tourist-arrivals

Trading Economics. (2021e). *Regulatory Quality.* Trading Economics. https://tradingeconomics.com/australia/regulatory-quality-percentile-rank-lower-bound-of-90percent-confidence-interval-wb-data.html

Trading Economics. (2021f). *Insurance and Financial Services (% of service exports).* Trading Economics. https://tradingeconomics.com/sri-lanka/insurance-and-financial-services-percent-of-service-exports-bop-wb-data.html

Transparency International. (2020). *Corruption Perception Index (CPI) scores.* Transparency International. https://www.transparency.org/en/cpi/2020/index/mus

Transparency Mauritius. (2014). *Towards transparent and accountable political financing.* Transparency Mauritius. https://www.transparencymauritius.org/wp-content/uploads/2014/10/Transparency-Mauritius_Pledge_HD.pdf

UNCLOS. (1982). *United Nations Convention on the Law of the Sea.* United Nations. https://www.un.org/depts/los/convention_agreements/texts/unclos/unclos_e.pdf

UNEP. (2021). *Nairobi Convention.* United Nations Environment Programme. https://www.unep.org/nairobiconvention/

UNFCCC. (2018). *Health, Climate and Small Island States.* United National Framework Convention on Climate Change. https://unfccc.int/news/health-climate-and-small-island-state

UNFCCC. (2021). *Most Vulnerable Countries Leading Climate Response*. United National Framework Convention on Climate Change. https://unfccc.int/news/most-vulnerable-countries-leading-climate-response

World Bank. (2020). *Easy of Doing Business*. World Bank. https://data.worldbank.org/indicator/IC.BUS.EASE.XQ?locations=MU

Worldometers. (2021). *Sri Lanka*. Worldometers. Retrieved October 14, 2021, from https://www.worldometers.info/coronavirus/country/sri-lanka

XE. (2021). *Australian Dollar to US Dollar Exchange Rate Chart*. XE. Retrieved October 14, 2021, from https://www.xe.com/currencycharts/?from=AUD&to=USD&view=10Y

Zhang, T. (2020). *Global and Asia Economic Outlook: Greater Bay Area Chief Economist Forum*. IMF. https://www.imf.org/en/News/Articles/2020/07/10/sp071020-speech-on-the-global-and-asia-economic-outlook

ADDITIONAL READING

Mead, L. (2021). *Small Islands, Large Oceans: Voices on the Frontlines of Climate Change*. IISD. https://www.iisd.org/system/files/2021-03/still-one-earth-SIDS.pdf

Meddeb, R. (2021). *Small island developing states do not have the luxury of time*. UNDP. https://www.undp.org/blog/small-island-developing-states-do-not-have-luxury-time

UNDP. (2021). *Nationally Determined Contributions Global Outlook Report 2021: The State of Climate Ambition*. United Nations Development Programme. http://climatepromise.undp.org/sites/default/files/research_report_document/State-of-Climate-Ambition-UNDP-r2.pdf

KEY TERMS AND DEFINITIONS

Blue Economy: An emerging concept which aims to improve human wellbeing and social equity, while reducing environment risks related of our ocean.

Global Trading Partnership: This refers to bilateral trade agreements between the small islands and other international trading partners.

SDGs-14: This Sustainable Development Goal refers to life under water, with the goal of conserving and sustainably using the oceans, seas, and marine resources for sustainable development.

SIDS: Small Island Developing States represent a specific group of 38 United Nations member states and 20 non-UN members, faced with economic, social, and environmental issues.

Sustainability: It is defined as meeting today' needs without compromising the ability of future generations to meet theirs, with a focus on economic, social and environmental needs.

Chapter 6
Bilateral Cooperation Between Australia and Bangladesh in Diverse Areas:
An Analysis to Cope With the COVID-19 Aftermath

Muhammad Mahboob Ali
Dhaka School of Economics, University of Dhaka, Bangladesh

ABSTRACT

This chapter discussed the multi- sectoral bilateral cooperation between Australia and Bangladesh during and post-COVID-19-related to interregional trade, foreign investment, ready-made-garments export, education, blue economy, microfinance, tourism, renewable energy, and finally, fulfillment of targets of SDGs. How do diverse areas of bilateral cooperation between Bangladesh and Australia become more efficient and effective in resource utilization and bring socio-economic benefits? Advancement in economic cooperation in both the countries may be improved from trade and investment, enhancement of education using Australian model, improvement and enhancement in energy, blue economy, education, health, and RMG sector. Australian partnership will be helpful for government agencies, policy makers, and associated stakeholders of Bangladesh for future improvements and development interventions in diverse multisector areas. Emphasis needs to be given to ecofriendly sustainability as suggested by the author to meet the climate change and sustainability goals.

INTRODUCTION

Bangladesh is a country which is gradually trying to develop her economy from the least developed country (LDC) to a upper middle-income country by 2031. Hopefully by the 2026.Australian economy is one of the advanced economic countries of the globe. There is a wide scope of common standard of bilateral collaboration between the process of socio-economic expansion between Australia and Bangla-

DOI: 10.4018/978-1-7998-8657-0.ch006

desh in multi-sectoral areas through diversity of cultural attainment by bilateral cooperation. Australia and Bangladesh do have dynamic characteristics with the opportunities of equity and performing well such as to mitigate goals of Commonwealth, World Trade Organizations and United Nations. Australia takes mutual areas together with human rights, egalitarianism, the rule of law, reasonable expansion atmosphere, gender fairness, women's authorization, and international peace and security. According to Gross National Income per capita in 2019 Australia was ranked 14 with USD 55,100 (Atlas methodology) while Bangladesh was 151 with USD 1940 (Atlas methodology) and Australia was raked 23 in terms of PPP with 51,680(Purchasing power parity) and Bangladesh was ranked 145 with USD 5,200considering purchasing power parity(World Bank, 2021a). n the year 2022, Bangladesh and Australia will celebrate Fifty years of diplomatic relationship.

The world is going through a grim situation due to the COVID-19 pandemic. Not only people from all over the countries are dying but its impacts are also felt socially and on the global economies with the dysfunctional macroeconomic scenario, markets, and disrupted global supply-chains. Both aggregate supply and aggregate demand shocks have become acute due to COVID-19. Inadequate supply of essential medicines, food crisis, unemployment and increasing government debts are creating alarming situations across the world. The people's purchasing power has been diminishing day by day. The informal sector has also been impacted compared to the formal sector.

The Business Standard newspaper (2021) reported that Bangladesh and Australia had signed a Trade and Investment Framework Arrangement (TIFA) agreement, the first of its kind between the two countries on 14th September 2021.Thc newspaper reported that the framework was expected to provide a platform for institutional economic interaction and open new opportunities for trade and investment between the two countries. And the daily newspaper also commented that under the agreement, a joint working group will be formed keeping representation from related sectors and sub-sectors. Australia had proposed hosting an inaugural meeting of the working group in early 2022.Australia is the member of the Quadrilateral Security Dialogue (QUAD) which is a strategic dialogue among the United States, India, Japan and Australia.Yilmazkuday(2019) argued that any policy analysis should be achieved at the disaggregated level and then aggregated up to obtain macro propositions for the purpose country; otherwise, the upper-tier macro elasticity measures can be misleading due to the way that foreign products are aggregated at the destination country.

When the financial crisis started in USA, Australia did not get under recession due to appropriate policy's applicability's. Bangladesh has been receiving Australia's aid from mid-seventies though it is an insignificant in real terms. Trade and investment normally can be done with wider areas and in right direction so that it benefits both the countries. However, Bangladesh is still a developing country, so it gets wider opportunity to improve her economy. Gradually Australia's relationship with Bangladesh is strengthening. Strengthening the relationship between trade and investment will bring pareto optimality between two countries. Earlier Australian Bank ANZ Grindlays worked in Bangladesh. The bank created lot of entrepreneurs still mid-eighties. However, gradually trade and investment has strengthen which will ultimately bring fruitful results for both the countries. This will assist to raise economic growth and productivity of the country, improving standard of living and ultimately work as a push factor for economic development of Bangladesh. Ready Made Garment (RMG) sector of Bangladesh has a lion share in the Australian market.

There is a wide scope in the field of education, health, tourism sector, renewable energy sectors, fulfillment of funding of SDGs, micro financing, as well as normal businesses expansion. Moreover, disadvantaged group of people of the country can get wider scope to do business with Australia in future. Diversification of the products, successful utilization of 4th industrial revolution also needs to be addressed. Knowledge and skill prove better way to run organization during pandemic as well as world is passing through a volatile, uncertain, and complex times. Improving scenario due to COVID 19 pandemic may also be another part of interest to study where interchange of the ideas, creativity, innovation and adaption may act. Mutual education in the field of employability skill developed from Australian educations system for Bangladesh may act as advantageous. New sort of products including infrequent produce product which is necessary for human development may also gain popularity among two countries for which research and development is being needed. Cottage and Micro level entrepreneurs especially women entrepreneurs who are working in this sector need to get special preferential treatment.

Bangladesh economy is gradually developing business deals with the performance to create trading goods and services to maximize profits in cash or kind and minimizeproduction cost. Strategy refers to the ability to prepare, process and acts considering short,mid and long-term scenarios to mitigate in a conflicting or peaceful situation. COVID-19 created global healthcare emergency which was urgently addressed. Sustainability refers to 3Ps – people, planet, and profit (triple bottom line i.e. social, environmental, and financial). The government of Bangladesh whose leader is Prime Minister Sheikh Hasina has so far decided to distribute Bangladesh Tk. 103,117 crore, besides 19 packages which are 3.7% of the GDP to overcome the situation of an epidemic and guard citizens from the disaster in the year 2020.

Besides the Government of Bangladesh has been trying to provide more financial stimulus packages to different segments to conquer the pandemic situation especially giving more importance on agricultural sector of the country. However, Bangladesh needs multisectoral areas and bilateral cooperation between the country and Australia with COVID-19 and aftermath in the field of fulfillment of trade and investment, education, tourism and renewable-energy as well as NGO sector to meet the UNSDGs. Ahmed (2004) argued that the basis of Australia-Bangladesh relations hinges primarily on economic and political pursuits, and mutual interests since 1971 independence of Bangladesh.

Australia was the fourth country, and the first among developed nations, to recognize Bangladesh's independence in 1971. Australia's backing to Bangladeshis bring into line with the Bangladesh Government's vision, drew in its Seventh Five Year Plan 2016–2020, in which the Bangladesh Government has dedicated to enhancing economic progress and allow people as portion of the Government's long-term vision for removing poverty. In Bangladesh 8th five year plan was started in the month of July 2020 and will continue till June 2025 which mainly focuses on laid an all-encompassing basis for progressive development and to attain the maximum important goals, such as, upgrading in the better stages of living, health and education of the people, full employment, elimination of poverty etc. Australia also funded for higher education of Bangladeshi people which helps the country. Further, RMG sector, light engineering and pharmaceuticals, tourism sector, and maritime areas need to be developed. To attain demographic dividend, Bangladesh needs knowledge and skill manpower where the country needs international collaboration and effective utilization of political economy. Foreign funding for execution of targets of sustainable development goals are being required in Bangladesh. Australia's imports from Bangladesh are apparel knitted, apparel not knitted, other made-up textile, Headgear, footwear, leather and leather related products, Frozen Fish, Jute Carpets Pharmaceutical products, Ceramic products Plastics and articles, Toys etc. Australia's exports to Bangladesh are cotton, edible vegetables, Cereals, copper, Iron and steel, Paper, Zinc, Dairy products, Lead, Raw hides and skins, Machinery, Tanning or dyeing extracts, Electrical machinery and equipment, Sugars, Aluminum Preparations of cereals, flour, starch or milk, Edible fruit and nuts, Miscellaneous chemical Plastics and Vehicles, Pharmaceutical products, Oil, seeds, Optical, and photographic equipment etc.

Figure 1. Map South Asia and Australia
(Source: Google)

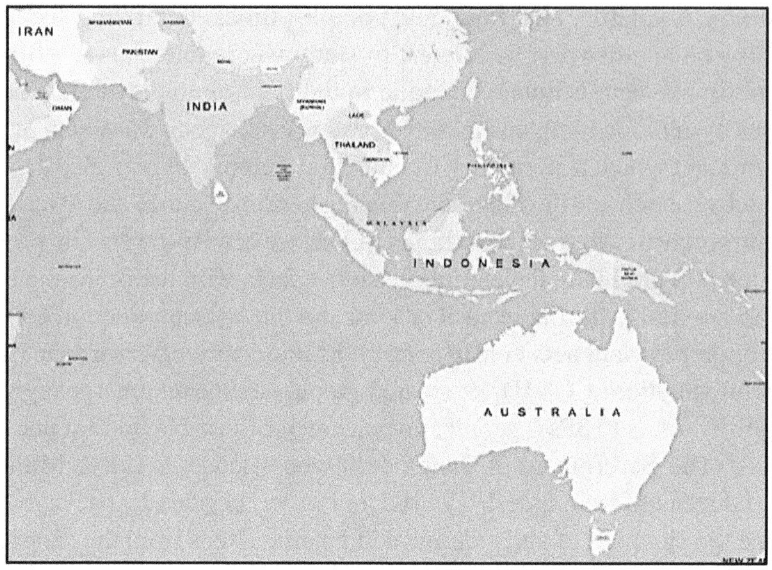

Under the COVID-19 Pandemic situation, we are moving towards "New Normal" situation which refers to the scenario where citizens have to become accustomed to the separation, maintaining social distancing, locked down, has a physical and psychological impact on individuals. Arrangements need to communicate, connect and converse with the community through the Internet and ICT technology platform, which as a human being is tough to quickly adapt to the "New Normal". Lockdown, curfew, shutdown, significant quarantines, tour limitations, social isolation, maintaining distance, staying at home etc. resulted in a quick fall in consumption and production activity hampering overall socioeconomic structure of the global economy. "New Normal" does not refer to return to the pre-pandemic situation. Staying at home, mostly doing official work, attending classes and meetings virtually from the home of individuals are creating mentally weak. This would not be possible without the Internet and virtual platforms like Zoom, meet Google, Google class, Skype, whose demands and stock prices have increased since March 2020.

Online education is getting more importantance. As such Bangladesh Government has decided to give student loan for purchasing the smart phone and providing Internet through SIM operator Tele-talk at a minimal cost. However, due to the current situation, exam system may be arranged online with a webcam through a remote online protected exam to observe whether the examinee is giving exam by the real examinee or arranging open book exam methods. Moreover, for practical purpose maintaining social distance practical labs need to be arranged. Hope that by the 2026 Hope that by 2026, Bangladesh can graduate from a Least Developed Country (LDC) and thereafter it will have to face post- LDC graduation issues. Land offices in Bangladesh is the main obstacle in context of ease of going business for local firms and people. Figure 1. illustrates the Map of Australia and South Asia including Bangladesh and the geographical distance.

Brewster(2021, p.4) argued that "Enhanced engagement on defence and security should be accompanied by initiatives to develop relationships with Bangladesh think tanks and other influential elements of Bangladesh civil society. The sponsorship of Track 1.5 security dialogues among leading think tanks is a useful way of developing relationships, sharing perspectives and generating ideas. An exchange of strategic insights involving officials and leading analysts would help promote the relationship and build shared perspectives on developments in the region". Australia has been currently supportive to the subsequent generation of energy technologies with an extra $1.62 billion for the Australian Renewable Energy Agency (ARENA) to invest, and expansionary emphasis of ARENA and the Clean Energy Finance Corporation (CEFC) to support new technologies that will cut emissions in agriculture, manufacturing, industry and transport sector(Prime Minister of Australia,2020). The buying of the Global Grindlays Business and merger with the branches of ANZ Grindlays Bank Limited in Bangladesh, it was renamed as Standard Chartered Grindlays Bank PLC on 1 August 2000.

BACKGROUND

This chapter will discuss the multi-sectoral bilateral cooperation with diversity between Bangladesh and Australia during and post-COVID-19 between Bangladesh and Australia in interregional trade, foreign investment, connectivity, education, tourism, targets of SDGs, micro finance, blue economy and renewable energy. Bilateral cooperation between Bangladesh and Australia become more efficient and effective in resources utilization and bring socio-economic benefits maybe a part of discussion. Advancement in the process of economic development, both the country may be improved from trade and investment bilaterally, enhancement of tertiary education using Australian model, improvement and enhancement in energy security and accessibility and mitigation of climate change are some of the key drivers of rapid development of renewable energy. Good governance mechanism can be arranged in different sectors in Bangladesh with the help of Australian model with transforming towards Bangladesh. Demand for labor both blue collar and white collar of Australia can be fulfilled by the Bangladeshi labor supply which needs skilling of labors for optimal utilization. Australian agricultural innovation can be helpful for Bangladesh if technological changes can be successfully transformed. Entrepreneurial steps in agricultural technology can be properly utilized in Bangladesh. In the health sector, entrepreneurial development may be developed. Bangladesh can take lesson from Australia to develop her tourism sector. Australian tourism sector was developed nicely before COVID -19.

Besides trade and investment, most important sector of cooperation is education sector, help to attain sustainable development goal by 2030, tourism sector, blue economy sector and renewable energy sector for the people in Bangladesh. Only TIFA sign is not a solution but to properly developing strategies in different sectors with proper economic diplomacy from the Bangladesh embassy at Australia is very much important. After math of COVID-19 cooperation between two countries will rise and also after LDC graduation by the Bangladesh, needs Australian help for recovering from bigger challenges.

Research question arises How bilateral cooperation between Bangladesh and Australia in multi-sectoral areas, will help to cope with the post-COVID-19 impact?

This chapter will discuss how Bangladesh can be benefitted from Australia and pareto optimality between two countries can prevail in different areas of socio-economics, political, cultural and promote, cooperation among two countries through collaborative efforts.

OBJECTIVES OF THE CHAPTER

Objectives of the Chapters are:

1. To assess how Bangladesh economy can benefit by bilateral cooperation between the two countries in diverse areas.
2. To investigate whether and how multi-sectoral areas bilateral cooperation can be arranged;
3. To examine the bilateral trade change between Australia and Bangladesh over the time period.
4.. To provide some suggestions for collaborative effort during ongoing COVID-19 and aftermath.

LITERATURE REVIEW

Australia and Bangladesh can mutually benefit, if they both work dynamically in various sectors of the economy as described in the literature review:

Ready Made Garments (RMG) Sector

According to World Bank (2021b) Bangladesh had remarkable pathway of growth and poverty reduction which has been among the fastest growing economies in the world over the past decade, supported by a demographic dividend, strong ready-made garment (RMG) exports, and stable macroeconomic conditions. Continued recovery in exports and consumption will help growth rates pick up to 6.4 percent in fiscal year 2021-22. Ali and Medhekar(2016) described that rehabilitation program of the unemployed person from RMG the export sector of the country, owing to the exit from the garments business should be taken as a preventive factor in Bangladesh for which training and development program for the garments workers is necessary so that if they fall victim of retrenchment from the job, then they can find alternative way for their livelihood. RMG sector is still key export sector of the country.

Education Sector

Keating(2003) argued that Australian educational qualification framework had a rigid and semi-regulatory role within the Vocational Education and Training (VET) awards and quality assurance systems. Pearson(2015) argued that Australia as one of the donor countries in Bangladesh with the toughest emphasis on education and health. Students in Bangladesh are increasingly misusing the freedom offered by online examinations that can be taken from remote locations such as home to make impersonators take the test on their behalf. Online ID authentication provides universities and corporate the option to switch on candidate authentication while configuring exam proctoring setting; Secure Browser may assist to avert dishonesty; Auto proctoring engages practice of a proctoring software that check the candidate's actions and their laptop/mobile action via audio and video recording previous to and throughout the examination to notice whichever doubtful movement that can be construe as corruption. Record & Review Proctoring offers the safety of respire proctoring but at a great deal reasonable way. Live proctoring can be used as mixture of auto and person proctoring, wherever the examinee is giving the exam is at the same time keep an eye on real-time by a live proctor and proctoring software which reports examinees and their online exam. movement earlier than and process throughout in the examination. Proctoring with 360-degree

Camera is also helpful. As such for governance in online education system in Bangladesh may be arranged online exam. security 'procedure, if needed any new rule is adopted in the education procedure which can be developed in accordance with Australian education system branding with Bangladesh after tailor made for quality increase of education with synchronization of technological. Australian education providers in Bangladesh were growing before COVID19, as collaboration in research and vocational education and training areas were very helpful to build educated human resources. Bangladeshi people are entitled to apply for Australia Awards Scholarships, Endeavour Scholarships and Fellowships and short-term Awards. Solar Energy has been the energetic strength towards the expansion of Bangladesh's green personnel as the country has deficit in HRM. International education engagement through quality education can play a vital role to keep economic progress of the country after COVID-19. Collaboration between Victoria University Melbourne, Australia, and Dhaka Study Center was a good example but now it does not exist. The Australian International School- Dhaka was established in the year 2002. It is the first and only international school in Dhaka that offers the comprehensive Australian Curriculum Accredited by the Government of Australia for students aged 3 (Early childhood) to 18 years (Year 12) (Australian International School-Dhaka,2021).Universal College Bangladesh (UCB)'s official campus inaugurated which is the exclusive partner of Monash College, Australia, and the only Ministry of Education-approved international education benefactor in Bangladesh (Universal College Bangladesh,2021). Murshid et al. (2019) commented that it was vital that policymakers should put emphasis on bigger consideration to quality of education and creation of a skilled, well-motivated work force in order to advantage from growth and also need to refrain from the attitude of backing and that was applied to avoid the formal structure of employment and disruption.

Blue Economy

Bangladesh has untapped resources in the 'Blue Economy, where Australia can help the country.Islam,& Mostaque(2018) described that blue economy of the country could wrap aquaculture, wild fisheries, marine biotechnology and other areas also add value considerably to the economy in Australia for which necessary collaborative effort was required. Wenhai et al.(2019) depicted that 'Blue Economy' is an integration of sustainable development and green growth which highlights an overall-planning and coordinated development between marine ecosystem and ocean and coastal zone economic system. Sadekin(2021) commented that the stress on the Blue Economy will ultimately be paid off by allowing economic development to flourish with environmental sustainability .As such to fulfillment of sustainable goals and its target, Australia can help through funding and technology transfer. Bangladesh may take appropriate technological changes with execution to utilize her blue economy.

Renewable Energy Sector

Gain(2002) described that energy, industrialization, and industrial pollution, air pollution, and disasters of clusters of issues which elaborate the environmental issues and concerns that Bangladesh, and its people encounter in their daily life. Sharif et al. (2018) argued that extra significance be supposed to be prearranged on renewable such as solar energy because it is the budding renewable energy segment of the country which has possible to get together the bulk of the energy and power demand of country's inhabitants. Kibria, Haroon, and Nugegoda (2018) described that investments in renewable energy (RE) technologies were essential for energy access, energy security, reduce dependency on fossil fuels, mitigating climate change and low-carbon economic growth and prosperity, in addition to creating new job opportunities in local areas. Barua et al. (2019) pronounced that how a developing country and developed countries managed their electricity generation sector via several fuel sources that can assist other countries to plan their generation strategy outline. Brewster (2019) depicted that Bangladesh required huge foreign investment in power generation and transport infrastructure to nurture her exports and required trustworthy sources for imports of raw materials and energy to feed an export economy. Blakers (2019) depicted that Australia was on track for deep and rapid greenhouse emissions reductions through deep renewable electrification, at approximately zero net cost. Karim et al. (2019) argued that to mitigate climate degradation and to achieve the SDG goals, Bangladesh should lead its energy sector into renewable sources. Uddin et al. (2019) argued that the government of Bangladesh must determination with international advanced technology via human intellectuals of the country for energy sustainability for which renewable energy can be measured as a possible alternative to conventional energy that comes from fossil fuel. Masud et al.(2020) opined that Bangladesh was heavily (62%) relying on natural gas although government had already taken steps to generate electricity from renewable energy sources. Simsek et al. (2020) found that the total additional energy requirements to meet energy-relate SDGs for Chile is compared to Indonesia results and Indonesia requires much more effort than Chile to meet energy related sustainable development goals (P.12). Siddique et al. (2021) opined that solar, wind, hydro and nuclear energy are the most reliable energy sources, other than fossil fuels.

Travel and Tourism Sector

Knoema(2019)described that in 2019, contribution of travel and tourism to GDP (% of GDP) for Australia was 10.9%. Travel Weekly (2021) informed that Australia's borders will probably stay closed pending mid-2022 due to COVID-19, while the International Air Transport Association (IATA) has indicated that air travel won't start again to pre-pandemic levels awaiting 2024. Islam,& Akter(2021) described that in Bangladesh investments in tourism and the development of infrastructure has to be ensured immediately as these will led to the expansion of tourism. Cumilla airport was closed in Bangladesh which is a drawback for travelling in the area and foreign tourists to visit historical places.

Microfinance Sector

Microfinance can be divided into four segments: microcredit, micro insurance, micro savings, and transfer of money. Mallick (2002) argued that microcredit has been introduced to rural communities in Bangladesh as a means of economic and social development, but there are increasing doubts about its effectiveness and suggestions that it causes domestic abuse. Dougherty (2013) argued that Microcredit and micro -insurance programs should be expanded to encourage small business development in areas losing their risk-tolerant and well educated to emigration. Ahshan et al. (2013) observed that micro insurance is looked upon as a potential means of minimizing the risk of future poverty in the wake of personal disasters related to various idiosyncratic shocks. Burkot(2015) reported that BRAC was also recognized as a global leader in several of the Australian aid program's priority areas – including innovation, gender and social enterprise development – and maintained an active program of research and evaluation.

Sustainable Development Goals (United Nations, 2017).

The Sustainable Development Goals (SDGs) define global sustainable development priorities and aspirations for 2030 and seek to mobilize global efforts around a common set of goals and 169 targets of SDGS. The SDGs call for worldwide action among governments, business and Civil Society to end poverty and create a life of dignity and opportunity for all, within the boundaries of the planet. Goals are explained given below and shown in Figure-1.

Goal 1: End poverty in all its forms everywhere
Goal 2: End hunger, achieve food security and improve nutrition and promote sustainable agriculture.
Goal 3: Ensure healthy lives and promote well-being for all at all ages
Goal 4: Ensure inclusive and equitable quality education and promote lifelong learning opportunities for all.
Goal 5: Achieve gender equality and empower all women and girls
Goal 6: Ensure availability and sustainable management of water and sanitation for all
Goal 7: Ensure access to affordable, reliable, sustainable and modern energy for all
Goal 8: Promote sustained, inclusive and sustainable economic growth, full and productive employment and decent work for all
Goal 9: Build resilient infrastructure, promote inclusive and sustainable industrialization and foster innovation
Goal 10: Reduce inequality within and among countries
Goal 11: Make cities and human settlements inclusive, safe, resilient and sustainable
Goal 12: Ensure sustainable consumption and production patterns
Goal 13: Take urgent action to combat climate change and its impacts
Goal 14: Conserve and sustainably use the oceans, seas and marine resources for sustainable development
Goal 15: Protect, restore and promote sustainable use of terrestrial ecosystems, sustainably manage forests, combat desertification, and halt and reverse land degradation and halt biodiversity loss
Goal 16: Promote peaceful and inclusive societies for sustainable development, provide access to justice for all and build effective, accountable and inclusive institutions at all levels
Goal 17: Strengthen the means of implementation and revitalize the global partnership for sustainable development.

Due to fund shortage all the 169 targets against SDGs cannot be implemented in Bangladesh though govt. is trying to implement at least two targets of each goal before COVID-19, within the constraint of the funds. A lion share of the fund now is being required to purchase anti COVID-19 vaccine in Bangladesh from abroad to save the life of people. Munir (2019) argued that to attain SDGs for all countries additional global investments of $5 trillion to $7 trillion per annum up to 2030 will be necessary .General Economics Division (GED) (2019) argued that the 17 SDGs and its associated 169 targets aimed at ending poverty, hunger and inequality; acting on climate change and the environment; improvement to access to health and education sector; caring for people and the planet; and building strong institutions and partnerships.

Figure 2. Sustainable development goals
(Source: Alam , 2016)

Other Sectors

Almost 30,000 Bangladeshi-born people live in Australia, and the community has been growing strongly during recent years. The personal ties between Australia-Bangladesh, forged by family, business, education — and by two countries shared love for cricket — are prominent (Australia Bangladesh Chamber of Commerce and Industry, 2021).Bangladesh possesses labor-intensive industry which need to be developed as know growing demand of applicability of artificial intelligence, blockchain technology, robotics, Internet of Thinking (IoT), where Australian investors can invest. Table:1(a), the study has shown FDI stock classified by major countries and major sectors in Bangladesh.

On the basis of Table:1(a) the author computed percentage of Foreign Direct Investment (FDI)) in Table:1(b)

From the aforesaid 1(b) table the study found that FDI from Australia to Bangladesh in terms of Total FDI stocks in percentage was 18.81% of Gas & Petroleum; .0046% of Textile & Weaving; .084% of Chemicals; Agriculture & Fishing was.18%, Leather & Leather Products was .37%;0.25% of Other Sectors while 4.22% of total Foreign direct stock by Australia in Bangladesh.

Table 1.

FDI stock classified by Major Countries and Major Sectors as on End of Mar'2021

(In million US$)

Sector / Country	Gas & Petroleum	Textile and Wearing	Banking	Power	Telecommunication	Food	Trading	Construction	Chemicals and Pharmaceuticals	Agriculture and Fishing	Leather and Leather Products	Insurance	Cement	NBFI	Metal and Machinery Products	Other sectors	Total FDI Stock
United States of America (USA)	2924.50	76.94	189.55	205.12	6.61	3.62	70.61	2.30	0.37	1.78	0.03	261.24	0.00	24.56	0.04	61.05	**3828.35**
United Kingdom (UK)	0.00	374.30	1275.50	124.17	0.32	252.56	-4.12	-0.69	139.79	59.80	0.25	0.00	0.00	20.52	2.57	90.02	**2335.02**
Netherlands	8.46	78.65	0.00	346.54	-0.20	907.66	72.52	12.53	0.36	0.05	21.75	0.00	125.05	0.00	0.00	107.63	**1681.00**
Singapore	226.90	169.56	9.35	404.54	186.05	69.22	98.82	27.86	11.21	37.27	0.01	0.00	0.00	92.43	0.00	342.88	**1676.10**
Korea, Republic of	0.00	893.94	101.91	0.13	0.00	0.12	48.88	1.32	-0.15	0.00	106.44	0.00	9.26	0.00	0.03	49.80	**1211.68**
China People's Republic (P.R)	0.00	236.66	0.00	442.67	0.00	0.66	58.88	28.87	2.82	1.19	12.12	0.00	0.00	0.00	1.44	245.36	**1030.67**
Hong Kong: SAR Of China	0.00	511.43	96.53	62.20	0.28	0.70	41.34	0.06	0.00	1.33	58.92	0.00	49.82	0.88	0.77	180.48	**1004.74**
Australia	840.14	0.16	0.00	0.00	0.00	0.00	0.03	0.00	0.26	0.53	1.01	0.00	0.00	0.00	0.00	5.24	**847.37**
Malaysia	0.01	18.85	0.00	3.09	727.67	0.41	0.29	25.24	3.06	0.00	0.13	0.00	0.00	3.86	0.00	26.13	**808.74**
India	-1.08	112.96	175.52	83.62	-0.28	19.08	26.62	3.18	33.25	7.29	0.69	7.24	0.00	0.00	0.09	221.81	**689.99**
Canada	423.42	33.20	30.25	0.01	0.00	0.00	0.56	0.23	0.04	0.00	0.00	0.00	0.00	0.04	45.29	12.23	**545.27**
United Arab Emirates (UAE)	3.31	10.35	49.83	146.71	-0.14	0.72	23.55	67.81	0.05	0.00	0.00	0.00	22.95	11.47	5.64	86.36	**428.61**
Norway	0.00	0.00	33.91	0.00	349.87	0.00	4.07	0.00	0.00	0.00	0.00	0.00	0.32	0.00	0.00	14.59	**402.76**
Japan	21.17	51.35	2.22	25.77	0.00	4.12	14.77	38.29	10.19	-1.30	10.28	0.00	0.00	0.00	11.25	209.04	**397.15**
Sri Lanka	0.00	77.05	175.30	76.84	0.00	1.97	1.92	1.68	0.75	0.00	0.00	0.00	0.00	11.17	0.00	28.34	**375.02**
British Virgin Islands	0.00	206.86	0.00	3.66	0.00	0.00	3.06	0.00	1.06	-0.02	0.00	0.00	0.00	7.54	0.00	126.19	**348.35**
Thailand	0.00	0.87	0.00	0.00	0.00	17.93	0.45	90.05	0.71	162.66	0.00	0.00	33.45	0.47	0.00	35.83	**342.42**
Mauritius	0.00	180.23	0.00	76.72	7.41	0.00	2.34	3.50	0.02	14.86	0.00	0.00	0.00	0.00	0.00	26.22	**311.30**
Taiwan: Province of China	0.00	122.47	0.00	0.00	0.00	2.57	28.03	2.82	0.22	0.04	46.00	0.00	0.00	0.00	11.82	69.86	**283.83**
Saudi Arabia	0.01	0.13	218.26	0.00	0.00	0.00	0.02	0.00	0.00	0.00	0.00	0.00	0.00	42.84	0.00	0.03	**261.29**
Other Countries	18.35	325.21	248.69	144.21	110.39	34.53	24.46	6.80	105.67	5.47	14.95	0.01	9.58	7.44	26.78	177.65	**1260.19**
Total FDI Stock	**4465.22**	**3481.17**	**2606.85**	**2146.00**	**1387.98**	**1315.87**	**517.10**	**311.85**	**309.68**	**290.95**	**272.58**	**268.49**	**250.43**	**223.22**	**105.72**	**2116.74**	**20069.85**

Source: Foreign Investment & External Debt (FIED) Management Cell, Statistics Department, Bangladesh Bank

Ahmad (1992) depicted that the utilization of foreign assistance, foreign private investment and remittances suggests that foreign capital inflow had positive effects of all categories of imports. Bhattacharya(1993) observed that the countries in the region had failed, despite the size of their populations and potential for economic growth, to attract significant amount of FDI in the past, to a large extent, because of policy induced problems, including discriminations against foreign ownership. Bhuyan(2011) observed that Bangladesh offered opportunities to foreign investors for investing in the country's basic infrastructure, apart from the three traditional sectors-primary, manufacturing and service sectors. Rahim (2011) opined that practical standard in trade strategies throughout the early phases of high performing Asian economies had a huge plea to a quantity of afresh emerging economies. Husain (2012) commented that the most vital requirement for harmony edifice in foreign policy was that the essential modification in the politician cognizance and political determination of the country, which was inseparably linked up with the excellence of political leadership.

Table 2. FDI from Australia to Bangladesh in terms of Total FDI stocks in percentage

Sectors	Gas & Petroleum	Textile & Weaving	Banking	Power	Tele Communication	Food	Trading	Construction	Chemicals & Pharmaceuticals	Agriculture & Fishing	Leather & Leather Products	Insurance	Cement	NBFI	M&MP	Other Sectors	Total FDI Stock
Stock (%)	18.81	0.0046	0	0	0	0	0.0058	0	0.084	0.18	0.37	0	0	0	0	0.25	4.22

(Source: Computed by the author)

Murad (2012) commented that overall trade balance was an aggregation of bilateral trade balance; hence, any change of bilateral trade influenced the aggregate trade balances. However, due to heterogeneity among trading nations, the determinants of overall trade balance might lose its essence for bilateral trade balances. Bartelmus(2013) described seven conclusions out of which most important was sustainability of the economy and generate benchmarks for prudent environmental and economic behavior and policies. Islam et al. (2013) depicted that though Bangladesh was operating under free floating exchange rate system, but the country might be able to avoid a major shock -both internal and external sector as long as it can be managed through floating exchange rate policy properly. Littleboy (2016) commented that ethical decision-making and effective decision making were alike in that each needs due regards for the consequences.

Pramanic(2016) observed that political stability was a major factor in determining whether a country will experience economic growth or not. Ahmad (2018) depicted that there must be a political and administrative commitment to developing a suitable technological system for the country for self-reliant and people-oriented development and to establishing an appropriate national institutional network charged with their responsibility. Khan, Wong, &Sultan (2020) discussed on value in the context of international marketing considering four models, these were schools of thought who include cost leadership school of thought, superior product school of thought, relationship school of thought, and culture school of thought. Rahman, & Akter(2020) opined that among Australia and Bangladesh the bilateral trade ratio had improved over time in favor of Bangladesh. Intra-industry trade between the two countries had increased in disaggregated commodity categories, rather than in broad commodity items. They also commented that Australia provided a duty-free and quota-free (DFQF) facility to Bangladesh for all export items, whereas Bangladesh still applies most-favored nation (MFN) duty on products imported from Australia.Augustin(2021) commented that unless the business communities and political leadership of both the countries seize the opportunity, the TIFA will end up being symbolic and left on the shelf of unmet expectations. Kraiwanit(2021) described that CT infrastructure development should be prioritized for ease of e-consumption with human skills need to be improved and e-retail should be encouraged. Khan &Teicher(2021) argued about sustainable global value chain through the integration of Closed Loop Supply Chains and traditional supply management can lead to more sustainable international supply chain management by improving the international supply chain agility during and post-COVID-19 type future global crisis. Hossain et al. (2021) found that the policy makers in Bangladesh should think about environment friendly technologies to emit less $C0_2$. Islam(2021) expressed view that in between Bangladesh and Australia trade scene there was a potentiality of trade for amounting USD 5.0 billion per annum. Medhekar(2021) described that economic significant of bilateral trade relationship between Australia and India, opportunities and challenges faced by the two countries with focus on education, tourism, health agri-business, alternative energy and mining sectors to meet the demand and supply gap and the sustainable development goals is essential.

PROBLEMS

Most of the literatures were discussed on particular area but there was scanty research work on diverse areas of collaboration between two countries Australia and Bangladesh for which this chapter has been designed. How can both the countries utilize their resources in diverse sectors for the betterment of their communities, economic growth and application of capability approach in real life scenario needs to be discussed. Recent TIFA agreement between the two countries gives wider scope and range for investment in diverse sectors of the Bangladesh economy.

Table 3. Shows descriptive statistics of export and import between two countries.

Descriptive Statistics	Mean	Std. Deviation	N
Export	184972.9547	259210.85320	32
Import	279422.72	239628.558	32

(Source: Computed by the author)

Table 4. Pearson correlations between export and import data

Correlations		Export	Import
Export	Pearson Correlation	1	.899**
	Sig. (2-tailed)		.000
	Sum of Squares and Cross-products	2082898258972.736	1730802694273.150
	Covariance	67190266418.475	55832344976.553
	N	32	32
Import	Pearson Correlation	.899**	1
	Sig. (2-tailed)	.000	
	Sum of Squares and Cross-products	1730802694273.150	1780077220676.496
	Covariance	55832344976.553	57421845828.274
	N	32	32
**. Correlation is significant at the 0.01 level (2-tailed).			

(Source: Computed by the author)

Table 5. Partial correlation between export and import data

Control Variable			Export	Import
Year	Export	Correlation	1.000	.647
		Significance (2-tailed)	.	.000
		df	0	29
	Import	Correlation	.647	1.000
		Significance (2-tailed)	.000	.
		df	29	0

(Source: Computed by the author)

Table 6. Descriptive statistics

Descriptive Statistics	Mean	Std. Deviation	N
Year	07/01/04	3426 07:32:38.711	32
Export	184972.9547	259210.85320	32
Dummy variable	.50	.508	32

(Source: Computed by the author)

Table 7. R square value and F change

R	R Square	Adjusted R Square	Std. Error of the Estimate	Change Statistics				
				R Square Change	F Change	df1	df2	Sig. F Change
.935[a]	.874	.865	1258 19:49:15.814	.874	100.330	2	29	.000

(Source: Computed by the author)

METHODOLOGY OF THE STUDY

The study will use mixed method both quantitative and qualitative analysis. Exact sources will be discussed. Two case studies will be discussed how Bangladeshi students got benefit from Australian education and put their potentialities in Bangladesh economy.

For the period of 1988 to 2019 the study collected data of export and import proceeds between two countries as shown in the following regression equations:

$Y_{t1}=a+bX_1+Dm+\mu$

$Y_{t2}= a+b_{M1}+Dm+\mu$

Where Y_{t1}=Year

X_1=Export
M_1=Import
Dm=Dummy Variable

Table 8. Indicated analysis of variance.

Model- ANOVA		Sum of Squares	df	Mean Square	F	Sig.
1	Regression	2373662391512624600.000	2	1186831195756312320.000	100.330	.000[b]
	Residual	343049512866255810.000	29	11829293547112270.000		
	Total	2716711904378880500.000	31			

a. Dependent Variable: Year
b. Predictors: (Constant), Dummy variable, Export
(Source: Computed by the author)

Table 9. Indicated regression results

Model		Unstandardized Coefficients		t	Sig.	Collinearity Statistics	
		B	Std. Error			Tolerance	VIF
1	(Constant)	13043309122.976	27288156.147	477.984	.000		
	Export	516.863	97.257	5.314	.000	.600	1.666
	Dummy Variable	338208706.590	49625921.214	6.815	.000	.600	1.666

(Source: Computed by the author)

Table 10. Descriptive statistics

Descriptive Statistics	Mean	Std. Deviation	N
Year	07/01/04	3426 07:32:38.711	32
Dummy variable	.50	.508	32
Import	279422.72	239628.558	32

(Source: Computed by the author)

From 1988 to 2007 the study will use Dm=0 to assess there is no change in the trading pattern while Dm=1 to assess there is change in the trading pattern due to export and import respectively

μ-Error term

The study will determine the Variance Inflation Factor (VIF) to test multicollinearity problem. The study will also examine Pearson correlation and also partial correlation between import and export series. For partial correlation year has been kept as a constant. Furthermore, the study also determined % of FDI from Australia t Bangladesh in terms of percentage in Table:1(b).

Time period of the study is March 2021 to July 2021 considering data from 1988 to 2019.

ESTIMATED RESULTS

Note all tables in the result section are computed by author.

Table 3 shows mean value and standard deviation of export and import between the two countries.

Table 11. R square value and F change

R	R Square	Adjusted R Square	Std. Error of the Estimate	Change Statistics				
				R Square Change	F Change	df1	df2	Sig. F Change
.945[a]	.892	.885	1161 17:39:44.640	.892	120.325	2	29	.000

(Source: Computed by the author)

Table 12. Indicated analysis of variance

ModelANOVA[a]		Sum of Squares	df	Mean Square	F	Sig.
1	Regression	242453873739685680 0.000	2	1212269368698428420.000	120.325	.000[b]
	Residual	292173166982023620.000	29	10074936792483570.000		
	Total	2716711904378880500.000	31			

a. Dependent Variable: Time
b. Predictors: (Constant), Import, Dummy variable
(Source: Computed by the author)

From the aforesaid Table: 4, it was observed that there was a correlation between both export and import between Australia and Bangladesh.

From theTable:5, the study observed that when the study consider year as controlling variable then export and import both become significant.

1st Regression Equation

In Table 6 descriptive statistics were given which included mean value and standard deviation.

Now R square value and F change is shown in Table:7

In Table 7, the study observed that R square and adjusted R square indicated how well terms fit the regression line. F change is also significant which was indicated that the variables added in that step significantly improved the prediction.

Through the table 8 the study observed that there were not statistical differences between the means of two independent groups as F stat. was significant at 0.01 level of significance.

From the aforesaid Table 9, the study indicated that constant term, export and dummy variable were significant at 99% confidence interval. Dummy variable was significant at 0.01 level of significance, which implies that structural change in trading pattern, had occurred over the time period. The Variance Inflation Factor indicated that no multicollinearity problem existed.

As such the regression equation of Export between Australia and Bangladesh could be written as:

$$Y_{t1}=13043309122.976+516.863X1+338208706.590$$

2nd Regression equation is shown in Table 10.

Table 13. Indicated regression results

Model		Unstandardized Coefficients		t	Sig.	Collinearity Statistics	
		B	Std. Error			Tolerance	VIF
1	(Constant)	12983014336.896	27702162.567	468.664	.000		
	Dummy Variable	263934156.373	52718317.271	5.006	.000	.453	2.207
	Import	690.845	111.760	6.181	.000	.453	2.207

(Source: Computed by the author)

In Table 10 descriptive statistics were given which included mean value and standard deviation. Now R square value and F change is shown in Table:6b

In Table 11, the study observed that R square and adjusted R square indicated how well terms fit the regression line. F change was also significant which indicated that the variables added in that step significantly improved the prediction.

Through the Table 12 the study observed that there are not statistical differences between the means of two independent groups as F stat. is significant at 0.01level of significance.

From the aforesaid Table 13, the study indicated that constant term, import and dummy variable are significant at 99% confidence interval. Dummy variable is significant at 0.01 level of significance, which implied that structural change had occurred. The Variance Inflation Factor indicated that no multicollinearity problem existed.

As such the regression equation of Import between Australia and Bangladesh can be written as:

$$Y_{t2}=12983014336.896+690.845M_1+263934156.373$$

Qualitative Analysis (Considering Impact Assessment of Education) *

Case Study: 1

One of the most successful management teachers and serving as a Chairperson of the Department of Business Administration of a private university was now middle aged in Bangladesh, who had been serving in a very good standard private university went to Australia to acquire higher education at the Macquarie university. There she did her PhD degree and due to family reasons, her time to complete PhD degree took more than 11 years. On return to Bangladesh now she is serving very nicely and also became Associate Professor and currently being Chairperson of the Department of the Business Administration. She is a good researcher and also published her research works in different reputed journals. While talking with the researcher she said that Australian education gave her best effort to deal with modern teaching learning system and her professional life was nicely motivated by the Australian University.

Case Study: 2

An indigenous lady went to Australia for higher education and training. She did her Masters in Community Planning and Development from La Trobe university, Australia. Now she is working successfully as a communication officer of an international organization. Currently nicely doing communications activities of the organization and tried to do planning, design and implementation of internal and external strategies for communications and outreach programs of the international organization. She felt that her education in Australia transformed her more successful to work in the international organization professionally with ethically, effectively and efficiently.

**Note: Both the cases were prepared by the author of the chapter.*

DISCUSSION

Interregional trade, foreign investment, and connectivity between two countries may play vital role for good relationship. Through quantitative analysis the study found that: Pearson correlation is significant at 99% level for import and export. Partial correlation keeping year as constant is also significant at 99% level of significance. From regression equation the study found that Dummy variable is significant at 1% level of significance, which implies that structural change has occurred. Moreover, both import and export are significant at 99% level of significance. For qualitative analysis, two case studies were prepared it was observed that Australian education helped for better human resource management. As per Yilmazkuday(2019) view proper macro elasticity measures of the upper-tier needs to be estimated by the Bangladesh Bureau of statistics ethically and morally. Successful business model between two countries may work for long run sustainability with competitiveness so that strategic cooperation and partnership can work. Under new normal situation both the country can help jointly for removing disparity and attaining social justice. Sustainable development can be viewed as a service industry where a set of variable actions based on the nature of development needs to be performed on a sustainable basis through long term competency for the advancement of the society. This notion of sustainable development addressed concerns about the relationship between human society and the environment and has been framed in terms of economic growth, ecological balances and societal progress. This chapter aimed at exploring the role of renewable energy in the context of sustainable development for Bangladesh and Australia in terms of current status, future prospects and challenges. In addition, a comparative analysis of both countries' renewable sectors will be made to identify the gaps in policies and implementation strategies in Bangladesh. Sustainable development first and foremost engaged economic expansion and robustly correlates with rise in energy habit (fossil fuels e.g. coal, gas) and augmented greenhouse gas (GHG) discharged. Renewable energy resources come into view to be one of the most useful and well-organized resolution to overcome such impediment. Therefore, present is an unlocking link between renewable energy and sustainable development. Progression in economic expansion, development and enrichment in energy security and accessibility and mitigation of climate change are some of the key drivers of rapid development of renewable energy. Recommendations based on the analysis of outcome and Australia's advancement will be helpful for government agencies, policy makers and associated stakeholders of Bangladesh for future improvements and development interventions in the renewable energy sector. In the field of education also there is every chance to improve quality education with the help of Australia. To fulfill all the targets of the sustainable development goals Bangladesh needed foreign funding where Australia can help to donate to remove poverty, removing gender inequality, decent works and arranging environmental development etc. Bangladesh needs foreign funds to implement sustainable developments goals and their all targets to fulfill for which guidelines are mentioned in the publication General Economics Division (GED)(2019) of the Planning ministry of government of Bangladesh.

However, Bangladesh embassy in Australia needs to be more proactive so that trade and investment between two countries can be raised. Though they have web page, but for this research work twice I sent emails to the embassy of Bangladesh with some questions and to access to get data for doing more in-depth study, but they did not reply which implies non respect to a citizen of the country. Persons to persons, Business to Business and Government to Government relationships are needed to act as a significant module of two-side of the coin. Both the countries collaborate thoroughly to endorse harmony and safety, counting to stop asymmetrical relocation and to counter fierce radicalism. COVID-19 and after math especially new normal situation has created challenges for Bangladesh which has deepened pre-existing humanitarian and economic challenges from donor agencies or entrance to get new market opportunities in Australia. Bangladesh may think about Kraiwanit(2021)'s view for Bangladesh's economic development. However, in the name of microcredit using new liberal technique women must not be repressed by the NGOs. Specialized banks like Bangladesh Krishi bank, RAKUB and Bangladesh development bank need to come forward to provide microfinance in the country along with Palli Karma-Sahayak Foundation (PKSF) and Bangladesh NGO Foundation(BNF).Behavioral economics may also be applied for the betterment of the people of both the countries and free trade agreement may be executed properly.

Australia cares in teaching, well-being, scarcity reduction of resources, preservation and females enable management and leadership value. Both the country might respectively add value in relations to catastrophe and environmental modification. Australia can help livestock businesses to the Bangladeshi entrepreneurs by providing upgrading technology and supply chain procedures in Bangladesh. Australia may nourish Bangladesh to upsurge the procedural assistances of its enormous populace and advance the human source of competencies. Australia has enormous natural resources and unfilled up land zone while Bangladesh has enormous populace. Both the countries might attain their requirements by dispersion the collaboration of each-other. Interdependence and economic co-operation remain nowadays widespread. The biosphere low-cost is nowadays gradually noticeable by interdependence. The dogmatic and financial necessities, the essential for nationwide safety and expansion and additional forces in the stage of globalized free market economy remain the main causes of current inter-state relationships. Medhekar(2021) comments on the relationship between Australia and India can also be considered as a model for developing ties between Bangladesh and Australia. Bangladesh as said by Blakers(2019) can follow the Australian track and transition quickly to renewable by subsequent huge evasion of forthcoming greenhouse secretions. From Figures 1 and 2 the study indicated that Australia has immense scope to invest through FDI from Australia to Bangladesh in terms of Total FDI stocks in percentage. There are no investments by Australia such as power sector, banking sector, telecommunication sector, food, construction, insurance, cement, non-bank financial institutions and metal and machinery products etc. For the expansion of blue economy of Bangladesh also in the literature indicated that Australia could invest in blue economy of the country and can help the country to fulfill Sustainable development goals through funding and investments. Bangladesh accreditation Board may work to improve educational structure of the country following Australian structure. Barua et al.(2019) viewed can be followed by the policy makers of the country for improvement of electricity. Technological transfer from the Australia can help the economy with modernization in the era of the 4th industrial revolution. Moreover, expansion of the exportable commodities in the Australia can help to attain the economic development of Bangladesh. All sectors such as manufacturing, service, industrial, health, renewable energy sector, blue economy, and education had been hit hard due to the pandemic situation in Bangladesh though economy is now recovering. Need based development for both the countries required. Tariff structure between both the countries need to be assesses. Scope for tourism in Australia and learning from Australian tourism sector in Bangladesh is required.

FUTURE RESEARCH DIRECTIONS

In depth study both using qualitative and quantitative analysis with more time and preparing questionnaires and collective proper sample size in different sectors may be analyzed. In this case structural equation model may be used through using panel data. Under new normal situation, the economy of the country may change. As such with 2/3 years gap, may another study be prepared by using PESTEL analysis, VRINE model to assess forthcoming economic and managerial scenario. Furthermore, ARIMA model may be used to forecast about trade and investment scenario. A real observation about utilization of 'Blue Economy', Tourism sector and also renewable energy, how Australia can help Bangladesh, may be another way to find through research work. How Australia can transfer technology in the health sector in Bangladesh may also be an interesting study in future? Benefits of trade and investment may also be studied with deep assessment on the basis of sector wise evaluation of two countries economy so that win -win situation can prevail for both of them. A detailed study on TIFA agreement between two countries and its impact on both the countries and applicability may be done a research on at different levels of expansion, trade and investment so that policy makers can get a real strategy formulation and execution to improve the ties between both the countries.

CONCLUSION

Australia can help Bangladesh through technological transfer and financial donation for fulfillment of SDGs' targets. Bilateral relationship and free trade agreement between two countries need to be executed properly. Victoria University, Australia can start a study center in Bangladesh. More training and education centers through online and physically need to ensure in Bangladesh by the Australian universities and colleges and schools so that skill and knowledge may be ensured which may help for human resource management. This may help for international collaborative education in the field of technological and industry-based education under the fourth industrial revolution. Modern technology transfer for agricultural production process for sustainable development may be ensured in Bangladesh. In the field of blue economy, Australia can go for foreign direct investment. Similarly Australia can help for expansion of QUAD by political and motivational diplomatic strategy by expanding member countries like Bangladesh, United Kingdom, France, New Zealand, Thailand, Vietnam, Canada, Sri Lanka, Nepal,Bhutan. Bilateral supply chain among both the countries may be strengthened and bilateral cooperation may be much needed as foreign direct investment is relatively low. Post pandemic small and medium enterprises may get more assistance from Australia and market for selling the products in Australia under free trade agreement is much needed. Numerous help for further expediting digitization processes and also subcontracting amenities may be strengthen by providing to Bangladesh after arranging Australian commercial system through at fair pricing.

With Australian collaboration, Bangladesh can improve her sports in different areas such as Rugby, golf, athletics, tennis and swimming etc. Similarly, Bangladesh's traditional sports such as Kabaddi, Boli Khela, Lathi Khela etc. may be arranged to give learning to Australia. Though Bangladesh already is doing well in cricket but ICC men's T-20 world cup Bangladesh did extremely worst for which Australia can help our young cricket players. As such more cricket matches between two counties can be arranged. For the RMG sector of Bangladesh, Australia can arrange to purchase more products as the product will add value to the poor. Though 7th October, 2021,Australia became the first team to win 11 games on the trot in the same World Cup qualifying campaign after beating Oman 3-1 in Qatar so Bangladesh also take help from the Australia to improve her quality of football game. As Australia is three times hockey champion so Bangladesh can take lesson to improve its hockey team. For moral education, removing child marriage and creation and cooperation in the digital process of small businesses along with microfinance

Australia can through their govt. and private sector help Bangladesh so that economically vulnerable groups can be come out from the vicious circle of poverty. Bangladesh embassy in Australia should play their due role to assess the market need of the Australia and also collaborative effort to export more products in a diversified manner for which they must recommend to the government of Bangladesh for taking necessary steps. Employees of Bangladesh embassy should behave like professional diplomat with the motto to serve the country through economic diplomacy and obey the present government's development policies rightly.

The risk may arise under new normal situation through engaging appropriate technologies, persisting change, sound values and staying together. This will lead to debacle of the domestic, regional and global value chain. Production in agriculture, services and industrial sectors have been greatly hampered. Consumer durables cannot be utilized properly. Digital policy, robotics, use of artificial intelligence and innovative skills may help to build mass employment and enhance the value for ICT and computer-savvy employees. The unemployment rate has increased, and people are getting frustrated. Due to the pandemic impact, global and national leaders need to work collaboratively to assist businesses facing an economic and financial crisis. The inadequacy of the accommodative fiscal policy reforms has failed to stop the financial harm to the economic disorder. However, the monetary policy will relatively work better than the Fiscal policy does.

Microsoft had recently found that when organizations have prioritized technology adoption to enable remote working environments and overall business transformation, the change was not driven through technology alone. Emphasis should be given on import substitution, domestic production, consumption, industrialization process and strengthening local level economy based on competitive advantage. Measures are being needed to have an all-inclusive policy and remove the negative environmental impact. Measures are needed, especially for women and children as they are more susceptible to economic shocks due to financial, natural and COVID-19 pandemic effects. It has become imperative and need of the hour for the IT professionals to design and develop the cyber secured way of transactions, information exchange etc., to cope up with the "New Normal" scenario. Customers also need to be kept safe from fraudulent activities from electronic devices, especially in the case of electronic fund transfer.

Supply chain management is gradually changing from conventional to the batch-based planning course of action, to a complementary active route entrenched in real-time information, with the ambition of escalating alertness. Large and middle-companies may adapt to process quickly; but it is difficult for nano, micro and small companies to assess the process. Employment creation for the younger generation by the public-private partnership is an important factor. More products from Bangladesh can be exported to Australia especially RMG goods by the will be helpful for Bangladesh economy to thrive in the real world as it will have positive impact on various sectors of the country as well as help to attain gender equality .Holistic approach via public-private-partnership, which is an extremely genuine occasion for adopting an optimistic; missing from neo-liberal ascendancy to a planet with stronger community values and morality and must concentrate on the local economy. Traditional economic system won't work in the "New Normal" situation.

More emphasis should be put on the local economy: "grow, produce and consume local with expansion and sustainability of green growth in Bangladesh". The financial sector, NGOs and social development should work with innovative ideas for social welfare. The informal sector should get a special financial package and minimize corruptions in the case of distribution of relief fund. Food security needs to be arranged by a combined effort of all parties – political leaders and administrative staff. The agricultural sector and agro-based industries need uninterrupted mechanisms – which is possible with a focus on adding local and national value. Technological awareness, innovation and dissemination of skill with remote, rural and urban areas are needed. Cumilla airport in Bangladesh needs to be started urgently for which huge investment and infrastructures are being required to increase travelling in the area as there are quite good number of tourist spots in Cumilla District from the ancient period.

Organization's scarce resources need to be utilized efficiently and effectively. Moral hazard should be reduced so that the danger of a rivalry is not generated or proved deceptive in turn concerning its possessions, legal responsibilities, or praiseworthy ability among the nations. Nano and micro-business personnel should have ability, boldness, expertise, expected acceptance competence to receive inventive private enterprise and encourage females in the countryside to adapt to "New Normal" and ICT. Work-life balance for maintaining a healthy lifestyle is important. An integrated effort among the worldwide nations as a part of the globe is needed to stop greediness and put emphasis on the collaborative effort to reverse the decrease of cumulative demand and supply. Even in the rural areas and for urban poor those who are competent in nano and micro private enterprises could be trained in a business model including operative competence and cost-cutting techniques under "New Normal".

The procedure of national and international combined incentive schemes may inspire prominence, elevation and linkage so that inventive business-persons can progress with further enthusiasm, eagerness, ability and expertise. Information symmetry should be readily available to save human of the world, and market imperfection should be reduced or eliminated. Along with the Bangladesh government and the governments of other countries in the world, scientists, doctors, economists, business personnel, producers, agriculturalists, sociologists, environmentalists, entrepreneurs should work to save the world and humanity from the grim situation. Without global collaboration, the world economic order cannot be improved and come out of the present socio-economic situation which has been worsening inequality and the macroeconomic de-stabilization process. This has already started due to global pandemic and restrictions for travel, tourism, businesses and social distancing to prevent the spread and stop the deadly virus. Travel and tourism sector with the security of human being should get special attention. Without arranging security for the tourist, as a tourist-one will be in danger to tour one place to another. In that case, travelers will feel insecure. Security must be ensured. The global problem of drugs should be stopped with and social -political desires are taking help of law and order forces. The situation should be well designed and if necessary high-powered committee may be established so that innocent people cannot be the victim.

WHO's protocol must be based on scientific reasoning. Vaccine's innovation should not be kept for a few people; it should be given to the global people. In the meantime, Russia claimed that they invented COVID-19 vaccine. If their claim is true, Bangladesh should negotiate for the free production of the vaccine with the help of local pharmaceuticals. Behavioral economics will be more valuable rather than mainstream economics to get rid of this calamity. Free from frustration, mental and physical wellbeing and to maintain socializing with physical distance is important. New Normal creates opportunities, as well as threats to shift their business processes and become accustomed to innovative preparations, evaluate circumstances, rethinking appropriate strategies. After fully started tourism sector of post pandemic period in Australia, Bangladesh can learn how to develop her tourism sector in post pandemic period along with developing new tourist spots and human resources.

Bangladesh is in the right path to overcome the crisis originated from the COVID -19 under the leadership of the Prime Minister Sheikh Hasina. However, after math of COVID-19,it is a challenging for the country to return to the previous situation of 2019 which is not impossible, if present government's strong political will for welfare of the masses remain constant and corruption, nepotism and one group of actress, model's rude and king-queen type behavior with the public places with harassment towards masses along with bureaucratic mannerism can be driven out. Strong action against these types of so-called actors and actresses who use false monogram like Bangladesh channel- i (TV channel) in the car along with young gang try to kill masses by accident with the help of car driver as a fun should be stopped for which law and enforcement agencies need to be vigilant especially such criminal actor or actress who might be as law is equal for all. Sometimes parents are giving false identification to protect criminal minded young children's and drug addict person which is tantamount to unscrupulous behavior. People's safety from these sorts of criminal minded people in Bangladesh should be driven out. Those who did communalism in Bangladesh are also criminal. Learning from Australia to maintain cultural diversity and religious harmony is being needed in Bangladesh.

Everyone should work as per Honorable Prime Minister's directives to come out from the post COVID-19 crisis. Junior, mid and upper level management should coordinate top-down approach and bottom-up approach. Too effectively need to combat this pandemic and its related issues for the making of a better and a safer disease-free world. Due to COVID -19, trade and investment opportunity becomes hampered. Though we are calling new normal situation but it won't come so soon. But after 2/3 years gap, considering new normal situation of trade and investment relationship between Australia and Bangladesh will be further strengthened when worldwide people will adjust with the new normal situation especially in the multi-sectoral areas through bilateral cooperation. In diversity areas, both the country can act for the strengthening pledges of the social values, norms, improvement of livelihoods, fulfillment of basic needs and removing ultra-poor after math of COVID-19 impact. More emphasis needs to be given to eco-friendly sustainability in all sectors of the economy.

REFERENCES

Ahmad, S. (1992). Foreign Capital inflow and economic growth in Bangladesh. University of Dhaka.

Ahmed, K. U. (2004). Three Decades of Australia-Bangladesh Relations 35 three decades of Australia - Bangladesh relations: Future directions and potentials. *Journal of International Affairs*, *8*(1&2), 35–38.

Ahsan, S. M. (2013). The Microinsurance Market in Bangladesh: An Analytical Overview. *Bangladesh Development Studies*, *36*, 1–54.

Alam, S. (2016). *Development Planning in Bangladesh: 7th Five Year Plan and SDG Implementation. General Economics Division, Planning Commission*. Government of the People's Republic of Bangladesh, June.

Augustin, B. (2021, Sept. 29). Australia–Bangladesh: A booster dose for trade diversity? *The Daily Star*.

Australia Bangladesh Chamber of Commerce and Industry. (2021). *Australia Bangladesh Relation*. Retrieved from https://abccibd.com/project/startups-consulting/

Australian International School-Dhaka. (2021). Retrieved from https://www.ausisdhaka.net/

Bartelmus. (2013). *Sustainability economics-An introduction*. Routledge.

Barua, M. (2019). A Survey of Cross-Country Generation Mix - Opportunities and Challenges: Bangladesh, Australia, and the U.S.A Perspectives. *International Conference on Electrical, Computer and Communication Engineering (ECCE)*, 1-6. 10.1109/ECACE.2019.8679344

Bhattacharya, D. (1993). Competing for global resources: Perspective on Foreign investment in South Asia. *Bank Parikrama*, *17*(3&4), 104–114.

Bhuyan,M.A.(2012). Performance of the Bangladesh Economy during FY2011-12 and outlook for the near term. *Thoughts on Economics*, *22*(3).

Blakers, A. (2019). *An Australian model for the renewable-energy transition*. Retrieved from https://www.lowyinstitute.org/the-interpreter/australian-model-renewable-energy-transition

Brewster, D. (2021). *New Indo-Pacific Partnership: Building Australia-Bangladesh Security Ties policy options paper no. 20*. Retrieved from https://nsc.crawford.anu.edu.au/sites/default/files/publication/nsc_crawford_anu_edu_au/2021-06/nsc_policy_options_paper_bangladesh_web_1.pdf

Brewster. (2019). *Australia should pursue opportunities in a booming Bangladesh*. Retrieved from https://www.lowyinstitute.org/the-interpreter/australia-should-pursue-opportunities-booming-bangladesh

Burkot, C. (2015). *BRAC and the Australian aid program*. Retrieved from https://devpolicy.org/brac-and-the-australian-aid-program-20150602/

Dougherty, M. L. (2013). Work, mobility and livelihoods in a changing rural Latin America. In Handbook of Rural Development. Edward Elgar Publishing.

General Economics Division (GED). (2019). *Prospects and Opportunities of International Cooperation in Attaining SDG Targets in Bangladesh*. Bangladesh Planning Commission Ministry of Planning Government of the People's Republic of Bangladesh.

Husain, S. A. (2012). Bangladesh Foreign policy: A framework for consensus building in regional cooperation and Globalisation, Bangladesh, South Asia and beyond. The University Press Limited.

Islam, F. (2013). Income terms of trade and Trade Balance: The long run evidence from Bangladesh. *Bangladesh Development Studies*, *36*(2), 109–122.

Islam, M., & Mostaque, L. Y. (2018). Blue economy and Bangladesh: Lessons and Policy implications. *BIISS Journal*, *39*(2), 135–162.

Islam, M. N., & Akter, S. R. (2021). Problems and Prospects of Tourism Industry in Bangladesh: A Study on Cumilla District. *South Asian Journal of Social Studies and Economics*, *10*(4), 27–35. doi:10.9734ajsse/2021/v10i430271

Islam, S. (2021, Aug. 27). Bangladesh, Australia going to TIFA deal. *The Financial Express*.

Keating, J. (2003). Qualifications Frameworks in Australia. *Journal of Education and Work*, *16*(3), 271–288. doi:10.1080/1363908032000099449

Khan, S. I., & Teicher, J. (2021). Sustainable global supply chain management model post-Covid-19. In M. A. Marinov & S. T. Marinova (Eds.), *Covid-19 and international business: Change of era* (pp. 205–224). Routledge. Retrieved from https://www.routledge.com/

Khan, S. I., Wong, H. Y., & Sultan, P. (2020). A critical review of the concept of value in the international marketing context. In M. A. Marinov (Ed.), *Value in marketing: Retrospective and perspective stance* (pp. 126–144). Routledge. doi:10.4324/9780429264337

Kibria, G., Haroon, A. K. Y., & Nugegoda, D. (2018). Low-Carbon Development (LCD) Pathways in Australia, Bangladesh, China and India-A Review. *Journal of Climate Change*, *4*(1), 49–61. doi:10.3233/JCC-180006

Knoema. (2019). *Australia - Contribution of travel and tourism to GDP as a share of GDP*. Retrieved from https://knoema.com/atlas/Australia/topics/Tourism/Travel-and-Tourism-Total-Contribution-to-GDP/Contribution-of-travel-and-tourism-to-GDP-percent-of-GDP

Kraiwanit, T. (2021). A multiplier of e-consumption: The study of the developing economy. *Journal of Governance & Regulation*, *10*(3), 85–92. doi:10.22495/jgrv10i3art7

Littleboy, B. (2016). Development planning under strategic uncertainty. In M. Allaudin, M. K. Mujeri, & D. K. Nath (Eds.), *Bangladesh Yesterday, Today, tomorrow, Essays in Honor of Professor Sanat Kumar Saha* (p. 76). Shahitya Prakash.

Mallick, R. (2002). Implementing and Evaluating Microcredit in Bangladesh. *Development in Practice*, *12*(2), 153–163. doi:10.1080/09614520220127676

Masud, M. H., Nuruzzaman, M., Ahamed, R., Ananno, A. A., & Tomal, A. N. M. A. (2020). Renewable energy in Bangladesh: Current situation and future prospect. *International Journal of Sustainable Energy*, *39*(2), 132–175. doi:10.1080/14786451.2019.1659270

Medhekar, A. (2021). Australia-India: Bilateral Trade Opportunities and Challenges. In A. Hooke, H. Vachharajani, H. Kaur, & K. Dow (Eds.), Emerging Business and Trade Opportunities Between Oceania and Asia (pp. 57-86). IGI Global. doi:10.4018/978-1-7998-4126-5.ch004

Munir, M.M.H. (2019).*Bangladesh Needs to Fight against Illicit Finance Flow and to Achieve SDGs*. Social Watch. Retrieved from https://www.socialwatch.org/node/18286

Murad, S. M. W. (2012). Bilateral Export and Import Demand Functions of Bangladesh: A Cointegration Approach. *Bangladesh Development Studies*, *35*(1), 43–60.

Murshid, K. A. S. (2019). Employment and Unemployment amongst Educated Youth in Bangladesh: An Exploratory Analysis. *Bangladesh Development Studies*, *42*(4), 1–49.

Pearson, E. (2015). *How Australia can help end child marriage in Bangladesh*. Women's Agenda. Retrieved from, https://www.hrw.org/news/2015/06/24/how-australia-can-help-end-child-marriage-bangladesh

Prime Minister of Australia. (2020). *Investment in new energy Technology*. Prime Minister, Minister for Energy and Emissions Reduction, Media Release 17 September. Retrieved from https://www.pm.gov.au/media/investment-new-energy-technologies

Rahim, M. (2011). Initial Trade Policy Focus of the High Performing Asian Economies: A Critical Assessment. *Bangladesh Development Studies*, *34*(1), 87–102.

Rahman, S. M., & Akter, H. (2020). Bilateral trade relation between Bangladesh and Australia. In The Economic Development of Bangladesh in the Asian Century Prospects and Perspectives. Routledge.

Sadekin, M.N. (2021, July 30). Potentials of Blue Economy in Bangladesh. *Daily Asian Age*.

Sharif, S. I. (2018). The Prospect of Renewable Energy Resources in Bangladesh: A Study to Achieve the National Power Demand. *Energy and Power*, *8*(1), 1–6. doi:10.5923/j.ep.20180801.01

Siddique, A. H., Tasnim, S., Shahriyar, F., Hasan, M., & Rashid, K. (2021). Renewable Energy Sector in Bangladesh: The Current Scenario, Challenges and the Role of IoT in Building a Smart Distribution Grid. *Energies*, *14*(16), 5083. doi:10.3390/en14165083

Simsek, Y. (2020). An analysis of additional energy requirement to meet the sustainable development goals. *Journal of Cleaner Production*, *272*(122646), 1-14. doi:10.1016/j.jclepro.2020.122646

The Business Standard. (2021, Sept. 15). *Bangladesh, Australia ink first Tifa agreement*. Author.

Travel Weekly. (2021). *Australia's tourism sector bouncing back "Stronger than expected" says new government report*. Retrieved from https://www.travelweekly.com.au/article/australias-tourism-sector-bouncing-back-stronger-expected-says-new-government-report/

Uddin, M. N., Rahman, M. A., Mofijur, M., Taweekun, J., Techato, K., & Rasul, M. G. (2019). Renewable energy in Bangladesh: Status and Prospects. *Energy Procedia*, *160*, 655–661. doi:10.1016/j.egypro.2019.02.218

United Nations. (2017). *Resolution adopted by the General Assembly on 6 July 2017, Work of the Statistical Commission pertaining to the 2030 Agenda for Sustainable Development*. Retrieved from https://ggim.un.org/documents/a_res_71_313.pdf

Universal College Bangladesh. (2021). Retrieved from https://ucbbd.org/

World Bank. (2021a). *Gross national income per capita 2019, Atlas method and PPP, World Development Indicators database*. Retrieved from https://databank.worldbank.org/data/download/GNIPC.pdf

World Bank. (2021b). *The World Bank in Bangladesh, Overview*. Retrieved from https://www.worldbank.org/en/country/bangladesh/overview#1

World Integrated Trade Solution. (2021). *Australia Product exports and imports to Bangladesh 2019*. Retrieved from https://wits.worldbank.org/CountryProfile/en/Country/AUS/Year/2019/TradeFlow/EXPIMP/Partner/BGD/Product/all-groups

Yilmazkuday, H. (2019). Understanding the international elasticity puzzle. *Journal of Macroeconomics*, *59*, 140-153. doi:10.1016/j.jmacro.2018.11.010

ADDITIONAL READING

Ali, M. M. (2020). Digitization of the emerging economy: An exploratory and explanatory case study. *Journal of Governance & Regulation*, *9*(4), 25–36. doi:10.22495/jgrv9i4art2

Ali, M. M. (2021). Digital opportunities in the healthcare enterprises during COVID-19: An empirical analysis of the developing country. *Corporate Governance and Organizational Behavior Review*, *5*(2), 44–55. doi:10.22495/cgobrv5i2p4

Ali, M. M., Khanna, P., & Kraianit, T. (2020).New normal and COVID-19,Impact on Education, Economic, Business strategies and management of supply chain, Mauritius, East Africa: LAP Lambert publishing.

Brewster, D. (2013). India-Australia security engagement: Opportunities and challenges, Gateway House. Retrieved from,https://www.gatewayhouse.in/india-australia-opportunities-and-challenges/

Mahajan, A. (2021).India-Bangladesh relations: A robust history and optimistic future,*WION Web Team, March 24,*Retrieved from,https://www.wionews.com/south-asia/india-bangladesh-relations-a-robust-history-and-optimistic-future-372759

Shah, M.H., Sarwar, M.H.,& Iqbal, S.(2021).China-Pakistan economic corridor: prospects and challenges for economy of Pakistan. *Pakistan Journal of International Affairs,* 4(3).

Wallis, J. (2021). Contradictions in Australia's Pacific Islands discourse. *Australian Journal of International Affairs*, *75*(5), 487–506. doi:10.1080/10357718.2021.1951657

KEY TERMS AND DEFINITIONS

Bilateral Collaboration: A type of long-standing collaboration on expansion among between government agencies and private sectors area significant and realistic fraction of bilateral collaboration.

Blue Economy: Association with the marine, creating impetus to plan the phases to enlarge economic affluences and maritime rebuilding.

Corporate Governance: Rules to converse with engage and defend shareholders including transparencies, accountabilities, and fairness.

Diversity: Mixture of differentiation that form sight of the planet with point of views and approaches.

Microfinance: Financial services afford to low-income persons which includes micro credit, micro insurances, micro savings, and financial transactions.

Multi-Sectoral: The partnership among organizations in diverse areas of rules, and unusual sectors, as well as societies and populace, operational jointly to attain rule results.

Political Economy: Interdisciplinary stem of the study that focal point on the interrelationships surrounded by persons, governments, public policy, private sector as well as foreign sector.

Renewable Energy: Renewable energy originates from bases or procedures that are continually replenished.

TIFA: Trade and Investment Framework Agreements (TIFAs) afford planned outlines and viewpoints for negotiating on trade and investment related issues between two or more countries under the agreement.

APPENDIX

Table 14. Bangladesh- Australia Trade (Value in Thousand USD)

Year	Bangladesh Export to Australia	Bangladesh Import from Australia
1988	19442.96	36391.27
1989	16807.56	74609.31
1990	20194.18	47530.9
1991	19791.74	65437.95
1992	13945.85	50364.62
1993	13102.4	40126.71
1994	15808.82	67541.82
1995	18328.44	77905.13
1996	16973.92	123461.76
1997	36736.33	148961.16
1998	27722.81	143228.56
1999	26659.81	115163.96
2000	46428.42	186596.32
2001	27659.44	181173.84
2002	27866.69	175363.97
2003	31718.8	146266.39
2004	37747.42	198077.14
2005	39008.53	179349.1
2006	31671.95	138686.21
2007	35183.68	165242.42
2008	49498.2	215368.07
2009	124514.96	321319.14
2010	140517.94	535489.98
2011	250948.01	598029.37
2012	387157.15	506985.65
2013	447817.45	546530.89
2014	502176.36	494882.96
2015	635556.93	520293.26
2016	659,789.43	616109.88
2017	665043.22	915790.4
2018	734980.29	673372.43
2019	798334.86	635876.49

(Source: World Integrated Trade Solution, 2021).)

Chapter 7
India and Australia's New Education Policy:
Lessons for SAARC Nations

Manisha Goswami
https://orcid.org/0000-0003-4033-5772
Agra University, Mathura, India

ABSTRACT

Nepal, Bangladesh, and Indian education sectors suffer from limited foreign collaborations; less research orientation; redundant and obsolete curricula; and less relevance of courses with job opportunities available. Especially in the case of India, few initiatives were taken to improve quality of education. India adopted new education policy that opened the doors to strategic collaboration with international universities, as India has begun to concentrate on vocational education and training for the first time. This research examines the scope and restrictions of institutional partnerships between India, other SAARC nations, and Australian higher education institutions. This study is based on the analysis of data presented in the different case studies like Rajasthan Royals and Deakin Australian Universities, IIT Bombay and Monash Australian, Indian Academy of Science and Innovation Research (AcSIR) and RMIT Australian University.

INTRODUCTION

Education is universally acknowledged as a critical factor in promoting economic, social, and personal growth (OECD, 2016). A well-educated and intellectual workforce is seen as a catalyst for success and has become a marketable commodity (Phale et al., 2021). Under the World Trade Organization, traded education services have become one of the most important international trade-in services (WTO). In the Asia-Pacific, four main exporters dominate education services trade: The United States, Canada, the United Kingdom, and Australia. Even though these nations have surplus education services, Australia is the most competitive exporter in terms of "revealed comparative advantage in selling education

DOI: 10.4018/978-1-7998-8657-0.ch007

services," with the Asia-Pacific area accounting for 75% of international students studying in Australia (Larsen et al., 2002).

This wealth creation in human skills and abilities gives Australia a competitive advantage in the area when it comes to selling educational resources. While Australia has an overflow of educational services, India has an overabundance of demand for high-quality education and training. India's extensive economic reforms and rapid growth necessitate a highly efficient and knowledge-based workforce, which means it is quickly becoming a significant importer of education services in the area. India has been identified as the possibly largest new market for Western institutions, according to a joint analysis by the British Council and the Economist Intelligence Unit (The Economist, 2010). India would gain from merging its education program trade with Australia for competitive and comparative advantage reasons.

The fast expansion of several higher education institutions in the Asia-Pacific area is a key trend, driven by ever social demand, the democratization of secondary education, and the expanding prosperity of many nations. As higher education institutions grow, there is a pressing need to find new finance and resources. Higher education institutions from various countries are forming and developing strategic cooperation and collaboration to mobilize resources, facilitate academic exchanges, and offer joint programs to increase information and communication technologies advancement and student and staff mobility (Lee, 2012).

The SAU first welcomed students in 2010 and now provides graduate and doctorate degrees in Mathematics, Biotechnology, Computer Science, Development Economics, International Relations, Law, and Sociology to residents of all SAARC nations. SAU envisions three primary aims as a SAARC regional-level initiative: building a culture of understanding and regional consciousness; nurturing a liberal, brilliant, and quality leadership; and building regional scientific and technology capabilities (SAU, 2015). According to the university requirements, at least 80% of faculty seats must be filled by professors from the eight SAARC nations, with the remaining places accessible to faculty from other countries.

SAARC is a geostrategic association made up of eight nations in South Asia. SAARC's mission is to foster regional economic development and collective self-reliance. One of the association's main objectives was to promote and stimulate cultural interchange throughout the area, particularly via promoting South Asian arts, including music, dances, creative arts, handicraft, poetry, and literature. SAARC has established substantial diplomatic relationships with the European Union, the United Nations, and several other international organizations throughout the years. (Bajaj, et al., 2016).

The social constitution of SAARC educational provision proposed four objectives. These include increasing universal access to primary and secondary education for all children, regardless of gender, primary completion rates, young adult literacy rates, and learning quality at the basic, secondary, and vocational levels (SAARC, 2014). SAARC currently oversees several educational initiatives, including fellowship and scholarship programs, open and distance learning programs, efforts to standardize curricula, mutual recognition, and accreditation of higher education courses, credit transfer between accredited universities in member countries, and the formation of teacher forums for the exchange of educational ideas and values across the region. The development of the South Asian University (SAU) in New Delhi, on the other hand, is an educational endeavour that best symbolizes SAARC's ideological promise.

Furthermore, the Indian Ministry of Education has announced the National Education Policy 2020 (NEP 2020) to improve education standards and vocational training at all levels, from primary to university, as it has been observed that India's education sector suffers from limited foreign collaborations, a lack of research orientation, redundant, obsolete curriculum, and a lack of relevance of courses with job opportunities. Australia and India have signed a new Memorandum of Understanding on Collaboration in

Vocational Education and Training to establish new links of cooperation in policy creation, programme implementation, and information sharing as India pursues its ambitious skills reform agenda. Additionally, the Independent Tertiary Education Council of Australia (ITECA) welcomes the Australian Government new plan, stating that doing so will foster an atmosphere that will facilitate foreign student enrolment hike with autonomous higher education and vocational training providers. The federal government unveiled its 10-year international education plan, with the goal of positioning the country for a strong pandemic recovery and "creating new chances" to promote a more varied and sustainable industry. The Australian Strategy for Foreign Education 2021-2030 not only examines methods to encourage the rapid return of international students when borders reopen on December 1 this year, but it also details strategies to make the industry more viable in the longer term.

Education, research, and talents are all important aspects of the connection. India and Australia agreed that they undergird nations' progress and growth paths, and that the interchange of students and scholars between the countries fosters significant people-to-people connections. They agree to continue, to put efforts to increase engagement in these areas, including research collaboration.

This research examines the scope and restrictions of institutional partnerships between India, other SAARC nations, and Australian higher education institutions. This study is based on the analysis of data presented in the different case studies like Rajasthan Royals and Deakin Australian Universities, IIT Bombay and Monash Australian, Indian Academy of Science and Innovation Research (AcSIR) and RMIT Australian University, An Indian Economic Strategy to 2035 report submitted to Australian Government, other Government-funded research on India Australia Bilateral relationship and press release on Australia-India Knowledge partnership-a key aspect of our bilateral and multilateral ties. The case studies included analysing pertinent documents available on the networks, which gave perspectives into a plethora of partnerships and collaborative relationships. They also assisted in evaluating a rich and complicated image of why collaborations are perceived to be appealing, the different motives that encourage them, the challenges they face, and the methods that make for effective and enduring alliances.

This study's first section gives an overview of the larger circumstances within which higher education institutions in India, other SAARC nations, and Australia presently exist, relying on this thorough conceptual study. It discusses the disparities in attitudes about the opportunities of organizational partnerships between the two nations and the strategies involved. It continues over some of the major roadblocks to forming and maintaining collaborative relationships. The study's final section discusses the circumstances whereby bilateral relationships among Indian and Australian higher education institutions may be established and sustained while adhering to usefulness, assurance, and mutuality standards. It concludes with a few comprehensive suggestions for practitioners and researchers in higher education on maximizing the opportunities of institutional partnerships.

BACKGROUND LITERATURE REVIEW

South Asian countries recognize education as a basic right (Batra, 2017). Education was proclaimed as a fundamental right in Sri Lanka three years before independence in 1945, Bangladesh in 1993, Nepal in 1990, India in 2009, and Pakistan in the subsequent year. Except for Sri Lanka and the Maldives, whose literacy rates are 93 and 99 percent, literacy rates in other South Asian nations range from 38 percent in Afghanistan to 72 percent in India (Census of India, 2011). Although South Asia's adherence to children's right to free and obligatory primary education, injustice exists in and via education due to differences within each nation. In South Asia, for example, rapid economic expansion did not result in a considerable rise in per-student spending (Rama, 2014a, p. 115). India spends the least per person on elementary education of any country, notably for the poorest quintile.

In the past few decades, the number of out-of-school children of primary school age has declined by more than 40%, from 99 million in 2000 to 58 million in 2019. Girls made up 54 percent of the children who were not in school. Despite this great achievement, the world must speed up the decrease of out-of-school children, which has remained steady for more than a decade (UNICEF, 2021). Afghanistan, India, Bangladesh, and Pakistan have the highest out-of-school children (UIS, 2012).To achieve universal primary and secondary education in South Asia by 2030, an additional 15 million teachers would be needed. The countries with the greatest inequalities are Afghanistan, Bangladesh, India, and Pakistan (UNESCO, 2016). According to research, teacher absenteeism is frequent in India and Pakistan, and many teachers in Bangladesh, India, and Pakistan know little more than their students (Dundar, 2014).

After embarking on education for all roads, certain South Asian countries are confronted with the problem of insufficient educational reforms, which have resulted in increased rates of school failure and poor learning outcomes. Critical voices from the South have questioned the relevance and appropriateness of notions that have led these shifts. The sheer expanse and diversity of the region provide both considerable challenges and opportunities for contextual innovation. Governments in South Asia are taking remedial action as a consequence of insufficient international cooperation and collaboration, a lack of research orientation, repetitious, old, and outdated curriculum, and fewer course relevancies, and numerous initiatives are now being performed by these governments, notably in India, which is implementing a new education strategy in the year 2020.

The National Education Policy 2020: Pathways for the Future

The NEP 2020 places a strong emphasis on increasing international student mobility in India. While this will be difficult in the post-COVID-19 environment, the aim is noteworthy; it correctly underlines the need for Indian schools to improve their capacity to host students. Twinning programs, semester abroad, internships, and other immersion programs for Indian undergraduate and graduate students are encouraged under the NEP 2020. This opens up huge possibilities for globalizing Indian education, forming foreign academic relationships, and increasing teacher and scholar mobility. These are all positive steps; not only will these agreements allow Indian students to explore international education, but they will also allow Indian educators to collaborate with foreign peers and bring the greatest internationalization methods to India. The NEP 2020 makes a path-breaking recommendation of allowing foreign universities (ranked top 100 globally) to operate out of India. While many academics, researchers, and thought leaders in India support this idea, it would need a broad-based consultation process, a thorough regulatory framework, political will, and bureaucratic commitment to carry it through (Chakraborty, 2020; Tilak 2020). India is the world's largest democracy and a 1.3 billion-person market. Its young population, diverse economy, and rapid development give tremendous opportunities for Australian businesses, particularly in education, agriculture, energy, resources, tourism, healthcare, financial services, infrastructure, research and innovation, and sport.

Australian Strategy for International Education 2021-2030

Focus primarily on more diversified student from different parts of world specially India and other SAARC nations; to improve the transparency and diversity foreign students; Australian Government will be increasing the diversification Index.

Independent Tertiary Education Council of Australia (ITECA) applauds the new approach, which will be crucial in assisting independent higher education and vocational training providers that serve foreign students. "They've been pummelling over the last eighteen months, so the unveiling of the new plan couldn't have come at a better moment (Australian Strategy for International Education 2021-2030).

Australian International education system is the biggest service exporter and Australian is known for its world class education but because of COVID'19 international footfall of the international students have significantly declined which need to be revived by the Australian Government (Ghosh, 2021). New strategy, aiming to set the country for a strong pandemic recovery and "create new chances" to develop a more varied and sustainable sector.

Existing Collaborations Between India and Australia and Other SAARC Nations

The economic connection between Australia and India has enormous potential. Smart business people in Australia and India recognize this and are working hard to strengthen their ties (Medhekar, 2021). Australian enterprises excel in areas where India's growth is a priority.

In recent years, a slew of collaborative partnerships between Indian and Australian higher education institutions have evolved, spanning a wide range of disciplinary subjects, motivated by several factors, and now in varying negotiation and development stages. Australian Education International (AEI) undertook a partial analysis of existing university linkages and discovered approximately 380 current collaborations in cooperative research, academic exchange, and student exchange (Walters, 2012). However, several Australian delegations have visited India but have frequently returned without committing to pursue a specific joint practice. Similarly, Indian delegations have been let down by some of their efforts. Visiting vice-chancellors, high-ranking universities, or government officials may sign a Memorandum of Understanding (MoU) or announce a cooperative effort, but no further action is taken. Nonetheless, many Australian and Indian colleges' websites have a variety of similar configurations, some of which are seen below.

Academic Initiatives and Connections

The way to get involved in regional educational services is to invest intra-regionally. In the same way, as student mobility is predominantly from other nations to India, investment flows are primarily in one direction, from India to other South Asian countries. However, these investments have been quite restricted to date in terms of sectoral focus and institution range. They are largely limited to Medical Education and Information Technology, with a few Indian colleges like Manipal, NIIT, and Aptech thrown in for good measure. There have been few such operations at the school level in Kathmandu, such as the Delhi Public School franchise.

The Manipal College of Medical Science (MCOMS), Pokhra, founded in Nepal in 1994 in conjunction with the Government of 36 Nepal and is affiliated with Kathmandu University, is one of the most famous examples of regional investment and collaboration in education. The Indian software and computer training organization National Institute of Information Technology (NIIT) has developed branches in Sri Lanka, Nepal, Bhutan, and Bangladesh in information technology. These institutes are either operated by NIIT directly or collaborated with local institutions. The institution is not just present in cities, but it has also served the rural inhabitants of these nations. Further, Indian IT education firm, Aptech, had also launched a branch in Bangladesh, serving 40% of the country's IT training market in 2006-07. The 2.5 million Ngultrum "complete solution" project 39, financed by India, is also significant in Bhutan.

Most Australian universities have endeavoured to form academic networks with Indian higher education institutions, resulting in various activities centered on mutual interests, such as conferences and projects. RMIT collaborated on a significant initiative in Kolkata in the late 1990s with several institutions, non-governmental organizations (NGOs), and labour unions. Tramjatra was created to investigate the many ways in which trams play an essential economic and cultural role in Melbourne and Kolkata's social lives. Moreover, Deakin University has collaborated with Hyderabad to host an international relations conference. Artistic partnerships have resulted in public exhibits and performances as other intellectual initiatives. Development initiatives in rural and distant parts of India have also come from collaborative efforts. It is worth noting that there has been an emphasis on public health. However, these have frequently been one-off projects that have not resulted in long-term collaborations, despite the greatest intentions.

OBJECTIVE OF THE CHAPTER

The main objective of this chapter is to identify the scope and restrictions of institutional partnerships between India, Australia and other SAARC nations higher education institutions. This study is based on the extensive conceptual review of case studies like Rajasthan Royals and Deakin Australian Universities, IIT Bombay and Monash Australian, Indian Academy of Science and Innovation Research (AcSIR) and RMIT Australian University. For analysing the data conclusion has been drawn based on the existing literature; Stake (1995) defines analysis as "adding meaning to first impressions as well as finding; compilations." However, as Bassey (1999) warns, "case study work frequently creates a large amount of raw data." This was also true for this investigation. Case analysis yielded massive amounts of data. Concurrently, these were evaluated and triangulated. For analysis and presentation of data, Bereday's framework of comparison (1964) was constantly resorted to.

EDUCATION COLLABORATION AND PARTNERSHIP PROJECTS BETWEEN AUSTRALIA AND INDIA

Through the AISRF, the Australian and Indian governments have funded 93 high-quality joint projects and 15 collaborative conferences in a wide range of scientific fields, and a fellowship program for scientist exchange. The AISRF has brought together over 90 premier universities and research institutes from both sides, as well as hundreds of academics, to assist in addressing today's great concerns, such as food and water security, the environment, health, and energy. Following Myanmar's visit to India in 2020, the Advanced Centre for Agricultural Research and Education (ACARE) in Naypyidaw was created under an MoU. (Mishra & Das, 2020)

1. Enunciation and Collaboration

Informally, several enunciation agreements have been made between Australian universities and several private Indian higher education institutions (Deuchar & Freeman, 2021). These agreements call for Australian institutions to acknowledge studies completed at an Indian university. This is a one-way agreement because Indian universities have no system to recognize credits earned at other schools in India or abroad. However, with the reforms in Education Policy, such difficulties have been rectified.

2. Faculty and Students Exchange

Several student and staff exchange arrangements have also been developed. However, they have proven difficult to maintain after one or two exchange cycles. Internships, study trips, and cultural programs for overseas students, such as the University of Hyderabad's Study in India Program (SIP). The Australian Department of Industry, Innovation, Science, Research and Tertiary Education offers a study abroad short-term mobility program for qualified Australian university students to increase collaboration across the higher education sector.

The Australian Government has also just announced the Asia Bound Grants Program, which will provide financial assistance to more than 10,000 Australian students who wish to study in Asia. In terms of aim, institutional commitment, depth of involvement, and frequency and duration of the program, the specifics of these partnerships vary substantially. The staff has also had the opportunity to go to partner universities to participate in collaborative conferences, seminars, and exhibitions, some of which are regular, recurrent activities, and others that are ad hoc or one-time. Longer sabbaticals are still uncommon. Staff visits can also occur due to — or as part of — joint research.

Every year, around 3,000 scholarships/seats are awarded to Nepalese nationals through the Indian embassy in Kathmandu for study at the plus-2 level, as well as undergraduate and postgraduate courses in engineering, medicine, agriculture, pharmacology, veterinary sciences, computer application, business administration, music, and fine arts. The bilateral BP. Koirala India–Nepal Foundation was established in 1991 to foster educational collaboration. India provided Nepal with INR 3 crores for the construction of an educational facility in the Udaipur district (Saroha, 2020).

3. Collaboratively Supervised Ph.D. Programs

Joint research programs, in which Ph.D. students are collaboratively supervised by participating universities, have shown to be the most effective type of collaborative program. An Australian institution usually confers the degree. Students spend most of their time studying in India, with a semester or year in Australia thrown in for good measure. Many of these kinds of agreements are now thriving. Deakin and RMIT universities are, for example, collaborating with universities such as the University of Hyderabad; public institutions, such as the Indian Institute of Chemical Technology (IICT) Hyderabad, the Centre for Cellular and Molecular Biology (CCMB) Hyderabad, and the Jawaharlal Nehru Centre for Scientific Research (JNCASR) Bangalore; public-private institutions such as the Public Health Foundation of India (PHFI); NGOs such as HelpAge India and Business Community Foundation (BCF); research institutes such as The Energy Research Institute (TERI), and corporations such as VIMTA, Biocon, Tata Steel, and ABB Corporate Research Centre, Bangalore.

The normal financing patterns that support this concept are scholarships awarded by Australian institutions that include tuition price waivers and a fully financed six-month to one-year stay in Australia. In exchange, the Indian partner accommodates the student for the duration of his or her candidature, offers joint supervision, and pays for research supplies. All parties engaged exchange research outcomes, with universities in both countries particularly interested in publication outputs and Ph.D. completions. The concept has already resulted in several key co-authored publications, patents, and other academic research. However, disagreements over intellectual property rights can arise from time to time (IP).

4. University-Industry Partnerships

This style of collaboration has already resulted in several substantial alliances, allowing Indian and Australian institutions to interact with commercial laboratories or corporate research and development wings to work on mutually beneficial research. Ph.D. students from the participating university are frequently involved in such endeavours. The student is typically a company employee who wishes to pursue a higher degree that corresponds to the company's long-term human resource development strategy. Part-time off-campus PhDs have not been available in India. Therefore, this partnership allows industry employees to get a Ph.D. while still working. This concept assists firms in retaining good staff and developing their R&D program. This concept assists firms in retaining good staff and developing their R&D program.

5. Joint Degrees

A program that results in a degree that participating universities jointly grant is perhaps the most formal partnership model. South Asia University (SAU) degrees are recognized by all SAARC member countries, pursuant to an inter-governmental agreement signed by the foreign ministers of the eight SAARC member countries. South Asian University mostly recruits students from the eight SAARC countries, but students from other continents also attend. There is a country quota system in place for student admission. SAU administers entrance tests at numerous locations across all eight nations every year.

However, the best-known and most successful example of such partnership is the IITB-Monash Academy, a collaboration between two prestigious universities to develop research capability in both nations through a combined Ph.D. program (Rizvi, et al., 2013). The AISRF was the first to endorse this collaboration. Bombay's Indian Institute of Technology is home to the IITB-Monash Academy. Students in this program are co-supervised by advisors in India and Australia, and they spend a semester or a year at Monash University in Australia. Students who complete their PhDs through this program will get a jointly honoured degree.

Most RMIT, Deakin, and Monash universities' collaborative research initiatives are in science and technology, and they are increasingly interdisciplinary and entail efforts to tackle problems crucial to new sectors. Nanotechnology, infrastructure engineering, biotechnology and stem cell research, water, clean energy, advanced computational engineering, and materials engineering have been important areas of joint endeavour during the last decade.

Collaborative activities in the social sciences based on this paradigm have yet to be formed, despite the approach's obvious promise. Until now, engagement between Indian and Australian higher education appears to have pursued a distinct path in the social sciences, with the formation of academic networks that foster collaboration on global challenges. Traditionally, social scientific collaborations have focused on jointly hosted conferences, occasionally resulting in publication. Moreover, multilateral cooperation and partnership can occur among more than three nations, where the nations agree to reduce and dismantle their tariff and non-tariff barriers (Krugman et al., 2020; Medhekar, 2021).

These collaboration examples indicate that there is no single strategy for developing relationships between Indian and Australian higher education and that many successful practices have arisen. Collaborative practices centered on research training and higher degrees by research appear to have been the most fruitful in recent years. However, joint awards of Bachelors or Masters Degrees, as well as vocational and skills education, have yet to be developed in any systematic form. There is a higher interest in contributing finances in research partnerships, and the projected returns are long-term rather than monetary. In contrast, the incentive for some programs is commercial, and immediate profits are expected.

There is much debate between Indian and Australian institutions regarding the possibilities of new technologies and online learning in creating collaborative relationships in teaching and research. However, this debate is still in its early stages. It is focused not just on academic and practical difficulties but also on misunderstandings around government policy regarding the approval required for abroad universities to offer online programs in India. While the internet and new communication media are frequently utilized in research to stay in touch, the more far-reaching uses of new technologies in data collection and mining and the creation of new information are still being investigated. So, while the possible advantages of the partnership via new technologies are generally acknowledged, the systems required to realize this promise have yet to be built (Planning Commission of India).

ECONOMIC BENEFITS FROM EDUCATIONAL PARTNERSHIP

The advantages of a partnership between Indian, SAARC, and Australian higher education institutions would, of course, differ across nations and between different types of institutions. In India, institutional collaboration is increasingly seen as a crucial tool for dealing with the numerous issues the Indian higher education system faces. The most critical of these problems, as previously stated, is the need to meet rapidly increasing demand by widening the number of learning options accessible to students.

With rapid evolution of expertise creation and trade, evolving requirements from a dispersed and multifaceted student body, and changing pedagogy possibilities latest technology and media, Indian authorities recognised the need to engage in innovative practises and have brought about a radical shift in Indian Education Policy, for the very first time focusing on vocation. They have suggested international cooperation in research, particularly in research training, as another option for universities in both Australia and India to create research capability, work on regional and global challenges, and discover and pool resources needed to remain competitive.

International collaboration is not only necessary but also extremely desirable. As a result of cooperation, nations' progress is becoming more diverse and comprehensive. Collaboration has resulted in the establishment of totally new institutions, such as the IITB-Monash Academy in Mumbai, the Deakin India Research Initiative (DIRI) in Delhi, the IICT-RMIT center Hyderabad, and the Deakin research centers and SAU (South Asian University). They have resulted in increased financing opportunities. International consortia can vie for higher financing amounts, allowing for the establishment of large-scale initiatives, particularly if procedures and bureaucratic structures are well established, as with mature research institutes. Grant proposals can be made more competitive by collaborating across big institutions.

CHALLENGES IN COLLABORATIVE PARTNERSHIP

Crippling poverty, growing disparity in social and gender discrimination, famine, high maternal and infant mortality, and regional and socioeconomic imbalances on nearly all health and education indicators are key issues for most South Asian nations (Batra, 2019). Among the world's poorest population quintiles, the area has some of the lowest human development results. Stunting affects up to 50% of children under the age of five in Bangladesh and Nepal, and 60% of children under the age of five in India. Pakistan and India have the highest rates of neonatal mortality in the region.

Despite the effective performing nations, such as Bhutan, Maldives, and Sri Lanka, have lower human opportunity indices than other unequal countries like Brazil and South Africa. There is much disparity in educational achievement. While the Maldives and Sri Lanka have the smallest educational attainment discrepancies, Nepal, Afghanistan, and Pakistan have significant gaps.

One important cause for this is a lack of investment in education. Bangladesh devotes 2.2 percent of its GDP to education, while India devotes 3.3 percent, Pakistan devotes 2.4 percent, and Sri Lanka devotes 2%. This investment is unequally distributed: in 2010, the poorest 40% of Bangladesh's population got 50% of primary public expenditure, while the richest 40% received 80% of public higher education spending. This is also true for Pakistan and India (Rama et al., 2014).

India has lately been a focus of attention for many institutions globally due to its supply of brilliant students, notably in the sciences, and given India's rising economic influence. When there is a choice of institutions from across the world to collaborate, cooperation with Australia may encounter hurdles due to a view of Australian universities and society among some in India. Even though half of Australia's universities are highly ranked, institutions in the United States of America and the United Kingdom are frequently seen as more renowned or of greater quality in India. Furthermore, certain sections of the Indian media have portrayed Australian society as unwelcoming. However, Indians have represented the biggest proportion of new immigrants and the second-highest number of overseas students visiting Australia in recent years. These views may potentially stymie collaboration between the two countries.

Challenges for India and Australia Partnerships Regarding New Education Policy and Post-Covid-19, Collaboration Need to Be Enhanced

Australia and India must turn their intentions into action and capitalise on the numerous opportunities available in various areas as shown in Table 1. Australian universities higher education sector has suffered with falling international student numbers due to border closures. Governments and stakeholders are recommended to explore the following priority action area in order to reduce the potentially disastrous repercussions of the COVID-19 pandemic.

SOLUTIONS AND RECOMMENDATIONS

It is critical to have a solid and innovative set of administrative processes in place and appropriate and devoted administrative professionals focused on troubleshooting and removing impediments. Just as academic staff must establish a personal connection, it would be an enormously beneficial investment for employees to move to the collaborating countries and interact with individuals working in the other institution personally. An office in India, as "Deakin University" does, tends to pay significant rewards

Table 1. Priority action areas

Priority Action Areas		Recommendations
1	Joint Education PhD programs	That Australian institutions, in collaboration with established Australia-India academies, launch a combined Education PhD programme.
2.	Education-discipline focused international research collaboration	That Australian universities foster international research linkages between Australia and India in education (schools, VET, higher education) and education policy.
3.	Australia-India academies	That Australian institutions with established Australia-India joint PhD academies serve as mentors to other Australian universities interested in investing in similar collaborations.
4.	Collaborations in higher education teaching	Universities Australia and the Australia India Institute will hold a series of seminars to look into ways to expand university education learning partnerships, including TNE through offshore and online education.
5.	Connections to international offices	That Australian university international offices engage with existing and rising Indian HEI international offices in order to share best practises and foster professional interactions.
6.	Application based higher education	That (dual sector and other) Australian universities and other degree-accredited providers (including TAFE institutions) seek options for collaboration with Indian HEIs delivering applied higher education programmes.
7.	School/university/ researcher networks	That Australian schools have had interaction, practicum education student deployments, and/or education research partnerships with Australian universities to give Education PhDs to Indian foreign students via Australia-India alliances.

Source: India's National Education Policy 2020 And Australia's Education Engagement: Key Findings from Roundtables

for Australian universities. It has helped Deakin University build a variety of relationships, but it has also increased the university's profile and prestige in India. Office people have evolved into cultural dragomans and ambassadors, making it easier for those interested in partnerships and those striving to establish them.

Strategies for improving joint student supervision must also be examined to reduce stress on students and guarantee that students in collaborative arrangements have optimal circumstances. Joint supervision tactics are expected to improve over time – most collaborative Ph.D. programs are still in their early stages, and everyone engaged is still figuring out how to do things. Educators associated with a single university, on the other hand, struggle with supervision arrangements at times — and strategies for eliciting student feedback are ineffective, given the misalignments between students' and supervisors' situations, and problems can be magnified when students work all over diversified institutional structures, preconceptions, societies, and conflicting interests.

The Indian Government's strategy to lure overseas students is not motivated by a desire to play a more dominating role globally and strengthen diplomatic ties with source nations (Varghese, 2020).

Public and private Indian colleges recruiting overseas students should consider the following issues: Can the worth of overseas students be judged just in economic terms, or do these students contribute to the intellectual life of the campus and classroom? What type of evaluation criterion (academic, personality, or holistic) is utilized to choose these students to offer value to the institution's general culture?

The following areas that university leaders and Indian authorities should address while encouraging internationalization. Improving Mobility Increasing foreign student flow to Indian universities would need a focused institutional strategy and implementation plan and expenditures in faculty, facilities, and aggressive marketing. At most Indian universities, academics also serve as foreign student coordinators. They are responsible for various activities, including orienting incoming international students, troubleshooting their day-to-day difficulties, serving as academic advisers, and ensuring that they attend courses.

This is an unsustainable business model. Suppose India wants to become a strong player in inbound international student mobility, including the West and the Global South. In that case, it must encourage public and private institutions to invest in professional teams that recruit, enroll, and provide various services to international students, scholars, and faculty. The prestige of the host country, post-education career opportunities, highly rated educational institutions, cultural and social experience, and the potential to develop English language abilities are some of the most often stated aspects that attract international students.

Subjective understanding and perception of religion and safety and peer and family influence are other essential considerations (Wilkins & Epps, 2011). International students have specific requirements, and there is no one-size-fits-all approach to international student recruitment and retention. India will need to build a strong brand around 'Study in India,' similar to the Ministry of Culture's tourism-focused 'Incredible India' campaign.

These efforts will involve more than merely sending marketing agents to recruiting fairs in South Asia, the Middle East, and Africa; each institution will need to have a well-thought-out internationalization plan. This would entail:

- Working on recruitment plans for specific source countries;
- Creating or improving international student housing;
- Implementing campus-safety strategies utilizing technology;
- Training and fostering a cadre of international student advisers;
- Online learning platforms;
- Academic writing centers;
- Moreover, an institutional culture that supports international students.

1. Conducive Environment

Careful evaluation and reaction to unique constraints to international student mobility might help India portray itself as an appealing study abroad destination. First and foremost, India must address the robust rule of law enforcement. Second, reports of sexual exploitation, such as those recently at one of Delhi University's affiliated women's colleges, do not bode well for student and faculty mobility. Third, the presence of campus police or a group of campus safety guards is unavoidable to ensure the protection of foreign nationals from all nations (developed or developing). Institutional leadership will need to invest extensively in the initiative in terms of time and money.

This may involve the construction of new infrastructure or the renovation of existing infrastructure, such as student accommodation, cafeterias or mess halls, recreational centres, health, and emergency services, patrols, and campus policing, to mention a few examples. Once these fundamentals are addressed, colleges must build a globally relevant and current curriculum, well-equipped laboratories and other research facilities, and academic writing centres. This is a multi-year endeavour, and before India can begin to recruit overseas students, it must verify that all boxes are checked.

For internationalization to flourish, a friendly campus where international students feel appreciated and embraced and all stakeholders respect diversity and inclusiveness is required. India's administrators and academics must note that students from source nations will have distinct ethnoreligious origins, economic profiles, learning demands, and even sexual orientations and gender identities. Any Indian institution genuinely interested in internationalization must have an open and accepting character. Indian institutions can benefit greatly from the suggestions made by Knight (1994) in a research that discovered that the most important duties of an international relations office were

- The institution's senior leadership, faculty, and staff's dedication,
- Appropriate internal and external finance, and
- The presence of an international office with experienced employees.

As a result, the availability of these three organizational characteristics at the institutional level is critical to the success of internationalization activities. In times of catastrophe, public health crisis, conflict, and other contingency scenarios, Indian institutions must build frameworks for the well-being and security of overseas students. This will give prospective overseas students confidence and establish India as a significant regional higher education powerhouse.

2. Employability Skill

Australia's universities are perceived to have weak connection with business. When it comes to university options, Indian students prioritise employability. Numerous Indian scholars say that Australian institutions lack tight linkages to industry, especially when compared to competitors such as Canada, who have highly established partnership programs for students to obtain business experience as part of their coursework. • Indian students in Australia say they are missing out on practical chances that would help them advance in their careers. This also means that, despite the fact that visa laws enable foreign students to work and form people-to-people interactions while studying, Australian firms are missing out on a large talent pool of abroad students due to a lack of exposure. India has made a firm commitment to sharing the advantages of technological advancements with neighbouring countries.

3. Deepening Bilateral Programs

Another facet of internationalization is the movement of research scholars and professors and research collaborations. We believe that research scholar and faculty mobility is most conceivable and is currently taking place. Examples include the Fulbright-Nehru Fellowships administered by the United States-India Educational Foundation (USIEF), the Erasmus program of the European Union (EU), the EU's Horizon 2020, and other bilateral initiatives. Many of these scholar mobility initiatives have been running for decades with great success.

Some of India's finest institutions, such as the Indian Institute of Science (IISC), work on collaborative research projects supported by both governments. Strong cooperation is being promoted in public health, renewable energy, genetics, and cancer therapies. Global Initiatives for Academic Networks (GIAN) (IIT Kharagpur, 2020), Scheme for Promotion of Academic and Research Collaborations (SPARC)

(IIT Kharagpur, 2020), and Visiting Advanced Joint Research (VAJRA) (Department of Science and Technology, 2020) are excellent examples of senior scholar and faculty mobility. The GIAN curriculum is now available in 203 Indian universities, most of which are elite. GIAN and other projects covered in this part are a positive step toward sustaining economic development and increasing competitiveness in the global market.

The Indian Government might give such programs a stronger push and expand them outside the IITs, IIMs, and other prestigious universities to encourage collaborative research and academic activity (Rajkhowa, 2016). Many high-quality Indian institutions might be encouraged to collaborate on research with overseas universities and colleges. This will contribute to the advancement of Indian universities' research and innovation outputs and the overall quality of higher education. The benefit of research is that it will eventually enhance the lives of Indian communities across a wide range of impact areas. There is also a potential for Australian virtual learning suppliers to collaborate with India's huge multinational conglomerates to prototype innovative education technologies with Australian content, which can then be scaled up in India as a road to global markets (Varghese, 2018).

4. Reconfiguring Technology in Education in a Post-COVID-19 Era

Following the COVID-19 global pandemic crisis, India could work toward developing an education technology platform that allows Indian institutions to collaborate with their foreign counterparts to develop e-learning opportunities such as remote synchronous and online asynchronous courses, as well as the ability to offer accredited joint online degrees. This program will disseminate global expertise among Indian students engaged in tertiary education, and this would also benefit Indian universities by avoiding recreating the wheel.

While there are numerous Massive Open Online Courses and current Government of India programs such as Study Webs of Active-Learning for Young Aspiring Minds (SWAYAM) and National Program on Technology Enhanced Learning (NPTEL), joint online degrees will inject a much-needed international perspective into university curricula while also developing Indian faculty expertise and knowledge. These collaborations may pave the way for other types of cooperation as well.

As a result of COVID-19, the world's finest institutions have already gone online, delivering their courses through Learning Management Systems (LMS) such as Canvas, Blackboard, and Google Classroom and, in many cases, assessing students online as well (Nanda, 2020). While most Indian colleges lack an LMS infrastructure, these overseas collaborations can help Indian universities begin adjusting to a post-COVID-19 world. To benefit from this global collaboration, the Indian Government and its higher education administration bodies, such as the Ministry of Education, the University Grants Commission, or the All-India Council for Technical Education, will need to be open and flexible in regards to these requirements, as well as allow for reasonable conditions.

With the development of digitization and more intelligent social robots, the outlines of forthcoming schooling are becoming clear. Future education will need totally new knowledge and skill sets in order to prepare pupils to be global citizens. More innovative, intellectual capacity, critical thinking, enthusiasm, and benevolence will be required in prospective schooling. Technological disruptions will occur in the future, and content will be publicly available, opening the path for a new university system that is ready for the Industry revolution. It should be technologically enabled, adaptable, modular, collaborative, cross-institutional, and cross-cultural, with learners having an important role as knowledge makers, challenging instructors' monopoly. AI, Machine Learning (ML), deep learning, cybernetics, and robots will soon dominate educational content and delivery.

NEW EDUCATION POLICY IMPLICATIONS FOR AUSTRALIA-INDIA AND LESSONS FOR SAARC NATIONS

The New Education Policy of India allows institutions rated among the top 100 in the world to set up shop in India. In the end, this may encourage some Australian institutions to open offices in India. However, this will need the enactment of new legislation, and foreign organisations are unlikely to establish new facilities in India in the near future.

In the near and medium term, it is more probable that Universities of Australia would embrace the National Education Policy, with a focus on globalisation and adaptability, as a chance to strengthen partnership in specific areas such as:

- Co-creation of new themes and programmes
- Co-creation of public and remote learning goods and services, such as online schools
- Increased engagement among Indian and Australian researchers in PhD guidance.
- The establishment of cross-national post-doctoral research areas, following the lead of the Australia India Institute's Nextgen Partnership.
- Improved research collaboration in mutually advantageous areas such as irrigation, healthcare, education, electricity, and information technology, as well as effective execution of the Sustainable Development Goals
- Greater emphasis on how universities link with industry, government, and the community among Australian and Indian academic institutions
- Using India's philosophy as a "Vishwa Guru," Australian educators and administrators could investigate what may be gained from India's educational history.

India has strong bilateral ties with Afghanistan, Bangladesh, Bhutan, the Maldives, Nepal, and Sri Lanka. As part of our 'Neighbourhood First' policy, India is an active development partner in these nations, participating in a number of initiatives. India's involvement with these nations is consultative, non-reciprocal, and result-oriented, with a focus on providing advantages such as increased connectivity, enhanced infrastructure, stronger development cooperation in many areas, security, and expanded people-to-people relations. India has been strong in its commitment to sharing the benefits of technology developments with neighbouring countries as well. This form of collaboration has the potential to improve the quality, variety, and significance of academic research and education in India, Australia, and the other SAARC countries. It has the potential to broaden countries' awareness of the other's global contributions.

FUTURE RESEARCH DIRECTIONS AND LIMITATIONS

India is progressively, but unilaterally, opening its education services sector, as seen by its 2005 modified offer. Further liberalisation is expected to widen new opportunities for academic service providers to nurture dynamic productivity gains, increased market competition, learning by doing in exports, and FDI, all of which will help stimulate economic growth in both nations and improve right to schooling in India. It is vital for both countries to demonstrate that, via bilateral trade in education services, they can act as collaborators in creating national capacities and development rather than as a threat to each other's national suppliers.

Given the current glacial pace of global trade liberalisation in education services, a bilateral approach appears to be an intuitively appealing and viable choice. The development experience of Australia and India is likely to have a bigger cascade impact on others, functioning as a Given the current glacial pace of global trade liberalisation in education services, a bilateral approach appears to be an intuitively appealing and viable choice. The development experience of Australia and India is likely to have a bigger cascade impact on others, functioning as a compatible and adaptive intermediate step toward WTO-mandated international trade liberalisation of education services. and responsive intermediate step toward WTO-mandated international trade liberalisation of education services.

Higher education is a significant factor in determining a country's economy, social prestige, technological adoption, and healthy human behaviour. The government's education department is responsible for improving GER in order to include everyone in the country in higher education possibilities. The National Education Policy of India 2020 works toward this aim by establishing new regulations to improve quality, attractiveness, affordability, and supply by opening higher education to the commercial sector while maintaining stringent quality controls in all higher education institutions.

NEP-2020 is anticipated to achieve its goals by 2030 by empowering credence admissions with unrestricted and fellowships, performance based continuous performers as academic staff, performance-based proven figureheads in regulating bodies, and stringent quality tracking through biennial accreditation based on self-declaration of progress through technology-based monitoring. All higher education institutions with the current nomenclature of affiliated colleges will either develop as multi-disciplinary standalone institutions with degree - granting competence in their identities or become component colleges of their affiliated institutions.

An unbiased organization, The National Research Foundation, will provide funding for creative initiatives in the fundamental sciences, applied sciences, and social sciences, and humanities, which are priority research areas. The higher education system will become more student-centred, with the ability to select core and related studies within and across fields. Faculty members are also granted autonomy under the limitations of the regulatory regime, in curriculum design, method, pedagogy, and evaluation systems.

These modifications will begin in 2021-22 and will last until 2030 when the first stage of transition is noticeable. As a result, the system of higher learning in India is shifting from teacher-centred to student-centred, information-focused to knowledge-focused, marks-centric to skills-centric, examination-centric to experimental-centric, learning-centric to research-centric, and choice-centric to competency-centric

CONCLUSION

This research looked at various questions, including the prospective opportunities and challenges of institutional partnership between India, other SAARC countries, and Australian university education. It implies that, both India and Australia recognize the importance of globalization's political processes in restructuring and redesigning their universities and colleges, their ideas on international collaboration differ, as do their aims and competencies.

These distinctions have resulted in widely disparate conceptions of the benefits of academic collaboration. As a result, there is a necessity to provide venues for people to learn about the similarities, differences, and places of confluence between the two higher education systems. The development of collaborative arrangements based on the doctrine of reciprocity and mutual benefit necessitates a greater awareness of the growing modalities of cooperation, the challenges that are constantly encountered, and the larger conditions of success. There is also a need to recognize that there is no one formula for success and that fruitful cooperation requires perseverance, conviction, and a long-standing commitment to considerate discourse and experimentation.

Multinational firms value cross-cultural communication abilities, behavioral and attitude skills, the capacity to adapt and modify, and critical thinking (Ghosh, 2004). The internationalization of Indian education would allow India's economy and vast youth population to compete in the global free-market economy. Further Australia can also benefit from exporting its international education to SAARC countries, and also develop campus in India, through a partnership arrangement.

Because more than half of India's population is under 25 years old, and the NEP 2020 has established a goal of increasing the gross enrolment ratio (GER) to 50%, India has to enhance access to excellent higher education for its youthful population at a quick pace. Internationalization may help India improve the quality of higher education through academic and research collaborations, virtual and physical institutions, and academic programs. Internationalization provides many benefits for Indian institutions, the economy, society, and scholarship.

Other significant difficulties may be tackled through academic and research collaborations, such as public health crises such as epidemics and pandemics, international terror networks, climate change, and sustainable agriculture, as described throughout this article. For India to embrace broad internationalization, great political will, a comprehensive regulatory framework, institutional leadership, and a well-defined national policy and the institutional plan would be required.

Currently, India spends 4.4 percent of its GDP on education, and this has to be increased to increase access and improve education quality. Financing will need to be improved at the national, state, and institutional levels to support full internationalization. Institutional autonomy and the admission of authorized and internationally-minded foreign universities will be critical to achieving internationalization goals. India benefits much from a balanced and iterative approach to internationalization, provided all stakeholders collaborate. The Government chooses an open and flexible approach, and much-needed investments are made in the industry.

Efforts were made to discover the techniques and practises that underlying the operation of university-based education at a world-class institution. It is anticipated that the findings and implications given in this study will be useful to anybody who has an interest in how universities develops significant collaborations. The case study and related studies are expected to serve as a mirror, allowing anybody with an interest in this process to consider how their own policies and practises could evolve.

REFERENCES

Bajaj, M., & Kidwai, H. (2016). *Human rights and education policy in South Asia*. Academic Press.

Bassey, M. (1999). *Case Study Research in Educational Settings*. Open University Press.

Batra, P. (2017). Imperatives of comparative and international education: Some reflections from the south. In A. W. Wiseman (Ed.), *Annual review of comparative and international education*. Emerald Publishing Ltd.

Batra, P. (2019). *Comparative Education in South Asia: Contribution*. Contestation, and Possibilities., doi:10.1108/S1479-367920190000036011

Bryman, A. (1988). *Quantity and Quality in Social Research*. Routledge.

Census of India. (2011). *Census of India 2011. Provisional Population Totals*. New Delhi: Office of the Registrar General & Census Commissioner, Government of India. Retrieved from http:// www.censusindia.gov.in/2011census/c-01.html

Chakraborty, A. (2020). *Foreign partnerships in Indian higher education: Significance, challenges and concerns*. Globalization, Societies, and Education. https://www.tandfonline.com/doi/pdf/10.1080/14767724.2020.1861439

Department of Science and Technology, Government of India. (2020). *About VAJRA*. https://www.vajra-india.in/index.php/about-vajra

Deuchar, A., & Freeman, B. (2021). *Deepening collaboration and strengthening opportunities for Australia-India research and engagement*. Australia India Institute.

Ghosh, A. K. (2021, February 5). Education today needs more funds, not less. *The Statesman*.

Ghosh, R. (2004). Globalization in the North American region: Towards renegotiation of cultural space. *McGill Journal of Education*, *39*(1), 87–101.

Indian Institute of Technology Kharagpur. (2020a). *Global initiative for academic networks*. https://gian.iitkgp.ac.in/

Indian Institute of Technology Kharagpur. (2020b). *Scheme for promotion of academic and research collaborations*. https://sparc.iitkgp.ac.in/

Jha, J., Minni, P., & Ahmed, M. (2020). *Teachers and Teaching Profession in South Asia*. Working Paper. Centre for Budget and Policy Studies (CBPS).

Knight, J. (1994). *Internationalization: Elements and checkpoints*. Canadian Bureau of International Education. https://files.eric.ed.gov/fulltext/ED549823.Pdf

Larsen, K., Martin, P. J., & Morris, R. (2002). Trade in education services: Trends and emerging issues. *World Economy*, *25*(6), 854, 857, 867. doi:10.1111/1467-9701.00466

Medhekar, A. (2021). Australia-India: Bilateral Trade Opportunities and Challenges. In *Emerging Business and Trade Opportunities between Oceania and Asia*. IGI Global Publishing. doi:10.4018/978-1-7998-4126-5.ch004

Mishra, I. (2020, March 13). Study in India: Is India ready to be a destination for foreign students? *The Bastion*. https://thebastion.co.in/politics-and/study-in-india-is-india-ready-to-be-a-destinationfor-foreign-students/

Mishra, V., & Das, S. (2020). *Education as a Pivot in India's Cooperation with BISMTEC Countries. ORF Issue Brief No. 418*. Observer Research Foundation.

Molly, N. N. (2012). Regional cooperation in higher education in Asia and the Pacific. *Asian Education and Development Studies, 1*(1), 18–23. doi:10.1108/20463161211194432

Nanda, P. K. (2020, June 18). *Govt to allow colleges, varsities to offer 40% of coursework online*. https://www.livemint.com/education/news/govt-to-allow-colleges-varsities-tooffer-40-of-coursework-online-1159242573470

OECD. (2016). *Innovating Education and Educating for Innovation: The Power of Digital Technologies and Skills*. OECD Publishing.

Phale, K., Li, F., Adjei, M., Omari-Sasu, A. Y., & Musah, M. (2021). Knowledge-Based Economy Capacity Building for Developing Countries: A Panel Analysis in Southern African Development Community. *Sustainability, 13*(5), 2890. doi:10.3390u13052890

Rajkhowa, G. (2016, September 3). *Internationalising Indian universities – The way forward*. University World News. www.universityworldnews.com/ post.php?story=20160903061847638

Rama, M., Béteille, T., Li, Y., Mitra, P. K., & Newmann, J. L. (2014). *Addressing Inequality in South Asia*. World Bank Publications. doi:10.1596/978-1-4648-0022-1

Rizvi, F., Gorur, R., & Reyes, C. (2013). *India-Australia Institutional Collaborations in Higher Education: Potential, Problems, Promises. A report for the Australia India Education Council. Project Report*. Australia-India Education Council.

SAARC. (2014). *Areas of cooperation Education*. South Asian Association of Regional Cooperation. Retrieved from https://www.saarc-sec.org/areaofcooperation/cat-detail.php?cat_id=53

Sakshi S. (2019). *India extends 30 million aid to Nepal to build educational institution*. Academic Press.

SAU. (2015). *South Asian University*. Retrieved from http://www.sau.ac.in/

Stake, R. E. (1995). *The Art of Case Study Research*. SAGE Publication.

The Economist. (2010). Learning without frontiers: Globalisation and higher education. *The Economist, 397*(8706).

Tilak, J. B. (2020, August 9). A policy with a right intention. *The Hindu*. https://www.thehindu.com/opinion/op-ed/a-policy-with-many-a-right-intention/article32254650.ece

UIS. (2012). *Online database and glossary*. UNESCO Institute for Statistics. Retrieved from http://www.uis.unesco.org

UNESCO. (2015). *Adult literacy rate, population 15+ years (both sexes, female, male)*. UIS Data Centre. Retrieved from http://data.uis.unesco.org/Index.aspx? DataSetCode=EDULIT_DS&popupcustomise=true&lang=en#

Varghese, N. V. (2020). Internationalisation and cross-border mobility in Indian higher education. International Journal of African Higher Education.

Walters, C. (2012). *A Focus on Quality and a Long Term Strategy*. Australian Education International.

Wilkins, S., & Epps, A. (2011). Student evaluation web sites as potential sources of consumer information in the United Arab Emirates. *International Journal of Educational Management, 25*(5), 410–422. doi:10.1108/09513541111146341

ADDITIONAL READING

A Weekly Journal of Higher Education. (2021). Published by the Association of Indian Universities, Vol 58, No-33, special issue on Reimagining Indian University.

Department of Education and Training (AU). 2016 International Student Survey. Canberra AU: The Commonwealth of Australia; 2016.

National Education Policy. (2020). https://www.mhrd.gov.in/sites/upload_files/mhrd/files/nep/ NEP_Final_English.pdf referred on 10/08/2020.

The global outlook for international higher education strengthens [Internet]. (2018) Available from: http://www.hsbc.com/news-and-insight/media-resources/mediareleases/2017/the-global-outlook-forinternational-higher-education-strengthens

Varghese, P. N. (2018). An India Economic Strategy to 2035, Navigation from potential to Delivery. A report to Australian Government, Retrieved from http://indiaeconomicstrategy.dfat.gov.au

World University Rankings [Internet]. Times Higher Education (THE). 2018 [cited 4 April 2018]. Available from: https://www. timeshighereducation.com/world-universityrankings/2018/world-ranking

KEY TERMS AND DEFINITIONS

Academic Collaboration: The collaboration between academic institutions for improving skills, increasing visibility, and making network for further growth and development.

Bilateral Programs: Bilateral Programs exist between two nations like India and Australia have IIT Bombay and Monash Australian, Indian Academy of Science and Innovation Research (AcSIR), and RMIT Australian University as Bilateral programs.

Conducive Environment: Right condition for establishing the bilateral or multilateral academic relation between nations.

Education Policy: It consists of the principle and policies on educational system.

Employability Skills: Employability Skills are the set of transferable skills, which is required by a job seeker to make themselves 'employable'.

Post COVID-19: During the COVID-19 pandemic, the term new normal has been increasingly used to refer to the changes of human behavior during, or after the pandemic.

SAARC Nations: SAARC is a geostrategic association made up of eight nations in South Asia. SAARC's mission is to foster regional economic development and collective self-reliance.

Chapter 8
Strategic Partnership of Bangladesh With Australia to Protect From Possible Debt Trap and Diseconomies of Scale of One-Belt One-Road: Lessons for SAARC Nations

S. Jobayear Ahmed
https://orcid.org/0000-0001-6356-2666
Bangladesh Rural Advancement Committee (BRAC), Bangladesh

ABSTRACT

Bangladesh is a developing nation that is about to complete its Golden Jubilee partnership by 2022 with Australia, a country that has been supporting Bangladesh through aid, assistance, grant, loan, trade, scholarship, etc. Recently, the regional and global superpower China has increased its influence in the Indian Ocean region both through its military and through the OBOR or BRI where it has also shown interest to work with Bangladesh in both fronts. Bangladesh is a very small country but strategically very important, with access to the Indian Ocean. Therefore, it is important to check whether the OBOR initiatives put any negative impact on the neighboring SAARC nations and partner states. The study therefore attempted to identify the potential diseconomies of scale and the solutions Australia-Bangladesh relations might offer.

INTRODUCTION

Bangladesh gained independence in 1971 after a 'war of liberation' (CIA, 2020). Bangladesh is about to celebrate its 50th year of diplomatic relationship with Australia, which is one of the first few countries, which recognized Bangladesh in 1972 (Chowdhury, 2019). Bangladesh is a riverine South Asian

DOI: 10.4018/978-1-7998-8657-0.ch008

country with a Population of 163.0 million growing at the rate of 0.98% annually. The total Area of the country is: 148,460 square kilometers where Land area is: 130,170 square kilometers and Water area is: 18,290 square kilometers. The rate of literacy is 73.9% and rate of urbanization is 38.2% (CIA, 2021). The country has a GDP (PPP) of $838.6 billion with a 7.9% growth, the compound 5-year annual growth is 7.5% 5-year compound annual growth, $4,951 per capita, an unemployment rate of 4.2%, inflation (CPI) rate of 5.7% and FDI Inflow of $1.6 billion. Bangladesh's economic freedom score is 56.5, making its economy the 120th freest in the 2021 Index. Its overall score has increased by 0.1 point, primarily because of an improvement in the tax burden score. As of December 1, 2020, 6,675 deaths had been attributed to the pandemic in Bangladesh, and economic growth was forecast to decline to 3.8 percent for the year. (Country Rankings: World & Global Economy Rankings on Economic Freedom, 2021).

The country observed enormous economic growth since 1971 and will achieve the Lower Middle Country Status by 2026. In order to proceed beyond Bangladesh will need to invest in human capital, enhance female labour force participation and their productivity, continue sound macroeconomic management, and implement structural reforms (The World Bank, 2020). The country is expected to return to a 6 percent growth if supported by favorable domestic economic recovery and global economic conditions (IMF, 2020) even after the COVID. A concentric Ready Made Garments (RMG) Export based national income posed significant risks (Rasul, 2020) for the country and therefore it has attempted to diversify and create a risk hedge though attracting various foreign investments in the energy, power, telecommunication and infrastructure. But the analysis of the Ease of Doing Business Index shows that it ranks 168(Trading Economics, 2021), one of the lowest in the world and therefore necessitate the country to undertake various infrastructural and policy reform often financed by the aid and loans sourced from the international organizations and developed countries.

Recently the evolvement of China, as a global development partner (where Bangladesh has also become a part), through its One-Belt One-Road (OBOR) or Belt and Road Initiative (BRI) has attracted undivided global attention. The aim of BRI is to improve connectivity and cooperation on a transcontinental scale as an open arrangement in which all countries are free to join. The BRI's impacts were assessed by World Bank (based on 70 countries with 35% of global foreign direct investments and 40% of global merchandise exports) particularly on BRI's links to trade, investment, debt, procurement, environment, poverty reduction and infrastructure (World Bank, 2018). The estimated cost of the project is US$575 billion which will reduce the travel time by 12%, increase trade and income up to 9.7% and 3.4% and uplift 7.6 million people from extreme poverty. But the associated risks are: debt risks, governance risks (corruption and procurement), stranded infrastructure, environmental risks and social risks (World Bank, 2018).

But the gradual increase in the Bangladesh debt to China has raised a certain question whether Bangladesh will fall into a debt trap like some other countries like few African countries, Srilanka and Pakistan which have already fallen victim to the Chinese Debt Trap Diplomacy (Chellaney, 2017). Therefore it necessitates to identify whether there is adequate scope to promote bilateral strategic partnership with Bangladesh's long held ally, Australia to enhance Bangladesh's maritime power, to minimize the risk factors of OBOR and avoid debt trap. The chapter contains the following sections: a background outlines the literature review and the research gap, that is followed by the objectives, research questions, methods followed by the main focus of the chapter. In the main focus both the historic and the current engagement of the countries with Bangladesh has been discussed elaborately. After that the OBOR has been discussed, followed by the dilemma of Bangladesh and in search of a question whether Bangladesh is falling into the debt trap. After that the potential diseconomies of scale have been identified and ways have been identified on how the relationship with Australia may help Bangladesh and also SAARC countries to avoid the diseconomies of scale OBOR-Road Debt Trap.

BACKGROUND

Bangladesh is growing fast and is on its way to becoming the next Asian Tiger in spite of various natural disasters, political unrests and diffusion of economic policies and reforms, in the last few decades. The country achieved a growth above 7% in GDP from a GDP of 3.7% back in 1980 and thereby turning the development "basket case" into the "development surprise" through particular progress in per capita income as well as social and development sectors. Currently the 41st largest economy, Bangladesh will be the 25th largest economy by 2035 (Ali, 2020). Its per-capita income rose to $2,227 per capita GNI in FY 2020-21 from around $100 in the early 1970s, and the country has achieved food self-sufficiency. The country achieved Millennium Development Goals (MDGs) and also has implemented structural adjustment reforms supported by the World Bank and the IMF through adopting key exchange and trade system liberalization policies, policies in project management, procurement and implementation(*International Monetary Fund Bangladesh: Letter of Intent and Memorandum of Economic and Financial Policies*, 2015). Macro-economic reforms are required such as, reduction in fiscal and trade deficits to sustainable level, increase in the savings and investments, withdrawal of food and agricultural subsidies, privatization of state owned enterprises, financial liberalization, and withdrawal of quantitative import restrictions, moving towards an open economy and introduction of value added tax led to growth.

The growth has also been supported by the government's digital transformation programme, more than 90 million unique of mobile phone users (Okeleke, 2021), increase in the remittance and the export particularly the RMG. Currently the country has $44 billion in Foreign Exchange reserve, 5.56% inflation reserve. Bangladesh is the world's 7th most populated country with about 170 million people, 45% of whom are aged below 24 years and 70% aged below 40 years of age, 2.3 million young professionals joining workforce every year(BIDA, 2021). On the contrary high population, poverty, scarce land and natural resources, associated with growing crops, livestock, fisheries and forests, upstream water withdrawal and climate change on the ecology, biodiversity and environment are a few challenges for Bangladesh. Specifically, the female headed households in remote areas, and households consisting of socially excluded and other vulnerable people, fall victims of poverty, inequality and deprivation. Bangladesh, therefore, stands at the juncture of making both ends by ensuring the optimum utilization of her scarce resources and attempting to ensure uniform developments across all sectors and actors. The riverine country is gifted with the connectivity to the sea which supports its international trade. The country has got 580 km coastline, 10 active land ports linking various states of neighboring India, 90% international trade done via Chittagong and Mongla ports Deep-sea ports - Matarbari and Payra Ports to be completed by 2025, 3 international and 5 domestic airports, 22,418 km of highways, 2,955 km of railways, 3 Asian highways- AH1, AH2 and AH41 connecting India and Myanmar and the Part of regional highway corridors like SASEC, BIMSTEC and SAARC (BIDA, 2021). In pursuance of the development initiatives the country has taken an aspirant endeavor to develop the critical infrastructure with the support of various donor agencies and developed countries. Therefore, Bangladesh has undertaken various measures to meet the infrastructural gaps with the support of its development partners.

President Xi Jinping first announced his five point proposal for the New Silk Road economic belt during a speech in Astana, Kazakhstan and again during a Shanghai Cooperation Organization (SCO) summit (Szczudlik-Tatar 2013). OBOR is a continuation of Deng Xiaoping Theory, a series of economic reforms which began in the late 1970s, eventually developing into the Shenzhen special economic area. This reform work was continued through the term of Zhang Jemin with his going out strategy. OBOR can be seen as the pinnacle of going out, as China seeks to become a world economic power (Johnson, 2016). The aspirant project that involves majority of the world's population, resources, coverage and trade is often termed for promoting debt trap for countries through extensive use of soft power. Kukreja and Upadhyay (2019) believes that, usually a debt trap results from the failure to repay loan and its responsibility of interests and as a result it often circulates, even after refinancing as well. The model is mostly factual in developing countries where public debt remains a major accountability. The High debt servicing costs consume a lion's share of national income and therefore the nation is often deprived of the critical avenues like the issues of economic, infrastructural and social development.

In current decades, unsustainable debt – mostly external – has brought country after country into deep economic crisis, with dramatic social consequences for their populations. Molson (2021) observed the advantage of the Chinese foreign policy and the challenges posed therefrom, which might result in China's domination in many strategic arms of their governance and decision-making process to trade freely and openly with other countries. Bokhari (2017) identified that: China's One Belt, One Road, a much-touted initiative to connect the country with Europe, the Middle East, Africa and other parts of Asia, is facing resistance from states whose cooperation Beijing needs to build its highly ambitious infrastructure projects. Akram and Scholar (2018) noted that: one of the common reservations expressed regarding China Pakistan Economic Corridor (CPEC) is that it lacks transparency and non-availability of complete data. But Ranasinghe (2019), argued that: Chinese loans are not the primary cause of the Sri Lankan debt crisis. (ISSAfrica.org, 2018) noted that Africa's growing public debt has sparked a renewed global debate about debt sustainability on the continent. Will (2015) also notes that based on the consensus that it is the high debt rate causes the 2015 Chinese stock crash, thereafter, explained the logic that how credit, and debt may influence the market and attempted to investigate what was behind the rise of high debt rate before the Chinese stock crash.

In 2016 during that visit of Chinese President, China announced huge investments in various sectors of Bangladesh. The implementation of those investment projects is now in full swing. Among the ongoing projects are the Padma Multipurpose Bridge Project (Hauxia, 2021;Yukun et al., 2019), Karnafuli Tunnel (Suman, 2021), Dhaka-Chittagong Highway Four Lane Up gradation, (Hauxia 2021a), Payra Port Development (Fairman, 2019), Chittagong-Cox's Bazar Railway Project, (*Chittagong-Cox's Bazar Railway Line - Railway Technology*, n.d.), Power Grid Network Strengthening Project, (Rahman, 2020), Dhaka-Ashulia Elevated Expressway (Mamun, 2021), Dhaka-Sylhet Four Lane Highway (Byron, 2021). Recently, there have been reports of China's cooperation in the overall development of the Teesta basin (Modak, 2020), which, if implemented, could radically change certain sectors, including agriculture and industry, in a large area of North Bengal. The Chinese President pointed out the commonality Bangladeshi dreams with the Chinese dream of national renewal and underscored that the dream of the people of Bangladesh, as we are on the way to achieving the goal of becoming a middle income country by 2021 and a developed country by 2041 can be materialized through joint efforts, develop and maintain practices and policies, (Sakhawat, 2020). Therefore it is imperative to identify the bottlenecks and risk factors prevalent therein from an objective point of view.

OBJECTIVE OF THE STUDY

In pursuance of the scenario mentioned above the chapter would like to be guided based on the following objectives:

Broad Objective

The broad objective of the chapter includes exploring the potentials of Strategic Partnership in between Bangladesh and Australia to safeguard from the possible 'Debt Trap' and Diseconomies of Scale of OBOR and highlight the case studies of SAARC Countries.

Specific Objectives

The specific objectives of the chapter are to:

- Understand the possibility of debt trap for Bangladesh due to the One belt One road initiative
- Identify the diseconomies of scale of the One belt One road initiatives and to cite the examples from the SARC countries
- Explore the potentials of safeguarding Bangladesh through its Strategic Partnership in with Australia
- Identify the lessons for the SAARC Nations from the potential diseconomies of scale due to OBOR debt trap

Research Questions

The chapter will answer the following research questions:

- Whether there is any possibility of debt trap for Bangladesh due to the OBOR initiative?
- What are the diseconomies of scale of the OBOR initiatives?
- What are the potentials of safeguarding Bangladesh through its Strategic Partnership in with Australia?
- What lessons the SAARC Nations can take from the potential diseconomies of scale?

RESEARCH METHODOLOGY

The chapter is based on an explorative study of secondary literature. The information attained from different sources generated further information and insight of the topic. The data collected and generated was analyzed using thematic approach along with graphical presentation. The thematic approach of data analysis was used as it is recognized as the most common (Guest, 2012) and foundational (Holloway & Todres, 2003) method of qualitative data analysis. The method emphasizes on the content of a text, 'what' is said more than 'how' it is said, the 'told' rather than the 'telling' (Riessman, 2006). The categories and analytical codes have been drawn in alignment with the objectives set. The research questions and conceptual framework had generated an initial start list of analytical codes, which were developed during data analysis. Besides the themes were patterns across data sets that were important to the description of a phenomenon. The themes became the categories for analysis (Fereday & Muir-Cochrane, 2006). Triangulation permitted the search for convergence and divergence in the multiple sources of information gathered in order to develop and confirm (or disconfirm) the analytic themes (Creswell, 2003). The study followed ethical guidelines given by (Berg, 2001; Miles & Huberman, 1994) in case of necessity. The Verbatim data, having been collected, has been converted into logical clusters and framed into different categories. The ethical considerations of this chapter have been - assuring the privacy of the research and appropriate use of it; including no harmful issues which affects individual or a community and society; following human and property rights carefully during data collection and other field techniques and issues which can have adverse impact on the bio-physical environment has been evaded.

MAIN FOCUS OF THE CHAPTER

Country Profile

China: The People's Republic of China (Wilbur, 2021) is a Communist state that has a capital housed in Beijing, (Capital, 2014, August 26) and a population of (2019): 1,400,050,000 with a rapid economic growth of GDP (gross domestic product) averaging 10 percent per year and has become the second-largest economy in the world and is increasingly playing an influential role in the global economy (World Bank, 2018). COVID-19 had a huge impact on the world's economy in 2020 where China took solid steps to stabilize its employment, finance, foreign trade, foreign investment, domestic investment and market expectations, and fully safeguard residential employment, people's livelihood, market entities, food and energy security, stability of industrial and supply chains and operations at grassroots levels. In 2013, President Xi Jinping unveiled China's ambitious infrastructure and economic development strategy known Belt and Road Initiative (Chronology of China's Belt and Road Initiative, 2015). China is spending around US$150 billion a year to connect more than 60 countries that have signed up to the scheme who will be connected through a network of railways, roads, pipelines and utility grids linking China with Central Asia, West Asia and parts of South Asia. The BRI is currently developing six international economic cooperation corridors, including the New Eurasian Land Bridge, China–Mongolia–Russia, China–Central Asia–West Asia, China Indochina Peninsula, China–Pakistan, and Bangladesh–China–India–Myanmar (The Belt and Road Initiative, 2018).

Australia*:* Australia is one of the wealthiest Asia–Pacific nations and has enjoyed more than two decades of economic expansion. Australia is internationally competitive in financial and insurance services, technologies, and high-value-added manufactured goods. Mining and agriculture are important export sectors. Australia's 15 free-trade agreements include FTAs with the U.S., China, Japan, South Korea, and the Association of Southeast Asian Nations. Negotiations on similar agreements are ongoing with the European Union and expected to begin with the United Kingdom now that it has left the EU. The population of Australia is 25.4 million, GDP (PPP): $1.4 trillion, 1.8% growth in 2019, 5-year compound annual growth 2.4%, $53,320 per capita, unemployment: 5.3% inflation (CPI): 1.6% FDI inflow: $36.2 billion public debt: 45.0% of GDP (Country Rankings: World & Global Economy Rankings on Economic Freedom, 2021).

Table 1. Socio economic indicators

Name of Indicator	China	Australia	Bangladesh
Population(Million)	1440	25.68	165
Unemployment rate (%)	4.9	4.6	5.3
GDP Annual growth rate (%)	4.9	9.6	5.47
Inflation rate (%)	2.3	3	5.7
Interest rate (%)	3.85	0.1	4.75
Government debt to GDP (%)	66.8	24.8	31.7
Corporate tax rate (%)	25	30	32.5
Competitiveness Rank	28	16	105
Corruption Rank	78	11	146
Ease of doing business	31	14	168
Coronavirus vaccination rate	178	122	64.08

Source: Trading Economics (2021)

Inter Country Comparison of Socio Economic Indicators

The socio economic indicators of China, Australia and Bangladesh presented in Table-1, exhibit that the population of China is the highest among the three countries. It also shows that Bangladesh has the highest unemployment percentage, while the GDP growth is the highest in Australia, but the interest rate is the lowest. The country also ranks highest in the competitiveness, corruption and Ease of Doing Business, China has got the lowest in the percentage of Corporate Tax and highest Coronavirus Vaccination Rate (see Table-1).

History of Relationship With China and Australia

- ***Sino Bangladesh Relationship:*** China and Bangladesh are neighbors with resplendent and long-standing civilizations, which naturally led to communication for over 2500 years. China and Bangladesh connect through the centuries-old Southern Silk Road where cultural interactions brought together by Southern Silk Road, Fa Xian, Xuan Zang & Yi Jing, Atisha Dipankar, visit of Zheng He, twice in Bengal in the 13th Century. The communication remained infrequent till the 1950s and 1960s when Chinese Premier Zhou Enlai visited East Pakistan. Bangabandhu Sheikh Mujibur Rahman, in 1952, also visited China twice and formed close friendship with Mao Zedong, Zhou Enlai, Zhu De, Liu Shaoqi and other Chinese leaders, which laid a solid foundation for the establishment of diplomatic relations (Embassy of China, 2011), which was delayed by Chinese actions and inactions, between the two countries in 1975.

Mahanty (1983) has highlighted the double standard played by China before and after the liberation war of Bangladesh. China opposed the independence of Bangladesh, tilted towards Pakistan in the context of the Cold War and Sino-Soviet conflict, vetoed and blocked Bangladesh's UN membership in 1972. China even delayed its recognition to Bangladesh until October 1975 and thereby hurdled the establishment of smooth diplomatic relation is spite of the relentless efforts from the leadership of Bangabandhu who could not see the diplomatic relationship in his lifetime (Sakhawat, 2020). Despite such Chinese Opposition, over the decades relations have grown in a positive direction and has been termed as 'all weather friendship' which has been bolstered by Bangladesh's support for the 'One China Policy' and support for China in different multi-national forums and thereby establishing a mutual trust and interests based stable and continuous bilateral cooperation (Uddin & Bhuiyan, 2011).

After a long gap of 30 years the 24 Hours long visit of the Chinese President Xi Jinping to Bangladesh in 2016 bore significance due to the large package of Projects, signing of extensive and varied Memorandum of Understanding (MOU) and thereby beginning of a 'Strategic Partnership of Cooperation'. Chinese Ambassador proposed Belt and Road mechanism for Bangladesh in 2018. China's encouragement for cross border direct engagement, Bangladesh's location in the Bay of Bengal and has been planned to be connected by means of the BCIM (Bangladesh, China, India, & Myanmar) was mooted by Beijing to connect Yunnan province with India, Bangladesh and Myanmar wherein China expects and Bangladesh, that finds BRI offering the chances to extend the prospects beyond neighborhood and thus intends to be an important player. Apart from active participation the Bangladeshi Prime Minister encourages India to participate in the OBOR and finds that BRI could have a significant impact on Bangladesh from an economic and connectivity perspective and the Chittagong Port can act as a central hub to connect Northeast India, Myanmar, Southeast China, Bhutan, Nepal, and Bangladesh, (Datta, 2019; Mohan, 2011).

- ***Australia Bangladesh Relationship:*** Australia was among the first countries to recognize the newly independent Bangladesh in 1971 and establish diplomatic relation since early 1972 (2022 will be the 50th year of relationship) (Chowdhury, 2019). Australia and Bangladesh are old friends, sharing commonwealth ties, democratic traditions and people-to-people links. The strong moral support of the Australia's mass media to the liberation struggle of Bangladesh in 1971 was depiction of Australia's sympathy towards the liberation struggle. The goodwill and friendly gestures had inevitable positive implications as was praised through an editorial in *The Canberra Times* while and also the recognition by Australia was described as "useful and imaginative piece of diplomacy" (Stockwin 1972, p. 341). Subsequently, the harmony was reflected in Australian humanitarian and development assistance and reconstruction efforts for the war-ravaged country (Kamal & Ahmed, n.d.) through US$14 million of economic assistance for rehabilitation and reconstruction of the economy during 1972-75, continuing supporting Bangladesh's development efforts and providing maximum of Australian Aid to Bangladesh making it atop any other country. Australia and Bangladesh intend to pursue new opportunities to promote trade and investment in order to ensure the support for a shared economic recovery from COVID-19.

Investment and Financial Integration

China: The size of the infrastructure investment (wherein the transport and the power sector are the most priority sector) will fall and is predicted to be around 1% of total GDP in Bangladesh on the eve of the economic development of the country. It has been predicted that the sectorial needs for energy and transport sectors will be the major area demanding the fund wherein the BRI could be a replacement. Particularly the FDI generated from the Chinese investors show an upward moving trend while in the first quarter of the fiscal year 2019, Chinese net FDI inflow amounted to $396.99mn, which was 38.34%.

Figure 1. Sector wise Chinese and Australian investment in Bangladesh in 2020
Source: Author Based on Bangladesh Bank Report 2020

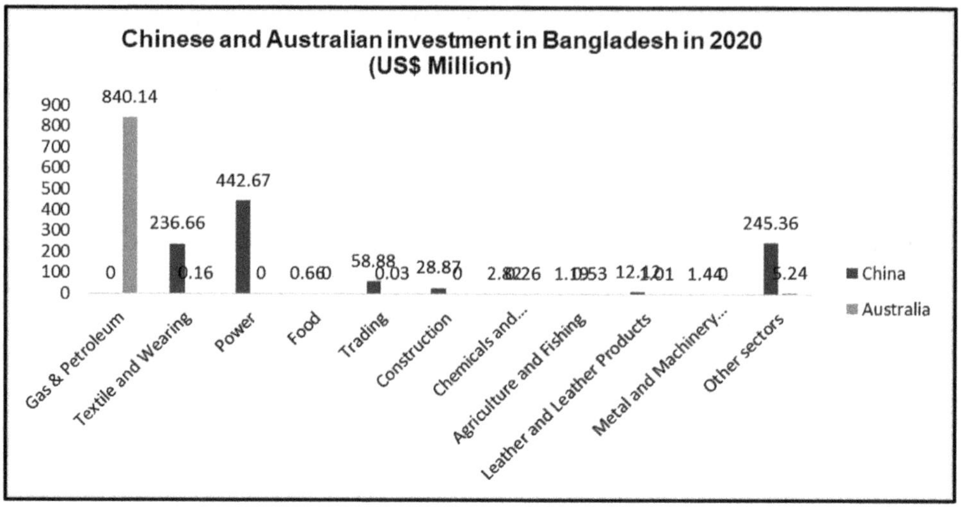

Trade and Economic Relation

- ***China:*** Bangladesh is the third largest trade partner of China in South Asia, has a complementary economic relationship with plenty of cheap labour and raw materials while China possesses latest technology and huge amount of capital. Although China has bolstered its economic aid to Bangladesh to address trade imbalance, but Bangladesh needs to diversify its export baskets, remove its structural problems, be competitive and seek for greater amount of Chinese investment to expand and sustain in Chinese market. China's major exports to Bangladesh include textiles, machinery and electronic products, cement, fertilizer, tire, raw silk, maize, etc. Most of the products that people use in Bangladesh are from China,(Faiz, & Maitra,2020). On the other hand, China mainly imports raw materials from Bangladesh like leather, cotton textiles, fish, etc. Trade was at over $16 billion in 2017, which grew by 17.6 percent in 2018. The trade between China and Bangladesh has been increasing gradually since 2010 overtaking the place previously held by India, although there is a wide gap in between the states in terms of trade. China shared 18.94% of total trade of Bangladesh which was two times more than that of India and more than that of US and Germany combined. Recently Chinese government has declared duty of access of 97% Bangladeshi Products (8256 products) in the Chinese Market which targets to acquire at least 1% of the 40 trillion dollar domestic market of China (Target 1% of China market for smooth LDC graduation: Experts, 2021).
- ***Australia:*** The total trade between the two countries soared from A $2.7 million in 1972 to A$350.1 million in 2000 while between 2001 and 2018, trade value grew over 440% to $1.9 billion in 2018, (Chowdhury, 2019). In 2018-19, Australia's two-way goods and services trade with Bangladesh grew to over $2.5 billion (goods valued at $1.9 billion), whereas Australia mainly exports agricultural products and cotton and imports clothing and textiles. Bangladesh, a Least Developed Country, whose products get duty-free and quota-free access to Australian Markets offer an increasing long-term commercial opportunities in education services, food and bever-

ages, agribusiness and energy and minerals. Bangladesh enjoys duty and quota free access to the Australian Markets subject to the fulfillment of Rules of Origin (RO) criteria since July 1, 2003. Although the weak infrastructure, skills shortages and the governance environment are certain constraints but the country's geographic position including the seaports offers it a certain level of dividend. Bangladesh's export to Australia mainly consists of readymade garments, woven fabrics, knitwear, textile manufactures, home textile, leather goods and footwear, processed food, fish, jute goods etc. Major Australian export consists of wheat, vegetables, lentil and pulses, milk, cream and other dairy products, cotton, fertilizers, oil seeds, primary plastic products, machinery and transport equipment, scraps and some other industrial raw materials. Bangladesh also offers commercial opportunities to Australian companies in energy, telecom, transport, textiles, education and mining sectors (Consulate General of Bangladesh, 2021).

As seen from Table-2, Australia is one of the important trading partners for Bangladesh with bilateral trade of over one billion US dollar annually, with the balance of trade remaining slightly in favors of Australia. Table-2 shows that the bilateral trade in between Australia and Bangladesh was always in favor of Bangladesh in between the years 2014 and 2019 with the exception of 2017. On the other hand the China Bangladesh Trade observed that China had always been in a favourable position. Besides in comparison to the import and export from Australia and China it was observed that both export and import are growing but the ratio of export in the last five years(2014 to 2019) show that the total Bangladeshi export to Australia is less than four fifth of its export to China. On the other hand the comparison of the import shows that the total import from Australia was less than 6-7% of what the Country imported from China.

Official Development Assistance

- China: China has so far provided US $ 48.5 million in grants assistance and US $ 3165.3 million as loan aid. The grants aid comprised US $ 6.2 million in Food Aid, US$ 42.4 in Project and of the loan aid US $ 8.5 million in Food Aid, US $ 14.5 million in Commodity, US$ 3142.4 Million in Project aid (Economic Relations Division, 2020).
- Australia: Australia has so far provided a total of US$ 73047.8 Million in ODA of which 27.89% was in between 1990-2000 with an annual average of US$ 1851.6 Million per year, 33.58% was in between 2001-2010 with an annual average of US$ 2472.8 Million per year and 38.3% in between 2011-2018 with an average of US$ 3494.10 Million per year (Figure-2) (Economic Relations Division, 2020).

- **Development Aid(Loan):** The development partners(both organizations and countries), as seen in Figure-3, have provided a total of US$ 60239.1 Million in development aid to Bangladesh wherein the contribution of China was 5.26% (Economic Relations Division, 2020).

- ***People to people and Cultural Exchange***

China: Cultural exchange being a component of the BRI goes through knowledge sharing, research collaboration, and strengthening of people-to-people bonds. There has been a steady increase in the

Table 2. Bangladesh's import and export from and to Australia and China

Year	Export to Australia	Import from Australia	Favourable Position (Bangladesh/Australia)	Export to China	Import from China	Favourable Position (Bangladesh/China)	Export Ratio (Australia/China)	Import Ratio (Australia/China)
2000	46428.42	186596.32	Australia	13901.21	856965.01	China	3.34	0.22
2001	27659.44	181173.84	Australia	10301.48	894090.8	China	2.69	0.21
2002	27866.69	175363.97	Australia	23892.02	824962.82	China	1.17	0.22
2003	31718.8	146266.39	Australia	25955.35	1113457.51	China	1.23	0.14
2004	37747.42	198077.14	Australia	57500.3	1580186.51	China	0.66	0.13
2005	39008.53	179349.1	Australia	65197.86	2002263.07	China	0.6	0.09
2006	31671.95	138686.21	Australia	776651.55	2570789.91	China	0.05	0.06
2007	35183.68	165242.42	Australia	222217.89	2750202.2	China	0.16	0.07
2008	49498.2	215368.07	Australia	92915.57	4561176.38	China	0.54	0.05
2009	124514.96	321319.14	Australia	118276.46	3837205.09	China	1.06	0.09
2010	140517.94	535489.98	Australia	259158.15	5323341.57	China	0.55	0.11
2011	250948.01	598029.37	Australia	382895.52	3610348.88	China	0.66	0.17
2012	387157.15	506985.65	Australia	431774.73	6477949.4	China	0.9	0.08
2013	447817.45	546530.89	Australia	485505.37	7219305.08	China	0.93	0.08
2014	502176.36	494882.96	Bangladesh	761107.88	11782272.27	China	0.66	0.05
2015	635556.93	520293.26	Bangladesh	816845.19	13894707.66	China	0.78	0.04
2016	659789.43	616109.88	Bangladesh	869397.55	14300635.41	China	0.76	0.05
2017	665043.22	915790.4	Australia	875144.72	15169021	China	0.76	0.07
2018	734980.29	673372.43	Bangladesh	985405.47	17759539.78	China	0.75	0.04
2019	798334.86	635876.49	Bangladesh	1036436.11	17335124.03	China	0.78	0.04

Source: World Bank (2020)

number of scholarships offered to foreign students, number of foreign students in China, establishment of Confucius centers(increased about one fifth within five years) and classrooms(doubled within five years). The number of Bangladeshi students in China increased in China by 4,905 in 2016 compared to the previous year, a Confucius institute was established, and the number of students increased. Currently there are about 12000 students studying in China with different scholarships (Tithila, 2021).

Australia: Bangladeshi-Community in Australia has been growing strongly during recent years forged by the personal ties regarding family, business, education and sports particularly cricket. The number of Bangladeshi born citizens increased in Australia as 2016 Census recorded 41,233 people from Bangla-

Figure 2. Australian official development assistance to Bangladesh
Source: Economic Relations Divisions, Ministry of Finance, Bangladesh,2020- (Economic Relations Division, 2020)

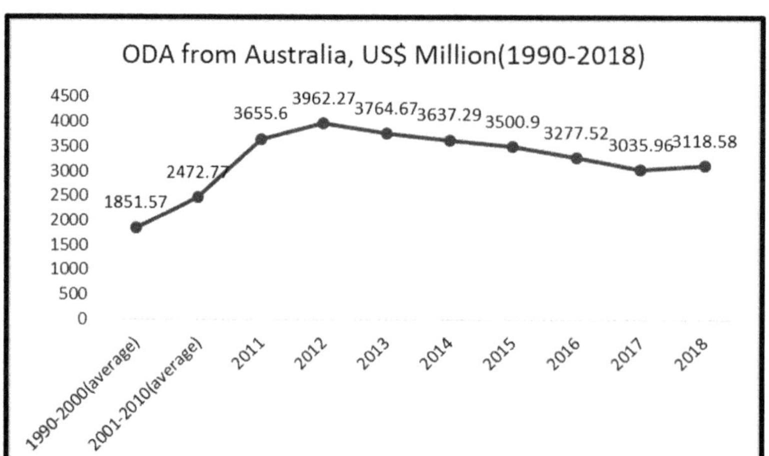

Figure 3. Bangladesh partner wise development aid (loan) percentage 1972-2021
Source: Economic Relations Divisions, Ministry of Finance, Bangladesh (2020)

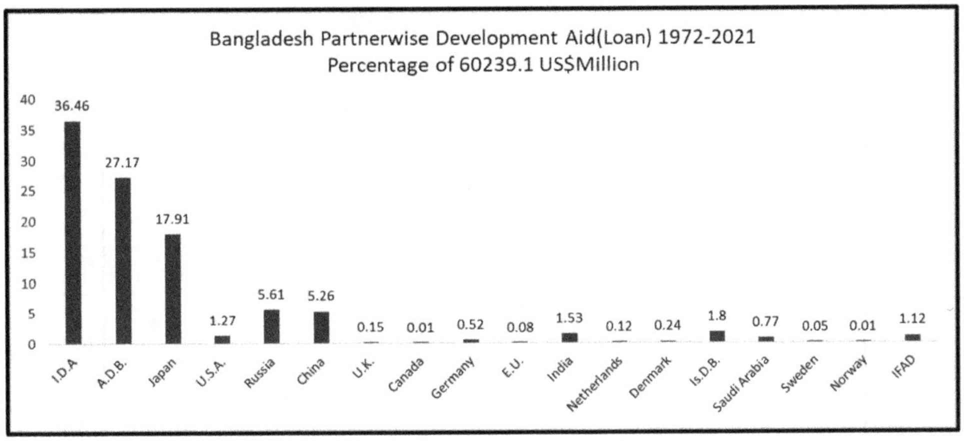

desh living in Australia, up from 27,808 recorded in the 2011 Census. In 2018, about 7,000 Bangladeshi students enrolled to study in Australia (an increase of 26% from 2015) (DFAT, 2021).

Healthcare Support During COVID-19

- ***China:*** China, against the backdrop of the COVID-19 global pandemic, provided Bangladesh with, 40,500 test kits, 15,000 surgical N95 masks, 300,000 medical masks, 10,000 protective gowns and 1000 infrared thermometers to Bangladesh to address COVID-19 pandemic which was further reaffirmed by the Chinese President including sending a medical expert team to Bangladesh. (Hossain & Islam, 2021).
- ***Australia:*** Australian provided medical equipment, training, hygiene and community awareness services; constructed 1900 bed hospital and emergency food and income to vulnerable people across Bangladesh in COVID response. It will also continue to partner with Australian, Regional and Global NGOs, World Health Organization, GAVI, the Vaccine Alliance, and the Global Fund to Fight AIDS, Tuberculosis and Malaria programmes and meet basic needs in nutrition, education, protection and hygiene services (DFAT, 2021).

Military Weaponry, Logistics and Treaties

- ***China:*** Defense cooperation occupies a significant aspect of Bangladesh–China relations wherefrom Bangladesh Armed Forces (Army, Navy and Air Force) have been using weaponry (tanks, frigates, submarines, missile boats and fighter jets) for decades. China, in between 2008 and 2017, provided US$1.86 billion of weapons to Bangladesh, constituting 71.9% of Bangladesh's military acquisitions over this period (China Power, 2018), supported by offering generous loans and competitive pricing. Bangladesh Air Forces' main interceptor aircraft F-7 is supplied by China wherefrom Bangladesh also procured seven Chinese-made K-8W training aircraft under an agreement (The Daily Star, 2020) the country has received two China-made Type-035G Ming-class submarines for just over US$100 million each in 2017 (Cited in Azim, 2019, p. 127).

Figure 4. One Belt One Road, country wise Chinese investments and major projects of BRI
Source: China Trade: Balancing Opportunities & Risks in One Belt One Road, (2018)

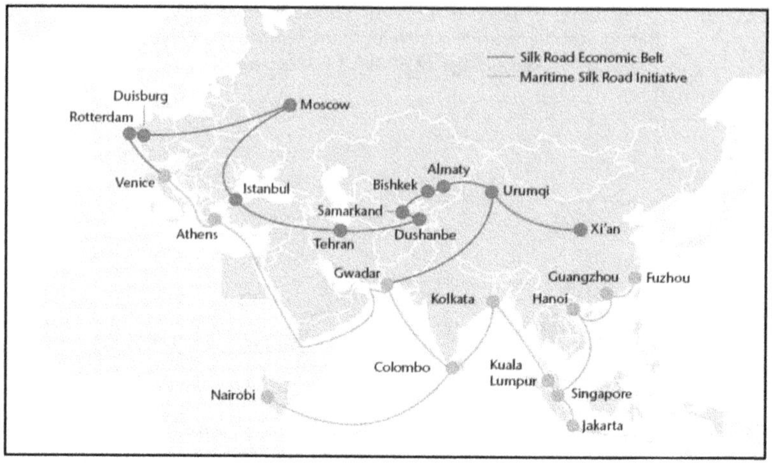

- ***Australia:*** Although Australia does not have any major military or strategic relationship with Bangladesh, but the countries are related with QUAD and Indian Ocean Rims Association (IORA). Besides Australia has also been a strong advocate of peaceful, Free and Open Indo Pacific region with democratic values and vows after the US, Japan, India bloc for Indio-Pacific Strategy (*Joint Statement from Quad Leaders*, 2021).

THE ONE BELT ONE ROAD

One Belt One Road is the Chinese plan to rebuild connectivity and cooperation across six main economic corridors through the land network connecting China to Europe via Central Asia ("One Belt") and the maritime route from China to Southeast Asia, South Asia, the Middle East, and Eastern Africa ("One Road"), see figures (4 & 5). The one belt one road which includes the China-Bangladesh-India-Myanmar (BCIM) Economic Corridor connecting Bangladesh, is renamed as Belt and Road Initiative (BRI), having signed by a total of 136 countries and 30 international organizations had joined through 194 cooperation documents till July 2019. The BCIM corridor covers 1.65 million square kilometers, and includes about 440 million people and connects China's Yunnan province, Bangladesh, Myanmar, and Kolkata in India through road, rail, water, and air linkages Khatun & Saadat, (2020) and thereby build regional cooperation through building an economic corridor connecting the sub-regions of South Asia, Southeast Asia, and East Asia and potential for benefiting from the blue economy and international maritime trade through the Bay of Bengal, the Indian Ocean, and the Andaman and Nicobar Islands. An amount of US $24.45bn was in bilateral assistance for infrastructure projects and US $13.6bn in joint ventures. In addition, US $20bn in loan agreements was committed.

In 2016, Bangladesh and China signed eight projects costing more than US $9.45bn financed by China including: Padma Bridge rail link worth US $3.3bn; the power plant in Payra worth US $1.9bn; digital connectivity worth US $1bn, and power grid network strengthening project worth US $1.32bn (Figure-5). As part of Bangladesh government's initiative on establishing Special Economic Zone (SEZ),

Figure 5. One Belt One Road, country wise Chinese investments and major projects of BRI
Source: China Trade: Balancing Opportunities & Risks in One Belt One Road, (2018)

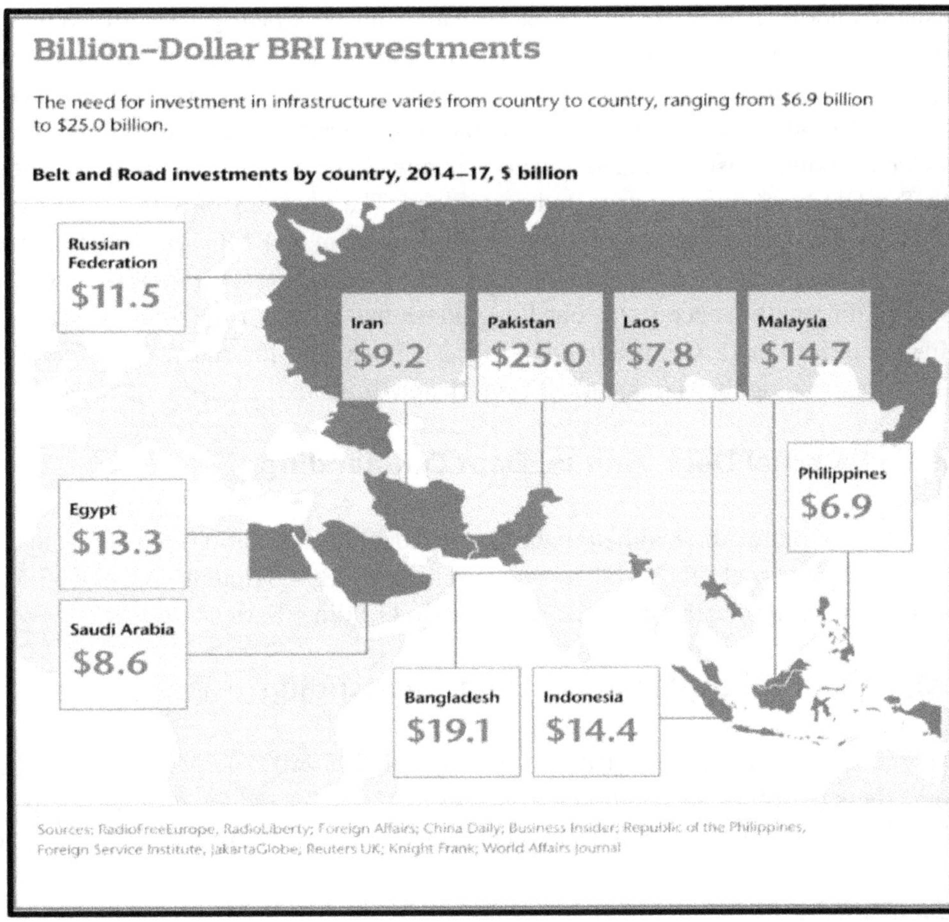

Chinese Economic and Industrial Zone (CEIZ) is being developed in Anwara Upazila of Chittagong district on a land of 783 acres. State-run China Harbour Engineering Company holds 70% share in the joint venture (Khatun & Saadat, 2020).

Bangladesh's Projects Under OBOR/BRI Initiative

According to the news published in the newspaper on June 7, 2020, the government of Bangladesh has undertaken 17 development projects on a priority basis by China-Bangla Investment Corporation for the first time which are mostly the BRI projects. The major projects include the Padma Bridge Rail Link, establishing the ICT infrastructure, railway projects, elevated expressways, tunnel under the Karnaphuli River etc. Altogether the estimated budget is US$ 21429.33 Million.

Case Study: Sri Lanka

Sri Lanka became middle income country in 1997. The country is facing economic downturn due to wrong economic policies. Recently, Bangladesh has agreed to lend $200 million to debt-ridden Sri Lanka which is struggling to maintain a moderate foreign exchange reserve. Undoubtedly, it is a matter of pride for Bangladesh. At the same time, Bangladesh should take lessons from Sri Lanka for upcoming days to avoid unexpected economic crisis. Bangladesh and Sri Lanka have similar economic weak point. In both countries, the Tax-GDP ratio is not at expected percentage. The economy of both countries depends on a single product, for example- Bangladesh's economy is dependent on RMG and Sri Lankan economy is dependent on tourism industry (Maritime Gateway, 2021). The good news for Bangladesh is that, though Sri Lanka is struggling with its economy, but Bangladesh has enough time to confront the upcoming challenges. In case of Sri Lanka, China agreed in July 2017 to a debt-for-equity swap for $8nn loan and a 99-year lease for managing the Hambantota Port (Khatun & Saadat, 2020).

Bangladesh's External Debt: Annual Debt Outstanding

Figure 6 shows that, for Bangladesh, although the external debt to GDP ratio is reduced, but the absolute amount of outstanding external debt has also increased from $19354.81mn in 2007 to $33,511.83mn in 2018, for Bangladesh has gradually increased over a period of time (Sarwar, 2020).

Bangladesh's External Debt: Annual Debt Outstanding

The figure-7 shows that in 2019-20 Bangladesh had a total of US$ 44095.12 Million and its highest loan was with World Bank (37.65%), second highest with ADB (24.43%) and the third with Japan(17.06%), relative to China's 6.81%, much lower than Bangladesh (Ministry of Finance, Bangladesh, 2020).

- ***Bangladesh's Dilemma***

Intense power competition, worsened ties between Beijing and New Delhi and the influence of the critical role of Japan and the United States altogether stiffened Bangladesh's act of balancing interests. Dependence on USA for export, in Japan for infrastructure, on China for Raw Materials and on India for geo-strategy has juxtaposed a serious dilemma for Bangladesh to proceed confronting the country with a less favorable strategic and economic environment in the future and therefore demands a very calculative action the absence of which due to miscalculation and polarization might jeopardize the country's hard-earned achievements (*Bangladesh at 50: Navigating Strategic Survival*, 2021). A calculative and neutral approach might help Bangladesh reap the benefits of relations with all major powers, contrary to the popular theoretical expectations, which can be bolstered through stable, confident and experienced leadership adept to deal with the major powers. Apart from nearly no security threat from China, Bangladesh at the same times embraces the Chinese narrative. Bangladesh is also rejecting the Chinese-centric notion of a 'community of shared destiny'. Against small states' interest, competing connectivity strategies feed into the fragmentation of multilateralism that seems to be one of the hallmarks of multi polarity, that favours exclusive regional and global great power clubs and has put the legitimacy and effectiveness of global governance are under stress. Although the BRI may eventually breed cooperation

Table 3. China funded projects in Bangladesh in 2020

Name of Project	Value(US$million)
Padma Bridge Rail Link	2667.93
Dhaka–Sylhet four-lane highway	2110.00
Development of the national ICT infra-network	156.56
Construction of tunnel under Karnaphuli River	705.80
Installation of Single Point Mooring (SPM)	500.47
Rajshahi WASA Surface Water Treatment Plant	350.00
System loss reduction	165.98
Expansion and strengthening of the Power System Network under DPDC area	1650.51
Power Grid Network Strengthening Project under PGCB	1321.83
Construction of Dhaka–Ashulia elevated expressway	1393.98
Establishing six full-fledged TV stations of Bangladesh Television	127.88
Modernisation of telecommunication network for digital connectivity	231.00
Construction of a dual-gauge track parallel to the existing Joydebpur–Mymensingh–Jamalpur section	581.26
Construction of double line between Joydebpur and Ishurdi sections	752.79
Establishing digital connectivity	1000.00
Marine Drive Expressway and coastal protection works from Sitakunda–Chittagong–Cox's Bazar	2856.56
Expansion and modernisation of Mongla port facilities	249.17
Extension of underground mining operations of Barapukuria Coal Mine	256.41
Gazaria 350 MW coal-fired power plant	433.00
Conversion of MG railway track to DG railway track in the Akhaura–Sylhet section	1756.05
Prepayment metering project for Bangladesh Power Development Board's (BPDP) distribution zone	521.56
New inland container port near Dhirasram railway station	200.00
Replacement of overloaded distribution transformer to provide reliable electricity to the RE region	230.59
Water supply, sanitation, drainage, and solid waste management for small municipalities	150.00
Modernisation and expansion of public sector jute mills of Bangladesh	280.00
Chinese economic and industrial zone in Chittagong	280.00
Modernisation of rural and urban lives through ICT	500.00

The Author's contribution based on, Datta, (2021)

Figure 6. Bangladesh's annual debt outstanding (1971-2020) in US$ million
Source: Source: Economic Relations Divisions, Ministry of Finance, Bangladesh (2020)

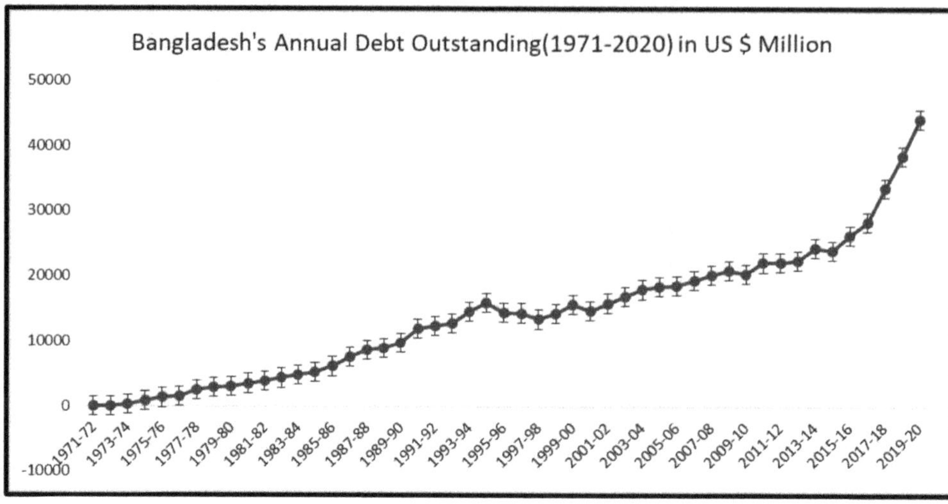

amongst major powers overlapping interests in increasing connectivity regionally and the helpfulness of Chinese funding for this may make it happen (Plagemann, 2021).

Is Bangladesh in a Debt Trap?

Due to the LDC status Bangladesh avails loans and credits on easier terms, lower interest rates and longer grace periods, which till the graduation from LDC (in 2026) will continue benefitting Bangladesh. The benefits, such as lowest interest rate; longer grace period, that Bangladesh receives as a LDC from different donor organizations like World Bank (WB), International Monetary Fund (IMF), Japan International Cooperation Agency (JICA) etc. will be available till 2027.Besides the country is going to

Figure 7. Development partner wise debt distribution percentage 2019-20 in US$ million
Source: Source: Economic Relations Divisions, Ministry of Finance, Bangladesh (2020)

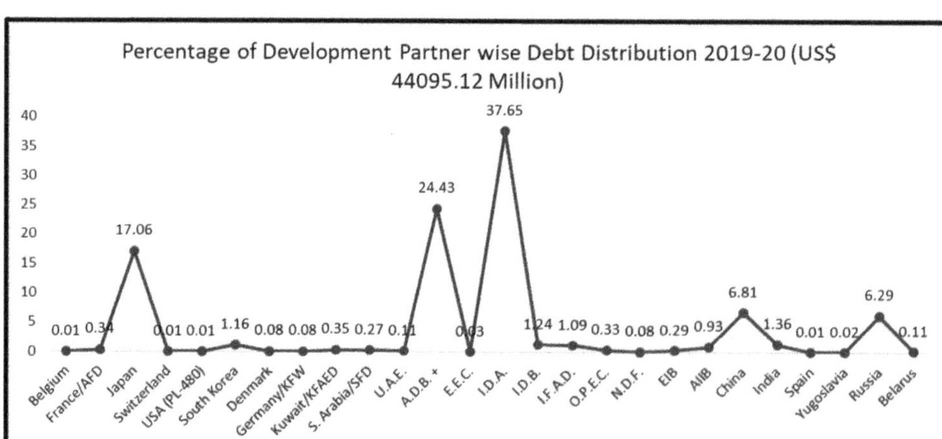

graduate soon therefore the development works must be completed soon, otherwise the projects might stiffen the development processes by increasing the cost (Maritime Gateway, 2021). According to Economic Relations Department's (ERD) 'Flow of External Resources into Bangladesh' report, in 2019-20 fiscal years, total external debt outstanding of Bangladesh was USD 4409.51 crore which is equal to BDT 3,74,898.35 crore in local currency. According to this figure, the per capita loan is BDT 23,425 considering the total population as 16 crores. According to IMF and World Bank's Standard, it is only dangerous for an economy if its external debts exceed 40% of GDP while Bangladesh's total external debts is less than 15% of GDP which is far from danger mark. In the current fiscal year, Bangladesh has taken 38% from World Bank, 24.5% from Asian Development Bank, 17% from Japan, 3% from China and 1% from India as external debt. Bangladesh has taken 80% of total external debt from WB, ADB and JICA. Therefore the likelihood of the debt trap might not be true (Maritime Gateway, 2021). Besides the alternative sources of flexible funding opportunity Chinese Development Finances (DFIs) have created competition in the market and has increased the buyer power and thereby the development partners like: Japan, India etc have to offer flexible terms.

DISECONOMIES OF SCALE OF ONE BELT ONE ROAD (OBOR)

Debt Issue

Chinese government has provided debt relief to countries whereas China has approached debt issues in various countries (at least 28 heavily indebted poor countries (HIPC)) which have been suffering from debt distress, on a case-by-case manner, including 100% forgiveness for several (for example, Burundi, Afghanistan, and Guinea). In case of Sri Lanka, China agreed in July 2017 to a debt-for-equity swap for $8nn loan and a 99-year lease for managing the Hambantota Port (Khatun & Saadat, 2020).

Environmental Concerns

OBOR/BRI is likely to cause irreversible damage to the environment as the infrastructure may threaten the eco-systems and the livelihoods of the people who depend on environmental resources surrounding them. Although China has been promoting green financing system but the need for clear definitions, strategy, legal framework, enforcement, overlapping regulations, environmental liability insurance, legality of emission rights and the supervision, reporting and authentication systems, necessary policies to stimulate development of green financial products and capacity in financial institutions are a few challenges (Kidney & Oliver, 2014).

Transparency

Lack of open, transparent, and competitive procurement processes can lead to poor performance of projects in terms of missing timeline, cost overrun, and low quality services. The Corruption Perceptions Index (CPI) score of Transparency International indicates that the perceived corruption in the Belt and Road corridor economies is higher than the global average and higher among lower middle and low income countries. In comparison with the two countries Bangladesh scored lower in Corruption Perception and thus scored low. Therefore it is possible that corruption might take place in BRI supported projects in

Bangladesh. Sakib (2019) found association between OBOR and organized crime and corruption in Bangladesh, and what Bangladesh can learn through OBORization.

Addressing Political Risk Across Countries

It is important for business leaders to assess, understand and develop clear risk management strategies regarding the cross border political risk before making significant investment in countries historically prone to political or economic volatility. Due diligence at the start is critical to developing clear risk-management strategies to address the potential impacts of these risks on their business. Uncertainty about the future of trade relationships – how contracts will be affected, implications to supply chain and a business's overall ability to market in certain geographies – can make business decisions much more complex.

Security Perils Along the Route

The companies operating on BRI-linked projects face various security-related perils including the physical assets to employees who can be exposed to threats of kidnap for ransom, illegal detention and extortion along these routes which may not be solved employing the local security force alone. Awareness of these risks and the need to implement preventative measures based on worst case scenario analysis and assurance of reaching out the world class experts for a successful resolution.

Free Trae Agreement (FTA)

Bangladesh has been signing a lot of free trade agreements which it is highly likely to have idea about the project is that it will probably fail. Due to the higher mechanization and the economies of scale the developed countries will benefit which get cost advantage over Bangladesh. Therefore ultimately the companies of Bangladesh will be harmed.

Extinction of the Local Industries

Higher extent of mechanization in the developed countries will also challenge the local industries of Bangladesh, since the operating and production costs will rise, which lead towards the extinction the local industries.

Contention Over the Rohingya Issues

As with India, Bangladesh–China relations face challenges. The Rohingya crisis is a bone of contention as Bangladesh enormously suffers from it. It is strongly felt in Bangladesh that China has been shielding Myanmar in the United Nations Security Council and outside. It is reported in a daily in Dhaka, China's role as the savior of Myanmar just never ends. China, instead of taking a role in stopping Myanmar, discouraged to "internationalize" the Rohingya crisis. Beijing has been one of the few backers of Myanmar who played down the Rohingya repression in Rakhine as Myanmar's internal issues (The Business Standard, 2020).

OFFERINGS OF AUSTRALIA: TO AVOID POTENTIAL DISECONOMIES OF SCALE OF ONE BELT ONE ROAD (OBOR)

The three Ps of Bangladesh-Australia relations are: potential for growth, pragmatism and people-centricity based on the Commonwealth values including human rights, democracy, the rule of law, sustainable development environment gender equality and women's empowerment, education and health; and international peace and security. Australia will seek to deepen economic and development cooperation and bilateral trade with Bangladesh from shedding light on global issues. The countries would focus on the Rohingya crisis, migration, climate change, cooperation on transnational crime (since 2015) (DFAT, 2021) and strategic interests in Indian Ocean Rim Association (IORA) chaired by Bangladesh since October 2021 (IORA, 2021). Australia is the third popular destination for Bangladeshi students with about 50,000 Bangladeshis living in Australia. Australia is also an observer in SAARC where Bangladesh is a member. The basis of Australia-Bangladesh relations hinges primarily on economic(particularly FDI, imports and exports), political pursuits, and mutual interests complemented by Australian humanitarian and development assistance program which seems marginal if compared to other partners of Bangladesh like: Japan, USA, UK, Germany, and People's Republic of China (PRC) (Kamal & Ahmed, n.d.).

Diplomatic Relation (Regional Engagement of Australia)

Australia would continue to support Bangladesh in the ongoing crisis by providing humanitarian assistance, advocate for accountability in the Rakhaine state and work with Myanmar, Bangladesh and other partners for a durable solution. Besides the country could support Bangladesh through its response and recovery from COVID-19 particularly the intensified pre-existing humanitarian and economic challenges (DFAT, 2021). A history of cooperation and friendship should lead to reliable partnership in between the two countries for trade and investment.

Australian Aid to Development (Emphasis on Post COVID Aid)

Australia will continue to support the densely populated Bangladesh through its response to climate change, natural disasters and recovery from COVID-19, that intensified pre-existing humanitarian and economic challenges, particularly in Cox's Bazar where almost 1.3 3 million people(855,000 Rohingya refugees and 444,000 local Bangladeshis) depend on humanitarian assistance. The country will continue partnering with Bangladesh Government and other donors to support health security, stability and economic recovery, emphasizing on protecting the most vulnerable, especially women and girls and people with disabilities. The 2021-22 bilateral allocation [budget estimate] $30.8 million, 2021-22 total Australian ODA [budget estimate] $133.8 million and 2019-20 total Australian ODA [budget estimate] $70.1 million (DFAT, 2021).

Strategic Cooperation in Defense and Security

Australia could develop a long-term engagement on transnational security issues and initiatives including: defense relationships; enhancing maritime capabilities; regional security engagement and building relationships with Bangladesh civil society. The Australian Defense Force (ADF), the Department of Foreign Affairs and Trade (DFAT) and other agencies can play important roles in this regard(Brewster,

2021). Australia could also build strong personal relationship and network with Bangladesh Military by posting Military Lecturers/ Officers/Defense Advisors (DA) to Dhaka, to the Defense Services Command and Staff College and the National Defense College which will improve Australia's visibility of security developments in Bangladesh. Exchanges of military personnel Networks, military professional training and Graduate education on Warfare, national security, maritime governance, Technology Management, project management, sustainment, logistics and defense acquisitions and inviting the Bangladesh Military Officers to share their experiences in the UN Peace Keeping Operations, shared security and maritime concerns. Besides there might be mutual exchanges between the Bangladesh Institute of Peace Support Operations Training and Australia's Peace Operations Training Centre. Also there could be a Naval Visit including offshore exercises to promote the future Indo Pacific Endeavour activity in the northeast Indian Ocean. This altogether should include opportunities for Australia as a potential supplier in niche defense technologies or surplus equipment in light of the Bangladesh military's major modernization program (Brewster, 2021).

Stability

Australia is partnering with Bangladesh to support greater social cohesion and address food security risks exacerbated by COVID-19, reform the systems underpinning the National Social Security Strategy, supporting nutrition services and agricultural research partnerships, support inclusive education and skills development. Australia's humanitarian assistance will support initiatives that build the resilience, social cohesion and self-reliance and support inclusive education and skills development with the World Food Programme, ACIAR, CSIRO and Australian NGOs, Underprivileged Children's Educational Program (UCEP), Australia Awards, and the Global Partnership for Education. Australia will work with Bangladesh (DFAT, 2021) to support stability and economic growth in the Indian Ocean Region, including through the Indian Ocean Rim Association (IORA).

Economic Recovery

Australia will support Bangladesh's longer-term economic recovery, including investing in human capital and job creation, develop transport and energy infrastructure, and revitalize, diversify and promote trade and investment, private and multilateral development bank finance, climate and disaster resilience, low-carbon and inclusive development and improve regional connectivity, new opportunities through Australia's new Emerging Markets Impact Investment Fund, the Business Partnerships Platform with CSIRO (DFAT, 2021).

Partnership

There has been ample scope of partnership and cooperation on the technology and cyber support, since Australia has made significant investment in digital infrastructure, stay competitive by gaining market intelligence, identifying growth opportunities, designing innovative goods and services, improving pricing, and operating, accessing the global digital economy through people, digital enterprises, government on a digital platform.

Engagement on Regional Security

Bangladesh should connect as an instrument of enhanced regional engagement in the northeast Indian Ocean area with combined activities with Sri Lanka, Maldives and, potentially, India.

IORA AS A PLATFORM FOR REGIONAL COLLABORATION

Bangladesh is a leader in Blue Economy and the Chair of the Indian Ocean Rim Association (IORA) in 2021 which gives Bangladesh a valuable opportunity to frame the relationship, in co-sponsorship with Australia on maritime safety and security, the blue economy and environmental security, blue carbon, fisheries and ocean renewables.

Engage With BIMSTEC

Australia should review options for formal or informal engagement with BIMSTEC as an observer that would express the country's interest and offering a platform for sharing perspectives.

Relationships With Bangladesh Civil Society

Enhanced engagement on defense and security should be accompanied by an exchange of strategic insights involving officials, leading analysts, Bangladesh think tanks and other influential elements would help promote the relationship and build shared perspectives on developments in the region.

Relationship With IORA

Bangladesh should feature strongly in the list of countries which can potentially provide that additional bandwidth for more trade diversity amidst Australia's ever-growing challenges with China

SAARC COUNTRIES: SOCIO ECONOMIC INDICATORS

The socio economic indicators, shown in Table 4, indicate that India has got the highest (1347 million) population while Maldives has the lowest (0.56 million) population, Afghanistan has the highest rate of unemployment (11.2%) while Pakistan has the lowest rate (4.4%). India has the highest (8.4%) annual growth rate of the GDP growth rate while Bhutan has the lowest (-10.08%). Pakistan has the highest rate of inflation (11.5%) while Maldives has the lowest rate (-0.2%). Pakistan has the highest rate of interests (9.75%) while Afghanistan has no interest (0%) rate. Bhutan has the highest rate of debt to GDP percentage (121%) while Afghanistan has the lowest percentage (7.8%) rate. Pakistan has the highest rate of corporate taxes (29%) while Maldives has the lowest (15%) rate. India ranks upmost in the competitiveness rank (68) while Afghanistan ranks the lowest(165). Bhutan ranks upmost in the corruption rank (24) while Pakistan ranks the lowest(124). India ranks best in the Ease of Doing Business competitiveness rank(68) while Afghanistan ranks the lowest(173). India ranks best in the Ease of Doing Business competitiveness rank(68) while Afghanistan ranks the lowest(173). Maldives and Sri Lanka got the highest in the Corona Virus vaccination rate(144%) and Afghanistan ranks the lowest(13.13%) (Trading Economics, 2021a)

Table 4. Socio economic indicators of the SAARC countries

Name of Indicator	Afghanisthan	Bhutan	India	Maldives	Nepal	Pakistan	Sri Lanka
Population(Million)	33.2	0.77	1347	0.56	29.13	221	21.92
Unemployment rate (%)	11.2	5	6.9	6.4	4.44	4.4	5.1
GDP Annual growth rate (%)	-1.93	-10.08	8.4	-8.6	4	3.94	4.3
Inflation rate (%)	1.56	4.97	4.91	-0.2	4.24	11.5	9.9
Interest rate (%)		7.14	4	7	5	9.75	5
Government debt to GDP (%)	7.8	121	73.95	52.6	37.7	87	101
Corporate tax rate (%)	20		25.17	15		29	24
Competitiveness Rank	165	82	68		108	110	84
Corruption Rank		24	86	75	117	124	94
Ease of doing business	173	89	63	147	94	108	99
Coronavirus vaccination rate	13.13	148	95.4	144	64.56	59.87	144

Source: Trading Economics (2021a)

COMMONALITY AND VULNERABILITY OF THE SAARC COUNTRIES

The socio economic indicators shown in table 4 indicate that each SAARC country except has a certain limitation in the socio economic indicators. Kalra (2009) found that, Affordability, accessibility and timeliness of short-term and export credits, timely payments, technology upgradation, right manpower, poor quality control, limited business information. Apart from this, poor infrastructure facilities, airports, ports, roads, power, low internet connectivity, inadequate information, about rules and regulations governing trade between SAARC countries and time consuming procedures for export and import which increase the transaction cost of business also are some the common obstacles that they face (Kalra, 2009).

LESSONS FOR THE SAARC COUNTRIES

The SAARC countries may adopt the following initiatives to avoid the potential debt trap and diseconomies of scale:

- Adopting a diversified development partnership.
- To separate the development partnership from the trade relationship.
- To control the debt to GDP ratio and to keep the external debt below 40% of the GDP.
- To seek for low interest and long term credit facilities.
- To revise the cost structure associated with the development projects to keep the costs minimum and to finish the development work quickly.
- To distribute the infrastructural development work to as many developers as possible.

DISCUSSION

Therefore it can be assumed that if the three Ps of Bangladesh-Australia relations, namely: potential for growth, pragmatism and people-centricity based on the Commonwealth values are observed that might facilitate the deepening the economic and development cooperation and bilateral trade with Bangladesh from shedding light on global issues. The countries will focus on the Rohingya crisis, migration, climate change, cooperation on transnational crime (since 2015) and strategic interests in Indian Ocean Rim Association (IORA) chaired by Bangladesh since October 2021. Australia is the third popular destination for Bangladeshi students with about 50,000 Bangladeshis living in Australia. Australia is also an observer in SAARC where Bangladesh is a member. The basis of Australia-Bangladesh relations hinges primarily on economic(particularly FDI, imports and exports), political pursuits, and mutual interests complemented by Australian humanitarian and development assistance program which seems marginal if compared to other partners of Bangladesh like: Japan, USA, UK, Germany, and People's Republic of China (PRC) (Kamal & Ahmed, n.d.).

FUTURE RESEARCH DIRECTION

This study will enable a great opportunity to the other researchers, government and NGOs to take the knowledge further by conducting various studies on Bangladesh and Australia relation in particular. Further the debt-trap impact of the One-belt and road initiative on Bangladesh or Srilanka and lessons for the SAARC nations can be studied to make SAARC functional to help each other in infrastructure development with strategic partnership with Australia in trade, investment and security.

LIMITATION

The study is based on secondary literature. Therefore, some of the information may be subjected to the subjective judgment and critique by the author.

CONCLUSION

Therefore the study would propose that the Bangladesh should take the opportunity partnership with Australia will be very significant in case of Bangladesh particularly for skill enhancement, trade facilitation, technology transfer, learning and innovation and many more. Bangladesh's success has attracted many other partners, and the landscape is competitive. The Australian government, including through Export Finance Australia and Austrade, should consider some of the policies other countries have already used to develop market share in Bangladesh to grow Australia's presence. While it does have significant structural issues to address, many observers are cautiously optimistic that Bangladesh will be able to move up the manufacturing value chain. Australia is well placed to supply the country with natural resources and value-added inputs, as it has done elsewhere in the region as countries industrialized. Australia is also well suited to providing to a greater range and level of services, as has been done in the education sector where Australia has an established brand name in country.

Bangladesh understands the need to both attract new investment and diversify its economy in order to lessen its dependence on the ready-made garment sector, remittances from its large diaspora, and some light manufacturing. The country has been increasingly active in looking at how it can attract the necessary investment, both to help in this diversification push and to modernize its infrastructure. Australian investors, especially those with an appetite for – and experience in – investing in Asian infrastructure, should take note.

Both countries are also wary of being dominated by larger and more assertive neighbours. And Bangladesh is rising in prominence as a potential partner on strategic issues in the region. While there are some tensions between Bangladesh and India, the relationship is sturdy, and increased cooperation between Bangladesh and Australia in this area is unlikely to draw ire from Quad partner India, (Augustin, 2021). In last 50 years Bangladesh got a versatile growth wherein the contribution of Australia was remarkable. At present with the onset of COVID 19, the global tension in the pacific, influence of the rising China it is important to look for alternative choices to forge a sustainable solution for the coming days. Therefore, it is likely that the relations will proceed further if the interests like Strategic partnership of Australia and Bangladesh can be nurtured to curb the Maritime Power, One-Belt One-Road and Debt Trap of the rising China, and the lessons for SAARC nations.

ACKNOWLEDGMENT

The author is grateful to Professor Dr. Mahboob Ali and Entrepreneurship Economics Programme, Dhaka School of Economics, University of Dhaka Bangladesh for their guidance and support throughout the study.

REFERENCES

Akram, M., & Scholar, M. P. (2018). *Chinese investment in Asian country beneath the Umbrella of CPEC: A Blessing or Debt entice*. The Islamia University of Bahawalpur.

Ali, M. (2020, December 27). Bangladesh's economy to be 25th largest by 2035 [Review of *Bangladesh's economy to be 25th largest by 2035*]. *The Business Standard*. https://www.tbsnews.net/economy/bangladeshs-economy-be-25th-largest-2035-177334

Asia-Pacific Trade and Investment Report 2016. (2016). Retrieved from https://repository.unescap.org/bitstream/handle/20.500.12870/155/ESCAP-2016-FS-APTIR-executive-summary.pdf?sequence=5&isAllowed=y

Augustin, B. (2021, September 24). *Australia–Bangladesh: A Booster Dose for Trade Diversity?* [Review of *Australia–Bangladesh: A Booster Dose for Trade Diversity?*]. Australia Outlook; Australian Institute of International Affairs. https://www.internationalaffairs.org.au/australianoutlook/australia-bangladesh-a-booster-dose-for-trade-diversity/

Australia Awards Global Tracer Facility Bangladesh Case Study: Economic Development. (2019). https://www.dfat.gov.au/sites/default/files/australia-awards-global-tracer-facility-bangladesh-alumni-case-study.pdf

Australia's development partnership with Bangladesh. (n.d.). *Australian Government Department of Foreign Affairs and Trade*. Retrieved from https://www.dfat.gov.au/geo/bangladesh/development-assistance/development-assistance-in-bangladesh

Azim, M. A. (2019). Bangladesh-China economic relations: Opportunities and challenges. In D. Hossain (Ed.), *Bangladesh-East Asia relations: Changing scenarios and evolving linkages* (pp. 119–141). East Asia Study Center, University of Dhaka.

Bangladesh at 50: Navigating Strategic Survival. (2021, April 26). *War on the Rocks*. https://warontherocks.com/2021/04/bangladesh-at-50-navigating-strategic-survival

Bangladesh Military Strength. (2021). www.globalfirepower.com. https://www.globalfirepower.com/country-military-strength-detail.php?country_id=bangladesh

Barua, M., Mutsuddy, S., Mohammad, N., & Razak, M. A. (2019, February). A Survey of Cross Country Generation Mix-Opportunities and Challenges: Bangladesh, Australia, and the USA Perspectives. In *2019 International Conference on Electrical, Computer and Communication Engineering (ECCE)* (pp. 1-6). IEEE. 10.1109/ECACE.2019.8679344

Berg, B. (2001). *Qualitative research methods for the social sciences* (4th ed.). Allyn & Bacon.

BIDA. (2021). *Why Bangladesh* [Review of *Why Bangladesh*]. Bangladesh Investment Development Authority; Government of the People's Republic of Bangladesh. https://bida.gov.bd/

Bokhari, K. (2017, November 21). *China's One Belt, One Road Faces Pushback*. Geopolitical Futures. https://geopoliticalfutures.com/chinas-one-belt-one-road-faces-pushback/

Brahma Chellaney. (2017, January 23). *China's debt-trap diplomacy*. The Strategist. https://www.aspistrategist.org.au/chinas-debt-trap-diplomacy/

Brewster, D. (2021). New Indo-Pacific Partnership: Building Australia-Bangladesh Security Ties [Review of *New Indo-Pacific Partnership: Building Australia-Bangladesh Security Ties*]. In *Australian National University* (pp. 1–4). National Security College, Australian National University. https://nsc.crawford.anu.edu.au/sites/default/files/publication/nsc_crawford_anu_edu_au/2021-06/nsc_policy_options_paper_bangladesh_web_1.pdf

Byron, R. K. (2021, February 17). Dhaka-Sylhet Highway: Big plan for wider road [Review of *Dhaka-Sylhet Highway: Big plan for wider road*]. *The Daily Star*. https://www.thedailystar.net/backpage/news/dhaka-sylhet-highway-large-plan-big-stretch-2046049

Capital. (2014, August 26). *The State Council, The People's Republic of China*. Retrieved from http://english.www.gov.cn

Chellaney, B. (2017, January 23). *China's Debt-Trap Diplomacy*. Project Syndicate. https://www.project-syndicate.org/commentary/china-one-belt-one-road-loans-debt-by-brahma-chellaney-2017-01

China Power. (2018). *How dominant is China in the global arms trade?* https://chinapower.csis.org/china-global-arms-trade/

China Trade: Balancing Opportunities & Risks in One Belt One Road. (2018, December 12). *The One Brief.* https://theonebrief.com/chinas-global-ambition-balancing-opportunities-and-risks-in-one-belt-one-road/

China's trade ties with Bangladesh are deepening. (2021, July 14). *Dhaka Tribune*. https://www.dhakatribune.com/business/economy/2021/07/14/china-s-trade-ties-with-bangladesh-are-deepening

Chinese Ambassador Proposes belt and Road mechanism for Bangladesh. (2018). https://bdnews24.com/neighbours/2018/09/11/chinese-ambassador-proposesbelt-and-roadmechanismfor-bangladesh

Chittagong-Cox's Bazar Railway Line - Railway Technology. (n.d.). Retrieved November 20, 2021, from https://www.railway-technology.com/projects/chittagong-coxs-bazar-railway-line/

Chowdhury, M. B. (2019). Australia Bangladesh trade and investment potential. *ABBC Business Journal*, 64-68.

Chronology of China's Belt and Road Initiative. (2015, March 28). *The State Council, The People's Republic of China.* Retrieved from http://english.www.gov.cn

CIA. (2021, March 11). *The World Factbook.* Www.cia.gov. https://www.cia.gov/the-world-factbook/

Consulate General of Bangladesh. (2021). *Bangladesh-Australia Trade Relations* [Review of Bangladesh-Australia Trade Relations]. Consulate General of Bangladesh, Sydney; Government of People's Republic of Bangladesh. https://cgbdsydney.gov.bd/trade-and-investment/trade/

Creswell, J. W. (2003). *Research design: Qualitative, quantitative, and mixed methods approach.* SAGE.

Datta, S. (2019). *Bangladesh: Leveraging Its Locational Advantage.* Vivekananda International Foundation. https://www.vifindia.org/print/5757

Datta, S. (2021). Bangladesh and Belt Road Initiative: Unfolding Possibilities [Review of *Bangladesh and Belt Road Initiative: Unfolding Possibilities*]. *National Security, 4*(3), 254–271. https://www.vifindia.org/sites/default/files/national-security-vol-4-issue-3-article-Sreeradha Datta.pdf

DFAT. (2021). *Australia's development partnership with Bangladesh* [Review of *Australia's development partnership with Bangladesh*]. Development Assistance in Bangladesh; Department of Foreign Affairs and Trade, Australian Government. https://www.dfat.gov.au/geo/bangladesh/development-assistance/development-assistance-in-bangladesh

Dull, J. L. (2021, January 26). China. In *Encyclopedia Britannica.* Retrieved from https://www.britannica.com

Economic Relations Division. (2020). Flow of External Resources into Bangladesh [Review of *Flow of External Resources into Bangladesh*]. In *Bangladesh National Portal.* Ministry of Finance, Government of the People's Republic of Bangladesh. https://erd.gov.bd/site/page/565de360-e511-4758-a966-459d0dc1acfa/Flow-of-External-Resources-2019-20

Elliott, J. A. (2013). *An Introduction to Sustainable Development* (4th ed.). Routledge.

Embassy of China. (2011, May 19). *History and Legend of Sino-Bangla Contacts* [Review of *History and Legend of Sino-Bangla Contacts*]. Embassy of China; Government of the People's Republic of China. https://www.mfa.gov.cn/ce/cebd//eng/sbgx/t823712.htm

Fairman, C. (2019, August 23). Payra Seaport Won't Be Another Chinese "Pearl" [Review of *Payra Seaport Won't Be Another Chinese "Pearl"*]. *The Diplomat*. https://thediplomat.com/2019/08/payra-seaport-wont-be-another-chinese-pearl/

Faiz, M., & Maitra, P. (2020). Concentration and Diversification of Export Economy of Bangladesh: Comparison and Policy Implication with Other Asian Countries. *South Asian Journal of Social Studies and Economics*, 19-36.

Faruqui, G. A., Ara, L. A., & Acma, Q. (2015). TTIP and TPP: Impact on Bangladesh and India Economy. *Pacific Business Review International*, *8*(2), 59–67.

Fereday, J., & Muir-Cochrane, E. (2006). Demonstrating rigor using thematic analysis: A hybrid approach of inductive and deductive coding and theme development. *International Journal of Qualitative Methods*, *5*(1), 80–92.

Guest, G. (2012). *Applied thematic analysis*. Sage Publications.

Haider, A. Q. (2021, June 4). China: A development partner of Bangladesh [Review of *China: A development partner of Bangladesh*]. *The Financial Express*. https://thefinancialexpress.com.bd/views/china-a-development-partner-of-bangladesh-1622824911

Hauxia. (2021, November 10) a. Bangladesh approves Chinese-funded highway project in capital Dhaka [Review of *Bangladesh approves Chinese-funded highway project in capital Dhaka*]. *Xinhuanet*. http://www.news.cn/english/2021-11/10/c_1310303258.htm

Hauxia. (2021, September 26). *Bangladeshis to see end of boats-only experience in river-crossing traffic as China helps build new bridge* (Hauxia, Ed.) [Review of *Bangladeshis to see end of boats-only experience in river-crossing traffic as China helps build new bridge*]. Xinhuanet. http://www.xinhuanet.com/english/asiapacific/2021-09/26/c_1310211100_2.htm

Health Silk Road of China: A New "Debt-Trap Health Diplomacy" in Making. (n.d.). *Diplomatist*. Retrieved from https://diplomatist.com/2020/06/29/health-silk-road-of-china-a-new-debt-trap-health-diplomacy-in-making/

Holloway, I., & Todres, L. (2003). The status of method: Flexibility, consistency and coherence. *Qualitative Research*, *3*(3), 345–357.

Hossain, D., & Islam, M. S. (2021). Understanding Bangladesh's relations with India and China: Dilemmas and responses. *Journal of the Indian Ocean Region*, *17*(1), 42–59.

International Monetary Fund. (2020). *Helping Bangladesh Recover from COVID-19* [IMF News]. https://www.imf.org/en/News/Articles/2020/06/11/na-06122020-helping-bangladesh-recover-from-covid-19.

International Monetary Fund Bangladesh. (2015). *Letter of Intent and Memorandum of Economic and Financial Policies*. https://www.imf.org/external/np/loi/2015/bgd/100515.pdf

ISSAfrica.org. (2018, February 21). *Lessons from Sri Lanka on China's "debt-trap diplomacy."* ISS Africa. https://issafrica.org/iss-today/lessons-from-sri-lanka-on-chinas-debt-trap-diplomacy

Johnson, C. (2016). *President Xi Jinping's Belt and Road initiative, A Practical Assessment of the Chinese Communist party's Road Map for China's Global Resurgence*. A Report of the CSIS Freeman Chair in China Studies.

Joint Statement from Quad Leaders. (2021, September 25). *The White House*. https://www.whitehouse.gov/briefing-room/statements-releases/2021/09/24/joint-statement-from-quad-leaders/

J.P. (2017, May 15). What is China's belt and road initiative? *The Economist*. Retrieved, from https://www.economist.com

Kalra, K. (2009, October 31). Tackling the common problems in Saarc nations [Review of *Tackling the common problems in Saarc nations*]. *Financial Express*. https://www.financialexpress.com/archive/tackling-the-common-problems-in-saarc-nations/534963/

Kamal, U., & Ahmed. (n.d.). *Three Decades of Australia -Bangladesh Relations: Future Directions and Potentials*. http://www.biliabd.org/article%20intl/Vol-08/Kamal%20Uddin%20Ahmed.pdf

Khatun, F., & Saadat, S. Y. (2020, November 19). How can Bangladesh benefit from the Belt and Road Initiative? [Review of *How can Bangladesh benefit from the Belt and Road Initiative?*]. *Dhaka Tribune*. https://www.dhakatribune.com/opinion/op-ed/2020/11/19/op-ed-how-can-bangladesh-benefit-from-the-belt-and-road-initiative

Kidney, S., & Oliver, P. (2014). Greening China's financial markets. *Growing a Green Bonds Market in China*.

Kukreja, M.D., & Upadhyay, H. (2019). *A Study of External Debt Trap Threat Faced by Indian Economy*. Academic Press.

Mahanty, J. N. (1983). China and the Emergence of Bangladesh: Role of Great Power Global Perceptions. *India Quarterly*, *39*(2), 137–158.

Mamun, S. (2021, February 17). Construction of Dhaka-Ashulia Elevated Expressway finally set to begin [Review of *Construction of Dhaka-Ashulia Elevated Expressway finally set to begin*]. *Dhaka Tribune*. https://www.dhakatribune.com/bangladesh/2021/02/17/construction-of-dhaka-ashulia-elevated-expressway-finally-set-to-begin

Maritime Gateway. (2021, June 9). *Will Bangladesh be a victim to China's debt trap?* [Review of *Will Bangladesh be a victim to China's debt trap?*]. Maritime Gateway. https://www.maritimegateway.com/will-bangladesh-be-a-victim-to-chinas-debt-trap/

Miles, M., & Huberman, A. (1994). *An expanded sourcebook: qualitative data analysis*. Sage Publications.

Modak, S. (2020, November 11). *The Teesta quagmire: India's missed opportunity?* [Review of *The Teesta quagmire: India's missed opportunity?*]. Observer Research Foundation. https://www.orfonline.org/research/the-teesta-quagmire-indias-missed-opportunity/

Mohan, C. R. (2011). South Asia Rising. *The Indian Express*. https://indianexpress.com/article/opinion/columns/south-asia-rising/

Molson, M. (2021). China's Foreign Policy of giving huge loans to developing countries, whether it is an advantageous practice to fund development or a form of debt trap policy. *Moko Molson*. https://www.academia.edu/43317139/Chinas_Foreign_Policy_of_giving_huge_loans_to_developing_countries_whether_it_i

Okeleke, K. (2021). Achieving mobile-enabled digital inclusion in Bangladesh [Review of *Achieving mobile-enabled digital inclusion in Bangladesh*]. In *GSMA* (pp. 6–7). GSMA (Swedish International Development Cooperation Agency, Sida). https://www.gsma.com/mobilefordevelopment/wp-content/uploads/2021/03/Achieving-mobile-enabled-digital-inclusion-in-Bangladesh.pdf

One Belt, One Road (OBOR) Initiative: How Bangladesh can benefit through the new horizon of regional co-operation. (2017, June 19). *Light Castle Partners*. https://www.lightcastlebd.com/insights/2017/06/one-belt-one-road-obor-initiative-bangladesh-can-benefit-new-horizon-regional-co-operation

OP-ED: How do we attract FDI in the time of corona? (2020, May 28). *Dhaka Tribune*. https://www.dhakatribune.com/opinion/op-ed/2020/05/28/a-realignment-of-priorities-in-light-of-covid-19

Pitman, A. (n.d.). *Why Bangladesh has been ignoring India's warnings about the Chinese "debt trap."* Scroll.in. Retrieved from https://scroll.in/article/997715/why-bangladesh-has-been-ignoring-indias-warnings-about-the-chinese-debt-trap

Plagemann, J. (2021). Small states and competing connectivity strategies: What explains Bangladesh's success in relations with Asia's major powers? *The Pacific Review*, 1–29.

Rahman, M. M. (2020, August 10). BD gets $1.0b China loan to improve power grid [Review of *BD gets $1.0b China loan to improve power grid*]. *The Financial Express*. https://thefinancialexpress.com.bd/trade/bd-gets-10b-china-loan-to-improve-power-grid-1596857911

Rahman, S. M., & Akter, H. (2020). Bilateral trade relation between Bangladesh and Australia. In *The Economic Development of Bangladesh in the Asian Century* (pp. 29–62). Routledge.

Ranasinghe, K. (2019). Chinese loans are not the primary cause of the Sri Lankan debt crisis [Review of *Chinese loans are not the primary cause of the Sri Lankan debt crisis*]. *Ceylon Today*. https://www.academia.edu/38868730/Chinese_loans_are_not_the_primary_cause_of_the_Sri_Lankan_debt_crisis

Rasul, S. N. (2020, May 28). How do we attract FDI in the time of corona? [Review of *How do we attract FDI in the time of corona?*]. *Dhaka Tribune*. https://www.dhakatribune.com/opinion/op-ed/2020/05/28/a-realignment-of-priorities-in-light-of-covid-19

Riessman, C. (2006). Narrative analysis. In V. Jupp (Ed.), *The sage dictionary of social research methods* (pp. 186–189). Sage Publications.

Sakhawat, N. (2020, October 6). China-Bangladesh relations stronger than ever before [Review of *China-Bangladesh relations stronger than ever before*]. *The Daily Star*. https://www.thedailystar.net/opinion/news/china-bangladesh-relations-stronger-ever-1972993

Sakib, A. N. (2019). Corruption and organized crime in Bangladesh. In *Organized Crime and Corruption Across Borders* (pp. 241–256). Routledge.

Sarker, P. C. (2019). One Belt one road project is a driving force for holistic development of Eurasian region: challenges to Bangladesh. In *Silk Road to Belt Road* (pp. 279–291). Springer.

Sarwar. (2020, November 19). *How can Bangladesh benefit from the Belt and Road Initiative? - Fahmida Khatun and Syed Yusuf Saadat - CPD*. Centre for Policy Dialogue (CPD). https://cpd.org.bd/how-can-bangladesh-benefit-from-the-belt-and-road-initiative/

Scutaru, L. (2013). Economic Development versus Sustainable Development. *ECOFORUM, 1*(2), 35-40.

Shazzad, H. (2021, November 8). Is Bangladesh at risk of falling into the Chinese debt trap? *The Daily Star*. https://www.thedailystar.net/views/opinion/news/bangladesh-risk-falling-the-chinese-debt-trap-2224391

Similarities And Differences Between Australia and Bangladesh. (n.d.). Retrieved from https://www.cram.com/essay/Similarities-And-Differences-Between-Australia-And-Bangladesh/P3SPYFFNB5ZQ#google_vignette

Suman, M. (2021, October 9). Tunnel of hope: Breakthrough achieved in construction under Karnaphuli. *The Daily Star.* https://www.thedailystar.net/news/bangladesh/transport/news/tunnel-hope-2193871

Szczudlik-Tatar, J. (2013). *China's New Silk Road Diplomacy*. Polish Institute of International Affairs.

The Belt and Road Initiative. (2018, May 3). *HKTDC Research*. Retrieved January 26, 2021, from https://research.hktdc.com/en/

The BRI in Bangladesh. (2021). *"Win-Win" or a "Debt Trap"?* Retrieved from https://thediplomat.com/2021/11/the-bri-in-bangladesh-win-win-or-a-debt-trap/

The Business Standard. (2020, July 9). *Will China Deliver on its Rohingya Assurance?* https://tbsnews.net/opinion/will-china-deliver-its-rohingya-assurance

The Business Standard. (2021). https://www.tbsnews.net/economy/target-1-china-market-smooth-ldc-graduation-experts-329260

The Daily Star. (2020, October 15). *Seven BAF training aircraft procured from China arrive*. https://www.thedailystar.net/seven-baf-training-aircraft-procured-from-china-arrive-1978617

The Financial Express. (n.d.). *Harnessing benefits from OBOR initiative*. Retrieved from https://thefinancialexpress.com.bd/views/harnessing-benefits-from-obor-initiative-1553962144

Tithila, K. K. (2021, October 13). Higher studies in China: A new horizon for Bangladeshi students [Review of *Higher studies in China: A new horizon for Bangladeshi students*]. *Dhaka Tribune*. https://www.dhakatribune.com/bangladesh/education/2021/10/13/higher-studies-in-china-a-new-horizon-for-bangladeshi-students

Tripathi, S. (2021). *Bangladesh's Long Journey From "Basket Case" to Rising Star*. Foreign Policy. Retrieved from https://foreignpolicy.com/2021/04/10/bangladesh-independence-anniversary-basket-case-rising-star/

Uddin, M. J., & Bhuiyan, M. R. (2011). Sino-Bangladesh Relations: An Appraisal. *Strategic Analysis, 32*(1), 1–24.

Were, A. (2018). *Debt trap? Chinese loans and Africa's development options*. Academic Press.

WilburC. M. (2021). https://www.britannica.com/place/China

Will, X. W. (2015). *A Story of Doomed Bulls: On the Cause of High Debt Rate Behind 2015 Chinese Stock Crash*. Academic Press.

World Bank. (2018, March 29). *Belt and Road Initiative*. World Bank. https://www.worldbank.org/en/topic/regional-integration/brief/belt-and-road-initiative

World Bank. (2018). *The World Bank*. Retrieved from http://www.worldbank.org

Yukun, L., Kun, L., & Lihua, Z. (2019, July 23). Chinese firm progressing with Padma Bridge project [Review of *Chinese firm progressing with Padma Bridge project*]. *China Daily*. http://www.chinadaily.com.cn/a/201907/23/WS5d366fa8a310d83056400807.html

ADDITIONAL READING

Chowdhury, M. B. (2019). Australia Bangladesh trade and investment potential. *ABBC Business Journal*, 64-68.

Chronology of China's Belt and Road Initiative. (2015, March 28). *The State Council, The People's Republic of China*. Retrieved from http://english.www.gov.cn

Rahman, S. M., & Akter, H. (2020). Bilateral trade relation between Bangladesh and Australia. In *The Economic Development of Bangladesh in the Asian Century* (pp. 29–62). Routledge. doi:10.4324/9781003088165-4

Sarker, P. C. (2019). One Belt one road project is a driving force for holistic development of Eurasian region: challenges to Bangladesh. In *Silk Road to Belt Road* (pp. 279–291). Springer. doi:10.1007/978-981-13-2998-2_16

KEY TERMS AND DEFINITIONS

Australian Aid: Australian Aid is the brand name used to identify projects in developing countries supported by the Australian Government. The Department of Foreign Affairs and Trade has been responsible for Australia's official development assistance to developing countries. The fundamental purpose of Australian aid is to help people overcome poverty. This also serves Australia's national interests by promoting stability and prosperity both in our region and beyond.

Belt Road Initiative: The BRI is an ambitious plan to develop two new trade routes connecting China with the rest of the world. But the initiative is about far more than infrastructure. It is an effort to develop an expanded, interdependent market for China, grow China's economic and political power, and create the right conditions for China to build a high technology economy.

Debt Trap Diplomacy: Debt-trap diplomacy is a concept in international finance used to describe a powerful lending country or institution extending debt to a borrowing nation partially or solely for the lender to increase its political leverage.

Defence/Security: Defense is the resistance against danger, attack, or harm; protection. a person or thing that provides such resistance. a plea, essay, speech, etc, in support of something; vindication; justification. Usually, the Military forces in any country are deployed to safeguard the national assets.

Free Trade Agreement: A free trade agreement is a pact between two or more nations to reduce barriers to imports and exports among them. Under a free trade policy, goods and services can be bought and sold across international borders with little or no government tariffs, quotas, subsidies, or prohibitions to inhibit their exchange.

Partnership: A partnership is a formal arrangement by two or more parties to manage and operate a business and share its profits. There are several types of partnership arrangements. In particular, in a partnership business, all partners share liabilities and profits equally, while in others, partners may have limited liability.

SAARC Nations: The South Asian Association for Regional Cooperation (SAARC) is an economic and political organization of eight countries in South Asia. It was established in 1985 when the Heads of State of Bangladesh, Bhutan, India, Maldives, Nepal, Pakistan, and Sri Lanka formally adopted the charter.

Chapter 9
Medical, Pharmaceutical, and Healthcare Trade Relationships Between Australia and South Asian Nations

Ahmad A. Okasha
https://orcid.org/0000-0002-3769-1066
Canadian University Dubai, UAE

Eman Zabalawi
Amity University, Dubai, UAE

ABSTRACT

The global coronavirus (COVID-19) pandemic shocked the whole world. It had a disastrous impact on the economies and the healthcare systems of South Asian countries. Australia was able to minimize the COVID-19 impact by imposing a strict lockdown. The healthcare system and the healthcare industry in Australia are advanced and provide high quality pharmaceutical products and healthcare services. Australia has a lot to offer to South Asian countries in public health programs, quality of healthcare, complementary medicine products, clinical data management and development, and drug developments. Healthcare systems in South Asian countries vary significantly. Australia can play a significant role in developing the healthcare systems of South Asia. For instance, Australia can provide the traditional medicine sectors in South Asian countries with scientifically effective complementary medicines. Improving healthcare bilateral investment and the trade relationship between South Asia countries and Australia is a win/win partnership for SAARC nations post pandemic.

INTRODUCTION

Australia has robust health, medical, and pharmaceutical sectors and well-respected health care providers. Australia's healthcare and social assistant programs employ more than 1.7 million people (Health,

DOI: 10.4018/978-1-7998-8657-0.ch009

2021). The healthcare market industry in Australia is expected to grow to reach US$42.5 Billion (Drug-dev.com, 2021). In 2019, the value of the pharmaceutical industry global exports overall was US$3.85 billion (Statista.com). In addition, Australia's nutrition supplement sector continues to grow, and currently, it is valued at US$3.9bn per year. Exports grew by another 15% to US$766 million (Tingming, 2021). The health insurance market in Australia is estimated at US$26 billion. With the relative decline of the United States global economic power and the shift of global economic power towards the east, Australia realized the importance of countries in South Asia countries. South Asian countries formed the South Asian Association for Regional Cooperation (SAARC), including Bangladesh, Bhutan, India, Maldives, Nepal, Pakistan, and Sri Lanka. SAARC countries are also eager for Australia's involvement in economic development, including healthcare (Rozman & Liow, 2018).

The pandemic shocked the whole world and disrupted many aspects of our lives. COVID 19 pandemic also provided an opportunity for healthcare services growth. Australia has a lot to offer to South Asian Countries in public health programs, quality of healthcare, complementary medicine products, clinical data management and development, and drug developments.

South Asian countries have a high percentage of infectious and non-communicable diseases, with tuberculosis, diarrhoea, and pneumonia. They also have a high percentage of non-communicable diseases such as cardiovascular and mental health disorders. Approximately one-third of the world's child deaths occur in South Asian countries. Three-quarters of these deaths are due to diarrheal diseases, pneumonia, and neonatal conditions (Dhillon, et al., 2012).

This chapter starts with overall descriptions of healthcare systems in South Asia and Australia. Then it discusses the pharmaceutical and medical devices sectors in both Australia and South Asia. The chapter then analyzes the Impact of COVID-19 on South Asia and Australia, followed by analyzing issues, challenges that hinder improving bilateral trade relationships between South Asia and Australia. The chapter also analyses opportunities and recommends solutions and policy implications to improve the bilateral trade relationship between South Asia and Australia. Finally, the chapter discusses future research directions.

HEALTHCARE SYSTEMS IN SOUTH ASIA

South Asia is home to more than 24.8% of the world population (World Bank, 2020) and 40% of the poor in the world and 30% of the global disease burden (Dhillon, et al., 2012). The healthcare systems in SAARC countries vary. For instance, the Maldives enjoys a sound healthcare system and better overall health indicators than other South Asian countries. Alternatively, India, Pakistan, and Bangladesh have very high infant mortality and maternal mortality rates. The maternity and mortality indicators give a picture of the development of a healthcare system in a country.

LITERATURE REVIEW

Health Sector Overview: Australia and South Asian Countries

From a public health point of view, the risk factors for the high burden of diseases are low access to clean water, unavailable sewage systems, low sanitation, inadequate hygiene, limited access to healthcare

Table 1. Health indicators for South Asian countries

Indicator/ Country	Australia	Afghanistan	Bangladesh	Bhutan	India	Maldives	Nepal	Pakistan	Sri Lanka
Population in millions	25.6	38,9	164,7	0.771	1,380	.450	29.1	220.9	21.9
Life expectancy	83	63.2	74.3	73.1	70.8	79.6	70.9	65.6	76.9
Healthy life expectancy	83		56	55	56	75	55	56	63
Infant mortality rate (1000 live births)	3	45	22	20	27	5	23	56	6
Maternal mortality rates (100,000 live births)	6	638	173	183	145	53	186	140	36
Gross Domestic Product per capita	51812	509	1968	3122	1900	7455	1155	1193	3682
Health expenditures per capita	5187	49.8	41.1	102.7	72.8	973.5	57.8	42.8	157
Primary Education completion (%)	N/A	86	68	100	92	92	100	73	100

Sources: (World Bank, 2020), (Who 2019), (Statista.com, 2020), (World Bank, 2017). Healthy life expectancy is for 2012).

workers, and low awareness about personal health. Many people in South Asian countries travel a long distance to access a medical centre or a hospital.

South Asian countries account for 40% of the world's poor. The poor in those countries face multiple challenges: poverty, education, unemployment, gender inequalities, access to safe drinking water and sanitation, migration, urbanization, and globalization (Dhillon et al., 2012).

In most South Asian countries, there is a lack of hospital beds, physicians, medical equipment, and essential medications. In addition, only two countries have adequate universal healthcare coverage: Sri Lanka and Maldives (Hashim et al., 2012). COVID-19 came like a nightmare to Southeast Asia. It overwhelmed the healthcare systems in these countries. For instance, the Number of COVID-19 cases in India has reached 32 million, and deaths have reached 429,000. In Bangladesh, the total number of COVID-19 cases reached 1.47 million, and the number of deaths reached 25,153 (JHU CSSE COVID-19 Data, 2021).

According to the World Bank (2020), The COVID 19 situation in South Asia countries is hitting low-income workers hard. The healthcare systems in South Asia countries varies significantly. Table 1. shows Life expectancy for South Asian countries, ranging from 63.2 in Afghanistan to 79.6 in the Maldives. South Asia faces similar healthcare problems such as high incidence of infectious diseases, high maternal mortality rates, and low access to medical care.

Healthcare System Comparisons Between South Asian Countries

1. Afghanistan Healthcare System

Afghanistan healthcare system has been growing steadily over the last 17 years. A total of 3135 healthcare facilities were functional in the country in 2018 (World Health Organization, Afghanistan, 2021). As Table 1 above shows, Afghanistan has the lowest life expectancy in South Asian Countries. Decades of instability in the country have a toll on the population's health and the healthcare system in general. The recent withdrawal of the US troops from Afghanistan left the healthcare system under pressure.

Table 2. Selected healthcare indicators for South Asian countries

Indicator/ Country	Australia	Afghanistan	Bangladesh	Bhutan	India	Maldives	Nepal	Pakistan	Sri Lanka
Hospital beds per 1000 people	3.8	0.4*	0.8*	1.7*	0.5*	4.3*	0.3*	0.6*	4.2*
Physician per 1000 people	3.7	0.3*	0.5*	0.4*	0.8*	3.7*	0.9*	1.0*	0.9*
Hospitals	1350	150***	5816****	31****	2800****	21****	125****	1970****	628****
Basic Health Centers		873***	12527****	746****	200000****	62****	198****	5518****	474***
Community health workers per 1000 people		n/a	0.4*	0.1*	0.5*	1.8*	0.7*	0.1*	n/a
Nurses and midwives per 1000 people	12.6	0.2*	0.4*	1.9*	1.7*	6.4*	3.1*	0.7*	2.2*
Surgical procedures per 100,000 population	10156	n/a	161*	2639*	n/a	n/a	209*	n/a	4943*
Percentage of population using safe drinking water	100	n/a	55*	36*	n/a	n/a	27*	35*	n/a

Source: *: Word bank, 2017), (na: not available)
***Word Health Organization (WHO) 2020
**** Ministry of health data

Many healthcare workers have left the country to other neighboring countries. At the time of writing this chapter, it is unclear how the healthcare system will unfold.

2. Bangladesh Healthcare System

The healthcare system in Bangladesh is comprised of public and private healthcare services. There are three levels of care provided for government healthcare services: primary, secondary, and tertiary. The primary care is delivered through the Upazila Health Complexes (UHC) has 30 beds. The UHC hospitals are being upgraded to 50-80 bed hospitals. According to the Ministry of Health in Bangladesh, the secondary level district hospitals range from 100 beds to 250 beds and provide specialized care and primary care. The government has upgraded district hospitals from 100 beds to 150/200/250 beds. Regional Hospitals, Medical College Hospitals, and Specialized Hospitals (250-1700 beds) provide specialized and super-specialized services at the regional and central levels. Some of the regional hospitals also serve as teaching hospitals. Most of the secondary and tertiary level hospitals are linked with other hospitals as referral centres to coordinate the provision of Comprehensive Emergency Obstetric Care (Bangladesh Ministry of Health).

3. Bhutan Healthcare System

The Ministry of Health primarily drives the Bhutan healthcare system. Bhutan life expectancy has been improving significantly in the last 40 years as it is provisioned through three tiers. The first tier provides primary care level. The primary care level constitutes of basic health unit (BHU), sub-posts, and outreach clinics. The second tier is secondary care, which is provided through secondary or district hospitals. And the third tier is tertiary care which is provided through referral hospitals. Bhutan has difficult terrains and a dispersed population. The village health workers (VHWs) play a crucial role in health promotion and linking the community to the healthcare system (Bhutan Ministry of Health, 2010).

The primarily free healthcare services in Bhutan have focused on primary, prevention, and public health. The top three conditions in Bhutan are gastritis, neurological disorder, and arthritis. The country is also facing a rise in crime, substance abuse, and suicide cases.

The practice of medicine and healthcare workers are regulated by Bhutan Medical and Health Council (BMHC). The country had formulated a malpractice and negligence law. Medications, medical products, and medical technology are regulated through the Drug Regulatory Authority (DRA).

Bhutan has made great strides in developing comprehensive and up-to-date health information systems for its hospitals and clinics. The government has started a program to build electronic healthcare records for its citizens linking all hospitals and clinics. The country has established several telemedicine centres to improve access to the population living in remote areas.

Private sector participation is limited to retail pharmacies. However, the government is pondering how much it should let the private sector participate in healthcare services. Under Bhutan law, accessible primary healthcare services are mandated by the constitution.

4. India Healthcare System

Healthcare has become one of India largest industry sectors. The healthcare industry in India is expected to reach $198.3 billion (India Brand Equity Foundation, 2021). The Healthcare sector includes hospitals, medical devices, clinical trials, outsourcing, telemedicine, medical tourism, health insurance and medical equipment.

In Indian, healthcare services are provided through public and private organizations. The public healthcare services are delivered mainly through the government is limited to secondary and tertiary care organizations in key cities. The public healthcare sector includes basic healthcare facilities in primary healthcare centres (PHCs) in rural areas. Contrary to Bhutan, the private sector in India provides the majority of secondary, tertiary care organizations. Private hospitals in India are concentrated in metros and large cities. India is witnessing an increase in the middle-class population, which caused an increased demand for overall healthcare services and quality healthcare services. Health insurance coverage has also seen a massive increase due to the growth in the middle-class population. India's competitive advantage lies in its large pool of well-trained medical professionals. India is also cost-competitive compared to its peers in Asia and Western countries. The cost of surgery in India is about one-tenth of that in the US or Western Europe. The private sector in India is vibrant and leading much new development in healthcare in India. These are some of the recent developments:

1. The number of telemedicine consultations at the Ministry of Health virtual consultation program reached more than 6 million.
2. By March 2021, India will be exporting more vaccines than it had administered to its citizens. India has exported 60 million doses to 76 countries. India administered 52 million doses to its citizens. In addition, COVID-19 treatment, Remdesivir, witnessed an uptrend in exports. For example, exports doubled in March 2021 to $14.8 million from $5.75 million in February 2021
3. In March 2021, gross written premiums of health insurance companies in the non-life insurance sector increased by 41% YoY to Rs. 2,185.05 crore (US$ 294 million), driven by rising demand for health insurance products amid the COVID-19 surge.

4. In March 2021, the Parliament passed the National Commission for Allied Healthcare Professions Bill 2021, which aims to create a body that will regulate and maintain educational and service standards for healthcare professionals.
5. In the Union Budget 2021, investment in health infrastructure expanded 2.37x or 137% YoY; the total health sector allocation for FY22 stood at US$ 30.70 billion.
6. The Government of India is planning to increase public health spending to 2.5% of the country's GDP by 2025.
7. As of June 15, 2021, 26, 69,14,930 COVID-19 vaccine doses have been administered across the country (India Brand Equity Foundation, 2021).

India healthcare sector is in the growth model. The Indian healthcare sector is diversified and full of opportunities in every segment, including providers, payers, and medical technology. With the opening of the economy and the increased competition, businesses are looking to explore the latest dynamics and trends that will positively impact their business. The hospital industry in India is forecast to increase to US$ 132.84 billion by FY22.

5. Maldives Healthcare System

The Maldives government spends 9% of its GDP on health, the highest in the South Asia Region. Health services in the Maldives are currently delivered by a four-tier referral system comprising of the island, regional and central level services. Each island in the Maldives has a primary healthcare centre. In addition, each inhabited island has a hospital. The Indira Gandhi Memorial Hospital in Male' serves as the tertiary referral hospital. Six regional and 14 atoll hospitals in strategic locations across the country serve as the first referral while each of the inhabitant islands has a fully functional health centre. The Maldives continues to rely heavily on expatriate health professionals, who account for 82% of physicians and 55% of nurses and faces the challenges of high turnover and assuring the quality of the health workforce. Managing logistics and supplies across the islands centres and hospitals are challenging, and optimal information and communication technology is continuously explored. The Maldives enjoys a universal health insurance system. The healthcare system in the Maldives relies largely on expatriate healthcare workers (WHO, 2017).

6. Nepal Healthcare System

Nepal has made progress in raising the health status of its citizens. Under-five Mortality has been reduced by 67% and infant mortality by 59% during the twenty years. Similarly, maternal mortality has been reduced significantly (56%) between the period 1996 and 2016. The immunization coverage since 2011 had consistently remained above 90% for diphtheria, tetanus toxoid and pertussis (DPT) and Polio. However, it slightly decreased during 2015 – 2016.

On the other hand, measles coverage has been improved and reached 88% in 2016 from 83% in 2014, which may be due to health sector efforts toward measles elimination. The country has achieved polio eradication, and measles elimination is targeted for 2019. The "Full Immunization Declaration" approach aims at immunizing all children through a robust community engagement. Leprosy is at the elimination stage, and malaria is in the pre-elimination phase. Considerable efforts have been made to halt and reverse the trends of tuberculosis and human immunodeficiency virus (HIV). New HIV infections have been significantly declined; however, the gap remains between the estimated and identified HIV infection, resulting in low treatment coverage of 30% in 2015. Despite the stable CPR, the Total Fertility Rate (TFR) declined significantly from 5 births per woman in 1990 to 2.6 in 2011 and 2.3 in 2016.

The increasing migration trend exposes labour migrants to certain health risks and poses an additional challenge to address their health needs. Tuberculosis (TB) remains a public health problem in Nepal. However, the program can achieve a high success rate for the treatment of TB, which was 90% for new and relapse cases in the last five-year period. In the urban areas, inadequate physical activity and rapid and unplanned urbanization pose many health challenges, including an increased risk of non-communicable diseases. Air pollution is becoming an ever-increasing problem in the Kathmandu Valley and the southern Terai Region. Mental health problems are also increasing and further aggravated by migration, ageing population, poverty and widespread unemployment.

Moreover, Nepal is prone to natural disasters, which pose health problems. Despite the significant increase in government expenditure on health, out-of-pocket expenditure remains high (60% in 2010/2011). The Current Health Expenditures (CHE) in 2015 were 6.15% of Nepal's GDP or 44.4 US$ per capita. Nepal has been gearing towards addressing equity gaps and increasingly focused on making services accessible to the population in need. It has introduced free health care programs, targeted health package schemes and a safe delivery incentive scheme to minimize the equity gap. However, despite this, the country still faces many health challenges. The recent "Nepal Health Facility Survey" clearly shows challenges in delivering quality health services, retaining appropriate skilled human resources, and maintaining regular availability of essential commodities to deliver basic (World Health Organization, Nepal, 2017).

7. Pakistan Healthcare System

Pakistan has witnessed improvements in its political, security and social system. Per capita, the gross domestic product had improved in the last two decades but has declined in the last few years. Enhanced investment in economic development and high political commitment to health has resulted in some progress on universal access to health care, and Pakistan has shown some recent achievements in health with improving maternal and child mortality rates. The country is committed to augmenting the success of its socio-economic development, including improving health and education and ensuring social security for those in need. (Eastren Miditerranean WHO, 2021).

Non-communicable diseases and mental health represent more than half of Pakistan burden of diseases. Pakistan is ranked seventh highest in the world for diabetes prevalence. Pakistan has high hypertension and smoking levels. 25% of the adult population are hypertensive, and 38% smoke (Eastren Miditerranean WHO, 2021).

Both government and the private sector deliver the healthcare system in Pakistan. A significant strength of the government's health care system in Pakistan is a community outreach primary health care delivered by 100,000 Lady Health Workers (LHWs). There is also an increasing number of community midwives (CMWs), and other community-based workers. Those healthcare workers have earned success and trust in the communities. Like other South Asian countries, complementary, alternative and traditional care systems are also popular in Pakistan (Eastren Miditerranean WHO, 2021). The government spending on healthcare, which is 0.6% of the GDP, is low compared to the international level. The government has set a goal to raise this percentage to 3% by 2025 (Eastren Miditerranean WHO, 2021).

Health information systems currently in use in Pakistan are fragmented and highly specialized, and functional. They are focused mainly on the program that they serve. There is little integration between all of these programs. Therefore, health indicator data collated through various systems sometimes give conflicting results (Eastren Miditerranean WHO, 2021).

8. Sri-Lanka Healthcare System

Sri Lanka has witnessed significant improvements in healthcare system indicators such as infant mortality rates and life expectancy at birth. The country eliminated infectious diseases such as malaria, filariasis, Polio and neonatal tetanus, yet is expected to eliminate other diseases such as measles, congenital rubella syndrome, lymphatic filariasis, and leprosy.

As the country has improved its healthcare system over the years, the top causes of death in Sri Lanka are chronic and non-communicable diseases such as Ischemic heart disease and diabetes mellitus (World Health Organization Regional Office for Sout, 2021).

Sri-Lanka national hospital data show declining admissions for gastrointestinal infections and parasitic diseases. However, there are increasing new infections such as dengue, epidemic influenza and leptospirosis, and tuberculosis. These emerging infectious diseases pose challenges to health (World Health Organization Regional Office for Sout, 2021). Lifestyle-related risk factor such as obesity is increasing in Sri-Lanka.

Government tax revenue and private spending are the two primary sources of health financing in Sri Lanka. The Sri Lankan health system comprises western allopathic and other systems, namely Ayurveda, Siddha, Unani, acupuncture and deshiya chikitsa. The government of Sri Lanka provides primary care and most of the curative care for free at the point of delivery. The government provides a free point of care access, and most of the services are covered at 95% for inpatient and 50% for outpatient services.

The private sector mainly provides ambulatory care, limited inpatient care and rehabilitative care of varying degrees of sophistication. Private-sector services are financed through out of pocket payments and limited insurance plans. Out-of-pocket payments are increasing in Sri Lanka and represent 51% of healthcare expenditures (World Health Organization Regional Office for Sout, 2021). The Sri Lanka public health information system primarily comprises data from state government hospitals and primary healthcare centres.

The national system includes hospital information, preventive health information, administrative and operational information system, population census, civil registration and vital statistic system, and other specific population surveys (World Health Organization Regional Office for Sout, 2021).

PHARMACEUTICAL SECTOR: LITERATURE ON SOUTH ASIAN AND AUSTRALIAN COUNTRIES

Pharmaceutical Sector: South Asian Countries

the countries in the South Asian pharmaceutical sectors are in the early development phase of the pharmaceutical sector. Yet, the focus on the Indian pharmaceutical sector since it has a global reach and its government pushed for increased nationalization, leading to increased interest in science, research, and development.

Two Indian pharmaceutical firms mark the start of the modern pharmaceutical industry. These firms are Bengal Chemical and Pharmaceutical Work (BCPW) Ltd and Alembic Chemical Works Co. Ltd. These firms were set up in 1901, and 1907 respectively (Khtar, 2013). Currently, the Indian pharmaceutical industry is the third-largest sector in the Indian economy. The pharmaceutical sector reached US$ 36.7 billion in December 2016 and is expected to expand to US$ 55 billion by 2020. (Das, 2017). One of the challenges of the pharmaceutical industry in India is nationally controlled prices. However, the industry overcoming the challenges in the local economy by leveraging exports. For instance, Cipla, an Indian pharmaceutical firm, exports to more than 80 countries (Cipla, 2021). Another Indian global firm is Poonawala Serum Institute which is the world largest producer of vaccines. The Indian firm acquired Bilthoven Biologicals, a Belgium company, which brought access to the latest technology in injectable Polio Vaccine, Salk (Serum Institute of India Pvt. Ltd, 2021).

In2018, Indian pharmaceutical sector exports to Australia reached US$ 253.80 million with 7.5% increase. Main pharmaceutical products exported were drug formulations and biologicals. (Pharmexci, 2021). India has a significant potential to increase this value by increasing cooperation with the Indian pharmaceutical industry.

Healthcare Market and Pharmaceutical Sectors: Australian

Australia enjoys a nationally-funded healthcare system, Medicare. Australian Medicare enables patients to receive care free of charge at public hospitals (Callander, Fox, & Lindsay, 2019). Three levels of government are responsible for universal healthcare, which are federal, state, and local. The federal government provides funding and indirect support through Medicare Benefits System (MBS) and Pharmaceutical Benefits System (PBS). Government funding is the primary driver of the healthcare and pharmaceutical sectors in Australia (Mossialos & Wenzl, 2016).

The Australian Pharmaceutical Industry

The Australian pharmaceutical industry is comprised of biomedical research organizations, biotechnology firms, original and generic medicine manufacturers, and wholesaling and retailing companies. The primary customer for the pharmaceutical industry is the Australian Federal government. The Pharmaceutical Benefits Schemes (PBS), which is a component of the Medicare program, provide individuals in Australia with access to a wide range of needed medication and cost-effective prescription medications (Drug-dev.com, 2021)

The Australian pharmaceutical market is expected to reach 32.1 billion USD, driven by universal coverage of the Australian Medicare program (Drug-dev.com, 2021).

Australian Complementary Medicine and Wellness

COVID 19 has increased the demand for healthcare products around the world. Asian countries also are solid markets for complementary medicine products (Commonwealth of Australia, 2017). In Australia, complementary medicines include food supplements such as vitamins, minerals and other nutritional products. It also includes herbal, homoeopathic and aromatherapy medicines. In addition, Australian complementary medicine includes traditional medicines, Chinese medicine, Ayurvedic, Indigenous and Western herbal medicines (Commonwealth of Australia, 2017). The value of complementary medicine is estimated to be $1.4. The complementary medicine industry is heavily export-oriented. Total exports of complementary medicine products are estimated to be $677 million.

For instance, Life Space is one of the most popular international probiotics in China. Life-Space product is produced by Evolution, a leading complementary medicine company in Australia (Commonwealth of Australia, 2017). Vitex Pharma is another example of complementary medicine companies exporting to Asia countries. The National Institute of complementary medicine (NCICM) is cooperating with the Nanjing University of Chinese Medicine, is a leader in the development of Traditional Chinese Medicine (TCM) education in the Western world (Commonwealth of Australia, 2017).

Medical Devises Industry

The medical devices and diagnostic industry has been developing at a rapid rate. The medical devices industry is witnessing strong growth in digital health technologies and devices using advanced materials, robotics, imaging, IT, design and adaptive diagnostic technology platforms (Australia Trade Commission, 2016).

The medical devices industry in Australia is valued at $11.8, with exports estimated at $2.1 billion in 2013 (Australia Trade Commission, 2016).

MAIN FOCUS OF THE CHAPTER

Issues, Controversies, Problems and Challenges

Different challenges can impede the bilateral trade relationship between South Asian countries and Australia. The development of SAARC was supposed to promote mutual trust and understanding in South Asia. However, the SAARC block has not lived up to its ambitious goals. SAARC member states have fallen into fluctuating economic growth and volatile ethnic and religious conditions (Paul, Regional Cooperation in South Asia: Exploring the Three Pillars of Regionalism and their Relevance, 2020). The SAARC countries need to overcome many challenges to work with neighbouring countries such as Australia to advance their economies and tackle the myriad social and economic challenges.

With the relative decline of the United States power, Australia has been improving its trade relationship with South Asia countries in terms of exports. For instance, Australia has been strengthening its relationship with India (Thakur & Sharma, 2018).

Australia is in an excellent position to share and cooperate with SAARC countries to develop national healthcare strategies. The healthcare systems in South Asia vary in level, government interventions, financing, and privatization. Another issue is the low level of national health expenditures on health care, driving economic growth and increased bilateral relationships. For instance, Pakistan has a deficient national healthcare expenditure compared to other countries (Eastren Miditerranean WHO, 2021).

Another potential challenge is the varying levels of privatization of the healthcare sector in South Asian countries. For instance, Bhutan has limited the role of the private sector to retail pharmacies. Other sectors are all governed by local the Ministry of health (Bhutan Ministry of Health, 2010).

The Impact of COVID-19 on South Asian Economies

The COVID-19 pandemic hit the economies of South Asia hard. The formal and informal economies in those countries were brought to a grinding halt. Many South Asian countries initiated massive vaccination programs through their regions. However, the second wave of COVID 19 hits the healthcare systems and the economies insignificant (United State Institute of Peach, 2021; Usman et al., 2020). South Asian countries were hit hard mainly due to their large populations, high poverty levels and poor social-economic conditions (Rasul, et al., 2021). Many development projects financed and managed by China have stopped, such as Bangladesh and Pakistan (Usman, Ali, Riaz, Riaz, & Zubair, 2020).

The United State Institute of Peace published a report on the Impact of COVID-19 on South Asia. The report highlights that there was an increase in the inequality between wealthy and poor people. There was also an increase in food prices. This increased the pressure on policymakers in these countries. In addition, the report maintained that In Bangladesh, the slow growth of exports posed a challenge to Sheikh Hasina's economic growth plans. However, Bangladesh is expected to return to a high level of economic growth in 2022 and beyond (United State Institute of Peach, 2021).

In India, the resurgence of COVID-19 cases brought the Indian economy to another collapse. Oxygen shortages were reported across the country, the healthcare system virtually collapsed, crematoriums ran out of space, and bodies were seen floating in rivers. India was labelled as a "failed state" according to the United States Institute of Peach (2021).

In Bangladesh, the Pro reform government in Bangladesh led by Sheikh Hasina brought the GDP of Bangladesh from 40% lower than Pakistan in 1971 to 40% higher in 2021 (United State Institute of Peach, 2021). The carry-over effect of the GDP improvement impacted the healthcare system in Bangladesh as well.

At the time when Bangladesh was making progress in improving the economy, the COVID-19 hit hard. The government responded with a strict lockdown. The COVID-19 cases led to an increase in poverty which hit 40% of the population. With the reopening of the Economy, Bangladesh exported millions of personal protective equipment such as masks and gloves to many countries, including Australia (United State Institute of Peach, 2021).

The poverty rate in Bangladesh increased as indicated above, and absolute poverty tripped, climbing from 9.5 in 2018 to 28.5 in 2020. Bangladesh needs to diversify away from the heavy reliance on ready garment exports to more value-added exports. This will affect Bangladesh by losing it status as one of the least developed countries. By graduating from the least developed countries, Bangladesh will also lose many preferential economic benefits (Berg et al., 2021).

In 2020, the Hasina government were under criticism due to the mishandling of COVID-19 testing. The government responded by imposing fines on airlines bringing passengers with PCR tests and reshuffling officials in the health departments (United State Institute of Peach, 2021).

In Pakistan, the first cases of COVID-19 were reported On February 26, 2020. Similar to many developing countries, the pandemic could not have come at a worse time. Pakistan was experiencing slow growth before the pandemic. New jobs were difficult to come by, and high inflations exasperated the problems by eroding the purchasing power of many Pakistani families. As the Economy in Pakistan reached a standstill in March 2020, the government pushed a stimulus package. More than 15 million families received cash funds through the stimulus program (United State Institute of Peach, 2021).

The government in Pakistan formed National Command Operation Center (NCOC) to coordinate the COVID-19 response between the federal government and the local governments. Local governments ignored the opposition party's effort to disrupt the federal governments worked continued to cooperate with the federal government regarding COVID-19 (United State Institute of Peach, 2021).

Pakistan has many challenges ahead that need to be addressed. Pakistan is lagging behind its neighbours in terms of human development. Pakistan is behind Indian and Bangladesh in terms of youth literacy which stands for Pakistan around 75% (United State Institute of Peach, 2021).

The Impact of COVID-19 on the Australian Economy

The number of COVID-19 cases in Australia stood at around 56,121, and the number of deaths was 1006 (worldmeter, 2021). Australia geographical location and its social and political systems enable it to minimize the Impact of COVID-19. 16% of the Australian population are considered at-risk population. 30.3% of the COVID-19 deaths in Australia were among individuals 60 years of age or more (O'Sullivan, Rahamathulla, & Pawar, 2020). The government has instituted a strict national lockdown. Australia was able to minimize the effect of a pandemic on its economy. The expected unemployment rate stood around 10% in 2020, and it's expected to be reduced to 6% in the next two years (O'Sullivan et al., 2020). COVID-19 revealed weaknesses in the public healthcare system in Australia. Due to COVID, many essential healthcare program resources were compromised due to most of the resources directed toward COVID-19. COVID-19 revealed that the Australian healthcare system is highly dependent on imported medical inputs from India and China. An available stockpile of surgical masks stood only at 12 million (Bashkar, et al., 2020). The Indian government has limited the export of active pharmaceutical products and closed its border. Consequently, there were disruptions to supply the public healthcare services (Parlimant of Australia, 2021).

COVID-19 have effects on both the supplies and the demand of products and services in Australia. Many factories were closed due to the lockdown. In addition, as the government instituted the lockdown, many entertainments, hospitality, restaurants, elective medical procedures, and personal care services were severely affected (Bashkar, et al., 2020; O'Sullivan et al., 2020).

Australia's exports held steadily to historical numbers despite the COVID-19. The total value of Australia's goods exports hit a record high in March 2020 of $35.3 billion. While goods export values then dropped back 11.3 per cent to $31.4 billion in April, these levels are still relatively high by historical standards. These numbers indicate a resilient overall performance (Parlimant of Australia, 2021).

MEDICAL, PHARMACEUTICAL TRADE RELATIONS BETWEEN SOUTHERN ASIAN COUNTRIES AND AUSTRALIA

Australia has a stable and advanced economy that can benefit the regional economies of South Asia. Australia enjoys competitive, solid medical services, complementary medicine, pharmaceutical, drug discovery and clinical trial, and information technology industry segments. Australia can leverage these segments to build cooperation ties with South Asian countries. For instance, the pharmaceutical industry and medical devices segment is proliferating in India. Australia expertise in drug development, clinical trial administration can support India growth plans in these areas. Australia has built a solid complementary medicine segment. Many countries in South Asia have long and historical disciplines in osteopathic and traditional medicine. Australia can cooperate with traditional institutions. Australia has already done this with the traditional Chinese medicine institute. Sales of vitamin C supplements grew by more than 100% in 2020, compared to 2019. The overall vitamins category grew by 20% and reached 3 billion pills in 2020. This reflects growing opportunities for Australian supplements exporters, many of which are expanding their presence in India. E-commerce is a proven route to market in this sector.

A recent conference organized by Austrade South Asia convened stakeholders from the Australian and Indian healthcare industries. Significant opportunities were identified, including clinical data management, the use of clinical decision support tools, healthcare quality standards, and healthcare training.

Deakin University has teamed with AIIMS Jodhpur and IIT Jodhpur to begin clinical trials of medical devices for patients with neurological disorders. The program is the result of a collaborative research program between Deakin and institutes in India. India's drug and vaccine manufacturing industry is interested in partnering with institutions in Australia for collaboration, in-licensing and research (Australia Trade Commission, 2016).

Clinical research and pharmaceuticals companies are showing renewed interest in conducting clinical trials and joint research in Australia. According to sources, Indian medical care organizations continue to be receptive to Australian digital health products. Meanwhile, clinical research companies are collaborating well with Australian universities. Regional proximity and variance degree of economies between Australia and South Asian countries provide excellent opportunities to strengthen trade cooperation in the medical care, pharmaceutical, and complementary medicine segments. It is a win/win situation for both sides. Australia will enjoy increased exports, increased influence, and better regional relationships with its neighbours. South Asian countries will benefit from the technology transfer, high-quality products, and improvement in delivering care to their populations (Parlimant of Australia, 2021).

OPPORTUNITIES FOR AUSTRALIA AND SOUTH ASIA

Due to global power shifting from the west to the east, there are bountiful opportunities for bilateral trade relations in Australia and South Asia's medical, pharmaceutical, and complimentary medicine sectors. Main opportunities are health information technology, clinical trial management for drug and medical device development, biologics, complementary medicine, and education and training healthcare professionals.

Australia enjoys an advanced healthcare information sector. The country has implemented a national healthcare electronic healthcare record system that includes more than 22.7 million individuals. In addition, the Australian government has created the Digital Health Agency, an agency dedicated to transforming the Australian healthcare system to digital health (Department of Health Australia, 2021). Since the pandemic, many governments have realized the importance of health information technology. South Asian countries can cooperate with Australia to leverage the advanced health information technology knowledge that Australia has built over the last 70 years.

Another opportunity for bilateral trade between Australia and South Asia is the management of clinical trials for drug and device development. Not all countries in South Asia are in a position to benefit from this cooperation. India can reap huge benefits from such cooperation. Australia has developed high-quality assurance standards, drug and device development, and management of clinical trials. Australia can support Indian pharmaceutical and medical device manufacturers to develop and gain international approvals (Parlimant of Australia, 2021). In addition, Australian private pharmaceutical and medical device manufacturers can benefit from partnering with Indian healthcare providers to access millions of Indian patients and healthcare professionals. In addition, India can increase its penetration of the Australian healthcare sector in biologics such as vaccines and enzymes (Cipla, 2021).

Australia has built a global complementary medicine industry (Tingming, 2021). South Asia culture adopt and encourage traditional medicine and herbal medicine practice. Australia's complementary medicine sector can build on this momentum and focus its marketing and education campaign to target the traditional medicine providers in South Asia.

Higher education in Australia is in par with the best English teaching international higher education institutes. Many international students select Australia to pursue higher medical education (Breen & Birrel, 2020). Australia has also developed an academic program for complementary and Traditional Chinese medicine (Commonwealth of Australia, 2017). Australia can also play a role in standardizing higher medical and nursing education in South Asian countries.

SOLUTIONS AND RECOMMENDATIONS

Regional cooperation between Australia and South Asian countries is crucial for improving bilateral trade relationships in the medical and pharmaceutical fields. Bilateral trade relationships cannot be done in a vacuum. Social and public health cooperation need to be considered, especially in the global pandemic such as COVID-19. There are mutual benefits for both South Asian countries and Australia. The level of mutual benefits will vary from one country to another.

During the pandemic, there was a disruption of the pharmaceutical supply chain in Australia (Parlimant of Australia, 2021). Prior planning and regional cooperation between Australia and Indian, for instance, would prevent this from happening in future public health pandemics. In addition, regional workforce cooperation and taskforces can better enable steady supplies of needed vaccines, medical supplies, and healthcare professionals between South Asia and Australia.

Policymakers in South Asia need to study a gradual opening of the healthcare markets to privatization or joint cooperation with Australia. Bhutan, the Maldives, and Pakistan can benefit from analyzing how Australia has encouraged the privatization of specific health care markets.

India needs to develop policy, standards, and clinical governance structure to develop the clinical trial and research and development sector. This would require cooperation with Australia, which has developed its regulations for proper governance of clinical trials.

FUTURE RESEARCH DIRECTIONS

While conducting this study of the existing literature on the bilateral trade relationship between South Asia and Australia, limited research is available. More research is needed on needed first on individual country trade volume with Australia with regard to medical, pharmaceutical, and medical devices. Second, more research is needed to harmonies health data standards and share public health data between South Asia and Australia. The same is needed to study data security challenges and how South Asia and Australia can work together to minimize the risk of data security breaches.

It would be beneficial to have future research studying the financing mechanism available and how Australia can help South Asia countries access global financial markets.

It would also be of great value to study how South Asia and Australia can work together in medical tourism. India for instance, can provide Australia with more value-based care for certain individuals who need care. Research is needed to analyze which specialties India has competitive advantages and which specialties Australia still has competitive advantages.

CONCLUSION

Even though COVID-19 brought the economies of South Asian countries to a grinding halt, it also highlighted an opportunity to increase regional cooperation. Australia's geographical proximity and advanced healthcare industry enables it to support the growth of South Asian countries' healthcare systems. Australia enjoys competitive advantages in public health programs, informatics, complementary medicine products, clinical data management and development, and drug developments. Leveraging these services, Australia can play a significant role in developing the healthcare systems of South Asia. The healthcare systems in South Asian are in different levels of development. Australia is in an excellent position to cooperate with each of the South Asian countries based on their unique needs. Improving the healthcare trade relationship between South Asia countries and Australia is a win/win relationship for both parties.

REFERENCES

ArmstrongS. (2011). Asian Trade structures and trade potential: An initial analysis of South and East Asian Trade. SSRN.

Australia Trade Commission. (2016). *Medical devices and diagnostics.* Sydney: Commonwealth of Australia.

Bank, W. (2017). *Number of Maternal deaths in South Asian Countries.* Retrieved from https://data.worldbank.org/indicator/SH.MMR.DTHS?locations=8S

Bashkar, S., Tan, J., Bogers, M., Minssen, M., Badarrudin, H., Isreali-Korn, S., & Chesbrough, H. (2020). At the Epicenter of COVID-19–the Tragic Failure of the Global Supply Chain for Medical Supplies. *Frontier in Public Health.*

Berg, A., Chhaparia, H., Hedrich, S., & Magnus, K.-H. (2021, March). *What's next for Bangladesh's garment industry, after a decade of growth?* Retrieved from https://www.mckinsey.com/: https://www.mckinsey.com/industries/retail/our-insights/whats-next-for-bangladeshs-garment-industry-after-a-decade-of-growth

Bhutan Ministry of Health. (2010). Health population & nutrition sector strategic plan (HPNSSP) 2011 – 2016. Ministry of Health.

Breen, K., & Birrel, B. (2020). Selling medical education to international students: Time for review. *Internal Medicine Journal, 50*(5), 635–637. doi:10.1111/imj.14821 PMID:32431028

Callander, E., Fox, H., & Lindsay, D. (2019). Out-of-pocket healthcare expenditure in Australia: Trends, inequalities and the Impact on household living standards in ahigh-income country with a universalhealth care system. *Health Economics Review*, *9*(1), 10. doi:10.118613561-019-0227-9 PMID:30859357

Carreno, I., Dole, T., Medina, L., & Brandenburger, M. (2020). The Implications of the COVID-19 Pandemic on Trade. *European Journal of Risk Regulation*.

Cipla. (2021, October). *About Us*. Retrieved from cipla.com: https://www.cipla.com/about-us

Commonwealth of Australia. (2017). *Complimentary medicine*. Commonwealth of Australia.

Das, S. (2017). Impact of intellectual capital on business performance: Evidence from Indian pharmaceutical sector. *Polish Journal of Management Studies*.

Department of Health Australia. (2021). *Health Technology*. Retrieved from heath.gov.au: https://www.health.gov.au/health-topics/health-technology

Dhillon, P. K., Jeemon, P., Arora, N., Mathur, P., Maskey, M., Sukirna, R., & Prabhakaran, D. (2012). Status of epidemiology in the WHO South-East Asia region: Burden of disease, determinants of health and epidemiological research, workforce and training capacity. *International Journal of Epidemiology*, *41*(3), 847–860. doi:10.1093/ije/dys046 PMID:22617689

Drug-dev.com. (2021, August 9). *Australia's Pharma Sector to Grow to $32.1 Billion*. Retrieved from Drug-dev.com: https://drug-dev.com/australias-pharma-sector-to-grow-to-32-1-billion/

Eastren Miditerranean, W. H. O. (2021). *Country Cooperation Strategy for WHO and Pakistan 2020-2025*. WHO.

Hashim, J., Chongsuvivatwong, V., Phua, K., Pocock, N., Teng, Y., Chhem, R., . . . Lopez, A. (2012). *Health and Healthcare Systems in Southeast Asia*. Retrieved from Und.edu: https://unu.edu/publications/articles/health-and-healthcare-systems-in-southeast-asia.html

India Brand Equity Foundation. (2021, August 19). *Healthcare Industry in India*. Retrieved from ibef.org: https://www.ibef.org/industry/healthcare-india.aspx

JHU CSSE COVID-19 Data. (2021, August 12). *India*. Retrieved from https://ourworldindata.org/coronavirus-data: https://ourworldindata.org/coronavirus-data

Khtar, G. (2013). Indian pharmaceutical industry: an overview. *OSR Journal of Humanities and Social Science*.

Mossialos, E., & Wenzl, M. (2016). *2015 International Profiles of Health Care Systems*. The Commonwealth Fund. doi:10.15868ocialsector.25100

National Industry Insights. (2021, March 22). *Health*. Retrieved from National Industry Insights.net.au: https://nationalindustryinsights.aisc.net.au/industries/health#:~:text=The%20Health%20Care%20and%20Social%20Assistance%20industry%20is%20the%20largest,than%201.9%20million%20by%202024

O'Sullivan, D., Rahamathulla, M., & Pawar, M. (2020). The Impact and implications of COVID-19: Australian Perspective. *The International Journal of Community and Social Development*, 134-151.

Parliament of Australia. (2021). *Effects of COVID-19 on Australia*. Retrieved from Parliament of Australia: https://www.aph.gov.au/Parliamentary_Business/Committees/Joint/Foreign_Affairs_Defence_and_Trade/FADTandglobalpandemic/Report/section?id=committees%2Freportjnt%2F024552%2F73973

Paul, A. (2020). Regional Cooperation in South Asia: Exploring the Three Pillars of Regionalism and their Relevance. *The Journal of Indian and Asian Studies*.

Pharmexci. (2021). *Pharmexcil's Business Delegation to Australia and New Zealand (22nd July-26th July 2019)*. Retrieved from Pharmexci.com: https://pharmexcil.com/circulars/pharmexcil%E2%80%99s-business-delegation-to-australia-and-new-zealand--22nd-july-26th-july-2019-/10260/d94f-0180777644b247efb4b3cf863912.html

Rasul, G., Nepa, A., Hussain, A., Maharjan, A., Joshi, S., Lama, A., . . . Sharma, E. (2021). Socio-Economic Implications of COVID-19 Pandemic in South Asia: Emerging Risks and Growing Challenges. *Frontiers in Sociology*.

Rozman, G., & Liow, J. C. (2018). *International Relations and Asia's Southern Tier*. Asan-Palgrave Macmillan Series. doi:10.1007/978-981-10-3171-7

Serum Institute of India Pvt. Ltd. (2021, October). *About Us*. Retrieved from https://www.seruminstitute.com: https://www.seruminstitute.com/about_us.php

Statista.com. (2021a, August). *Infant mortality rates in South Asia between 2020 and 2025, by country*. Retrieved from Statista.com: https://www.statista.com/statistics/590050/infant-mortality-rates-in-south-asia/

Statista.com. (2021b, August 9). *Total value of pharmaceutical product exports in Australia from 2008 to 2019*. Retrieved from Statista.com: https://www.statista.com/statistics/1199092/australia-value-of-pharmaceutical-exports/

Thakur, R., & Sharma, A. (2018). *India in Australia's Strategic Framing in the Indo–Pacific*. Strategic Analysis.

Tingming, K. (2021). *Maintaining momentum: Australian supplements sector secures domestic and exports growth*. Retrieved from nutraingredients-asia.com: https://www.nutraingredients-asia.com/Article/2020/06/09/Maintaining-momentum-Australian-supplements-sector-secures-domestic-and-exports-growth#:~:text=Maintaining%20momentum%3A%20Australian%20supplements%20sector%20secures%20domestic%20and%20exports%20gr

United State Institute of Peach. (2021). *The Impact of COVID-19 on South Asian Economies*. United State Institute of Peach.

Usman, M., Ali, Y., Riaz, A., Riaz, A., & Zubair, A. (2020). Economic perspective of coronavirus (COVID-19. *Journal of Public Affairs*.

WHO. (2017). *Country cooperation strategy*. WHO.

World Bank. (2020, April). *South Asia Must Ramp Up COVID-19 Action to Protect People, Revive Economies*. Retrieved from Worldbank.org: https://www.worldbank.org/en/news/press-release/2020/04/12/south-asia-must-act-now-to-lessen-covid-19-health-impacts

World Health Organization. (2017). *Nepal.* WHO.

World Health Organization. (2021, August 25). *Afghanistan.* Retrieved from http://www.emro.who.int/afg/programmes/health-system-strengthening.html

World Health Organization Regional Office for South. (2021). *Sri Lanka Health System Review.* World Health Organization.

Worldmeter. (2021, September 1). *Australia.* Retrieved from Worldmeters.info: https://www.worldometers.info/coronavirus/country/australia/

ADDITIONAL READING

Bashkar, S., Tan, J., Bogers, M., Minssen, M., Badarrudin, H., Isreali-Korn, S., & Chesbrough, H. (2020). At the Epicenter of COVID-19–the Tragic Failure of the Global Supply Chain for Medical Supplies. *Frontier in Public Health* .

Breen, K., & Birrel, B. (2020). Selling medical education to international students: Time for review. *Internal Medicine Journal*, *50*(5), 635–637. doi:10.1111/imj.14821 PMID:32431028

Deci, E. L., & Ryan, R. M. (1991). A motivational approach to self: Integration in personality. In *Proceedings of Nebraska Symposium on Motivation* (vol. 38, pp. 237-288). University of Nebraska Press.

Dhillon, P. K., Jeemon, P., Arora, N., Mathur, P., Maskey, M., Sukirna, R., & Prabhakaran, D. (2012). Status of epidemiology in the WHO South-East Asia region: Burden of disease, determinants of health and epidemiological research, workforce and training capacity. *International Journal of Epidemiology*, *41*(3), 847–860. doi:10.1093/ije/dys046 PMID:22617689

Hashim, J., Chongsuvivatwong, V., Phua, K., Pocock, N., Teng, Y., Chhem, R., . . . Lopez, A. (2012). *Health and Healthcare Systems in Southeast Asia.* Retrieved from Und.edu: https://unu.edu/publications/articles/health-and-healthcare-systems-in-southeast-asia.html

Mossialos, E., & Wenzl, M. (2016). *2015 International Profiles of Health Care Systems.* The Commonwealth Fund. doi:10.15868ocialsector.25100

National Industry Insights. (2021, March 22). *Health.* Retrieved from National Industry Insights.net.au: https://nationalindustryinsights.aisc.net.au/industries/health#:~:text=The%20Health%20Care%20and%20Social%20Assistance%20industry%20is%20the%20largest,than%201.9%20million%20by%202024

Patricia Ordoñez de Pablos. (2019). *Innovative Management and Business Practices in Asia (The University of Oviedo, Spain), Xi Zhang (Tianjin University, China) and Kwok Tai Chui.* The Open University of Hong Kong.

Paul, A. (2020). Regional Cooperation in South Asia: Exploring the Three Pillars of Regionalism and their Relevance. *The Journal of Indian and Asian Studies.*

Pharmexci. (2021). *Pharmexcil's Business Delegation to Australia and New Zealand (22nd July-26th July 2019)*. Retrieved from Pharmexci.com: https://pharmexcil.com/circulars/pharmexcil%E2%80%99s-business-delegation-to-australia-and-new-zealand--22nd-july-26th-july-2019-/10260/d94f-0180777644b247efb4b3cf863912.html

Rozman, G., & Liow, J. C. (2018). *International Relations and Asia's Southern Tier*. Asan-Palgrave Macmillan Series. doi:10.1007/978-981-10-3171-7

KEY TERMS AND DEFINITIONS

Bilateral Trade: The exchange of goods between two nations promoting trade and investment. The two countries will reduce or eliminate tariffs, import quotas, export restraints, and other trade barriers to encourage trade and investment.

Clinical Governance: The framework through which healthcare organizations are accountable for continuously improving the quality of their services and safeguarding high quality of care'. Leadership is required to ensure that clinical governance processes are embedded within service provision.

COVID-19: A large family of viruses that cause illness ranging from the common cold to more severe diseases. Also known as novel coronavirus (nCoV) is a new strain that has not been previously identified in humans.

Health System: Referred to as health care system or as healthcare system, is the organization of people, institutions, and resources that deliver health care services to meet the health needs of target populations.

Healthcare Services: The codification of a health policy will directly impact the kinds of health care services available in an area.

Healthcare Systems: Public healthcare services are administered by different regulatory authorities in each country.

Infant Mortality: The death of an infant before his or her first birthday. The infant mortality rate is the number of infant deaths for every 1,000 live births.

Maternal Mortality: Death of either a pregnant woman or death of a woman within 42 days of delivery, miscarriage, termination, or ectopic pregnancy providing the death is associated with pregnancy or its treatment.

Medical Standards: Standards are explicit statements of expected quality in the performance of a health care activity. They may take the form of procedures, clinical practice guidelines, treatment protocols, critical paths, algorithms, standard operating procedures, or statements of expected health care outcomes, among other formats.

Medical Tourism: The process of traveling outside the country of residence for the purpose of receiving medical care. Originally, the term referred to the travel of patients from less-developed countries to developed nations in pursuit of the treatments not available in their homeland.

Personal Health: The ability to take charge of your health by making conscious decisions to be healthy. It not only refers to the physical wellbeing of an individual, but it also comprises the wellness of emotional, intellect, social, economic, spiritual, and other areas of life.

Pharmaceutical Industry: The pharmaceuticals industry consists of drug manufacturers, biotechnology companies and the distribution and wholesale companies that handle the products produced.

Most of the revenues in the industry come from drug companies who make prescription, generic, and over-the-counter drugs for medical or veterinary use.

Referral Centers: A tertiary referral hospital (also called a tertiary hospital, tertiary referral center, tertiary care center, or tertiary center) is a hospital that provides tertiary care, which is a level of health care obtained from specialists in a large hospital after referral from the providers of primary care and secondary care.

SAARC: The South Asian Association for Regional Cooperation (SAARC) is an economic and political organization of eight countries in South Asia. It was established in 1985 when the Heads of State of Bangladesh, Bhutan, India, Maldives, Nepal, Pakistan, and Sri Lanka formally adopted the charter. What is the main purpose of SAARC? The main objectives of SAARC are to place regional cooperation on a firm foundation, accelerate the pace of social and economic development of the countries, and further the cause of peace, progress, and stability in the region.

Specialized Hospitals: Those offer focused services to treat medical conditions that require a particular subset of skills and technology. They have existed in various forms for many years as children's hospitals, psychiatric hospitals, rehabilitation hospitals, eye and ear hospitals, arthritis hospitals, and others.

Teaching Hospitals: A teaching hospital is a hospital or medical center that provides medical education and training to future and current health professionals.

Chapter 10
The Recycling of Australian Offshore Structures in Bangladesh:
Challenges and Opportunities

Mohammad Zulfikar Ali
https://orcid.org/0000-0002-5479-1755
Curtin University, Australia

Nahid Islam
Curtin University, Australia

ABSTRACT

The circular economy has emerged as a policy goal with respect to the trade relationships between developed and developing countries. The aim of the circular economy is to take responsibility for the costs involved in recycling by going away from the linear economic model, which is briefly stated as 'take-recycle-dispose' with unused materials in at one end and externalised the wastes at the other. Recycling numerous unused structures is a persisting problem for Australia that can be resolved following this circular economy approach. To that end, an underlying aim of this chapter is to propose a bilateral agreement between Bangladesh and Australia that aims at recycling offshore structures of Australian companies in Bangladesh's ship recycling industry (hereinafter referred to as recycling industry). This chapter also sheds light on the challenges for Bangladesh in recycling the offshore structures in a sustainable way but disputes that those offshore structures will only increase the waste burden for Bangladesh.

INTRODUCTION

Australia's offshore oil and gas infrastructure is ageing. Moreover, concentration on new Liquefied Natural Gas (LNG) production units is pushing the oldest oil-rigs, i.e., offshore structures, to be recycled (Wood Mackenzie, 2016). Recently, the Northern Endeavour, an abandoned oil production ship laying

DOI: 10.4018/978-1-7998-8657-0.ch010

far off the coast of Darwin has exposed Australia's challenges over decommissioning all types of end-of-life platforms (both floating and permanent) (Macdonand-Smith, 2020). The specific challenges for the offshore industries and the Australian government to dispose of these excess offshore structures include, limited onshore facility to dispose of the growing volume of end-of-life offshore structures, time constraint, and arrangement of logistics (Macdonand-Smith, 2020). Bangladesh, on the other side, can turn this overcapacity problem into an opportunity using their existing recycling industry. Bangladesh does not have a separate recycling industry for recycling oil and gas platforms, but Bangladesh's ship recycling industry (hereinafter referred to as recycling industry), in fact, recycles both oil and gas platforms, and old ships. Recycling Australian offshore structures in Bangladesh's recycling industry is therefore not only a reasonable solution, but also a new business idea for five reasons.

First, Bangladesh's labour cost is lot cheaper than Australia; second, Bangladesh has an established recycling industry; third, Bangladesh is a leading recycling country and fourth, its recent growth in steel consumption is indicative of the contribution of its recycling industry (Mohammad Sujauddin, 2017, p. 191). Fifth, since Bangladesh does not have iron ore to support its fast-growing steel demand, recycling of offshore structures of Australian companies is to contribute significantly to its demand. Recycling industry that recycles both offshore structures and end-of-life ships has therefore turned into its primary source contributing largely to the input needs for steel scraps (Mohammad Sujauddin, 2017, p. 192). The authors thus argue for a bilateral agreement between Bangladesh and Australia that aims at creating a legal foundation for recycling Australia's end-of-life offshore structures in Bangladesh.

In an economic sense, the proposed bilateral agreement for recycling Australia's end-of-life gas and oil platforms (both fixed and floating) is an idea to implement the well-known circular economy approach where both parties gain from the deal. A circular economy refers to a systemic approach to economic development designed to benefit, businesses, society, and the environment (Ellen Macarthur Foundation, n.d.). To that end, circular economy emphasises on the extension of material and resource circularity within the economic system. An appropriate circularity therefore requires minimising the potential adverse effects on the place where the process takes place (Kim, 2020). Recycling has taken a dominant position in applying this approach as it arguably allows reusing the original product and it negates the idea of 'dumping' recyclable materials from developed to developing countries. Recyclable materials have turned into economic opportunities for developing countries. However, for achieving higher value of the recycling option, it requires an extended producer's responsibility and establish monetary incentive approach (Rahman, 2019) so that recyclers do not follow their localised and harmful approach to recycling, taking advantage of the challenges of distance. Producer's responsibility and monetary incentive approaches require the operators of the offshore industry to provide financial and technical assistance to the recyclers so that they can overcome the challenges of distance of a recycling location from the operator of an offshore industry (Gregson, 2015).

The authors shed light on the business prospect of recycling the Australian end-of-life offshore structures in Bangladesh. The authors, however, acknowledge that recycling offshore structures is challenging with respect to health, safety of workers, but that can be addressed under the proposed agreement subject to incorporating mandatory requirements of financial and technical assistance as required under the producer's responsibility, and monetary incentive approaches. This Chapter proceeds by reviewing the relevant literature on Australia's offshore oil and gas industry and Bangladesh's recycling industry.

BACKGROUND LITERATURE

Considered further below in the section entitled, *Direction for Recycling the Offshore Structures in the Existing Legal Frameworks*, international laws that deal with inter-State wastes transfer do not ban the transboundary transfer of recyclable materials if the exporter can ensure their sound management during the process of recycling. Australia follows this approach (Fowler et al, 2014, p. 21) that can lead to transferring offshore structures to a foreign jurisdiction for the purpose of recycling. This is a right approach for Australia in the current context because Australia, as a host country responsible for disposing of its end-of-life offshore structures is not ready to recycle them in its jurisdiction cheaply. Australia does not have arrangements or facilities to dispose of these structures and its labour cost in this decommissioning sector is much higher than Bangladesh. Moreover, because of high volume of inbuilt hazardous materials contained in these structures and strict regulatory requirements for their sound management, Australia's expenditure for their decommissioning will be too high. On the other hand, Bangladesh can cheaply recycle these structures and make recycling a potential business because Bangladesh's labour cost is much cheaper than Australia's. Bangladesh also has enough recycling facilities. Bangladesh is recycling end-of-life offshore structures of the United Kingdom based offshore companies and this experience can put them into a competitive position. Considered further below, Australia has already developed a good trade relationship with Bangladesh, but bi-lateral trade in offshore industry has remained unexplored between Bangladesh and Australia. Sending offshore structures and investment from Australia will breach the gap. This will be a new approach to trade not only for Australia's interest but also for Bangladesh's benefit.

Literature review in this area suggests that Bangladesh has retained its top position in global recycling by offering high sale price to exporters of recyclable materials. The legal framework of Bangladesh is improving by active guidance from Bangladesh's Supreme Court.

Bangladesh's recycling industry contributes significantly towards socio-economic benefit of Bangladesh. Bangladesh is a developing country that has no iron ore deposits to support its fast-growing steel demand and as offshore structure offers a good amount of scrap steel for producing refined steel as furnished products in the country's steel industry; the Australian end-of-life offshore structures have a good demand in Bangladesh.

Recycling industry is a vital source of steel for Bangladesh's steel mills and construction industry. Bangladesh construction industry and re-rolling mills are largely dependent on the scrap supplied from the recycling industry (John, 2016). As Bangladesh construction industry mainly uses Roller Compacted Concrete (RCC) pillar for all high or low-rise building, this high demand reflects this construction model. Recycling industries supply the lion's share of the raw materials to run more than 350 re-rolling mills in Bangladesh (Hossain 2016, p. 86).

The high steel demand in fact, reflects the rapid development of infrastructure and high demand of steel scraps recycled from exported sources. Steel scraps are reproduced into refined and new steel materials. Table 1 below shows that between 2006 and 2010, the recycling industry contributed 81.2% to Bangladesh's total steel demand with the maximum of 95% in 2006. This is an indication that recycling business has significantly contributed to Bangladesh's national demand for steel (Golam Zakaria, 2012). Because of recycling old ships and offshore structures, Bangladesh does not need to import steel and that saves a substantial amount of foreign exchange.

The recycling industry also provides a vital source of employment. Recycling is a labour-intensive industry that requires thousands of workers to remove and process the steel. Bangladesh recycling industry

Table 1. Impact of recycling sector on the steel sector in Bangladesh

Year	Supply From Recycling Industry (in tonnes)	Contribution to Demand
2006	555,000	95%
2007	655,000	71%
2008	1,884,000	72%
2009	1,960,002	80%
2010	4,381,000	88%
		Average- 81.2%

Source- (Sujauddin, 2017, p. 198)

employed more than 25,000 workers in 2017 (Rahman, 2011). Some sources claimed that the number might be around 50,000 (Veritas). In addition, more than one million people are employed in retail shops and re-rolling mills that are dependent on its recycling industry (Sarraf, 2010, p. 27).

Recycling also benefits the local shipbuilding industry (Hossain, 2016), being the main source of annual steel supply to that industry. Bangladesh's shipbuilding industries add more than 200 ships each year to their local fleet and the recycling industries supply the basic raw materials for building these vessels (Hossain, 2016).

Recycling is a good source of tax revenue. Annually, Bangladesh's revenue earning from the recycling industry is more than USD 130 million (Hossain, 2015). In 2016, about fifteen per cent of the total tax revenue of Bangladesh came from the recycling industry (Rahman, 2017). The revenue is generated by imposing duties (7.5%), yard tax (2.5%), and other imposts (Rahman, 2011). Recycling is one of the top ten-billion-dollar businesses in Bangladesh (LensCulture, n.d.). Regular supply of offshore structures from Australia will add to this significantly.

As a potential source of steel, Bangladesh's recycling industry is keen to purchasing offshore structures from the UK and Norway oil and gas companies. As discussed later in this Chapter, the business however has raised several international concerns, namely selling offshore structures without ensuring sound management of the wastes involved in their body.

Against the backdrop, the aim of this Chapter is to examine the current trade relationship between Bangladesh and Australia, legal structure of inter-State transfer of offshore structures, and thus construct a legal avenue for the proposed agreement. The Chapter is premised on three additional objectives. First, this Chapter claims that recycling the offshore structures in Bangladesh is a better strategy than disposing of them in Australia because Bangladesh's labour cost is much less, than Australia and Bangladesh have experience and established industry to perform the task of recycling. Second, it argues that the proposed bilateral agreement will not only save billions of USD for Australia, but it will also earn millions of USD from the sale price of the offshore structures. Third, recognising the lack of capacity of Bangladesh, the Chapter argues that under the existing international laws, it is possible for Australia to remove the offshore structures and send them for recycling in Bangladesh, but considered further below, Australia should provide technical and financial assistance to ensure their sound management as required under the *Basel International Convention for Transboundary Movement of Wastes and other Materials*, 1992.

MAIN FOCUS OF THE CHAPTER

Australia's Offshore Structures: Overcapacity Crisis in Australia

Australia's position is at the bottom in a group of 30 Oil and gas producing nations that have a successful abandonment strategy (Natonal Energy Resources Australia, 2016) highlighting that overcapacity is a growing challenge for Australia (NOPSEMA, 2020). Although the offshore decommissioning wave is forming in Australia, it has already hit the UK. One study shows that between 2021 and 2026, the UK will need to remove 146 platforms that would cost them more than USD 66 billion or maybe twice this amount (Wilby, 2016). From the perspective of global expenditure on global offshore decommissioning projects, one study suggests that the cost would be around USD210 billion between 2010 and 2040 (Foxwell, 2016). Over the next fifty years, Australia would expect to share more than A$ 27 billion of this global cost for decommissioning its offshore structures and wells (Gourvenec, 2017, p. 422). This cost speculation indicates that while decommissioning was once a distant problem, Australian oil and gas industries cannot ignore the problem with the growing volume of unused assets now and in future (Gourvenec, 2017, p. 422).

One of the most preferred approaches to offshore decommissioning is to remove the structures completely and recycle, even though removal of old infrastructure from the harsh environment and their relocation offshore or disposal when brought to shore involves a high cost (Gourvenec, 2017, p. 422). Concerning the disposal of the facilities after removal, the Australian supply chain lacks vessels, tooling, disposal facilities or the trained workforce for offshore decommissioning. More than anything, Australia does not have suitable onshore facilities for recycling or scrapping large structures (Barrymore, 2017). The absence of available disposal facilities onshore to meet the capacity of the disposing current number of offshore structures is fatal for Australia.

Types of Offshore Structures

There are different types of Oil and Gas structures in Australia (see Figure 1 below) (Jenssen , Mork & Mulinaris, 2018). Fixed and floating are the two primary types of offshore structures. Concrete legs and steel of these fixed structures are attached to the seabed supporting the deck that remains over the water surface. Unlike the fixed structures, oil and gas industries also use floating structures to explore, produce, drill, and support the operation of the fixed offshore rigs (Jenssen et al, 2018). Specifically, the mobile offshore drilling unit (MODU) that refers to oil and gas drilling assets that float on water for their mobile nature can serve other production fields. MODU also has specific International Maritime Organisation number as ships and as discussed further bellow thus fall under the ship-related legislation.

Figure 2 shows that Australia's offshore structures are spread around the country, from Northern Caravan, and Gippsland to Perth and Bass. Australia also has both fixed and floating platforms. Table 2 shows that Australian end-of-life offshore structures are largely dominated by fixed structures, such as, Wells (subsea development, exploration, and appraisal), more than 1000 (1008). Australia also has a very good number of Subsea Structures (535) which refer to fixed platforms that are found at the heart of any subsea oil and gas field development and a small number of floating platforms, only 11. Moreover, Australia has 205 Flowlines that connect a single wellhead to a manifold or process equipment.

The types contribute to their decommissioning cost and option. Recycling fixed platforms is more expensive than floating platforms. Fixed platforms cost additional expense for their removal from the

Figure 1. Different offshore structures

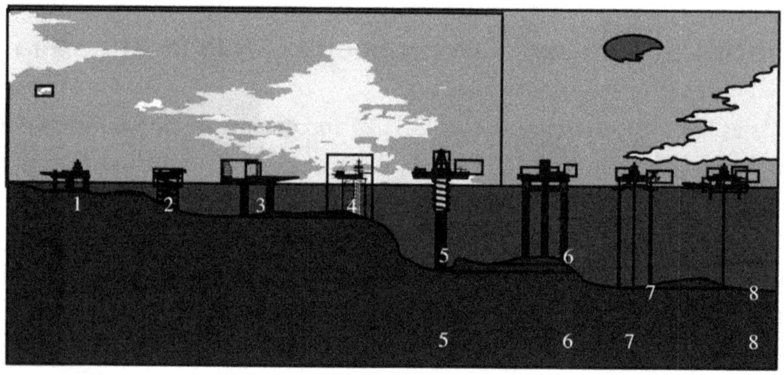

Figure 2. Australian offshore oil and gas asset stock by basin and types
(Source- Centre of Decommissioning Australia-2020)

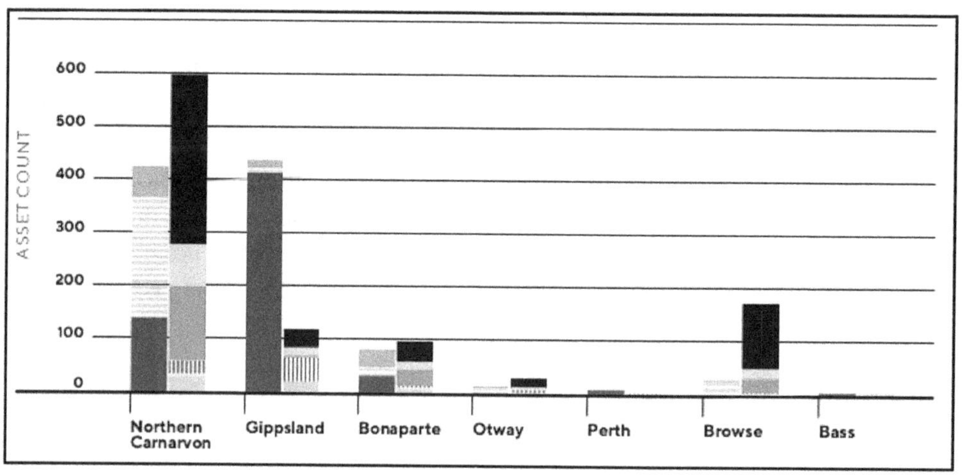

Table 2. Australian offshore oil and gas asset stock

Nature of the Offshore Structures	Numbers
Wells(subsea development, exploration, and appraisal)	1008
Floating Facilities (FPSO, FSOs and FLNG)	11
Infield Flow lines	205
Subsea Structures	535
Fixed Facilities	57
Export and inter-field pipelines	82
Static Umbilicals	130
Flexible Risers	126

(Source- Centre of Decommissioning Australia-2020)

seabed and transportation to onshore locations or recycling countries using expensive towing services, whereas floating structures can sail directly to a recycling yard (Jenssen et al, 2018).

Direction for Recycling the Offshore Structures in Bangladesh Under the Existing Legal Frameworks

Australia is a party to international laws that guide offshore decommissioning to follow the complete removal and disposal policy of the fixed platforms. The most basic international instrument is the *Geneva Convention on the Continental Shelf* (1958) that provides the requirement of complete removal of the end-of-life infrastructures in clear terms: '*any installation which is abandoned or disused must be entirely removed.* This is still binding on its Member States. Even partial removal of fixed platforms for disposal onshore is legally acceptable. In this context, partial removal means to remove the top side of the fixed platforms and send them for disposal onshore. The later *United Nations Convention on the Law of the Sea* 1982 (UNCLOS) provides an opportunity for the resource industry to derogate from the complete removal requirement. Art 60(3) of the UNCLOS provides:

Any installations or structures, which are abandoned or disused, shall be removed to ensure the safety of navigation, considering any generally accepted international standards established in this regard by the competent international organisation. Such removal shall also have due regard to fishing, the protection of the marine environment and the rights and duties of other states.

Different persons may interpret the above provision differently, but it is implicit that partial removal is possible in certain circumstances (Barrymore, 2017, p. 398). The two international laws provide two different directions, but as UNCLOS is a subsequent law on the same issue, the removal rule of the UNCLOS, would prevail. In practice, the relaxation of the removal obligation has allowed partial removal and their transboundary transfer. Some studies, however, suggest that such removal has been outdated especially after new scientific development, which suggests that rather than removing decommission in situ is the best option (Bond et al, 2018, p.53). This Chapter argues that such in situ decommission is not a popular approach in the UK and Norway (North Sea countries) who have the world's most aging offshore infrastructures. These North-Sea countries follow a partial removal method due to the potential dangers involved with navigation, in case of in situ decommission. Australia should learn lessons from these North Sea countries.

Another relevant and most recent international instrument is the *Convention for the Protection of the Marine Environment of the North-East Atlantic*, 1992 (OSPAR) that also allows partial removal of the offshore structures and their final disposal. All North Sea oil and gas producing countries are parties to OSPAR and therefore require following rigorous safety and environmental standards. OSPAR aims at regulating the decommissioning process of the fixed platforms that are partially dismantled on the spot; cut parts are then transported to a nearby scrapping site where the rest of the scrapping process continues, but it suggests nothing about the floating platforms.

The floating platforms are covered under the *Hong Kong Convention*, 2009 (Jenssen et al, 2018, p. 20). Presumably, the International Maritime Organisation introduced the Hong Kong Convention for exporting ships that also refer to offshore structures for breaking into foreign jurisdictions. Under Art 2 (7) of the *Hong Kong Convention*, "Ship" means a vessel of any type whatsoever operating or having operated in the marine environment and includes submersibles, floating craft, floating platforms, self-

Table 3. Direction under the international instruments

International Laws	Aims	Interpretation
Geneva Convention on the Continental Shelf (1958)	Complete removal of the end-of-life infrastructures in clear terms	All offshore structures must be removed completely from the sea. Australia follows this approach.
United Nations Convention on the Law of the Sea 1982 (UNCLOS)	Partial removal is possible in certain circumstances	Some parts of the structures can be kept on the seabed unless they create navigation problems. It means topside of the structures can be separated and sent for recycling.
Convention for the Protection of the Marine Environment of the North-East Atlantic, 1992 (OSPAR)	Allows partial removal of the offshore structures and their final disposal	As above. Australia is not a party to this instrument.
Hong Kong Convention, 2009	Allows floating structure to be recycled	It is the guiding international instrument that will allow Australia to remove the offshore structures from the seabed and sent for recycling

elevating platforms, Floating Storage Units (FSUs), and Floating Production Storage and Offloading Units (FPSOs), including a vessel stripped of equipment or being towed.' The *Hong Kong Convention* thus creates the legal scope for global offshore industries exporting offshore structures in the name of recycling. These regulatory requirements lead to a logical conclusion that no law restricts Australia exporting sending fixed or floating platforms to Bangladesh.

Another relevant international principle specific in this context is the *1996 Protocol to the Dumping Convention*, which prohibits the dumping of *'any wastes or other matter'* on the sea. Australia's legal framework also supports removal and their export impliedly. According to the Australian legal regime, it is recommended to remove all structures that are, and all equipment and other property that is, neither used nor to be used in connection with the operations in which the owner is engaged or will be engaged, but there is no direction about their location of disposal (Section 572 (3) of the *Offshore Petroleum and Greenhouse Gas Storage Act 2006* (Cth). Australian government and industries can breach the gap by forming the proposed agreement that aims at exporting the structures after removal to Bangladesh. Presently, because of the relatively young age of the Australian oil and gas industry, regulators have not assessed the proposal. Chandal et al. argue that the regulatory requirements in Australia are very clear concerning complete removal of offshore structures (Chandler et al., 2017), but not so clear to its alternatives, including the proposed bilateral agreement. Perhaps this is because Australian legal policy has not been tested considering the overcapacity crisis (Gourvenec, 2017, p. 422).

Evidence That Bangladesh Is Willing to Import Offshore Structures

The literature review on Bangladesh Ship recycling industry suggests that if Australia agrees to follow the law and export offshore structures, Bangladesh ship recycling industry is willing to import these offshore structures. Around 200 offshore structures have been identified as scrapped globally since 2015- and an estimated 20% of these assets ended up in Bangladesh (Jenssen et al, 2018, p. 6). Out of the 185 oil and gas assets that have been identified as broken up since 2015, 79 ended up on the beaches of South Asia, including Bangladesh, India, and Pakistan (Jenssen et al, 2018). Out of these 79 vessels, Bangladesh broke 18 assets including FPSO, jack-up, maintenance platform, FSO, semi-submersible, drilling ship and Pontoon (Jenssen et al, 2018). These were vessels in general, not fixed platforms. A question eventually will arise about the high expense of transferring the fixed platforms after removal from the seabed. Recognising the high cost of towing a reasonable expectation of the proposed bilateral agreement is that because of regular use of towing services under the proposed agreement, the price would gradually decrease in future.

New Investment Relationship

The decision to export offshore structures from Australian waters to Bangladesh leads to the necessity for Australia's investment in building green capacity of Bangladesh's recycling industry. The authors also recognise the questions to be asked in relation to Australia's investment in Bangladesh. For example, why Bangladesh needs to focus on such investment from Australia, going beyond Chinese investment; what dilemma the proposed agreement will create in Bangladesh political circle in the context of China; and why Australia will invest in Bangladesh. In response, the authors argue for the proposed agreement, being its potential for Bangladesh to get away from overreliance on Chinese investment and its potential long-term adverse effect.

Bangladesh has been heavily relying on Chinese investments even though Chinese investments in developing countries has been counterproductive (Jaganmohan, 2021). One problem with Chinese investment is that rather than assisting capacity development of a host country, China uses 'commercial loans to advance it's economic and geostrategic interests' (Pence, 2018). Because of these self-interests, sometimes, Chinese investments may cause loss and eventually form a 'debt trap' for developing countries. Sri Lanka's commercial loan of USD 5 billion (15 per cent of external debt) from China is an example of this debt trap. A loss project can also make a country 'vulnerable to Chinese influence' (Wignaraja, 2020, p. 11). Bangladesh should learn lesson from Sri Lanka, a neighbouring country and be cautious about the negative side effect, i.e., the debt trap, of Chinese investment.

The new investment relationship under the proposed agreement will not create dilemma in Bangladesh's political circle and policy making in the context of China. This is because since 2019, China has stopped recycling foreign vessel and offshore structure (Chockalingam & Sivasamy, 2021). Chinese recycling industry therefore does not import end of life vessels and offshore structures from Organisation of Economic Development (OECD) countries, which in contrast, creates a big opportunity for Bangladesh's recycling industry.

Further, Australia's incentive from the proposed agreement is to find Bangladesh, a new partner, in recycling. Since 2020, because of trade war with China that resulted in the rejection of import of Australian resources and agri-business products such as food and crops, Australia is looking for new trade partners. The proposed agreement will certainly help Australia in that direction. Importantly, both Australia and Bangladesh share common history of ex-British colony and democratic values and because of these commonalities, and to cope with the Chinese ban on many Australian products, the proposed agreement will be a step forward for Australia to overcome the crisis, specially, in its resource sector.

Existing Trade Between Bangladesh and Australia

The proposed agreement will also add to the existing trade between Bangladesh and Australia. Bangladesh is the 32nd largest trade partner of Bangladesh (Commission, n.d.). Bilateral trade between Bangladesh and Australia has increased six times over the last ten years reaching USD 2 billion from less than USD

300 million. Particularly, Australia's Duty-Free Quota Free (DFQF) facility to least developed countries (LDCs) has contributed to increasing export of Bangladeshi products to Australia in recent years (Commission, n.d.). According to Department of Foreign Affairs and Trade (DFAT), Australia and Bangladesh expect to pursue new opportunities to stimulate trade and investment so that both countries can leverage a shared economic recovery from COVID-19. In 2019, the report titled "Trade and Investment at a Glance 2019" by DFAT states that Australia's two-way merchandise trade valued at $37.2 billion with 36 ongoing bilateral development partner countries has increased by 3.1 per cent per annum. Overall, Australia's exports to the partnership countries grew by 4.1 per cent per annum, while imports grew by 2.1 per cent per annum over the same period. The partnership is ongoing and with the continuous business relationship with Australia, Bangladesh has played a substantial role in the merchandise trade. This is because, in 2018-19, Australia's two-way goods and services trade with Bangladesh grew to over $2.5billion, with two-way trade in goods valued at $1.9 billion.

Evaluation of Australia's Investment for Improving Standards of Bangladesh's Recycling Industry

From the perspective of Australia's investment in foreign jurisdiction, and especially in South Asia, the agreement will not be the first of that kind. Australia has already made significant progress in building trade relationship with South Asian countries, including India, Bangladesh, and Pakistan. One of the joint initiatives is to establish the International Ocean Rim Association (IORA) on 7 March 1997 that aims to promote sustained growth and balanced development within the Indian Ocean Region (IORA, n.d.).

IORA in fact strengthens cooperation and dialogue with its Member States, but despite being an active member of IORA, Bangladesh has not progressed more than India in attracting attention for recycling offshore structures. Until recently, Indian beach is the largest breaking spot for importing and recycling offshore units. Since 2015, India has recycled hundreds of offshore platforms on their beaches even though the beaches are not following adequate safety standards (Chockalingam & Sivasamy, 2021). Like India, Bangladesh recycling yards are located on the beaches and both Bangladesh and India follow the same standards for breaking the assets (Jenssen et al, 2018), but Bangladesh has not been successful enough because of having weak business relationship with countries having rich offshore industries (Cairns, 2007). Considered further below, the authors emphasise on two perspectives, namely regulatory and economic perspectives and argue why Bangladesh is a better option for recycling Australia's offshore structures and why Australia needs to step in improving technical capacity of Bangladesh's recycling industry.

Economic Perspective

In general, Bangladesh can offer a higher purchase price to Australia offshore industries for the offshore structures than India. Bangladesh's per capita consumption of steel is the highest in the world because of its high demand of steel for both domestic use and export. Recent purchase price of old ships for recycling has already demonstrated that market of scrap steel in Bangladesh is very high (Chockalingam & Sivasamy, 2021). One report suggests that per ton price of scrap steel has jumped to 600/ton in Bangladesh in 2021 from USD 400/ton in 2019 (Milad, 2021). According to this report, between 2019 and 2021 there is a 19.5% jump, in the price of steel scraps for increasing price of iron in global market (Milad, 2021). On the contrary, one report suggests that average scrap value in India is USD 400 ton which is 200/ton less than Bangladesh (Romanenko, 2021). Apart from this business perspective in selling offshore structures to Bangladesh, positive legal environment in Bangladesh is also an important factor why Bangladesh is a better option than India. Next Section explains this in detail.

Regulatory Perspective

In principle, Bangladesh has started following an environment and labour friendly approach especially after a recent decision given by Bangladesh's Supreme Court in the case of *Bangladesh Environmental Lawyers Association v Janata Steel and* Others (*Janata Steel*). On the contrary, India follows a pro-business approach following its national legislations on recycling that refers to prefer economic perspective to environment and human consequences. According to both Indian and Bangladeshi laws, floating platforms are referred to as ships. Therefore, legal frameworks that aim at regulating their ship recycling industry are also applicable to recycling offshore structures. A deficiency in the domestic laws of India is the limited power of the National Authorities to check inbuilt wastes of a ship, which is against the objective of promoting a responsible recycling industry and strengthening the national institutions in recycling States.

On the contrary, in relation to the local authority's power in assessing the in-built substances of a ship, Bangladesh's approach is superior to those of Pakistan and India. The Bangladesh Supreme Court in *Janata Steel* convincingly decided that before a shipbreaking yard can apply for beaching, the Department of Environment (DoE) must have the power of a formal and detailed assessment of the in-built and on-board hazardous materials or wastes of an end-of-life ship (*Janata Steel*, p. 73). The Court further ruled that after examining the hazardous wastes of a scrap vessel, including wastes in structures and on board, the DoE can agree or decline to issue an environmental clearance certificate prior to beaching. This decision is pivotal in ensuring that Bangladesh may be able to uphold the green recycling image and be more competitive for Australia in recycling offshore structures than India.

Potential Benefit for Australia and Bangladesh

Australia's Benefit Under the Proposed Agreement

Australia's offshore oil and gas industry's estimated cost for decommissioning stands at USD 40.5 billion (Centre of Decommissioning Australia, 2021, p. 3). According to a recent report, fixed structure is 81% of the total liability. The report also suggests that asset removal and transport cost is USD 5 billion of the liability (Centre of Decommissioning Australia, 2021, p. 9). As under the proposed agreement, Australia will need to spend anything except the removal and transportation cost, Australia will approximately save USD 35.5 billion by sending the offshore structures to Bangladesh. On top of that, Australian industry will earn millions of dollars from the sale price of the structures. Considered more below, that will increase competitiveness of Bangladesh's recycling industry.

Australian Offshore Industries

There is no available data to suggest the potential income for offshore industries from the proposed business. Nevertheless, Table 4 suggests that the global maritime industry yearly earns around 2500 million USD from selling ships for recycling in South Asia. The income depends on the price and weight of units. Subject to the amount and price of iron, the income of maritime industry this amount gives an

Table 4. Key indicators for Australia's profit

Year	Ships Broken in Million LDTs	Bangladesh Price in USD/LDT	Indian Price in USD/LDT	Pakistani Price in USD/LDT	Average Price in USD/LDT	Total Revenue
2007	1.9	500	470	460	476.66	905.65
2008	2.6	770	745	690	735	1911
2009	6.2	340	320	320	326.66	2025.35
2010	4.3	480	480	480	480	2064
2011	6.1	520	550	510	510	3111
2012	8.3	500	500	500	500	4150
2013	6.4	435	440	440	438.34	2805.38
2014	6	480	500	480	486.67	2920.02
2015	4.4	300	320	320	313.34	1378.70
2016	8.1	310	310	310	310	2511
2017	5.9	380	390	380	383.34	1955.03
2018	5.8	430	420	420	423.34	2455.34
Average income -- 2349.37						

Source of Data- (Mikelis, The Recycling of Ships, 2nd ed, 1 October 2019))

indication to offshore industries about the potential income from the transboundary transfer of offshore structures to Bangladesh's recycling industry. A better quality of iron found in offshore structures than the ships would also be a major factor concerning the potential business income for the offshore industries.

Evidence That the Agreement Will Facilitate Bangladesh's Steel Demand and Economic Growth

The proposed agreement will contribute to both steel export and economic growth of Bangladesh. Figure 3 shows that there is 83 percent increase in export during the July-January period in Bangladesh (Chakma, 2021). Due to pandemic, stimulus packages are in place and in turn, the demand for steel supply for infrastructural development has surged in the recent past around the world. Being a steel exporting country, Bangladesh has also contributed to this high global demand by exporting a substantial amount of steel.

This growing trend of steel export shows that recycling industry is not only meeting Bangladesh's national demand it is also contributing to its steel export substantially. Further, because of a substantial increase in global demand for steel export and supply from Bangladesh, it has experienced a 7% GDP growth recently. For maintaining the growth, importantly, Bangladesh government has adopted the 'Vision 2041' in line with 'Vision 2021' that provides impetus to such development of the nation. Bangladesh has also prepared the Perspective Plan 2021-2041 to translate the policies and programmes cherished in the Vision 2041 into development strategies (Bangladesh Planning Commission, 2020). This Vision 2041 relies on the four pillars. Figure 3 integrates the four pillars: (i) governance; (ii) democratization; (iii) decentralization and (iv) capacity building to pave the way to achieve the status of a

Figure 3. Steel export booming
(Source: The Daily Star 2021).

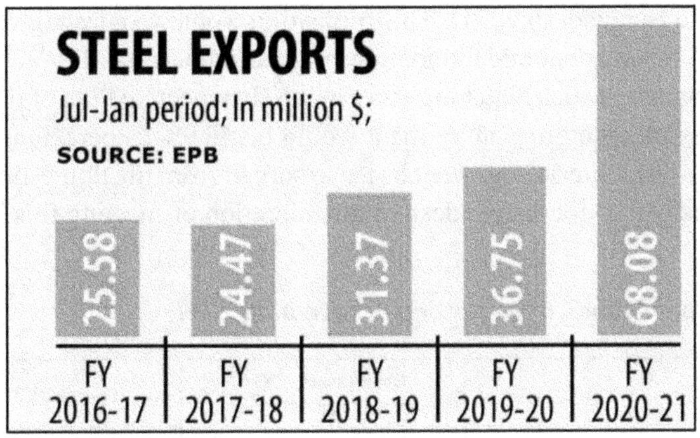

developed country with a per capita income of USD 12,500 or more (at 2019 USD) (Perspective Plan of Bangladesh 2021-2041).

Figure 4. Four institutional pillars of vision 2041.
(Source: Planning Commission, Bangladesh, p. 48).

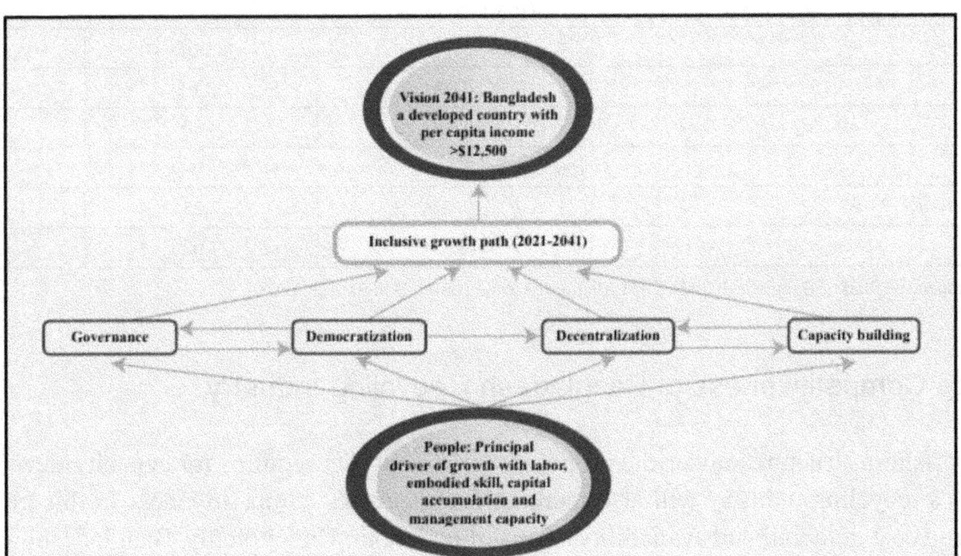

Bangladesh needs more recycling sources for meeting its growing domestic steel demand. The government in Bangladesh has expedited the mega projects like construction of Padma Bridge, Metrorail, Elevated Expressway, Karnaphuli Tunnel, Matarbari Thermal Power Station, Payra Seaport, 100 Special Private Economic Zones etc. that would create necessary physical infrastructure conducive to fostering both local and foreign investment. All these mega projects may be completed within few years. These projects are introduced to follow the projected key macroeconomic indicators that align with the Perspective Plan of Bangladesh 2021-2041 as outlined in Table 2 (the General Economics Division under the Planning Commission in Bangladesh 2021). This projection would require high and sustained long-run growth. The underlying macroeconomic foundations with sustained stability including internal and external would be the safeguard of such high long-run growth (Perspective Plan of Bangladesh 2021-2041). The projection indicates that the gross investment would be 46.9% as percentage of GDP benchmark. As such, the demand for raw materials for steel has also surged from the domestic market. The proposed agreement will be a timely step for Bangladesh to this direction of meeting this increasing demand.

Table 5. Key macroeconomic indicators for perspective plan 2041

	Benchmark FY20 (% of GDP)	**Target FY31**	**Target FY41**
Real GDP Growth (%)	8.19	9.0	9.9
CPI inflation (%)	5.5	4.7	4.5
	as % of GDP		
Gross Investment (%)	32.76	41.15	46.9
Gross National Savings (%)	31.31	37.18	43.95
Total government revenue (%)	10.47	19.55	24.15
Total government expenditure (%)	15.52	24.55	29.15
	Growth rate		
Exports	5.00	11.65	11.00
Imports	5.00	12.05	10.00
Remittances	9.00	4.50	2.00
	Poverty (headcount, %)		
Extreme poverty (%)	9.38	2.25	0.68
Poverty (%)	18.82	7.02	2.59

(Source: Perspective Plan of Bangladesh 2021-2041, Planning Commission, Bangladesh, p.65.)

Increasing Competitiveness of Bangladesh Recycling Industry

Recycling offshore structures under the proposed agreement that requires for capacity development of Bangladesh's recycling industry will also increase Bangladesh's competitiveness in this global sector with its cheap cost of labour and availability of unskilled labour. Undoubtedly, Bangladeshi workers can become a skilled workforce with proper training and awareness.

Bangladesh's labour cost is cheaper, only USD 17.9/per month, than Australia's cost of labour, which is around USD 2,276 per month (Country Economy, 2020). Bangladesh also has a good number of unskilled labour force with around 2823 million people are currently unemployed in Bangladesh (Country Economy, 2020). The unemployment rate rose substantially after Covid-19 pandemic. As recycling the offshore structures is a highly labour-intensive industry in Bangladesh with proper training and technical support from Australia, these large number of workforces can turn into an asset. Particularly, technical training to workers on environmental and labour safety will eventually improve capacity of the industry.

Bangladesh has skill shortage and recycling industry in Bangladesh does not use modern technology for recycling the structures. The investment from the Australian government for improving the green recycling capacity of Bangladesh's recycling industry is crucial for the business opportunity proposed in this Chapter. This also answers the question how Australia can support financially and technically without further harming the global and Bangladesh environment.

It is also an opportunity for Australia to become a global leader in the issue of offshore decommissioning; besides solving its own decommission related problems. By sending the end-of-life structures to Bangladesh, Australian companies would be able to externalise the technical, financial, and environmental costs involved in soundly managing the structures. However, the authors, along with Lloyd's Register Foundation, argue that decommissioning offshore structures is controversial in Bangladesh from the perspective of health and safety of workers and sound environmental management (Lloyd's Register Foundation, 2020).

Potential Challenges for Bangladesh in Recycling the Offshore Structures and Need for Investment

From the perspective of the sound environment, recycling is the best way of getting rid of offshore structures. One of the main reasons is its ability to reuse valuable resources as steel. Besides its significance to provide steel, recycling offshore structures is the same heavy and hazardous process as recycling that expose the workers, the environment, and communities to many risks. These include exposure to toxic materials- such as asbestos, heavy metal compounds, toxic residues- that may cause long-term health diseases and irreversible environmental damage (Jenssen et al, 2018).

Safe recycling of offshore structures is a problem in South Asia. NGO Ship recycling platform identifies beaching, being the main problem for Bangladesh. Beaching refers to laying a vessel or structure on a tidal mudflat for breaking (Jenssen et al, 2018). The industry uses High tide to ground the vessel and offshore structures and takes advantage of low tide to continue breaking operations on the coastal beach.

International Labour Organisation, a special agency of the United Nations has declared ship recycling the most dangerous job in the world (ILO, n.d.). Bangladesh ship recycling industry has poor occupational safety and environmental standards causing regular deaths and injuries. Although ship recycling supports the global maritime industry in getting rid of unwanted ships, the industry receives limited funding to improve the standards. That result in explosions, falling from heights and dropping steel parts. The situation has intensified for using the beaching practice (ILO, n.d.). Ambulances can hardly reach the ship recycling yards located on the beaches and due to the softness of the mudflat; it is not possible to use cranes or heavy lifting machines. Moreover, currents and tides spread the pollutants from the vessel to the surrounding environment (Jenssen et al, 2018). This eventually causes serious environmental harm and long-term issues to public and environmental health. Moreover, the use of oxy-torch cutting and burning of cable on-site cause air pollution alongside exposing workers to toxic fumes (Jenssen et al, 2018, p. 30).

Alongside the general problems in Bangladesh's ship recycling industry, there are some specific challenges in recycling oil and gas platforms. First, transportation of fixed platforms to Bangladesh is costly because they do not sail on international water autonomously and for transportation, they require towing by tugs or lifting on top of heavy lifting vessels. One estimate shows that due to the expensive amount of fuel and expensive insurances, towing and heavy lifting requires a cost of up to USD 1 million. However, according to industry sources, the price may go down when there is an increasing demand for heavy lifting vessels in this sector. This demand increase would increase the assets number for recycling in Bangladesh. NGO recycling Platform predicts that owners will send semi-submersible and jack-ups to beaching yards if their transportation cost goes down in future (Jenssen et al, 2018, p. 27).

Second, while there is no cost involved in exporting drill ships, FPSO and FSO to Bangladesh as unlike, mobile offshore drilling unit (MODUs), they can sail independently to Bangladesh, the workers need special knowledge and training for their recycling. The structures require a thorough cleaning process before they are ready to cut into pieces. Moreover, unlike ships, MODUs has no hull to provide any containment while breaking. The beaching of MODUs is also challenging as they include subsea structures. For example, in the absence of sufficient water depth at the arrival point, MODUs with cones mounted at the base of a jack-up render beaching highly risky, and even impossible (Jenssen et al, 2018).

Third, oil and gas extraction units have naturally occurred radioactive materials (NORM) coated inside of the storage, transportation, and production equipment. Unless the parts containing NORM have been cleaned, handled, and disposed of in a controlled manner at licenced facilities by skilled workers, exposure to NORM poses additional risks to workers' health, the public and the environment (Strand, 2017).

Fourth, not only NORM, the oil and gas units may also contain mercury in thermometers, electrical switches, level switches and light fittings. As even a low level of mercury vapour can cause serious health problems, such as kidney damage, the World Health Organisation considers Mercury as one of the top ten chemicals of major public health concern. Unless workers identify mercury before recycling risks for workers and the environment are very high (Jenssen et al, 2018, pp. 29-31).

Followed by Bangladesh's long time recycling experience, it can overcome the specific threats to the environment and workers in recycling oil and gas units, if Australia supports its capacity building in handling NORM, Mercury, establishing dock method for safer recycling and providing sophisticated training to workers for cutting the structures.

SOLUTIONS AND RECOMMENDATIONS

Recycling offshore structures in Bangladesh consists of both prospects and challenges of the circular economy approach. How Australia's financial and technical support can help Bangladesh in overcoming the challenges is mentioned below.

1. ***Central treatment, storage, and disposal facilities:*** One of the main problems for Bangladesh's recycling industry is not to have a central treatment, storage, and disposal facilities (TSDF) for storing the hazardous wastes found in offshore structures. Recently the International Maritime Organisation has introduced the SENSREC Phase III project in Bangladesh. This project costs USD 120 million and is mainly funded by Norway, a European Union nation to make Bangladesh recycling industries more durable in line with the TSDF system (IMO, 2020). An estimated cost of establishing TSDF is between USD 4.5 to 5 billion and if implemented, the industry's waste management system will allow sending to the central purification system (ED: shipbreaking to shipbuilding, 2021). Australia can contribute to this project providing financial support to this project.
2. ***Taking Responsibility for Sound Management*:** In practical terms, it means alongside sending the offshore structures to Bangladesh's recycling industry, it is for Australia to take responsibility and assist Bangladesh to maintain high standard in recycling the structures and support completing a

capacity building project, such as, the SENSREC Phase III project. Australia can achieve the goals by both financial and technical support under the proposed agreement. The proposed bilateral agreement will thereby apply the producers' responsibility and monetary incentive approach for recycling Australian offshore structures in Bangladesh.

3. ***Reliable Trading Partner in Indo-Pacific Region*:** Moreover, Australia's investment in this sector would put Australia in a competitive advantage in the Indo-pacific region. Australia is looking for new reliable trade partners as Australia is having a trade war with China after Covid pandemic, so, the bilateral agreement would turn into a good initiative for Australia not only for business but also for more maritime control over Indian and Indo-pacific region with Bangladesh's support. Besides investing billions of USD in energy and construction sectors, China has recently made a USD 1.6 billion investment in constructing the Payra Deep Sea Port in Bangladesh, the third-largest port in the country. China has got access to major seaports in Bangladesh, but by doing so, its aim is to gradually take control of maritime region of Indian Ocean (Samsani, 2021). China also has huge investment in Pakistan, Sri Lanka, Maldives, and Nepal. A study argues that these investments are eventually contributing to form a debt trap for these countries (Samsani, 2021). Therefore, the proposed agreement would take a shift away solely from Chinese investments in this region.
4. ***Resolving the Decommissioning Problem*:** The problem of decommissioning is a global issue and developed countries are finding the South Asian recycling yards, being a reasonable solution. The UK and EU are already in a trade relationship with Bangladesh and sending offshore structures to South Asia. Offshore structures are already on the beaches of Bangladesh from the UK and other EU countries for recycling (Foundation, 2020). However, media report notes that sending offshore structures from the UK or EU to Bangladesh is not beyond question (Foundation, 2020). NGO Ship recycling Platform has mainly raised this question because of the poor standards maintained in Bangladesh's recycling yards (Jenssen et al, 2018). Australia must concentrate on improving the standards in Bangladesh following internationally accepted legal principles.
5. ***Following the Environmentally Sound Management Approach under the International Environmental Law*:** International law in this context also has two directions- the waste regime and the ship recycling regime. *Basel Convention* covers the waste regime, which requires companies to take extended liability whereas the *Hong Kong Convention* establishing the ship recycling regime does not require the companies to take such extended liability. *The Hong Kong* Convention imposes no liability on exporter companies. In sharp contrast to the *Basel Convention* that does not support sending wastes to developing countries, the *Hong Kong Convention* developed the principle of exporting fixed platforms after removal and floating platforms 'as is' basis. As stated above, like the floating platforms, the fixed structures fall under the definition of the ship provided in the *Hong Kong Convention* because of their floating capacity when they are partially removed from the seabed.

Under the *Basel Convention* that aims at regulating the transboundary movement of wastes, transfer of wastes from OECD countries to developing countries is not allowed unless the importing states need them as raw materials and exporting states follow the basic principles of ensuring sound management of wastes in a foreign jurisdiction. On the other hand, the *Hong Kong Convention* shifts the expensive sound management liability of the structures to the importing countries and their industries. Moreover, the *Hong Kong Convention* is silent on the issue of transferring technology from developed to developing countries or providing funding to ship recycling countries to improve their standards. This is a significant legal gap in the law of ship recycling. Arguably, article 4 of the *Basel Convention* allows developed countries to export wastes in the name of ships because it aims to regulate rather than ban, the export of hazardous wastes. Linked to the shortcoming, the Convention does not impose liability on exporting companies, who are responsible for violating the Convention (Hackett, 1990, p. 321). Although the government of shipping companies can administer them, the administration is indirect. In a legal sense, the *Basel Convention* also allows offshore structures or ships in the broad sense to be sent to developing countries as raw materials (like steel plates for recycling or recovery industries) (*The Basel Convention* art 4(9)(b)) or where the exporters do not have the potential technology or facility to dispose of the waste in an environmentally sound manner (*The Basel Convention* art 4(9)(c).

Therefore, after the adoption of the *Basel Convention* transfer off offshore structures cannot be termed as dumping of wastes from developed countries if the developed countries take responsibility of their sound management. For Australia, it is a waste for not having adequate and established industry, but it is an opportunity for Bangladesh, a developing country. Alternatively, a good option is to take workers from Bangladesh to Australia, but the authors argue that taking workers from Bangladesh to Australia is not an appropriate option because it will still be very expensive for Australia because the country does not have an established industry such as Bangladesh and it will require spend billions of dollars to establish its new recycling industry for the offshore structures.

6. ***Responsible Recycling*:** Despite generating profit for both sides, this potential recycling pathway proposed in this Chapter raises some issues, including the responsibility of all parties to recycling workers in South Asia who may face deaths, injuries or suffer work-related diseases and the concerns related to environmental problems in their recycling. A safer approach for Australia would be to follow the *Basel Convention*'s requirements. This means Australia can send offshore structures to South Asia following the proposed bilateral agreement. At the same time, being an existing party to the *Basel Convention* Australia should ensure Sound management of the wastes in a foreign jurisdiction by investing in improving the standard of the importing states and by pre-cleaning the hazardous substances of the offshore structures.

FUTURE RESEARCH DIRECTION

The existing and upcoming decommissioning wave represents a perfect opportunity to apply this innovative idea proposed in this Chapter. This Chapter proposes that the Bangladesh's recycling industry could be the ultimate destination of Australian offshore infrastructure at their end of life. The vessels, like the Northern Endeavor, could end up in Bangladesh for recycling (Miline, 2021). As highlighted before selling the offshore structures would not only help the Australian industries earning high sale prices but the business opportunity would help them externalising the environmental and health risks in decommissioning the structures onshore, it is the best time for Australian scientists, legal researchers, and policy makers to think about the issue and the proposal in detail. It is important for the future researchers to examine the potential benefits of the bilateral agreement through the lens of cost and benefit. It is hoped that the Chapter's discussion of potential trade relationships in this sector will add value to the researchers, observers, and policy makers to research further, support and design and implement policies to create a conducive and effective environment to the industry.

It is also essential for future researchers to examine the workplace safety standards, Waste and Debris Management System, Skill Standard, efficiency level, health and environmental risk factors and mitigation strategy of Bangladesh recycling industry in detail. More so, an examination of the forward and backward integration of the industry, wage comparison of South Asian major recycling countries, laws/accords in tables, their wages, compliance and labour welfare standards, life insurance/health insurance and environmental damage Costs, and waste management methods can be undertaken by future research in this area.

CONCLUSION

National Energy Resources Australia (NERA) highlighted the necessity for an innovative recycling strategy, arguing that the increasing volume of unused offshore structures is not only 'a looming threat but also an opportunity (Natonal Energy Resources Australia, 2016). A report published by them notes that increasing the volume of end-of-life oil and gas infrastructures could be an opportunity to invest and build the relevant strategy before the wave of decommissioning activities starts (Natonal Energy Resources Australia, 2016; Gourvenec, 2017). As offshore structures are in high demand for their reusable steel, the study has suggested that by exporting and recycling the offshore structures in Bangladesh following the proposed bilateral agreement, Australia not only can externalise the risks of its own human and environment but also can earn huge revenue from the sale of the structures.

A brief analysis of the international mechanisms of recycling and decommissioning the offshore structures has exposed that neither international nor national laws put a restriction for Australia to form the bilateral agreement with Bangladesh that aims at transferring these oil and gas assets for recycling in Bangladesh.

Arguably, the proposed bilateral agreement would raise a global issue of environmental and human costs, which may require the Australian government and industries to invest in building technical capacity of the Bangladesh recycling industry for a safer and more sustainable management of the offshore assets. It is increasingly in the interest of both Australia and Bangladesh. This Chapter has broadly argued that unless exporting nations and their industries play an effective role in the recycling processes, it would not be a successful recycling pathway (Lloyd's Register Foundation, 2019). A shared responsibility to improve standards of Bangladesh's recycling industry, develop and adopt best practices to improve safety in recycling these structures should be the principal aim of the proposed bilateral agreement between Bangladesh and Australia.

ACKNOWLEDGMENT

This research was supported by the Curtin University (Curtin Publication Grant - 2021). The authors gratefully acknowledge receipt of funding for preparing this Book Chapter through a Curtin Publication Grant, 2021. The project satisfies the aim of the Grant, being the achievement of joint publications by Curtin University HDR students based on the PhD thesis.

REFERENCES

Barrymore, S. (2017). Decommissioning of Australia's oil and gas facilities in the 21st century. *APPEA Journal, 57*(2), 397. doi:10.1071/AJ16004

Bond, T., Partridge, J., Taylor, M., Langlois, T., Malseed, B., Smith, L., & McLean, D. (2018). Fish associated with a subsea pipeline and adjacent seafloor of the northwest shelf of western Australia. *Marine Environmental Research, 141*, 53–65. doi:10.1016/j.marenvres.2018.08.003 PMID:30107887

Cairns, G. (2007). Postcard from Chittagong: Wish you were here? *Critical Perspectives on International Business, 3*(3), 266–279. doi:10.1108/17422040710775030

Chakma, J. (2021, February 7). Steel exports jump 83pc. *The Daily Star*. https://www.thedailystar.net/business/news/steel-exports-jump-83pc-2040485

Chandler, J., White, D., Techera, E. J., Gourvenec, S., & Draper, S. (2017). Engineering and legal considerations for decommissioning of offshore oil and gas infrastructure in Australia. *Ocean Engineering, 131*, 338–347. doi:10.1016/j.oceaneng.2016.12.030

Chockalingam, G. C. G., & Sivasamy, D. K. (2021). A Perspective Study of Ship breaking in India and the Impact of International Conventions and Regulations. *IIRE Journal of Maritime Research and Development, 5*(1). https://ojsiire.com/index.php/IJMRD/article/view/168

Commission, B. P. (2020, March). *General Economic Division*. Www.plancomm.gov.bd. http://www.plancomm.gov.bd/sites/default/files/files/plancomm.portal.gov.bd/files/10509d1f_aa05_4f93_9215_f81fcd233167/2020-08-31-16-

Cullinane, B., & Gourvenec, S. (2017). Decommissioning – the next Australian oil and gas boom? *APPEA Journal, 57*(2), 421. doi:10.1071/AJ16203

Decommissioning Australia, C. of. (2021). *Reports and Publications (portal): NERA National Energy Resources Australia*. https://www.nera.org.au/Publications-and-insights

ED. From ship-breaking to ship-building. (2021, September 29). *Dhaka Tribune*. https://www.dhakatribune.com/opinion/editorial/2021/09/29/ed-from-ship-breaking-to-ship-building

Ellen Macarthur Foundation. (n.d.). *Explore the Circular Economy in Detail*. http://www.ellenmacarthurfoundaiton.org/explore/the-circular-economy-in-detail

Foxwell, D. (2016). *Decommissioning Market Growing Size and Complexity but Providers too Fragmented*. http://www.osjonline.com/news/veiw,decom-market-growing-size-and-complexity-but-providers-too-frgamanted_45672

Gregson, N., Crang, M., Fuller, S., & Holmes, H. (2015). Interrogating the circular economy: The moral economy of resource recovery in the EU. *Economy and Society, 44*(2), 218–243. doi:10.1080/03085147.2015.1013353

Hand, M. (2014, June 28). *Five workers dead in blast at Alang shipbreaking yard*. Sea trade Maritime; Maritime News. https://www.seatrade-maritime.com/asia/five-workers-dead-blast-alang-shipbreaking-yard

High Commission. (n.d.). *Bangladesh - Australia Trade and Investment Relations | Bangladesh High Commission Canberra*. https://www.bhcanberra.com/trade-investments/bangladesh-australia-trade-relations

Hossain, A. (2018). *Determination of reusable and waste material from ship recycling industry of Bangladesh by broad sampling of data*. SSRN Electronic Journal. doi:10.2139srn.3252979

Hossain, K. A. (2015). Overview of Ship Recycling Industry of Bangladesh. *Journal of Environmental & Analytical Toxicology*, *5*(5). Advance online publication. doi:10.4172/2161-0525.1000312

Hossain, M., Fakhruddin, A., Chowdhury, M., & Gan, S. (2016). Impact of ship-breaking activities on the coastal environment of Bangladesh and a management system for its sustainability. *Environmental Science & Policy*, *60*, 84–94. doi:10.1016/j.envsci.2016.03.005

ILO. (2009, June 15). *Ship-breaking: A hazardous work*. Www.ilo.org. https://www.ilo.org/safework/areasofwork/hazardous-work/WCMS_110335/lang--en

IMO. (2020, July 31). *Ship recycling in Bangladesh leaps forward with third phase of key project signed*. https://www.imo.org/en/MediaCentre/PressBriefings/pages/23-SENSREC-Phase-III.aspx

IORA. (n.d.). *About IORA*. https://www.iora.int/en/about/about-iora

Jaganmohan, M. (2021, June 1). *India: iron ore export volume 2020*. Statista. https://www.statista.com/statistics/1131708/india-iron-ore-export-volume/

Jenssen, I. (2020). Biennial Report- 2018-19. In *NGO Shipbreaking Platform*. NGO Shipbreaking Platform. https://www.shipbreakingplatform.org/wp-content/uploads/2020/06/NGOSBP-Bi-Annual-Report-18-19.pdf

Jenssen, I., Mulinaris, N., & Mork, M. (2019). Recycling Outlook: Decommissioning of North Sea Floating Oil and Gas Units. In *NGO Shipbreaking Platform*. KLP. https://www.shipbreakingplatform.org/wp-content/uploads/2019/09/Shipbreaking-OG-Report.pdf

Jenssen, I., & Puckett, J. (2020). *Contradiction in Terms: European Union Must Align Its Waste Ship Exports with International Law and Green Deal*. European Union. https://mk0eeborgicuypctuf7e.kinstacdn.com/wp-content/uploads/2020/09/Report-EU-SRR-Ban-Amendment-BAN-EEB-GP-SBP.pdf

John, J., & Kumar, S. (2016). A locational decision making framework for shipbreaking under multiple criteria. *International Journal of Strategic Decision Sciences*, *7*(1), 76–97. doi:10.4018/IJSDS.2016010104

LensCulture. (n.d.). *Ship Breaking in Bangladesh - Photographs and text by Jan Møller Hansen*. LensCulture. Retrieved October 14, 2021, from https://www.lensculture.com/articles/jan-moller-hansen-ship-breaking-in-bangladesh

Lloyds Register Foundation. (2020). *Safer Decommissioning of Offshore Structures and Ships*. Lloyd's Register Foundation. http://lrfoundation.org.uk

Macdonald-Smith, A. (2020, November 3). *Decommissioning crisis clouds oil M&A outlook*. Australian Financial Review. https://www.afr.com/companies/energy/decommissioning-crisis-clouds-oil-m-and-a-outlook-20201102-p56anf

McKay, S., Higgins, S. A., & Baker, P. (2020). NORM inventory forecast for Australian offshore oil and gas decommissioned assets and radioactive waste disposal pathways. *APPEA Journal*, *60*(1), 19–33. doi:10.1071/AJ19159

Mikelis, N. (2019, October). *The Recycling of Ships*. GMS. https://www.gmsinc.net/gms_new/assets/publications/pdf/2020-01-16rJU_org.pdf

Milad, M. (2021, July 9). 25 Years Old Ship, Cost 24.564 million. *Prothom Alo*.

Miline, P. (2021, August 23). *Government Hurries to Tow Northern Endeavor away by Mid-2023*. Boiling Cold. https://boilingcold.com.au

Mizanur Rahman, S., & Mayer, A. L. (2015). How social ties influence metal resource flows in the Bangladesh ship recycling industry. *Resources, Conservation and Recycling*, *104*, 254–264. doi:10.1016/j.resconrec.2015.07.022

NERA. (2016). *Oil and Gas Industry Competitiveness Assessment: Report on the Framework, Baseline Score, Insights and Opportunities*. www.nera.org.au

NOPSEMA. (2020). *Inside: Managing Ageing Infrastructure Stewarding Australia's offshore assets in later life*. NOPSEMA. https://www.nopsema.gov.au/sites/default/files/documents/2021-04/A720926.pdf

Pence, M. (2018). *Vice President Mike Pence's Remark on the Administration's Policy Towards China*. https://www.hudson.org/events/1610-vice-president-mike-pence-s-remarks-on-the-administration-s-policy-towards-china-102018

Rabbi, H., & Rahman, A. (2017). Ship breaking and recycling industry of Bangladesh; issues and challenges. *Procedia Engineering*, *194*, 254–259. doi:10.1016/j.proeng.2017.08.143

Rahman, S., & Kim, J. (2020). Circular economy, proximity, and shipbreaking: A material flow and environmental impact analysis. *Journal of Cleaner Production*, *259*, 120681. doi:10.1016/j.jclepro.2020.120681

Romanenko, M. (2021, January 13). *How to Scrap a Cruise Ship and What They Go For*. https://www.cruiseindustrynews.com/cruise-news/24172-how-to-scrap-a-cruise-ship-and-what-they-go-for.html

Samsani, S. (2021). *China–Bangladesh strategic linkages*. Observer Research Foundation. https://www.orfonline.org/expert-speak/china-bangladesh-strategic-linkages/

Sarraf, M., Stuer-Lauridsen, F., Dyoulgerov, M., Bloch, R., Wingfield, S., & Watkinson, R. (2010). *Ship Breaking And Recycling Industry In Bangladesh And Pakistan December 2010*. World Bank. https://documents1.worldbank.org/curated/en/872281468114238957/pdf/582750ESW0Whit1LIC1011098791web1opt.pdf

Shahnewaz, M. (2017). *The Effective Enforcement of National Ship Recycling Regulations in India* [Master's Thesis].

Strand, T. (2017). *NORM in the Norwegian Oil and Gas Industry -Activity Levels, Occupational Doses and Protective Measures*. https://www.ipen.br/biblioteca/cd/irpa/2004/files/5k14.pdf

Sujauddin, M., Koide, R., Komatsu, T., Hossain, M., Tokoro, C., & Murakami, S. (2016). Ship breaking and the steel industry in Bangladesh: A material flow perspective. *Journal of Industrial Ecology*, *21*(1), 191–203. doi:10.1111/jiec.12423

Techera, E. J., & Chandler, J. (2015). Offshore installations, decommissioning and artificial reefs: Do current legal frameworks best serve the marine environment? *Marine Policy*, *59*, 53–60. doi:10.1016/j.marpol.2015.04.021

The Offshore Petroleum and Greenhouse Gas Storage Act (2006).

Voinov Kohler, J. (2017). The Basel convention on the control of transboundary movements of hazardous wastes and their disposal 1989. In *Multilateral environmental treaties* (pp. 331–342). Edward Elgar Publishing. doi:10.4337/9781783477210.V.32

Wignaraja, G. W., Panditaratne, D., Kannangara, P., & Hundlani, D. (2020). *Chinese Investment and BRI in Srilanka*. Chatham House. https://www.chathamhouse.org/2020/03/chinese-investment-and-bri-sri-lanka

Wilby, D. (2016, February 1). *Douglas-Westwood: coming decommissioning boom to be driven by UK*. Oilfield Technology. https://www.oilfieldtechnology.com/offshore-and-subsea/01022016/douglas-westwood-coming-decommissioning-boom-to-be-driven-by-uk/

Wood Mackenzie. (2016). *Wood Mackenzie*. https://www.woodmac.com/web/woodmac/data

Zakaria, N., Ali, M., & Hossain, K. (2012). Underlying problems of ship recycling industries in Bangladesh and way forward. *Journal of Naval Architecture and Marine Engineering*, *9*(2), 91–102. doi:10.3329/jname.v9i2.10515

ADDITIONAL READING

Det Norske Veritas. (2001, February 13). *Study on the technological and economic feasibility of ship scrapping in Europe*. Internal Market, Industry, Entrepreneurship and SMEs - European Commission. https://ec.europa.eu/growth/content/study-technological-and-economic-feasibility-ship-scrapping-europe-0_en

Mikelis, N. (2018). The Recycling of Ships. In *gmsinc.net*. Global Marketing System. https://www.gmsinc.net/gms_new/assets/ads/folder.pdf

Petrig, A. (2020). Autonomous offender ships and international maritime security law. In *Autonomous ships and the law* (pp. 23–55). Routledge., doi:10.4324/9781003056560-5

Rahman, M. M. (2011). Shipbreaking Activities: Threat to Coastal Environment and Fish Biodiversity. In M. E. Y. Haroon & A. K. Hussain (Eds.), *Eco-system Health and Management of Pollution in the Bay of Bengal* (pp. 23–42). Bangladesh Fisheries Research Institute.

Sultana, M. (2013, January 11). *Equal Times*. https://www.equaltimes.org/wp-content/uploads/2013/01/Shipbreaking_021-WP.jpg

KEY TERMS AND DEFINITIONS

Bilateral Agreement: Agreement between two inter-State parties. Both parties make their own promises considering the object of the relationship and bring profit for both sides.

Decommissioning: Final stage of an energy project. It includes the abandoning of oil and gas wells and then remove and reprocess the structures at their end of life.

Offshore Industries: "Off the coast." It refers to subsea development of oil fields and natural gas deposits.

Offshore Structures: Offshore platforms. Special type of complex structures.

Recycling: Cutting the offshore structures into pieces, reprocessing, and reusing the original materials.

Recycling Industry: Industry that cuts the ships and oil platforms into pieces for scrap steels, using manual labours in India and Bangladesh. Recycling industry is the major source of steel industry in Bangladesh.

Waste Dumping: A decision to dispose of the hazardous materials or a ship, or an offshore structure that contains hazardous materials in its body.

Chapter 11
Review of Post-COVID-19 Tourism Marketing Partnership Opportunities Between Australia and Pakistan

Farooq Haq
https://orcid.org/0000-0002-1620-9226
Canadian University Dubai, UAE

Anam Syed Maheen
Canadian University Dubai, UAE

ABSTRACT

This chapter presents a deliberation on an opportunity for tourism marketing partnership between Australian and South Asia, with a focus on Pakistan. Tourism being the star performing industry across the globe has faced unprecedented crash due to COVID-19. Post-COVID-19 market opening relies heavily on the fundamental option of partnerships between governments and private players. The tourism demand has triggered partnerships between government and private agencies across various countries that have convergence in areas of culture, politics, and economy. Australia and Pakistan are among the countries who do not have geographical proximity, but they enjoy congruence in agriculture-based economy and sports-based entertainment. Moreover, both countries have diverse tourism resources serving travelers in hedonistic, mountain, snow, spiritual, sports, and events. This chapter highlights the types of tourism marketing that could be facilitated in a post-COVID-19 environment between Australia and Pakistan and phases involved in the partnership essential for meeting United Nations SDGs.

INTRODUCTION

COVID-19 pandemic has drastically changed the business structures and operations around the globe. Production of tangible items and food products suffered with sale drops and business declines. The service

DOI: 10.4018/978-1-7998-8657-0.ch011

industry has been the major victim of COVID-19, with all stakeholders from airlines to hotels losing businesses that were progressively running for many decades. Many governments and private agencies betting all their chips in tourism, faced the biggest loss during the financial disaster in 2020-21. After two years of COVID-19 regulations, lockdowns, precautions, various variants, 219 million infected and 4.55 million dead worldwide, the intensity seems to be weakening. The positive environment is opening opportunities for various industrial encouragement moving towards growth. Most service industries are ahead in the race to capitalize on the new COVID-19 free environment, the front runner being the tourism related services.

The post COVID-19 world presents a new business map with new opportunities, which can be capitalized with properly analyzed and sorted out partnerships. Moreover, the partnerships emerging now are going across geographical boundaries and beyond cultural convergences (Wyman, 2020). This chapter presents a conceptual study suggesting that post COVID-19 new opportunities could be observed and followed in tourism among Australia and South Asia. The South Asian countries are further narrowed down to Pakistan where a new partnership for tourism management and growth could be materialized. Apparently, Australia and Pakistan seem as two distant nations but the emergence of new tourism dimensions and tourism partnerships could be substantiated for bilateral benefits. Due to its past success in tourism, Australia could be considered as the leading partner taking the role of the teacher, while Pakistan could be the follower taking the role of the student.

This chapter illustrates the opportunity that could be recognized by Australia and Pakistan for tourism partnership based on an analysis of other partnerships in tourism involving these countries. Furthermore, both countries have a positive history of bilateral engagement in areas of agriculture, environment, sports, music, global peace and security (Haider, 2020). This chapter is structured as follows. The first section of the chapter introduces the changed business atmosphere related to global tourism based on partnerships after the COVID-19 pandemic. Section 2 provides the literature review studying the significance of Australia's tourism engagement with South Asia in general and a specific country such as Pakistan. Section 3 outlines Australia's tourism-based partnerships with other Asian countries and their outcomes. Section 4 delivers findings of this study indicating the phases involved in tourism partnerships between Australia and Pakistan. The final section 5 summarizes the research and concludes the chapter with identification of future research direction involving empirical research with tourists and tourism providers.

BACKGROUND

Pakistan, although not a well know tourism destination, it presents a diverse range of choices for various types of tourists. The country hosts one of the oldest human civilizations, hosts several locations of scenic beauty, range of highest mountains, many religious, spiritual, and historic places, unique arts and crafts, a multi-contextual culture and a rich heritage (Seraphim & Haq, 2019). About the Pakistani people, Ahmed (2021) reported that the British Backpacker Society ranked Pakistan as the world's top adventure travel destination in 2018, labeled the people as one of the friendliest nation, with countless mountain sceneries that could be described as beyond wildest imagination.

The TripAdvisor (2021) promoted Pakistan as stretched between Karakoram Mountain ranges in the North to the huge muddy delta of the Indus River in the South; Pakistan presents a land of super adventure and nature. Out of 18, ten mammalian orders are found in Pakistan with species ranging from the smallest mammals, the Mediterranean Pigmy Shrew, to the largest known mammal the blue whale.

The TripAdvisor (2021) further reported that Pakistan accommodates 108 peaks above 7,000 meters and more than 100 peaks above 6,000 meters, five of the 14 highest independent peaks known as the 8-thousanders stand in Pakistan, found in the surroundings of Concordia; the confluence of Baltoro Glacier and Godwin Austen Glacier. Seraphim & Haq (2019) found that Pakistan hosts six tangible heritage sites recognized by UNESCO: Archaeological Ruins at Moenjodaro (1980), Buddhist Ruins of Takht-i-Bahi and Remains at Sahr-i-Bahlol (1980), Fort and Shalamar Gardens in Lahore (1981), Historical Monuments at Makli, Thatta (1981), Rohtas Fort (1997) and Taxila (1980). There are some heritage sites that are hoping to be part of the formal recognition from World Heritage Centre includes: Badshahi Mosque, Lahore (1993), Wazir Khan's Mosque, Lahore (1993), and Tombs of Jahangir, Asif Khan and Akbari Sarai, Lahore (1993).

Collaborative tourism partnership opportunities come in a variety of types and brings in different perceived benefits. Previous research has extensively discussed Islamic spiritual tourism opportunities among Australia and Pakistan where various stakeholders are actively involved such as in public and private tourism providers, their agencies, transportation, and accommodation providers. According to this study, public-private partnerships are beneficial in a variety of business areas, and this public/private mix of partners has immense potential in spiritual tourism (Haq, 2014).

Previous studies have not looked at the development of tourism in Pakistan through modern logistics infrastructure and best environmental policies, and information is not widely available. As a result, current chapter, aims to address potential opportunities between Pakistan and Australia in order to develop the most effective strategies for the promotion of tourism in the country. There is no doubt that Pakistan and China have had a long and fruitful relationship through China-Pakistan Economic Corridor (CPEC) project that provides market for tourism of Pakistan with various green initiatives, and now other countries are trying to join the CPEC (Naz et al., 2019). Because of their close proximity, these two countries have strategic and social interests in common (Ullah, Khan, & Haq, 2018). Furthermore, Canada and Australia were the fastest-growing emerging destinations for Pakistani tourists (Ahmed, 2021). Improvements in tourism operations can spur the growth of related sectors, resulting in more direct and indirect employment.

The mountainous regions of Pakistan are said to have some of the world's most stunning and interesting landscapes and ecology offering the best tourism potential (Ullah, 2020). However, tourism in these areas is increasing strain on the local ecosystem, resulting in increased pollution, natural habitat loss, and endangered species pressure. These consequences have the potential to gradually deplete the environmental resources that tourism relies on (Ahmed, 2021). Pakistan features a diverse mountain scenery, with some of the world's highest peaks and longest glaciers. Mountain tourism is growing in popularity in Pakistan, and it has the potential to be a significant component of the economy in these areas, which offers a unique tourism experience that attracts travelers from developed countries including Australia. Moreover, an opportunity exists for Australia and Pakistan to collaborate in development and promoting environmental tourism resources should place an emphasis on environmental and cultural relic preservation, as well ensuring tourist safety. Pakistan's tourism infrastructure is currently incapable of handling a significant number of visitors in a short period of time and this is where Australia can help and be an effective teacher.

The ineffectiveness of governmental institutions as a result of the bureaucracy's limited capacity, corruption and over-politicization, is jeopardizing Pakistan's economic, social, and political development. Given the unavoidably political aspect of public service reform, far more focus should be placed on establishing political strategies and tactics to push reforms through, rather than addressing issues as purely technical. Another key obstacle to public service reform in Pakistan has been the country's recurrent political instability. Government's short tenures and frequent changes have contributed to a culture where the incentives are to focus on short-term political and financial gain rather than attaining mid- to long-term policy goals. The most important issue today for Pakistan's civil service is to restore constitutional security by the representative elected does not misuses their power and influence (Wilder, 2009).

LITERATURE REVIEW

Opportunities in Tourism Partnerships for Pakistan

The advancement of logistical infrastructure benefits the tourism industry both directly and indirectly and there is a strong connection between tourism business development and better logistics infrastructure (Selin, 1999). The vulnerable ecosystems of the Northern Areas can be irrevocably harmed by a single season of uncontrolled tourism. Ecological tourism, commonly known as 'eco-tourism', is a type of tourism in which visitors go with the goal of learning about the local environment and culture while avoiding any damage to it (Graci, 2013). It would, however, require commitments from all major stakeholders, including government officials, tour operators, local communities, tourists, and the hotel industry, to protect natural and cultural resources. In addition, Sustainable tourism is an area that can be explored to protect the environment and culture, it necessitates the implementation of certain norms and regulations. Australia can support to establish financial initiatives by creating policies with tour operators whilst maintaining the cultural heritage of the area.

The major challenge for tourism in Pakistan is the lack of infrastructure, particularly in natural landscapes that require effective planning before inviting international tourists (Sadaqat, 2021). The Pakistani Government is conscious about opening new tourism places to avoid encroachment and mushroom growth, while ensuring fair competition, organic growth, and preservation of the natural ecosystem (Sadaqat, 2021). Recently, Hilton brand announced a major tourism residence in Islamabad while many other hotel chains including Sheraton and the Intercontinental are also searching for options for new properties in Pakistan (Ahmed, 2021). Sadaqat (2021) reported that the government is seeking more partnerships to expand the tourism industry with more global hotels being invited to join the hospitality portfolio, since the government analyzes the Covid-19 pandemic as damaging yet offering an opportunity to excel in the upcoming global tourism markets.

China launched One Belt One Road (OBOR) in 2014, a huge economic development project, with a plan to invest over $3 trillion in infrastructure in 68 regions over the next several decades as part of this strategy (Economist, 2016). With the China-Pakistan Economic Corridor (CPEC), China has massively invested in Pakistan and because of this, it will have a multiplier effect on the country's economy, which needs infrastructural projects (Farr, 2017). The impact of the (OBOR) project has both positive and negative impact in the long run on the CPEC relationship between both countries. Industrial parks, agricultural fields, trains, airports, highways, a fiber-optic network, energy-generating projects and including one of the world's biggest solar farms are all part of CPEC initiatives which are already underway in some areas (Hali et al., 2015). A new telecommunications network will be built as part of the project, connecting Pakistan to China and then to Europe via China (Economist, 2016).

At the completion of the CPEC, it will provide much-needed infrastructure to Pakistan's underdeveloped areas rather than simply operating as a transit route for Chinese commodities (Farr, 2017). Foreign direct investment in the region will restore the economies of Pakistan's underdeveloped and neglected regions (Hali et al., 2015). Furthermore, the CPEC is an extension of the OBOR where the project has the support of Pakistan's political authorities. The real question is whether CPEC will help or impede Pakistan's progress. On one hand, the $60 billion investment will provide Pakistan with resources and beneficial economically, but it will involve a considerable financial burden for the country (Farr, 2017). Pakistan faces numerous challenges that will risk the CPEC project's viability, including regional and ethnic conflicts and rivalries, as well as the growing operations of Islamic extremist groups. Among the several problems cited, Pakistan's extremely hierarchical and corrupt class system may represent the greatest threat as highlighted by Wilder (2009).

Pakistan also offers a wide range of religious and spiritual tourism places and events (Haq & Medhekar, 2019). Based on multi-religious culture and society, there are several sacred destinations for Hindus, Buddhists and Sikhs in Pakistan (Haq & Wong, 2013). The government is actively promoting religious and spiritual tourism, due to the global growth of interest in spirituality and related matters, which could also be the last bridge between Indian and Pakistani Governments (Haq & Medhekar, 2019). In 2019, the Kartarpur Project, known as Sikhism followers' Makkah, was opened as a non-visa corridor for Sikh pilgrims and spiritual tourists coming to Pakistan (Haq & Jackson, 2021). The Pakistani Prime Minister Imran Khan was leader of the project that has drawn the attention of the Sikh community around the world, resulting in 83 percent of the eight million diaspora Sikhs residing outside India, 79 percent of the 20 million Indian Sikhs, showing their interest in visiting Pakistan (Haq & Jackson, 2021). The Sikh community is rapidly growing in Australia, which will be happy to visit Kartarpur in Pakistan (Wyeth, 2021). Similarly, the Frontier Province of Pakistan, bordering with Afghanistan, has been dotted with several Holy Buddhist sites supported by the World Bank to develop a Buddhist trail to attract Buddhists along with celebrated Buddhist Monks from all parts of the world.

Similarly, coastal tourism in Australia has been studied by several researches in the past where infrastructure concerns and growing population constraints in Western Australia, for example, have sparked a surge of interest in tourism and residential development ideas along the coast (Graci, 2013; Craik, 1995). Another public-private partnership can be encouraged in coastal tourism projects between the two countries. Alternative kinds of tourism, such as community-based ecotourism, should be investigated to prevent mass coastal tourism and environmental degradation. The government of Pakistan needs to take serious steps to improve the country's international image as a tourist destination (Ullah, Khan & Haq, 2018).

Cooperation and Partnerships Between Australia and Pakistan

The purpose of this proposal is to study the problems which Pakistani dairy farmers face when they are dealing with Australian businessmen via AUSTRADE and what initiatives should be taken by AUSTRADE to improve this relationship and create a equilibrium game.

Our study is mainly explanatory in its nature and exploratory to some extent. Data from literature was compared with on-ground situation and policy makers in AUSTRADE Pakistan were interviewed to get insight into their role in dealings between Pakistani and Australian dairy farmers; focusing on problems they face and steps to be taken to resolve the issues and improve the bilateral relations and conditions of Pakistani farmers. it has been educed that the fundamental roles of AUSTRADE should include Resolving Communication & Negotiation Problems (Seminars, Meetings, Workshops), Improving Conditions of Pakistani Dairy Farmers (Conversion to Formal Sector, Partnerships b/w Small Scale Farmers, Competitive

Environment, Effective Utilization of Resources, Improving Technical Skills via Workshops, Improving the Genetics of Farmers), Stakes of Australian Businessmen Formal (Sector+Partnerships+Improved Genetics= More Profitability) as a result Stakes of Australian Businessmen will rise leading towards a collaborative and a win-win situation.

The Australian government is committed to helping Pakistan in achieving economic development and stability. Haider (2020) reported that the Pakistani population living in Australian cities has enlarged to 91,000 in 2019, while at least 15000 Pakistani students are studying in various Australian Universities. Since 1984, Australian Centre for International Agricultural Research (ACIAR) has supported a research collaboration program with Pakistan, with recent projects focusing on the country's major fruit crops (mangoes and citrus), livestock (small holder farmers dairy), agricultural policy, and agricultural water management. ACIAR combines world-class research in Australia with Pakistani partners, assisting in the removal of production constraints and the deployment of productivity-boosting technology and innovation. ACIAR collaborates closely with the Pakistani government, non-governmental organizations (NGOs), and the corporate sector to support R&D and technical capacity building (Kazmi, 2017).

Under this, they began a four-year program known as Australia-Pakistan Agriculture Sector Linkages Program (ASLP) founded in 2006 to promote economic systems for Pakistan's rural population and to establish ties between Australia and Pakistan's agricultural sectors (Mitra, 2014). Pakistan is another example of partnership with ACIAR with goal of eliminating poverty and enhancing lives of many as a result of joint worldwide research that has resulted in more productive and sustainable agriculture (Mehdi, Ahmad & Ahsan, 2018). In Pakistan, there are a number of challenges where Australia is in a good position to help Pakistan improve irrigation, drainage, and salinity management in large agricultural areas, and this is a target of the research program (Mehdi et al., 2018; Badar, Ariyawardana, & Collins, 2015). Badar et al. (2015) also illustrated that regarding the Pakistani mango farming and selling value chains are not well structured and generally fragmented in nature, local government bodies are unable to support these chains through effective value chain enhancements and administration where Australian mentorship is required on an on-going basis.

On similar grounds, both countries have a bright history of regular engagements and competitions in various sports; cricket, squash and field hockey are some primary examples (Crowe & Middeldorp, 1996). A lot has been researched on cricket between Australia and Pakistan, with little cooperation in developing the game and events around it (Crowe & Middeldorp, 1996). Regarding the eco-tourism and green revolution for farming, Long Term Agronomic Experiments (LTAE) were initiated more than a century ago to assess the response of farming systems to new ideas and practices, seven of these are being implemented even today in Australia for nutrition and crop protection within modern farming systems (Norton, Perris & Armstrong, 2007). The benefits of LTAE have been shared by Australian farmers with other countries and Pakistan could one of the beneficiaries. The Australia and Pakistan based agricultural partnership indicates a positive history in the bilateral relationship. Although, it is no within the scope of this research paper, yet, the eco-tourism and green revolution can be applied to tourism partnership between both countries.

The green revolution is also gaining popularity in Pakistan especially due to the new Prime Minister Imran Khan; who started the 10 billion tree plantation drive since 2018, which has also inspired Saudi Arabia seeking collaboration for the Middle East Green Initiative (Naz et al., 2019). Moon, Mohel and Farooq (2021) examined the extended environmental theory of planned behavior among the university students of Pakistan to measure the green consciousness. Findings of the research indicated that the perceived gravity of environmental issues and sovereign self-construal were the most decisive determinants of green buying behavior among Pakistani university students. Moon et al. (2021) recommended that marketers could align green consumption with personal goals, while governments need to develop public awareness about the significance of environmental poverty to inspire pro-environmental consumption for all industries including tourism. Australian public and private tourism organizers could help the Pakistani counter parts in this segment of pro-environmental tourism promotion and practices.

In addition, AUSTRADE is the agency in-charge of The Australian Trade and Investment Commission, Australia. AUSTRADE has the primary mission is to support Australian businesses, educational institutions, tourism, government, and citizens in breaking into international markets, promoting international education, attracting foreign direct investment and improving the tourism industry (Ahmad, Hassan & Rizvi, 2017). They serve under the supervision of the Australian High Commission in Pakistan, with operations in Islamabad, Lahore, and Karachi. Pakistan, like other countries, seeks for and identifies potential opportunities for Australians in the country. AUSTRADE is working as a liaison between the two countries Australia and Pakistan by partnering with Pakistani dairy producers in their efforts to improve their industry (Ahmed et al., 2017). Likewise, Australia is known as beef capital of the world due to its superior cattle farming techniques (Walsh & Cowley, 2016), which also could be part of the AUSTRADE support to improve cattle farming in Pakistan.

The Australian government is attempting to tap the Pakistani dairy industry with the cooperation of AUSTRADE. Through this initiative, Pakistani farmers' overall productivity, development, and profits will increase, while Australian investors will benefit from and share those profits, and future relations will be developed. A partnership between countries for tourism is where Pakistan could be guided better by AUSTRADE in promoting their services and improving their image.

Tourism Based Partnerships Between Australia and Other Asian Countries

Historically, White Australia was the political philosophy of the country until 1975 that manifested the termination of the policy, which had its origins in racist theories aligned with its European and, more precisely, British origins, which moved the mindset towards part of Asia (Jupp, 1995). The globalization effect started in 1990s and the change in population, business, cultural exchange and capital movements in the region converted the White Australia into partnerships with Asian nations (Craik, 1995). Nevertheless, public opinion has yet to accept these changes fully, especially when they involve changing the ethnic character of the resident population. It is concluded that the generation which has grown up since 1945 and which is now starting to dominate politics and intellectual life will find it easier to reorient Australia than did the previous generation, despite continuing ambivalence in public attitudes. The presence in Australia of large numbers of permanent residents and citizens of Asian origin is a necessary factor in expediting change. Since the start of this century, Australia has been interested in social and business cooperation with South Asia and has been an observing member of the South Asian Association of Regional Cooperation (SAARC) (Hall & Page, 2000).

Tourism is a highly interdependent business in which the formation of collaborative partnerships such as networks is highly significant. For the past two decades, researchers have looked into the advantages of collaborations for private tourism providers (Scott, Baggio & Cooper, 2008). The tourism industry is also distinguished by its complementary business offerings. Tourists, for example, frequently use a variety of services such as air travel, vehicle rental, accommodation, and tours. Typically, a number of different organizations supply these services. A properly-designed website opens up potential for collaboration with a variety of affiliates and can help providers in arranging a variety of tourism and travel services, as well as consumers in making the best decisions possible, resulting in a more pleasant experience, a website can also serve as a travel service hub, allowing places to emerge and function as umbrella brands (Haq, 2014).

Partnerships supports relationship marketing to build operational efficiencies among the various players involved in the tourism business, the success depends on stakeholders on both the demand side and supply side must collaborate and benefit (Graci, 2013). The global tourism business operations generally include both vertical and horizontal partnerships with both forward and backward integration (Selin, 1999). Horizontal partnerships are based on cooperation between public and private operators and providers of spiritual tourism products and services, while vertical partnerships are the result of collaboration between the operators and various stakeholders, including transport companies, hotels, insurance companies, and financial providers, such as banks and credit card companies (Selin & Chavez, 1995).

Regional development has been regarded as a key driver for tourism. The type and quality of a region's natural assets, the management capacities of regional tourist organizations and operators, and the degree of support from governments at all levels may all influence the amount to which new opportunities are generated (Haq & Medhekar, 2019; Michael, James & Michael, 2018). For example, Adventure, culture, heritage, transportation, accommodation, retail, and hospitality are just a few of the products and services offered by the tourism business. Regional destination marketing organizations, also known as Destination Marketing Organizations (DMOs), are a part of this industry structure with the primary role of promoting tourism in a given region (Burgess, Parish & Alcock, 2011).

This capacity complements the traditional regional marketing locations across Australia and gives an alternate and more feasible contact point, especially for overseas visitors who are increasingly researching their vacation areas before arriving. In addition, over 350,000 tourism-related organizations operate in Australia, offering diverse tourism activities and products (Craik, 1995). The impact of tourism marketing and destination image on tourist behavior and perceptions is a topic that has received a lot of attention in the tourism research literature (Abodeeb, Wilson & Moyle, 2015; Haq & Medhekar, 2019). Australia has been aggressively marketing itself to the UAE/GCC as a preferred tourism destination with a variety of attractions in recent years.

Australia is one of the countries attempting to draw tourists from the Gulf Cooperation Council (GCC) by promoting itself as a competitive tourism destination capable of attracting visitors from a broad number of nations and cultures (Michael, Armstrong, Badran & King, 2011), For example, a particular study findings indicated that Emirati tourists preferred the cooler weather of Australia during the humid months in the UAE (Michael et al., 2018). Moreover, halal food or restaurants were easily available in Australia which shows the strong tourist infrastructure. This study concluded that Australia has well positioned itself as a safer, friendlier, Western culture destination that satisfy the needs of Emirati/GCC visitors. Some visitors expressed their emotions by identifying Australia as a safe, socially and culturally relaxing place where they may wear the Hijab (native female Emirati dress) or even regular casual clothing. In this study, it was found that Emirati tourists planned to return to Australia or suggest it to others, whether they were encouraged to go to Australia for a vacation by others (Michael et al., 2018).

MAIN FOCUS OF THE CHAPTER

Research Issues and Problems

The literature review has highlighted that there are many similarities between Australia and Pakistan, which includes Commonwealth membership, passion for sports mainly cricket, hockey and squash, agriculture based economy, government focus on tourism and green revolution (Crowe & Middeldorp, 1996; Haider, 2020; Mehdi et al., 2018). The Australian Government has been supporting Pakistan in various affairs as discussed in the preceding sections, however, tourism partnership has not been explored or examined earlier in theory or practice. This chapter attempts to work on this research objective or analysing the possibility of tourism partnership between both countries for bilateral benefits. Hence the chapter presents a conceptual study indicating the opportunities that could be capitalized by both countries to enter a sustainable partnership for tourism growth in mountain, green, spiritual and heritage tourism.

POST--COVID-19 DEVELOPMENTS IN TOURISM

Businesses and destinations will require significant government help to turn present constraints into opportunities for recovery in the current socio-economic climate and the ever-changing demand landscape. Globally, governments have already taken steps to mitigate COVID-19's impact on the travel and tourism industry, including easing travel restrictions, providing liquidity and monetary support, protecting workers, establishing health protocols with the private sector, promoting tourism, and investing and encouraging innovation (Ullah et al., 2021). Primarily, in the travel and tourism sector the demand has shifted among traveler's choices and behaviors. In the midst of stay-at-home orders, digital adoption and consumption are increasing, with consumers now demanding contactless technology, such as biometrics, as a minimum need for a safe and seamless travel experience (Wyman, 2020).

In addition, firms and destinations are grasping the opportunity to collaborate and build on their previous experiences in order to improve their strategy and assure the sector's long-term and inclusive recovery. To recover faster, the importance of a global coordinated approach involving public-private cooperation, enacting global health and hygiene protocols, to rebuild traveler trust, and embracing the acceleration of technological transformations have all been revealed (Augustyn & Knowles, 2000; Weidenfeld, 2018). A reflection on these occurrences indicate that they might either represent a temporary shift or have the potential to change the future landscape of travel and tourism.

The impact of the COVID-19 pandemic on Australia's and Pakistan's tourism industry are expected to last for years. Despite the uncertainties, it is anticipated that a slowing in the flow of tourism development moving forward. ACIAR might continue working with Pakistan ongoing projects or those at the proposal stage may postpone moving to the planning stage, which involves more financial investment, until COVID-19 situation normalizes. One major drawback of this outbreak was construction on new projects could have been suspended or slowed as a result of lockdowns and social distancing restrictions, or as a result of a lack of resources (Ullah et al., 2021). When it comes to addressing the pandemic's health and overall economic effects, Australia is in an enviable situation.

However, some segments of the tourism industry, including travel agencies and international aviation, have been adversely impacted and will continue to struggle to recover until the pandemic is gone. Others, on the other hand, have the opportunity to shift in order to increase domestic travel. Similarly, in 2020, the COVID-19 pandemic wreaked havoc on Pakistan's tourism industry which strengthened the local tourism business, despite the limited inbound of tourists from abroad. It can be implied that Pakistani government expects that, given the country's enormous tourism potential, all efforts should be made to expand the growing tourism sector and attract not only local tourists but visitors from all over the world once the pandemic has passed. This shows that for recovery development for the tourism sector post Covid-19 prevails in areas of eco-tourism, spiritual tourism and sustainable tourism partnerships among the two countries.

FINDINGS AND RECOMMENDATIONS

The conceptual study in this chapter that was constructed on the secondary data, indicates various dimensions of partnership for tourism between Australia and South Asia, with a focus on Pakistan. Graci (2013) researched on tourism partnership for sustainability and elaborated that in tourism partnership all partners are required to be interdependent; strategic decisions must have joint ownership; all partners assume collective responsibility for the future direction and the collaboration stays as a dynamic and emergent process. Gray (1989) is considered as a pioneer in tourism partnerships, arguing that partnerships must have a cohesive environmental vision, sharing information and increasing the environmental and social action during the tourism process. Gray (1996) crafted a three-phase framework for tourism partnerships, the first phase being the problem setting, second phase, of direction setting while the third and last phase being the implementation of the strategy for the partnership. This chapter focuses on first 2 steps of problem setting and direction setting.

It is understood that partnerships drive marketing to build operating efficiencies among various players or partners engaged in the tourism industry. The success of a tourism partnership will depend on the fact that it is advantageous for all partners on the demand side and supply side of the industry (Augustyn & Knowles, 2000; Haq, 2012). In the real business world, tourism industry covers both vertical and horizontal partnerships and aims for the forward and backward integration. The vertical partnership contains the expansion of the tourism product or service into a related service, for example a hotel also offering food packages (Weidenfeld, 2018). Horizontal partnerships indicate tourism business entering into partnership with a relevant business, for example a hotel acquiring or seeking a strategic alliance with a travel agency (Augustyn & Knowles, 2000; Weidenfeld, 2018).

Horizontal partnerships indicate the depth of cooperation with public and private operators and providers of various tourism products and services (Augustyn & Knowles 2000). Vertical partnerships indicate the depth of collaboration between tourism operators and various players, which may consist of transport businesses, hotels, media channels, insurance agencies, destination management and financial institutions such as banks and credit card companies (Augustyn & Knowles 2000). This study suggests that marketing tourism needs partnership between Australia and Pakistan in relation to their position on both vertical and horizontal axis. In the first phase of partnership, horizontal axis shall be focused to set a connection between the government departments and tourism agencies in both countries. Likewise, the transportation, food, safety and accommodation business could align with each other in both countries. In the second phase, the vertical axis shall be focused by analyzing and applying the stretch for all products and services involved in tourism, which have shown positive results based on the horizontal partnership.

The depth and width of a partnership will identify the number and variety of players and stakeholders. The scope of this chapter does not cover suggestions to identify and choose partners, but this study presents the phases involved in tourism partnership among Australia and Pakistan. This chapter agrees with the industry and earlier research, who have suggested various parameters for establishing fruitful partnerships in the tourism industry that could be adapted, including: reciprocal grounds, mutual goals, expert participation, developmental structure and sustainability (Augustyn & Knowles, 2000; Tilson, 2001; Weidenfeld, 2018).

Furthermore, Selin and Chavez (1995) further augmented the research of Gray (1989) and presented a framework for the evolution of tourism partnerships. The tourism partnerships were guided to proceed through five stages: antecedents, problem setting, direction setting, structuring and outcomes (Selin & Chavez 1995). This chapter focuses on first 3 stages of antecedents, problem setting, direction setting mapping with the first 2 phases of Gray (1996). Various types of tourism partnerships have been adapted in this research as presented in Table 1 labelled as tourism marketing partnership model for Australia and Pakistan.

Table 1. Tourism marketing partnership model for Australia and Pakistan

Types of Tourism	Role for Australia	Role for Pakistan	Partnership Phases
Mountain & snow	• Destination management support • Marketing & planning support • Visit as tourists	• Learn destination management • Learn safety and risk management • Attract tourists and trainers	➢ Horizontal partnership ➢ Research collaboration ➢ Goals and problem setting
Spiritual & Religious	• Learn place and event setting • Marketing & planning support • Visit as tourists – different religions	• Learn marketing and planning • Learn ticketing as commercialization • Attract tourists and religious leaders	➢ Horizontal partnership ➢ Research collaboration ➢ Goals and problem setting
Green	• Green eco-awareness campaign support • Publicity support • Marketing & planning support • Eco-tourism growth	• Learn public green awareness • Learn marketing and planning • Attract global experts and tourists	➢ Vertical partnership ➢ Research collaboration ➢ Direction setting to stretch tourism
Heritage	• Identify place and related event setting • Marketing & planning support • Relate heritage with modern tourism	• Learn heritage place, people and event setting, apply for recognition • Learn marketing and planning • Attract heritage experts and tourists	➢ Vertical partnership ➢ Research collaboration ➢ Direction setting to stretch tourism

Source: Designed for this paper

FUTURE RESEARCH DIRECTIONS

This chapter has presented a novel idea of tourism marketing partnership between two dissimilar countries: Australia and Pakistan. The chapter also highlights the post Covid-19 opportunity for collaboration between Australia and SAARC nations in general, specifically Pakistan for four special types of tourism where both players are suggested to play different roles. A future study based on the framework given in figure 1 is suggested to be conducted a qualitative research based on direct interviews with tourism providers, managers, related government officials, and special interest tourists in both countries. Likewise, a quantitative research could be organised by providing surveys to different population segments interested in tourism, to assess their tastes and preferences in order to sharply craft a tourism partnership between Australia and Pakistan. On a similar note, senior government officers working with ministry or department of tourism could also be engaged in research to learn about their insights into partnership in different styles and strategies tourism partnership for different countries.

CONCLUSION

While it is essential to minimize the politicization by restoring some protection under the law to the state bureaucracy, the political barriers in the way of achieving this reform goal are substantial. At present, the Pakistani Government of the Tehreek e-Insaaf party enjoys smooth relations with the military who is taking over civilian positions. These positions by military professionals indicate Pakistan's most powerful political interest group that could effectively block important reforms that are seen to be damaging its interests. There are several ways that more public support for civil service reform could be produced. The digital media sector's growing influence in Pakistan in terms of informing and shaping public opinion provides possibly the strongest opportunity to raise public awareness about the civil service's dilemma. The mutual relationship between Australia and Pakistan will only be beneficial until the crisis affecting the public service is properly communicated in Pakistan, and pressure for civil service reform comes from within Pakistan rather than from international contributors.

This research attempted to assess opportunities for tourism partnership between Australia and Pakistan, which seemed complex due to large imparity based on cultural, economic, political, and social structures and applications in both countries. However, the chapter highlighted four major types of tourism that could be the centre of any tourism partnership between both countries. These four types of tourism include: Mountain and snow, spiritual and religious, green, and heritage tourism. The authors of this paper also conclude that the tourism partnership for both countries will also have specific roles for each player. The roles move around the basic role of Australia as the senior partner and tourism teacher, while Pakistan could take the role of the student or follower to learn about the mechanics and tactics involved in the tourism marketing.

The chapter also highlights the post Covid-19 opportunity for collaboration between Australia and SAARC nations in general, specifically Pakistan for four special types of tourism where both players are suggested to play different roles. Other than the industrial and business support for tourism; this paper presents a unique opportunity for partnership between Australia and South Asian countries in general, and Pakistan in particular. The study recommends travel, tourism and hospitality based partnerships between Australia and SAARC nations in order to manage the Covid-19 damage and build a tourism collaboration to handle any future pandemics.

REFERENCES

Abodeeb, J., Wilson, E., & Moyle, B. (2015). Shaping destination image and identity: Insights for Arab tourism at the Gold Coast, Australia. *International Journal of Culture, Tourism and Hospitality Research*, *9*(1), 6–21. doi:10.1108/IJCTHR-06-2014-0051

Ahmad, A., Hassan, F., & Rizvi, S. J. (2017). A model for collaboration between Pakistani & Australian dairy farmers. *Journal of Strategy and Performance Management, 5*(1), 4–22.

Ahmed, A. (2021). *Tourism putting stress on Pakistan environment: Study*. Retrieved from https://www.dawn.com/news/1619551

Augustyn, M. M., & Knowles, T. (2000). Performance of tourism partnerships: A focus on York. *Tourism Management, 21*(4), 341–351. doi:10.1016/S0261-5177(99)00068-0

Badar, H., Ariyawardana, A., & Collins, R. (2015). Capturing consumer preferences for value chain improvements in the mango industry of Pakistan. *International Food and Agribusiness Management Review, 18*, 131-148.

Burgess, L., Parish, B., & Alcock, C. (2011). To what extent are regional tourism organisations (RTOs) in Australia leveraging the benefits of web technology for destination marketing and eCommerce? *Electronic Commerce Research, 11*(3), 341–355. doi:10.100710660-011-9077-1

Craik, J. (1995). Are there cultural limits to tourism? *Journal of Sustainable Tourism, 3*(2), 87–98. doi:10.1080/09669589509510713

Crowe, S. M., & Middeldorp, J. (1996). A comparison of leg before wicket rates between Australians and their visiting teams for test cricket series played in Australia, 1977–94. *The Statistician, 45*(2), 255–262. doi:10.2307/2988414

Economist. (2016). One Belt, One Road: An Economic Roadmap. *Economist Intelligence Unit*. https://www.eiu.com/public/topical_report.aspx?campaignid=OBORSept2016

Farr, G. (2017). *Pakistan's Role in China's One Belt One Road Initiative*. https://pdxscholar.library.pdx.edu/cgi/viewcontent.cgi?article=1141&context=soc_fac

Graci, S. (2013). Collaboration and partnership development for sustainable tourism. *Tourism Geographies, 15*(1), 25–42. doi:10.1080/14616688.2012.675513

Gray, B. (1989). *Collaborating*. Jossey-Bass.

Gray, B. (1996). Cross-sectoral partners: Collaborative alliances among business, government and communities. In C. Huxham (Ed.), *Creating Collaborative Advantage*. Sage. doi:10.4135/9781446221600.n4

HaiderT. (2020). *Pakistani Population in Australia*. Retrieved from https://www.sbs.com.au/language/english/pakistani-population-in-australia-increases-to-91-000

Hall, C. M., & Page, S. J. (2000). Developing tourism in South Asia: India, Pakistan and Bangladesh – SAARC and beyond. In C. M. Hall & S. J. Page (Eds.), *Tourism in South and Southeast Asia: Issues and cases* (pp. 197–224). Butterworth Heinemann.

Haq, F., & Jackson, J. (2021). Tourism Marketing Mix Applied for Inclusive Spiritual Tourists in Pakistan and Australia. *NUST Business Review, an International Journal, 2*(12), 30-46.

Haq, F., & Medhekar, A. (2019). Is Spiritual Tourism a Peace Vehicle for Social Transformation and Economic Prosperity in India and Pakistan. In A. Nedelea (Ed.), *Marketing Peace for Social Transformation and Global Prosperity* (pp. 189–211). IGI Global Publishing. doi:10.4018/978-1-5225-7464-4.ch010

Haq, F., & Wong, H. Y. (2013). Branding Islamic spiritual tourism: An exploratory study in Australia and Pakistan. *European Journal of Business and Management*, *5*(11), 154–162.

Haq, F. M. (2014). The significance of partnership as a marketing strategy for Islamic spiritual tourism. *Journal of Islamic Marketing*, *5*(2), 258–272. doi:10.1108/JIMA-11-2013-0079

Jupp, J. (1995). From 'White Australia' to 'part of Asia': Recent shifts in Australian immigration policy towards the region. *The International Migration Review*, *29*(1), 207–228. PMID:12319613

Kazmi, M. R. (2017). Australian Centre for International Agricultural Research (ACIAR) in Pakistan: 30 years of partnership in research for development. *ACIAR Technical Reports Series*, *91*, 24–3.

Medhekar, A. (2021). Australia-India: Bilateral Trade Opportunities and Challenges. In *Emerging Business and Trade Opportunities Between Oceania and Asia* (pp. 57–86). IGI Global. doi:10.4018/978-1-7998-4126-5.ch004

Mehdi, M., Ahmad, B., & Ahsan, M. B. (2018). 13. Value Chain Development and Social Upgrading: A Case of Pakistan's Mango Industry. *Labor and Globalization*, *1*(1), 273–290.

Michael, I., Armstrong, A., Badran, B., & King, B. (2011). Dubai outbound tourism: An exploratory study of Emiratis and expatriates. *Journal of Vacation Marketing*, *17*(1), 83–91. doi:10.1177/1356766710391448

Michael, N., James, R., & Michael, I. (2018). Australia's cognitive, affective and conative destination image: An Emirati tourist perspective. *Journal of Islamic Marketing*, *9*(1), 36–59. doi:10.1108/JIMA-06-2016-0056

Mitra, S. K. (2014, August). Mango production in the world–present situation and future prospect. In *XXIX International Horticultural Congress on Horticulture: Sustaining Lives, Livelihoods and Landscapes (IHC2014): IV 1111* (pp. 287-296). Academic Press.

Moon, M. A., Mohel, S. H., & Farooq, A. (2021). I green, you green, we all green: Testing the extended environmental theory of planned behavior among the university students of Pakistan. *The Social Science Journal*, *58*(3), 316–332. doi:10.1016/j.soscij.2019.05.001

Naz, A., Zaman, K., Yousaf, S. U., Nassani, A. A., Aldakhil, A. M., & Abro, M. M. Q. (2019). Saudi Arabia-China-Pakistan economic corridor: Intergovernmental green initiatives. *Environmental Science and Pollution Research International*, *26*(25), 25676–25689. doi:10.100711356-019-05843-2 PMID:31267397

Norton, R., Perris, R., & Armstrong, R. (2007). Learning from Long-term Experiments–What Do They Teach Us? The Healthy Soils Symposium. *Embrace Green Revolution, 1,* 113-160.

Sadaqat, R. (2021). *Unified tourism strategy to put Pakistan to global travel map*. Retrieved from https://www.khaleejtimes.com/business/global/unified-tourism-strategy-to-put-pakistan-to-global-travel-map

Scott, N., Baggio, R., & Cooper, C. (2008). *Network analysis and tourism: From theory to practice.* Channel View Publications.

Selin, S. (1999). Developing a typology of sustainable tourism partnership. *Journal of Sustainable Tourism*, *7*(3&4), 260–273. doi:10.1080/09669589908667339

Selin, S., & Chavez, D. (1995). Developing a collaborative model for environmental planning and management. *Environmental Management, 19*(2), 189–195. doi:10.1007/BF02471990

Seraphim, J., & Haq, F. (2019). Can design thinking enhance experiential heritage tourism in Pakistan. *NUST Business Review. International Journal (Toronto, Ont.), 1*(1), 1–11.

TripAdvisor. (2021). *Explore Pakistan. Tripadvisor has 74086 reviews of Pakistan Hotels, Attractions, and Restaurants.* https://www.tripadvisor.in/Tourism-g293959-Pakistan-Vacations.html

Ullah, Z., Khan, J., & Haq, Z. U. (2018). Coastal Tourism & CPEC: Opportunities and Challenges in Pakistan. *Journal of Political Studies, 25*(2), 261–272.

Ullah, Z., Naveed, R. T., Rehman, A. U., Ahmad, N., Scholz, M., Adnan, M., & Han, H. (2021). Towards the Development of Sustainable Tourism in Pakistan: A Study of the Role of Tour Operators. *Sustainability, 13*(9), 4902. doi:10.3390u13094902

Walsh, D., & Cowley, R. (2016). Optimising beef business performance in northern Australia: What can 30 years of commercial innovation teach us? *The Rangeland Journal, 38*(3), 291–305. doi:10.1071/RJ15064

Weidenfeld, A. (2018). Tourism diversification and Its Implications for smart Specialisation. *Sustainability, 10*(2), 319–331. doi:10.3390u10020319

Wilder, A. (2009). The politics of civil service reform in Pakistan. *Journal of International Affairs, 63*(1), 19–37.

Wyeth, G. (2021). What We Can Learn from Australia's Sikh Community. *The Diplomat.* https://thediplomat.com/2021/06/what-we-can-learn-from-australias-sikh-community/

Wyman, O. (2020). *To Recovery & Beyond: The Future of Travel & Tourism in the Wake of COVID-19.* https://tcmih.ku.ac.ke/handle/123456789/243

ADDITIONAL READING

Carson, D. B., & Taylor, A. J. (2008). Sustaining four wheel drive tourism in desert Australia: Exploring the evidence from a demand perspective. *The Rangeland Journal, 30*(1), 77–83. doi:10.1071/RJ07036

Hall, C. M., & Page, S. J. (Eds.). (2016). *The Routledge handbook of tourism in Asia.* Taylor & Francis. doi:10.4324/9781315768250

Hameed, R. (2017). Pakistan and China: Partnership, prospects and the course ahead. Policy Perspectives. *The Journal of the Institute of Policy Studies, 14*(1), 3–22.

Hunter-Jones, P. (2010). Consumer vulnerability and exclusion: A study of carers in the tourism marketplace. *Journal of Marketing Management, 27*(1-2), 165–180. doi:10.1080/02672571003737809

Khan, M. U. H. (2018). UAE-Pakistan: A Strategic Partnership. *Defence Journal, 22*(5), 72–2.

O'Neill, M. A., & Palmer, A. (2004). Wine production and tourism: Adding service to a perfect partnership. *The Cornell Hotel and Restaurant Administration Quarterly*, *45*(3), 269–284. doi:10.1177/0010880404263075

Rita, P. (2000). Internet marketing destinations in the global tourism marketplace. *Proceedings INET.* https://web.archive.org/web/20160103001309/http://www.isoc.org/inet2000/cdproceedings/

Stone, M., & Smith, D. (2006). An outline of Parks Victoria's tourism partnership strategy and challenges for sustainable park tourism in Australia. *Sustainable Tourism II*, *2*(1), 1125–1137. doi:10.2495/ST060031

Wang, Y. (2008). Collaborative destination marketing: Understanding the dynamic process. *Journal of Travel Research*, *47*(2), 151–166. doi:10.1177/0047287508321194

KEY TERMS AND DEFINITIONS

Post COVID-19: All business, social, economic, and political scenarios based on the time after the end of the COVID-19 Pandemic, assumed to be from the end of 2021.

SAARC: South Asian Association of Regional Cooperation includes seven countries: Bangladesh, Bhutan, India, the Maldives, Nepal, Pakistan, and Sri Lanka. SAARC was established in Kathmandu, Nepal, on 16 January 1987, and was inaugurated by King Birendra Bir Bikram Shah of Nepal.

Tourism Marketing: All business planning focused on the needs, wants, and demands of tourists, is called as tourism marketing, which provides sustainable competitive advantage to tourism agencies and destinations.

Tourism Partnership: Partnerships supports relationship marketing to build operational efficiencies among the various players involved in the tourism business, the success depends on stakeholders on both the demand side and supply side must collaborate and benefit. The global tourism business operations generally include both vertical and horizontal partnerships.

Chapter 12
Post-COVID-19 Australian and Indian Collaboration for Enhanced Effectiveness in the Resource Sector for Renewable Energy

Gayatri Gopidas Nair
Canadian University Dubai, UAE

Rahul Vinit Mehta
Canadian University Dubai, UAE

ABSTRACT

India and Australia have a diverse range of ties, spanning from geostrategic collaboration and trade to global influence. An initial period of warmth followed by decades of coldness characterizes the relationship between Australia and India. This chapter makes a case for improving resource sector related bilateral relations between New Delhi and Canberra to aim for a sustainable future through strategic collaboration in climate change and the renewable energy sector. Trade and investment possibilities exist between the two countries, and over the years, the engagements between countries have been neglected. The worldwide focus on renewable energy adoption through technological innovation and collaboration is thriving. This research focuses on understanding if there has been a change in the relationship between the two since the pandemic. Through the analysis and observation of qualitative data, suggestions with the current scenario and the future scope of both countries, particularly in the resources and energy sector, have been discussed in this chapter.

INTRODUCTION

India and Australia as well as their international and economical significance extend beyond bilateral

DOI: 10.4018/978-1-7998-8657-0.ch012

relations, with a considerable impact on issues affecting the Asia-Pacific region and the world at large (Star, 2019). Many nations are becoming more tactically and financially involved in the Pacific area as a result of the region's growth as a global economic hub and the shifting character of economic and political operations from the Atlantic to the Pacific. For decades, Australia has been involved in the Asia-Pacific area, notably with the East Asian economy heavyweights of Japan and South Korea, as well as China. Australia is pursuing a complete partnership with India, which may result in more trade and investment (Bhowmick, Saha, & Basu, 2019). Australia's foreign policy circle's support for the Indo-Pacific direction, as well as the concern of its sustainability, are pressing Australia to embrace India fully on the financial front (Gnanagurunathan, 2012). The development of the 'Indo-Pacific' area as a new geopolitical construct, a change from the 'Asia-Pacific' idea to cope with he strategic and economic reality in the region amidst China's ascent, has positioned India in a long-term strategic opportunity (Bhaskar, 2019). A few years ago, India was not even among the top business locations. India is now regarded as among the most attractive investment locations. India has grown and is being recognized on the world scene financially, politically, and strategically since the liberalization and economic reforms began in the 1990s (Bhowmick et al, 2019). From geostrategic cooperation and trade to soft power mechanisms like cricket and tourism, India and Australia have a wide range of relations (Smith, 2014). There are significant trade and business potential between the two nations, but their relationships have remained undeveloped throughout time (Hall, 2021). The focus on digital economies throughout the world, along with technical progress in both nations, is expected to improve marine connections and business climate.

The New Delhi-Canberra engagement is gaining traction as a key bilateral partnership, owing to shared interests in sectors such as academics regional stability, power and materials and global trade. Australia and India have a lot in common, both historically and in terms of geopolitics now (Brewster, 2014). In recent years, the shifting environment in the Indo-Pacific area has acted as a spur for closer connections (Bhowmick, et al., 2019). Australia and India are a perfect match for cooperation and collaboration since they share democratic ideals, a love of sport, and strategic and economic aspirations (Star, 2019). Both administrations have realized that the Australia-India connection must be prioritized in international relationships (Hall, 2021). Australia and India have maintained a friendly but distant relationship for a long time. There appears to be room to grow an economic alliance and improve regional integration (Smith, 2014). A strategic relationship, on the other hand, will not be easy to achieve it would need long institutional dedication from both sides (Brewster, 2014). This chapter focuses on understanding the strategic partnership between Australia and India on the front line of the resources and energy sector. With in-depth understanding and focused data collected from secondary sources, the chapter talks about how the relationship between both countries have evolved since the beginning. With the entire investigation taking place using secondary data, the data statistics and findings shown may lack the reality of the situation. This paper has considered the various relationships and plans of both countries from secondary data available from trusted resources which could lack the gravity of the situation and may not put the entire picture together. On the lines of other sectors, further research in this chapter shows how both countries have taken up various measures to strengthen their economies and how COVID-19 has impacted them. With the effect of COVID-19, just like all countries suffering the crisis, the chapter aims to learn in the following sections on how both countries are joining their hands together and reworking Free Trade Agreement (FTA) and other sector agreements to bring benefits and balanced outcomes to both countries.

BACKGROUND

The Canberra-New Delhi Connection

Since the First World War, India and Australia have had a long history of military collaboration. When Indian Prime Minister Narendra Modi visited Australia in November 2014, the two signed a benchmark contract to strengthen their defence partnership, as well as a paper issued by the Australian government offering a plan for broader engagement with Asian countries, including India (Hall, 2021). India's Look East Policy has also been broadened to include Australia as a priority. Enhancing bilateral connections between India and Australia has several benefits (Smith, 2014). In recent years, India and Australia have signed a series of agreements addressing various elements of their relations (Hall, 2021). India and Australia are natural allies in this respect, as fellow democracies with a common interest in the protection and maintenance of freedom of navigation and overflight in the Indo-Pacific. The region has the opportunity to let the two nations communicate and trade more easily (Bhowmick, et al., 2019).

Considering the transitions in the administrations of Australia and India, the two countries remain committed to strengthening their business and security relations. Varghese (2018) recommended that India be elevated to one of Australia's top three export markets. It also asks for India to become the third-largest market for Australian outbound investment in Asia. By reimagining their goods, resources, and organizational structure, India and Australia can extend their trading networks. India's economy is one of the world's fastest expanding, while Australia's economy is rising at its highest rate in over a decade (Varghese, 2018). To boost bilateral trade and FDI, both nations must make use of contemporary digital trade advances. In policy areas such as maritime security, climate change, energy security, law enforcement, governance, and the politics of security institutions, ASEAN, Australia, and India share a trilateral dynamic. Digital technologies, such as the digitization of maritime ties between the two nations and the rest of the globe, are part of the latter (Gnanagurunathan, 2012). In light of China's ambitious One Belt One Road (OBOR) project to improve global physical connectivity, Australia's High Commissioner to India recently emphasized the importance of joint infrastructure financing between India and Australia in the Indo-Pacific region to strengthen the region's economic order (Bhaskar, 2019). Finding the potential for India-Australia networks, on the other hand, would not only improve efficiency and performance but also create viable business and service conditions (Star, 2019).

The relationship between Australia and India has a long history, but it has been marked by periods of apathy punctuated with political irritants (Hall, 2021). The growth of India and the shifting balance of power in Asia have given the relationship a new dimension. Australia and India are more connected than they have ever been, with shared worries about China's influence and the territory's security and prosperity (Varghese, 2018). On all sides, there is a renewed ability to compromise and move beyond previous ideological divides. Participation, on the other hand, is only getting started, and collaboration must proceed towards a more tangible level. India has become one of Australia's most important resource and energy consumers as in economic and strategic aspects, the two markets are complimentary (Gnanagurunathan, 2012). India is a large and expanding export market that offers a chance to counterbalance China. There are several chances to expand two-way commerce and strengthen the investment connection. For India, Australia provides politically secure and trustworthy sources of power and resource that will aid in the country's economic development, hence over the previous decade, trade between Australia and India has increased considerably (Star, 2019). The trade balance favours Australia and is likely to continue that way for the years ahead. Indian firms are increasingly interested in resource investments as they seek vertically integrated initiatives. Bilateral trade is yet underdeveloped, which might be a cause of friction (Brewster, 2014). The Australian government website shows detailed statistics that in 2019-20, India was Australia's ninth biggest trading partner and third-largest services export market. In 2019-20, two-way goods and services trade totalled $26.2 billion, while two-way investment stock was $36.7 billion. Numerous Australian businesses want to engage in India's resources industry but are generally barred by the country's stringent investment laws. The economic connection is possibly unstable due to the lack of significant investment ties. For quite some time, a Comprehensive Economic Co-operation Agreement (CECA) has been in the works.

Over the recent decade, bilateral political conversations between Australia and India have grown significantly. However, they frequently look to lack genuine depth or adoption of the Indian half from an Australian standpoint. This reflects the political and bureaucratic restrictions in India. Over the last decade, the connection has grown significantly, indicating a converging of strategic ideas. For several years, Australia's unwillingness to sell uranium to India hampered the relationship. However, advances in the negotiation of uranium supply agreements and a shift in Australia's uranium policy in 2011 have essentially eliminated this obstacle to the partnership. In recent years, India and Australia have enjoyed a positive relationship, but there are still obstacles to overcome. India is a rising power with lofty ambitions, whereas Australia is dynamic medium power. Australia still has work to do to convince India that it is a vital partner. When making decisions concerning China or the Indian Ocean (Sharma, 2016). When it comes to security cooperation, Australia and India have quite distinct traditions and sensibilities. India tends to resist multilateral collaboration unless it is done under the unambiguous flag of the Co-operation, which bears the ideological blemish of jeopardizing India's geopolitical sovereignty Australia has a lengthy history of joining multinational coalitions, but India takes a more cautious strategy. India and Australia have been wary of allowing their relationship to be seen as anything resembling a sinaphobic alliance. Canberra, which is concerned about China's aggression in the South China Sea, is more receptive than New Delhi to the concept of enabling a role for China as a genuine participant in Indian Ocean security. Although India may perceive a strategic value in being able to control China's marine lines of communication, Australia may have a larger interest in facilitating China's position as a competent participant (Sharma, 2016).

Differences in legislative and geopolitical cultures must be bridged between Australia and India. There are numerous common interests and possibilities but overcoming them will need political will and determination. In the long run, New Delhi may discover that a positive bilateral partnership with Australia can help India achieve its wider strategic goals. The governmental website portal states that Australia and India had a diplomatic relationship before India was Independent. Let's have a look back into the history of the two from which their relationship was nurtured (Australia India Council (AIC), 2020). In 1941, The Indian General Consulate first opened its office in Sydney. In 1944, Australia's first High Commissioner Lieutenant-General Iven Mackay was appointed in India. In the same year, India's first High Commissioner R.R Saxena was appointed in Australia. It is to be noted that Australia and India have made necessary efforts and implemented plans that cover three main categories as Trade, Education and Defense. These three branches which are important for every nation has been carefully curated by the two countries allowing a win-win situation for the two under any circumstance. The Australia-India Council known as AIC was instituted in 1992 to help manage trade relations, foreign affairs, defence, etc. AIC (2020) has been organized to maintain a healthy relationship between the two countries and they focus on the following:

- To grow bilateral relationships among the two countries and raise awareness of their relationship to facilitate foreign investments.
- Foster collaboration between the two countries in areas of connection to the strategic partnership.
- Promote programs that exhibit Australia's commercial credentials to prominent Indian audiences. mobilize
- Gather the community and involve the private sector to support AIC's hardships to improve both the country's economy and broaden its relationship

The Australia Indian Education Council (AIEC) was formed to foster educational partnerships to encourage educational relationships among the two countries. The council helps in expanding collaboration in education, training, and research. They aim to set the diplomatic direction of the education, training and research partnerships and monitors the same to develop and shape their collaborative endeavours Australia and India have a positive defence relationship including a variety of conferences to develop strategic dialogue, regular interactions with the defence ministry of both countries and concentrating on training methods and other vital exchange of information. Australia and India have fostered a major military partnership that works strategically to ensure the protection of both countries if any of the countries face dangers (AIEC, 2021).

Apart from all the attention given to development, both countries have worked tirelessly to provide various overseas aid programs. Australia has taken up an interest in reducing poverty, unemployment, and underdevelopment of the economy of developing countries. India extends support to Australia for such programs through global and regional investments and technical support. An interesting area of the two countries is their mining and resources sector. Even before the pandemic, both countries were in this sector for a long time. India has the advantage of having minerals and other reserves. India's mining sector contributes 2.5% in 2020 to the country's GDP which has substantially grown from 1.4% which was the GDP contribution in 2019 (Bhaskar, 2019). Although we see this sector being developed, it is far away from what India's potential is. India has an underdeveloped mining resource when compared to Australia as Australia has utilized to a point where the country's economic growth was achieved alone with the development of the mining sector. India and Australia do not have any partnerships in this sector however with the common features shared by both countries such as geological resemblance, large reserves, critical mineral extractions and other factors, there is a lot of potential scope for both countries which will be seen in the later section of this chapter.

LITERATURE REVIEW

Agreements Between Australia and India

The relationship between both countries strengthned with Australia's White Paper on Foreign Policy that sees India in the front rank of International Partnerships in November 2017. It says, "Beyond an increasingly important economic relationship, our security interests are congruent, particularly concerning the stability and openness of the Indian Ocean. Both the countries have common interests in upholding international law, especially concerning freedom of navigation and maritime security" Rughani, 2021). Even looking at the bilateral trade agreements between the two, India is the 5th largest trade partner of Australia where the goods and services are estimated to be A$ 29 billion. This was a 3.6% share of

Australia's total trade in the year 2017-18. It includes the A$ 8 billion and A$ 21 billion as exports and imports respectively. Through the years, the overall trade percentage that increased was 13.1%, imports increased to 9.75 and exports increased fairly better at a rate of 23.3%. India's exports to Australia included refined petroleum, hover trains, pearls, gems, medicaments, textiles, gold, metal, vegetables, wool, fruits, nuts, and many more goods (Rughani, 2021).

India and Australia had also started discussing a Comprehensive Economic Cooperation Agreement (CECA) (established in 2011) focusing on improving both their economies. The head of Indian and Australian business among a broad number of sectors have joined to create an India-Australia CEO forum. This forum aims to grow businesses of both nations, engaging directly on ways to build a bilateral trade and investment relationship targeting foreign investment in both countries. The sector heads come from various sectors including energy, agricultural, financial, telecommunications, IT, and education (Australian Government Department of Foreign Affairs and Trade, 2020). In 2018, during the visit of the Indian Prime Minister Narendra Modi to Australia, this CEO Forum had held its meetings to indicate the plan and process of execution. The recent QUAD meeting that was held in September 2021 between the USA, India, Australia, and Japan sought a political commitment to maximizing the global and strategic policy frameworks. The main highlights of the meeting were on how the countries would pursue economic stability during the time of crisis and how bilateral basis would be continued as reported by the Atlantic Council (Atlantic Council, 2021). It is indicated that Japan and Australia would face greater challenges in reconciling the bilateral relationship with the USA and India. It is foreseen in the agreement that the bilateral relationship with China will be excluded, and stronger anger trade allies will be created to help each other and gravitate towards a moderate upgrading. Education has been the biggest intangible export of Australia to India and it is valued at about $6 billion (in 2020). Education being a channel of knowledge and plays a great part in both countries' economies, Australia stepped further to strengthen the partnership. The AIBX program (Australia India Business Exchange) provides all kinds of support to Australian businesses to establish their branches in India. India is one of the fastest-growing countries, it has its competitiveness and potential that can be accessed to improve both economies (Rughani 2021). The AIBX focuses on accessing potential opportunities and succeed in the Indian market. The AIBX's targeted industry in India includes the agriculture, infrastructure, education, medical and energy sectors.

Renewable Energy

In February 2016, the Minister of State (Coal, Power, and renewable energy) of India, Shri Piyush Goyal, and Mr Josh Frydenberg, the Minister of Resources and Energy in Australia jointly attended the roundtable discussion focusing on issues related to energy security and renewable energy. The discussion aimed to resolve and develop ways to save energy and cultivate clean energy to avoid its pollution on the environment of both countries (Sharma, 2014). This strategic partnership on energy grounds have developed both countries and have now been seen as a role model for the rest of the world. Renewable energy is at a crossroads, with solar and wind technologies at the vanguard of global energy system changes. Their increased use is essential for programs aimed at reducing greenhouse gas emissions, air pollution, and increasing energy supply. In the coming decade, renewable energy will continue to gain ground on fossil fuels, decreasing greenhouse gas emissions. Renewable energy provides reliable power and a wide range of fuels, increasing energy security and reducing the risk of fuel leaks while also reducing the need for imported fuels. Renewable energy also helps the country's natural resources to be conserved. Considering the renewable energy industry employs more people than the fossil fuel industry, more jobs are produced on average. The industry has a positive ripple effect through the renewable energy supply chain and into other businesses as a result of increased family wages (Buy Clean Energy, 2017).

Solar, wind, geothermal, and hydropower are examples of renewable energy sources that do not require fuel or transportation, resulting in more price stability. In practice, some electric providers factor this into their retail power pricing, exempting customers who buy renewable energy from some fuel-related taxes. Electricity generation produces 66 per cent of the nation's Sulphur dioxide, which causes acid rain. Electricity generation also accounts for 29% of nitrogen oxides. High NOx levels make people more susceptible to respiratory diseases, especially youngsters. Ozone is a useful gas that occurs naturally in the upper atmosphere. However, ozone in the lower atmosphere causes the haze we call smog in cities. Ground-level ozone is mostly caused by automobiles and energy sources. Breathing ozone can cause shortness of breath, lung inflammation, asthma episodes, and a higher chance of lifelong lung illness in children who grow up in places with high ozone pollution, according to the American Lung Association.

Particulate matter, more often known as soot, is a kind of air pollution. People with lung and heart illnesses are particularly vulnerable to particulate matter exposure. Carbon dioxide is a greenhouse gas that plays a role in global warming. Long-term consequences of fossil fuel combustion might be far more concerning than today's air pollution-related mortality. Tropical illnesses may thrive in the future as the world's temperature rises, and mortality from harsh weather conditions may arise. Mercury is an extremely hazardous metal emitted by coal-fired power plants (Buy Clean Energy, 2017).

India was among the first countries to join the Paris Climate accord in 2015. The country is currently the world's third-largest emitter of greenhouse gases after China and the US. Coal power plants, rice paddies, and cattle are major sources of steeply rising emissions levels. Per capita emissions continue to remain below the global average. The country is vulnerable to climate change because of their vast natural resources and ecological diversity; melting Himalayan glaciers and changing monsoons are posing threats to the region. India's GHG emissions have risen by 335.33% from 1990 to 2018, according to the International Energy Agency (IEA). According to the IEA, in 2018 India's emission level was 2307.78 MtCO2e, an increase of 335.34% compared to 1990. In 2015, India's per capita emissions are less staggering with measurements identifying those levels to be 2.7t CO2e 2015. As a country, however, they are trending quite poorly (Pandey, 2020). Before it can enhance its promises and submit its updated NDCs, India has to hear from industrialized countries about their plans to provide climate funding, green technology transfers and promised capacity building. By 2030, they want to have 40 per cent of their installed power come from renewable sources.

Furthermore, India has established a strategy to expand overall tree cover to produce a cumulative carbon sink of 2,500-3,000 MtCO2e by 2030, nearly equal to the country's entire annual emissions. Despite possessing the world's fourth-largest economy, India suffers from profound inequalities and unequal resource distribution (Sharma, 2014). The country's industrial and economic activity has recently surged due to investments in agriculture, infrastructure, electricity, manufacturing, and autos. India has increased its production to better provide for its 1.4 billion-strong population (Pachauri, 2021). Due to the economic effect of COVID-19, India's emission predictions in 2030 are 9-12 per cent lower than prior projections in 2019. Despite their lofty objective of 40% non-fossil fuel capacity share, India is presently on course to exceed its 2030 targets by a large margin. Because of the country's continuing commitment to the coal sector, emissions are expected to rise by 24-25 per cent above 2019 levels in 2030 under existing energy objectives and policies. A rise in emissions of this magnitude is incompatible with the Paris Agreement (Pandey, 2020). Domestic emissions must reach a peak and then begin to decline, with international assistance. Although India has taken appropriate steps to reduce its carbon-intensive economy, several current policy actions targeted at stimulating the economy are expected to result in increased carbon emissions. Clean energy resources may be extended through technical innovation, research, green employment creation, and clean energy production, as well as the implementation of coal-phase-out policies (Pandey, 2020).

Therefore, the two countries have grown towards each other's development with strategic partnership even at recent times indicating that even when times get rough, they have seen to have come up with ways to help each other. Through the different segments layered out, it has been observed that though a lot of the plans and actions have been implemented, India and Australia have a gap in the development process which will be discussed in the later sections of the paper.

METHODOLOGY

In order to understand the relationship between the two countries, it must be analyzed first. This research fully depends on the qualitative data achieved from secondary resources mostly retrieved from previously published articles, statistics and reports found on both countries' governmental portals. This research has been conducted through extensive use of different journals, articles and online information from government powered websites to enlighten the state at which the two countries were, are and will be. Since qualitative research focuses on comparisons and tends to be subjective, it is an efficient source of information that guided further analysis to come up with vital conclusions. Since this research uses the existing data as its base, the authors picked the most related and data that shows the clarity and the reality of the situations and relationships between the two countries.

Thematic analysis was adopted to analyze the qualitative data collected from secondary sources as identified above. The process of thematic analysis was applied as suggested by Lincoln and Guba (2003), which is based on a review of all relevant data in light of the research problem and goals and identifying the anchoring topics. These anchoring topics will become themes of this paper contributing towards the theory of partnership based on renewable energy between all countries in general, Australia and India in particular. To select the most suitable data, the researchers of the paper filtered numerous articles and journals that were related to both countries, Australia, and India, individually. It was then followed by assessing their previous relationship before the COVID-19 attack that laid a foundation to understanding whether there has been a change or not, which is the purpose of the research. The research data collected were also ensured that there was focus on the current situation and analysis of the present relationship status and how both countries are trying to maintain and improve their relationship. In this paper, with the help of the research, a deep understanding of the design and a vision of if things have changed between the two, and if so, how things have changed. However, the research is based on only the secondary data available with trusted sources, the research may still lack the reality and gravity of the situation, even though a general idea can still be figured out.

FINDINGS

The thematic analysis of the qualitative data resulted in the emergence of themes that are presented and explained separately below:

The Impact of COVID-19 Pandemic

The two countries' strategic partnership discussions have progressed quickly, with specific action plans being developed and implemented. During the COVID-19 epidemic, which has persisted for almost a year, both nations have faced challenging circumstances. The economic ties are excellent. In particular, India's foreign direct investment (FDI) system has been significantly liberalized, which bodes well for Australian entrepreneurs. For Indian firms, Australia's clear FDI system offers several options. India and Australia share strong cultural and aesthetic affinities. Indians are the most common source of immigration to Australia and many Indian students' study at Australian institutions under normal conditions (Sharma, 2016). The formalization of the QUAD partnership between Australia, India, the United States, and Japan was the pinnacle of official Australia-India ties. The conduct of joint naval exercises known as the Malabar exercises by the fleets of the four nations in late 2020 illustrated it. A few ideas that emerged from this research are Liberalization, Formalization, Implementation and Partnerships.

Most of the governmental protocols and other barriers have been eased and liberalized that has provided a better free trade environment for both countries which has resulted in increased exports and imports. The new plans and strategies have been discussed and listed down leading to the formalization of different committees indicating that both countries have seen a different issue that arose and affected their economies. Strategies were not simply made to just look at or publicize but to implement on the grounds of increasing the economic stability and capacity followed by immense support for each other and the rest of the world. This brings to the final theme that the research recognizes on the value of partnerships. The years have been tough and both countries have been taking joint decisions and extended their partnerships with each other and other countries to fulfil each other's priorities. Since Australia requested an independent investigation into the origins of the COVID-19 virus, ties between Australia and its largest trading partner, China, have deteriorated. China has imposed tariffs and limitations on several Australian exports. Since the last all-out conflict in 1962, relations between India and China have been tense. Relations between Australia and India are currently stronger than they have been in decades. It is necessary to take advantage of this goodwill and develop alternatives to China's concentration on industries and services. The Australian government must take advantage of the two nations' good relations by exploring methods to increase bilateral investment and trade.

With the defence accord and cooperation deal, India and Australia have agreed to improve their 2+2 discussion. The deal will allow the two nations to utilize one other's bases for supply maintenance and replenishment, as well as facilitate the expansion of overall defence collaboration and a separate pact on mining and rare earth minerals cooperation. India long remained largely reliant on China for essential minerals, but the deal will allow it to obtain them from Australia, which has one of the world's greatest strategic mineral deposits. COVID-19 disruption posed a danger to Australia's India Economic Strategy, which aimed to increase outbound investment to India by tenfold by 2035. In the long run, India has the potential to establish itself as a worldwide leader in cost-effective medical device and technology innovation. Building on existing research relationships and cooperation with India in a variety of fields, including healthcare, may also benefit Australia (Sharma, 2016).

India and Australia: The Resources Sector Performance

As we have seen, the business commitment initiatives, programs and strategies taken by Australia and India have been expanding in the past few years. In particular, the two-way prime ministerial visits in

2014 helped the India–Australia bilateral relationship gather more momentum, revitalizing ties between two countries that have long been thought of as being mutually indifferent. After all, even as Australia is one of India's extended neighbours, the two have historically not shared strong trading ties (Bhaskar, 2019). Historically, a few years before India's independence, we have seen how both countries have become each other's allies. India's strength includes having a powerful reserve of minerals and metals (including iron, zinc, and thermal coal). India is the second-largest global producer of thermal coal and the fourth-largest producer of iron (Pachauri, 2021). A fascinating detail is that India's planned geology is significantly familiar to that of Western Australia. While Australia has had the resources and the technology to explore its mineral sector, India has lacked the efforts to investigate its potential. However, this sector has been underdeveloped mostly due to the lack of capital, labour, safety conditions, pollution, and other prominent factors.

Australia's mining and resources sector is entirely and undoubtedly different, or rather opposite from India. The mining sector in Australia performed a vital role in developing the country and increasing its economic growth. Apart from the extraction, the development of METS (mining equipment, technology, and service) has changed the gameplay for Australia. An article in the Energy Government Australia (2021, p.3) reported: "Australia's minerals and mining equipment, technology and services (METS) sectors generated A$241.9-billion in value-added to the national economy in 2019/20, representing approximately 12.4% of the value of the Australian economy, a new analysis by Deloitte Access Economics has shown". The increasing rate and revenue from this sector, it has improved the standard and living conditions of Australians. The METS has gained a lot of attention due to the safety experience and the sustainable designs it has been created with (Pachauri, 2021). The advanced technology systems provided by the METS is inclusive of raising underground mining productivity and product quality.

Even with the pandemic, there has been a good amount of effort from both sides to increase the resource sector and maintain a stronger alliance. But with that said, there should be ways that both countries could improve their segments. Bhaskar (2019, p.2) adds: "The government's programmed such as "Make in India" (hike manufacturing share in the GDP from the current 17 per cent to 25 per cent by 2022), "Housing for all by 2022," smart cities, "power for all", modernization of the railways and aggressive highway construction targets will drive growth at a faster pace in end-user industries. Growth in these industries—including power, cement, construction and infrastructure—will, in turn, boost domestic mineral consumption." India's GDP is expected to grow, and the government's efforts are in encouraging domestic goods can potentially help increase the growth.

The Resources Sector Opportunities

In 2020, Prime Ministers Morrison and Modi decided to re-engage the Comprehensive Economic Cooperation Agreement (CECA) former known as the Free Trade Agreement (FTA) between the countries. They have continued to ensure that despite such tense times, both countries should also focus on strengthening their economy and advance themselves to progress in the future. An "Early Harvest Deal" has been decided by both countries as it is more practical and promising. The new reworked agreements between both countries depend on how Australia can align its export goals and how India can further expand its investment potential as priorities. The modern trade agreement between the two countries will seek beyond goods, services, and foreign investment. It aims to deepen the ties and secure trade and investments with balanced outcomes for both countries.

Figure 1. The demand for services in India
Source: IBEF, 2020

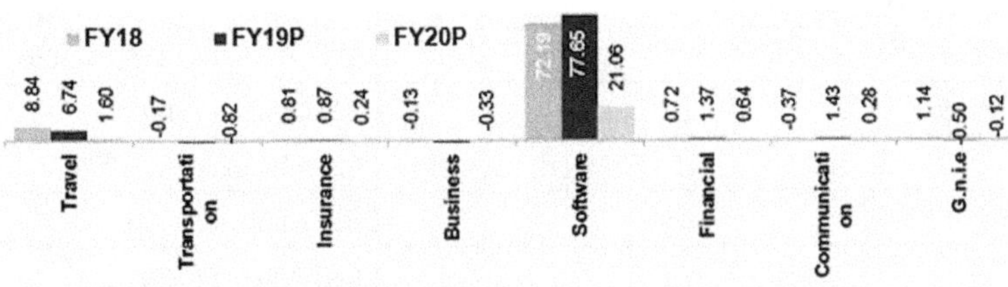

Figure 1 shows the services demand in India where travel, transportation, insurance, finance, business, software, etc. have been highlighted and forecasted. The current demand has been significant in the Software market as the increasing dependence on software has increased. With the pandemic, there has been an effect on travel due to which it has significantly decreased.

Figure 2 and 3 represents the physical and online market demand and potential in India respectively. From both figures, it can be observed that the offline and online market demand has great potential and will increase by 2025.

Figure 2. The demand for retail products in India
Source: IBEF, 2020

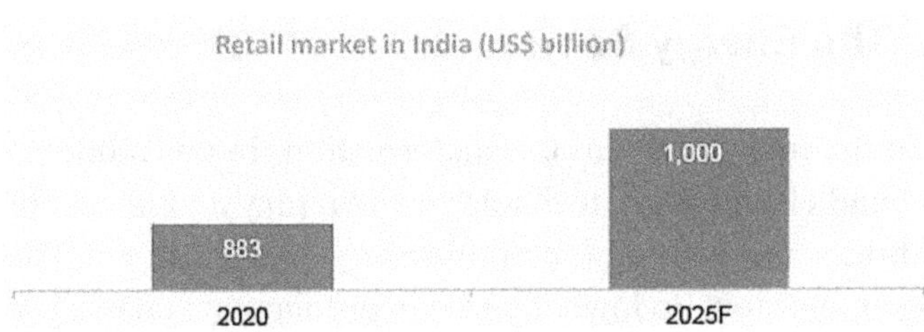

Figure 3. The demand for the e-commerce market in India
Source: IBEF, 2020

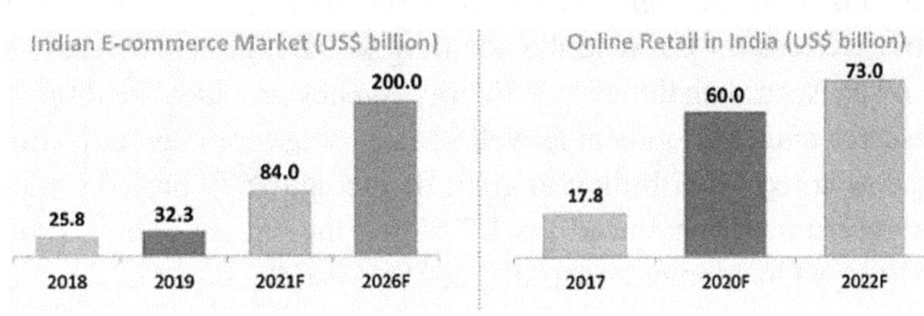

Table 1 shows the imports to Australia where the resources demand is about $ 208.2 billion. In the table, it can be observed that the highest demand Australia faces is in terms of machinery and vehicles that total up to $78.7 billion. This is a high demand rate for the country which is why they import many types of equipment.

Table 1. The demand for resources in Australia and the value of the imports

Resources Requirements	Imports
Machinery including computers	US$30.7 billion (15.1% of total imports)
Electrical machinery, equipment	$24.1 billion (11.9%)
Vehicles	$23.9 billion (11.8%)
Mineral fuels including oil	$16.9 billion (8.3%)
Pharmaceuticals	$8.7 billion (4.3%)
Gems, precious metals	$8.7 billion (4.3%)
Optical, technical, medical apparatus	$8 billion (4%)
Plastics, plastic articles	$6.2 billion (3%)
Furniture, bedding, lighting, signs, prefabricated buildings	$4.7 billion (2.3%)
Articles of iron or steel	$4.5 billion (2.2%)

Source: World Top Exports, 2019

The findings of the paper discussed three emerging themes based on India and Australia: the resources sector performance and opportunities and the in the pact of COVID-19. The results of this study are based on two major issues of the energy sector of India and Australia and their economic strategy for 2035. These results are further elaborated below:

India and Australia: The Energy Sector

The electrical market is in the midst of a major transformation. In our modern and dynamic electrical market, renewable energy and clean energy technologies will play an increasingly significant role. The government has put $1.4 billion on securing renewable energy and storing it. Australia is co-leading the creation of a clean hydrogen 'mission,' to lower hydrogen production and usage costs throughout supply chains (Energy Government Australia, 2021). Through loans and equity investments, the CEFC promotes energy efficiency, renewable energy, and low-emission energy projects. The CEFC has made investment commitments totalling more than $8.8 billion through more than 170 direct clean energy deals since its establishment in 2013. This comprises agreements with 13 co-finance counterparties that have completed over 20,000 smaller transactions across Australia, totalling $ 30.8 billion in investment (Energy Government Australia, 2021). The Australian Renewable Energy Agency provides grant financing for renewable energy technology research and development as well as early-stage commercialization. As of December 31, 2020, ARENA had awarded $1.67 billion in grant financing to 579 projects, totalling $6.84 billion in project value. The government announced a $ 1.9 billion investment plan in future technologies on September 17, 2020 (Energy Government Australia, 2021). Australia is one of the countries where fossil fuel energy resources are plentiful. Australia must restrict the usage of conventional energy and make every effort to replace it with renewable energy. Solar energy, biomass, wave energy, and wind energy are all examples of renewable energy resources in Australia. The contribution of the United States to global greenhouse gas emissions may be decreased by expanding the use of renewable energy resources (Energy Government Australia, 2021).

Figure 4 shows the demand for energy demand, supply, production and CO2emissionsn in India. As seen in the figure, it is evident that the demand for energy resources is likely to increase, making India's

Figure 4. The demand for energy resources in India
Source: IEA, 2018

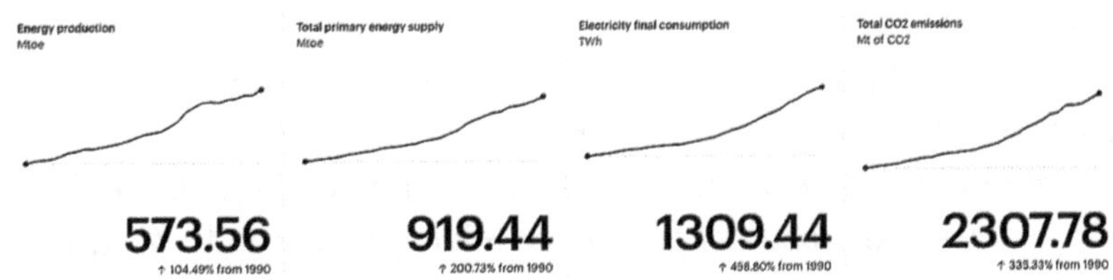

supply necessary to match the demand. With the demand increasing for considerably energy resources, it is evident that the CO2 emissions could also increase.

Table 2 shares the details of energy demand for Australia and its forecasted growth rate in 12years. As seen in the table, the demand for energy resources in Australia is likely to increase by 2030 which means that there would be a boom in the market for energy resources. Resources such as LNG, Aluminum and Metallurgical coal are expected to be the highest demanded resources while the rest provide a significant growth rate.

Table 2. The demand for energy resources in Australia and its expected growth rate

Energy Requirements	2018	2030	Growth
LNG (million tons)	318	530	+67%
Iron Ore (million tons)	2,107	2,372	+13%
Gold (thousand ounces)	148,620	172,906	+16%
Refined copper (thousand tones)	24,373	30,274	+24%
Finished nickel (thousand tones)	2,328	2,992	+29%
Aluminium (thousand tones)	62,382	94,884	+52%
Zinc (thousand tones)	14,664	18,858	+29%
Metallurgical Coal (million tons)	326	458	+41%
Thermal Coal (million tons)	1,053	1,214	+15%

Source: AME Group, 2019

INDIA AND AUSTRALIA ECONOMIC STRATEGY 2035

The India Economic Strategy is a bold strategy that seeks to change Australia's economic relationship with India until 2035. A rising India will require many of Australia's products and services during the next 20 years, including education, farming, energy, resources, travel, health, financial sectors, infrastructure, technology and development, and sport, getting the strategy right would enhance the Australian economy's resilience and contribute to (Pandey, 2020) India's goals. The IES2035 previously established an aim of India being one of Australia's top three export markets, India becoming the third-largest market in Asia for Australian outbound investment, $100 billion by 2035, and a larger, better trading basket with balanced trade ties between both nations (Bhaskar, 2020).

India's AES encompasses a wide variety of industries, considering the post-COVID recovery plan that both Australia and India will need to implement. Mining and Resources, Mining Equipment and Technology Services (METS), Critical minerals, Pharmaceutical, Medical Devices and Technology, Soil Mapping, Blue Economy, Sports Management and Sports Technology, Innovation and Research, Agri-tech, Health-tech, Water Management, Food Processing and Food Storage, Energy Efficiency and Renewables, Railways, Gems and Jewelry are among the sectors highlighted. India has urged Australia to take a more operationalized and granular approach to bilateral trade and investment. It requests sector-specific specialized delegation exchanges, increased nonstop flights between Australia and India's key corporate centres, and other things, as well as a renewed emphasis on negotiating the Free Trade Agreement (Bhaskar, 2020). Following the COVID-19 event, India's economic policy has primarily focused on substantial internal foundational and systemic changes across different sectors, as well as global engagement to attract foreign capital. The emphasis has been on land, labour, liquidity, and regulations that promote inbound capital by allowing FDI in most industries and generate employment.

Australia and India are located in the Indo-most Pacific's dynamic area, which is currently the centre of economic and strategic gravity. The year began with the Australia India Business Exchange (AIB-X), one of the largest commercial missions to India in the previous five years, led by Finance Minister Simon Birmingham and consisting of 120 members. A virtual summit between the Australian and Indian Prime Ministers resulted in the designation of this bilateral relationship as a Comprehensive Strategic Partnership, with agreements on cyber-enabled vital technology collaboration, cooperation in mineral processing of crucial minerals, contracts on defence, scientific research, and technology collaboration, and joint logistics sharing. The Indo-Pacific region serves as a meeting ground for Australian and Indian interests, as evidenced by the Supply Chain Resilience Initiative (Australia, India, and Japan) and Quad (United States, India, Japan, and Australia), which broadens the scope of India's evolving strategic alignment and is supplemented by Australia's recent participation in Malabar exercises (Bhaskar, 2020). India and Australia must be aware of their current reality, requirements, constraints, and limits to overcome the sticking issues in their Free Trade Agreement (FTA). Textiles, apparel, car components, and jewellery will benefit from goods, services, and investment-focused FTA with Australia. It will also make investment flows easier with Australia, which manages the world's third-largest pool of investment money. A free trade agreement (FTA) might boost company confidence in the operating environment. According to the Joint Study Group (JSG), the FTA's welfare gains may be between 0.15 and 1.14 per cent of GDP for India and 0.23 and 1.17 per cent of GDP for Australia. As part of 'Make in India 2.0' which covers areas like robots, Artificial Intelligence, Genomics, chemical feedstock, and electric storage, India may investigate opportunities with Australia in high tech manufacturing. Australia's advanced manufacturing experience can help India construct its export-led growth plan. Advanced manufacturing technologies are critical for achieving global expense, efficiency, creativity, reliability, and competitiveness.

Australia leads the world in Mining Equipment and Technology Services (METS), whereas India lags behind other mining nations. The Australian METS sector has several comparative advantages that, if properly exploited, may supply India's mining industry with a range of solutions. The first India-Australia Joint Working Group on Critical and Strategic Minerals met in November 2020 and decided on actions and future steps for the coming year. India and Australia have signed a Memorandum of Understanding (MoU) on Essential Minerals. The availability of these critical minerals is crucial for India's e-mobility and renewable energy ambitions. Mobile phones and computers, flat-screen displays, wind turbines, electric automobiles, photovoltaic systems, battery packs, space, and defence-industry technologies and goods all utilize these minerals. These assets may be used by India's public and private sectors, as well as its government consortia on essential minerals, to ensure future supply and develop an efficient energy economy. Because of its favourable economic climate and policy stability, Australia's mining and resources industry is the most attractive to foreign investors. Australia has also issued a list of 24 important vital minerals where India may emerge as a prospective supplier (Bhaskar, 2020).

According to the Indian and Australian governments, India and Australia can benefit from each other's experience in several critical sectors, including Agri-tech, energy efficiency, and renewables, and combine it with their respective skills in data analytics, biotech, and mobile apps. Australia's hydrogen sector experience might complement India's National Hydrogen Mission. The Hydrogen RD&D Foreign Collaboration Program, which will run for two years, will foster engagement between Australian and international research organizations while also facilitating R&D collaboration with partner nations.

India and Australia have agreed to continue their Energy Dialogue, which will focus on pumped hydro storage, cost-effective battery technology, hydrogen and coal gasification, renewable energy technology adoption, fly ash management, and solar forecasting and scheduling. Both nations pledged to continue working together on climate change, energy security, and other regional and global challenges, particularly through the International Solar Alliance (ISA) and the Coalition for Disaster Resilient Infrastructure (CDRI) (Australian Government Department of Foreign Affairs and Trade, 2020).

An Australian specialist has been assigned to the ISA Secretariat, and a working group of Australian business representatives will be formed to encourage commercial engagement in ISA initiatives. Australia will continue to lobby for India to be admitted to the International Energy Agency on a full membership basis (Government response to An India Economic Strategy to 2035, 2020). The Brookings Institution India has been tasked with looking at India's evolving gas policy landscape and determining the consequences of planned reforms for overseas providers. The research will give evidence to the Australian government and business parties who are considering gas export and investment collaboration with India (Government response to An India Economic Strategy to 2035, 2020). India will continue to rely on imports for most of its energy needs until 2035. The prospects for Australian energy commodity exports to India are not as promising as for non-energy resource commodities. India is looking for ways to improve its energy efficiency, and there's a growing market for technology and services that may assist. Government intervention is prompted by political sensitivities around the provision of inexpensive power. Australia should encourage India's increasing links with the international energy policy framework, engage on regulatory obstacles, and build a deeper bilateral knowledge relationship to enable larger economic engagement with India in the energy sector. In this area, we should also aim to strengthen our bilateral investment partnership, notably Indian participation in Australian renewable energy sources.

RECOMMENDATIONS

From the above sections, a relative picture of the relationship between the two countries can be observed. With the growing effects of the pandemic and overall economic stress, it can be observed that the two countries have tried to fill the gap caused but have a lot more to do in terms of partnerships and implementation. After analyzing the scenario between the two countries in the resources and energy sector, the research comes to the vital stage of suggestions that the two can consider helping grow each other.

1. Bhaskar (2020) mentions that the Australian machines and equipment and other related services are designed and produced to provide productive, cleaner, and safer mining and extraction facili-

ties in India. Australian resources and technology are advanced, sustainable, adaptive, and safe for use. If METS is utilized and promoted in India, Australia can increase its revenue in exports the technology and India can fully develop its mining industry.

2. Mining does affect the environment around and to conduct mining, various types of clearances require reports on environmental and wildlife protection. Usually, these take a lot of time as the clearance issue runs from the district, state, and central levels. India should facilitate a faster clearance process where the system investigates the environmental sustainability and use of the latest technology and the equipment which can be provided by Australia. India could also give exclusivity and clearances if there is the use of METS as the equipment is reliable and environment friendly.
3. Since India also lacks in exploring its mineral potential, partnering with Australian forces and the department of Mining can help discover India's geological depth. This should also include understanding the Indian geography, architecture and detecting mineral reserves. The level of significance of rare materials and vital minerals has increased and with the assistance of Australia, India could rediscover and extract them through this way.
4. India and Australia have been partnering for a long time and India needs to improve a lot and reach its potential. India should learn and understand the ways Australia has modularized its sector and work towards the strategies to improve its mining and resources sector. Australia having abundant resources and technology puts the country at a good advantage especially when it comes to India. India also has the opportunity and privilege to utilize METS. The scope for the resources sector for both countries seems favourable if well established and properly employed. This could be done through mineral alliance, geological exploration and research, and other ways. With the employment of such strategies and stronger partnerships between the two countries, both can get benefited and carry their friendship for longer years and more generations.
5. The future of energy supply will rise as Australia's and the world's populations continue to grow and live increasingly energy-dependent lives. Under the Look East and now Act East policies, India's economic and security relations with Australia have gotten a boost. Australia is eager to deepen its ties with India, which is seen as one of the most promising countries in terms of economic growth and geopolitical importance. Energy ties between the two nations have been improving in recent years and are expected to continue to improve in the future.
6. Growing energy demands in India, transitions from fossil fuels to renewables, climate change concerns, and population growth are all variables that influence the overall energy relationship between India and Australia. Australia possesses the world's greatest uranium, gas, and coal reserves, and is on the verge of becoming the world's largest LNG provider. Australia may become a major thermal coal supplier to India. The majority of India's power plants are built to run solely on imported coal. India is one of Australia's largest importers of coking coal. This means that India will need to import gas to satisfy its needs, and Australia may be able to help.
7. Australia has much higher concentrated uranium reserves, and its deposits, unlike India's, are closer to the surface. Because it does not employ nuclear power, Australia sells all of its uranium. In the foreseeable future, India's nuclear demands are expected to be largely fulfilled by imports, which presents an opportunity for Australia. In 2011, Australia lifted its restriction on exporting uranium to India. Australia may potentially provide India with up to 300 tons of uranium each year, according to estimates (Hazarika & Pathak, 2019).
8. With the support of technology transfer and financial aid from foreign sources such as the Green Climate Fund, India hopes to reach about 40% electric power installed capacity from renewable

resources by 2030. Solar energy is an essential component that, according to predictions, will play a major role by 2040. The National Solar Mission of India intends to promote solar energy as a component of electricity generation while also making it cost-competitive with fossil fuels. The mission's goal is to lower the cost of solar power generation through investing in research and development, as well as local raw material and component manufacture (Hazarika & Pathak, 2019).

FUTURE RESEARCH

Australia and India have a thriving relationship and being each other's allies for a long time have been a great achievement for both countries. The vast complementarities that exist between the two countries can act as a catalyst for increased bilateral commerce and information exchange. flow. Furthermore, there is a trilateral network between India and Australia, as well as the ASEAN, in the Indo-Pacific. The two countries' economic ties are strong, with Australia's position as an energy provider to India becoming increasingly crucial and greater attention on the undeveloped security cooperation is required due to mutual strategic objectives in Asia, the Indian Ocean and counterterrorism, especially if China is in the equation. The focus on their economies and the assistance each other have given to build their resources and energy sector is indeed a noticeable and remarkable fact. The world went through the COVID-19 pandemic and still recovering even in the current year. From this research, it is evident that both countries even though faced their challenges still try to support each other and themselves. The effect of the pandemic is on different levels. This research has been conducted through extensive use of data collected from journals, published books, government portal websites, etc. The research focused on understanding the scenario between the two and the data that has been interpreted can have its limits and variations.

Looking deeper into the relation shared by the two countries, the entire research is based on the data available from trusted resources which indicates that the research may lack the reality of the situation with all the information and material being referred are from secondary sources. With these findings from the research, there may always be gaps as these sources are secondary information found on different journals, government data, statistics, and other mediums. With new trends and changing environment, there may be other opportunities for both countries to explore which can also be the future scope of this research. Therefore, the future scope of the research would be to try to analyze quantitative data with a large number of business entrepreneurs working in the resources and energy sector to understand the behaviour and trends.

CONCLUSION

The Dialogue aims to enhance the nations' institutional structure as well as their interaction across all areas of the energy value chain. India is one of the world's fastest-growing rising economies, with a growing need for low-cost, environmentally friendly energy. Access to India's massive energy market will benefit Australian firms substantially. By 2030, Indian industries have pledged to use renewable energy to supply 50% or possibly 100% of their electricity. As a result, the benefits to Australian firms from such initiatives and commitments in India are enormous (Hazarika & Pathak, 2019). Australia's desire for greater economic cooperation with India coincides with its desire for a stronger strategic and military tie with the country. Australia's susceptibility to China manifests itself in a variety of ways, ranging from political to economic. The economic and military growth of China, notably in the Indo-Pacific area, has forced India and Australia to consider deeper alliances. Energy cooperation is a crucial component of such collaboration. India plans to satisfy its energy needs through expanding domestic production, imports, pipelines, and collaboration with states to benefit from technological knowledge and financial incentives. As a storehouse of natural reserves as well as having experience in the creation of solar energy, Australia would be able to play a significant role in assisting India in meeting its energy security goals. If prices decrease and India decides to diversify its gas import sources, Australia may become a key destination for future gas imports for India.

There are several uncertainties in Australia's energy cooperation with India. The growing import of Australian energy resources may be hampered by India's commitment to renewable energy and investment in local reserves. Technological advancements, price reductions, and other energy supplies may all influence Australia's chances of becoming a major energy supplier for India. India might establish something akin to the Australia–China Joint Research Centre for Energy. The centre serves as a key platform for Australia and China to collaborate on science and research in the field of energy science and engineering, with an emphasis on both renewable and fossil fuels. Intensifying collaboration between India and Australia along these lines will benefit both countries. Australia is well-positioned to play a big role in non-renewable energy imports, which will continue to be a large component of India's energy requirements. Over the last few years, the Australian government has collaborated extensively with the Indian government to create new renewable energy projects.

REFERENCES

Australia India Business Exchange. (2021). *Austrade*. https://www.austrade.gov.au/australia-india-business-exchange

Australia-India Comprehensive Economic Cooperation Agreement (AI-CECA). (2020). *Australian Government Department of Foreign Affairs and Trade*. https://www.dfat.gov.au/trade/agreements/negotiations/aifta/australia-india-comprehensive-economic-cooperation-agreement

Australia-India Council. (2020). *Australia and India. A dynamic mix*. https://www.dfat.gov.au/people-to-people/foundations-councils-institutes/australia-india-council/adynamicmix/Pages/default

Australian Government Department of Foreign Affairs and Trade. (2014). *The Lessons of European Integration for the Indo Pacific*. https://www.dfat.gov.au/news/speeches/Pages/140616_anu

Bhaskar, N. J. (2019). *Examining the potential of India–Australia partnerships in mining*. Observer Research Foundation. https://www.orfonline.org/research/examining-the-potential-of-india-australia-partnerships-in-mining-49983/

Bhaskar, N. J. (2020). *India's Australia Economic Strategy: A big push to bilateral trade*. Business Today. https://www.businesstoday.in/opinion/columns/story/india-releases-australia-economic-strategy-to-give-a-big-push-to-bilateral-trade-between-both-countries-282654-2020-12-26

Bhowmick, S., Saha, R., & Basu, P. (2019). *India and Australia: From 4000 Nautical Miles to 22 Yard*. Observer Research Foundation. https://www.orfonline.org/wp-content/uploads/2019/10/ORF_OccasionalPaper_219_India-Australia.pdf

Brewster, D. (2014). *Australia-India Strategic Relations: The Odd Couple of the Indian Ocean?* Future Directions International Associate Paper. https://www.futuredirections.org.au/wp-content/uploads/2014/05/Australia-India_Strategic_Relations_-_The_Odd_Couple_of_the_Indian_Ocean_.pdf

Business Opportunities in India: Investment Ideas, Industry Research, Reports. (n.d.). https://www.ibef.org

Department of Foreign Affairs and Trade. (2018). *An India Economic Strategy To 2035.* https://www.dfat.gov.au/geo/india/ies/index.html

Department of Foreign Affairs and Trade. (2018). *Energy Sector - An India Economic Strategy To 2035.* https://www.dfat.gov.au/geo/india/ies/chapter-7.html

Energy Government Australia. (2021). *Clean energy and the electricity market.* https://www.energy.gov.au/government-priorities/energy-supply/clean-energy-and-the-electricity-market

Gnanagurunathan, D. (2012). India-Australia in the Indo-Pacific: a blossoming partnership. *Viewpoint (Indian Council of World Affairs), 21.* https://www.futuredirections.org.au/wp-content/uploads/2013/03/VPIndopacific.pdf

Government response to An India Economic Strategy to 2035. (2020). *Australian Government Department of Foreign Affairs and Trade.* https://www.dfat.gov.au/about-us/publications/Pages/government-response-india-economic-strategy

Hall, I. (2021, February 2). *Australia and India in the Modi era: An unequal...* International Politics. https://link.springer.com/article/10.1057/s41311-020-00278-w?error=cookies_not_supported&error=cookies_not_supported&code=ef481862-2c59-46d4-aa7f-b52630f6643b&code=7a4f4e59-0c6c-4775-af28-92750484e8a4

Hazarika, O. B., & Pathak, S. (2019). Energy Security Dynamics in India–Australia Relations. *Jadavpur Journal of International Relations*, *23*(1), 26–47. doi:10.1177/0973598418803480

India - Countries & Regions. (n.d.). https://www.iea.org/countries/india

Indian Brand Equity Foundation IBEF. (2021). *Renewable Energy Industry in India: Overview, Market Size & Growth.* https://www.ibef.org/industry/renewable-energy.aspx

Joint Statement on a Comprehensive Strategic Partnership between Republic of India and Australia. (n.d.). *Australian Government Department of Foreign Affairs and Trade.* https://www.dfat.gov.au/geo/india/joint-statement-comprehensive-strategic-partnership-between-republic-india-and-australia

Lincoln, Y. S., & Guba, E. G. (2003). Paradigmatic controversies, contradictions, and emerging confluences. In The Landscape of Qualitative Research: Theories and Issues (2nd ed., pp. 253-291). London: Sage.

Pachauri, R. K. (2021). Oration 11: 2007 KR Narayanan Oration. Coping with Climate Change: Is Development in India and the World Sustainable? In *Twenty KR Narayanan Orations: Essays by Eminent Persons on the Rapidly Transforming Indian Economy*. ANU Press. doi:10.22459/TKRNO.2021.11

Pandey, P. C. (2020, December 18). *India Has Seen Greenhouse Gas Emissions Increase by a Staggering 335% Since 1990.* Climate Scorecard. https://www.climatescorecard.org/2020/12/india-has-seen-greenhouse-gas-emissions-increase-by-a-staggering-335-since-1990/

Rughani, D. (2021, September 4). *Realising an 'early harvest' for Australia–India trade.* East Asia Forum. https://www.eastasiaforum.org/2021/09/04/realising-an-early-harvest-for-australia-india-trade/

Sharma, A. (2016). *Australia-India relations: trends and the prospects for a comprehensive economic relationship* (No. 2016-02). The Australian National University, Australia South Asia Research Centre. https://acde.crawford.anu.edu.au/sites/default/files/publication/acde_crawford_anu_edu_au/2016-09/asarc_wp_2016-02_sharma.pdf

Smith, R. F. I. (2014). India and Australia: Closer and Closer? *Politico (Pavia, Italy), 127.* http://politicosse.in/uploads/Politico_2014_Vol-2_No-22.pdf#page=147

The Australian resources sector - significance and opportunities. (n.d.). https://www.industry.gov.au/data-and-publications/australias-national-resources-statement/the-australian-resources-sector-significance-and-opportunities

Trivedi, A. (2021, September 22). *Experts: September 2021 White House QUAD meeting.* https://www.atlanticcouncil.org/uncategorized/experts-react-the-september-2021-white-house-quad-meeting/

Workman, D. (2021, March 16). *Australia's Top 10 Imports.* https://www.worldstopexports.com/australias-top-10-imports/

ADDITIONAL READING

Cho, S. W. S., & Yoon, G. (2013). Sectoral analysis of an Australia–India free trade agreement. *Journal of the Asia Pacific Economy, 19*(2), 205–229. doi:10.1080/13547860.2013.820469

Duggal, M. K. (2021). Emerging Business and Trade Opportunities Between India and Australia. *Emerging Business and Trade Opportunities Between Oceania and Asia*, 144–178. doi:10.4018/978-1-7998-4126-5.ch007

Jayasuriya, S., & Panza, L. (2011). Will India Be the Next China? Challenges, Prospects and Implications for Australia. *The Australian Economic Review, 44*(4), 446–456. doi:10.1111/j.1467-8462.2011.00659.x

Mayer, P., & Jain, P. (2010). Beyond Cricket: Australia–India Evolving Relations. *Australian Journal of Political Science, 45*(1), 133–148. doi:10.1080/10361140903517759

Medhekar, A. (2021). Australia-India. *Emerging Business and Trade Opportunities Between Oceania and Asia*, 57–86. doi:10.4018/978-1-7998-4126-5.ch004

Mishra, R. (2012). India–Australia Strategic Relations: Moving to the Next Level. *Strategic Analysis, 36*(4), 657–662. doi:10.1080/09700161.2012.689537

Panda, R., & Baruah, P. (2010). India–Australia Strategic Partnership. *India Quarterly. Journal of International Affairs, 66*(2), 203–221. doi:10.1177/097492841006600205

Shekhar, V. (2010). India and Australia in the Twenty-first Century. *India Quarterly. Journal of International Affairs*, *66*(4), 397–412. doi:10.1177/097492841006600405

KEY TERMS AND DEFINITIONS

Bilateral Relations: The process of encouraging commerce by entering into agreements governing the quantity and price of commodities that are equally enforceable on both parties.

Climate Change: A shift in global climate patterns, particularly one seen from the middle to late twentieth century and primarily ascribed to rising amounts of carbon dioxide in the atmosphere caused by the use of fossil fuels.

Geopolitical: Concerning politics, particularly international relations as impacted by geographical variables.

Greenhouse Gas: Gases that absorbs infrared light and so contributes to the greenhouse effect, greenhouse gases include carbon dioxide and chlorofluorocarbons.

Liberalization: The elimination or relaxation of constraints on something, usually a political or economic system.

Renewable Energy: It is the energy derived from naturally renewing but flow-limited sources; renewable resources are practically limitless in terms of duration but restricted in terms of energy available per unit of time.

Resources Sector: An sector that manufactures and resells products and services using natural resources as raw materials.

Chapter 13
New Trade Frontiers Between India and Australia:
Challenges and Opportunities Post COVID-19

Risha Khandelwal
JECRC University, India

Princi Gupta
JECRC University, India

ABSTRACT

The rising geopolitical tensions between China and Australia can develop new trade frontiers between India, Australia, and the South Asian region as a whole. With this view, the chapter aims to study the present state of bilateral trade relations between India-Australia, identify obstacles that hindered the growth of trade relations between India-Australia in the past, understand the impact of comprehensive economic cooperation for free trade agreement between the two countries. The chapter further discusses the challenges that COVID-19 has posed for trade between Australia and China as well as the future opportunities for bilateral trade between India and Australia. The 2020-21 Australia-India Joint Statement on Comprehensive Strategic Partnership and Comprehensive Economic Cooperation agreement is a step forward in a positive direction in meeting many of the UN SDGs. This chapter is essential for understanding the complexities of "trade creation" between (India and Australia) and "trade diversion" between (China and Australia).

INTRODUCTION

Bilateral relations between Australia and India during the post-war period were marked by "strategic apathy," if not "strategic detachment". While Australia had shifted its alliance preferences from England to the United States, India has carved a non-aligned path while keeping a close relationship with the erstwhile Soviet Union (Smith, 2010). Now, Asia has become the new Europe when the Cold War ended,

DOI: 10.4018/978-1-7998-8657-0.ch013

and the post-Cold War period lasted far into the second decade of the new century. Asia has emerged as the launching point for everything that signifies growth and development (Ranjan, 2016). The idea that the Asians own the twenty-first century has become a common theme in policy circles around the world. In 2018, Australia published "An India Economic Strategy to 2035," a document that outlined the strategic sectors where the country should invest in. The document stated that by 2035, Australia wants India to be its third largest export market.

India is likewise enthusiastic about its relationship with Australia. "Modi's Act East policy has enlarged the canvas by putting Australia at the centre of India's eastern strategy and the South Pacific back on India's political radar". Furthermore, Modi's November 2014 visit to Australia was the first by an Indian Prime Minister in nearly three decades, and it held a lot of promise. Modi stated that Australia was no longer on the outside of New Delhi's "vision," but rather "in the centre of our ideas." He promised to work with Canberra at the G20 and regional multilateral forums, to strengthen the bilateral security collaboration, and to reach an agreement on a free trade agreement (Bajpaee, 2017).

But, only a few of these commitments were kept. Within and beyond the Quad, progress was achieved in defence and security cooperation, but a free trade agreement proved too difficult. "India was Australia's eighth-largest trading partner and fifth-largest export market in 2018-19, driven by coal and international education". Bilateral "trade with India was $30.3 billion in 2018-19, and the level of investment was $30.7 billion in 2018"(The Economic Times, 2021). "While China is Australia's largest two-way trading partner in goods and services, accounting for 29 per cent of Australia's trade with the world". Bilateral trade reached $251 billion in 2019-20"(The Hindustan Times, 2021). Their "exports to China grew by 9 per cent to reach $168 billion". China remained "Australia's biggest services export market, particularly in education and tourism" (Jaishankar, 2020).

Australia is the 34th most popular destination for India's total exports. India, on the other hand, is Australia's fourth-largest export market. Pharmaceuticals, textiles, jewelry, automobiles, and mineral fuels are among India's biggest exports to Australia; followed by computer and information services, as well as tourism, in top service exports (Chakraborty et al.,2019). Nevertheless, Australia sees India as a potential significant market for its products. Coking coal is Australia's most important export to India, accounting for 65 percent of all exports to India(Business Standard, 2021). Gold, copper, aluminum, and petroleum products are among India's other Australian imports (Chakraborty et al.,2019). India imports significant quantities of coal since it does not manufacture high- quality coal. Australia could potentially be a supplier of high-quality coal, which would aid India's carbon reduction efforts. Hence, Australia has the potential to be India's strategic energy partner.

To meet domestic demand, Indian corporations have engaged in coal mining in Australia. Lanco Infratech Limited for example made the greatest such strategic investment in 2010. It is noteworthy that India has huge potential for Australian exports, but Australia is still not a big market for Indian items. Not surprisingly, the bilateral defence and security collaboration was elevated to a Comprehensive Strategic Partnership (CSP) at the June 2020 Morrison-Modi virtual summit, with both sides committing to 'deepen and broaden' defence co-operation within the partnership. Morrison said the CSP will "increase the level of trust required" to promote trade and investment flows between Australia and India, which are currently "not where both would like them to be," The broad aims of the joint strategy were to resolve the economic and social effects of Covid-19; each has signed CSPs with a number of other nations (Sarma, 2020)

Following a trade war with China, Australia, which is emerging as a key partner of India in the Indo-Pacific region, is in talks with New Delhi to expand their partnership beyond security and defence. Australia is in talks with New Delhi to enter into a trade agreement to boost its mining sector and wine sales. According to reliable sources, Australia is attempting to entice India to replace the void left by China in its mining industry investments and wine imports. The firms, particularly Coal Indian corporations, are being pushed to invest in coal, iron ore, and vital minerals exploration and mining.

The goal of this chapter is to better comprehend India's and Australia's bilateral trade and geopolitical interactions. It also addresses the efforts made by the governments of India and Australia to improve their bilateral commerce connections through the signing of free trade agreements, as well as how the two nations are trying to strengthen their defence relationships.

In addition, the chapter discusses the challenges that Covid-19 has produced for commerce between Australia and China, as well as how this can benefit India. Finally, it discusses the problems that India and Australia are facing in developing their strong connections.

LITERATURE REVIEW

Background on India- Australia Bilateral Relations – Past and Present

The Australian government, led by Prime Minister Scott Morrison, is negotiating a Free Trade Agreement with India in order to expand trade relations. This comes on the heels of India, Australia, and Japan launching a robust supply chain plan last year (Kaul, 2000). According to Economic times, China has blocked the import of Australian coal, and the Australian government is looking at ways for wine producers who have been affected by China's trade restrictions to enter the Indian market. In the Indo-Pacific area, Australia has been feeling the heat from China. China has previously indicated that it intends to maintain a permanent military presence in the region. This might give Beijing the potential to put pressure on island states and Australia, as well as cut off vital supply routes to the US. Australia is strengthening its defence cooperation with other countries in the region, particularly India. Experts say Australia has been the target of cyber-attacks, influence operations, trade boycotts, diplomatic threats, and espionage. Following a low in Beijing's ties with Canberra, India and Australia are looking into early harvest trade accords (Chadha et al.,2019). Agriculture, health, education and training, the digital economy, and defence are all areas where India and Australia are looking for opportunity (Athukorala, 2020).

India's geology is similar to Western Australia's, and it possesses undeveloped resources. The Australian mining equipment, technology, and services industry has enormous prospects to collaborate with India's resources and rare earths industries. The ambassadors' and parliamentarians' language has been anything but diplomatic and certainly not parliamentary (Maurya, 2017). The heated debates that were traditionally held behind closed doors have spilled out into the open, been shown on television, and printed in newspapers. The fraught relationship between Australia and China reached a new low this week, with a deteriorating conflict arising, apparently, from Australia's desire for an international, independent study into the origins of the Covid-19 outbreak, which has killed more than 230,000 people so far. China and Australia, on the other hand, see this investigation as two distinct entities, despite the fact that the idea is still amorphous. When the Consulate General of India opened as a Trade Office in Sydney in 1941, the two countries established diplomatic relations before independence. In 1945, the first Indian High Commissioner to Australia arrived in Canberra. Lieutenant-General Iven Mackay was named Australia's first High Commissioner to India in March 1944 (Chao & Yoon,2014).

Australia-India Council

Following an inquiry of Australia's relations with India, the Senate Standing Committee on Foreign Affairs, Defence, and Trade recommended that the AIC) be founded on May 21, 1992. The AIC works to strengthen the relationship between Australia and India by increasing awareness and encouraging interactions (Tahir et al.,2016).

Education

The education cooperation between Australia and India is critical for generating participation, collaboration, and constructing a bridge between our two countries. The Australia India Education Council (AIEC), which is unique among India's education partners, is a ministerial-led policy forum that provides a platform for ministerial interaction on policy and operational concerns across education. The AIEC is co-chaired by both countries' education ministries and includes members from government, academia, and industry (Timsina & Culas, 2020).

Defence

The 2006 Memorandum on Defence cooperation and the 2009 Joint Declaration on security cooperation establish positive defence cooperation between India and Australia. The defence cooperation has developed to include a variety of platforms for strategic engagement, as well as frequent encounters between our respective services through senior visits, staff talks, and training exchanges, after the signing of a bilateral Framework for Security Cooperation in 2014 (Timsina & Culas,2020).

Development Assistance

The Australian government's overseas aid programme serves the national interest of Australia by supporting developing countries in reducing poverty and achieving economic development. While Australia does not have a bilateral development cooperation programme with India, we do support the country through our global and regional aid investments and technical assistance. Here you will find information on Australia's development programme. The South Asia Regional Program aims to strengthen Australia's economic participation in the region by tackling significant regional hurdles to long-term economic growth (Timsina & Culas,2020).

DOOR FOR INDIA TO JOIN REGIONAL COMPREHENSIVE ECONOMIC PARTNERSHIP (RCEP) REMAINS FIRMLY OPEN: AUSTRALIAN

India has opted out of the RCEP. That door, in Australia's opinion, remains firmly open. Whatever India's final choice is, we accept it and will continue to support India's engagement in the Indo-Pacific region(Panda,2014). According to Australian Minister Simon Birmingham, the door for India to join the fifteen-member Regional Comprehensive Economic Partnership (RCEP) agreement remained firmly o en from Australia's perspective, and the country was also looking forward to re engagement on the bilateral free trade agreement. The Minister was addressing at the CII partnership summit's virtual introduction of the Australia Economic Strategy Report. Birmingham expressed his eagerness for the two countries to reengage on the India-Australia Comprehensive Economic Cooperation Agreement (CECA). "Let us knock the ball for six by obtaining speedy movement on this accord and scoring some quick runs as our countries meet on the cricket field," he remarked (Zreik,2021).

Due to a variety of discrepancies between the two countries, notably in areas such as agriculture and services, the CECA negotiations, which began in 2011, were halted.However, as part of Prime Minister Narendra Modi and his Australian counterpart Scott Morrison's comprehensive joint strategic partnership announced in June this year, it was decided to re-engage on the CECA.

The decision was made in part because India had withdrawn from the Regional Comprehensive Economic Partnership (RCEP), a free trade agreement involving the ten member ASEAN, China, Australia, New Zealand, Japan, and South Korea, due to worries about China.According to the Australian Minister, bilateral trade in products and services has increased in the last five years, and India was Australia's eighth-largest trading partner and fifth-largest export market in 2019, with $29 billion in two-way trade and services (Hsu,2013). While Australia was a valued trading partner, India's exports to the country were moderate, according to Commerce and Industry Minister Piyush Goyal, and discussions were underway to offer more chances for India to grow its footprints in the country and bridge the gap.

While mining had been the mainstay of India's relationship with Australia, he noted that additional fields of collaboration were growing including power, railway, gems, and jewellery, auto, pharmaceutical, healthcare, and agribusiness (Gurry, 2012). He believes the Australia-India trade basket must grow, improve, and become more balanced. According to Goyal, the India Economic Strategy report and the Australia Economic Strategy report can give a good middle ground for talks and define areas of cooperation (Deb, 2020). Goyal is optimistic regarding the new trade relations evolving between India and Australia. He stated that Australia and India have been cooperating even more closely on the strategic front, whether it is through Malabar exercises, QUAD (quadrilateral security dialogue) groups, or strategic alliances in a variety of areas (Graham, 2018).

This strong cooperation will continue to benefit our economic alliance in the years ahead, he said. The trading connection between India and Australia has grown significantly in recent years, owing to numerous complementarities between the two economies (Gopal & Ahlawat, 2015). The value of two-way products and services trade has increased from $13.6 billion in 2007 to $24.3 billion by 2020 (Das & Dubey,2020). India is the world's largest democracy and a 1.3 billion-strong market. Education, agriculture, energy, mining, tourism, healthcare, financial services, infrastructure, research and innovation, and sport are all areas where Australia's youthful population, diversified economy, and growth trajectory present substantial opportunities for Australian businesses (Taylor & Taylor, 2017). In May 2011, Australia and India began talks on a Comprehensive Economic Cooperation Agreement. After nine rounds of talks, both countries agreed to put the talks on hold in September 2015, pending the conclusion of other multilateral regional talks.

Comprehensive Strategic Partnership between India and Australia, while appropriately considering earlier bilateral discussions, where a mutually agreed way forward can be found. Australia is willing to spend millions of dollars in South-East Asia and wants to give new directions to the existing bilateral relations between the two regions (Roy,2018).

Australian Prime Minister Scott Morrison's government has been under fire from domestic critics who say the country's investment in Southeast Asia is insufficient and that it does not pay enough attention to the region. Most of the opponents blamed China's growing influence in the region for their remarks (Brewester,2010). The government documents pertaining to this alleged proposal have yet to be revealed. Australia, as a major economy, has long been involved in the development of Southeast Asia and has a significant investment presence in the region. From 2018 to 2019, Australia-Southeast Asia economic and trade cooperation totalled AUD $123.7 billion (US$88 billion), accounting for 13.9 percent of Australia's total trade (The Herald Sun, 2021).

Australia has historically been a source of support to Southeast Asia. Its assistance to the region is provided through ASEAN or APEC. Education, health, humanitarianism, disaster relief and rehabilitation, infrastructure, agriculture, fisheries, and water support are all areas where aid is concentrated. Southeast Asia is also major recipient of Australian aid. Between 2018 and 2019, the aid from Australia to Southeast Asian countries (except Singapore, Malaysia, and Thailand) amounted to AUD$ 841 million(The Herald Sun, 2021). From 2016 to 2020, Australia's budget of multilateral aid to ASEAN and the Mekong region rose from AUD$29.6 million to AUD$38.4 million, respectively (Panda,2020).

Over the last two years, Australia has kept a close eye on Southeast Asia, seeing the region as a key pillar in the Indo-Pacific Strategy's advancement. ASEAN has built cooperative frameworks with countries such as China, Japan, South Korea, Australia, the United States, Russia, and the European Union. The region has emerged as a key investment destination for the world's major economies. Competition between rival powers is unavoidable, regardless of economics, commerce, or aid. Positive competition will encourage more cooperative behaviours and increase the impact of aid. Regional development and prosperity are hampered by fierce rivalry. into pawns for sacrifice (Buruah,2018). Logic of an agreement with India and Australia partnership, is the improved and legally-binding access to such a huge market would result in significant economic gains, particularly for commodity and service exports. In the Indo-Pacific area, India is the only of Australia's main markets where trade is still conducted on non-preferential terms. India has been less enthused, but two major factors are giving the CECA talks fresh energy (Miller, 2018).

First, the competition between the United States and China, as well as India's own concerns about China, have encouraged India to strengthen its strategic and economic ties as a buffer against potential risk. An upscaling in bilateral defence linkages is ongoing, as evidenced by the recent Australia-India 2+2 ministerial meetings, paving the way for a high-trust strategic (World Trade Organization [WTO], 2020). alliance. It's also worth observing what's going on in the economy. India is accelerating its economic and technical self-reliance, according to Prime Minister Narendra Modi's "Make in India" campaign. Although starting from different places, both Australia and India are working to broaden their trade and investment links. A trade agreement with India would be a major victory for the Morrison government's economic diversification goal (The Economic Times,2021). Second, the economic impact of Covid-19 on India's economy has prompted the country to place a considerable emphasis on identifying new markets to aid its post-pandemic recovery. India is putting a premium on market access. Some Indians have openly discussed the chances that China's economic coercive campaign against Australia could provide for India.

These are encouraging signs, but any appraisal of India's trade strategy must be founded. Early harvests in trade talks are politically appealing, but they are generally impossible to achieve. Professional negotiators embrace the "single undertaking" negotiating paradigm, which states that nothing is agreed upon until everything is agreed upon. This methodology avoids cherry-picking from the market access component to preserve as much scope as possible to produce a balanced and comprehensive agreement. Market access issues, notably in agriculture and services, have played a key role in the CECA negotiations' deadlock (Pereira, 2021). India's main concern has been the liberalisation of "mode 4" services, notably the short-term entry of businesspersons. India has claimed that Australia's Short-term business visitor legislation is impending India's service exports. Australia has resisted these demands, citing concerns about the implications for the labour market. The Australian side's pragmatism was palpable in the Tehan- Goyal statement, which omitted any mention of "ambitious", a constant in most Australian pronouncements of intentions in FTA negotiations .

Given the significant stakes in agriculture and services, however, it is unlikely that either side would give up key negotiation leverage in an early harvest package.More than likely, the early harvest will be populated from the various country's economic initiatives, such as fintech, investment promotion, essential minerals and skills, education, and capacity-building.There is substantial possibility for win-win results on these topics on any objective basis, but trade discussions are hard-fought exchanges of concessions.Brinkmanship is an unavoidable aspect of them, and given the stakes, it's unlikely that the current negotiations will go smoothly (Irwin,2020). India have been strained by a trade war. China has put high tariffs on Australian barley and wine exports, as well as creating trade hurdles for timber and coal. The economic partnership between Australia and India, as well as the ambitious interim and final trade agreements, were at the forefront of his discussions with commerce. Even though both sides were approaching the negotiations with a "win-win" mindset, he admitted it would be difficult for the two parties to reach an interim trade agreement in just three months. There has been "a lot of movement" in cooperation with India on rare earth minerals, with a key development being Prime Minister Scott Morrison's announcement last week about Export Finance Australia establishing a $2 billion critical minerals facility to assist with mineral exploration and processing, as well as the development of supply chains for exports to countries like India" (The Heraldsun, 2021). This will assist Australia and India in developing that important mineral partnership. Also, a clean technology deal between Australia and India, which may also help in the critical minerals field.

Even before the Covid-19 controversy, the two countries were discussing the potential of cooperating in the mining and processing of rare earth metals including lithium, neodymium, and dysprosium, for which Australia has the world's sixth greatest reserves. India has been attempting to diversify its supplies of rare earth metals, which it buys from China for more than 90% of its requirements. Imports from China totalled $3.4 million in 2016 (The Hindustan Times, 2021). The use of merino wool in India's textile industry, phytosanitary measures for the export and import of fruits and vegetables, and Australian investments in the Indian food processing sector. E-commerce negotiations will have to wait till India approves significant legislation on the subject, but that it will be included in the final trade agreement.

Misra and Choudhary (2020)studied the impact of increased tariffs on trade of other nations. The study examined the possible economic impacts of these two large economies' significant tariff hikes on Brazil, Russia, India, China, and South Africa, with a focus on India. According to the study, the trade war between the United States and China may give some chances for India in the short to medium term since gains from trade deflection would outweigh losses from trade contraction. However, future tariff increases will have a negative impact on the global economy in the long run. A defining element of the post-global financial crisis world has been an increased predisposition for protectionism in recent years (Siddiqui & Singh.,2021) .In this context the results of Sanyal (2021) shows that there will be a significant trade diversion to India in case of trade war between US and China.

Figure 1. Exports from India to Australia (2014-20)
Source: tradingeconomics.com

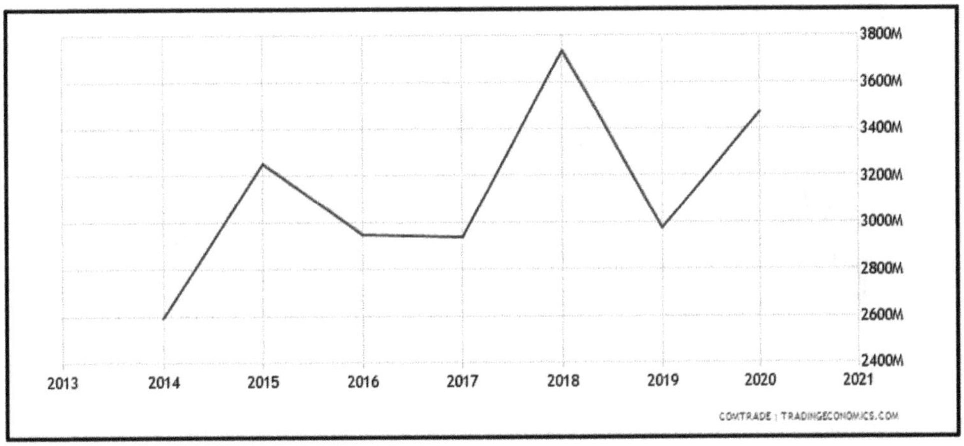

BILATERAL TRADE RELATIONS BETWEEN INDIA AND AUSTRALIA

Exports From India to Australia

Exports to Australia in India averaged 7.49 INR Billion from 1991 until 2021, reaching an all-time high of 51.87 INR Billion in August of 2021 and a record low of 0.25 INR Billion in May of 1991(The Economic Times, 2021). This page includes a chart with historical data for India Exports to Australia. India Exports to Australia - values, historical data, and charts - was last updated in October of 2021.

Figure 1 illustrates that, due to the trade war between China and Australia, India's exports to Australia increased dramatically during the period 2019-20. Although the export scenario from India to Australia is highly variable, it is reasonable to assume that the situation would not remain unchanged in the future, as both economies seek strong trade links. Australia Exports to India was US$6.89 Billion during 2020, according to the United Nations COMTRADE database on international trade. Australia Exports to India - data, historical chart, and statistics - was last updated in October of 2021. Imports from Australia in India decreased to 85.44 INR Billion in August from 85.93 INR Billion in July of 2021(The Economic Times,2021)

Figure 2 illustrates that, an increase in exports from India to Australia, which also shows an increase in exports from Australia to India. Australia exports coal and wine to China, but owing to sanctions, the country was unable to continue. As a result, India stepped in to help Australia by acquiring the same commodities and meeting its need.

COVID-19 AND TRADE IMPACT ON AUSTRALIAN EXPORTS

Covid has severely affected the trade of various countries, but it even resulted into trade war for some nations like Australia and China. As it is visible from the graph that there is a sudden decline in the export trade from Australia to India from 2019 to 2020.

Figure 2. Exports from Australia to India (2014-20)
Source: tradingeconomics.com

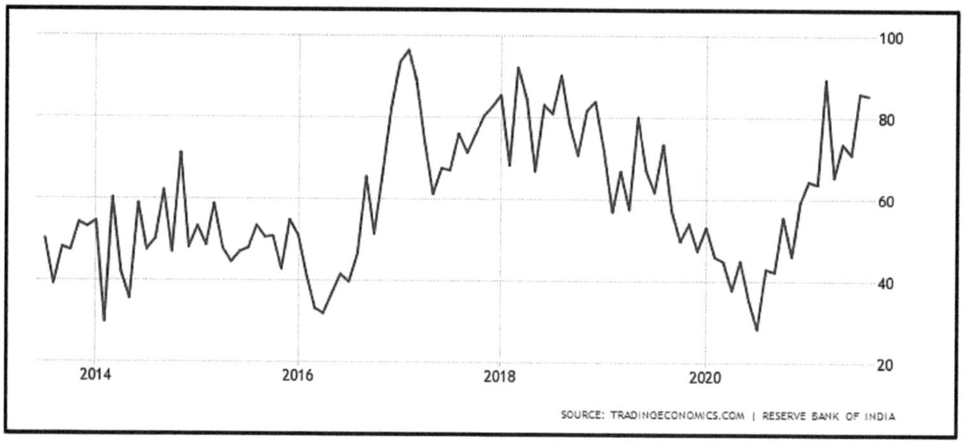

Table 1. Items wise composition of products exported and imported by India and Australia

Major Exports From Australia to India		Major Exports From India to Australia	
Item	**Percentage**	**Item**	**Percentage**
Coal Briquettes	47.4%	Refined petroleum	27.3%
Gold	38.2%	Medicaments	7.8%
		Gems and Jewellery	5.3%

Source: https://oec.world/

Figure 3. Impact of Covid on Australian Exports to China
Source: tradingeconomics.com

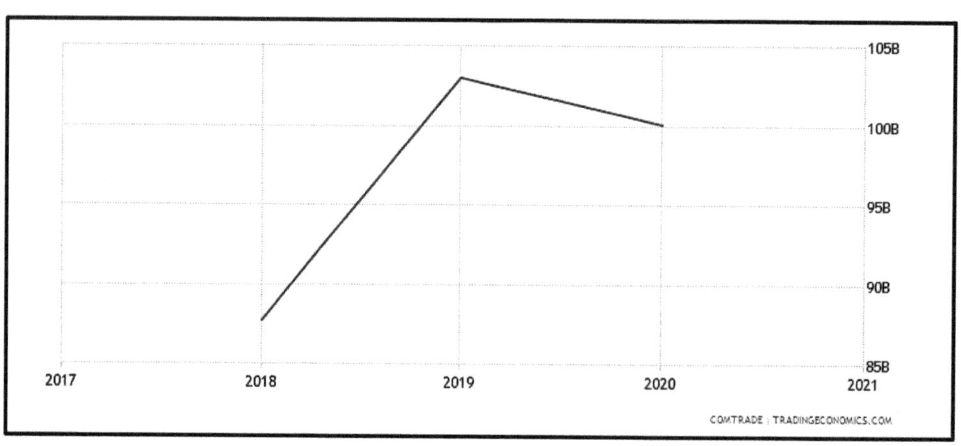

Impact of COVID on Trade-A Case of China and Australia

The imposition of tariff has a direct impact on goods production and flows; it employs input–output analysis to assess indirect effects on GDP, exports, and employment; and it permits trade to be diverted to other producers (Shah et al.,2021)· China sees Australia as leading the charge — once again, in Beijing's eyes – on an issue designed to isolate, criticise, and humiliate the country. It claims that the investigation is a political witch hunt orchestrated by Washington (Timsina & Culas, 2021).

The Chinese response looks to be a disproportionate overreaction to an entirely reasonable international worry about the origins of the Covid-19 epidemic, in Australia's opinion. To Canberra, the response appears to be an attempt to deflect accountability, or worse, to shift blame elsewhere. The decision by Australia to exclude Huawei from the 5G network rollout. China is under intense pressure to defend its handling of the Covid-19 outbreak, not so much for its suppression of the virus (which it did, albeit with far more draconian measures than any liberal democracy would consider), but rather for accusations that it initially misled the world about the virus's seriousness, costing the international community valuable weeks to prepare a response .China is eager for the world to read the conclusion of its Covid-19 storey; it does not want anyone to go back to the beginning. Australia isn't the only country that has been chastised, criticised, and threatened because it has demanded Beijing's accountability. China has chastised the US for blaming it for the spread, even publishing a weird Lego propaganda video called "Once Upon a Virus" set to the tune of The Entertainer through its Xinhua news agency (Alam et al., 2013).

Despite product bans, Australian firms say there are evidence that the trading relationship with China will not collapse, since exports and imports between the two countries remain thriving. According to Chinese data released on Monday, China's total imports from Australia in May increased by more than 55% from the previous month to US$13.6 billion, while exports increased by just over 1% to US$4.9 billion. In the end, ongoing trade disputes between the world's two largest economies will continue to put downward pressure on international commerce while accelerating pre-existing tendencies like supply chain diversification (Anukoonwattaka et al., 2021).

The expansion is a continuation of the two countries' brisk trading pattern, which has remained resilient despite continued bilateral tensions thanks to the iron ore trade. On the other hand, was not the catalyst for the worsening of China-Australia relations, which had been building for some time. According to China, Australia is closely following the United States in applying geopolitical pressure on China, particularly in relation to the Hong Kong and South China Sea conflicts (Kaliranjan,2000). Australia is a strong supporter of the Indo-Pacific policy to counterbalance China, has barred Huawei from engaging in its 5G deployment in non-market ways, and has campaigned for holding China accountable for the COVID-19 outbreak. Concerns about these issues have sparked a lot of tension between the two countries (Qi & Jhang 2018).

Each country's economy will undoubtedly suffer as geopolitical relations deteriorate. China and Australia, despite their current enmity, have highly substantial and deep trading ties. According to figures, the trade volume between China and Australia in 2019 was around $158 billion, with a trade surplus of close to $50 billion for Australia. Last year, Australia's exports to China were $102.90 billion, accounting for 39 percent of the country's overall exports. China contributed $55.07 billion to Australia's total imports, or 25.8% of total imports, an increase of 1.4 percentage points over the previous year. Australia's most important trading partner, export destination, and import supplier is still China (Xiang et al., 2017).

The Australian economy is heavily reliant on the Chinese market. As a result, many ordinary Chinese are perplexed by Australia's political stance toward China. Many Chinese are perplexed as to why

Australia acts in this manner, given that it is not a global hegemon like the US. This widespread view in Chinese society impacts public opinion, which in turn has a significant impact on Chinese policy. As the two nations' relations have deteriorated, the trade war between Australia and China has worsened this year. China slapped an anti-dumping tax of 73.6 percent and an anti-subsidy penalty of 6.9 percent on Australian barley in May, following examinations under WTO rules and domestic legislation. According to Bloomberg, China will begin a legal assault on seven categories of Australian exports on November 6, including coal, barley, copper ore and copper concentrate, sugar, wood, wine, and lobster (www.wto.org).

China's Ministry of Commerce announced on November 27 that some Australian wines had been dumped in China, causing considerable damage to the country's wine industry. As a result, tariffs ranging from 107 percent to 212 percent were imposed on the dumped Australian wines. This move, which has taken Australia by surprise, will almost certainly be a blow for China-Australia economic and trade relations. In addition, there are strong indications that the coal trade has been banned. On October 9, four Chinese state-owned utilities received verbal instruction from China's customs to immediately block imports of Australian coking and thermal coal, according to foreign media (The Hindustan Times,20121).

Since then, China's coal imports from Australia have plummeted, from 9.44 million tonnes in May to 5.17 million tonnes in October and 1.79 million tonnes in November.

Will Australia sever economic and trade ties with the United States? Because bilateral trade between China and Australia accounts for 11% of Australia's GDP, the short-term economic impact on Australia would be severe in that extreme scenario (Business Standard,2021).

There are also significant signs that the coal trade has been prohibited. On October 9, China's customs issued a verbal order to four Chinese state-owned utilities to immediately stop importing Australian coking and thermal coal, according to foreign media. Since then, China's coal imports from Australia have plummeted, from 9.44 million tonnes in May to 5.17 million tonnes in October and 1.79 million tonnes in November (O'Connell et al.,2018).

The damage to China- As international tensions worsen, Australia's business and trade partnerships are a done deal. However, geopolitical games are rarely played to their logical conclusion, and the two countries have not yet been entirely split apart. Most likely, the two sides will escalate to the point where the economic costs outweigh the geopolitical benefits. The two parties may then decide to call a halt to the fighting and seek a strategy adjustment. Nonetheless, China-Australia relations will be severely harmed. After a succession of trade sanctions and suspensions, China. Australia trade relationship, in our opinion, faces the risk of a hard "reset." It will not return to its previous levels. Australia anticipates structural changes in some commodity trade between Australia and China (for example, wine and coal), as well as some degree of trade substitution. Excessive reliance on the Chinese market will also be a serious concern for Australian manufacturers and dealers. There are nevertheless some industries that will be unaffected, most notably the iron ore industry. Mineral exports, primarily metal ores, have been the foundation of Australia's exports to China, with a total value of $71.39 billion in 2019, up 29.0 percent from the previous year. Minerals made for 68.7% of Australia's overall exports to China last year (The Hindu, 2021).

BHP and Rio-Tinto Group are Australia's two largest mineral exporters. As a result, if mineral exports are harmed, the impact will be considerable in terms of trade volume but small in terms of the number of enterprises affected. BHP and Rio Tinto Group are Australia's two largest mineral exporters. As a result, if mineral exports are harmed, the impact will be considerable in terms of trade volume but small in terms of the number of enterprises affected. Disruptions to Australian iron ore shipments, on the other hand, would have a higher impact on Chinese businesses, as in 2019, China imported 665 million tonnes of iron ore from Australia, accounting for 67 percent of total imports. If iron ore imports are disrupted, several Chinese steel mills may encounter supply disruptions, which could have a significant impact on the domestic steel industry (WTO,2020). A disruption in iron ore trade would be devastating to China Australia commerce, and it is unlikely that either country would initiate it. The deteriorating geopolitical relationship between China and Australia is having a substantial impact on the trade relationship between the two countries, which is expected to be structurally harmed and "reset" to some extent. A reset does not mean that trade is completely halted, but it also does not mean that relations are restored to their prior state. Many organisations' agility in responding to changing conditions was emphasised as a general observation. Business paradigms were shifting, and entrepreneurs were embracing innovation (Hanami,2008).

After China put significant tariffs and restrictions on many Australian export goods amid a deterioration in relations with Beijing, India's trade minister has said that India may become the next big trade destination for Australian exporters. Last year, Australia's economic relations with China deteriorated when it backed a request for an international investigation into China's handling of COVID-19, which was initially disclosed in the Chinese city of Wuhan. China imposed a slew of restrictions on Australian imports, ranging from new taxes to outright bans. Several Australian commodities, including barley, lumber, coal, cotton, wine, and lobster, have been subjected to Chinese bans and tariffs. Australia, for its turn, has asked the World Trade Organization to mediate in their dispute over China's high tariffs on Australian barley (McVey,2018).

While exploring for new trade prospects throughout the world, Australia's Trade Minister Dan Tehan highlighted India as a major priority on Wednesday. Australia haven't had a formal trade ministers meeting with China in over three years, and we've been trying to engage constructively with China for that long (The Economic Times, 2021).

Japan, Vietnam, and the next US administration of Joe Biden all give many chances for Australia, and that will be focusing on, along with constructive engagement with the Chinese. Australia needs to be patient with its India relationship, which is quite important to Australia and is something which is needed to be prioritise. It is keen to be noted that China is Australia's greatest commercial partner, accounting for more than a third of all export's worth more than 150 billion Australian dollars annually, while trade with India is valued more than 30 billion Australian dollars (The Economic Times, 2021).

CHALLENGES AND PROBLEMS FOR INDIA AND AUSTRALIA

Can Australia diversify into other markets, such as India, which has the world's second-largest population, as the trade conflict with China over its coal ban escalates? The current Commerce and trade data of Australia with India is only a tenth of what Australia deal with China, it's difficult to imagine India ever displacing China in the near or even medium term. However, examining the products on China's "restricted" list reveals possible avenues for Australia to investigate and grow its trade with India. China consumes 51% of all coal consumed globally, whereas India consumes only 12%. With such low consumption and the Indian government's goal of self-sufficiency, much more of coal is unlikely to find a market there (Haski-Leventhal & Mehra, 2016). Barley used to be a key export for Australia to India, and it got a boost recently when India accepted malting barley. Sugar, on the other hand, is already produced in great amounts in India and is one of the country's main exports, so there are few chances there for us. In India, beef is a "no go" zone due to religious and cultural reasons, but Australian lamb could be a growing market as interest in Western cuisines grows, particularly among the young, urban middle class. Growing desire for Western-style furniture from the same group could open doors for Australia to ship to India, which is one of the world's major timber importers.

Similarly, wine is a major "status" commodity for India's young, urban population, with 5.2 million litres worth roughly $40 million imported in 2018 (Bloomberg, 2021). However, Australia fell behind France, Chile, and the United States in this market. The most significant wine potential in India includes the tremendous growth in all types of online sales, particularly for some mid-tier priced wines, as well as the desire for wine education. Copper ore and concentrates are also in high demand in India, with around 90% of it coming from abroad. While Australia is listed as a supplier, it is not near the top of the list. India has contributed significantly to Australia's tourist and education sectors, and both countries might work hard to extend this as China's interest wanes. Australia's "clean and green" horticultural products are one of the most promising segments in India. Food imports in India tripled in the last decade and are expected to increase even more in the next, thanks to the urban middle class, e-commerce, and supermarkets (O'Connell et al.,2018).

It is apparent that Australia has a lot of room to grow in India. However, to balance trade dependency on China, Australia needs "think big" about dramatically transforming their approach to trade, which has mostly been a transactional relationship sensitive to shock shifts. Australia has traditionally concentrated on the Pacific Ocean, with major economic partner such as China, the United States, Japan, and South Korea, as well as its most important strategic defence alliance, all present. By combining this vision with a concentration on the Indian Ocean, Australia can maintain the best of what it now has while also taking the lead in establishing a new regional participant in global trade and defence (Roy et al.,2018). It would provide some protection against Chinese trade retaliation, which Australia has seen in recent months. It also has the potential to earn more respect in Beijing. India can play a role in resolving Australia's trade dispute with China, but it will never be able to fully replace it. As a result, taking a regional strategy makes sense (O'Connell et al.,2018.

OPPORTUNITIES FOR NEW TRADE FRONTIERS BETWEEN INDIA AND AUSTRALIA

The forum heard that because of COVID-19, a complex dynamic was unfolding in both Australia and India, with different sectors being impacted at different levels of severity, resulting in varied recovery periods for each. While both countries' short- and medium-term economic outlooks were bleak, this did not necessarily imply that the relationship's longer-term growth tendencies would fundamentally shift. It was discovered that, rather than creating new history, crises tend to accelerate it. However, because things change so quickly, it's difficult to anticipate the near future, and doing so would be highly hypothetical. The travel prohibitions in place have, of course, put a halt to tourism and restricted the mobility of overseas students. Both industries are vital to Australia's and India's trade and investment relations. Education is Australia's greatest service export to India, worth AU$5.5 billion in 2019, with around 115,000 Indian students studying in Australia (Qi & Jhang, 2018).

COVID19 is posing significant difficulties to our education industry, including highlighting our responsibility to international students, putting pressure on future enrolments, and requiring current students to work in distant, online contexts. It was noted that international students, including those from India, were something of a 'lost tribe' at the time, and that Australia needed to position itself as a country with a heart when it came to enticing students back, rather than being seen as a country only interested in recouping lost revenue. India is Australia's seventh-largest tourism market and, prior to the epidemic, our fastest-growing, with 350,000 visitors last year, up 53% from the previous year. Current limits prevent corporate travel as well, but once the restrictions are relaxed, there is optimism for a rather speedy recovery (The Hindustan Times, 2021). Physical constraints have accelerated digitisation and online shopping, as well as a greater focus on innovation, in the context of trade and business more broadly.

In the long run, India has the potential to position itself as a worldwide leader in cost-effective medical device and technology innovation. India, for example, has retooled its automobile manufacturers to make affordable ventilators in response to global demand, with the country aiming to produce 50,000 ventilators per month by the end of May, up from 5,580 units in March. For Australia, expanding on current research relationships and cooperation with India in a variety of fields, including healthcare, is a possibility. A fundamental component of Australia's India Economic Strategy to 2035 (IES) was to increase outbound investment to India by tenfold, and COVID-19 disruption posed a risk to attaining this goal, according to Narayanamurti (The Guardian, 2021).

India, for example, has retooled its automobile manufacturers to make affordable ventilators in response to global demand, with the country aiming to produce 50,000 ventilators per month by the end of May, up from 5,580 units in March. However, on a more upbeat note, he believes superannuation funds can improve their thinking when it comes to allocating capital to longer-term assets, such as infrastructure projects in India. The meeting also heard that Austrade was doing everything it could to ensure that air and shipping freight could continue to flow freely between our two countries (Moreton, 2020), The value of engagements like the recent Australia India Business Exchange (AIBX) expedition to India was emphasised, with disappointment that the momentum from the mission was unable to continue owing to the pandemic. Many organisations' agility in responding to changing conditions was emphasised as a general observation. Business paradigms were shifting, and entrepreneurs were embracing innovation. The meeting also heard that Austrade was doing everything it could to ensure that air and shipping freight could continue to flow freely between our two countries. The value of engagements like the recent Australia India Business Exchange (AIBX) expedition to India was emphasised, with disappointment that the momentum from the mission was unable to continue owing to the pandemic.

QUADRILATERAL SECURITY DIALOGUE (QUAD): CHINA A FEAR FOR AUSTRALIA

The Quadrilateral Security Dialogue (Quad) is an informal strategic dialogue involving India, the United States, Japan, and Australia, with the goal of ensuring and supporting a "free, open, and prosperous" Indo-Pacific. Shinzo Abe, the Japanese Prime Minister, proposed the Quad concept in 2007. However, the plan was thwarted when Australia withdrew, ostensibly owing to Chinese pressure (Stevenson & Envall, 2019). China's violations of international conventions, particularly the development of military installations on reclaimed islands in the South China Sea, as well as its expanding military and economic strength, have posed a strategic threat to India in recent years (Haski-Leventhal & Mehra, 2016).

Given China's strategic importance, India is carefully balancing China on the one hand and the United States on the other by maintaining strategic autonomy for China, which has proven to be reassuring to China. India has also refused to allow Australia to join in the Malabar Trilateral Maritime Exercises with India, the United States, and Japan, fearing that it would send the wrong message to China, which is cautious of the exercise. The recent Mamallapuram meeting between President Xi Jinping and Prime Minister Modi is a positive development that both parties regard as critical in providing strategic counsel to stakeholders on both sides.

SOLUTIONS AND RECOMMENDATIONS

It's popular to be negative about the strategic cooperation between India and Australia. Most strategic analysts in Canberra and New Delhi would describe the relationship as long on promises and short on deliverables. Much of it stems from the two countries' tumultuous pasts. India and Australia talked past one other for more than half a century following India's independence in 1947. Antiquated stereotypes linger, and ties continue to be subjected to some irrational expectations. Now the question arises that When will India, like China, become a driver of the Australian economy and Why is India so averse to joining the US alliance network in Asia?"

The connection, on the other hand, has some difficulties. Because of their differing histories, geography, and economics, the two countries inevitably have different priorities and worldviews. They also have various abilities, which can sometimes complement one other. Their strategic and economic ties are also diverse, with Australia relying on the US for security and China for economic growth far more than India in both cases. It is not impossible to overcome these obstacles. However, now that a platform for strategic cooperation between two strong and capable democratic powers in the Indo-Pacific has been built, the two countries have the potential to build on it. One solution is to make their consultation procedures a priority, especially given their recent proliferation. Given restricted capacity and schedules, the breadth of working-level, bilateral, and trilateral conversations will be challenging to sustain. Improving interoperability will be a second focus. This may necessitate, for example, the signing of a secure communications agreement, as India has done with the United States. Beyond that, additional efforts can be done to strengthen the strategic connection, such as collaboration on defence technologies, commercial and trade ties, and social contacts. If India-Australia ties continue to grow at their current rate, the relationship might become one of the Indo-most Pacific's important regional partnerships.

FUTURE RESEARCH DIRECTIONS

Some limitations may limit the generalizability of the findings. Only the World Trading Organization, the Director General of Foreign Trade, newspapers, and other associated literature on India's and Australia's trade systems are available. As a result, the study's findings can be utilised to guide similar investigations in the countries analysed. As a result, future research could look at additional influencing factors on international trade systems as well as other geographical locations in a larger sense.

Future research might analyse and contrast the impact of the US-China trade war on India with the trade war between China and Australia. Quantitative and qualitative research may be used in the future to better understand the impact of trade wars on nations' trade. Secondary data can be analysed using a variety of econometric tests, which can aid in improving trade dynamics between India and the other sample countries. Furthermore, a review of the literature suggests that the trade war between China and the United States has a significant impact on other nations, but the same has not been studied in the case of China and Australia. As a result, Future Research may address this issue and propose relevant solutions.

CONCLUSION

The chapter is essential for understanding the complexities of "trade creation between (India and Australia) "and "trade diversion between (China and Australia)".

This chapter highlights influence of China's trade war with Australia on India's and Australia's trade dynamics. Both, India and Australia did not have strong trading connections. They always have a low intension for trade. Covid has sparked a desire in Australia to explore new trading routes, such as those in Southeast Asia like India. Moreover, Covid has shed some light on the situation by providing India with a trade diversion opportunity i.e. from China).

The chapter further studies the present state of bilateral trade relations between India –Australia. It identifies obstacles that hindered the growth of trade relations between India- Australia in the past. It also focuses on the impact of comprehensive economic cooperation free trade agreement on trade of India and Australia. The chapter aims at identifying the challenges that Covid has posed for trade between Australia and China, as well as the opportunities for trade between India and Australia.

India may be able to benefit from the trade battle between China and Australia. The study concludes that aside from economic benefits, stronger links will provide strategic political benefits to both countries- India and Australia. Unlike China, India and Australia have much in common. Both countries are federal democracies with English as the primary language of both foreign ministries. These parallels go a long way toward assuring easy diplomatic communication between the two governments, which has been a stumbling block in the Australia-China relationship in the past. If India were to enter the picture, Australia wouldn't have to worry about picking sides. Instead, Australia might take advantage of the situation and cooperate cooperatively with both countries.

Australia remains preoccupied with China, as China accounts for more than 30% of Australian exports, while India only accounts for 5%. In the 2017 Foreign Policy White Paper, China was mentioned 112 times and got its own sub-chapter. India, on the other hand, was only referenced 60 times. The "Rise of China" is frequently mentioned in Australian foreign policy circles, but India should be seen in the same light. In the Indo-Pacific, India is on the rise geopolitically. Like the rise of Chinese influence in Pacific Island countries, Australia often overlooks the fact that India is also playing this game with other countries in the region, much to Beijing's chagrin. The space competition and cyber security will become increasingly important in the coming decade, with India looking to play a key role in both. In terms of rising power status and strategic importance, India has a lot in common with China. Australia has yet to acknowledge this, and prioritising China over India is not in Australia's strategic interests. Being a member of QUAD, India and Australia can explore more bilateral ties between them with the goal of ensuring and supporting a "free, open, and prosperous environment. Moreover, with India's global expansion, Australia has a unique opportunity to improve its economic and strategic reliance.

REFERENCES

Alam, S., Mukhopadhya, P., & Islam, M. R. (2013). The Australia India proposed Free Trade Agreement and trade in agriculture: Opportunities and challenges. *The Journal of World Investment & Trade*, *14*(1), 167–197. doi:10.1163/22119000-01401006

Anderson, J. E., & Yotov, V. (2016). Terms of trade and global efficiency effects of free trade agreements,1990–2002. *Journal of International Economics*, *99*, 279–298. doi:10.1016/j.jinteco.2015.10.006

Anukoonwattaka, W., Romao, P., & Lobo, R. S. (2021). If the US-China trade war is here to stay, what are the risks and opportunities for other GVC economies outside the war zone? (No. 209). *ARTNeT Working Paper Series*.

Athukorala, P. C. (2020). Trump's Trade War: An Indian Perspective. *Asian Economic Papers*, *19*(1), 92–109. doi:10.1162/asep_a_00749

Bajpaee, C. (2017). Dephasing India's look East/Act east policy. *Contemporary Southeast Asia*, *39*(2), 348–372. doi:10.1355/cs39-2d

Bandara, J., & Yu, W. (2003). How Desirable Is the South Asian Free Trade Area? A Quantitative Economic Assessment. *World Economy*, *26*(9), 1293–1323. doi:10.1046/j.1467-9701.2003.00574.x

Bloomberg. (2021). *India, Australia Deepen Defense, Trade Ties Amid China Tensions*. https://www.bloomberg.com/news/articles/2021-0

Brewster, D. (2010). The Australia–India Security Declaration. *Security Challenges*, *6*(1), 1–9.

Chadha, R., Pohit, S., & Pratap, D. (2019). The US-China Trade War: Impact on India and Its Policy Choices (No. 119). New Delhi: National Council of Applied Economic Research.

Chakraborty, D., Chaisse, J., & Xu, Q. I. A. N. (2019). Is it finally time for India's free trade agreements? the ASEAN "Present" and the RCEP "Future". *Asian Journal of International Law*, *9*(2), 359–391. doi:10.1017/S2044251319000043

Cho, S. W., & Yoon, G. (2014). Sectoral analysis of an Australia–India free trade agreement. *Journal of the Asia Pacific Economy*, *19*(2), 205–229. doi:10.1080/13547860.2013.820469

Das, R. U., & Dubey, J. D. (2020). *Mechanics of Intra-Industry Trade and FTA Implications for India in RCEP*. Academic Press.

Deb, R. (2020). Is RCEP a Panacea for India? *The Indian Economic Journal*, *68*(4), 659–666. doi:10.1177/0019466221998626

Gopal, D., & Ahlawat, D. (2015). Australia–India Strategic Relations: From Estrangement to Engagement. *India Quarterly*, *71*(3), 206–220. doi:10.1177/0974928415584022

Graham, E. (2018). The Quad deserves its second chance. *Debating the Quad*, 4.

Gurry, M. (2012). India, the new centre of gravity: Australia–India relations under the Howard government. *South Asia*, *35*(2), 282–305. doi:10.1080/00856401.2011.633299

Haski-Leventhal, D., & Mehra, A. (2016). Impact measurement in social enterprises: Australia and India. *Social Enterprise Journal*.

Hsu, K. (2013). The RCEP: Integrating India into the Asian Economy. *Indian Foreign Affairs Journal*, *8*(1), 41–51.

Jaishankar, D. (2020). *The Australia-India Strategic Partnership: Accelerating Security Cooperation in the Indo-Pacific*. Lowy Institute for International Policy.

Kalirajan, K. P. (2000). Trade flows between Australia and India: An empirical analysis. *International Journal of Commerce and Management*, *10*(2), 32–49. doi:10.1108/eb047401

Kaul, M. M. (2009). The Indian diaspora in Australia and New Zealand: Challenges and the way forward. *Diaspora Studies*, *2*(2), 187–201.

MauryaA. (2017). US China trade war: Opportunities for India. *Available at* SSRN 3043699. doi:10.2139/ssrn.3043699

Miller, J. B. (2018). *The Quad: security cooperation between the US.*

Misra, R., & Choudhry, S. (2020). Trade war: Likely impact on India. *Foreign Trade Review*, *55*(1), 93–118. doi:10.1177/0015732519886793

Panda, J. P. (2014). Factoring the RCEP and the TPP: China, India and the Politics of Regional Integration. *Strategic Analysis*, *38*(1), 49–67. doi:10.1080/09700161.2014.863462

Panda, J. P. (2020). India, the blue dot network, and the 'Quad Plus' calculus. *Air Force J. Indo-. Pacific Affairs*, *3*, 4–22.

Pereira, A., Biddington, B., Rajagopalan, R., & Suzuki, K. (2021, March). The Quad: Implications for Space. In 2021 IEEE Aerospace Conference (50100) (pp. 1-15). IEEE.

Qi, C., & Zhang, J. X. (2018). The economic impacts of the China-Australia Free Trade Agreement-A general equilibrium analysis. *China Economic Review*, *47*, 1–11. doi:10.1016/j.chieco.2017.11.002

Raja Mohan, C. (2014, Nov. 22). Not so easy to Act East. *The Indian Express*. https://indianexpress.com/article/opinion/columns/not-so-easy-to-act-east/

Ranjan, V. (2016). Australia and India in Asia: When 'Look West 'Meets Act East. *Strategic Analysis*, *40*(5), 425–439. doi:10.1080/09700161.2016.1209906

Roy-Chaudhury, R., & de Estrada, K. S. (2018). India, the Indo-Pacific and the Quad. *Survival*, *60*(3), 181–194. doi:10.1080/00396338.2018.1470773

Saha, S., & Zhang, Z. (2013). Do exchange rates affect consumer prices? A comparative analysis for Australia, China and India. *Mathematics and Computers in Simulation*, *93*, 128–138. doi:10.1016/j.matcom.2012.11.002

Sanyal, A. (2021). *Impact of US-China Trade War on Indian External Trade*. Academic Press.

Sarma, N. (2020). Free Trade after RCEP: What Next for India? *ORF Issue Brief*, (353).

Shah, M. I., Ullah, I., Xingjian, X., Haipeng, H., Rehman, A., Zeeshan, M., & Afridi, F. E. A. (2021). Modeling Trade Openness and Life Expectancy in China. *Risk Management and Healthcare Policy*, *14*, 1689–1701. doi:10.2147/RMHP.S298381 PMID:33935523

Siddiqui, A. A., & Singh, P. (2021). US-China trade war: Impact on chemical exporting firms from India to US. *Corporate Governance*, (1), 75–84.

Smith, G. (2010). Australia and the Rise of India. *Australian Journal of International Affairs*, *64*(5), 566–582. doi:10.1080/10357710903544114

Stevenson, K., & Envall, H. D. P. (2019). The 'quad 'and disaster management: An Australian perspective. *International Disaster Response: Rebuilding the Quad*, 13-23.

Tahir, M., Estrada, M. R., Khan, I., & Afridi, M. A. (2016). The role of trade openness for industrial sector development: Panel data evidence from SAARC region. *Journal of Asia Business Studies*, *10*(1), 93–103. doi:10.1108/JABS-01-2015-0007

Taylor, S., & Taylor, M. (2017). The aroma of opportunity: The potential of wine geographical indications in the Australia-India comprehensive economic cooperation agreement. *The Importance of Place: Geographical Indications as a Tool for Local and Regional Development*, 81-107.

The Business Standard. (2021). *With China relationship on the rocks*. https://www.business-standard.com/article/international/with-china-relationship-on-the-rocks-australia-eyes-india-for-trade-120091600276_1.html

The Economic Times. (2021). *Australia eyes closer economic ties*. https://economictimes.indiatimes.com/news/international/world-news/australia-eyes-closer-economic-ties-with-india-after-trade-row-with-china/articleshow/81384874.cms?from=mdr

The Guardian. (2021). *Australia vows to 'vigorously defend' itself*. https://www.theguardian.com/australia-news/2021/jun/24/australia-vows-to-vigorously-defend-itself-against-china-wto-complaint

The Herald-Sun. (2021). *China complains to WTO over Australia's trade measures*. https://www.heraldsun.com.au/news/world/china-complains-to-wto-over-australias-trade-measures/news

The Hindustan Times. (2021a). *India shares challenges that prompted us to join AUKUS: Australian envoy*. https://www.hindustantimes.com/india-news/india-shares-challenges-that-prompted-us-to-join-aukus-australian-envoy-101631859734070.html

The Hindustan Times. (2021b). *Australia looking to diversify trade ties*. https://www.hindustantimes.com/world-news/australia-looking-to-diversify-trade-ties-amid-difficulties-with-china-trade-minister-dan-tehan-101633107517025.html

The World Trade Organization. (2020a). *China — Anti-dumping and countervailing duty measures on barley from Australia*. https://www.wto.org/english/tratop_e/dispu_e/dispu_status_e.htm

The World Trade Organization. (2020b). *United States — Tariff Measures on Certain Goods from China*. https://www.wto.org/english/tratop_e/dispu_e/cases_e/ds543_e.htm

Timsina, K. P., & Culas, R. (2021). Australia's Free Trade Agreements (FTAs) and Potentiality of Wheat Exports: A Panel Gravity Model Approach. *Journal of East-West Business*, 1–28. doi:10.1080/10669868.2021.1974640

Timsina, K. P., & Culas, R. J. (2020). Do free trade agreements increase Australian trade: An application of Poisson pseudo maximum likelihood estimator? *Journal of East-West Business*, *26*(1), 56–80. doi:10.1080/10669868.2019.1685056

Xiang, H., Kuang, Y., & Li, C. (2017). Impact of the China–Australia FTA on global coal production and trade. *Journal of Policy Modeling, 39*(1), 65–78. doi:10.1016/j.jpolmod.2017.01.001

Zreik, M. (2021). The Regional Comprehensive Economic Partnership and Its Impact on the US-China Trade War. *Journal of Asia Pacific Studies, 6*(3).

ADDITIONAL READING

Hanami, T. (2008). *Industrial Conflict Resolution in Market Economies: A Study of Australia*. Kluwer Law and Taxation Publishers.

Irwin, H. (2020). *Communicating with Asia: Understanding people and customs*. Routledge. doi:10.4324/9781003134763

McVey, R. (2018). Globalization, marginalization, and the study of Southeast Asia. In *Southeast Asian Studies* (pp. 37–64). Cornell University Press. doi:10.7591/9781501719400-002

Moreton-Robinson, A. (2020). I still call Australia home: Indigenous belonging and place in a white post-colonizing society. In *Uprootings-Regroundings Questions of Home and Migration* (pp. 23–40). Routledge. doi:10.4324/9781003087298-3

O'Connell, J. F., Allen, J., Williams, M. A., Williams, A. N., Turney, C. S., Spooner, N. A., Kamminga, J., Brown, G., & Cooper, A. (2018). When did Homo sapiens first reach Southeast Asia and Sahul? *Proceedings of the National Academy of Sciences of the United States of America, 115*(34), 8482–8490. doi:10.1073/pnas.1808385115 PMID:30082377

Roy, S. K., Balaji, M. S., Soutar, G., Lassar, W. M., & Roy, R. (2018). Customer engagement behavior in individualistic and collectivistic markets. *Journal of Business Research, 86*, 281–290. doi:10.1016/j.jbusres.2017.06.001

KEY TERMS AND DEFINITIONS

Act East Policy: The policy that places the Eastern region at the centre of economic activity for India, as it has been neglected for the past decades.

Embargo: Embargo is defined as a complete trade ban between two nations.

Free Trade Agreement: A free trade agreement removes trade barriers and promotes free trade between importing and exporting countries.

Look East Policy: A policy framed by the government to strengthen strategic and economic ties with the South-East Asia members.

Non-Tariff Barriers: A type of barrier which is imposed on imported goods by the importing nations, but it can't be quantified as tariff barriers. examples are subsidies, quota, embargo, etc.

QUAD: The Quadrilateral Security Dialogue (Quad) is an informal strategic dialogue involving India, the United States, Japan, and Australia, with the goal of ensuring and supporting a "free, open, and prosperous" Indo-Pacific.

Regional Economic Comprehensive Partnership: An agreement between ASEAN and its free trade agreement partners.

Tariffs: The duties imposed on the imported goods by the government of importing nations.

Trade Creation: An outcome of a free trade agreement through which trade flow are redirected for the member nations.

Trade Diversion: An outcome of free trade agreement which leads to diversion of trade from an efficient exporter to an inefficient exporter.

Trade War: A condition in which a country ban the trade with other country by way of tariffs.

Chapter 14
Australia's Trade and Investment Strategy in the Post-COVID-19 Era:
Prospects for Australia-Bangladesh Partnership

Mamta B Chowdhury
Western Sydney University, Australia

Ataus Samad
Western Sydney University, Australia

Md Sayfullah
https://orcid.org/0000-0003-2627-4491
Bangladesh High Commission, Canberra, Australia

ABSTRACT

This chapter examines how the trade and investment relationship between Australia and the Asia-Pacific nations has been evolving over the past decades. The chapter also reflects on the gradual shift of trade and diplomatic relationships in this region since the outbreak of the COVID-19 pandemic. The ongoing global pandemic has not only been disrupting the global economic and geopolitical environment but also reshaping the trade relationship in the region. The chapter explores the greater trade and investment opportunities between Australia and South Asia with a special emphasis on the increased potential bilateral trade partnership with Bangladesh. Following the neoclassical comparative advantage theories, this study suggests that long-run economic benefits and synergies can be enhanced by utilising the ample trade opportunities created by the COVID-19 pandemic to achieve numerous UNSDGs. Therefore, strengthening further trade and diplomatic alliances between Australia and Bangladesh will be mutually beneficial and generate positive growth and development effects for both countries.

DOI: 10.4018/978-1-7998-8657-0.ch014

INTRODUCTION

Australia's uninterrupted annual average growth above 3% over the last three decades with strong economic fundamentals made the country significant among the developed nations. Although Australia has been maintaining its longstanding common democratic values, diplomatic, security, trade and investment relationship with Europe and America since the beginning of the 20th Century, however, it has established close economic relationship with countries in the East, mainly with Asia-Pacific nations over the last three decades. The growing demand for Australian mineral resources, agricultural products, education and tourism from the high-growth Asia-Pacific countries made Australia change its trade and investment focus gradually towards the region over the last three decades. China accounted for 33% of all Australia's trade in 2020, which is more than its combined trade with Japan, South Korea, the US and India (Australian Bureau of Statistics (ABS), 2020). Nonetheless, the current diplomatic and trade tensions between Australia and some of its significant trade partners, especially with China on security and COVID-19 origin inquiries and the recent Australia-France rift over the $90 billion submarine deal have brought opportunities for the South Asian countries to strengthen the trade and diplomatic relationship with Australia.

This chapter discusses Australia's gradual shift in international trade and investment focus towards the Asia-Pacific countries from its traditional allies of the United States (US) and United Kingdom (UK) and other Western countries since the early 1990s. The chapter further explores the trade relationship between Australia and South Asian countries and focuses on the existing and potential trade prospects between Australia and Bangladesh, especially after the COVID-19 pandemic.

South Asia[1] is the home of almost two billion or one-fourth of the world's population and one of the significant two-way trade partners of Australia. Given the current regional geopolitical disquiet, it would be advantageous for Australia to proactively strengthen its trade ties with the South Asian nations who are rapidly becoming emerging markets. South Asian countries have also established regional cooperation since the middle of the 1980s, which is commonly known as the South Asian Association of Regional Cooperation (SAARC). Among the South Asian countries, Bangladesh is one of the most emerging countries with its vast consumer market, rising middle-income people, large young working-age population.

Bangladesh had one of the fastest-growing gross domestic product (GDP) of over 8% in 2019 and was the best-performing country among the 46 countries in the region until September 2020. Asian Development Bank (ADB) has predicted remarkable growth for Bangladesh economy in the Asia-Pacific region in 2021 followed by Maldives, India and China (The Business Standard, 2021). Apart from the economic sector, Bangladesh has progressed significantly in other socio-economic measures and achievement of the UN Millennium Development goals over the past few decades. While there are huge potentials for expansion of bilateral trade and investment between Australia and Bangladesh, there also exist some challenges. These challenges lie mostly on the non-alignment of priority trade and investment areas which need to be addressed and improved through close coordination between these countries.

The demand for Australian products are growing in recent years and the exports from Bangladesh to Australia are also increasing at a faster rate. Bangladesh can further avail the opportunity to enter into the Australian market with its comparative advantage in labour-intensive products, especially in ready-made garments (RMG), pharmaceutical products, light engineering products, jute and leather items as well as information communication technology (ICT) related products and services. Further collaboration between sectors such as Education (i.e., Technical and Further Education or TAFE, Universities), Science and Technology (i.e., Commonwealth Scientific and Industrial Research Organisation or CSIRO), energy sector and primary and construction industries (agricultural mineral resources and infrastructure development) can add value to the effort for greater economic collaboration between the countries.

The recently signed Trade and Investment Framework Arrangement (TIFA) between Australia and Bangladesh would further strengthen and expand the trade and investment opportunities between these two countries (Shams, 2021). Having access to Bangladesh's market of 165 million people and assisting to increase the capacity building of the nation will be mutually beneficial in the long run for Australia and Bangladesh.

Therefore, the objective of the study is to review Australia's ongoing shift of trade and investment relationship towards the Asia-Pacific countries and examine the existing trade and investment partnership between Australia and Bangladesh. The chapter further attempts to explore the opportunities to expand this relationship, especially in the post-COVID-19 era where the new possibilities can be utilised fully by both nations. Since there are no comprehensive studies on this topic, this study will significantly contribute to the Australia-Bangladesh trade literature. The framework of the study is based on the effect of comparative advantage in international trade on the economic growth of trading partners.

The chapter is organised as follows: following the introduction, a brief literature review provides the analytical framework of the study. The chapter then presents the background of the study. The focus of the chapter begins with a brief overview of Australia's international trade through time, followed by a discussion of Australia's changing trade relationship with the Asia-Pacific region. The chapter proceeds with a presentation of the trend and developments of Australia's trade relationships with South Asian countries. The chapter then launches a special focus on Australia-Bangladesh existing and potential trade and investment partnership. The chapter lays out some challenges in regards to Australia-Bangladesh trade expansion and suggests possible recommendations by indicating opportunities and further trade collaborations between these two countries. Finally, the chapter proposes future research directions and completes the study with a brief conclusion.

LITERATURE REVIEW

International trade plays a vital role in economic growth and development through specialisation and exchange according to the comparative advantage of the production of goods and services, which is mutually beneficial for both trading partners. International trade is a fundamental part of global economic activities and has grown rapidly since the onset of the most recent globalisation from the mid-1980s. The value of global exports to the share of GDP increased from 8% in 1950 to 17% in 1980 and then to 26% in 2008. The world trade and GDP have both increased by 26% since 2008 (World Trade Organisation, 2019). Thus, the relationship between international trade and economic growth has drawn researchers and policymakers to focus on the importance of international trade and investment, especially in a more liberalised trade setting.

The analytical framework of this chapter is based on the export-led growth effect of international trade in a more open trade regime. The theoretical model of international trade of the study follows the Ricardian and Heckscher-Ohlin comparative advantage theories. Ricardo's (Ricardo, 1817) comparative advantage theory explains if the ability of a country to produce a good at a lower opportunity cost than others, the country will have a comparative advantage in producing that good. The country should specialise and produce that product and export the surplus products in exchange for the products where it does not have a comparative advantage. A more flexible model of comparative advantage was postulated by the

Heckscher-Ohlin model which allows for the difference in the factor endowment of a country (Ohlin, 1933). The Heckscher-Ohlin model explains that a country will produce and export goods and services that use locally abundant factors intensively, which is a major source of comparative advantage over another country. For example, Australia will have a better comparative advantage in producing minerals or other professional services, as the country is endowed with these resources. Whereas, a country like, Bangladesh, which is endowed with a large young population, can gain comparative advantage in producing and exporting labour-intensive products and import goods and services where the country does not have a comparative advantage. Since international trade is a major component of aggregate demand (AD) of a country, increased net export (value of exports - value of imports) will stimulate economic growth.

Empirical literature also illustrates that international trade and investment positively affect economic growth through expanding the market for its goods and services across the borders and importing essential inputs, goods and services at a competitive price than the domestic substitutes (Frankel & Romer, 1999; OECD, 2003). The dynamics of international trade are much significant than stimulating the short-run economic activities. Increased international trade not only adds to the domestic economic growth by increasing export values but also facilitates the long-run growth by importing essential raw materials, technology, medicine, expertise in education, health, finance and priority skill-building areas of a country. Foreign direct investment (FDI) and portfolio investment create a spill-over effect and facilitate technological diffusion as well as supply of needed capital for the capital-starved developing countries, which in turn enhances labour productivity and long-run economic growth (Adnan, et. al, 2020). International trade can greatly assist higher and faster economic growth in a more open trade regime (Balassa, 1986).

BACKGROUND

An unexpected break out of the Covid-19 pandemic from late 2019 has not only created an unprecedented global health crisis but also brought various challenges for the world economy. The current ongoing pandemic has been disrupting the global business, diplomatic and bilateral trade and investment opportunities, besides adversely impacting both the demand and supply sides of the global real economy. As a result, both developed and developing countries are facing various economic challenges and implementing policies to have economic recovery while combating the virus.

Australia is a major Asia-Pacific country with a population of 24.6 million of which 28% population are foreign-born (Australian Bureau of Statistics (ABS), 2021a). Australia's Human Development Index (HDI) is 0.939 in 2019, globally ranking the country at third position followed by Norway and Switzerland in first and second position respectively. In 2020, Australia's GDP accounted for A$1.95 trillion and GDP per capita of above A$80,000 (i.e., US$57520 in 2019). It is the second wealthiest nation in terms of wealth per adult after Switzerland. Australia's current unemployment rate in July, 2021 was 4.6%, very close to its full-employment level (ABS, 2021b).

International trade has significant implications for Australia's economy as it contributed 46% to the country's GDP in 2019. Australia's major trading partners are the Asia-Pacific countries, which constitutes 74% of Australia's trade in 2020. Among them, China has been the major trading partner of Australia over the last decade and accounts for over 29% of total two-way trade with Australia in 2020, which is more than its combined trade with Japan, South Korea, the US and UK (DFAT, 2021).

Australia has been adopting an open economy and integrated with the global economy via its international trade and investment. Australia is the third most open economy with 15 free trade agreements across Asia and North and South America in 2021 (Tang, 2021). Australia has been engaged in Asia-Pacific free trade agreements (FTA) with the major East and Southeast Asian countries such as China, South Korea, Japan, Singapore, Hong Kong, Thailand, Malaysia, and Indonesia as well as with the South American countries of Peru and Chile (Department of Foreign Affairs and Trade (DFAT), 2021a). Australia signed a Trade and Investment Framework Arrangement (TIFA), with Bangladesh in September, 2021,

Australia-China trade and the diplomatic relationship started deteriorating in early 2020 due to Australia's call for an independent inquiry into the origin of the COVID-19 pandemic, disapproval of Chain's presence in the South China Sea and Australia's diplomatic claim about espionage interference threatening its national security. Besides reinforcing its existing relationship with the US and its Western allies, Australia joined a diplomatic network 'The Quadrilateral Security Dialogue' (QSD, also known as the Quad) with the US, India and Japan. These issues have accelerated the tense diplomatic relationship further between these two significant nations in the Asia-Pacific basin.

China took retaliatory measures against Australia by curtailing the importation of Australian goods, such as barley, wine, lobster, meat, timber and coal. It is reported that Chinese international students' recruitment agents are asked to divert the Chinese students to other countries than Australia (Hare, 2021). Apart from the current strained Australia-China trade relationship, the diplomatic relationship between Australia and its significant European ally France has become tensed recently as Australia withdrew from $90 billion submarine building contract with French Shipbuilder Naval Group (Tillett & Cranston, 2021). As a result of these changing diplomatic and trade relationships with some of Australia's existing significant trade partners, it is necessitated the emergence of greater diversification of trade relationships with other countries in South Asia. Bangladesh with its large market and competitive labour intensive production capability may be explored as a reliable trade partnership with Australia during and after the post-COVID-19 era.

Australia and Bangladesh are celebrating 50 years' trade and diplomatic relationship in 2021, which commenced right after the independence of Bangladesh in 1971. Australia was one of the first countries to recognise Bangladesh and established its resident mission in Dhaka in 1972. The bilateral relationship between these two nations was started based on development assistance to Bangladesh, a war-torn county in the early 1970s, which then steadily replaced with the trade and investment partnership. Australia's official development assistance (ODA) to Bangladesh significantly fell since 2018. It can be observed that Bangladesh has reduced its dependency on Australian ODA, instead engaged in trade with Australia, in an attempt to enhance the economic growth and development of the country and strengthen the long-run strategic and diplomatic relationship.

The trade relationship between these two countries also goes back to the early 1970s and grew rapidly since the mid-1990s. The total value of trade between these two nations increased from A$2.7 million in 1972 to A$350.1 million in 2000. In the next two decades from 2001 to 2020, trade value grew over 467% to $2.4 billion in 2020 with a sharp increase in exports from Bangladesh to Australia since 2007 (ABS, 2021). Among the SAARC countries, Bangladesh is a net exporter with Australia in international trade, suggesting a solid trade relationship between these two countries.

COVID-19 has created the demand for various goods and specific services related to health care, which brought opportunities for both Australia and Bangladesh to expand their trade and investment based on their comparative advantage. While there are huge potentials for Bangladesh to produce health care and ICT products and services utilising its relatively cheaper labour resources. Bangladesh government can take initiative to provide vocational and technical training to its young labour force in the areas of health services, ICT, and data input activities to engage in services trade-related to longer-run COVID management. Australia can also utilise its high standard consultancy services in the health care, education, vocational training, and other priority areas in Bangladesh. The collaboration and trade will add greater value to the economic benefits of both countries.

Australia's trade and investment trend over time and its significant shift from the West to the Asia-Pacific neighbouring countries and South Asian region would be discussed in the next Section.

AUSTRALIA'S INTERNATIONAL TRADE AND INVESTMENT THROUGH TIME

Australia is recognised as a trading nation over the last 120 years and international trade contributes significantly to the GDP of the nation. However, the contribution and composition of trade has been changed significantly since the Federation to the Second World War (WW2) and then to the new millennium of 2000 (DFAT, 2021b). Since the beginning of the last century, the total trade has been contributing above 40% of GDP, which reached 46% in 2019 and directly supported one in five jobs of the economy (DFAT, 2021a).

Agricultural products and minerals, including wheat, wool, beef, sugar, butter, and Zinc dominated Australia's exports until the middle of the 20th century. In 1913, Australia exported 50% of zinc in the world market. Australia produced and supplied a record amount of wool to the world market between 1920 and 1971. Australia supplied all wool to the UK during the second WW. In the 1970s, Australia started exporting more minerals to the world market, including coal, iron ore, natural gas and gold. From the late 1980s, Australia further diversified its exports, including services exports of travel and tourism, international education, and financial services. In addition, Australia's exports include other non-organic chemicals, machinery, and computers, electrical equipment, optical, technical, and medical apparatus along with other agricultural and mineral items in 2019. Australia's export earnings reached $370 billion in 2019 from $52 billion in 1985 (ABS, 2021c).

Australia's imports dominated capital and intermediate goods over the first half of the 20th century. Textiles and apparels were the largest shares of imports for Australia in 1906. In the 1960s, Australia's imported items included vehicles, parts, petroleum, timber, sugar, metals, footwear, iron, steel, and mercenary. The major imports in 2019 were petroleum and crude oil, vehicles and delivery trucks, smartphones, and phone system devices, computers, and optical readers, pharmaceuticals, gold, and electro-medical equipment. Tourism and travelling abroad have also been a significant item in Australia's services imports list over the last fifteen years to 2019 until the COVID-19 pandemic struck the world and disrupted international travelling since early 2020.

Australia relied on the UK, US, and other European and American countries for its imports, and more than 70% of its imports were supplied by these two regions in the mid-1960s. However, in 2013-14, Australia's 57% of imports were sourced from China, Japan, and other Asian countries and remained the same until the end of the decade in 2019. It is interesting to note that Japan's contribution to imports and absorbing Australia's exports remained almost similar from the mid-1960s to 2019.

Figure 1 shows Australia's export value has been increasing above the import value since the early 1970s. However, between 2007 to 2015, the total value of imports exceeded the value of exports and created a trade deficit over those years. Nonetheless, the country experienced a trade surplus since 2016, although both exports and imports declined, mainly due to the global pandemic in 2020.

In 1901, two-way merchandise trade accounted for about 73% GDP of Australia, which fell sharply due to the protectionist measures during the height of the Great Depression to 25.7% in 1931-32. How-

Figure 1. Australia's Exports, Imports and Trade Balance 1960-2020
Source: Contracted by the authors using ABS National Income Accounting data (various years)

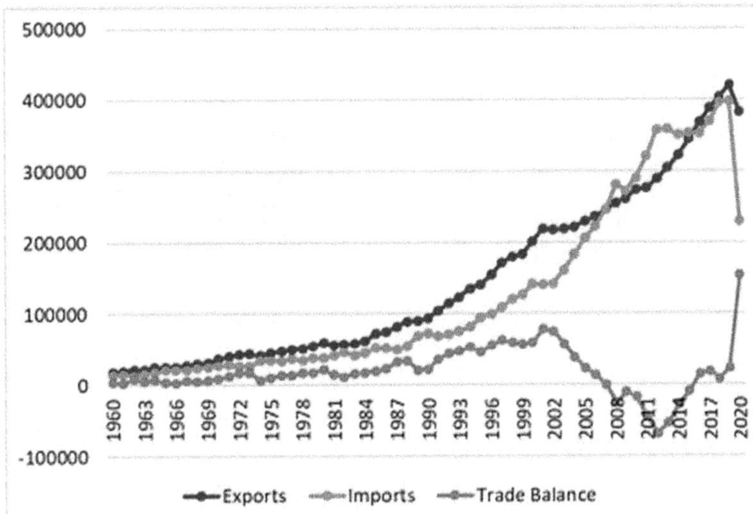

ever, the contribution of total trade to the GDP reached its highest level of 56.3% in 1950-51 during the Korean War commodity boom. By the early 1970s trade to GDP fell its lowest to 24.9% in 1971-72 as Australia took import substitution policies to promote its domestic industries (DFAT, 2016). However, the trade liberalisation policies were undertaken since the mid-1980s, which reversed the trend and the contribution of trade increased to 46% in 2019 but fell again to 31.7% in 2020 as the Covid-19 global pandemic hit the economy since early 2020.

Change in Australia's International Trade From West to the East

Australia's composition of two-way trade partnerships has also changed over the years since the beginning of the last century. The focal shift in Australia's two-way trade with the rest of the world can be seen in Figure 2 and 3 since the new millennium. The UK was the key trading partner of Australia from 1901 to 1964-65. The UK was also the major source (60%) of all imports and destination of about 62% of Australian exports (Figure 2 and 3). Since the mid-1970s, the US became the major source of imports, which was replaced by Japan in the mid-1980s. In 2013-14, Australia's 57% of imports were sourced from China, Japan, and other Asian countries and remained the same until the end of the decade in 2019.

The US, UK, and other American and European countries absorbed about 60% of Australia's exports in 1963-64 when China's share for Australian exports was only about 8%. Japan also became the number one destination of Australian exports over the next three decades until the mid-2000s. China overtook Japan's position as the number one export market of Australia in 2009 and accounted for 37% of all exports in 2013-14 (Figure 2). Within half a century the trade relationship reversed when the US and UK's combined share drastically fell to 5.3% and China and other Asian countries accounted for 65% of all Australia's exports in 2013-14. China accounted for 33% of all Australian exports in 2019, followed by Japan (13%), South Korea (6.2%), the US (5%), and India (5%) in 2019 as shown in Figure 4. However,

Figure 2. Direction of Merchandise Exports by Selected Country/Region
Source: Department of Foreign Affairs and Trade, 2014

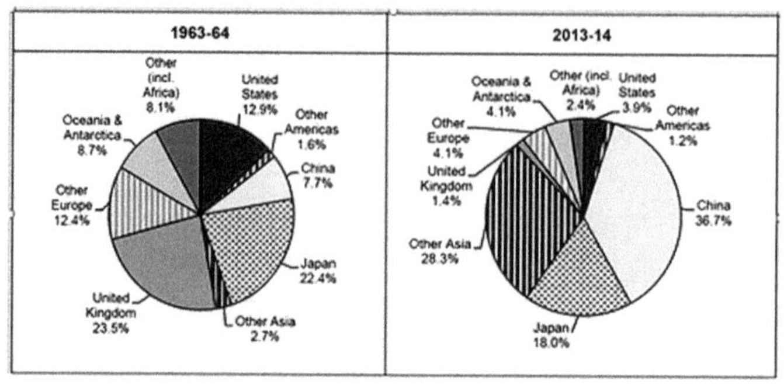

by January 2021, Australia's exports to China declined by 8% driven by the fall in metalliferous ores (-5%), cereals (-77%), and meat (-41%) (ABS, 2021d).

Australia's top ten two-way trade partners are shown in Figure 5, where it can be observed that about 73.2% of Australia's trade was with the Asia Pacific Economic Cooperation (APEC[2]) in 2018-19. By 2020, Australia's two-way trade with the Asia Pacific region (APEC, ASIAN and SAARC) increased to 85% from 78% in 2001 shown in Figure 6. However, China remained the number one two-way trade partner of Australia over the twelve years from 2009 to 2020.

It is interesting to note that while the major share of Australia's bilateral trade is with APEC countries, Australia's outbound investment is focused on the US, UK, Japan and other developed countries. The US and UK are the top two sources and destinations of Australia's foreign investment, followed by Japan, which was the third-largest destination and fourth-largest source of foreign investment (Figure 7). About 40% of the FDI went to the mining industries, followed by the manufacturing, real estate, financial and insurance industries in 2017 (DFAT, 2020b).

Figure 3. Direction of Merchandise Imports by Country/Region
Source: Department of Foreign Affairs and Trade, 2014

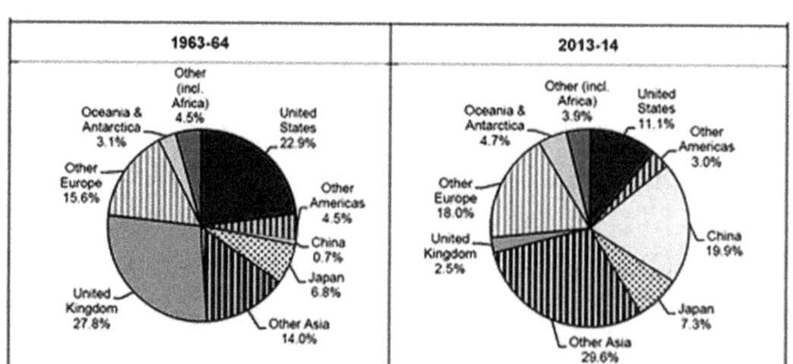

Figure 4. Top Five Export Markets for Australia 2019
Source: Constructed by the authors using Australian Government, DFAT data, 2020b

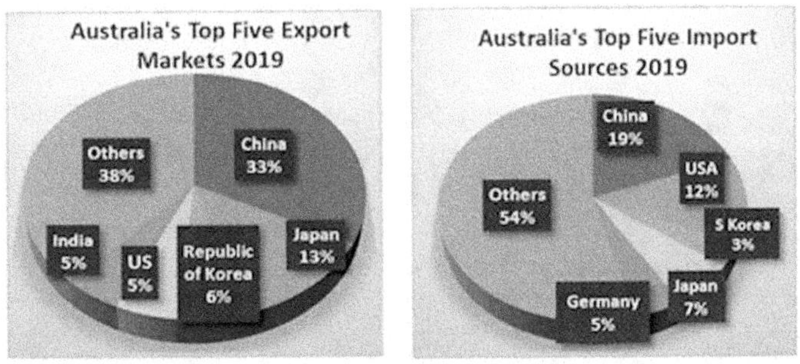

Figure 5. Australia's Top Ten Two Way Trade Partners 2018-19
Source: Constructed by the authors using Australian Government, DFAT data, 2021a

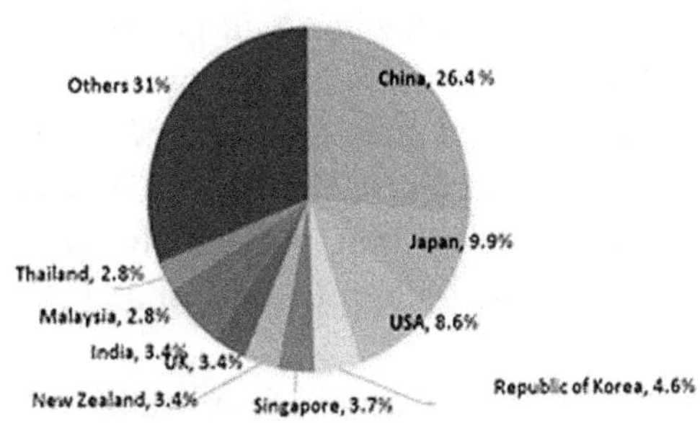

Figure 6. Australia's two-way Trade by Region 2001 and 2020
Source: Constructed by the authors using Australian Government, DFAT data

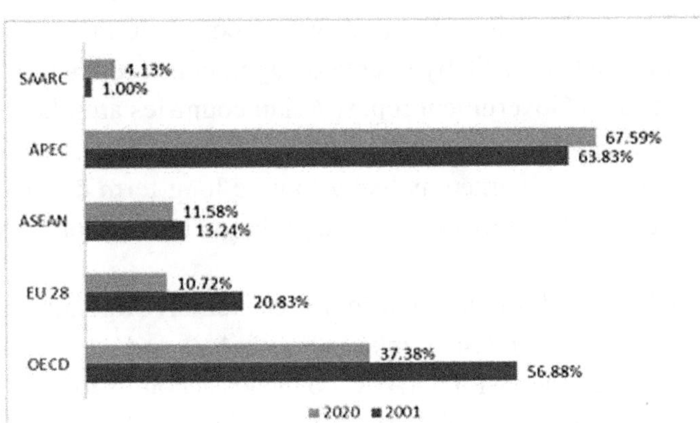

Figure 7. Australia's Foreign Investment Destinations and Sources 2018-19
Source: Constructed by the authors using Australian Government, DFAT data, 2020a

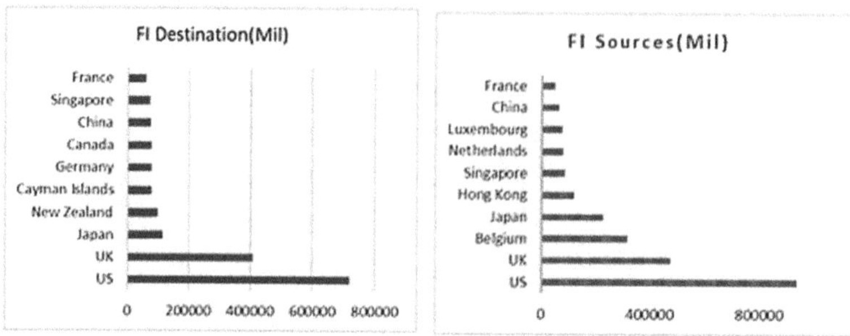

IMPORTANCE OF SOUTH ASIA IN AUSTRALIA'S INTERNATIONAL TRADE

Australia is uniquely positioned in the fastest growing Asia-Pacific region of the world currently. Over the last three decades, China and India have been expanded by seven times in terms of GDP (adjusted by PPP) and their share of the global economy increased to 26%. The other ASEAN and South Asian countries are also growing significantly. It is expected by IMF (2019) that the Asia-Pacific region would contribute over 45% of the world's economic output by the early 2020s. Realising the potential of the region, Australia has been strengthening its trade relationship and alliance with the region since the mid-1980s.

Although, China is still the largest trading partner of Australia in 2021, and the export of iron ore increased by $1.3 billion to $10.1 billion in March 2021, however, Australia needs to diversify its trade dependency away from China to other Asian countries. Given the current geopolitical situation, Australia can focus on strengthening its trade ties with South Asian fast-growing nations that are becoming emerging markets for trade and investment.

South Asia is one of the fastest-growing regions in the world in 2019 with a large young population of about 1,836 million, which is 23.91% of the total world population (World Bank data 2019). The recent dynamic in the Asian countries is likely to create huge opportunities for Australia in the coming years. According to an Australian Government report Asian countries are likely to deliver two-third of the overall global growth by 2030 (DFTA, 2020a).

Having access to these emerging markets is likely to give long-term dividends for Australia. Australia's bilateral trade in goods and services across the globe including South Asia and Bangladesh is shown in Table 1.

The SAARC is a regional union of South Asian countries, namely Afghanistan, Bangladesh, Bhutan, India, The Maldives, Nepal, Pakistan and Sri Lanka in South Asia and was founded in Dhaka on 8 December 1985. Australia's bilateral trade with SAARC countries accounts for 4.1% of total trade. Table 2 shows bilateral trade between Australia and SAARC nations. Among the SAARC countries, Australia's trade engagement with India was 72.8%, Nepal 9% and Bangladesh 7.3%. However, the trade between Bangladesh and Australia grew at around 23% over the last ten years, which is higher than Australia China trade growth of 18% (Table 1). Bangladesh was the net exporter to Australia in the financial year 2019-20 (DEFT 2021b). Stronger trade ties and more trading partnerships with the region will be beneficial

Table 1. Australia's trade in goods and services (A$ millions) 2009-2020 (Selected countries and regions)

Australia's Bilateral Trade With	2009-10	2014-15	2019-20	Annual Average Growth (Over Last 10 Years) (%)
World	528,938	674,118	873,145	6.51
China	90,572	144,587	251,073	17.72
Japan	58,978	67,734	79,113	3.41
Republic of Korea	26,178	35,725	38,890	4.86
Association of southeast Asian Nations (ASEAN)	80,004	101,124	*113,914*	4.24
Europe 28	80,702	88,748	*115,286*	4.29
South Asia (7 countries)	26,141	23,686	35,961	3.76
India	22,619	18,454	26,227	1.60
Bangladesh	799	1,768	2,626	22.87

Source: Constructed by the authors using DFAT data, 2021b.

for both Australia and SAARC region. Bangladesh is one of the fastest-growing countries in the South Asian region and can offer competitive potential trade and investment partnerships further with Australia.

Table 2. Bilateral trade between Australia and SAARC nations 2019-20 (A$ million)

Particulars	Australia Exported (Goods and Services) to SAARC Countries in 2019-20	Australia Imported (Goods and Services) From SAARC Countries in 2019-20	Bilateral Trade Between Australia and SAARC Countries in 2019-20
All Countries	475,240	397,905	873,145
SAARC Countries	25,587	10,458	36,045
Afghanistan	10	71	81
Bangladesh	1,117	1,450	2,627
Bhutan	197	5	202
India	18,618	7,609	26,227
The Maldives	60	69	129
Nepal	3,086	145	3,231
Pakistan	1,302	534	1,836
Sri Lanka	1,137	575	1,712

Source: Constructed by the authors using DFAT data, 2021b.

Foreign investment plays a key role in the Australian economy in terms of generating employment, bringing new skills and technology, and assisting growth. Foreign direct investment (FDI) was $132 billion and supported one in ten jobs in Australia in 2014-15 (DFAT, 2020a, p.38).

In 2018, Australia's two-way investment accounted for $3.5 trillion, while Australia invested $2.5 trillion in foreign countries, which increased to $3.1 trillion including $15.4 billion in India and $444

Table 3. Australian investment position in selected Asia-Pacific countries (A$ million)

Countries	2016	2017	2018	2019	2020
China	-83,040	-77,308	-79,146	-85,268	-64,029
India	-10,382	-13,902	-15,579	-19,912	-15,403
Indonesia	-9,301	-10,792	-5,631	-8,158	-3,172
Vietnam	-1,877	-2,277	-2,411	-2,927	-1,383
Thailand	-4,608	-4,647	-3,887	-4,795	-4,144
Bangladesh	-215	-218	-323	-444	-435
Total	-2,274,165	-2,369,431	-2,547,688	-2,953,056	-3,043,697

Source: International Investment Position, Australia: Supplementary Statistics, ABS, 2021c

million in Bangladesh in 2020 (Table 3). The largest type of Australia's foreign investment was portfolio investment followed by FDI and other investments.

POTENTIAL TRADE AND INVESTMENT PARTNERSHIP BETWEEN AUSTRALIA AND BANGLADESH

Australia and Bangladesh are two heterogeneous countries in terms of their resource endowment and socio-political-cultural characteristics, however, both countries are prominent in terms of their economic activities and international trade in the Asia-Pacific basin. COVID-19 pandemic and the associated deterioration of Australia-China trade and diplomatic relationship has provided Australia and Bangladesh to strengthen their trade and investment relationship further. Bangladesh can engage in trade with various manufacturing goods and light technological products as well as various other COVID-19 recovery and management related health and ITC services at a competitive price, which are discussed in the following sections.

The COVID-19 pandemic brought health as well as economic challenges for the Australian government and a total of A$291 billion in economic support has been provided by the government to the economy since the beginning of the pandemic. An additional $41 billion economic support has been committed in the 2021-22 budget to stimulate the economy with a $7.4 billion tax cut and $110 billion in a 10-year infrastructure investment pipeline. The Reserve Bank of Australia (RBA) also takes an expansionary monetary policy to stimulate the economy by slashing the cash rate few times since June 2019 to a record low of 0.01% in July 2021. However, the inflation rate rose suddenly to 3.8% in July from 1.1% in June 2021. However, it has been seen as a one-off temporary increase caused by the increase in petroleum price. Nonetheless, the RBA and most economists believe the inflation will stay around 2% through 2021 and may fall to 1.5% in 2022 (Hawkins, 2021).

The United Nations declared that Bangladesh will be considered as a developing nation effective from 2026 from a least developed country (Byron & Mirdha 2021). Bangladesh's economic status improved over the last three decades driven by export-led growth and consumer spending. Bangladesh's strong and steady average growth of above 6% over the last 25 years created opportunities for its trading partners, especially for Australia to explore and expand its trade potential with Bangladesh further.

Figure 8. GDP Growth rate in Australia and Bangladesh 2007-2018
Source: Constructed by the Author using World Bank Data.2021a

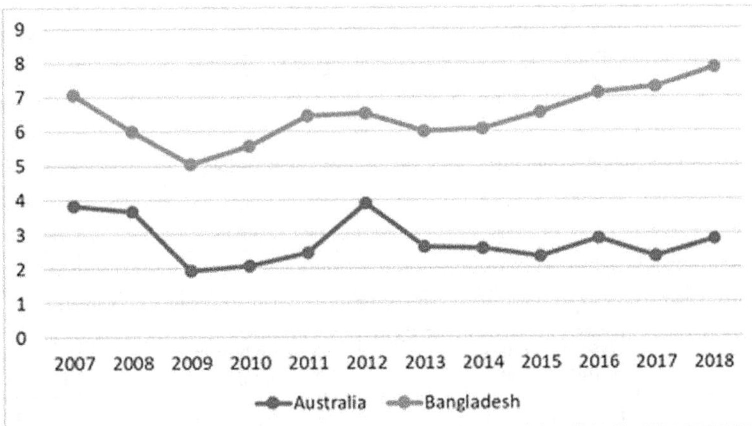

Several key sources such as PricewaterhouseCoopers (PwC) and HSBC (2018) also forecasted Bangladesh's future in the coming decades. For example, while BRIC (Brazil, Russia, India, and China) could be among the four most dominant economies by 2050, Bangladesh, with a large population of about 160 million people, will be among the Next Eleven (N11) emerging markets besides Egypt, Indonesia, Iran, Mexico, Nigeria, Pakistan, Philippines, Turkey, South Korea, and Vietnam (PwC, 2015). It is further projected that Bangladesh's GDP could surpass that of Australia within 20 years to 2030 (PwC, 2015). HSBC (2018) also projected that Bangladesh to be one of the fastest risers in rank on a GDP basis and becoming the 26th large economy in the world from its current standing of 42. In 2020, Bangladesh's GDP accounted for US$330 billion and the country ranks 38th largest economy with a population of 160 million. GDP grew spectacularly with a growth rate of 8.2 and Bangladesh became the world's fifth fastest-growing economy indicated by the World Bank (World Bank, 2019). GDP per capita for Bangladesh improved significantly and was valued at $5,083 in terms of PPP (international dollar) in 2020. The unemployment rate was 4.3%, the inflation rate was 5.4%, and the real interest rate was 3.9% in 2019.

Bangladesh became an example of export-led growth and accounting for an annual average growth rate of GDP was 6.4% over 2007 and 2018 mainly supported by ready-made garments exports and workers' remittances along with growth in domestic industrial production. Figure 8 compares Australia and Bangladesh's GDP growth over 2007 and 2018. Bangladesh's total trade has grown considerably over the last two decades. The total value of exports was US$30 billion and imports US$46 billion in 2020. The main export from Bangladesh is ready-made garments, which accounted for 86% of total exports in 2020. Other exports include foot ware, leather, fish, tobacco, paper yarn, rawhides. Bangladesh imports refined petroleum, raw cotton and textile, wheat, raw sugar and machinery and other appliances. The US is the largest export destination for Bangladeshi products as 17% of total exports are bought by the US. The major import sources for Bangladesh are China (21.5%), India (12.2%), Singapore (9.2%), EU (6.2%) and Hong Kong (5.5%).

In 2020-21, Bangladesh also earned US$20.7 billion from workers' remittances with a growth of 26% from 2020 which contributed 6.7% to the GDP during the height of the global Covid-19 pandemic. The economic fundamentals of Bangladesh are shown in Table 4.

Table 4. Economic fundamentals of Bangladesh

Particulars	2013	2018	2020
GDP (nominal)	US$ 150 billion	US$ 274 billion	US$ 330 billion
Forex reserve	US$ 21.51 billion (7 Months of import bill)	US$ 32.92 billion (8 Months of import bill)	US$ 41 billion (9 Months of import bill)
Domestic resource mobilisation	28.69% of GDP Tk 3,876 billion	31.23% of GDP Tk 7,028 billion,	31.56% of GDP Tk 8,004 billion,
Foreign aid Net Foreign Aid	US$ 2.14 billion (1.43% of GDP)	US$ 4.62 billion (1.64% of GDP)	US$ 4.96 billion (1.55% of GDP)
Debt to GDP, %	32.4%	27.9%	35%
Foreign Debt to GDP, %	14.9%	12.7%	12.5%
Remittances	US$ 14.23 billion (8.19% of GNI)	US$ 14.98 billion (5.47% of GNI)	US$ 16.42 billion (4.81% of GNI)
FDI stock in Bangladesh	US$ 8.60 billion	US$ 17.06 billion	US$ 18.72 billion

Source: Constructed by the authors using Bangladesh Bank Data 2021

Bangladesh introduced gradual outward-looking trade policies since 1985 and the liberalisation effort gained impetus from the mid-1990s as Bangladesh continues to reduce both tariff and quantitative restrictions under the South Asian Preferential Trading Agreement (SAPTA) launched by SAARC in April 1995 (Chowdhury, 2005). This agreement is considered to be the major stepping-stone towards a higher level of intra-regional trade liberalisation and economic cooperation among the member countries. As a result, intra-regional as well as international trade outside the region increased at a rapid pace and the country gained spectacular export growth over the last two decades (Chowdhury, 2005).

Australia-Bangladesh Trade and Investment Partnership

Bangladesh's strong and steady growth of above 6% over the last 25 years created opportunities for its trading partners, especially for Australia to explore and expand its trade with Bangladesh further. The total value of Australia-Bangladesh trade has grown significantly over the last four and half decades from A$2.7 million in 1972 to A$2.7 billion in 2019. The total value of Australia's exports to Bangladesh increased from A$92.2 million in 1995 to A$1.1 billion in 2018 and then fell slightly to $941 million in 2020.

Figure 9 shows the Australia-Bangladesh bi-lateral trade, aid, exports and imports value over 1972-2020. Exports from Australia to Bangladesh were A$1194 million in 2017, consisting of cotton, vegetables, wheat, lentil and pulses, seed oil, milk, cream, and other dairy products, plastic products, industrial raw materials, transport equipment, machinery, and scraps. Bangladesh is one of the top three importers of Australia's cotton with an import value of A$297 million, which is 32% of all export earnings from Bangladesh to Australia in 2017. Australia has further opportunity to expand its cotton exports to Bangladesh as cotton is one of the major inputs for Bangladesh's top exports of textile and garments. International education is the top services export for Australia over the last decade, earning over A$40.3 billion in 2019. This outcome has been supported by the education-related travel expenses by the international students and the visitors related to them. Bangladeshi students' enrolments to Australia increased from 57,860 persons in 2015 to 82,984 persons in 2020. Over 75% of these total enrolments

Figure 9. Bi-lateral Trade and Aid Between Bangladesh and Australia 1971-2020 (A$ million)
Source: Constructed by the Authors using data from DFAT data, Australian Government.

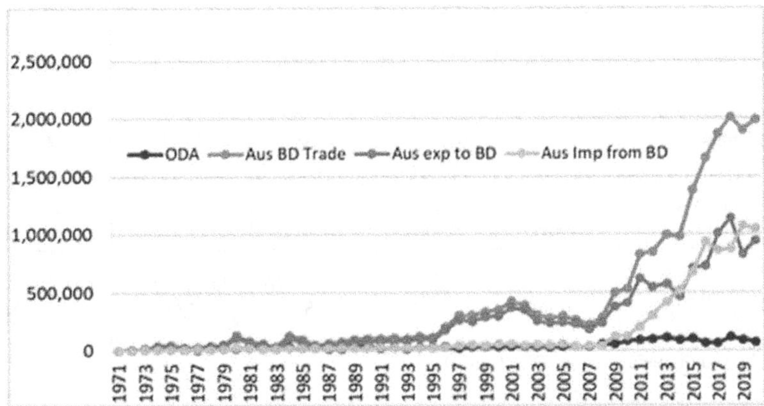

were counted for higher education. However, the total student number fell significantly in 2021 to 33,705 as a result of the COVID-19 breakout and Australian border closure (Department of Education, Skills and Employment (DESE), 2021).

Bangladesh's Exports to Australia

Bangladesh's trade with Australia has increased about five times in the last ten years. As a Least Developed Country (LDC), Bangladesh has been availing the advantages of duty-free and quota-free (DFQF) accorded by Australia as an LDC since 1 July 2003. However, this privilege is soon going to be affected due to the elevation of Bangladesh from an LDC status to a Developing Nation effective from 2026 (Daily Star, 2019). Major exports from Bangladesh to Australia are consisting of ready-made garments, knitwear, headgear, textile manufactures, woven fabrics, footwear and leather goods, processed food, carpets, jute items, pharmaceutical products, ceramic products, and fish. The major competitors in the Australian market for Bangladesh are China, Vietnam, India, Indonesia, Thailand. The total bilateral trade between Australia and Bangladesh grown by 77%, whereas exports increased by 114% from 2013 to 2020 as shown in Table 5. The total value of exports from Bangladesh to Australia was A$21.0 million in 1995, which increased to A$773 million in 2018 and then increased further to A$1.12 billion in 2019 (DFAT, 2020b). It is notable that even amid the COVID-19 pandemic in 2020, Bangladesh's total exports to Australia fell only by 3% (Table 5).

Australia's foreign investment in Bangladesh has been small but increasing steadily since 2015, especially in the portfolio investment category as shown in Table 6. Australia's investment in Bangladesh reached A$444 million in 2019 of which 85% are in portfolio investment. Nonetheless, there are a number of areas where Australia's investors can explore the potential of FDI. There is a huge potential to invest in the food and beverage retail sector, restaurants, hotels, international fast-food franchise, supermarket, infrastructure, energy and telecommunication sectors in Bangladesh (Austrade, 2021).

Table 5. Bilateral trade between Australia and Bangladesh (selected years) Unit: A$ million

Particulars	2013	2015	2017	2019	2020	Growth of Total Exports, Imports and Trade Over 6 Years (%)
Bangladesh's Export to Australia Goods + (Services) = Total	465 (78) = 543	848 (82) =930	850 (102) =952	1,128 (132) =1,260	1,068 (94) =1,162	114%
Bangladesh's Import from Australia Goods + (Services) = Total	567 (259) =826	688 (321) =1,009	1,194 (378) =1,572	913 (524) =1,437	811 (451) =1,262	53%
Bilateral Trade between Australia and Bangladesh, Goods + (Services) = Total	1,032 (337) =1,369	1,536 (403) =1,939	2,044 (480) =2,524	2,041 (656) =2,697	1,879 (545) =2,424	77%

Source: Constructed by the authors using data of DFAT, 2021b

Table 6. Australian investment position in Bangladesh (selected years) (Amount in A$ million)

Particulars	2015	2016	2017	2018	2019	2020
Total investment in Bangladesh	-53	-215	-218	-323	-444	-435
FDI	-	-	-9	-56	-68	-55
Portfolio investment	Np	np	-209	-267	-376	-380

Source: ABS, 2021c

Challenges for Bangladesh in Attracting FDI From Australia

Bangladesh is yet to attract significant Australian investment, especially the FDI in the real sectors of the economy to absorb technological diffusion and increase employment creation. One of the reasons for the lower FDI flow from Australia to Bangladesh is that Australia's foreign investment interests are not currently aligned with Bangladesh's thrust sector. Bangladesh's major export sector is ready-made garments (RMG). However, Australia's current interest in FDI is mainly focussing on the exploration of mineral resources and metals offshore. Woodside, an Australian company, expressed its keen interest to engage in an exploration of gas offshore, which has recently opened its operation in Myanmar. Bangladesh may avail opportunities like this through effective lobbying and negotiations with its counterparts to go for a joint venture with Australian companies to explore LNG, where it has abundant unexplored potential.

The challenge associated with investing in the portfolio market is that Bangladesh's financial market is not matured enough to attract foreign investment. Bangladesh's demand for FDI and other forms of foreign capital is mainly in the manufacturing and infrastructure development sectors. Bangladesh authorities in the foreign trade offices have to provide readily available information and incentives to the Australian companies to assess the potential benefits in investing in Bangladesh, which are aligned with Australia's investment interest.

Another important issue relating to foreign investment and trade with Bangladesh is that Australian investors may feel comfortable in a predictable business environment governed by agreements such as ASEAN-Australia FTA, RCEP and TPP-11. Tariff liberalisation, lesser customs duty, mutually recognised standards and other procedures, supply chain, etc., are likely to be advantageous for Bangladesh's competitors who are members of these trading arrangements. Thus, to attract Australia's investment, Bangladesh has to provide a competitive and conducive business and investment environment to attract Australian investors. Bangladesh also needs to provide further improvement on the infrastructure, institutional qualities and competitive time of doing business to attract investment from Australia.

Table 7. Total international students to Australia 2015-2020

Intake Year	Enrolment (Total)	Commencements (Total)	Enrolment Growth (% Change)	Enrolment (Higher Education)	Commencements (Higher Education)	Higher Education Enrolment Growth (% Change)
2015	57866	18782	-	46261	12613	-
2016	60709	19693	5.0	50556	14640	9.28
2017	65629	21985	8.10	55708	16336	10.2
2018	73560	24096	12.1	62665	18156	12.5
2019	80282	24338	9.13	66712	16984	6.5
2020	82980	23172	3.4	65299	14287	-2.1

Source: Constructed by the authors using data from the Australian Department of Education, Skills and Employment, 2021

OPPORTUNITIES FOR FURTHER AUSTRALIA-BANGLADESH COLLABORATION

Trade and Investment Potential: Australia to Bangladesh

With rising per capita income and a growing middle-income people of 30 million, rapid urbanisation with an informed consumer base, Bangladesh can be a significant market for Australian products and services. Bangladesh is the 32nd trading partner of Australia and has been recognised as an important market for Australian international education. Total commencements of Bangladeshi students to Australian educational institutions increased from 13,063 in 2002 to 24,338 in 2019. The new enrolment by Bangladeshi students in the Australian education sector has increased to 7,878 in December 2020 from 7,839 in December 2019.

Considerably large middle-income group households of Bangladesh are opting for international education. Australia can foster its international education sector in the Bangladesh market as it has a growing number of middle-income people who value international education highly and the country has 30.6 million people aged between 15 and 24 years (UNESCO, 2019). Australia has already been a popular destination for Bangladeshi students for higher education besides other destinations such as the US, UK, Europe, China and India. The total international intake of Bangladeshi students' number shows a healthy growth over the recent years as shown in Table 7. Australia can pursue to expand its international education sector to Bangladesh as Bangladeshi students and parents are considering Australia for their international education destination country for its geographical proximity, warmer climate and the similarity of its flora and fauna, its commonwealth country bonding, and its stable socio-economic, political status.

Figure 10. Bangladesh LNG Import Demand Forecast
Source: Mackenzie, 2017

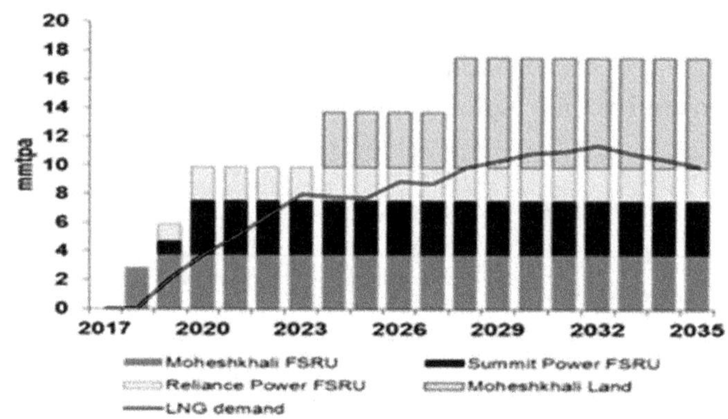

An Austrade (2021) study indicates that Bangladeshi consumers are increasingly informed about the quality of Australian products and Australian food franchises would be well received. Currently, Australia is the major supplier of dairy products, including milk powder, cheese, cream, butter, honey, and breakfast cereals. Australia is the second-largest supplier of fresh juice to Bangladesh. Australia's fresh fruit and vegetables are in good demand in Bangladesh. Thus, Australia can enter into joint ventures with Bangladeshi local companies in this area. Also, Australian companies can consider establishing food franchises in Bangladesh. Bangladesh has seen significant growth in the international food franchises, including KFC, Pizza Hut, Nandos, Krispy Kreme, Burger King. Australia's Gloria Jeans Coffee has had the second-largest operation in Bangladesh since 2012.

Bangladesh's retail modern food sector is expanding rapidly and accounted for US$16 billion in 2019. Over 200 supermarkets opened in the three large cities of Dhaka, Chittagong and Sylhet, which was expected to contribute $37 billion by 2020. There are 12 international chains of four- and five-star hotels in Bangladesh, including Hyatt Regency, West-Inn, JW Marriott, Holiday Inn, Radisson Blue, Hilton and Dusit, and Element Hotel. Australia can take the opportunity to invest in these areas of business in Bangladesh, which can bring economic benefit for both countries in terms of trade, investment, employment and growth. Austrade organises food promotion with mainstream local supermarkets and international five-star hotels every year under Australian Unlimited and Taste of Australia branding. Austrade also supports Australian companies to promote their products in such events in Bangladesh (Austrade, 2021).

Bangladesh's demand for energy will increase to maintain its growth trajectory for some years in the future. There is an increasing demand for Australian raw materials including coal, LNG, minerals, cotton in Bangladesh. For example, Bangladesh planned to generate between 10,000 megawatts (MW) and 12,000 MW of electricity from coal by 2030 (Shawon & Farhat, 2021). Figure 10 shows Bangladesh's LNG import demand forecast up to the year 2035. Bangladesh is importing fuel and coal from Indonesia, South Africa, India, Russian Federation, Malaysia, China and Australia. Australia can export low emission and high-performance coals at a competitive price and supports Bangladesh's effort to minimise carbon emission. Furthermore, Australia may also support Bangladesh with the technical know-how of high efficiency, low emissions (HELE) coal-fired plants.

Bangladesh government plans to develop the Matarbari Island area to build ports and facilities which allow imports of coals and liquefied natural gas (LNG) for power generations after 2021 and 2022, respectively. A 500 mmcfd LNG capacity floating storage and regasification unit is already operational. Bangladesh buys LNG from Qatar and Oman under a government-to-government (G2G) agreement. In 2017, Bangladesh signed a 15-year contract with RasGas of Qatar, which would supply 2.5 million tons of LNG every year (Paul, 2017).

Bangladesh government has a 10-year LNG import deal with Oman Trading International (Byron, 2018). There appears to be a deficit of at least 4 million tons of LNG/year by 2025. Australia being the world's largest gas exporter can take the advantage of exporting LNG to Bangladesh as the government of Bangladesh is going to buy LNG from the spot market to meet the growing demand alongside purchasing the LNG through long-term contracts.

Bangladesh has been emerging as an essential market for minerals and metals in particular for iron and steel. Steel production has already reached about 9 million tons annually and may go further in the next few years to meet increasing demand from the infrastructure sector. There is a growing demand for other non-ferrous metals. In 2019, Bangladesh's global importation of non-ferrous metals includes copper- US$200 million, zinc- US$157 million, lead- US$47 million, Aluminium - US$445 million (Trade Map, 2021). Australia is one of the major sources of these minerals and resources and can take the opportunity of exporting these to Bangladesh at a competitive price. Australia can also take its end-of-life offshore oil ridge structures and old ships to Bangladesh ship recycling companies to economically benefit both countries. Bangladesh well established and booming ship recycling industry can extract a large amount of iron and steel to support its ongoing demand for the steel industry and infrastructure development (Chakma, 2021).

Australian investment in Bangladesh stands at A$ 450 million from 2010 to 2019 (ABS, 2021d). Australia may further invest in Bangladesh including steel manufactures, pharmaceuticals and biotechnological items, medical equipment, IT and IT-enabled services, and the agri-business sector in addition to the energy sector, bond and security market.

Besides eight existing Export Processing Zones (EPZ), Bangladesh has taken initiatives to establish 100 Special Economic Zones (SEZs) by 2030, of which 70 Government Approved Economic Zones (EZ) and 30 Private Economic Zones. Japan, China and India showed their interest to develop G2G EZs. India has already signed an MoU to invest in two EZs. Chinese Economic and Industrial Zone in Anwara of Chattagrom and Japanese Economic Zone near Dhaka City in Arihajar Upazila of Naryanganj District have been already developed.

Bangladesh Economic Zones Authority signed a Joint Venture Agreement with Sumitomo Corporation of Japan for developing the Japanese Economic Zone in May 2019 which will attract 20-billion-dollar worth of foreign investment, most of which will be from Japan. A good number of other foreign companies, such as Honda Motors, Sumitomo Nippon, Asian Paint, Barger Paint, Adani Group, Wilmar, Yabang, Siam Group, TIC Group, Unilever, Sakata Inch and Chain Harbour are the major foreign investor in the special EZ in Bangladesh. There are ample opportunities for Australian investors to take their FDI to Bangladesh and utilise the large market and abundant low-cost workers to be more competitive.

Trade and Investment Potential: Bangladesh to Australia

While there are huge potentials for Australia to increase its trade and investment in Bangladesh, there are also avenues for Bangladesh to expand its trade and investment relationship with Australia. For

Table 8. Export potential for major exportable of Bangladesh to Australia

Particulars (Chapter)	Products Imported by Australia				Product-wise Main Exporting Countries to Australia (Unit: US $ million)
	From World		From Bangladesh		
	in 2017	in 2019	in 2017	Actual in 2019	
Knitted Apparel ('61)	3,088	3,226	350	400	China (63%), Bangladesh (12.4%), Viet Nam (4.3%), Cambodia (2.6%), India (3.1%)
Not Knitted Apparel ('62)	3,114	3,372	223	296	China (64%), Bangladesh (8.8%), Viet Nam (4.9%), Indonesia (4.3%)
Other made-up textile ('63)	1,359	1,385	46	37	China (63.4%), India (9.8%), Pakistan (6.4%), Bangladesh (2.8%),
Articles of Leather ('42)	1,323	1,452	3.26	16	China (48.1%), Italy (18.4%), France (10.4%), India (5.6%), Bangladesh (1.1%),
Footwear ('64)	1,669	1,781	3.07	8.88	China (50.1%), Viet Nam (22.35%), Italy (7.1%), Bangladesh (0.5%),
Headgear ('65)	208	218	6	5.8	China (67.9%), US (6.9%), Italy (3.6%), Bangladesh (2.7%)

Source: Source: Constructed by the authors using data of ABS 2021d

example, Bangladesh is the second-largest exporter of RMG and exported $400 million worth of knitted apparel to Australia in 2019 (Table 8). Bangladesh can further expand its market in Australia by exploring the particular requirements of Australian consumers. Bangladesh is one of the top importers of Australian cotton, which is one of the major inputs in the Bangladesh RMG industry. A collaborative Australia-Bangladesh forward and backward linkage RMG and cotton and wool industries can be a win-win business and trade between these two nations. Besides, RMG and apparel sector, Bangladesh has shown its competitiveness in jute products, processed foods, fish, leather goods, footwear, ITC products and pharmaceuticals.

Bangladesh has also earned A$132 million from its services exports in 2020 (DFAT, 2021c). Australia can further engage in trade with Bangladesh and import a range of products shown in Table 9, that Bangladesh has been exporting to other countries. The pharmaceutical industries and information communication technology (ICT) have been performing strongly and producing for the domestic and international market with proven price competitiveness. Among them, pharmaceuticals are notable, that

Table 9. Export potential for newer export items of Bangladesh to Australia

New Exportable Products	Product-wise Main Exporting Countries to Australia in 2019
Plastic products	China (5.8 b), US (715m), Viet Nam (65m), India (60m)
Pharmaceuticals (HS Code 3004)	US, Germany, Switzerland, India (300 m)
Furniture	China (3.1 b), Viet Nam (236m)
Toys	China (1.8 b), US (150 m), Viet Nam (60 m), India (21 m)
Electronics and electrical items	China (12.9 b), US (2.3 b), Viet Nam (1.5b), India (140 m)
Bicycle (H S code 8712)	China (106 m), Germany, US

Source: Constructed by the authors using data of ABS 2021d

earn $300 million from European countries as well as from India (Table 9). About 1200 pharmaceutical products have been registered for export to more than 100 countries, including the US, UK, Australia and Africa since 2018. Bangladesh government has declared the ICT export target at US$5 billion by 2021.

Australian companies can develop joint ventures with pharmaceuticals produces in Bangladesh, which can produce quality products at a competitive price for the world market. Bangladesh's plastic Industry has been performing well over the years with strong domestic demand and exports of US$1 billion in 2018. Plastic products are exported to over 68 countries such as the US, Canada, Europe, China and India. The plastic toy market has been growing at a rate of 161% and contributed US$40 million of export values in 2016 (DATABD.C, 2020). The furniture industry in Bangladesh has shown commendable growth for both domestic and international markets. It is one of the largest employment generating sectors in Bangladesh after the apparel sector. Bangladesh furniture sector exported over US$63 million worth of products to Canada, Nepal and Bhutan in 2018. Australian importers can explore the competitive source of these items in Bangladesh (DATABD.C, 2019). Further collaboration in agri-business, minerals and energy, research and development, science, technology, ICT, education and nursing may add value to the effort for greater economic collaboration between these two countries. Furthermore, proactive initiatives such as the withdrawal of air cargo restriction by Australia, initiating direct air connectivity between Dhaka-Sydney/Melbourne, the treaty on investment protection and the treaty on the elimination of double taxation may enhance bilateral trade between Bangladesh and Australia further.

FUTURE RESEARCH DIRECTIONS

This chapter suggests that the expansion of the Australia-Bangladesh trade relationship would be beneficial for both nations based on their complementary specialisations in mineral resources, technologies, expertise in research and development for Australia and comparative advantage in labour-intensive production and large market with increasing middle-income groups for Bangladesh. This study contributes significantly to the Australia-Bangladesh trade literature as there is limited literature on the trade nexus between these two nations in the Asia-Pacific region. However, the limitation of the study is not having an analytical model of the effect of Covid-19 on the trade prospects between Australia and Bangladesh due to data unavailability. A further study can develop an empirical analysis based on an analytical framework of international trade and investment. Time series analysis of cointegration and Error Correction Model can be used to examine the pre-and post-COVID-pandemic dynamic trade relationship between Australia and Bangladesh and its effect on the economic growth and development of these two countries. Additionally, future trade studies can be undertaken on the priority areas created by the COVID-19 pandemic, such as health care services, healthcare-related ICT products, pharmaceuticals. Also, in-depth analysis of trade and joint investment in the backward and forward linkage industries of existing sectors, like cotton, textile and RMGs, ship recycling, steel, energy or international education between Australia and Bangladesh can shed light on the expansion of future trade collaboration between these two countries.

CONCLUSION

This chapter provides an overview of Australia's international trade relationships, including Australia-Bangladesh trade, investment, and economic development. This study also identifies and suggests future opportunities for bilateral cooperation between these two countries in the current context of the geopolitical environment in the region. The study recommends the policymakers, practitioners, business community, observers, and academics to engage in further dialogues to enhance the bilateral relationship which can be beneficial for both countries, especially when both countries are putting their efforts to revive their economies with the support of international trade and investment based on their comparative advantage.

This chapter evaluates Australia's global trade and investment relationships and how they have been evolving from the early Federation years to the early 21st century. Although Australia has been having strong diplomatic, strategic, common values, shared heritage and trade and investment links with the UK, US, and the other Western countries since the early 20th century, however, its flow of international trade has gradually moved towards Asia-Pacific countries over the last fifty years (DFAT, 2016). Australia started securing its trade relationship with the emerging economies of Asia-Pacific as the demand for Australia's resources and quality products increased rapidly since the most current globalisation from the mid-1980s. Over the next three decades to 2020, Australia's three-fourth trade was exchanged with the APEC countries. However, the COVID-19 pandemic outbreak from early 2020 and the increasing geopolitical issues surfacing up in the region seem to start tarnishing Australia's trade and diplomatic relationship with its largest trading partner, China (Hare, 2021). Over-reliance on the Chinese market might have given some kind of trade stability to Australia, however, many critics believe that over-reliance on the Chinese market exposed the country to higher economic and security risks, especially when Australia demanded an independent inquire of the origin of the COVID-19. China has also taken punitive measures by cutting down on Australia's agricultural as well as some mineral and services exports (Chowdhury, 2021). This trade tension between Australia and China has heightened the emergence of diversification of Australia's international trade towards the fast-growing Asian nations, especially in South Asia. Strengthening and expanding the Australia-Bangladesh trade and investment by utilising a large young working population, rising middle-income consumers and investing in its priority areas relating to COVID-19, can cover the trade gap created by the Australia-China fallout. Australia and Bangladesh have ample opportunity to expand and strengthen their trade and investment relationship further to the sectors where it will benefit both countries and enhance the economic synergies. Australia and Bangladesh need to pursue new opportunities to promote trade and investment so that both countries can support quick economic recovery from the aftermath of COVID-19.

While challenges remain in doing business from both countries, Bangladesh offers increasing long-term commercial opportunities to Australian companies operating in food and beverages, agribusiness, education services, energy and minerals. Australian businesses are well placed to provide services, technical expertise and equipment for energy and infrastructure developments in Bangladesh. Bangladesh's geographic position, including its seaports, provides further economic opportunities through regional integration. Although, weak infrastructure, skills shortages and the governance environment remain as some concerns while doing business in Bangladesh, however, they can be overcome through collaborative supports, measures to uplift the skill base in the priority areas through education and training and strict implementation of investment conducive policies.

Bangladesh also has a liberal foreign investment regime, offering opportunities in textiles, ready-made garments, pharmaceuticals, telecommunication, ICT, energy and gas, infrastructure development, leather goods, plastic goods, jute goods, light engineering, ceramics, agro-processing, shipbuilding and recycling and various services sectors, including agricultural, construction, nursing, health-care services, skill development and education services and ICT. Australia can invest in Bangladesh as other foreign investors like Japan, China, India as the Bangladesh government has been supporting the congenial investment climate in the country. There are 56.7 million workable populations in Bangladesh who can be utilised in quality labour-intensive production and services with some training.

TIFA, a bilateral trade and investment arrangement between Australia and Bangladesh has been signed in September 2021 that provides the principles and strategic frameworks for further strengthening the trade and investment relationship between these two countries. Therefore, the governments and policymakers of Australia and Bangladesh should explore, guide, and support the business and investment-enhancing activities to harness the economic growth and development as well as reinforce the long-run strategic alliance between these two countries in the Asia-Pacific region.

REFERENCES

ABD sees robust growth for Bangladesh, fourth in Asia. (2021, September 18). *The Business Standard.* https://www.tbsnews.net/economy/adb-forecasts-68-percent-growth-bangladesh-current-fiscal-133039

Adnan, Z., Chowdhury, M., & Mallik, G. (2020). Determinants of total factor productivity in Pakistan: a time series analysis using ARDL approach. *International Review of Applied Economics.* https://www.tandfonline.com/doi/full/10.1080/02692171.2020.1792420?scroll=top&needAccess=true

Austrade. (2021). *Food and Beverage to Bangladesh: Trends and Opportunities.* Australian Government, Australian Trade and Investment Commission.

Australian Bureau of Statistics (ABS). (2020). *Australia's Trade in Goods with China in 2020.* https://www.abs.gov.au/articles/australias-trade-goods-china-2020

Australian Bureau of Statistics (ABS). (2021). *International Merchandise Trade, Preliminary, Australia.* https://www.abs.gov.au/statistics/economy/international-trade/international-merchandise-trade-preliminary-australia/jan-2021

Australian Bureau of Statistics (ABS). (2021a). *30% of Australia's Population Born Overseas, Preliminary, Australia.* https://www.abs.gov.au/media-centre/media-releases/30-australias-population-born-overseas

Australian Bureau of Statistics (ABS). (2021b). *Labour Force, Australia.* https://www.abs.gov.au/statistics/labour/employment-and-unemployment/labour-force-australia/latest-release

Australian Bureau of Statistics (ABS). (2021c). *Australia's National Accounts: National Income, Expenditure and Products.* https://www.abs.gov.au/statistics/economy/national-accounts/australian-national-accounts-national-income-expenditure-and-product/latest-release

Australian Bureau of Statistics (ABS). (2021d). *International Merchandise Trade*, Preliminary, Australia. https://www.abs.gov.au/statistics/economy/international-trade/international-merchandise-trade-preliminary-australia/jan-2021

Balassa, B. (1986). Policy responses to exogenous shocks in developing countries. *The American Economic Review*, *1986*(5), 75–78.

Bangladesh Bank. (2021). https://www.bb.org.bd/en/index.php

Bangladesh Government Power Division. (2021). *Annual Report 2019-20*. https://powerdivision.gov.bd/sites/default/files/files/powerdivision.portal.gov.bd/annual_reports/7d86d53d_5ebb_408d_8839_64d1a9eea653/ANNUAL%20REPORT-%202019-2020%20.pdf

Bangladesh has highest number of LEED platinum-rated garment factories. (2019, September 19). *Bangladesh Textile Today*. https://www.textiletoday.com.bd/topics/usgbc/

Bangladesh in Top Five Growing Economies: WB. (2019, April 4). *The Daily Star*. https://www.thedailystar.net/world/news/bangladesh-top-5-growing-economy-wb-1724815

Byron, R. K. (2018, September 4). LNG to come from Oman too. *The Daily Star*. https://www.thedailystar.net/frontpage/lng-come-oman-too-1564528

Byron, R. K., & Mirdha, R. U. (2021, September 4). Becoming a Developing Nation: Bangladesh Reaches A Mile Milestone. *The Daily Star.* https://www.thedailystar.net/frontpage/news/becoming-developing-nation-bangladesh-reaches-milestone-2052161

Chakma, J. (2021, February 7). Steel exports jump 83pc. *The Daily Star*. https://www.thedailystar.net/business/news/steel-exports-jump-83pc-2040485

Chowdhury, M. (2005). Trade reforms and economic integration in South Asia: SAARC to SAPTA. *Applied Econometrics and International Development*, *5*(4), 23-40.

Chowdhury, M. B. (2021). Internationalisation of education and its effect on economic growth and development. *World Economy*, *00*, 1–20. https://doi.org/10.1111/twec.13174

DATABD. (2019). *Timber and furniture*. https://databd.co/profiles/industries/profile-timber-and-furniture

DATABD. (2020). *Prospects of Plastics Sector: A Rarely Told Story*. https://databd.co/stories/prospects-of-plastics-sector-a-rarely-told-story-10507

Department of Education, Skills, and Employment (DFSE). (2021). *International student data 2021: Basic pivot table 2002 onwards*. https://internationaleducation.gov.au/research/international-student-data/Pages/InternationalStudentData2021.aspx

Department of Foreign Affairs and Trade (DFAT). (2014). *Fifty years of Australia's trade*. file://ad.uws.edu.au/dfshare/HomesK-W$/30053305/Downloads/fifty-years-of-Australias-trade%20(1).pdf

Department of Foreign Affairs and Trade (DFAT). (2016). *Australia's trade since federation*. https://www.dfat.gov.au/sites/default/files/australias-trade-since-federation.pdf

Department of Foreign Affairs and Trade (DFAT). (2020a). *Trade and Investment at a Glance 2020*. https://www.dfat.gov.au/publications/trade-and-investment/trade-and-investment-glance-2020

Department of Foreign Affairs and Trade (DFAT). (2020b). *Australia's free trade agreements (FTAs)*. https://www.dfat.gov.au/trade/agreements/trade-agreements

Department of Foreign Affairs and Trade (DFAT). (2021). *Trade and Investment at a Glance 2021.* https://www.dfat.gov.au/publications/trade-and-investment/trade-and-investment-glance-2021

Department of Foreign Affairs and Trade (DFAT). (2021a). *Australia's trade through time.* https://www.dfat.gov.au/publications/minisite/tradethroughtimegovau/site/index.html

Department of Foreign Affairs and Trade (DFAT). (2021b). *Trade, investment and economic statistics.* https://www.dfat.gov.au/trade/resources/trade-statistics/trade-statistics

Department of Foreign Affairs and Trade (DFAT). (2021c). *Bangladesh.* https://www.dfat.gov.au/sites/default/files/bade-cef.pdf

Hare, J. (2021). Chinese student numbers to free-fall in 2021. *Financial Review.* https://www.afr.com/policy/health-and-education/chinese-student-numbers-to-free-fall-in-2021-20210228-p576ji

Hawkins, J. (2021). Now that Australia's inflation rate is 3.8%, is it time to worry? *The Conversation.* https://theconversation.com/now-that-australias-inflation-rate-is-3-8-is-it-time-to-worry-165098

Hongkong and Shanghai Banking Corporation. (2018). *The world in 2030: Our long-term projection for 75 countries by Henry, J. & Pomeroy, J.* file://ad.uws.edu.au/dfshare/HomesK-W$/30053305/Downloads/HSBC-The-World-in-2030-Report.pdf

International Monetary Fund. (2019). *IMF, Executive Board Concludes 2018 Article IV Consultation with Australia.* https://www.imf.org/en/News/Articles/2019/02/21/pr1953-australia-imf-executive-board-concludes-2018-article-iv-consultation

Mackenzie, W. (2017). *Woodmac: Bangladesh's LNG demand to rise to 8 MMtpy by early next decade.* http://www.gasprocessingnews.com/news/woodmac-bangladeshs-lng-demand-to-rise-to-8-mmtpy-by-early-next-decade.aspx

OECD. (2003). *The Source of Economic Growth in OECD Countries.* Organization for Economic Co-operation and Development.

Ohlin, B. (1933). Interregional and International Trade. Harvard University Press.

Paul, R. (2017). Bangladesh set to sign 15-year LNG import deal with Qatar. *Reuters.* https://www.reuters.com/article/us-bangladesh-qatar-lng-idUSKCN1BO10P

PricewaterhouseCoopers. (2015). *The World in 2050: Will the shift in global economic power continue?* https://www.pwc.com/gx/en/issues/the-economy/assets/world-in-2050-february-2015.pdf

Ricardo, D. (1817). On the Principles of Political Economy and Taxation. London: John Murray.

Shams, M. (2021). Bangladesh, Australia sign TIFA: The pact will usher in trade and investment opportunities, says economist. *The Business Post.* https://businesspostbd.com/post/28128

Shawon, A. A., & Farhat, N. (2021, June 26). PM Hasina approves scrapping of 10 coal-fired power plant projects. *Dhaka Tribune.* https://www.dhakatribune.com/bangladesh/2021/06/26/pm-hasina-approves-scrapping-of-10-coal-fired-power-plant-projects

Tang, E. (2021). Australia has the third freest economy in the world, says US think tank. *Australian Trade and Investment Commission*. https://www.austrade.gov.au/news/economic-analysis/australia-has-the-third-freest-economy-in-the-world-says-us-think-tank

Tillett, A., & Cranston, E. (2021). Going nuclear: PM to announce $90b French submarine deal is dead. *Financial Review*. https://www.afr.com/politics/federal/speculation-pm-will-announce-90b-french-submarine-deal-is-dead-20210915-p58rzo

Trade Map. (2021). *Trade statistics for international business development Monthly, quarterly and yearly trade data. Import & export values, volumes, growth rates, market shares, etc*. https://www.trademap.org/Index.aspx

United Nations Educational, Scientific and Cultural Organization. (2019). *Sustainable Development Goals: Bangladesh*. http://uis.unesco.org/en/country/bd

World Bank. (2021a). *Data for Pakistan, India, Bangladesh, Sri Lanka, Nepal, Afghanistan*. https://data.worldbank.org/?locations=PK-IN-BD-LK-NP-AF

World Bank. (2021b). *GDP growth (annual %)*. https://data.worldbank.org/indicator/NY.GDP.MKTP.KD.ZG

World Economic Forum. (2021). *Global Results*. https://reports.weforum.org/global-gender-gap-report-2020/the-global-gender-gap-index-2020/results-and-analysis/

World Trade Organisation. (2019). *World Trade Statistical Review 2019*. https://www.wto.org/english/res_e/statis_e/wts2019_e/wts2019_e.pdf

ENDNOTES

1 South Asian countries includes Bangladesh, Bhutan, India, Pakistan, Nepal, Sri Lanka, Afghanistan and Maldives.

2 APEC's 21 Member Economies are Australia; Brunei Darussalam; Canada; Chile; People's Republic of China; Hong Kong, China; Indonesia; Japan; Republic of Korea; Malaysia; Mexico; New Zealand; Papua New Guinea; Peru; The Republic of the Philippines; The Russian Federation; Singapore; Chinese Taipei; Thailand; United States of America; Viet Nam. APEC Member Economies which are also members of ASEAN include: Brunei, Indonesia, Malaysia, Philippines, Singapore, Thailand, and Viet Nam.

Chapter 15
Exploring Partnerships Between Australia and South Asia for Crowdfunding Social Enterprises:
A Post-COVID-19 Strategy

Chureerat Haq
Charles Darwin University, Australia

Susan E. Bandias
Charles Darwin University, Australia

Faiz Shah
Asian Institute of Technology, Thailand

Rajeev Sharma
Charles Darwin University, Australia

ABSTRACT

Social enterprises have proven to be an effective mechanism for addressing economic, social, and environment problems in a number of countries. While conventional businesses have, in general, encountered difficult times during the COVID-19 pandemic, online businesses have tended to register success as a direct result of mobility constraints imposed on multinational or regional value-chains during this time. Social enterprises have continued to demonstrate their value as reservoirs of social and economic resilience during this unprecedented global crisis. Thought leaders like Muhammad Yunus see micro-economies, comprising locally focused social businesses linked digitally into distant value chains, as a viable strategy for economic growth in difficult times to achieve the SDGs. This chapter examines the potential of strategic business collaborations between social enterprises in Australia and South Asia that can leverage crowdfunding as a tool for mutual advantage and explores opportunities and challenges for Australian interests entering the financial services sector in South Asia.

DOI: 10.4018/978-1-7998-8657-0.ch015

INTRODUCTION

The COVID-19 pandemic has highlighted fundamental issues, particularly, uneven access to education, healthcare, food, and finance. Each of these is linked to three prevailing megatrends, namely, Globalisation, Urbanisation, and Digitalisation (Shah, 2021). Consolidating economic interests across diverse geographies as a result of globalising value-chains has contributed to a decline in self-reliance at the community level. With constraints on mobility, this vulnerability has increased. The consistently rising transfer of populations to urban communities with better job opportunities and infrastructure, has continued to deplete local communities of young, educated residents, who now face uncertainty because of changing patterns of employment. Affordable and ubiquitous information technologies have increasingly enabled secure and lightening-speed transactions, often obviating face-to-face engagement.

Mobility constraints, predicted as a feature of the Post COVID-19 "new normal" for the immediate future, are expected to accelerate the mainstreaming of online business models and services. At the same time, shrinking urban employment opportunities, and re-calibration of international value-chains to distribute and digitally connected models is likely to increase the pressure on grassroots communities to seek ways to rebuild social and economic resilience. Governments and corporations in Australia and South Asian countries often adopt a variety of approaches for strategic trade partnerships. This chapter explores the potential of crowdfunding social enterprises to energize grassroots micro-enterprises and social businesses as a strategy for Australia in developing bilateral partnerships in South Asia.

The chapter commences with the background and rationale for exploring this topic, and its aims and objectives. It proceeds to discuss Social Enterprise as a development approach, the demand for access to finance, and the role of crowdfunding in promoting Social Entrepreneurship. An overview of crowdfunding in Australia is followed by a discussion on access to impact finance in South Asia. The discussion references Yunus et al. (2010)'s Social Business Model Framework as the theoretical guideline, consisting of four key components, namely, value proposition, economic profit equation, value constellation, and social profit equation. The framework is adopted to analyse how value can be created, captured, and delivered from the partnerships. This analysis leads to identifying challenges for crowdfunding faced by South Asian social entrepreneurs, and proposes practical solutions within specific limitations. The chapter concludes with future research directions.

BACKGROUND LITERATURE

COVID-19 has created unprecedented damage to established global equilibrium. Apart from the drastic health crisis caused by the pandemic, 2020 saw the highest rise in the global extreme poverty rate in more than 20 years. Over 2.3 billion people are unable to eat a healthy balanced diet on a regular basis, while an additional 119 – 124 million people have been pushed into extreme poverty because of disruptions in education and job losses (UNSTATS, 2021). The pandemic has uncovered the deepening inequalities within and among countries (Jomo & Chowdhury, 2020, UNSTATS, 2021). The crisis underscores global interdependency as well as the interlinkages between health and well-being, social, economic, and environment, and international cooperation that serve to safeguard financial stability in a world of technological changes and innovations (Barua, 2021; United Nation, 2021; Vučinić, 2020). A disruption of this magnitude demands that innovative multinational measures to create future resilience be designed and implemented (Jomo & Chowdhury, 2020; Ziegler & Shneor, 2021).

There is agreement across diverse terminologies and operational practices, that a social enterprise is characterised by the social value it creates as a by-product of its business, and not merely personal or shareholder wealth (Austin et al., 2006; Teasdale, 2011; Yunus et al., 2010). This chapter defines social enterprise as an organisation whose commercial activities generate income to sustain their primary social mission. Social enterprise has emerged as a strategy for social, economic, and environmental improvement both nationally and internationally (Defourny & Nyssens, 2010; Mair et al., 2012).

Australia has created an eco-system of financial inclusion within the country that leverages technology-driven financial products and services (FinTech) that not only serve non-traditional clients, but also promise a better deal for investors and consumers (UNSGSA, 2019). Crowdfunding is an application of FinTech that has promise for social enterprises, particularly if it can be diverted into partnerships between Australia and South Asia. With crowdfunding in Australia energising social enterprises in South Asia, it is possible to create greater local economic resilience among grassroots communities, as well as provide Australian consumers with a greater selection of responsibly sources products. Implemented with vigour, this could be an effective post Covid-19 strategy that Australia could leverage to strengthen cooperation and partnerships with South Asian countries.

Fundamental to a financial inclusion strategy is access to finance (United Nations, 2021). Access to finance, in particular, can create circumstances for achieving significant numbers, the first nine of the United Nations Sustainable Development Goals (SDGs). These include alleviating extreme poverty, reducing hunger and promoting food security, improving health and well-being, accessing to quality education, achieving gender equality, accessing to clean water and sanitation, accessing to affordable and clean energy, promoting inclusive economic growth, and promoting industry innovation and infrastructure (Kara et al., 2021; Klapper et al., 2016). Perhaps the most commonly recognized access strategy is Microfinance, which is the provision of a small loans to people who may not have access to regular banking services due to the lack of traditional collateral in the banking system (Brau & Woller, 2004). But there are other access to finance initiatives that are gaining recognition, including, but are not limited to, impact investment and crowdfunding (Barraket et al., 2016; Castellas et al., 2018). Often social entrepreneurs are located in developing countries, where ready access to finance is a challenge. At the same time, social impact investors or philanthropic funders seeking to provide resources for worthwhile community initiatives are typically located in developed countries. This makes a strong case for creating bilateral crowdfunding partnerships between funding sources in Australia and social enterprises in South Asia. In addition to the Sustainable Development Goals (SDGs) highlighted by the United Nations, this approach can also contribute to achieving SDG 10 and SDG 17, which aims at reducing of inequity within and among countries, and enhance partnering for the Goals respectively.

Within the context of crowdfunding social enterprise in South Asia as a development strategy for Australia, this chapter has two objectives. First, it provides a discussion on exploring crowdfunding social enterprise as a strategy for Australia to develop partnerships with South Asia to mitigate the economic impact of COVID-19 at international levels. Second, it discusses challenges for implementation and presents a suggestion on solutions and recommendations on how Australia could collaborate with South Asian countries through using crowdfunding social enterprise as a strategy to develop partnerships.

The conceptual discussion in the chapter is built upon Yunus et al. (2010)'s Social Business Model Framework, which provides a comprehensive understanding of key factors and associations necessary for analysing the crowdfunding partnerships proposed. The framework consists of four key components, namely, value proposition, economic profit equation, value constellation, and social profit equation. Conceptual framework is an interlinked concepts that provides a comprehensive understanding of a phenomenon (Jabareen, 2009). Conceptual framework exhibits key factors and constructs and posits associations among them (Miles & Huberman, 1994). Considering the explorative nature of the book chapter, the adoption of Yunus et al. (2010)'s Social Business Model Framework deems appropriate for the analytical discussion.

Introduction to Social Enterprise

A social enterprise is a business that generates income by using innovation and entrepreneurship to financially sustain while business profits is channelled back for social aims, thus giving priority to social benefits over financial profits (DiDomenico et al., 2010; Mair et al. 2012). Social enterprises have been a key feature of economic activity in both developed and developing countries where policy makers and practitioners are increasingly aware of the social enterprise phenomenon (Barraket, Mason, & Blain, 2016; Defourny & Nyssens, 2010; Hoogendoorn et al., 2009; Leadbeater, 2007; Moizer & Tracey, 2010).

Social enterprises have experienced a rapid rise in deliberations in many countries such as the United Kingdom, the United States, Canada, New Zealand, and Australia (Gray, Healy, & Crofts 2003). Australian social enterprises are located in every state and territory in all areas including urban, regional, rural, and remote areas (Barraket et al., 2016). These social enterprises operate in every industry of the economy predominantly in local and regional markets, hence, focusing on local and regional targets accordingly (Barraket et al., 2016).

Within a domestic market, social enterprises have served as a strategy for achieving social and economic development in underprivileged communities, social procurement, skills and knowledge for employment (Barraket et al., 2016; Furneaux & Barraket, 2014; Loosemore, 2016). One of the concerns on social enterprise development in Australia has been on treating social enterprises as the welfare interventions (Barraket et al., 2016). Viewing from social work perspective, Gray et al., (2003) argued that social enterprises encourage effective community-business partnerships that lack in the social work field.

Social enterprises may be seen as an endeavour to respond to the influences of globalisation and centralisation to address their impact in local contexts (Gray et al., 2003). However, innovation and creativity that appear to embed within social enterprises enable them to seize on opportunities (Defourny & Nyssens, 2010; Gray et al., 2003). As a consequence, social enterprise has emerged as a strategy in public and academic debate for the betterment both nationally and internationally (Defourny & Nyssens, 2010; Mair et al. 2012). Although predominantly operate in local and regional domestic markets, certain social enterprises in Australia also operate in international markets and seek to respond to missions of international scope (Barraket et al., 2016).

After the 2008 financial crisis, public confidence in the financial industry was severely impacted (Brown, Rocha, & Cowling, 2020). Accordingly, one of the strategies that the investors adopted involved investing in socially related projects to reclaim their public image (Brown et al., 2020; Mitra, 2012). Since its outbreak in 2019, however, COVID-19 has created global unprecedented damage, especially in terms of economic and health (Agrawal & Hockerts, 2021; Farhoud et al., 2021; Moysidou & Hausberg, 2020; Ratten, 2020).

Identifying Crowdfunding Social Enterprise

Crowdfunding is an alternative finance that is enabled by technology and market-based funding outside the traditional financial system, hence a part of financial innovations enabled by technological advancements known as FinTech (European Commission, 2016). Crowdfunding is generally categorised according to incentives or enticement that backers or investors obtain or expect for their contributions, for instance, donation, reward, lending, and equity with common elements of the funds being raised in small to medium amounts by using digital technology to reach out to a number of backers at a relatively lower costs and time (Bruton et al., 2015; De Luca et al., 2019; Scataglini & Ventresca, 2019; Shneor, 2020; Theerthaana & Manohar, 2021).

This terminology largely consistent across academic and practitioner discussions, with relatively few variations. The literature refers to individuals or organisations that support or fund through crowdfunding are inconsistently termed as backers, funders, supporters, sponsors, investors, lenders, and donors, depending on the type of crowdfunding (Bruton et al., 2015; De Luca et al., 2019; Gray & Zhang, 2017; Scataglini & Ventresca, 2019; Shneor, 2020; Suresh, Øyna, & Munim, 2020; World Bank, 2019; Ziegler et al., 2021).

The emerging typology identifies the first type of crowdfunding as equity crowdfunding or equity-based crowdfunding (Shneor, 2020; Scataglini & Ventresca, 2019). In this typology, investors receive equity or shares of organisations whose products and services predictably are innovative (De Luca, 2019), and a share of the profits (Mitra, 2012). The second type, namely lending crowdfunding or lending-based crowdfunding, or loan-based crowdfunding (De Luca et al., 2019; Ziegler & Shneor 2021), has lenders providing funding as a loan with or without interest (Bradford, 2012). Lending crowdfunding is also known as peer-to-peer lending (P2P) crowdfunding (Shneor, 2020; Suresh et al., 2020). Crowd-based microfinance is considered as a part of this crowdfunding typology, specifically when the loans cater to financially marginalised individuals or groups (Shneor, 2020; Ziegler & Shneor 2021). In the lending crowdfunding, lenders lend directly to fundraisers or invest in debt obligations issued through a platform (Scataglini & Ventresca, 2019).

The third type is reward crowdfunding or reward-based crowdfunding (De Luca et al., 2019; Gray & Zhang, 2017), in which sponsors receive non-financial rewards, which may include early release of new products, exclusive access to a limited gifts, events, and experiences, in exchange for the investment or purchase (De Luca et al., 2019; Scataglini & Ventresca, 2019). This type of crowdfunding does not only offer initial funds for campaign creators, but also pre-orders, new opportunities and market testing because the campaign creators engage with backers and receive feedback for their new products (Gray & Zhang, 2017; Suresh et al., 2020).

The fourth type is donation crowdfunding or donation-based crowdfunding (De Luca et al. 2019; Gray & Zhang, 2017). Unlike other forms of crowdfunding, backers for this type of crowdfunding are often called donors who give money without expecting returns of finance or materials (De Luca et al., 2019, Scataglini & Ventresca, 2019). Rather, the donors receive non-material reward such as satisfaction from supporting something they consider worth their monetary contribution to recipients that could be a project, an individual, or a business, in which they may be passionate about (De Luca et al., 2019; Shneor, 2020). Ziegler and Shneor (2021) argue that the reward and donation crowdfunding models are most recognised by the public.

Belleflamme and Lambert (2016) suggest a distinction between investment model and non-investment model crowdfunding, describing it based on the nature of incentives expected by funders. Therefore, non-investment model crowdfunding may include reward and donation crowdfunding, while investment model crowdfunding include lending and equity models (Belleflamme & Lambert, 2016; Ziegler & Shneor, 2021). Crowdfunding value goes beyond a mere fundraising. Additional advantages or value of crowdfunding include market tests, feedback for products and services, engagement and building relationship with potential customers/donors, organisational promotion, financial and social inclusion (De Luca et al., 2019; Shneor, 2020). Crowdfunding typology could further develop, for instance, equity crowdfunding could later be more evolved and innovative in such a way that social enterprises could provide non-profit sharing equity through equity crowdfunding, if that is not already advancing amongst practitioners. Donation crowdfunding, crowdfunded microfinance, and reward crowdfunding have advantages as a means for people from lower income backgrounds or people who lack access to traditional financing (United Nations, 2021). Backers and donors associate a higher social and environmental value with reward and donation crowdfunding (Gray & Zhang, 2017).

According to Ziegler and Shneor (2021), global online alternative finance market has grown consistently over the past three years. The global volumes, excluding China, rose by three per cent from 89 billion USD in 2018 to 91 billion USD in 2019. Despite the COVID-19, in 2020, the global market volume rose a further 24 per cent year-on-year to reach 113 billion USD in 2020. Excluding China, peer-to-peer lending remained the largest model type both in 2019 and 2020, with a total volume of 33.6 billion USD, accounting for 37 per cent of the total global volume in 2019. The report argues that business funding was 38 per cent of the total volume in 2019, while business funding accounted for 47 per cent of the total volume in 2020. Equity-based model contributed 1.5 billion USD in 2019 and 2.2 billion USD in 2020, thus three per cent in 2019 and four per cent in 2020. Non-investment models accounted for 533 million USD in 2019 and 744 million USD in 2020.

On the other hand, donation crowdfunding has experienced high growth, accounting for 7 billion USD globally in 2020 (Ziegler & Shneor, 2021). The surge in growth of 160 per cent between 2019 and 2020 annually was detected as largely attached to the outbreak of COVID-19 related charitable, community and health-related online fundraising activities around the world (Ziegler & Shneor, 2021). Crowd-led microfinance served 72 per cent of clients identified as unbanked, and 27 per cent as underbanked. Largely, the percentage of female fundraisers has only slightly increased from 37.8 per cent in 2019 to 38.9 per cent in 2020. In regards to female market participation, it differs broadly across alternative finance models. Female participation for most models, whether as a fundraiser or funder remained to be below 40 per cent and further drops during 2020. The share of female fundraisers in peer-to-peer lending type reported the largest drop from 61 per cent in 2019 to 35 per cent in 2020. Donation crowdfunding, nevertheless, had the highest number of female fundraisers at 63 per cent across the models.

As such, certain types of crowdfunding, particularly lending, crowdfunded microfinance, and donation crowdfunding are social enterprises and rapidly growing as alternative strategies for individuals, social enterprises, non-profit organisations, and social investment units or corporate social responsibility (CSR) departments. Considering the growing attraction of crowdfunding as an alternative social investment strategy for Australian social impact investors, and the visible funding gaps confronting social business entrepreneurs in South Asia's developing economies, it appears worthwhile to explore the potential of collaboration between Australian social impact investors and South Asia's social business entrepreneurs as a mutually beneficial strategy for rebuilding social and economic resilience in the Post COVID-19 world.

SERVING THE DEMAND

Crowdfunding is growing in appeal across the social enterprise landscape, instead of depending on assessments made by a small group of investors and bank managers. Development projects or small businesses seeking funding are able to approach investors directly, and receive support with minimal process or regulatory intermediation. This innovative medium is successfully providing funding opportunities, in particular, for start-ups and small and medium enterprises (Belleflamme, Lambert, & Schwienbacher, 2010; Lehner, 2013; Moysidou & Hausberg, 2020).

Through crowdfunding platforms, crowd-funders are able to exercise independent control over decisions regarding financial commitment to socially beneficial projects with or without monetary incentives (Belleflamme et al., 2010). This is in line with the general concept of impact investment, which allows investors to receive financial returns with an accompanying answer to particularly pressing social problems (BuggLevine & Emerson, 2011). Businesses that co-create economic and social value have been seen to have played a significant role during the COVID-19 crisis by continuing to provide essential needs for populations isolated by public health regulations and long periods of diminished mobility (Farhoud et al., 2021; Ratten, 2020; Shah, 2021).

Emerging evidence indicates that social enterprises are globally resurgent and have a clear role in re-establishing economic momentum at the grassroots, where livelihoods continue to be under threat because of barriers to mobility, access to services, and brittleness of incomes. If social businesses and community-service enterprises are the answer to challenges of local socio-economic resilience, it can be safely assumed that the social enterprise sector would be in desperate need for financial support to sustain operations, and increase scale (Barraket et al., 2016; Battaglia et al., 2020; Farhoud et al., 2021). Steiner and Teasdale (2016) argue that although grants are frequently criticized as directing social enterprises to inefficiency and dependency, main stream funding options such as bank loans remain costly or not accessible for social enterprises. This means that crowdfunding is rightly recognized in academic research as an emerging financial service model that proposes a practical alternative for businesses to raise finance in relatively small units of funding drawn from a larger volume of independent funders using the Internet (Bruton et al., 2015; De Luca et al., 2019; Theerthaana & Manohar, 2021).

Studies also confirm that access to flexible loans and grants is a preferred alternative for social enterprises to develop the businesses (Agrawal & Hockerts, 2021; Steiner & Teasdale, 2016). On the other hand, empirical studies show a significant decrease in entrepreneurial finance since the COVID-19 pandemic (Brown, Rocha, & Cowling, 2020). This decrease, in particular, appears to affect start-ups, which in the case of the United Kingdom, have seen a decline in seed finance by almost 40 per cent in the first quarter of 2020 as compared to that of 2019 (Brown et al., 2020).

During the same period, according to the 2nd Global Alternative Finance Market Benchmarking Report from Cambridge Centre for Alternative Finance (CCAF), donation crowdfunding has increased by 160 percent, accounting for 7 billion USD globally (Ziegler & Shneor, 2021). The surge is largely attributed to COVID-19 related charitable, community and health-related online fundraising activities around the world (Ziegler & Shneor, 2021). Crowd-led microfinance served 72 per cent of clients identified as unbanked, and 27 per cent as underbanked. Largely, the percentage of female fundraisers has slightly increased from 37.8 per cent in 2019 to 38.9 per cent in 2020. In regards to female market participation, it differs broadly across alternative finance models. Female participation for most models, whether as a fundraiser or funder, remained below 40 per cent, and further dropped during 2020. The share of female fundraisers in peer-to-peer lending type reported the largest drop from 61 per cent in 2019 to 35 per cent in 2020. Donation crowdfunding, nevertheless, had the highest number of female fundraisers at 63 per cent across the models. This chapter examines possible proposals for Australia providing financial access to target populations in South Asia to the mutual benefit of each region.

An Overview of Crowdfunding in Australia

Equity crowdfunding has a significant presence in Australia for many years, however, it was restricted to professional investors and or high net worth investors, referred to as wholesale investors in Australia. In 2017, the crowdfunding registration included retail investors. Since then, the term crowd-sourced funding (CSF) and equity-based crowdfunding are used interchangeably (ASIC, 2021). In 2018, Birchal, Equitise, and OnMarket became the first group of licensed equity crowdfunding platforms to allow retail investors as individual Australian investors to purchase shares in private and unlisted public companies (Equitise, 2021, Onmarket, 2021; Birchal, 2021). According to the website of the crowdfunding platforms, Birchal has raised 50 million Australian Dollars for over 70 start-ups and small businesses, Equitise raised over AU$38 million (Equitise, 2021), OnMarket has raised over AU$150 million (Onmarket, 2021).

ReadyFundGo is a rewards and equity crowdfunding platform that collectively helped Australian businesses with seed, start-up and growth funding (ReadyFundGo, 2021). Gofundraise is a crowdfunding platform that campaigns for only not-for-profit Australian organisations towards charities/charitable events and does not allow personal causes (GoFundraise, 2021). Mycause is an Australian crowdfunding platform that allows individuals to raise money for all causes including personal, charities, or projects (Mycause, 2021).

Australia also experiences and appreciates crowdfunding platforms from overseas. AngelList is a crowdfunding platform from the United States that largely allows US-based startups to raise equity funding from remote investors. JustGiving is a crowdfunding platform headquartered in the United Kingdom that allows funders to participate from all over the world and runs bank account verification to ensure all donations are made to legitimate charities. Chuffed from the United Kingdom focuses on supporting campaigns that aim to raise funds for social, community or political causes. GoFundMe is a crowdfunding platform from the United States that allows individuals to raise funds for personal and group causes, ranging from education, sports, animals, medical, and more.

Access to Impact Finance in South Asia

South Asian countries, comprising Bangladesh, Bhutan, India, Nepal, Pakistan, and Sri Lanka, have a combined population of nearly 2 billion, with an expanding consumer class indicating an extensive untapped opportunity in the region (Suresh et al., 2020). Discussion in this section focuses on crowdfunding situations in Bangladesh, India and Pakistan. According to Suresh et al. (2020), all of the four major types of crowdfunding, namely, reward, equity, lending, and donation are prevalent in India, with a predominance of loan crowdfunding. Since 2016, equity and donation crowdfunding have grown steadily at a similar pace, while the volume of reward crowdfunding remains low. Between 2013 and 2017, crowdfunding volume in India reached 450 million USD, even though it was anticipated to reach USD 5 billion for the South Asia region (The World Bank, 2013 in Suresh et al., 2020). The crowdfunding industry promises tremendous growth, considering the volume of 268 million USD in a single year in 2017, with year-on-year growth of 116 per cent (Ziegler et al., 2018 in Suresh et al., 2020).

According to Suresh et al. (2020), the growth of non-financial return crowdfunding including donation and reward crowdfunding is driven by growth in charity and philanthropy in India, an increase in foreign donations, and support for new and innovative causes while growth in peer-to-peer lending is due to the credit gap and unbanked population. In Bangladesh, India, and Pakistan all the crowdfunding industry is driven by increased demand for alternative finance due to improved socio-economic status, significant increase of internet users, and complexity of lending from traditional financial institutions such as banks (Arshad, 2017; Suresh et al., 2020).

The concept of donation crowdfunding has gained vast attention as it joins donors from around the world in a short period of time at a relatively lower cost (Theerthaana & Manohar, 2021; Ziegler et al. 2018). Although donation crowdfunding concept is not new, it is still emerging in developing countries in South Asia including Bangladesh, India and Pakistan (Suresh et al., 2020; Khowaja et al., 2019). As compared to more advanced markets like China, the United States, United Kingdom, and Europe, countries in South Asia are behind in terms of awareness, acceptance, and usage of crowdfunding (Suresh et al., 2020). Considering large population and poverty levels of the countries, crowdfunding, especially, non-investment crowdfunding has the opportunity to create a substantial socio-economic impact (Arshad, 2017; Suresh et al., 2020)

In 2017, there were about 40 and 50 platforms adopting peer-to-peer (P2P) lending crowdfunding in India (Suresh et al., 2020). Donation crowdfunding was the second largest crowdfunding type by volume after peer-to-peer (P2P) lending crowdfunding in India with USD 21 million raised in 2017 (Suresh et al., 2020). As of May 2019, India has more than 25 donation crowdfunding platforms (Suresh et al., 2020). While donation crowdfunding, where backers donate products, meals, or medicine to non-governmental organisations through the crowdfunding platforms and pass them on to people in need, since 2017 medical crowdfunding has gaining momentum where donation platforms intermediate the fundraising for costly medical treatments (Suresh et al., 2020). India is an example of a crowdfunding platform that facilitates a vast variety of crowdfunding donation projects as well as individual, corporate donation, and monthly donation (Giveindia, 2021). Donation crowdfunding in India includes, but not limited to, medical, professional, personal, education, food and hunger, animals, women and girls, creative causes projects, and community development (Crowdfundingindia, 2021; Giveindia, 2021; Ketto, 2021).

India has around nine to ten reward crowdfunding as of May 2019, with approximately 5.3 million USD has raised between 2013 to 2017, 40 per cent of the amount raised was for business purposes (Suresh et al., 2020). Since the global financial crisis of 2008, financing through traditional means such as angel investors, private equity, or loan arrangements, became more challenging for small and medium enterprises, resulting in an enormous unmet debt demand (PWC, 2017). As a consequence, alternative finance such as crowdfunding has evolved to ease the establishment of start-ups that rapidly increased after the financial crisis in 2008 (Suresh et al., 2020). At the beginning of 2019, there has been around 15 crowdfunding platforms operating in India that facilitates the growth of the start-ups (Suresh et al., 2020).

A report from Ernst & Young published in 2017 indicated more than 40 per cent of the population and approximately 90 per cent of small businesses were not connected to formal financial institutions (EY, 2017 in Suresh et al., 2020). As a result of the unmet financial needs of Indian consumers and businesses from traditional finance access, alternative lending such as lending crowdfunding has emerged as one of the fastest growing segments in the Indian Fintech industry with over 225 alternative lending companies in India in 2017 (Suresh et al., 2020).

In Pakistan, the increase in crowdfunding has followed regulatory approval by the Securities and Exchange Commission of Pakistan in 2017. With the number of entrepreneurship initiatives increasing, and the start-up ecosystem maturing, the need for alternative funding approaches has been felt more and more (Ali, 2019; Arshad, 2017; Khowaja et al., 2019). A number of international platforms also operate in Pakistan, but like in India, the predominant type of crowdfunding remains donation-based. The most active crowdfunding platforms in Pakistan raise sector-specific funding targeting projects in healthcare, education, and social welfare. At least one of the country's leading platforms fills the need for Islamic-compliant investments, where backers can choose to deposit Zakat or faith-mandated alms contributions into a support fund for micro-entrepreneurs. Startup Pakistan, the government-supported enabler, reports a record 101 million USD raised in the first half of 2021, up from 66 million USD during 2020. The growth is significant, but still remains below expectations for a country with 220 million people and a growing enterprise sector.

It is imperative to ensure adequate finance access for micro, small and medium-sized enterprises in order to accelerating inclusive economic growth and achieving Bangladesh's goal of becoming a middle-income country by 2024 (United Nations, 2021). Although these enterprises play critical roles for the country, especially in terms of employment, they remain financially constrained, and predict to worsening due to the COVID-19 pandemic (United Nations, 2021).

Studies indicated that funding options have a direct impact on the start-ups social enterprises and the lack of available funding constraint the growth (Steiner & Teasdale, 2016; Sunley & Pinch, 2012). More needs to be done in relation to opening up access to support for social entrepreneurs from socially excluded backgrounds (Steiner & Teasdale, 2016). Practically, it is unrealistic to expect social enterprises to reach out or secure traditional financing, rather, social enterprises need flexible terms loans and support (Steiner & Teasdale, 2016; Sunley & Pinch, 2012).

Moreover, in Bangladesh, there has been a large financing gap and mismatch between demand and supply due to inadequate analysis and support, in particular, financing access for women entrepreneurs (United Nations, 2021). According to the United Nations report, further to limited crowdfunding services in Bangladesh, there is lack of policy and regulatory framework for the industry (United Nations, 2021).

THEORETICAL FRAMEWORK

In order to examine the potential of using social enterprise as a strategy through crowdfunding to develop Australia partnerships with South Asia, this chapter will adopt Yunus et al. (2010)'s Social Business Model Framework as the theoretical guideline. Figure 1 below demonstrates the four components of a social business model from the framework.

Value Proposition

According to the framework, the first key element is value proposition. Value proposition in the Yunus (2010)'s Social Business Model Framework includes stakeholders and products and services.

Stakeholders

Key players in social enterprise development, including government and policy makers, encourage the promotion of investment and access to finance for social development (Brown, Rocha & Cowling, 2020; United Nations, 2021). A review of the literature and observation of industry practices indicate key stakeholders in the crowdfunding consist of fundraisers and or beneficiaries, backers, intermediaries, and government bodies (Belleflamme et al., 2015; Ziegler & Shneor, 2021). Intermediaries in the crowdfunding context include the platform and financial intermediaries. The platform acts as an intermediary between fundraisers and backers that generates income by charging fees for the services from fundraisers (Belleflamme et al., 2015). The platform does not manage funding transactions by itself, otherwise it will

Figure 1. Four components of a social business model
Source: Yunus et al. (2010): Building Social Business Models: the Grameen Experience

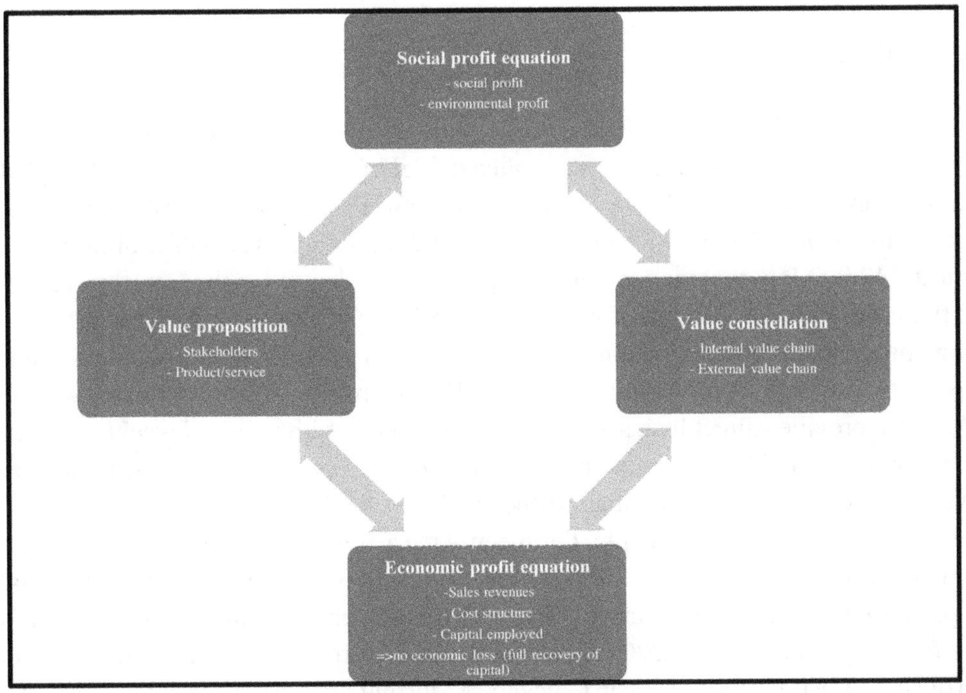

need to follow financial regulation rules (Scataglini & Ventresca, 2019). Therefore, the crowdfunding platform pays payment gateways fee to financial intermediaries or third party payment processors for funding transactions that use credit cards and third party payment (Scataglini & Ventresca, 2019). Key stakeholders that need finance access also include entrepreneurs, and organisations representing them including business chambers, trade bodies, and industry associations (United Nations, 2021). In a social enterprise context, key stakeholders include social entrepreneurs and innovators networks. Stakeholders in this proposed sector indicate a variety of groups of stakeholders that could benefit from the partnerships.

Australia's Value Proposition to the South Asian Markets

According to data reported earlier, Australia could play a vital role in providing crowdfunding services in countries in South Asia such as Bangladesh, India and Pakistan. In particular, there is a gap in loans for women entrepreneurship, social entrepreneurs, in particular, those from socially excluded backgrounds, and funding for micro, small, and medium enterprises. FinTech such as crowdfunding has changed consumer expectations and preferences, increasing user expectations of fast and easy access to services on mobile phones and other electronic devices (Vučinić, 2020). As discussed, although the concept of crowdfunding is not new, it is still in early stages, especially in developing regions such as South Asia (Suresh et al., 2020). Early entry to these markets will benefit Australia. Innovative virtual experimentation of certain social enterprises during the COVID-19 pandemic as to be discussed in the following section, value constellation, provides an insight and vision that crowdfunding social enterprises could be utilised as a strategy for Australia to develop partnership and has the ability to disrupt geographic barriers for long term relationship with South Asian countries.

Value Constellation

Yunus's (2010) Social Business Model Framework suggests value constellation as a key component for a social business model. Grameen America is a replica model of the Grameen Bank in Bangladesh which was founded by Nobel Laureate Professor Muhammad Yunus that applies several of the same principles and structure with 24 branches in 14 major cities in 2021, lending over half a billion dollars a year, serving almost 140,000 low-income women entrepreneurs (Esler & Krishnamurthy, 2021). Grameen America is the fastest and largest microfinance non-profit organisation in the United States providing loans, savings programs, credit formation and other financial services to women entrepreneurs living below the poverty line in the United States (Esler & Krishnamurthy, 2021; Grameen America, 2021). Grameen America provides direct loan access for entrepreneurs with required weekly financial training and help the borrowers build assets as well as build credit by opening savings accounts and teaching them to save every week (Esler & Krishnamurthy, 2021).

To cope with the COVID-19 pandemic, Grameen America introduced virtual center meetings with digital payments (Sharma, 2021). All Grameen America centers (2,700) hold weekly virtual meetings where groups of 30-35 entrepreneurs virtually meet for training and sharing and Grameen America team could attend from anywhere (Sharma, 2021; Esler & Krishnamurthy, 2021). Grameen America opened a new branch during COVID-19 pandemic in Chicago as a virtual branch with complete virtual operations, including opening ceremony, negotiations, training, and meetings (Sharma, 2021). During the outbreak of COVID-19, lending and repayment from borrowers of Grameen America went down significantly since 52 of borrowers passed away because of the COVID-19. However, the organisation has a 99.6 per cent repayment on recovery loans starting in August 2020 (Esler & Krishnamurthy, 2021; Sharma, 2021). Thus, value constellation from the key activities within the organisation and partnerships with key stakeholders during the pandemic was the result of digitisation. Digitisation includes virtual meetings as described earlier, loans repayment channels, and disperse loans directly to borrower accounts or onto disbursement cards, which are Grameen's proprietary cards issued and pre-planned by MasterCard to act almost like a debit card (Esler & Krishnamurthy, 2021).

Complimentary partnerships will play fundamental roles to create value constellation for Australian crowdfunding as platforms that create innovative alternative financial access to the underserved and or unserved markets. It is specifically important to have partnerships with local partners. An example could be drawn from the case of Kiva, a lending crowdfunding platform that originated from the United States. Kiva has provided loans to four million borrowers of which 81 per cent are women, from over 77 countries globally, 1.62 billion USD, or over 2.2 billion AUD was funded through the crowdfunding platform from 1.9 million lenders at 96.3 per cent repayment rate (Kiva, 2021). Kiva has partnered with over 3,000 field partners and trustees including microfinance institutes, foundations, and socially-driven enterprises, for instance, in Pakistan, the platform partners with the Kashf Foundation (Kiva, 2021).

Internal and external value chain created and captured from innovative virtual experimentation of certain social enterprises during the COVID-19 pandemic as discussed above supports findings from studies including UNSGSA (2019) that FinTech, such as crowdfunding social enterprise, directly promotes financial inclusion and exchange on financial innovation and has the ability to disrupt geographic barriers for long term relationship with South Asian countries.

Economic Profit Equation

This section discusses capital, costs, and revenues for crowdfunding businesses (Yunus et al., 2010). Sources of funding for crowdfunding platforms include grants, rewards, and private co-investment. In terms of costs, crowdfunding has high initial infrastructure costs, especially technology. Technology is a key element of crowdfunding platforms since it enables interactions between fundraisers, funders and a broader group of stakeholders (Scataglini & Ventresca, 2019).

Available data from crowdfunding websites indicates that crowdfunding platforms generate revenue from subscription fees and or service fees charging to each crowdfunding project in percentages starting from five per cent and often do not include transaction costs. While some donation crowdfunding platforms charge subscription fees, certain donation crowdfunding platforms, such as Taejai platform in Thailand, charge flat rate fees of ten per cent that cover everything including transaction costs and project performance appraisal (Taeja, 2021).

Lending-based crowdfunding's revenue is generated from both charging and no interest charging (Mitra, 2012). Under Kiva's revenue strategy, the crowdfunding receive free grants from various organisations and funding from a large number of lenders. Lenders of the platform do not receive interest, however, they receive their principle back through Kiva's field partners, or using money transfer platform PayPal (Kiva, 2021). The crowdfunding platform provides the received funds to its field partners who charge borrowers interest rates. Kiva charges platform fees from field partners (Kiva, 2021). Kiva collects the funds from individual lenders and transfers to appropriate field partners who then allocate the loans to borrowers. When borrowers repay the loans with interest, the field partners forward the funds back to Kiva. Lenders could use the repaid loans to fund new loans, donate, or withdraw the money from the crowdfunding platform (Kiva, 2021).

Despite initial high cost, FinTech such as crowdfunding social enterprise has proved to operate more efficiency and technology could further bring the cost low (UNSGSA, 2019). Findings from UNSGSA (2019) indicates specific initiatives in this context may include bilateral cooperation agreements between each country to facilitate information sharing and referral of innovation from one market to another. The agreements could be achieved on joint projects, including development of a regulatory framework on technology-led financial innovation. The cooperation will strengthen crowdfunding industry within Australia and scale up its crowdfunding industry as it expands into overseas markets.

Social Profit Equation

Access to finance has been considered as a critical factor that enables people to transform income, business, and improve quality of life (Burgess & Pande, 2003). Various types of crowdfunding platforms have attributed to socio-economic equality, meeting financial demand and inclusion (Suresh et al., 2020). In particular, considering the rapid growth of donation crowdfunding, especially during the COVID-19 pandemic, it improvises the potential for providing a sizable contribution to develop partnerships for both Australia and the South Asia region. Partnerships with South Asia in social enterprise crowdfunding will put Australia as a part of social enterprise ecosystem that alleviates economic, social and environment problems.

THE CHALLENGES

Regulations for Crowdfunding in Each Country

One of the major problems in crowdfunding complex ecosystem is the inter-agency coordination (Statistica, 2020). Crowdfunding platform business operation is directed by policy and regulatory bodies in each national sphere, in addition to self-regulation for their own procedures and individual platform members, resulting in restraint of developing into overseas markets (Shneor, 2020). Thus, most platforms remain their business operations at local with domestic focus or delimited international business activities (Shneor, 2020). That being said, donation crowdfunding is not regulated making it a global business (Scataglini & Ventresca, 2019).

Meanwhile, different alternative finance sectors are normally overseen by different regulators (World Bank & CCAF, 2019). Therefore, public authorities hold importance as a key stakeholder in terms of influencing how crowdfunding practices as an industry (World Bank & CCAF, 2019). Regulatory challenges for developing economies, especially to emerging and developing economies involves limited resources, hence technology–led innovations could create additional pressure (UNSGSA, 2019). Similar to most countries, countries in South Asia including Bangladesh and India, do not have suggested regulations for donation and reward crowdfunding (Suresh et al., 2020). Given the fact that these businesses do not offer financial return, they do not fall into regulators such as the securities market and the central bank and, instead come under other regulations related to the payment of donations and campaign content (Suresh et al., 2020). However, in India, all types of money lending, including equity and lending crowdfunding are regulated by the Reserve Bank of India, which is the central bank of India (Suresh et al., 2020). Pakistan, however has created regulatory guidelines for promoting crowdfunding, beginning with regulatory sandbox in 2017, and a formal notification in October, 2020 allowing crowdfunding.

The Issue of Trust

According to Kshetri (2015) and Suresh et al. (2020) in societies like Bangladesh, India and Pakistan, people are likely to hold a low degree of trust between strangers, hence they are less likely to contribute or invest in fundraising by strangers. While the campaign owner being friends and family is believed to positively associated with intention to support for a backer in a country context, the quality of the campaign with better media coverage may consider to be more important in another country's context (Baber, 2019; Munim et al., 2020). Ghemawat (2007) and Scataglini and Ventresca (2019) argue that countries that are closer in terms of culture, organisational administration, and level of economy could play a role in terms of a degree of challenges and trust for the crowdfunding businesses.

Mistrust could emerge from customer's doubt in relation to mission drift in a crowdfunding platform. Kiva experienced the issue with trust from social media exposure in 2009 when lenders came to know that while they willingly did not receive interests to lend money to the underprivileged in different countries in the world, the local partners of Kiva charged relatively high interests to administer the loans (Schwittay, 2019). The fact that Kiva used intermediary microfinance organisations that receive high interest rates created upset among its lenders (Schwittay, 2019). Furthermore, loans were given in advance to the person on Kiva's platform while the campaign was still running. Kiva was forced to explain and indicate explicitly in its platform that the loans backfilling and interest payments to its local partners is deemed necessary to smooth a provision of much needed loans and cover the high operation costs for microfinancing in developing markets (Kiva, 2021; Schwittay, 2019).

Financial Viability

A study on unsuccessful funded projects on crowdfunding platform Kickstarter, as of November 2020, reveals that approximately 62.8 per cent of donation crowdfunding campaigns fail and stay unfunded (Statistica, 2020). In addition, there have been concerns over infrastructure, access to, and the stability of Internet in certain areas of target population, hence the worthiness of business investment that may result in a decision not to provide services to the most needed groups (Scataglini & Ventresca, 2019).

Furthermore, rationale for the financial viability challenging crowdfunding platforms has been hinted over two different approaches termed as all or nothing and take it all (Shneor, 2020). The terms refer to the way the crowdfunded would be awarded. The first approach involved fundraisers receiving all the amount funded, also known as take it all where fundraisers take all money raised regardless of the amount (Shneor, 2020). The second approach is called all or nothing where fundraisers receive the funds raised only if the campaign has achieved minimum goal. The all or nothing approach may impose higher risks for campaigners, however, it encourages higher levels of commitment from fundraisers, hence greater success rates, whereas take it all is a popular approach in donation and other non-investment crowdfunding where certain development is preferable to none (Shneor, 2020). Crowdfunding businesses significantly sustain from fees charges, as a consequence, funding failures challenge financial viability of organisations.

SOLUTIONS AND RECOMMENDATIONS

This section considers solutions and recommendations on how Australia could collaborate with South Asian countries to provide financial assistance through using crowdfunding social enterprise as a tool to develop partnerships.

There is a strong need at government policy level to enhance ecosystem by appointing focal point to enhance policy coherence (United Nations, 2021). This is an opportunity for Australia to strengthen existing crowdfunding ecosystem in the country. Special attention could be paid to incubation and acceleration support for crowdfunding women businesses and social enterprises. Crowdfunding platforms, especially non-investment types such as donation, reward, and crowdfunded micro loans and key players should be provided with intensive support.

National policy should respond to enticements specialisation in required areas such as women owned businesses (United Nations, 2021). A variety of strategies could be applied, for instance, a focus on enterprises owned by women, businesses that provide products and services to women and girls to advance gender equality, a focus on women's participation in their workforce. The expected outcomes are to see increased number of women as recipients of alternative investments, women investors and entrepreneurs (United Nations, 2021). This could be done by building a prototype to build an initial group of crowdfunding platforms that the authority bodies plan to support for overseas expansion and then pilot the prototype carefully but rapidly to consolidate lessons and develop patterns with a focus in a single country first and gradually develop the ecosystem (Scataglini & Ventresca, 2019).

Furthermore, since there is a general lack of policy and regulatory framework in crowdfunding industry, Australia could play an important role in offering the services to mutually develop policy and regulatory framework for the industry in relevance countries. Consideration could be made to look into linking with Australian social organisations already established in different countries. This strategy does not consider only for easing the partnership development but also for cultural adjustment, considering cultural differences in the target countries.

FUTURE RESEARCH DIRECTIONS

Future research could consider strategies involved in expanding social enterprises from Australia and how they could create economic, social, and environment benefits for both Australia and the counterparts. Empirical study including case study could also be conducted to investigate lessons learned from the practitioners and key stakeholders from adopting the strategies.

From a business model perspective, research could be conducted on how social enterprises could be more innovative in providing financial access at international collaboration. How risks could be managed while exposing to opportunities. In-depth study could be conducted to examine challenges that social enterprise encountered in order to operate successfully at international level. Innovative regulatory policies development in crowdfunding services in a country, for instance, could accelerate learnings for the same in other countries.

Limitations

This study is based on conceptual research. As a consequence, it lacks empirical evidence. Delimitation is managed by providing evidence found from literature and industry practices.

CONCLUSION

Following the crisis emerging from the COVID-19 pandemic, this research paper aims to explore and posit crowdfunding social enterprise as a unique approach to create and enhance partnerships between Australia and South Asia to mitigate the economic impact of COVID-19. Financial inclusion solution such as crowdfunding social enterprise could create circumstances for achieving significant numbers, the first nine of the United Nations Sustainable Development Goals (SDGs). Bilateral crowdfunding partnerships between funding sources in Australia and social enterprises in South Asia as proposed in this chapter could also contribute to achieving SDG 10 and SDG 17, which aims at reducing of inequity within and among countries, and enhance partnering for the Goals respectively.

The rapid growth of crowdfunding could potentially serves as business area that creates, captures, and delivers value for Australia and South Asia. The analysis using Social Business Model Framework as the theoretical guideline implies potential benefits from the bilateral partnerships. This includes value being proposed to a diverse and large group of stakeholders, exchange on information and financial innovation between the regions, and referral of innovation from one market to another. Social profit equation analysis indicates partnerships could contribute to socio-economic equality, responding to financial demand, and financial inclusion.

Challenges for the implementation are recognised in the areas of regulations for crowdfunding social enterprise in each country, the issue of trust, and financial viability.

ACKNOWLEDGMENT

This research received no specific grant from any funding agency from the public, commercial, or not-for-profit sectors.

REFERENCES

Agrawal, A., & Hockerts, K. (2021). Impact Investing: Review and Research Agenda. *Journal of Small Business and Entrepreneurship, 33*(2), 153–181. doi:10.1080/08276331.2018.1551457

Ali, H. M., & Williams, R. (2019). *Stakeholder Perceptions and Influence of Crowdfunding as a Source of Entrepreneurial Funding: The Case of Pakistan. ISBE Conference.*

America, G. (2021). *Board of Directors.* Accessed date 31 August 2021 from https://www.grameenamerica.org/board

Arshad, N. (2017). Contextualizing Crowdfunding in Low-Income Countries: the Case of Pakistan. In *Contextualizing Entrepreneurship in Emerging Economies and Developing Countries.* Edward Elgar Publishing. doi:10.4337/9781785367533.00018

ASIC. (2021). *Crow-sourced-funding. Australian Securities and Investments Commission.* Accessed date 4 September from https://asic.gov.au/regulatory-resources/financial-services/crowd-sourced-funding/

Austin, J., Stevenson, H., & Wei-Skillern, J. (2006). Social and commercial entrepreneurship: Same, different, or both? *Entrepreneurship Theory and Practice, 30*(1), 1–22. doi:10.1111/j.1540-6520.2006.00107.x

Barraket, J., Douglas, H., Eversole, R., Mason, C., McNeill, J., & Morgan, B. (2017). Classifying social enterprise models in Australia. *Social Enterprise Journal, 13*(4), 345–361. doi:10.1108/SEJ-09-2017-0045

Barraket, J., Mason, C., & Blain, B. (2016). *Finding Australia's social enterprise sector 2016: Final Report.* Social Traders and Center for Social Impact Swinburne.

Barraket, J., Muir, K., Lasater, Z., Dunkley, M., Mason, C., Joyce, A., Giuntoli, G., Salignac, F., Foenander, E., & Blain, B. (2016). *Social Enterprise Development & Investment Funds (SEDIF): Evaluation Report.* Department of Employment, Canberra.

Barua, S. (2021). Understanding Coronanomics: The economic implications of the covid-19 pandemic. *Journal of Developing Areas, 55*(3), 435–450. doi:10.1353/jda.2021.0073

BattagliaF.BusatoF.ManganielloM. (2020). Equity crowdfunding: brave market or safe haven for the crowd during the Covid-19 crisis? https://ssrn.com/abstract=3666021 doi:10.2139/ssrn.3666021

Belleflamme, P., Lambert, T., & Schwienbacher, A. (2010). *Crowdfunding: An Industrial Organization.* Working Paper.

Birchal. (2021). *Overview.* Accessed date 31 August 2021 from https://www.birchal.com/company/birchal

Brau, J. C., & Woller, G. M. (2004). Microfinance: A comprehensive review of the existing literature. *Journal of Entrepreneurial Finance and Business Ventures, 9*(1), 1–28.

Brown, R., Rocha, A., & Cowling, M. (2020). Financing entrepreneurship in times of crisis: Exploring the impact of COVID-19 on the market for entrepreneurial finance in the United Kingdom. *International Small Business Journal: Researching Entrepreneurship, 38*(5), 380–390. doi:10.1177/0266242620937464

Bruton, G., Khavul, S., Siegel, D., & Wright, M. (2014). New financial alternatives in seeding entrepreneurship: Microfinance, crowdfunding, and peer-to-peer innovations. *Entrepreneurship Theory and Practice, 39*(1), 9–26. doi:10.1111/etap.12143

Bugg-Levine, A., & Emerson, J. (2011). Impact investing transforming how we make money while making a difference. *Innovations, 6*(3), 9–18. doi:10.1162/INOV_a_00077

Burgess, R., & Pande, R. (2003). *Do rural banks matter? Evidence from the Indian social banking experiment*. Discussion Paper No. DEDPS/40.

Castellas, E. I.-P., Ormiston, J., & Findlay, S. (2018). Financing social entrepreneurship: The role of impact investment in shaping social enterprise in Australia. *Social Enterprise Journal, 14*(2), 130–155. doi:10.1108/SEJ-02-2017-0006

Crowdfundingindia. (2021). *How crowdfunding in India works*. Accessed date 30 August 2021 from https://www.crowdfundingindia.org/

De Luca, V. V., Margherita, A., & Passiante, G. (2019). Crowdfunding: A systemic framework of benefits. *International Journal of Entrepreneurial Behaviour & Research, 25*(6), 1321–1339. doi:10.1108/IJEBR-11-2018-0755

Defourny, J., & Nyssens, M. (2010). Conceptions of social enterprise and social entrepreneurship in Europe and the United States: Convergences and divergences. *Journal of Social Entrepreneurship, 1*(1), 32–53.

Equitise. (2021). *Equity crowdfunding*. Accessed date 31 August 2021 from https://equitise.com/equity-crowdfunding-au

Esler, J., & Krishnamurthy, D. (2021). Grameen America: Microfinancing Having a Macroeconomic Impact - An Interview with Andrea Jung. *Social Impact Review*. Harvard Advanced Leadership Initiative. Accessed date 31 Aug. 2021 at https://sir.advancedleadership.harvard.edu/news/grameen-america-microfinancing-having-macroeconomic-impact-interview-andrea-jung?admin_panel=1

European Commission. (2016). *Crowdfunding in the EU Capital Markets Union*. Author.

Farhoud, M., Shah, S., Stenholm, P., Kibler, E., Renko, M., & Terjesen, S. (2021). Social enterprise crowdfunding in an acute crisis. *Journal of Business Venturing Insights, 15*(1), 1–6. doi:10.1016/j.jbvi.2020.e00211

Furneaux, C., & Barraket, J. (2014). Purchasing social good(s): A definition and typology of social procurement. *Public Money & Management, 34*(4), 265–272. doi:10.1080/09540962.2014.920199

Giveindia. (2021). *About Us*. Accessed date 30 August 2021 from https://www.giveindia.org/aboutus

Gofundraise. (2021). *About us*. Accessed date 17 Aug. 21 from https://www.gofundraise.com.au/articles/about-us/

Gray, M., Healy, K., & Crofts, P. (2003). Social enterprise: Is it the business of social work? *Australian Social Work*, *56*(2), 141–154. doi:10.1046/j.0312-407X.2003.00060.x

Gray, M., & Zhang, B. (2017). Crowdfunding: Understanding Diversity. In R. Martin & J. Pollard (Eds.), *Handbook on the Geographies of Money and Finance*. Edward Elgar Publishing. doi:10.4337/9781784719005.00034

Jabareen, Y. (2009). Building a Conceptual Framework: Philosophy, Definitions, and Procedure. *International Journal of Qualitative Methods*, *8*(4), 49–62. doi:10.1177/160940690900800406

Jomo, K. S., & Chowdhury, A. (2020). COVID-19 Pandemic Recession and Recovery. *Development*, *63*(1), 226–237. doi:10.105741301-020-00262-0 PMID:33223764

Kara, A., Zhou, H., & Zhou, Y. (2021). Achieving the United Nations' sustainable development goals through financial inclusion: A systematic literature review of access to finance across the globe. *International Review of Financial Analysis*, *77*(1), 1–16. doi:10.1016/j.irfa.2021.101833

Ketto. (2021). *Fundraisers*. Accessed date 30 August 2021 from https://www.ketto.org/crowdfunding/fundraisers

Khowaja, A., Khan, U., Arain, A. M., Naim, W. S., Ashraf, N. S., & Kandhro, A. I. (2019). Need of a Localized Social Network Platform for Crowdfunding in Pakistan. *International Journal of Computer Science and Network Security*, *19*(9), 210–215.

Kiva. (2021). *About Kiva*. Accessed date 1 September 2021 from https://www.kiva.org/about

Klapper, L., El-Zoghbi, M., & Hess, J. (2016). *Achieving the Sustainable Development Goals: The Role of Financial Inclusion. United Nations Secretary General's Special Advocate for Inclusive Finance for Development*. UNSGSA.

Kraus, S., Palmer, C., Kailer, N., Kallinger, F. L., & Spitzer, J. (2018). Digital entrepreneurship: A research agenda on new business models for the twenty-first century. *International Journal of Entrepreneurial Behaviour & Research*, *25*(2), 353–375. doi:10.1108/IJEBR-06-2018-0425

Lehner, M. O. (2013). Crowdfunding social ventures: A model and research agenda. *Venture Capital*, *15*(4), 289–311. doi:10.1080/13691066.2013.782624

Loosemore, M. (2016). Social procurement in UK construction projects. *International Journal of Project Management*, *34*(1), 133–144.

Miles, M. B., & Huberman, A. M. (1994). *Qualitative data analysis: An expanded source book* (2nd ed.). Sage.

Milian, E. Z., Spinola, M. D. M., & Carvalho, M. M. D. (2019). Fintechs: A literature review and research agenda. *Electronic Commerce Research and Applications*, *34*(1).

Mitra, D. (2012, July - December). The role of crowdfunding in entrepreneurial finance. *Delhi Business Review*, *13*(2), 67–72. doi:10.51768/dbr.v13i2.132201218

Moysidou, K., & Hausberg, J. P. (2020). In crowdfunding we trust: A trust-building model in lending crowdfunding. *Journal of Small Business Management, 58*(3), 511–543. doi:10.1080/00472778.2019.1661682

Mycause. (2017). *Top crowdfunding sites in Australia.* Accessed date 17 Aug. 21 at https://www.mycause.com.au/blog/top-crowdfunding-sites-in-australia

Onmarket. (2021). *What we do.* Accessed date 31 August 2021 from https://www.onmarket.com.au/about-us/what-we-do/

Parthiban, R., Qureshi, I., Bandyopadhyay, S., Bhatt, B., & Jaikumar, S. (2020). Leveraging ICT to overcome complementary institutional voids: Insights from institutional work by a social enterprise to help marginalized. *Information Systems Frontiers, 22*(1), 633–653. doi:10.100710796-020-09991-6

PWC. (2017). *Crowdfunding: Unleashing female entrepreneurial potential.* The Crowdfunding Center. PricewaterhouseCoopers.

Ratten, V. (2020). Coronavirus (covid-19) and social value co-creation. *International Journal of Sociology and Social Policy.*

ReadyFundGo. (2021). *Crowdfunding in Australia.* Access date 17 August 2021. From website https://readyfundgo.com/crowdfunding-in-australia/

Scataglini, M., & Ventresca, J. M. (2019). *Funding the UN Sustainable Development Goals: Lessons from donation-based crowdfunding platforms.* University of Oxford Said Business School Working paper, February 2019.

Schwittay, A. (2019). Digital mediations of everyday humanitarianism: The case of Kiva.org. *Third World Quarterly, 40*(10), 1921–1938. doi:10.1080/01436597.2019.1625267

Shah, F. H. (2021). *Producing Grassroots Social Business Changemakers for Smart Communities.* Keynote at the Global Smart Education Conference, Beijing Normal University.

Sharma, E. K. (2021). *Interview: Muhammad Yunus on micro-credit & social impact models for a changed world.* https://www.financialexpress.com/economy/interview-muhammad-yunus-on-micro-credit-social-impact-models-for-a-changed-world/2207167/

Shneor, R. (2020). Crowdfunding models, strategies, and choices between them. In *Advances in Crowdfunding Research and Practice.* Palgrave Macmillan. doi:10.1007/978-3-030-46309-0_2

Shneor, R., & Zhang, Z. B. (2020). The Global Status of the Crowdfunding Industry Tania Ziegler. *Advances in Crowdfunding Research and Practice.* doi:10.1007/978-3-030-46309-0

Shneor, R., & Zhao, R. (2020). Fundamentals to Advances in Crowdfunding Research and Practice. In *Advances in Crowdfunding Research and Practice.* Palgrave Macmillan.

Steiner, A., & Teasdale, S. (2016). The playground of the rich? Growing social business in the 21st century. *Social Enterprise Journal, 12*(2), 201–216. doi:10.1108/SEJ-12-2015-0036

Sunley, P., & Pinch, S. (2012). Financing social enterprise: Social bricolage or evolutionary entrepreneurialism? University of Southampton, Southampton, UK. *Social Enterprise Journal*, *8*(2), 108–122. doi:10.1108/17508611211252837

Suresh, K., Øyna, S., & Munim, Z. H. (2020). Crowdfunding prospects in new emerging markets: the cases of India and Bangladesh. In *Advances in Crowdfunding Research and Practice* (pp. 297–318). Palgrave Macmillan. doi:10.1007/978-3-030-46309-0_13

Taejai. (2021). *About*. Accessed date 1 September 2021 from https://taejai.com/en/

Teasdale, S. (2011). What's in a name? Making sense of social enterprise discourses. *Public Policy and Administration*, *27*(2), 99–119. doi:10.1177/0952076711401466

Theerthaana, P., & Hansa Lysander Manohar, L. H. (2021). How a doer persuade a donor? Investigating the moderating effects of behavioral biases in donor acceptance of donation crowdfunding. *Journal of Research in Interactive Marketing*, *15*(2), 243–266. doi:10.1108/JRIM-06-2019-0097

United Nations. (2021). *Economic and Social Commission for Asia and the Pacific, Micro, Small and Medium sized Enterprises' Access to Finance of in Bangladesh*. MSME Financing Series No. 5. Available at https://www.unescap.org/kp/2021/micro-small-and-medium-sized-enterprises-access-finance-bangladesh

UNSGSA FinTech Working Group and CCAF. (2019). *Early Lessons on Regulatory Innovations to Enable Inclusive FinTech: Innovation Offices, Regulatory Sandboxes, and RegTech*. Office of the UNSGSA and CCAF.

UNSTATS. (2021). *The Sustainable Development Goals Report 2021*. Access dated 13 October 2021 from https://unstats.un.org/sdgs/report/2021/The-Sustainable-Development-Goals-Report-2021.pdf

Volunteer, Go. (2021). *About Volunteering*. Accessed date 10 August 2021. https://govolunteer.com.au/about-volunteering/

Vučinić, M. (2020). Fintech and Financial Stability Potential Influence of FinTech on Financial Stability, Risks and Benefits. *Journal of Central Banking Theory and Practice*, *2*(2), 43–66. doi:10.2478/jcbtp-2020-0013

World Bank & CCAF (2019). *Regulating Alternative Finance: Results from a Global Regulator Survey*. Author.

Yunus, M. (2006). *Social Business Entrepreneurs Are the Solution, Skoll World Forum on Social Entrepreneurship*. Said Business School. Oxford University.

Yunus, M., Moingeon, B., & Lehmann-Ortega, L. (2010). Building social business models: Lessons from the Grameen experience. *Long Range Planning*, *43*(2), 308–325. doi:10.1016/j.lrp.2009.12.005

Ziegler, T., & Shneor, R. (2020). *The Global Alternative Finance Market Benchmarking Report: Trends, Opportunities and Challenges for Lending, Equity, and Non-Investment Alternative Finance Models. Cambridge Centre for Alternative Finance*. University of Cambridge.

Ziegler T., Shneor R. (2021). *The 2nd Global Alternative Finance Market Benchmarking Report*. Cambridge Centre for Alternative Finance. University of Cambridge.

ADDITIONAL READING

Demirgüç-Kunt, A., Klapper, L., Singer, D., Ansar, S., & Hess, J. (2018). *The Global Findex Database 2017: Measuring Financial Inclusion and the Fintech Revolution*. World Bank. doi:10.1596/978-1-4648-1259-0

KEY TERMS AND DEFINITIONS

Crowdfunding: Funding a project contributing from a number of people through the internet.

Digital Inclusion: inclusiveness of everyone to use online technology to improve quality of life and promote knowledge and wellbeing of the whole society.

Microfinance: A provision of small amount of loans to people who may not have access to regular banking services.

Social Enterprise: An organisation operating with an element of commercial activities to generate a considerable amount of income to sustain their primary social mission.

Social Enterprise Ecosystem: Contextual structures and functions in the society that could support or deteriorate social enterprise development.

Stakeholder: A group of people who may gain advantages or disadvantages from an issue of interest.

Value Constellation: Interactive activities that create value, especially among internal and external stakeholders.

Compilation of References

ABD sees robust growth for Bangladesh, fourth in Asia. (2021, September 18). *The Business Standard*. https://www.tbsnews.net/economy/adb-forecasts-68-percent-growth-bangladesh-current-fiscal-133039

Abodeeb, J., Wilson, E., & Moyle, B. (2015). Shaping destination image and identity: Insights for Arab tourism at the Gold Coast, Australia. *International Journal of Culture, Tourism and Hospitality Research*, *9*(1), 6–21. doi:10.1108/IJCTHR-06-2014-0051

ADB. (2020). *Maldives: Economic Update 2019*. Asian Development Bank. Retrieved from https://www.adb.org/sites/default/files/institutional-document/544946/maldives-economic-update-2019.pdf

Adnan, Z., Chowdhury, M., & Mallik, G. (2020). Determinants of total factor productivity in Pakistan: a time series analysis using ARDL approach. *International Review of Applied Economics*. https://www.tandfonline.com/doi/full/10.1080/02692171.2020.1792420?scroll=top&needAccess=true

Adnan, M., Abir, N., & Rahman, T. (2018). Energy scenario of Bangladesh and future challenges. *International Journal of Scientific and Engineering Research*, *9*(3), 1001–1005.

AfricLaw. (2021). *Is Covid-19 bringing out the inequalities in the delivery of health services in Mauritius?* AfricLaw. Retrieved from https://africlaw.com/2021/10/11/is-covid-19-bringing-out-the-inequalities-in-the-delivery-of-health-services-in-mauritius/#more-2391

Agrawal, A., & Hockerts, K. (2021). Impact Investing: Review and Research Agenda. *Journal of Small Business and Entrepreneurship*, *33*(2), 153–181. doi:10.1080/08276331.2018.1551457

Ahmad, S. (1992). Foreign Capital inflow and economic growth in Bangladesh. University of Dhaka.

Ahmad, A., Hassan, F., & Rizvi, S. J. (2017). A model for collaboration between Pakistani & Australian dairy farmers. *Journal of Strategy and Performance Management*, *5*(1), 4–22.

Ahmadzai, S., & McKinna, A. (2018). Afghanistan electrical energy and trans-boundary water systems analyses: Challenges and opportunities. *Energy Reports*, *4*, 435–469. doi:10.1016/j.egyr.2018.06.003

Ahmar, M. (2011). 'China in SAARC? To What Effect?': A Pakistani Perspective. *Strategic Analysis*, *35*(3), 508–510. doi:10.1080/09700161.2011.559996

Ahmed, A. (2021). *Tourism putting stress on Pakistan environment: Study*. Retrieved from https://www.dawn.com/news/1619551

Ahmed, K. U. (2004). Three Decades of Australia-Bangladesh Relations 35 three decades of Australia - Bangladesh relations: Future directions and potentials. *Journal of International Affairs*, *8*(1&2), 35–38.

Ahsan, S. M. (2013). The Microinsurance Market in Bangladesh: An Analytical Overview. *Bangladesh Development Studies, 36*, 1–54.

AIMS. (2020). *AIMS Index of Marine Industry 2020 report.* Australian Institute of Marine Science. Retrieved from https://www.aims.gov.au/aims-index-of-marine-industry

Akram, M., & Scholar, M. P. (2018). *Chinese investment in Asian country beneath the Umbrella of CPEC: A Blessing or Debt entice.* The Islamia University of Bahawalpur.

Alam F., Alam Q, Reza S, Khurshid-Ul-Alam S M, Saleque K, & Chowdhury H. (2017). Sourcing green power in Bhutan: a review. *Energy Procedia, 110*(December), 586–591. doi:10.1016/j.egypro.2017.03.189

Alam, S. (2016). *Development Planning in Bangladesh: 7th Five Year Plan and SDG Implementation. General Economics Division, Planning Commission.* Government of the People's Republic of Bangladesh, June.

Alam, S., Mukhopadhya, P., & Islam, M. R. (2013). The Australia India proposed Free Trade Agreement and trade in agriculture: Opportunities and challenges. *The Journal of World Investment & Trade, 14*(1), 167–197. doi:10.1163/22119000-01401006

Aldrighetti, R., Zenmaro, I., Fianco, S., & Battini, D. (2019). Healthcare Supply Chain Simulation with Disruption Considerations: A Case Study from Northern Italy. *Global Journal of Flexible Systems Managment, 20*(1), S81–S102. doi:10.100740171-019-00223-8

Ali, M. (2020, December 27). Bangladesh's economy to be 25th largest by 2035 [Review of *Bangladesh's economy to be 25th largest by 2035*]. *The Business Standard.* https://www.tbsnews.net/economy/bangladeshs-economy-be-25th-largest-2035-177334

Ali, H. M., & Williams, R. (2019). *Stakeholder Perceptions and Influence of Crowdfunding as a Source of Entrepreneurial Funding: The Case of Pakistan. ISBE Conference.*

Al-Mulali, U., Fereidouni, H. G., Lee, J. Y., & Sab, C. N. B. C. (2013). Examining the bi-directional long run relationship between renewable energy consumption and GDP growth. *Renewable & Sustainable Energy Reviews, 22*, 209–222. doi:10.1016/j.rser.2013.02.005

America, G. (2021). *Board of Directors.* Accessed date 31 August 2021 from https://www.grameenamerica.org/board

Anderson, J. E., & Yotov, V. (2016). Terms of trade and global efficiency effects of free trade agreements,1990–2002. *Journal of International Economics, 99*, 279–298. doi:10.1016/j.jinteco.2015.10.006

Anolick, N., Batten, J. A., Kinateder, H., & Wagner, N. (2021). Time for gift giving: Abnormal share repurchase returns and uncertainty. *Journal of Corporate Finance, 66*(101787), 101787. Advance online publication. doi:10.1016/j.jcorpfin.2020.101787

Anukoonwattaka, W., Romao, P., & Lobo, R. S. (2021). If the US-China trade war is here to stay, what are the risks and opportunities for other GVC economies outside the war zone? (No. 209). *ARTNeT Working Paper Series.*

Anwar, A., Arshed, N., & Nabeela Kousar, N. (2017). Renewable Energy Consumption and Economic Growth in Member of OIC Countries. *European Online Journal of Natural and Social Sciences*, 111–129.

Apergis, N. & Danuletiu, D. C. (2014). Renewable energy and economic growth: Evidence from the sign of panel long-run causality. *International Journal of Energy Economics and Policy,* 578-587.

Apergis, N., & Payne, J. E. (2010). Renewable energy consumption and economic growth: Evidence from a panel of OECD countries. *Energy Policy, 38*(1), 656–660. doi:10.1016/j.enpol.2009.09.002

Apergis, N., & Payne, J. E. (2012). Renewable and non-renewable energy consumption-growth nexus: Evidence from a panel error correction model. *Energy Economics*, *34*(3), 733–738. doi:10.1016/j.eneco.2011.04.007

ARENA. (2021). *Renewable Energy*. ARENA. Retrieved from https://arena.gov.au/renewable-energy/ocean/#main

ArmstrongS. (2011). Asian Trade structures and trade potential: An initial analysis of South and East Asian Trade. SSRN.

Aronshtam, L., Shrot, T., & Shmallo, R. (2021). Can we do better? A classification of algorithm run-time-complexity improvement using the SOLO taxonomy. *Education and Information Technologies*, *1*(5), 1–22. doi:10.100710639-021-10532-0

Arshad, N. (2017). Contextualizing Crowdfunding in Low-Income Countries: the Case of Pakistan. In *Contextualizing Entrepreneurship in Emerging Economies and Developing Countries*. Edward Elgar Publishing. doi:10.4337/9781785367533.00018

Asialink. (2019). *Where we Live*. Address to Asialink PM Scott Morrison. Retrieved from https://asialink.unimelb.edu.au/stories/australia-and-the-indo-pacific-an-address-by-prime-minister-scott-morrison

Asian Development Bank and United Nations Development Program. (2017). *Assessment of Sri Lanka's power sector: 100% electricity generation through renewable energy by 2050*. Retrieved from https://www.adb.org/publications/electricity-generation-renewable-energy-2050-sri-lanka

Asian Development Bank. (2017). *Nepal energy sector assessment, strategy, and roadmap*. doi:10.22617/TCS178936-2

Asian Development Bank. (2020). *A Brighter Future for Maldives Powered by Renewables: Road Map for the Energy Sector 2020–2030*. Retrieved from https://www.adb.org/sites/default/files/publication/654021/renewables-roadmap-energy-sector-maldives.pdf

Asia-Pacific Trade and Investment Report 2016. (2016). Retrieved from https://repository.unescap.org/bitstream/handle/20.500.12870/155/ESCAP-2016-FS-APTIR-executive-summary.pdf?sequence=5&isAllowed=y

ASIC. (2021). *Crow-sourced-funding. Australian Securities and Investments Commission*. Accessed date 4 September from https://asic.gov.au/regulatory-resources/financial-services/crowd-sourced-funding/

Asif, M., & Barua, D. (2011). Salient features of the Grameen Shakti renewable energy program. *Renewable & Sustainable Energy Reviews*, *15*(9), 5063–5067. doi:10.1016/j.rser.2011.07.050

Athukorala, P. C. (2020). Trump's Trade War: An Indian Perspective. *Asian Economic Papers*, *19*(1), 92–109. doi:10.1162/asep_a_00749

Augustin, B. (2021, Sept. 29). Australia–Bangladesh: A booster dose for trade diversity? *The Daily Star*.

Augustin, B. (2021, September 24). *Australia–Bangladesh: A Booster Dose for Trade Diversity?* [Review of *Australia–Bangladesh: A Booster Dose for Trade Diversity?*]. Australia Outlook; Australian Institute of International Affairs. https://www.internationalaffairs.org.au/australianoutlook/australia-bangladesh-a-booster-dose-for-trade-diversity/

Augustyn, M. M., & Knowles, T. (2000). Performance of tourism partnerships: A focus on York. *Tourism Management*, *21*(4), 341–351. doi:10.1016/S0261-5177(99)00068-0

Austin, J., Stevenson, H., & Wei-Skillern, J. (2006). Social and commercial entrepreneurship: Same, different, or both? *Entrepreneurship Theory and Practice*, *30*(1), 1–22. doi:10.1111/j.1540-6520.2006.00107.x

Austrade. (2021). *Food and Beverage to Bangladesh: Trends and Opportunities*. Australian Government, Australian Trade and Investment Commission.

Austrade. (2021). *Growth and opportunity in Australian international education.* Retrieved from: https://www.austrade.gov.au/australian/education/services/australian-international-education-2025/growth-and-opportunity

Australia Awards Global Tracer Facility Bangladesh Case Study: Economic Development. (2019). https://www.dfat.gov.au/sites/default/files/australia-awards-global-tracer-facility-bangladesh-alumni-case-study.pdf

Australia Bangladesh Chamber of Commerce and Industry. (2021). *Australia Bangladesh Relation.* Retrieved from https://abccibd.com/project/startups-consulting/

Australia India Business Exchange. (2021). *Austrade.* https://www.austrade.gov.au/australia-india-business-exchange

Australia Trade Commission. (2016). *Medical devices and diagnostics.* Sydney: Commonwealth of Australia.

Australia's development partnership with Bangladesh. (n.d.). *Australian Government Department of Foreign Affairs and Trade.* Retrieved from https://www.dfat.gov.au/geo/bangladesh/development-assistance/development-assistance-in-bangladesh

Australia-India Comprehensive Economic Cooperation Agreement (AI-CECA). (2020). *Australian Government Department of Foreign Affairs and Trade.* https://www.dfat.gov.au/trade/agreements/negotiations/aifta/australia-india-comprehensive-economic-cooperation-agreement

Australia-India Council (AIC). (2019). *Australia-India Council.* Retrieved from dfat.gov.au/people-to-people/foundations-councils-institutes/australia-india-council/governance/Pages/australia-india-council-strategic-plan-2017-2020.aspx

Australia-India Council. (2020). *Australia and India. A dynamic mix.* https://www.dfat.gov.au/people-to-people/foundations-councils-institutes/australia-india-council/adynamicmix/Pages/default

Australian Bureau of Statistics (ABS). (2020). *Australia's Trade in Goods with China in 2020.* https://www.abs.gov.au/articles/australias-trade-goods-china-2020

Australian Bureau of Statistics (ABS). (2021). *International Merchandise Trade, Preliminary, Australia.* https://www.abs.gov.au/statistics/economy/international-trade/international-merchandise-trade-preliminary-australia/jan-2021

Australian Bureau of Statistics (ABS). (2021a). *30% of Australia's Population Born Overseas, Preliminary, Australia.* https://www.abs.gov.au/media-centre/media-releases/30-australias-population-born-overseas

Australian Bureau of Statistics (ABS). (2021b). *Labour Force, Australia.* https://www.abs.gov.au/statistics/labour/employment-and-unemployment/labour-force-australia/latest-release

Australian Bureau of Statistics (ABS). (2021c). *Australia's National Accounts: National Income, Expenditure and Products.* https://www.abs.gov.au/statistics/economy/national-accounts/australian-national-accounts-national-income-expenditure-and-product/latest-release

Australian Bureau of Statistics (ABS). (2021d). *International Merchandise Trade*, Preliminary, Australia. https://www.abs.gov.au/statistics/economy/international-trade/international-merchandise-trade-preliminary-australia/jan-2021

Australian Digital Health Agency (ADHA). (2019). *My Health Record.* Retrieved from https://www.myhealthrecord.gov.au/for-you-your-family/what-is-my-health-record

Australian Government Department of Foreign Affairs and Trade. (2014). *The Lessons of European Integration for the Indo Pacific.* https://www.dfat.gov.au/news/speeches/Pages/140616_anu

Australian Government Medicare. (2021). *Medicare Services in Australia.* Retrieved from https://www.health.gov.au/health-topics/medicare

Australian Government. (2021). *COVID-19 Corona Vaccine rollout strategy*. Retrieved from https://www.australia.gov.au/covid19vaccines

Australian International School-Dhaka. (2021). Retrieved from https://www.ausisdhaka.net/

Azim, M. A. (2019). Bangladesh-China economic relations: Opportunities and challenges. In D. Hossain (Ed.), *Bangladesh-East Asia relations: Changing scenarios and evolving linkages* (pp. 119–141). East Asia Study Center, University of Dhaka.

Badar, H., Ariyawardana, A., & Collins, R. (2015). Capturing consumer preferences for value chain improvements in the mango industry of Pakistan. *International Food and Agribusiness Management Review, 18*, 131-148.

Bajaj, M., & Kidwai, H. (2016). *Human rights and education policy in South Asia*. Academic Press.

Bajpaee, C. (2017). Dephasing India's look East/Act east policy. *Contemporary Southeast Asia*, *39*(2), 348–372. doi:10.1355/cs39-2d

Bakas, D., & Triantafyllou, A. (2020). Commodity price volatility and the economic uncertainty of pandemics. *Economics Letters*, *193*(109283), 109283. Advance online publication. doi:10.1016/j.econlet.2020.109283

Balassa, B. (1986). Policy responses to exogenous shocks in developing countries. *The American Economic Review*, *1986*(5), 75–78.

Bandara, J. S., & Smith, C. (2002). Trade Policy Reforms in South Asia and Australia-South Asia Trade: Intensities and Complementarities. *South Asia Economic Journal*, *3*(2), 177–199. doi:10.1177/139156140200300204

Bandara, J., & Yu, W. (2003). How Desirable Is the South Asian Free Trade Area? A Quantitative Economic Assessment. *World Economy*, *26*(9), 1293–1323. doi:10.1046/j.1467-9701.2003.00574.x

Bangladesh at 50: Navigating Strategic Survival. (2021, April 26). *War on the Rocks*. https://warontherocks.com/2021/04/bangladesh-at-50-navigating-strategic-survival

Bangladesh Bank. (2021). https://www.bb.org.bd/en/index.php

Bangladesh Government Power Division. (2021). *Annual Report 2019-20*. https://powerdivision.gov.bd/sites/default/files/files/powerdivision.portal.gov.bd/annual_reports/7d86d53d_5ebb_408d_8839_64d1a9eea653/ANNUAL%20REPORT-%202019-2020%20.pdf

Bangladesh has highest number of LEED platinum-rated garment factories. (2019, September 19). *Bangladesh Textile Today*. https://www.textiletoday.com.bd/topics/usgbc/

Bangladesh in Top Five Growing Economies: WB. (2019, April 4). *The Daily Star*. https://www.thedailystar.net/world/news/bangladesh-top-5-growing-economy-wb-1724815

Bangladesh Military Strength. (2021). www.globalfirepower.com. https://www.globalfirepower.com/country-military-strength-detail.php?country_id=bangladesh

Bank, W. (2017). *Number of Maternal deaths in South Asian Countries*. Retrieved from https://data.worldbank.org/indicator/SH.MMR.DTHS?locations=8S

Barraket, J., Mason, C., & Blain, B. (2016). *Finding Australia's social enterprise sector 2016: Final Report*. Social Traders and Center for Social Impact Swinburne.

Barraket, J., Muir, K., Lasater, Z., Dunkley, M., Mason, C., Joyce, A., Giuntoli, G., Salignac, F., Foenander, E., & Blain, B. (2016). *Social Enterprise Development & Investment Funds (SEDIF): Evaluation Report*. Department of Employment, Canberra.

Barraket, J., Douglas, H., Eversole, R., Mason, C., McNeill, J., & Morgan, B. (2017). Classifying social enterprise models in Australia. *Social Enterprise Journal, 13*(4), 345–361. doi:10.1108/SEJ-09-2017-0045

Barrymore, S. (2017). Decommissioning of Australia's oil and gas facilities in the 21st century. *APPEA Journal, 57*(2), 397. doi:10.1071/AJ16004

Bartelmus. (2013). *Sustainability economics-An introduction*. Routledge.

Barua, M. (2019). A Survey of Cross-Country Generation Mix - Opportunities and Challenges: Bangladesh, Australia, and the U.S.A Perspectives. *International Conference on Electrical, Computer and Communication Engineering (ECCE)*, 1-6. 10.1109/ECACE.2019.8679344

Barua, S. (2021). Understanding Coronanomics: The economic implications of the covid-19 pandemic. *Journal of Developing Areas, 55*(3), 435–450. doi:10.1353/jda.2021.0073

Bashkar, S., Tan, J., Bogers, M., Minssen, M., Badarrudin, H., Isreali-Korn, S., & Chesbrough, H. (2020). At the Epicenter of COVID-19–the Tragic Failure of the Global Supply Chain for Medical Supplies. *Frontier in Public Health*.

Basray, R., Malik, A., Waqar, W., Chaudhry, A., Malik, M. W., Kham, M. A., Ansari, J. A., & Ikram, A. (2021). Impact of environmental factors on COVID-19 cases and mortalities in major cities of Pakistan. *Journal of Biosafety and Biosecurity, 3*(1), 10–16. doi:10.1016/j.jobb.2021.02.001 PMID:33786420

Bassey, M. (1999). *Case Study Research in Educational Settings*. Open University Press.

Batra, P. (2017). Imperatives of comparative and international education: Some reflections from the south. In A. W. Wiseman (Ed.), *Annual review of comparative and international education*. Emerald Publishing Ltd.

Batra, P. (2019). *Comparative Education in South Asia: Contribution*. Contestation, and Possibilities., doi:10.1108/S1479-367920190000036011

BattagliaF.BusatoF.ManganielloM. (2020). Equity crowdfunding: brave market or safe haven for the crowd during the Covid-19 crisis? https://ssrn.com/abstract=3666021 doi:10.2139/ssrn.3666021

Bauso, A. O. (2021). *25 Most Beautiful Beaches in the World*. Travel + Leisure. Retrieved from https://www.travelandleisure.com/trip-ideas/beach-vacations/most-beautiful-beaches-in-the-world

BBC. (2021). *Mauritius reopens to fully vaccinated tourists*. BBC. Retrieved from https://www.bbc.com/news/topics/cdl8n2edxept/mauritius

Belleflamme, P., Lambert, T., & Schwienbacher, A. (2010). *Crowdfunding: An Industrial Organization*. Working Paper.

Berg, A., Chhaparia, H., Hedrich, S., & Magnus, K.-H. (2021, March). *What's next for Bangladesh's garment industry, after a decade of growth?* Retrieved from https://www.mckinsey.com/: https://www.mckinsey.com/industries/retail/our-insights/whats-next-for-bangladeshs-garment-industry-after-a-decade-of-growth

Berg, B. (2001). *Qualitative research methods for the social sciences* (4th ed.). Allyn & Bacon.

Bhaskar, N. J. (2019). *Examining the potential of India–Australia partnerships in mining*. Observer Research Foundation. https://www.orfonline.org/research/examining-the-potential-of-india-australia-partnerships-in-mining-49983/

Bhaskar, N. J. (2020). *India's Australia Economic Strategy: A big push to bilateral trade*. Business Today. https://www.businesstoday.in/opinion/columns/story/india-releases-australia-economic-strategy-to-give-a-big-push-to-bilateral-trade-between-both-countries-282654-2020-12-26

Bhatacharya, S., Hossain, M. M., & Singh, A. (2020). Addressing the shortage of personal protective equipment during the COVID-19 pandemic in India-A public health perspective. *AIMS Public Health*, *7*(2), 223–227. doi:10.3934/publichealth.2020019 PMID:32617351

Bhattacharya, N. (2021, May 18). *China's warning to Bangladesh on the Quad*. Retrieved from https://thediplomat.com/2021/05/chinas-warning-to-bangladesh-on-the-quad/

Bhattacharya, D. (1993). Competing for global resources: Perspective on Foreign investment in South Asia. *Bank Parikrama*, *17*(3&4), 104–114.

Bhosale, S. (2018). Why India is Emerging as Australia's Natural Ally. *The Sydney Moring Herald*. Retrieved from https://www.smh.com.au/world/asia/why-india-is-emerging-as-australia-s-natural-ally-20180905-p501yp.html

Bhowmick, S., Saha, R., & Basu, P. (2019). *India and Australia: From 4000 Nautical Miles to 22 Yard*. Observer Research Foundation. https://www.orfonline.org/wp-content/uploads/2019/10/ORF_OccasionalPaper_219_India-Australia.pdf

Bhutan Ministry of Health. (2010). Health population & nutrition sector strategic plan (HPNSSP) 2011 – 2016. Ministry of Health.

Bhuyan,M.A.(2012). Performance of the Bangladesh Economy during FY2011-12 and outlook for the near term. *Thoughts on Economics*, *22*(3).

BIDA. (2021). *Why Bangladesh* [Review of *Why Bangladesh*]. Bangladesh Investment Development Authority; Government of the People's Republic of Bangladesh. https://bida.gov.bd/

Biggs, J. (2003). *Teaching for quality learning at university: What the student does*. Society for Research into Higher Education & Open University Press.

Biggs, J., & Collins, K. F. (1982). *Evaluating the Quality of Learning: The SOLO Taxonomy*. Academic Press.

Biggs, J., & Tang, C. (2007). *Teaching for quality learning at university*. Open University Press.

Bilgili, F., & Ozturk, I. (2015a). Biomass energy and economic growth nexus in G7 countries: Evidence from dynamic panel data. *Renewable & Sustainable Energy Reviews*, *49*, 132–138. doi:10.1016/j.rser.2015.04.098

Bilgili, F., & Ozturk, I. (2015b). Economic growth and biomass consumption nexus: Dynamic panel analysis for Sub-Sahara African countries. *Applied Energy*, 110–116.

Birchal. (2021). *Overview*. Accessed date 31 August 2021 from https://www.birchal.com/company/birchal

Blakers, A. (2019). *An Australian model for the renewable-energy transition*. Retrieved from https://www.lowyinstitute.org/the-interpreter/australian-model-renewable-energy-transition

Bloomberg Economics. (2021, April 28). Australia, Japan, and India form Supply Chain initiative to counter China. *Bloomberg*.

Bloomberg. (2021). *India, Australia Deepen Defense, Trade Ties Amid China Tensions*. https://www.bloomberg.com/news/articles/2021-0

Bokhari, K. (2017, November 21). *China's One Belt, One Road Faces Pushback*. Geopolitical Futures. https://geopoliticalfutures.com/chinas-one-belt-one-road-faces-pushback/

Bond, T., Partridge, J., Taylor, M., Langlois, T., Malseed, B., Smith, L., & McLean, D. (2018). Fish associated with a subsea pipeline and adjacent seafloor of the northwest shelf of western Australia. *Marine Environmental Research, 141*, 53–65. doi:10.1016/j.marenvres.2018.08.003 PMID:30107887

Borden, N. H. (1964). The concept of the marketing mix. *Journal of Advertising Research, 1*(1), 2–7.

Brahma Chellaney. (2017, January 23). *China's debt-trap diplomacy*. The Strategist. https://www.aspistrategist.org.au/chinas-debt-trap-diplomacy/

Brau, J. C., & Woller, G. M. (2004). Microfinance: A comprehensive review of the existing literature. *Journal of Entrepreneurial Finance and Business Ventures*, *9*(1), 1–28.

Breen, K., & Birrel, B. (2020). Selling medical education to international students: Time for review. *Internal Medicine Journal*, *50*(5), 635–637. doi:10.1111/imj.14821 PMID:32431028

Brewster, D. (2014). *Australia-India Strategic Relations: The Odd Couple of the Indian Ocean?* Future Directions International Associate Paper. https://www.futuredirections.org.au/wp-content/uploads/2014/05/Australia-India_Strategic_Relations_-_The_Odd_Couple_of_the_Indian_Ocean_.pdf

Brewster, D. (2021). New Indo-Pacific Partnership: Building Australia-Bangladesh Security Ties [Review of *New Indo-Pacific Partnership: Building Australia-Bangladesh Security Ties*]. In *Australian National University* (pp. 1–4). National Security College, Australian National University. https://nsc.crawford.anu.edu.au/sites/default/files/publication/nsc_crawford_anu_edu_au/2021-06/nsc_policy_options_paper_bangladesh_web_1.pdf

Brewster, D. (2021). *New Indo-Pacific Partnership: Building Australia-Bangladesh Security Ties policy options paper no. 20.* Retrieved from https://nsc.crawford.anu.edu.au/sites/default/files/publication/nsc_crawford_anu_edu_au/2021-06/nsc_policy_options_paper_bangladesh_web_1.pdf

Brewster. (2019). *Australia should pursue opportunities in a booming Bangladesh.* Retrieved from https://www.lowyinstitute.org/the-interpreter/australia-should-pursue-opportunities-booming-bangladesh

Brewster, D. (2010). The Australia–India Security Declaration. *Security Challenges*, *6*(1), 1–9.

Brookfield, S. D., & Preskill, S. (1999). *Discussion as a way of teaching: Tools and techniques for democratic classrooms*. Jossey-Bass.

Brown, R., Rocha, A., & Cowling, M. (2020). Financing entrepreneurship in times of crisis: Exploring the impact of COVID-19 on the market for entrepreneurial finance in the United Kingdom. *International Small Business Journal: Researching Entrepreneurship*, *38*(5), 380–390. doi:10.1177/0266242620937464

Bruton, G., Khavul, S., Siegel, D., & Wright, M. (2014). New financial alternatives in seeding entrepreneurship: Microfinance, crowdfunding, and peer-to-peer innovations. *Entrepreneurship Theory and Practice*, *39*(1), 9–26. doi:10.1111/etap.12143

Bryman, A. (1988). *Quantity and Quality in Social Research*. Routledge.

Bugg-Levine, A., & Emerson, J. (2011). Impact investing transforming how we make money while making a difference. *Innovations*, *6*(3), 9–18. doi:10.1162/INOV_a_00077

Burgess, R., & Pande, R. (2003). *Do rural banks matter? Evidence from the Indian social banking experiment*. Discussion Paper No. DEDPS/40.

Burgess, L., Parish, B., & Alcock, C. (2011). To what extent are regional tourism organisations (RTOs) in Australia leveraging the benefits of web technology for destination marketing and eCommerce? *Electronic Commerce Research, 11*(3), 341–355. doi:10.100710660-011-9077-1

Burke, W., Oseni, T., Jolfraei, A., & Gongal, I. (2019). Cybersecurity Indexes for eHealth. *Proceedings of the Australasian Computer Science Week Multiconference*, 1-18. 10.1145/3290688.3290721

Burkot, C. (2015). *BRAC and the Australian aid program.* Retrieved from https://devpolicy.org/brac-and-the-australian-aid-program-20150602/

Business Opportunities in India: Investment Ideas, Industry Research, Reports. (n.d.). https://www.ibef.org

Byron, R. K. (2018, September 4). LNG to come from Oman too. *The Daily Star*. https://www.thedailystar.net/frontpage/lng-come-oman-too-1564528

Byron, R. K. (2021, February 17). Dhaka-Sylhet Highway: Big plan for wider road [Review of *Dhaka-Sylhet Highway: Big plan for wider road*]. *The Daily Star*. https://www.thedailystar.net/backpage/news/dhaka-sylhet-highway-large-plan-big-stretch-2046049

Byron, R. K., & Mirdha, R. U. (2021, September 4). Becoming a Developing Nation: Bangladesh Reaches A Mile Milestone. *The Daily Star.* https://www.thedailystar.net/frontpage/news/becoming-developing-nation-bangladesh-reaches-milestone-2052161

Cairns, G. (2007). Postcard from Chittagong: Wish you were here? *Critical Perspectives on International Business, 3*(3), 266–279. doi:10.1108/17422040710775030

Callander, E., Fox, H., & Lindsay, D. (2019). Out-of-pocket healthcare expenditure in Australia: Trends, inequalities and the Impact on household living standards in ahigh-income country with a universalhealth care system. *Health Economics Review, 9*(1), 10. doi:10.118613561-019-0227-9 PMID:30859357

Capital. (2014, August 26). *The State Council, The People's Republic of China.* Retrieved from http://english.www.gov.cn

Carreno, I., Dole, T., Medina, L., & Brandenburger, M. (2020). The Implications of the COVID-19 Pandemic on Trade. *European Journal of Risk Regulation.*

Castellas, E. I.-P., Ormiston, J., & Findlay, S. (2018). Financing social entrepreneurship: The role of impact investment in shaping social enterprise in Australia. *Social Enterprise Journal, 14*(2), 130–155. doi:10.1108/SEJ-02-2017-0006

Census of India. (2011). *Census of India 2011. Provisional Population Totals.* New Delhi: Office of the Registrar General & Census Commissioner, Government of India. Retrieved from http:// www.censusindia.gov.in/2011census/c-01.html

Chadha, R., Pohit, S., & Pratap, D. (2019). The US-China Trade War: Impact on India and Its Policy Choices (No. 119). New Delhi: National Council of Applied Economic Research.

Chakma, J. (2021, February 7). Steel exports jump 83pc. *The Daily Star*. https://www.thedailystar.net/business/news/steel-exports-jump-83pc-2040485

Chakraborty, A. (2020). *Foreign partnerships in Indian higher education: Significance, challenges and concerns.* Globalization, Societies, and Education. https://www.tandfonline.com/doi/pdf/10.1080/14767724.2020.1861439

Chakraborty, D., Chaisse, J., & Xu, Q. I. A. N. (2019). Is it finally time for India's free trade agreements? the ASEAN "Present" and the RCEP "Future". *Asian Journal of International Law, 9*(2), 359–391. doi:10.1017/S2044251319000043

Chandler, J., White, D., Techera, E. J., Gourvenec, S., & Draper, S. (2017). Engineering and legal considerations for decommissioning of offshore oil and gas infrastructure in Australia. *Ocean Engineering, 131*, 338–347. doi:10.1016/j.oceaneng.2016.12.030

Changoiwala, P. (2020, June 23). *Why South Asia's COVID-19 Numbers Are So Low (For Now)*. Retrieved from https://www.quantamagazine.org/why-south-asias-covid-19-numbers-are-so-low-for-now-20200623/

Chang, T., Gupta, R., Inglesi-Lotz, R., Simo-Kengne, B., Smithers, D., & Trembling, A. (2015). Renewable energy and growth: Evidence from heterogeneous panel of G7 countries using Granger causality. *Renewable & Sustainable Energy Reviews, 52*, 1405–1412. doi:10.1016/j.rser.2015.08.022

Chellaney, B. (2017, January 23). *China's Debt-Trap Diplomacy*. Project Syndicate. https://www.project-syndicate.org/commentary/china-one-belt-one-road-loans-debt-by-brahma-chellaney-2017-01

China Power. (2018). *How dominant is China in the global arms trade?* https://chinapower.csis.org/china-global-arms-trade/

China Trade: Balancing Opportunities & Risks in One Belt One Road. (2018, December 12). *The One Brief*. https://theonebrief.com/chinas-global-ambition-balancing-opportunities-and-risks-in-one-belt-one-road/

China's trade ties with Bangladesh are deepening. (2021, July 14). *Dhaka Tribune*. https://www.dhakatribune.com/business/economy/2021/07/14/china-s-trade-ties-with-bangladesh-are-deepening

Chinese Ambassador Proposes belt and Road mechanism for Bangladesh. (2018). HTTPS://BDNEWS24.COM/NEIGHBOURS/2018/09/11/CHINESE-ambassador-proposesbelt-and-roadmechanismfor-bangladesh

Chittagong-Cox's Bazar Railway Line - Railway Technology. (n.d.). Retrieved November 20, 2021, from https://www.railway-technology.com/projects/chittagong-coxs-bazar-railway-line/

Cho, S., Heo, E., & Kim, J. (2015). Causal relationship between renewable energy consumption and economic growth: Comparison between developed and less-developed countries. *Geosystem Engineering*, 284-291.

Chockalingam, G. C. G., & Sivasamy, D. K. (2021). A Perspective Study of Ship breaking in India and the Impact of International Conventions and Regulations. *IIRE Journal of Maritime Research and Development, 5*(1). https://ojsiire.com/index.php/IJMRD/article/view/168

Cho, S. W., & Yoon, G. (2014). Sectoral analysis of an Australia–India free trade agreement. *Journal of the Asia Pacific Economy, 19*(2), 205–229. doi:10.1080/13547860.2013.820469

Chowdhury, M. (2005). Trade reforms and economic integration in South Asia: SAARC to SAPTA. *Applied Econometrics and International Development, 5*(4), 23-40.

Chowdhury, M. B. (2019). Australia Bangladesh trade and investment potential. *ABBC Business Journal*, 64-68.

Chowdhury, M. B. (2021). Internationalisation of education and its effect on economic growth and development. *World Economy, 00*, 1–20. https://doi.org/10.1111/twec.13174

Chronology of China's Belt and Road Initiative. (2015, March 28). *The State Council, The People's Republic of China*. Retrieved from http://english.www.gov.cn

CIA. (2021, March 11). *The World Factbook*. Www.cia.gov. https://www.cia.gov/the-world-factbook/

Cipla. (2021, October). *About Us*. Retrieved from cipla.com: https://www.cipla.com/about-us

Clean Energy Council (CEC). (2020). *Clean Energy Australia Report 2020*. Retrieved from https://assets.cleanenergycouncil.org.au/documents/resources/reports/clean-energy-australia/clean-energy-australia-report-2020.pdf

COMESA. (2021). *Common Market for Eastern and Southern Africa*. https://www.comesa.int/members/

Commission, B. P. (2020, March). *General Economic Division*. Www.plancomm.gov.bd. http://www.plancomm.gov.bd/sites/default/files/files/plancomm.portal.gov.bd/files/10509d1f_aa05_4f93_9215_f81fcd233167/2020-08-31-16-

Commonwealth of Australia. (2017). *Complimentary medicine*. Commonwealth of Australia.

Consulate General of Bangladesh. (2021). *Bangladesh-Australia Trade Relations* [Review of Bangladesh-Australia Trade Relations]. Consulate General of Bangladesh, Sydney; Government of People's Republic of Bangladesh. https://cgbdsydney.gov.bd/trade-and-investment/trade/

Contu, D., Elshareif, E. E., & Gurrib, I. (2021). Assessing Views towards Energy Sources with Social Media Data: The Case of Nuclear Energy in the UAE. *Processes (Basel, Switzerland)*, *9*(11), 1945. doi:10.3390/pr9111945

Craik, J. (1995). Are there cultural limits to tourism? *Journal of Sustainable Tourism*, *3*(2), 87–98. doi:10.1080/09669589509510713

Creswell, J. W. (2003). *Research design: Qualitative, quantitative, and mixed methods approach*. SAGE.

Creswell, J. W. (2014). *Qualitative Inquiry and Research Design: Choosing Among Five Approaches* (3rd ed.). SAGE.

Crowdfundingindia. (2021). *How crowdfunding in India works*. Accessed date 30 August 2021 from https://www.crowdfundingindia.org/

Crowe, S. M., & Middeldorp, J. (1996). A comparison of leg before wicket rates between Australians and their visiting teams for test cricket series played in Australia, 1977–94. *The Statistician*, *45*(2), 255–262. doi:10.2307/2988414

Cullinane, B., & Gourvenec, S. (2017). Decommissioning – the next Australian oil and gas boom? *APPEA Journal*, *57*(2), 421. doi:10.1071/AJ16203

D'Ambrogio, E. (2021). The Quad: An emerging multilateral security framework of democracies in the Indo-Pacific region. *European Parliament Research Services*. Available at https://www.europarl.europa.eu/RegData/etudes/BRIE/2021/690513/EPRS_BRI(2021)690513_EN.pdf

Dallimore, E. J., Hertenstein, J. H., & Platt, M. B. (2006). Nonvoluntary Class Participation in Graduate Discussion Courses: Effects of Grading and Cold Calling. *Journal of Management Education*, *30*(2), 354–377. doi:10.1177/1052562905277031

Das, R. U., & Dubey, J. D. (2020). *Mechanics of Intra-Industry Trade and FTA Implications for India in RCEP*. Academic Press.

Das, S. (2017). Impact of intellectual capital on business performance: Evidence from Indian pharmaceutical sector. *Polish Journal of Management Studies*.

DATABD. (2019). *Timber and furniture*. https://databd.co/profiles/industries/profile-timber-and-furniture

DATABD. (2020). *Prospects of Plastics Sector: A Rarely Told Story*. https://databd.co/stories/prospects-of-plastics-sector-a-rarely-told-story-10507

Datta, S. (2019). *Bangladesh: Leveraging Its Locational Advantage*. Vivekananda International Foundation. https://www.vifindia.org/print/5757

Datta, S. (2021). Bangladesh and Belt Road Initiative: Unfolding Possibilities [Review of *Bangladesh and Belt Road Initiative: Unfolding Possibilities*]. *National Security*, *4*(3), 254–271. https://www.vifindia.org/sites/default/files/national-security-vol-4-issue-3-article-Sreeradha Datta.pdf

Davis. (1989). Technology Acceptance Model. *MIS Quarterly, 13*(3), 319-340. Retrieved from: https://www.jstor.org/stable/249008

Day, C. (2000). Teachers in the twenty-first century: time to renew the vision. *Teacher and Teaching: Theory and Practice, 6*(1), 101-115.

De Luca, V. V., Margherita, A., & Passiante, G. (2019). Crowdfunding: A systemic framework of benefits. *International Journal of Entrepreneurial Behaviour & Research, 25*(6), 1321–1339. doi:10.1108/IJEBR-11-2018-0755

Dearing, R. (1997). Higher Education in the Learning Society, Report of the National Committee of Inquiry into Higher Education, London: HMSO.

Deb, R. (2020). Is RCEP a Panacea for India? *The Indian Economic Journal, 68*(4), 659–666. doi:10.1177/0019466221998626

Deccan Herald. (2021, April 1). *India to Counter China's foray in Bay of Bengal with BIMSTEC meet, 5 nation navy drill.* https://www.deccanherald.com/national/india-to-counter-chinas-foray-in-bay-of-bengal-with-bimstec-meet-5-nation-navy-drill-968854.html

Deccan Herald. (2021, April 1). *India to Counter China's foray in Bay of Bengal with BIMSTEC meet, 5 nation navy drill.* Retrieved from https://www.deccanherald.com/national/india-to-counter-chinas-foray-in-bay-of-bengal-with-bimstec-meet-5-nation-navy-drill-968854.html

Decommissioning Australia, C. of. (2021). *Reports and Publications (portal): NERA National Energy Resources Australia.* https://www.nera.org.au/Publications-and-insights

Defourny, J., & Nyssens, M. (2010). Conceptions of social enterprise and social entrepreneurship in Europe and the United States: Convergences and divergences. *Journal of Social Entrepreneurship, 1*(1), 32–53.

Deloitte. (2021). *RegTech Universe 2021: Take a closer look at who is orbiting in the RegTech space*. Deloitte. Retrieved from https://www2.deloitte.com/lu/en/pages/technology/articles/regtech-companies-compliance.html

Department of Education, Skills, and Employment (DFSE). (2021). *International student data 2021: Basic pivot table 2002 onwards.* https://internationaleducation.gov.au/research/international-student-data/Pages/InternationalStudentData2021.aspx

Department of Foreign Affairs and Trade (DFAT). (2014). *Fifty years of Australia's trade.* file://ad.uws.edu.au/dfshare/HomesK-W$/30053305/Downloads/fifty-years-of-Australias-trade%20(1).pdf

Department of Foreign Affairs and Trade (DFAT). (2016). *Australia's trade since federation.* https://www.dfat.gov.au/sites/default/files/australias-trade-since-federation.pdf

Department of Foreign Affairs and Trade (DFAT). (2020a). *Trade and Investment at a Glance 2020.* https://www.dfat.gov.au/publications/trade-and-investment/trade-and-investment-glance-2020

Department of Foreign Affairs and Trade (DFAT). (2020b). *Australia's free trade agreements (FTAs).* https://www.dfat.gov.au/trade/agreements/trade-agreements

Department of Foreign Affairs and Trade (DFAT). (2021). *Trade and Investment at a Glance 2021.* https://www.dfat.gov.au/publications/trade-and-investment/trade-and-investment-glance-2021

Department of Foreign Affairs and Trade (DFAT). (2021a). *Australia's trade through time.* https://www.dfat.gov.au/publications/minisite/tradethroughtimegovau/site/index.html

Department of Foreign Affairs and Trade (DFAT). (2021b). *Trade, investment and economic statistics.* https://www.dfat.gov.au/trade/resources/trade-statistics/trade-statistics

Department of Foreign Affairs and Trade (DFAT). (2021c). *Bangladesh*. https://www.dfat.gov.au/sites/default/files/bade-cef.pdf

Department of Foreign Affairs and Trade. (2018). *An India Economic Strategy To 2035*. https://www.dfat.gov.au/geo/india/ies/index.html

Department of Foreign Affairs and Trade. (2018). *Energy Sector - An India Economic Strategy To 2035*. https://www.dfat.gov.au/geo/india/ies/chapter-7.html

Department of Health Australia. (2021). *Health Technology*. Retrieved from heath.gov.au: https://www.health.gov.au/health-topics/health-technology

Department of Industry, Science, Energy & Resources. (2019). *Collaborating with India on Science and Research*. Retrieved from www.industry.gov.au/funding-and-incentives/science-and-research/collaborating-with-india-on-science-and-research

Department of Industry, Science, Energy and Resources. (2020). Australian Energy Update 2020: Australian Energy Statistics, September. Author.

Department of Innovation Industry & Science (DIIS). (2019). *Collaborating with India on Science and Research*. Retrieved from www.industry.gov.au/funding-and-incentives/science-and-research/collaborating-with-india-on-science-and-research

Department of Renewable Energy B. (2016). *Bhutan energy directory 2015*. Author.

Department of Science and Technology, Government of India. (2020). *About VAJRA*. https://www. vajra-india.in/index.php/about-vajra

Deuchar, A., & Freeman, B. (2021). *Deepening collaboration and strengthening opportunities for Australia-India research and engagement*. Australia India Institute.

DFAT. (2018). *Indian Economic Strategy 2035*. Department of Foreign Affairs and Trade. Retrieved from https://dfat.gov.au/geo/india/ies/index.html

DFAT. (2020). *Joint Statement on a Comprehensive Strategic Partnership between Republic of India and Australia*. https://www.dfat.gov.au/geo/india/Pages/joint-statement-comprehensive-strategic-partnership-between-republic-india-and-australia

DFAT. (2020). *Joint Statement on a Comprehensive Strategic Partnership between Republic of India and Australia*. Retrieved from https://www.dfat.gov.au/geo/india/Pages/joint-statement-comprehensive-strategic-partnership-between-republic-india-and-australia

DFAT. (2021). *Association of Southeast Asian Nations (ASEAN)*. Retrieved from: https://www.dfat.gov.au/international-relations/regional-architecture/asean

DFAT. (2021). *Australia's development partnership with Bangladesh* [Review of *Australia's development partnership with Bangladesh*]. Development Assistance in Bangladesh; Department of Foreign Affairs and Trade, Australian Government. https://www.dfat.gov.au/geo/bangladesh/development-assistance/development-assistance-in-bangladesh

DFAT. (2021). *Maldives Brief*. Department of Foreign Affairs and Trade. Retrieved from https://www.dfat.gov.au/geo/maldives/maldives-country-brief

DFAT. (2021a). *Australia-Singapore Digital Economy Agreement: summary of key outcomes*. Retrieved from: https://www.dfat.gov.au/trade/services-and-digital-trade/australia-singapore-digital-economy-agreement-summary-key-outcomes

DFAT. (2021b). *Australia-Singapore Digital Economy Agreement*. Retrieved from: https://www.dfat.gov.au/trade/services-and-digital-trade/australia-and-singapore-digital-economy-agreement

Dhaka Tribune. (2021, April 15). *COVID-19 deaths per million: Bangladesh's rate is third lowest in South Asia*. Retrieved from www.dhakatribune.com/bangladesh/2021/04/15/covid-deaths-per-million-bangladesh-6th-in-s-asia

Dhillon, P. K., Jeemon, P., Arora, N., Mathur, P., Maskey, M., Sukirna, R., & Prabhakaran, D. (2012). Status of epidemiology in the WHO South-East Asia region: Burden of disease, determinants of health and epidemiological research, workforce and training capacity. *International Journal of Epidemiology*, *41*(3), 847–860. doi:10.1093/ije/dys046 PMID:22617689

Dhume, S. (2021, March 8). *India Beats China at Vaccine Diplomacy*. Retrieved from https://www.wsj.com/articles/india-beats-china-at-vaccine-diplomacy-11616086729

DII. (2021). *Digital Inclusion Index. About Digital Inclusion in Australia*. Retrieved from: https://digitalinclusionindex.org.au/about/about-digital-inclusion/

Dixit, S. K., & Sambasivan, M. (2018). A review of the Australian healthcare system: A policy perspective. *SAGE Open Medicine*, *6*, 1–14. doi:10.1177/2050312118769211 PMID:29686869

Dougherty, M. L. (2013). Work, mobility and livelihoods in a changing rural Latin America. In Handbook of Rural Development. Edward Elgar Publishing.

Drug-dev.com. (2021, August 9). *Australia's Pharma Sector to Grow to $32.1 Billion*. Retrieved from Drug-dev.com: https://drug-dev.com/australias-pharma-sector-to-grow-to-32-1-billion/

DTA. (2021). *Common Pain Points*. Retrieved from: https://www.dta.gov.au/our-projects/govx/common-pain-points

Duan, C., Kotey, B., & Sandhu, K. (2021). Ecosystem Strategies for Transnational Digital Entrepreneurship: A Conceptual Framework of Three Ecosystems. In *Disruptive Technology and Digital Transformation for Business and Government*. IGI Global. Retrieved from: https://www.igi-global.com/book/disruptive-technology-digital-transformation-business/271732

Duan, C., Kotey, B., & Sandhu, K. (2021). Integrated Business Strategies for Transnational Digital Entrepreneurship: Case Studies for Immigrant Startups. In *Handbook of Research on Management and Strategies for Digital Enterprise Transformation*. IGI Global. Retrieved from: https://www.igi-global.com/book/handbook-research-management-strategies-digital/244649

Duckett, S. (2018). Expanding the breadth of Medicare: Learning from Australia. *Health Economics, Policy, and Law*, *13*(3-4).

Dull, J. L. (2021, January 26). China. In *Encyclopedia Britannica*. Retrieved from https://www.britannica.com

Eastren Miditerranean, W. H. O. (2021). *Country Cooperation Strategy for WHO and Pakistan 2020-2025*. WHO.

Economic Relations Division. (2020). Flow of External Resources into Bangladesh [Review of *Flow of External Resources into Bangladesh*]. In *Bangladesh National Portal*. Ministry of Finance, Government of the People's Republic of Bangladesh. https://erd.gov.bd/site/page/565de360-e511-4758-a966-459d0dc1acfa/Flow-of-External-Resources-2019-20

Economist. (2015). *Ocean Prosperity Roadmap: Fisheries and Beyond*. The Economist https://www.greengrowthknowledge.org/sites/default/files/downloads/resource/1.-Ocean-Prosperity-Roadmap-Synthesis-Report-5.30.15A.pdf

Economist. (2016). One Belt, One Road: An Economic Roadmap. *Economist Intelligence Unit*. https://www.eiu.com/public/topical_report.aspx?campaignid=OBORSept2016

Economy Next. (2021). *Sri Lanka generation plan renewable power share for 2030 equal to Germany: CEB engineers*. Retrieved from https://economynext.com/sri-lanka-generation-plan-renewable-power-share-for-2030-equal-to-germany-ceb-engineers-84506/

ED. From ship-breaking to ship-building. (2021, September 29). *Dhaka Tribune*. https://www.dhakatribune.com/opinion/editorial/2021/09/29/ed-from-ship-breaking-to-ship-building

EDB. (2019). *Industry Capability Report: Sri Lankan Fisheries Sector*. Export Development Board. https://www.srilankabusiness.com/ebooks/fish---fishery-products---industry-capability-report---december-2019.pdf

Eichenbaum, M., Rebelo, S., & Trabandt, M. (2020). *The Macroeconomics of Epidemics*. National Bureau of Economic Research. Working Paper 26882. doi:10.3386/w26882

Ellen Macarthur Foundation. (n.d.). *Explore the Circular Economy in Detail*. http://www.ellenmacarthurfoundaiton.org/explore/the-circular-economy-in-detail

Elliott, J. A. (2013). *An Introduction to Sustainable Development* (4th ed.). Routledge.

Embassy of China. (2011, May 19). *History and Legend of Sino-Bangla Contacts* [Review of *History and Legend of Sino-Bangla Contacts*]. Embassy of China; Government of the People's Republic of China. https://www.mfa.gov.cn/ce/cebd//eng/sbgx/t823712.htm

Energy Government Australia. (2021). *Clean energy and the electricity market*. https://www.energy.gov.au/government-priorities/energy-supply/clean-energy-and-the-electricity-market

Equitise. (2021). *Equity crowdfunding*. Accessed date 31 August 2021 from https://equitise.com/equity-crowdfunding-au

Esler, J., & Krishnamurthy, D. (2021). Grameen America: Microfinancing Having a Macroeconomic Impact - An Interview with Andrea Jung. *Social Impact Review*. Harvard Advanced Leadership Initiative. Accessed date 31 Aug. 2021 at https://sir.advancedleadership.harvard.edu/news/grameen-america-microfinancing-having-macroeconomic-impact-interview-andrea-jung?admin_panel=1

ESMA. (2020). *ESMA Report on Trends, Risks and Vulnerabilities*. European Securities and Markets Authority. https://www.esma.europa.eu/sites/default/files/library/esma_50-165-1287_report_on_trends_risks_and_vulnerabilities_no.2_2020.pdf

European Commission. (2016). *Crowdfunding in the EU Capital Markets Union*. Author.

European Commission. (2021a). *EU rules to combat IUU fishing*. European Commission. https://ec.europa.eu/oceans-and-fisheries/fisheries/rules/illegal-fishing_en

European Commission. (2021b). *The EU enhances collaboration with Sri Lanka's innovation and start-up ecosystem actors*. European Union. https://eeas.europa.eu/delegations/sri-lanka/105377/eu-enhances-collaboration-sri-lanka%E2%80%99s-innovation-and-start-ecosystem-actors_en

Evans, C. (2021). Exploiting students' part-time work to enhance learning, teaching and assessment. *Industry and Higher Education*, *35*(1), 10–13. doi:10.1177/0950422220930182

Ewens, W. (2000). Teaching using discussion. In R. Neff & M. Weimer (Eds.), *Classroom communication: Collected readings for effective discussion and questioning* (pp. 21–26). Atwood.

Fairman, C. (2019, August 23). Payra Seaport Won't Be Another Chinese "Pearl" [Review of *Payra Seaport Won't Be Another Chinese "Pearl"*]. *The Diplomat*. https://thediplomat.com/2019/08/payra-seaport-wont-be-another-chinese-pearl/

Faiz, M., & Maitra, P. (2020). Concentration and Diversification of Export Economy of Bangladesh: Comparison and Policy Implication with Other Asian Countries. *South Asian Journal of Social Studies and Economics*, 19-36.

Farabi-Asl, H. (2019). *Energy challenges for clean cooking in Asia, the background, and possible policy solutions*. doi:10.1007/978-1-349-67278-3_116

Farhoud, M., Shah, S., Stenholm, P., Kibler, E., Renko, M., & Terjesen, S. (2021). Social enterprise crowdfunding in an acute crisis. *Journal of Business Venturing Insights*, *15*(1), 1–6. doi:10.1016/j.jbvi.2020.e00211

Farr, G. (2017). *Pakistan's Role in China's One Belt One Road Initiative*. https://pdxscholar.library.pdx.edu/cgi/viewcontent.cgi?article=1141&context=soc_fac

Faruqui, G. A., Ara, L. A., & Acma, Q. (2015). TTIP and TPP: Impact on Bangladesh and India Economy. *Pacific Business Review International*, *8*(2), 59–67.

FATF. (2020). *Mauritius: 3rd enhanced follow-up report and technical compliance re-rating*. Financial Action Task Force. https://www.fatf-gafi.org/media/fatf/documents/reports/fur/ESAAMLG-3rd-Follow-Up-Report-Mauritius-2020.pdf

Fereday, J., & Muir-Cochrane, E. (2006). Demonstrating rigor using thematic analysis: A hybrid approach of inductive and deductive coding and theme development. *International Journal of Qualitative Methods*, *5*(1), 80–92.

Fernando, S., & Camilleri, E. (2020). *New perspective on Australia-South Asia foreign policy*. http://dspace.jgu.edu.in:8080/jspui/bitstream/10739/3365/1/New%20perspective%20on%20Australia.pdf

Ferrer, M. V., & Medhekar, A. (2012). The Factors Impacting on the Management of Global Medical Tourism Service Supply Chain. *Journal of Global Business Review*, *2*(2), 206–211. doi:10.5176/2251-3426_THoR1212

Fotourehchi, Z. (2017). Clean Energy Consumption and Economic Growth: A Case Study for Developing Countries. *International Journal of Energy Economics and Policy,* 61-64.

Foxwell, D. (2016). *Decommissioning Market Growing Size and Complexity but Providers too Fragmented*. http://www.osjonline.com/news/veiw,decom-market-growing-sizc-and-complexity-but-providers-too-frgamanted_45672

Furneaux, C., & Barraket, J. (2014). Purchasing social good(s): A definition and typology of social procurement. *Public Money & Management*, *34*(4), 265–272. doi:10.1080/09540962.2014.920199

General Economics Division (GED). (2019). *Prospects and Opportunities of International Cooperation in Attaining SDG Targets in Bangladesh*. Bangladesh Planning Commission Ministry of Planning Government of the People's Republic of Bangladesh.

Ghimire, P. C. (2007). Final report on technical study of biogas plants installed in Pakistan. *Asia/Africa biogas programme*.

Ghosh, A. K. (2021, February 5). Education today needs more funds, not less. *The Statesman*.

Ghosh, R. (2004). Globalization in the North American region: Towards renegotiation of cultural space. *McGill Journal of Education*, *39*(1), 87–101.

Gibb, S. (2020). Digital Transformation in Southeast Asia. *Medium*. Retrieved from: https://medium.com/endeavour-ventures/digital-transformation-in-southeast-asia-4f9682c568e3

Giveindia. (2021). *About Us*. Accessed date 30 August 2021 from https://www.giveindia.org/aboutus

Gnanagurunathan, D. (2012). India-Australia in the Indo-Pacific: a blossoming partnership. *Viewpoint (Indian Council of World Affairs), 21*. https://www.futuredirections.org.au/wp-content/uploads/2013/03/VPIndopacific.pdf

Gofundraise. (2021). *About us*. Accessed date 17 Aug. 21 from https://www.gofundraise.com.au/articles/about-us/

Gokhale, A. A. (1995). Collaborative learning enhances critical thinking. *Journal of Technology Education*, *7*(1), 22–30. doi:10.21061/jte.v7i1.a.2

Golechha, M. (2015). Healthcare agenda for the Indian government. *The Indian Journal of Medical Research*, *141*(2), 151–153. doi:10.4103/0971-5916.155541 PMID:25900948

Gopal, D., & Ahlawat, D. (2015). Australia–India Strategic Relations: From Estrangement to Engagement. *India Quarterly, 71*(3), 206–220. doi:10.1177/0974928415584022

Government of the People's Republic of Bangladesh. (2012). *Bangladesh country action plan for clean cook stoves*. Author.

Government response to An India Economic Strategy to 2035. (2020). *Australian Government Department of Foreign Affairs and Trade*. https://www.dfat.gov.au/about-us/publications/Pages/government-response-india-economic-strategy

Graci, S. (2013). Collaboration and partnership development for sustainable tourism. *Tourism Geographies, 15*(1), 25–42. doi:10.1080/14616688.2012.675513

Graham, E. (2018). The Quad deserves its second chance. *Debating the Quad*, 4.

Graham, J. (2021). *New report reveals Australia's major digital skills gap*. RMIT University. Retrieved from: https://www.rmit.edu.au/news/all-news/2021/feb/digital-skills-gap-report

Gray, B. (1989). *Collaborating*. Jossey-Bass.

Gray, B. (1996). Cross-sectoral partners: Collaborative alliances among business, government and communities. In C. Huxham (Ed.), *Creating Collaborative Advantage*. Sage. doi:10.4135/9781446221600.n4

Gray, M., Healy, K., & Crofts, P. (2003). Social enterprise: Is it the business of social work? *Australian Social Work, 56*(2), 141–154. doi:10.1046/j.0312-407X.2003.00060.x

Gray, M., & Zhang, B. (2017). Crowdfunding: Understanding Diversity. In R. Martin & J. Pollard (Eds.), *Handbook on the Geographies of Money and Finance*. Edward Elgar Publishing. doi:10.4337/9781784719005.00034

Greg, J. (2021). *Australia joins US, India, and Japan in 'unprecedented' deal for coronavirus vaccines after historic QUAD meeting*. Retrieved from https://www.abc.net.au/news/2021-03-13/QUAD-australia-us-india-japan-in-massive-covid-vaccine-deal/13245198

Gregson, N., Crang, M., Fuller, S., & Holmes, H. (2015). Interrogating the circular economy: The moral economy of resource recovery in the EU. *Economy and Society, 44*(2), 218–243. doi:10.1080/03085147.2015.1013353

Guest, G. (2012). *Applied thematic analysis.* Sage Publications.

Gurrib, I. (2018a). Can an energy futures index predict US stock market index movements? *International Journal of Energy Economics and Policy, 8*(5), 230–240. https://www.econjournals.com/index.php/ijeep/article/view/6622/3947

Gurrib, I. (2018b). The relationship between the Nasdaq Composite Index and energy futures markets. *Investment Management and Financial Innovations, 15*(4), 1–16. doi:10.21511/imfi.15(4).2018.01

Gurrib, I. (2019). Can energy commodities affect energy blockchain based cryptos? *Studies in Economics and Finance, 36*(4), 682–699. doi:10.1108/SEF-10-2018-0313

Gurrib, I. (2021). Early COVID-19 Policy Response on Healthcare Equity Prices. *Studies in Economics and Finance, 38*(5), 987–1006. doi:10.1108/SEF-02-2021-0075

Gurrib, I., Kweh, Q. L., Contu, D., & Kamalov, F. (2021). COVID-19, Short-selling Ban and energy Stock Prices. *Energy Research Letters, 1*(4). Advance online publication. doi:10.46557/001c.18562

Gurry, M. (2012). India, the new centre of gravity: Australia–India relations under the Howard government. *South Asia, 35*(2), 282–305. doi:10.1080/00856401.2011.633299

Haider, A. Q. (2021, June 4). China: A development partner of Bangladesh [Review of *China: A development partner of Bangladesh*]. *The Financial Express.* https://thefinancialexpress.com.bd/views/china-a-development-partner-of-bangladesh-1622824911

HaiderT. (2020). *Pakistani Population in Australia.* Retrieved from https://www.sbs.com.au/language/english/pakistani-population-in-australia-increases-to-91-000

Hall, I. (2021, February 2). *Australia and India in the Modi era: An unequal…* International Politics. https://link.springer.com/article/10.1057/s41311-020-00278-w?error=cookies_not_supported&error=cookies_not_supported&code=ef481862-2c59-46d4-aa7f-b52630f6643b&code=7a4f4e59-0c6c-4775-af28-92750484e8a4

Hall, C. M., & Page, S. J. (2000). Developing tourism in South Asia: India, Pakistan and Bangladesh – SAARC and beyond. In C. M. Hall & S. J. Page (Eds.), *Tourism in South and Southeast Asia: Issues and cases* (pp. 197–224). Butterworth Heinemann.

Hall, I. (2015). Is a 'Modi doctrine' emerging in India's foreign policy? *Australian Journal of International Affairs, 69*(3), 247–252. doi:10.1080/10357718.2014.1000263

Hand, M. (2014, June 28). *Five workers dead in blast at Alang shipbreaking yard.* Sea trade Maritime; Maritime News. https://www.seatrade-maritime.com/asia/five-workers-dead-blast-alang-shipbreaking-yard

Handforth, C., & Tan, S. (2021). *Mapping the Waypoints in Asia's Digital Future.* UNDP Global Centre for Technology, Innovation, and Sustainable Development. Asia and the Pacific. Retrieved from: https://www.asia-pacific.undp.org/content/rbap/en/home/presscenter/articles/2021/mapping-the-waypoints-to-asias-digital-future-.html

Haq, F., & Jackson, J. (2021). Tourism Marketing Mix Applied for Inclusive Spiritual Tourists in Pakistan and Australia. *NUST Business Review, an International Journal, 2*(12), 30-46.

Haq, F. M. (2014). The significance of partnership as a marketing strategy for Islamic spiritual tourism. *Journal of Islamic Marketing, 5*(2), 258–272. doi:10.1108/JIMA-11-2013-0079

Haq, F., & Medhekar, A. (2019). Is Spiritual Tourism a Peace Vehicle for Social Transformation and Economic Prosperity in India and Pakistan. In A. Nedelea (Ed.), *Marketing Peace for Social Transformation and Global Prosperity* (pp. 189–211). IGI Global Publishing. doi:10.4018/978-1-5225-7464-4.ch010

Haq, F., & Wong, H. Y. (2013). Branding Islamic spiritual tourism: An exploratory study in Australia and Pakistan. *European Journal of Business and Management, 5*(11), 154–162.

Hare, J. (2021). Chinese student numbers to free-fall in 2021. *Financial Review.* https://www.afr.com/policy/health-and-education/chinese-student-numbers-to-free-fall-in-2021-20210228-p576ji

Hashim, J., Chongsuvivatwong, V., Phua, K., Pocock, N., Teng, Y., Chhem, R., … Lopez, A. (2012). *Health and Healthcare Systems in Southeast Asia.* Retrieved from Und.edu: https://unu.edu/publications/articles/health-and-healthcare-systems-in-southeast-asia.html

Haski-Leventhal, D., & Mehra, A. (2016). Impact measurement in social enterprises: Australia and India. *Social Enterprise Journal.*

Hauxia. (2021, November 10) a. Bangladesh approves Chinese-funded highway project in capital Dhaka [Review of *Bangladesh approves Chinese-funded highway project in capital Dhaka*]. *Xinhuanet.* http://www.news.cn/english/2021-11/10/c_1310303258.htm

Hauxia. (2021, September 26). *Bangladeshis to see end of boats-only experience in river-crossing traffic as China helps build new bridge* (Hauxia, Ed.) [Review of *Bangladeshis to see end of boats-only experience in river-crossing traffic as China helps build new bridge*]. Xinhuanet. http://www.xinhuanet.com/english/asiapacific/2021-09/26/c_1310211100_2.htm

Hawkins, J. (2021). Now that Australia's inflation rate is 3.8%, is it time to worry? *The Conversation*. https://theconversation.com/now-that-australias-inflation-rate-is-3-8-is-it-time-to-worry-165098

Hazarika, O. B., & Pathak, S. (2019). Energy Security Dynamics in India–Australia Relations. *Jadavpur Journal of International Relations*, *23*(1), 26–47. doi:10.1177/0973598418803480

Health Silk Road of China: A New "Debt-Trap Health Diplomacy" in Making. (n.d.). *Diplomatist*. Retrieved from https://diplomatist.com/2020/06/29/health-silk-road-of-china-a-new-debt-trap-health-diplomacy-in-making/

Heath, K. (2011). The classical definition of a pandemic is not elusive. *Bulletin of the World Health Organization*, *89*(7), 540–541. doi:10.2471/BLT.11.088815 PMID:21734771

Henneberg, S. C. (2008). An Epistemological Perspective on Research in Political Marketing. *Journal of Political Marketing*, *7*(2), 151–182. doi:10.1080/15377850802053158

Henneberg, S. C., & O'Shaughnessy, N. (2009). Political Relationship Marketing: Some Micro/Macro Thoughts. *Journal of Marketing Management*, *25*(1/2), 5–29. doi:10.1362/026725709X410016

High Commission. (n.d.). *Bangladesh - Australia Trade and Investment Relations | Bangladesh High Commission Canberra*. https://www.bhcanberra.com/trade-investments/bangladesh-australia-trade-relations

Holloway, I., & Todres, L. (2003). The status of method: Flexibility, consistency and coherence. *Qualitative Research*, *3*(3), 345–357.

Hongkong and Shanghai Banking Corporation. (2018). *The world in 2030: Our long-term projection for 75 countries by Henry, J. & Pomeroy, J.* file://ad.uws.edu.au/dfshare/HomesK-W$/30053305/Downloads/HSBC-The-World-in-2030-Report.pdf

Hossain, A. (2018). *Determination of reusable and waste material from ship recycling industry of Bangladesh by broad sampling of data*. SSRN Electronic Journal. doi:10.2139srn.3252979

Hossain, D., & Islam, M. S. (2021). Understanding Bangladesh's relations with India and China: Dilemmas and responses. *Journal of the Indian Ocean Region*, *17*(1), 42–59.

Hossain, K. A. (2015). Overview of Ship Recycling Industry of Bangladesh. *Journal of Environmental & Analytical Toxicology*, *5*(5). Advance online publication. doi:10.4172/2161-0525.1000312

Hossain, M., Fakhruddin, A., Chowdhury, M., & Gan, S. (2016). Impact of ship-breaking activities on the coastal environment of Bangladesh and a management system for its sustainability. *Environmental Science & Policy*, *60*, 84–94. doi:10.1016/j.envsci.2016.03.005

Hostetter, L. R. Jr. (2017). Teaching Innovations in Marketing: A Brand-Based Student-Led Inquiry of Marketing Concepts and Practices. *Marketing Education Review*, *27*(2), 1–6. doi:10.1080/10528008.2016.1274633

Hsu, K. (2013). The RCEP: Integrating India into the Asian Economy. *Indian Foreign Affairs Journal*, *8*(1), 41–51.

Husain, S. A. (2012). Bangladesh Foreign policy: A framework for consensus building in regional cooperation and Globalisation, Bangladesh, South Asia and beyond. The University Press Limited.

ILO. (2009, June 15). *Ship-breaking: A hazardous work.* Www.ilo.org. https://www.ilo.org/safework/areasofwork/hazardous-work/WCMS_110335/lang--en

IMO. (2020, July 31). *Ship recycling in Bangladesh leaps forward with third phase of key project signed.* https://www.imo.org/en/MediaCentre/PressBriefings/pages/23-SENSREC-Phase-III.aspx

India - Countries & Regions. (n.d.). https://www.iea.org/countries/india

India Brand Equity Foundation. (2021, August 19). *Healthcare Industry in India.* Retrieved from ibef.org: https://www.ibef.org/industry/healthcare-india.aspx

Indian Brand Equity Foundation IBEF. (2021). *Renewable Energy Industry in India: Overview, Market Size & Growth.* https://www.ibef.org/industry/renewable-energy.aspx

Indian Institute of Technology Kharagpur. (2020a). *Global initiative for academic networks.* https:// gian.iitkgp.ac.in/

Indian Institute of Technology Kharagpur. (2020b). *Scheme for promotion of academic and research collaborations.* https://sparc.iitkgp.ac.in/

Ingram, G. (2020). The digital world. In *Development in Southeast Asia: Opportunities for donor collaboration.* Center for Sustainable Development at Brookings. Retrieved from: https://www.brookings.edu/wp-content/uploads/2020/12/Development-Southeast-Asia-Ch2-Digital.pdf

International Energy Agency (IEA). (2020). *World Energy Outlook 2020.* IEA. Retrieved from https://www.iea.org/reports/world-energy-outlook-2020

International Monetary Fund Bangladesh. (2015). *Letter of Intent and Memorandum of Economic and Financial Policies.* https://www.imf.org/external/np/loi/2015/bgd/100515.pdf

International Monetary Fund. (2019). *IMF, Executive Board Concludes 2018 Article IV Consultation with Australia.* https://www.imf.org/en/News/Articles/2019/02/21/pr1953-australia-imf-executive-board-concludes-2018-article-iv-consultation

International Monetary Fund. (2020). *Helping Bangladesh Recover from COVID-19* [IMF News]. https://www.imf.org/en/News/Articles/2020/06/11/na-06122020-helping-bangladesh-recover-from-covid-19.

International Trade Administration. (2021). *Country Commercial Guides – Sri Lanka: Energy.* Retrieved from https://www.trade.gov/country-commercial-guides/sri-lanka-energy

IOMOU. (2020). *2019 Report.* Indian Ocean memorandum of understanding on port state control. https://safety-4sea.com/wp-content/uploads/2020/05/Indian-Ocean-MoU-Annual-Report-2019-2020_05.pdf?__cf_chl_jschl_tk__=pmd_2tIrQZ8mF0Gp_WgWlKdV0JkYs02Ok.dUG_ZJXQumYlo-1634549871-0-gqNtZGzNAlCjcnBszQi9

IORA. (2015). *Declaration of the Indian Ocean Rim Association on enhancing Blue Economy Cooperation for Sustainable Development in the Indian Ocean Region.* Indian Ocean Rim Association. https://www.iora.int/media/8216/iora-mauritius-declaration-on-blue-economy.pdf

IORA. (n.d.). *About IORA.* https://www.iora.int/en/about/about-iora

IRENA. (2019). *Renewable's readiness assessment: Kingdom of Bhutan.* Issue December.

Irfan, M., Zhao, Z. Y., Panjwani, M. K., Mangi, F. H., Li, H., Jan, A., Ahmad, M., & Rehman, A. (2020). Assessing the energy dynamics of Pakistan: Prospects of biomass energy. *Energy Reports*, *6*, 80–93. doi:10.1016/j.egyr.2019.11.161

Islam, S. (2021, Aug. 27). Bangladesh, Australia going to TIFA deal. *The Financial Express.*

Islam, F. (2013). Income terms of trade and Trade Balance: The long run evidence from Bangladesh. *Bangladesh Development Studies*, *36*(2), 109–122.

Islam, M. N., & Akter, S. R. (2021). Problems and Prospects of Tourism Industry in Bangladesh: A Study on Cumilla District. *South Asian Journal of Social Studies and Economics*, *10*(4), 27–35. doi:10.9734ajsse/2021/v10i430271

Islam, M., & Mostaque, L. Y. (2018). Blue economy and Bangladesh: Lessons and Policy implications. *BIISS Journal*, *39*(2), 135–162.

ISSAfrica.org. (2018, February 21). *Lessons from Sri Lanka on China's "debt-trap diplomacy."* ISS Africa. https://issafrica.org/iss-today/lessons-from-sri-lanka-on-chinas-debt-trap-diplomacy

ITU. (2021). Digital trends in Asia and the Pacific 2021. In *Information and communication technology trends and developments in the Asia-Pacific region, 2017-2020*. ITU Switzerland. Retrieved from: https://www.itu.int/dms_pub/itu-d/opb/ind/D-IND-DIG_TRENDS_ASP.01-2021-PDF-E.pdf

Iyenger, K. P., Vaishya, R., Bahl, S., & Vaish, A. (2020). Impact of the coronavirus pandemic on the supply chain in healthcare. *British Journal of Healthcare Management*, *26*(6), 1–4. Advance online publication. doi:10.12968/bjhc.2020.0047

J.P. (2017, May 15). What is China's belt and road initiative? *The Economist*. Retrieved, from https://www.economist.com

Jabareen, Y. (2009). Building a Conceptual Framework: Philosophy, Definitions, and Procedure. *International Journal of Qualitative Methods*, *8*(4), 49–62. doi:10.1177/160940690900800406

Jaganmohan, M. (2021, June 1). *India: iron ore export volume 2020*. Statista. https://www.statista.com/statistics/1131708/india-iron-ore-export-volume/

Jain, E., & Lamba, J. (2021). Management and Digitalization Strategy for Transforming Education Sector: An Emerging Gateway Persuaded by COVID-19. In *Emerging Challenges, Solutions, and Best Practices for Digital Enterprise Transformation*. IGI Global. Retrieved from: https://www.igi-global.com/book/emerging-challenges-solutions-best-practices/271733

Jaishankar, D. (2020). *The Australia-India Strategic Partnership: Accelerating Security Cooperation in the Indo-Pacific*. Lowy Institute for International Policy.

Jenssen, I. (2020). Biennial Report- 2018-19. In *NGO Shipbreaking Platform*. NGO Shipbreaking Platform. https://www.shipbreakingplatform.org/wp-content/uploads/2020/06/NGOSBP-Bi-Annual-Report-18-19.pdf

Jenssen, I., & Puckett, J. (2020). *Contradiction in Terms: European Union Must Align Its Waste Ship Exports with International Law and Green Deal*. European Union. https://mk0eeborgicuypctuf7e.kinstacdn.com/wp-content/uploads/2020/09/Report-EU-SRR-Ban-Amendment-BAN-EEB-GP-SBP.pdf

Jenssen, I., Mulinaris, N., & Mork, M. (2019). Recycling Outlook: Decommissioning of North Sea Floating Oil and Gas Units. In *NGO Shipbreaking Platform*. KLP. https://www.shipbreakingplatform.org/wp-content/uploads/2019/09/Shipbreaking-OG-Report.pdf

Jha, J., Minni, P., & Ahmed, M. (2020). *Teachers and Teaching Profession in South Asia*. Working Paper. Centre for Budget and Policy Studies (CBPS).

JHU CSSE COVID-19 Data. (2021, August 12). *India*. Retrieved from https://ourworldindata.org/coronavirus-data: https://ourworldindata.org/coronavirus-data

Jian, Z. (2021). *World Economic Situation and Prospects*. United Nations. Retrieved from https://www.un.org/development/desa/dpad/wpcontent/uploads/sites/45/WESP2021_CH3_SA.pdf

John, J., & Kumar, S. (2016). A locational decision making framework for shipbreaking under multiple criteria. *International Journal of Strategic Decision Sciences*, *7*(1), 76–97. doi:10.4018/IJSDS.2016010104

Johnson, C. (2016). *President Xi Jinping's Belt and Road initiative, A Practical Assessment of the Chinese Communist party's Road Map for China's Global Resurgence*. A Report of the CSIS Freeman Chair in China Studies.

Joint Statement from Quad Leaders. (2021, September 25). *The White House*. https://www.whitehouse.gov/briefing-room/statements-releases/2021/09/24/joint-statement-from-quad-leaders/

Joint Statement on a Comprehensive Strategic Partnership between Republic of India and Australia. (n.d.). *Australian Government Department of Foreign Affairs and Trade*. https://www.dfat.gov.au/geo/india/joint-statement-comprehensive-strategic-partnership-between-republic-india-and-australia

Jomo, K. S., & Chowdhury, A. (2020). COVID-19 Pandemic Recession and Recovery. *Development*, *63*(1), 226–237. doi:10.105741301-020-00262-0 PMID:33223764

Jupp, J. (1995). From 'White Australia' to 'part of Asia': Recent shifts in Australian immigration policy towards the region. *The International Migration Review*, *29*(1), 207–228. PMID:12319613

Kalirajan, K. P. (2000). Trade flows between Australia and India: An empirical analysis. *International Journal of Commerce and Management*, *10*(2), 32–49. doi:10.1108/eb047401

Kalra, K. (2009, October 31). Tackling the common problems in Saarc nations [Review of *Tackling the common problems in Saarc nations*]. *Financial Express*. https://www.financialexpress.com/archive/tackling-the-common-problems-in-saarc-nations/534963/

Kamal, U., & Ahmed. (n.d.). *Three Decades of Australia -Bangladesh Relations: Future Directions and Potentials*. http://www.biliabd.org/article%20intl/Vol-08/Kamal%20Uddin%20Ahmed.pdf

Kanitkar, T. (2021, April 25). *COVID-19 vaccine day analysis*. Retrieved from www.firstpost.com/india/covid-19-vaccine-data-analysis-at-current-rate-of-2-2mn-doses-per-day-india-can-only-cover-30-population-by-end-2021-9562811.html

Kara, A., Zhou, H., & Zhou, Y. (2021). Achieving the United Nations' sustainable development goals through financial inclusion: A systematic literature review of access to finance across the globe. *International Review of Financial Analysis*, *77*(1), 1–16. doi:10.1016/j.irfa.2021.101833

Karan, A., Negandhi, H., Hussain, S., Zapata, T., Mairembam, D., ... Zodpe, S. (2021). Size, composition, and distribution of health workforce in India: Why and where to invest? *Human Resources for Health*, *19*(39), 1–14. doi:10.118612960-021-00575-2 PMID:33752675

Katekar, V. P., Asif, M., & Deshmukh, S. S. (2021). Energy and Environmental Scenario of South Asia. *Energy and Environmental Security in Developing Countries*, 75-103.

Kaul, M. M. (2009). The Indian diaspora in Australia and New Zealand: Challenges and the way forward. *Diaspora Studies*, *2*(2), 187–201.

Kazmi, M. R. (2017). Australian Centre for International Agricultural Research (ACIAR) in Pakistan: 30 years of partnership in research for development. *ACIAR Technical Reports Series*, *91*, 24–3.

Kearns, M. (2015). *EU fishing ban takes its toll on Sri Lanka*. Seafood Source. https://www.seafoodsource.com/news/supply-trade/eu-fishing-ban-takes-its-toll-on-sri-lanka

Keating, J. (2003). Qualifications Frameworks in Australia. *Journal of Education and Work*, *16*(3), 271–288. doi:10.1080/1363908032000099449

Kelegama, S., & Karunaratne, C. (2013). *Experiences of Sri Lanka in the Sri Lanka – India FTA and the Sri Lanka – Pakistan FTA. United Nations Conference on Trade and Development. https*://unctad.org/system/files/official-document/ecidc2013misc1_bp10.pdf

Kemmis, S., Marginson, S., Porter, P., & Rizvi, F. (2009). *Enhancing Diversity in Australian higher Education.* Paper presented to the University of Western Australia by Stephen Kemmis Research & Consulting Pty ltd.

Ketto. (2021). *Fundraisers.* Accessed date 30 August 2021 from https://www.ketto.org/crowdfunding/fundraisers

Khan, S. I., & Teicher, J. (2021). Sustainable global supply chain management model post-Covid-19. In M. A. Marinov & S. T. Marinova (Eds.), *Covid-19 and international business: Change of era* (pp. 205–224). Routledge. Retrieved from https://www.routledge.com/

Khan, S. I., Wong, H. Y., & Sultan, P. (2020). A critical review of the concept of value in the international marketing context. In M. A. Marinov (Ed.), *Value in marketing: Retrospective and perspective stance* (pp. 126–144). Routledge. doi:10.4324/9780429264337

Khan, T. M. (2021). Use of social media and WhatsApp to conduct teaching activities during the COVID-19 lockdown in Pakistan. *International Journal of Pharmacy Practice, 29*(1), 90–90. doi:10.1111/ijpp.12659 PMID:32715575

Kharbanda, V. K., & Panda, R. R. (2016). *Report on regional energy/electricity regulatory institutional mechanism in South Asia: South Asia forum of electricity/energy regulators.* SAFER.

Khatun, F., & Saadat, S. Y. (2020, November 19). How can Bangladesh benefit from the Belt and Road Initiative? [Review of *How can Bangladesh benefit from the Belt and Road Initiative?*]. *Dhaka Tribune.* https://www.dhakatribune.com/opinion/op-ed/2020/11/19/op-ed-how-can-bangladesh-benefit-from-the-belt-and-road-initiative

Khowaja, A., Khan, U., Arain, A. M., Naim, W. S., Ashraf, N. S., & Kandhro, A. I. (2019). Need of a Localized Social Network Platform for Crowdfunding in Pakistan. *International Journal of Computer Science and Network Security, 19*(9), 210–215.

Khtar, G. (2013). Indian pharmaceutical industry: an overview. *OSR Journal of Humanities and Social Science.*

Kibria, G., Haroon, A. K. Y., & Nugegoda, D. (2018). Low-Carbon Development (LCD) Pathways in Australia, Bangladesh, China and India-A Review. *Journal of Climate Change, 4*(1), 49–61. doi:10.3233/JCC-180006

Kidney, S., & Oliver, P. (2014). Greening China's financial markets. *Growing a Green Bonds Market in China.*

Kilian, L. (2009). Not all oil price shocks are alike: Disentangling demand and supply shocks in the crude oil market. *The American Economic Review, 99*(3), 1053–1069. doi:10.1257/aer.99.3.1053

Kiva. (2021). *About Kiva.* Accessed date 1 September 2021 from https://www.kiva.org/about

Klapper, L., El-Zoghbi, M., & Hess, J. (2016). *Achieving the Sustainable Development Goals: The Role of Financial Inclusion. United Nations Secretary General's Special Advocate for Inclusive Finance for Development.* UNSGSA.

Knight, J. (1994). *Internationalization: Elements and checkpoints.* Canadian Bureau of International Education. https://files.eric.ed.gov/fulltext/ED549823.Pdf

Knoema. (2019). *Australia - Contribution of travel and tourism to GDP as a share of GDP.* Retrieved from https://knoema.com/atlas/Australia/topics/Tourism/Travel-and-Tourism-Total-Contribution-to-GDP/Contribution-of-travel-and-tourism-to-GDP-percent-of-GDP

KPMG. (2021). *Mauritius Budget Highlights 2021/22.* KPMG. https://assets.kpmg/content/dam/kpmg/mu/pdf/2021/mu-Mauritius-Budget-Highlights-2021-2022.pdf.

Kraiwanit, T. (2021). A multiplier of e-consumption: The study of the developing economy. *Journal of Governance & Regulation*, *10*(3), 85–92. doi:10.22495/jgrv10i3art7

Kraus, S., Palmer, C., Kailer, N., Kallinger, F. L., & Spitzer, J. (2018). Digital entrepreneurship: A research agenda on new business models for the twenty-first century. *International Journal of Entrepreneurial Behaviour & Research*, *25*(2), 353–375. doi:10.1108/IJEBR-06-2018-0425

Krugman, P. R., Obstfeld, M., & Melitz, M. J. (2020). *International Trade Theory and Policy* (11th ed.). Pearson Education.

Kukreja, M.D., & Upadhyay, H. (2019). *A Study of External Debt Trap Threat Faced by Indian Economy*. Academic Press.

Kutan, A. M., Paramati, S. R., Ummalla, M., & Zakari, A. (2018). Financing renewable energy projects in major emerging market economies: Evidence in the perspective of sustainable economic development. *Emerging Markets Finance & Trade*, *54*(8), 1761–1777. doi:10.1080/1540496X.2017.1363036

Lam, N. L., Upadhyay, B., Maharjan, S., Jagoe, K., Weyant, C. L., Thompson, R., Uprety, S., Johnson, M. A., & Bond, T. C. (2017). Seasonal fuel consumption, stoves, and end-uses in rural households of the far-western development region of Nepal. *Environmental Research Letters*, *12*(12), 125011. Advance online publication. doi:10.1088/1748-9326/aa98cc

Larsen, K., Martin, P. J., & Morris, R. (2002). Trade in education services: Trends and emerging issues. *World Economy*, *25*(6), 854, 857, 867. doi:10.1111/1467-9701.00466

Laurillard, D. M. (2002). *Rethinking University teaching* (2nd ed.). Routledge Falmer. doi:10.4324/9780203160329

Leach, M., & Deshmukh, S. (2012). Sustainable energy law and policy. *Environ Energy Law,* 122–138.

Lee, E. V., Ferdinand, P., Benecke, B., Mason, J., & Burel, G. (2013). Advancing Public Health and Medical Preparedness with Operations Research. *Journal on Applied Analytics*, *43*(1), 79–98. Advance online publication. doi:10.1287/inte.2013.0676

Lees-Marshment, J. (2001). The marriage of politics and marketing. *Political Studies*, *49*(4), 692–713. doi:10.1111/1467-9248.00337

Lehner, M. O. (2013). Crowdfunding social ventures: A model and research agenda. *Venture Capital*, *15*(4), 289–311. doi:10.1080/13691066.2013.782624

LensCulture. (n.d.). *Ship Breaking in Bangladesh - Photographs and text by Jan Møller Hansen*. LensCulture. Retrieved October 14, 2021, from https://www.lensculture.com/articles/jan-moller-hansen-ship-breaking-in-bangladesh

Lescaroux, F., & Mignon, V. (2009). On the influence of oil prices on economic activity and other macroeconomic and financial variables. *OPEC Energy Review*, *32*(4), 343–380. doi:10.1111/j.1753-0237.2009.00157.x

Lincoln, Y. S., & Guba, E. G. (2003). Paradigmatic controversies, contradictions, and emerging confluences. In The Landscape of Qualitative Research: Theories and Issues (2nd ed., pp. 253-291). London: Sage.

Lincoln, Y. S., & Guba, E. G. (2003). Paradigmatic controversies, contradictions, and emerging confluences. In N. K. Denzin & Y. S. Lincoln (Eds.), *The Landscape of Qualitative Research: Theories and Issues* (2nd ed., pp. 253–291). Sage.

Ling, P. (2008). Political marketing in Australia. *IMC Journal*, *7*(1), 15–20.

Littleboy, B. (2016). Development planning under strategic uncertainty. In M. Allaudin, M. K. Mujeri, & D. K. Nath (Eds.), *Bangladesh Yesterday, Today, tomorrow, Essays in Honor of Professor Sanat Kumar Saha* (p. 76). Shahitya Prakash.

Lloyds Register Foundation. (2020). *Safer Decommissioning of Offshore Structures and Ships*. Lloyd's Register Foundation. http://lrfoundation.org.uk

Loosemore, M. (2016). Social procurement in UK construction projects. *International Journal of Project Management, 34*(1), 133–144.

Macdonald-Smith, A. (2020, November 3). *Decommissioning crisis clouds oil M&A outlook.* Australian Financial Review. https://www.afr.com/companies/energy/decommissioning-crisis-clouds-oil-m-and-a-outlook-20201102-p56anf

Mackenzie, W. (2017). *Woodmac: Bangladesh's LNG demand to rise to 8 MMtpy by early next decade.* http://www.gasprocessingnews.com/news/woodmac-bangladeshs-lng-demand-to-rise-to-8-mmtpy-by-early-next-decade.aspx

Mahanty, J. N. (1983). China and the Emergence of Bangladesh: Role of Great Power Global Perceptions. *India Quarterly, 39*(2), 137–158.

Maldives Customs Service. (2019). *Total Imports 2019.* Retrieved from https://www.customs.gov.mv/Media/Documents/downloads

Malik, A., Parks, B., Russell, B., Lin, J., Walsh, K., Solomon, K., Zhang, S., Elston, T., & Goodman, S. (2021). *Banking on the Belt and Road: Insights from a new global dataset of 13,427 Chinese development projects.* AidData at William & Mary.

Mallick, R. (2002). Implementing and Evaluating Microcredit in Bangladesh. *Development in Practice, 12*(2), 153–163. doi:10.1080/09614520220127676

Mamun, S. (2021, February 17). Construction of Dhaka-Ashulia Elevated Expressway finally set to begin [Review of *Construction of Dhaka-Ashulia Elevated Expressway finally set to begin*]. *Dhaka Tribune.* https://www.dhakatribune.com/bangladesh/2021/02/17/construction-of-dhaka-ashulia-elevated-expressway-finally-set-to-begin

Marcus, B. C. L. (2021). *How the Maldives became the biggest 2020 international tourism success story.* CNN. Retrieved October 14, 2021, from https://edition.cnn.com/travel/article/maldives-tourism-arrivals-coronavirus-intl-hnk/index.html

Maritime Gateway. (2021, June 9). *Will Bangladesh be a victim to China's debt trap?* [Review of *Will Bangladesh be a victim to China's debt trap?*]. Maritime Gateway. https://www.maritimegateway.com/will-bangladesh-be-a-victim-to-chinas-debt-trap/

Marques, A. C., & Fuinhas, J. A. (2012). Is renewable energy effective in promoting growth? *Energy Policy, 46*, 434–442. doi:10.1016/j.enpol.2012.04.006

Marton, F., & Saljo, R. (1976). On qualitative differences in learning. I - Outcome and Process. *The British Journal of Educational Psychology, 46*(1), 4–11. doi:10.1111/j.2044-8279.1976.tb02980.x

Masud, M. H., Nuruzzaman, M., Ahamed, R., Ananno, A. A., & Tomal, A. N. M. A. (2020). Renewable energy in Bangladesh: Current situation and future prospect. *International Journal of Sustainable Energy, 39*(2), 132–175. doi:10.1080/14786451.2019.1659270

MauryaA. (2017). US China trade war: Opportunities for India. *Available at* SSRN 3043699. doi:10.2139/ssrn.3043699

McCarthy, E. J. (1964). *Basic Marketing: A Managerial Approach.* Richard D. Irwin, Inc.

MCCI. (2021). *Mauritius Chamber of Commerce and Industry.* President Report. https://www.mcci.org/president-report-2021/

McCubbin, A., Hammer, S., & Ayriss, P. (2021). Learning and teaching benchmarking in Australian universities: The current state of play. *Journal of Higher Education Policy and Management, 1*, 1–18. doi:10.1080/1360080X.2021.1934244

McKay, S., Higgins, S. A., & Baker, P. (2020). NORM inventory forecast for Australian offshore oil and gas decommissioned assets and radioactive waste disposal pathways. *APPEA Journal, 60*(1), 19–33. doi:10.1071/AJ19159

McRae, H. (1995, Feb. 26). The privilege of unemployment, *Independent on Sunday*, p. 4. https://www.independent.co.uk/news/business/the-privilege-of-unemployment-the-economy-analysis-1574883.html

McSharry, G., & Jones, S. (2000). Role-play in science teaching and learning. *The School Science Review*, *82*(298), 73–82.

Medhekar, A. (2019). Emerging Trends of Wellness and Medical Tourism in India. In S. Paul & S.K. Kulshreshtha (Eds.), Global Developments in Healthcare and Medical Tourism. IGI Global. doi:091218-104208

Medhekar, A. (2021). Australia-India: Bilateral Trade Opportunities and Challenges. In *Emerging Business and Trade Opportunities between Oceania and Asia*. IGI Global Publishing. doi:10.4018/978-1-7998-4126-5.ch004

Medhekar, A., & Kaur, H. (2022). Look-East Act-East Policy: India and South East Asian Economic Cooperation. In A. Medhekar & H. Kaur (Eds.), *Evaluating Trade and Economic Relations Between India and Southeast Asia* (pp. 1–22). IGI Global Publishing., doi:10.4018/978-1-7998-5774-7.ch001

Medhekar, A., Wong, H. Y., & Hall, J. E. (2019). Factors influencing inbound medical travel to India. *Journal of Health Organization and Management*, *33*(2), 155–172. doi:10.1108/JHOM-08-2018-0234 PMID:30950309

Mehdi, M., Ahmad, B., & Ahsan, M. B. (2018). 13. Value Chain Development and Social Upgrading: A Case of Pakistan's Mango Industry. *Labor and Globalization*, *1*(1), 273–290.

Melville, A. (2021). The Global Digital Infrastructure Survey 2021. *IJ Global, Project Finance and Infrastructure Journal*. Retrieved from: https://ijglobal.com/articles/155544/the-global-digital-infrastructure-survey-2021

Menon, S. (2021, April 29). *India Coronavirus: can it make enough vaccines to meet demand?* Retrieved from https://www.bbc.com/news/world-asia-india-55571793

Ments, M. V. (1999). *The effective use of role play*. Kogan Page Publishers.

Michael, I., Armstrong, A., Badran, B., & King, B. (2011). Dubai outbound tourism: An exploratory study of Emiratis and expatriates. *Journal of Vacation Marketing*, *17*(1), 83–91. doi:10.1177/1356766710391448

Michael, N., James, R., & Michael, I. (2018). Australia's cognitive, affective and conative destination image: An Emirati tourist perspective. *Journal of Islamic Marketing*, *9*(1), 36–59. doi:10.1108/JIMA-06-2016-0056

Mikelis, N. (2019, October). *The Recycling of Ships*. GMS. https://www.gmsinc.net/gms_new/assets/publications/pdf/2020-01-16rJU_org.pdf

Milad, M. (2021, July 9). 25 Years Old Ship, Cost 24.564 million. *Prothom Alo*.

Miles, M. B., & Huberman, A. M. (1994). *Qualitative data analysis: An expanded source book* (2nd ed.). Sage.

Miles, M., & Huberman, A. (1994). *An expanded sourcebook: qualitative data analysis*. Sage Publications.

Milian, E. Z., Spinola, M. D. M., & Carvalho, M. M. D. (2019). Fintechs: A literature review and research agenda. *Electronic Commerce Research and Applications*, *34*(1).

Miline, P. (2021, August 23). *Government Hurries to Tow Northern Endeavor away by Mid-2023*. Boiling Cold. https://boilingcold.com.au

Miller, J. B. (2018). *The Quad: security cooperation between the US*.

Ministry of Fisheries. (2020). *Fisheries Statistics 2020*. Ministry of Fisheries. https://www.fisheriesdept.gov.lk/web/images/Statistics/FISHERIES-STATISTICS--2020-.pdf

Ministry of Foreign Affairs. (2017). *Joint Declaration on Enhanced Cooperation between Australia and Sri Lanka*. Ministry of Foreign Affairs. https://mfa.gov.lk/jd-a-sl/

Mishra, I. (2020, March 13). Study in India: Is India ready to be a destination for foreign students? *The Bastion*. https://thebastion.co.in/politics-and/study-in-india-is-india-ready-to-be-a-destinationfor-foreign-students/

Mishra, V., & Das, S. (2020). *Education as a Pivot in India's Cooperation with BISMTEC Countries. ORF Issue Brief No. 418*. Observer Research Foundation.

Misra, R., & Choudhry, S. (2020). Trade war: Likely impact on India. *Foreign Trade Review*, *55*(1), 93–118. doi:10.1177/0015732519886793

Mitra, S. K. (2014, August). Mango production in the world–present situation and future prospect. In *XXIX International Horticultural Congress on Horticulture: Sustaining Lives, Livelihoods and Landscapes (IHC2014): IV 1111* (pp. 287-296). Academic Press.

Mitra, D. (2012, July - December). The role of crowdfunding in entrepreneurial finance. *Delhi Business Review*, *13*(2), 67–72. doi:10.51768/dbr.v13i2.132201218

Mizanur Rahman, S., & Mayer, A. L. (2015). How social ties influence metal resource flows in the Bangladesh ship recycling industry. *Resources, Conservation and Recycling*, *104*, 254–264. doi:10.1016/j.resconrec.2015.07.022

MNRE G 2019–20. (2020). *Annual report 2019–20*. Ministry of New and Renewable Energy, Government of India.

Modak, S. (2020, November 11). *The Teesta quagmire: India's missed opportunity?* [Review of *The Teesta quagmire: India's missed opportunity?*]. Observer Research Foundation. https://www.orfonline.org/research/the-teesta-quagmire-indias-missed-opportunity/

Mohan, C. R. (2011). South Asia Rising. *The Indian Express*. https://indianexpress.com/article/opinion/columns/south-asia-rising/

Molly, N. N. (2012). Regional cooperation in higher education in Asia and the Pacific. *Asian Education and Development Studies*, *1*(1), 18–23. doi:10.1108/20463161211194432

Molson, M. (2021). China's Foreign Policy of giving huge loans to developing countries, whether it is an advantageous practice to fund development or a form of debt trap policy. *Moko Molson*. https://www.academia.edu/43317139/Chinas_Foreign_Policy_of_giving_huge_loans_to_developing_countries_whether_it_i

Moon, M. A., Mohel, S. H., & Farooq, A. (2021). I green, you green, we all green: Testing the extended environmental theory of planned behavior among the university students of Pakistan. *The Social Science Journal*, *58*(3), 316–332. doi:10.1016/j.soscij.2019.05.001

Moss, S., & Sandhu, K. (2020). A Study of Factors Influencing Digital Accounting Software Selection in Thailand. In *Digital Transformation and Innovative Services for Business and Learning*. IGI Global. Retrieved from: https://www.igi-global.com/book/digital-transformation-innovative-services-business/245338

Mossialos, E., & Wenzl, M. (2016). *2015 International Profiles of Health Care Systems*. The Commonwealth Fund. doi:10.15868ocialsector.25100

Moysidou, K., & Hausberg, J. P. (2020). In crowdfunding we trust: A trust-building model in lending crowdfunding. *Journal of Small Business Management*, *58*(3), 511–543. doi:10.1080/00472778.2019.1661682

Munir, M.M.H. (2019).*Bangladesh Needs to Fight against Illicit Finance Flow and to Achieve SDGs*. Social Watch. Retrieved from https://www.socialwatch.org/node/18286

Murad, S. M. W. (2012). Bilateral Export and Import Demand Functions of Bangladesh: A Cointegration Approach. *Bangladesh Development Studies*, *35*(1), 43–60.

Murshid, K. A. S. (2019). Employment and Unemployment amongst Educated Youth in Bangladesh: An Exploratory Analysis. *Bangladesh Development Studies*, *42*(4), 1–49.

Mycause. (2017). *Top crowdfunding sites in Australia.* Accessed date 17 Aug. 21 at https://www.mycause.com.au/blog/top-crowdfunding-sites-in-australia

Nanda, P. K. (2020, June 18). *Govt to allow colleges, varsities to offer 40% of coursework online.* https://www.livemint.com/education/news/govt-to-allow-colleges-varsities-tooffer-40-of-coursework-online-1159242573470

National Aeronautics and Space Administration. (2021). *Global Climate Change: Vital Signs of the Planet.* Retrieved from https://climate.nasa.gov/vital-signs/global-temperature/

National Centres for Environmental Information. (2021). *Assessing the Global Climate in June 2021.* Retrieved from https://www.ncei.noaa.gov/news/global-climate-202106

National Industry Insights. (2021, March 22). *Health.* Retrieved from National Industry Insights.net.au: https://nationalindustryinsights.aisc.net.au/industries/health#:~:text=The%20Health%20Care%20and%20Social%20Assistance%20industry%20is%20the%20largest,than%201.9%20million%20by%202024

Navpreet. (2020). Potential and Prospects for Regional Power Cooperation in the SAARC Region. *Journal of Critical Reviews, 7*(11).

Naz, A., Zaman, K., Yousaf, S. U., Nassani, A. A., Aldakhil, A. M., & Abro, M. M. Q. (2019). Saudi Arabia-China-Pakistan economic corridor: Intergovernmental green initiatives. *Environmental Science and Pollution Research International*, *26*(25), 25676–25689. doi:10.100711356-019-05843-2 PMID:31267397

Naz, S., Page, A., & Agho, K. E. (2017). Household air pollution from use of cooking fuel and under-five mortality: The role of breastfeeding status and kitchen location in Pakistan. *PLoS One*, *12*(3), 1–14. doi:10.1371/journal.pone.0173256 PMID:28278260

NERA. (2016). *Oil and Gas Industry Competitiveness Assessment: Report on the Framework, Baseline Score, Insights and Opportunities.* www.nera.org.au

Ngaibiakching & Pande, A. (2020). India's Act East Policy and ASEAN: Building a Regional Order Through Partnership in the Indo-Pacific. *International Studies, 57*(1), 67-78.

NITI, Aayog, & IEEJ. (2017). *Energizing India.* A Joint Project Report of NITI Aayog and IEEJ. doi:10.1016/j.ijcard.2017.07.068

Nix, J. M. L. (2021). Co-teachers' perceptions of collaborative EFL teaching: A case study in Taiwan. *Asia Pacific Education Review*, *1*(4), 1–14. doi:10.100712564-021-09684-y

NOPSEMA. (2020). *Inside: Managing Ageing Infrastructure Stewarding Australia's offshore assets in later life.* NOPSEMA. https://www.nopsema.gov.au/sites/default/files/documents/2021-04/A720926.pdf

Northrop, E., Konar, M., Frost, N., & Hollaway, E. (2020). *A Sustainable and Equitable Blue Recovery to the COVID-19 Crisis: Summary for Decision Makers, Secretariat of the High-Level Panel for a Sustainable Ocean Economy.* World Resources Institute. https://oceanpanel.org/sites/default/files/2020-09/20_HLP_Report_COVID_Blue_Recovery.pdf

Norton, R., Perris, R., & Armstrong, R. (2007). Learning from Long-term Experiments–What Do They Teach Us? The Healthy Soils Symposium. *Embrace Green Revolution, 1,* 113-160.

O'Cass, A. (1996). Political marketing and the marketing concept. *European Journal of Marketing, 30*(10/11), 37–53. doi:10.1108/03090569610149782

O'Sullivan, D., Rahamathulla, M., & Pawar, M. (2020). The Impact and implications of COVID-19: Australian Perspective. *The International Journal of Community and Social Development*, 134-151.

OECD. (2003). *The Source of Economic Growth in OECD Countries*. Organization for Economic Cooperation and Development.

OECD. (2016). *Innovating Education and Educating for Innovation: The Power of Digital Technologies and Skills*. OECD Publishing.

Offner, K. L., Sitnikova, E., Joiner, K., & MacIntyre, C. R. (2020). Towards understanding cybersecurity capability in Australian healthcare organisations: A systematic review of recent trends, threats, and mitigation. *Intelligence and National Security, 35*(4), 556–585. doi:10.1080/02684527.2020.1752459

Ohlin, B. (1933). Interregional and International Trade. Harvard University Press.

Okeleke, K. (2021). Achieving mobile-enabled digital inclusion in Bangladesh [Review of *Achieving mobile-enabled digital inclusion in Bangladesh*]. In *GSMA* (pp. 6–7). GSMA (Swedish International Development Cooperation Agency, Sida). https://www.gsma.com/mobilefordevelopment/wp-content/uploads/2021/03/Achieving-mobile-enabled-digital-inclusion-in-Bangladesh.pdf

One Belt, One Road (OBOR) Initiative: How Bangladesh can benefit through the new horizon of regional co-operation. (2017, June 19). *Light Castle Partners*. https://www.lightcastlebd.com/insights/2017/06/one-belt-one-road-obor-initiative-bangladesh-can-benefit-new-horizon-regional-co-operation

Onmarket. (2021). *What we do*. Accessed date 31 August 2021 from https://www.onmarket.com.au/about-us/what-we-do/

OP-ED: How do we attract FDI in the time of corona? (2020, May 28). *Dhaka Tribune*. https://www.dhakatribune.com/opinion/op-ed/2020/05/28/a-realignment-of-priorities-in-light-of-covid-19

Ormrod, R. P., & Henneberg, S. C. (2010). Strategic Political Postures and Political Market Orientation: Towards an Integrated Concept of Political Marketing Strategy. *Journal of Political Marketing, 9*(1), 294–313. doi:10.1080/15377857.2010.518106

Pachauri, R. K. (2021). Oration 11: 2007 KR Narayanan Oration. Coping with Climate Change: Is Development in India and the World Sustainable? In *Twenty KR Narayanan Orations: Essays by Eminent Persons on the Rapidly Transforming Indian Economy*. ANU Press. doi:10.22459/TKRNO.2021.11

Panda, A. (2017, Nov. 13). US, Japan, India, and Australia hold working-level Quadrilateral meeting on regional cooperation: The 'QUAD' is back. *The Diplomat*. Retrieved from https://thediplomat.com/2017/11/us-japan-india-and-australia-hold-working-level-QUADrilateral-meeting-on-regional-cooperation/

Panda, J. P. (2014). Factoring the RCEP and the TPP: China, India and the Politics of Regional Integration. *Strategic Analysis, 38*(1), 49–67. doi:10.1080/09700161.2014.863462

Panda, J. P. (2020). India, the blue dot network, and the 'Quad Plus' calculus. *Air Force J. Indo-. Pacific Affairs, 3*, 4–22.

Pandey, P. C. (2020, December 18). *India Has Seen Greenhouse Gas Emissions Increase by a Staggering 335% Since 1990*. Climate Scorecard. https://www.climatescorecard.org/2020/12/india-has-seen-greenhouse-gas-emissions-increase-by-a-staggering-335-since-1990/

Pandey, B., & Bajgain, S. (2007). Feasibility study of domestic biogas in Pakistan. *RSPN*, (July), 1–38.

Parliament of Australia. (2021). *Effects of COVID-19 on Australia.* Retrieved from Parliament of Australia: https://www.aph.gov.au/Parliamentary_Business/Committees/Joint/Foreign_Affairs_Defence_and_Trade/FADTandglobalpandemic/Report/section?id=committees%2Freportjnt%2F024552%2F73973

Parthiban, R., Qureshi, I., Bandyopadhyay, S., Bhatt, B., & Jaikumar, S. (2020). Leveraging ICT to overcome complementary institutional voids: Insights from institutional work by a social enterprise to help marginalized. *Information Systems Frontiers, 22*(1), 633–653. doi:10.100710796-020-09991-6

Paudyal, M. (2013). *Role of Private Sector in the Growth of Power Infrastructure in South Asia.* Investment Board, Government of Nepal.

Paul, A. (2020). Regional Cooperation in South Asia: Exploring the Three Pillars of Regionalism and their Relevance. *The Journal of Indian and Asian Studies.*

Paul, R. (2017). Bangladesh set to sign 15-year LNG import deal with Qatar. *Reuters.* https://www.reuters.com/article/us-bangladesh-qatar-lng-idUSKCN1BO10P

Pavithra, V., & Chandrasekaran, J. (2021). Developing Security Solutions for Telemedicine Applications: Medical Image Encryption and Watermarking. In *Research Anthology on Telemedicine Efficacy, Adoption, and Impact on Healthcare Delivery* (pp. 612-631). Retrieved from www.igi-global.com/chapter/developing-security-solutions-for-telemedicineapplications/

Pearson, E. (2015). *How Australia can help end child marriage in Bangladesh.* Women's Agenda. Retrieved from, https://www.hrw.org/news/2015/06/24/how-australia-can-help-end-child-marriage-bangladesh

Pence, M. (2018). *Vice President Mike Pence's Remark on the Administration's Policy Towards China.* https://www.hudson.org/events/1610-vice-president-mike-pence-s-remarks-on-the-administration-s-policy-towards-china-102018

Pereira, A., Biddington, B., Rajagopalan, R., & Suzuki, K. (2021, March). The Quad: Implications for Space. In 2021 IEEE Aerospace Conference (50100) (pp. 1-15). IEEE.

Phale, K., Li, F., Adjei, M., Omari-Sasu, A. Y., & Musah, M. (2021). Knowledge-Based Economy Capacity Building for Developing Countries: A Panel Analysis in Southern African Development Community. *Sustainability, 13*(5), 2890. doi:10.3390u13052890

Pharmexci. (2021). *Pharmexcil's Business Delegation to Australia and New Zealand (22nd July-26th July 2019).* Retrieved from Pharmexci.com: https://pharmexcil.com/circulars/pharmexcil%E2%80%99s-business-delegation-to-australia-and-new-zealand--22nd-july-26th-july-2019-/10260/d94f0180777644b247efb4b3cf863912.html

Pitman, A. (n.d.). *Why Bangladesh has been ignoring India's warnings about the Chinese "debt trap."* Scroll.in. Retrieved from https://scroll.in/article/997715/why-bangladesh-has-been-ignoring-indias-warnings-about-the-chinese-debt-trap

Plagemann, J. (2021). Small states and competing connectivity strategies: What explains Bangladesh's success in relations with Asia's major powers? *The Pacific Review,* 1–29.

Prabheesh, K. P., Padhan, R., & Garg, B. (2020). COVID-19 and the oil price–stock market nexus: Evidence from net oil-importing countries. *Energy Research Letters, 1*(2), 13745. doi:10.46557/001c.13745

Preiss, R. M. (2019). Sri Lanka's Market: An Investment Gem Hidden in Too Much Pessimism. *Forbes.* Retrieved October 14, 2021, from https://www.forbes.com/sites/rainermichaelpreiss/2019/08/07/sri-lankas-market-an-investment-gem-hidden-in-too-much-pessimism/?sh=521f301d5df6

Presidential Secreteriat. (2021). *A multi-day fishing vessel monitoring system from Australia to Sri Lanka. Presidential Secretariat.* https://www.presidentsoffice.gov.lk/index.php/2021/07/16/a-multi-day-fishing-vessel-monitoring-system-from-australia-to-sri-lanka/

PricewaterhouseCoopers. (2015). *The World in 2050: Will the shift in global economic power continue?* https://www.pwc.com/gx/en/issues/the-economy/assets/world-in-2050-february-2015.pdf

Prime Minister of Australia. (2020). *Investment in new energy Technology.* Prime Minister, Minister for Energy and Emissions Reduction, Media Release 17 September. Retrieved from https://www.pm.gov.au/media/investment-new-energy-technologies

PWC. (2017). *Crowdfunding: Unleashing female entrepreneurial potential.* The Crowdfunding Center. Pricewater-houseCoopers.

PWC. (2021). *National lockdown in Mauritius until 30 April 2021.* Price Waterhouse Coopers. https://www.pwc.com/mu/en/about-us/press-room/lockdown-communique.html

Pyper, J. (2021). *How India's Renewable Energy Sector Survived and Thrived in a Turbulent 2020.* Published Online at GreenTech Media. Retrieved from https://www.greentechmedia.com/articles/read/india-solar-energy-transition-pandemic-2020

Qi, C., & Zhang, J. X. (2018). The economic impacts of the China-Australia Free Trade Agreement-A general equilibrium analysis. *China Economic Review, 47*, 1–11. doi:10.1016/j.chieco.2017.11.002

Rabbi, H., & Rahman, A. (2017). Ship breaking and recycling industry of Bangladesh; issues and challenges. *Procedia Engineering, 194*, 254–259. doi:10.1016/j.proeng.2017.08.143

Rahim, M. (2011). Initial Trade Policy Focus of the High Performing Asian Economies: A Critical Assessment. *Bangladesh Development Studies, 34*(1), 87–102.

Rahman, M. M. (2020, August 10). BD gets $1.0b China loan to improve power grid [Review of *BD gets $1.0b China loan to improve power grid*]. *The Financial Express.* https://thefinancialexpress.com.bd/trade/bd-gets-10b-china-loan-to-improve-power-grid-1596857911

Rahman, S. M., & Akter, H. (2020). Bilateral trade relation between Bangladesh and Australia. In The Economic Development of Bangladesh in the Asian Century Prospects and Perspectives. Routledge.

Rahman, S. M., & Akter, H. (2020). Bilateral trade relation between Bangladesh and Australia. In *The Economic Development of Bangladesh in the Asian Century* (pp. 29–62). Routledge.

Rahman, S., & Kim, J. (2020). Circular economy, proximity, and shipbreaking: A material flow and environmental impact analysis. *Journal of Cleaner Production, 259*, 120681. doi:10.1016/j.jclepro.2020.120681

Raja Mohan, C. (2014, Nov. 22). Not so easy to Act East. *The Indian Express.* https://indianexpress.com/article/opinion/columns/not-so-easy-to-act-east/

Rajkhowa, G. (2016, September 3). *Internationalising Indian universities – The way forward.* University World News. www.universityworldnews.com/ post.php?story=20160903061847638

Rama, M., Béteille, T., Li, Y., Mitra, P. K., & Newmann, J. L. (2014). *Addressing Inequality in South Asia.* World Bank Publications. doi:10.1596/978-1-4648-0022-1

Ramsden, P. (2008). *Learning to teach in Higher Education.* Routledge Falmer.

Rana, M. (2018). Transformation of Indo-Bangladesh Relations: From Insecurity to Cooperation in Northeast India. *Strategic Analysis*, *42*(6), 559–577. doi:10.1080/09700161.2018.1559976

Ranasinghe, K. (2019). Chinese loans are not the primary cause of the Sri Lankan debt crisis [Review of *Chinese loans are not the primary cause of the Sri Lankan debt crisis*]. *Ceylon Today*. https://www.academia.edu/38868730/Chinese_loans_are_not_the_primary_cause_of_the_Sri_Lankan_debt_crisis

Ranjan, V. (2016). Australia and India in Asia: When 'Look West' Meets Act East. *Strategic Analysis*, *40*(5), 425–439. doi:10.1080/09700161.2016.1209906

Rasul, G., Nepa, A., Hussain, A., Maharjan, A., Joshi, S., Lama, A., . . . Sharma, E. (2021). Socio-Economic Implications of COVID-19 Pandemic in South Asia: Emerging Risks and Growing Challenges. *Frontiers in Sociology*.

Rasul, S. N. (2020, May 28). How do we attract FDI in the time of corona? [Review of *How do we attract FDI in the time of corona?*]. *Dhaka Tribune*. https://www.dhakatribune.com/opinion/op-ed/2020/05/28/a-realignment-of-priorities-in-light-of-covid-19

Ratten, V. (2020). Coronavirus (covid-19) and social value co-creation. *International Journal of Sociology and Social Policy*.

Ravenhill, J. (1997). *From paternalism to partnership: Australia's relations with ASEAN*. Australian National University Research Publications. https://openresearch-repository.anu.edu.au/handle/1885/40378

Rayburn, S. W., Anderson, S., & Sierra, J. J. (2020). Future thinking continuity of learning in marketing: A student perspective on crisis management in higher education. *Marketing Education Review*, *1*, 1–15.

RBA. (2021a). *Cash Rate Target*. Reserve Bank of Australia. https://www.rba.gov.au/statistics/cash-rate/

RBA. (2021b). *Statement by Philip Lowe, Governor: Monetary Policy Decision*. https://www.rba.gov.au/media-releases/2021/mr-21-19.html

ReadyFundGo. (2021). *Crowdfunding in Australia*. Access date 17 August 2021. From website https://readyfundgo.com/crowdfunding-in-australia/

Regan, H. (2020, May 6). *Billions of people could live in areas too hot for humans by 2070*. CNN.

Reliefweb. (2020). *Mauritius: MV Wakashio Oil Spill - Aug 2020*. Reliefweb. https://reliefweb.int/disaster/ac-2020-000180-mus

Report, B. (2008). *Review of Australian Higher Education*. Final report, 2008, Department of Education, Employment and Workplace Relations, Canberra.

Resource and Energy Quarterly. (2020). Office of the Chief Economist.

Ricardo, D. (1817). On the Principles of Political Economy and Taxation. London: John Murray.

Riessman, C. (2006). Narrative analysis. In V. Jupp (Ed.), *The sage dictionary of social research methods* (pp. 186–189). Sage Publications.

Ritchie, H. (2020). *Sector by sector: Where do global greenhouse gas emissions come from?* OurWorldInData.org.

Ritchie, H., & Roser, M. (2020). *Environmental impacts of food production*. Retrieved from: https://ourworldindata.org/environmental-impacts-of-food

Ritchie, H., Mathieu, E., Rodés-Guirao, L., Appel, C., Giattino, C., Ortiz-Ospina, E., Hasell, J., Macdonald, B., Beltekian, D., & Roser, M. (2020). *Coronavirus Pandemic (COVID-19)*. Our World in Data. https://ourworldindata.org/coronavirus

Rizvi, F., Gorur, R., & Reyes, C. (2013). *India-Australia Institutional Collaborations in Higher Education: Potential, Problems, Promises. A report for the Australia India Education Council. Project Report*. Australia-India Education Council.

Romanenko, M. (2021, January 13). *How to Scrap a Cruise Ship and What They Go For*. https://www.cruiseindustrynews.com/cruise-news/24172-how-to-scrap-a-cruise-ship-and-what-they-go-for.html

Roy-Chaudhury, R., & de Estrada, K. S. (2018). India, the Indo-Pacific and the Quad. *Survival*, *60*(3), 181–194. doi:10.1080/00396338.2018.1470773

Rozman, G., & Liow, J. C. (2018). *International Relations and Asia's Southern Tier*. Asan-Palgrave Macmillan Series. doi:10.1007/978-981-10-3171-7

Rughani, D. (2021, September 4). *Realising an 'early harvest' for Australia–India trade*. East Asia Forum. https://www.eastasiaforum.org/2021/09/04/realising-an-early-harvest-for-australia-india-trade/

Ruiz Estrada, M. A., Koutronas, E., & Lee, M. (2020). Stagpression: The Economic and Financial Impact of COVID-19 Pandemic. SSRN *Electronic Journal*. doi:10.2139/ssrn.3593144

SAARC Energy Centre. (2018). *SAARC Energy Outlook 2030*. CRISIL Ltd. Retrieved from https://www.saarcenergy.org/wp-content/uploads/2019/05/SAARC-Energy-Outlook-2030-Final-Report-Draft.pdf

SAARC. (2014). *Areas of cooperation Education*. South Asian Association of Regional Cooperation. Retrieved from https://www.saarc-sec.org/areaofcooperation/cat-detail.php?cat_id=53

Saavedra, A., Kotey, B., & Sandhu, K. (2020). The Digital Value Propositions for Virtual Business Incubators. In *Digital Innovations for Customer Engagement, Management, and Organizational Improvement*. IGI Global. Retrieved from: https://www.igi-global.com/book/digital-innovations-customer-engagement-management/245337

Sadaqat, R. (2021). *Unified tourism strategy to put Pakistan to global travel map*. Retrieved from https://www.khaleej-times.com/business/global/unified-tourism-strategy-to-put-pakistan-to-global-travel-map

SADC. (2020). *SADC Facts and Figures*. Southern African Development Community. https://www.sadc.int/about-sadc/overview/sadc-facts-figures/

Sadekin, M.N. (2021, July 30). Potentials of Blue Economy in Bangladesh. *Daily Asian Age*.

Sadorsky, P. (2009). Renewable energy consumption and income in emerging economies. *Energy Policy*, *37*(10), 4021–4028. doi:10.1016/j.enpol.2009.05.003

Saha, S., & Zhang, Z. (2013). Do exchange rates affect consumer prices? A comparative analysis for Australia, China and India. *Mathematics and Computers in Simulation*, *93*, 128–138. doi:10.1016/j.matcom.2012.11.002

Sajjanhar, A. (2016, May). Taking Stock of India's 'Act East Policy'. *Observer Research Foundation*, (142), 1–6.

Sakhawat, N. (2020, October 6). China-Bangladesh relations stronger than ever before [Review of *China-Bangladesh relations stronger than ever before*]. *The Daily Star*. https://www.thedailystar.net/opinion/news/china-bangladesh-relations-stronger-ever-1972993

Sakib, A. N. (2019). Corruption and organized crime in Bangladesh. In *Organized Crime and Corruption Across Borders* (pp. 241–256). Routledge.

Sakshi S. (2019). *India extends 30 million aid to Nepal to build educational institution*. Academic Press.

Salim, R. A., & Rafiq, S. (2012). Why do some emerging economies proactively accelerate the adoption of renewable energy? *Energy Economics*, *34*(4), 1051–1057. doi:10.1016/j.eneco.2011.08.015

Samsani, S. (2021). *China–Bangladesh strategic linkages.* Observer Research Foundation. https://www.orfonline.org/expert-speak/china-bangladesh-strategic-linkages/

Sandhu, K. (2020). Advances for Artificial Intelligence in Health Data Analytics to Drive Digital Systems Innovation. In *Opportunities and Challenges in Digital Healthcare Innovation.* IGI Global. Retrieved from: https://www.igi-global.com/book/opportunities-challenges-digital-healthcare-innovation/241178

Sandhu, K. (Ed.). (2021). Advancing Cybersecurity for Digital Transformation: Opportunities and Challenges. In Handbook of Research on Advancing Cybersecurity for Digital Transformation. IGI Global. doi:10.4018/978-1-7998-6975-7

Sanyal, A. (2021). *Impact of US-China Trade War on Indian External Trade.* Academic Press.

Sarker, P. C. (2019). One Belt one road project is a driving force for holistic development of Eurasian region: challenges to Bangladesh. In *Silk Road to Belt Road* (pp. 279–291). Springer.

Sarma, N. (2020). Free Trade after RCEP: What Next for India? *ORF Issue Brief,* (353).

Sarraf, M., Stuer-Lauridsen, F., Dyoulgerov, M., Bloch, R., Wingfield, S., & Watkinson, R. (2010). *Ship Breaking And Recycling Industry In Bangladesh And Pakistan December 2010.* World Bank. https://documents1.worldbank.org/curated/en/872281468114238957/pdf/582750ESW0Whit1LIC1011098791web1opt.pdf

Sarwar. (2020, November 19). *How can Bangladesh benefit from the Belt and Road Initiative? - Fahmida Khatun and Syed Yusuf Saadat - CPD.* Centre for Policy Dialogue (CPD). https://cpd.org.bd/how-can-bangladesh-benefit-from-the-belt-and-road-initiative/

SAU. (2015). *South Asian University.* Retrieved from http://www.sau.ac.in/

Scammell, M. (2015). Politics and image: The conceptual value of branding. *Journal of Political Marketing, 14*(1-2), 7–18. doi:10.1080/15377857.2014.990829

Scataglini, M., & Ventresca, J. M. (2019). *Funding the UN Sustainable Development Goals: Lessons from donation-based crowdfunding platforms.* University of Oxford Said Business School Working paper, February 2019.

Schwittay, A. (2019). Digital mediations of everyday humanitarianism: The case of Kiva.org. *Third World Quarterly, 40*(10), 1921–1938. doi:10.1080/01436597.2019.1625267

Scott, N., Baggio, R., & Cooper, C. (2008). *Network analysis and tourism: From theory to practice.* Channel View Publications.

Scutaru, L. (2013). Economic Development versus Sustainable Development. *ECOFORUM, 1*(2), 35-40.

Scuzzarello, S. (2020). Practising privilege. How settling in Thailand enables older Western migrants to enact privilege over local people. *Journal of Ethnic and Migration Studies, 46*(8), 1606–1628. doi:10.1080/1369183X.2020.1711570

SDG. (2016). *Partnerships for SDGs - 2016 special report.* United Nations Department of Economic and Social Affairs. https://sustainabledevelopment.un.org/content/documents/2329Partnership%20Report%202016%20web.pdf

Sebri, M., & Ben-Salha, O. (2014). On the causal dynamics between economic growth, renewable energy consumption, CO2 emissions and trade openness: Fresh evidence from BRICS countries. *Renewable & Sustainable Energy Reviews, 39,* 14–23. doi:10.1016/j.rser.2014.07.033

Selin, S. (1999). Developing a typology of sustainable tourism partnership. *Journal of Sustainable Tourism, 7*(3&4), 260–273. doi:10.1080/09669589908667339

Selin, S., & Chavez, D. (1995). Developing a collaborative model for environmental planning and management. *Environmental Management, 19*(2), 189–195. doi:10.1007/BF02471990

Sen, S., Ganguly, S., Das, A., Sen, J., & Dey, S. (2015). Renewable energy scenario in India: Opportunities and challenges. *Journal of African Earth Sciences.* Advance online publication. doi:10.1016/j.jafrearsci.2015.06.002

Seraphim, J., & Haq, F. (2019). Can design thinking enhance experiential heritage tourism in Pakistan. *NUST Business Review. International Journal (Toronto, Ont.), 1*(1), 1–11.

Serum Institute of India Pvt. Ltd. (2021, October). *About Us.* Retrieved from https://www.seruminstitute.com: https://www.seruminstitute.com/about_us.php

Shah, F. H. (2021). *Producing Grassroots Social Business Changemakers for Smart Communities.* Keynote at the Global Smart Education Conference, Beijing Normal University.

Shahbaz, M., Raghutla, C., Chittedi, K. R., Jiao, Z., & Vo, X. V. (2020). *The Impact of Renewable Energy Consumption on Economic Growth: Evidence form the Renewable Energy Country Attractive Index.* MPRA Paper No. 101168

Shahid, M. N., Hassan, W., & Sadaf, L. (2021). Exploring the Political Co-Brand Image & Positioning from External Stakeholder's Perspective in Pakistan. *Journal of Political Marketing, 1*(1), 1–30. doi:10.1080/15377857.2021.1930328

Shah, M. I., Ullah, I., Xingjian, X., Haipeng, H., Rehman, A., Zeeshan, M., & Afridi, F. E. A. (2021). Modeling Trade Openness and Life Expectancy in China. *Risk Management and Healthcare Policy, 14*, 1689–1701. doi:10.2147/RMHP.S298381 PMID:33935523

Shahnewaz, M. (2017). *The Effective Enforcement of National Ship Recycling Regulations in India* [Master's Thesis].

Shams, M. (2021). Bangladesh, Australia sign TIFA: The pact will usher in trade and investment opportunities, says economist. *The Business Post.* https://businesspostbd.com/post/28128

Sharif, S. I. (2018). The Prospect of Renewable Energy Resources in Bangladesh: A Study to Achieve the National Power Demand. *Energy and Power, 8*(1), 1–6. doi:10.5923/j.ep.20180801.01

Sharma, A. (2016). *Australia-India relations: trends and the prospects for a comprehensive economic relationship* (No. 2016-02). The Australian National University, Australia South Asia Research Centre. https://acde.crawford.anu.edu.au/sites/default/files/publication/acde_crawford_anu_edu_au/2016-09/asarc_wp_2016-02_sharma.pdf

Sharma, A. (2021). *The first summit QUAD meeting Reaffirms a free, open, and secure Indo pacific.* Retrieved from https://www.internationalaffairs.org.au/australianoutlook/the-first-summit-QUAD-meeting-reaffirms-a-free-open-and-secure-indo-pacific/

Sharma, E. K. (2021). *Interview: Muhammad Yunus on micro-credit & social impact models for a changed world.* https://www.financialexpress.com/economy/interview-muhammad-yunus-on-micro-credit-social-impact-models-for-a-changed-world/2207167/

Sharma, A., Gupta, P., & Jha, R. (2020). COVID-19: Impact on Health Supply Chain and Lessons to be Learnt. *Journal of Health Management, 22*(20), 248–261. doi:10.1177/0972063420935653

Shawon, A. A., & Farhat, N. (2021, June 26). PM Hasina approves scrapping of 10 coal-fired power plant projects. *Dhaka Tribune.* https://www.dhakatribune.com/bangladesh/2021/06/26/pm-hasina-approves-scrapping-of-10-coal-fired-power-plant-projects

Shazzad, H. (2021, November 8). Is Bangladesh at risk of falling into the Chinese debt trap? *The Daily Star.* https://www.thedailystar.net/views/opinion/news/bangladesh-risk-falling-the-chinese-debt-trap-2224391

Shehzad, K., Xiaoxing, L., & Kazouz, H. (2020). COVID-19's disasters are perilous than Global Financial Crisis: A rumor or fact? *Finance Research Letters*, *101669*, 101669. Advance online publication. doi:10.1016/j.frl.2020.101669 PMID:32837374

Shneor, R. (2020). Crowdfunding models, strategies, and choices between them. In *Advances in Crowdfunding Research and Practice*. Palgrave Macmillan. doi:10.1007/978-3-030-46309-0_2

Shneor, R., & Zhang, Z. B. (2020). The Global Status of the Crowdfunding Industry Tania Ziegler. *Advances in Crowdfunding Research and Practice*. doi:10.1007/978-3-030-46309-0

Shneor, R., & Zhao, R. (2020). Fundamentals to Advances in Crowdfunding Research and Practice. In *Advances in Crowdfunding Research and Practice*. Palgrave Macmillan.

Shringla, H. V. (2018). India–Bangladesh Relations: An Indian Perspective. *Strategic Analysis*, *42*(5), 524–528. doi:10.1080/09700161.2018.1523080

Shukla, A. K., Sudhakar, K., & Baredar, P. (2017). Renewable energy resources in South Asian Countries: Challenges, policy and recommendations. *Energy Centre, Resource-efficient Technologies*, *3*(3), 342–346. doi:10.1016/j.reffit.2016.12.003

Sibal, S. (2021, April 27). Retrieved from https://www.dnaindia.com/world/report-covid-19-crisis-australia-announces-support-pm-scott-calls-situation-heartbreaking-2888102

Siddique, A. H., Tasnim, S., Shahriyar, F., Hasan, M., & Rashid, K. (2021). Renewable Energy Sector in Bangladesh: The Current Scenario, Challenges and the Role of IoT in Building a Smart Distribution Grid. *Energies*, *14*(16), 5083. doi:10.3390/en14165083

Siddiqui, A. A., & Singh, P. (2021). US-China trade war: Impact on chemical exporting firms from India to US. *Corporate Governance*, (1), 75–84.

Similarities And Differences Between Australia and Bangladesh. (n.d.). Retrieved from https://www.cram.com/essay/Similarities-And-Differences-Between-Australia-And-Bangladesh/P3SPYFFNB5ZQ#google_vignette

Simsek, Y. (2020). An analysis of additional energy requirement to meet the sustainable development goals. *Journal of Cleaner Production*, *272*(122646), 1-14. doi:10.1016/j.jclepro.2020.122646

Smith, A. (1776). *An Inquiry into the nature and causes of the Wealth of Nations*. Retrieved from https://www.econlib.org/library/Smith/smWN.html

Smith, G. (2010). Australia and the Rise of India. *Australian Journal of International Affairs*, *64*(5), 566–582. doi:10.1080/10357710903544114

Smith, R. F. I. (2014). India and Australia: Closer and Closer? *Politico (Pavia, Italy)*, *127*. http://politicosse.in/uploads/Politico_2014_Vol-2_No-22.pdf#page=147

Somani, S. (2021). *Emerging infrastructure trends in Asia Pacific. A look at the future of the sector.* KPMG International entities. Retrieved from: https://home.kpmg/xx/en/blogs/home/posts/2021/05/emerging-infrastructure-trends-in-asia-pacific.html

Speed, R., Butler, P., & Collins, N. (2015). Human branding in political marketing: Applying contemporary branding thought to political parties and their leaders. *Journal of Political Marketing*, *14*(1-2), 129–151. doi:10.1080/15377857.2014.990833

Stake, R. E. (1995). *The Art of Case Study Research*. SAGE Publication.

Statista.com. (2021a, August). *Infant mortality rates in South Asia between 2020 and 2025, by country*. Retrieved from Statista.com: https://www.statista.com/statistics/590050/infant-mortality-rates-in-south-asia/

Statista.com. (2021b, August 9). *Total value of pharmaceutical product exports in Australia from 2008 to 2019*. Retrieved from Statista.com: https://www.statista.com/statistics/1199092/australia-value-of-pharmaceutical-exports/

Steiner, A., & Teasdale, S. (2016). The playground of the rich? Growing social business in the 21st century. *Social Enterprise Journal, 12*(2), 201–216. doi:10.1108/SEJ-12-2015-0036

Stevenson, K., & Envall, H. D. P. (2019). The 'quad 'and disaster management: An Australian perspective. *International Disaster Response: Rebuilding the Quad*, 13-23.

Strand, T. (2017). *NORM in the Norwegian Oil and Gas Industry -Activity Levels, Occupational Doses and Protective Measures*. https://www.ipen.br/biblioteca/cd/irpa/2004/files/5k14.pdf

Sujauddin, M., Koide, R., Komatsu, T., Hossain, M., Tokoro, C., & Murakami, S. (2016). Ship breaking and the steel industry in Bangladesh: A material flow perspective. *Journal of Industrial Ecology, 21*(1), 191–203. doi:10.1111/jiec.12423

Suman, M. (2021, October 9). Tunnel of hope: Breakthrough achieved in construction under Karnaphuli. *The Daily Star.* https://www.thedailystar.net/news/bangladesh/transport/news/tunnel-hope-2193871

Sunley, P., & Pinch, S. (2012). Financing social enterprise: Social bricolage or evolutionary entrepreneurialism? University of Southampton, Southampton, UK. *Social Enterprise Journal, 8*(2), 108–122. doi:10.1108/17508611211252837

Suresh, K., Øyna, S., & Munim, Z. H. (2020). Crowdfunding prospects in new emerging markets: the cases of India and Bangladesh. In *Advances in Crowdfunding Research and Practice* (pp. 297–318). Palgrave Macmillan. doi:10.1007/978-3-030-46309-0_13

Sutrisno, A., & Pillay, H. (2015). Knowledge transfer through a transnational program partnership between Indonesian and Australian universities. *Asia Pacific Education Review, 16*(3), 379–388. doi:10.100712564-015-9384-7

Szczudlik-Tatar, J. (2013). *China's New Silk Road Diplomacy.* Polish Institute of International Affairs.

Taejai. (2021). *About.* Accessed date 1 September 2021 from https://taejai.com/en/

Tahir, M., Estrada, M. R., Khan, I., & Afridi, M. A. (2016). The role of trade openness for industrial sector development: Panel data evidence from SAARC region. *Journal of Asia Business Studies, 10*(1), 93–103. doi:10.1108/JABS-01-2015-0007

Tandon, A. (2016). India's Foreign Policy Priorities and the Emergence of a Modi Doctrine. *Strategic Analysis, 40*(5), 349–356. doi:10.1080/09700161.2016.1209909

Tang, E. (2020). Australia's 'Big Five': The Dynamic Industries that power trade & Investment. *Australian Trade and Investment Commission - Economic Analysis.* Retrieved from https://www.austrade.gov.au/news/economic-analysis/australias-big-five-the-dynamic-industries-that-power-trade-investment

Tang, E. (2021). Australia has the third freest economy in the world, says US think tank. *Australian Trade and Investment Commission.* https://www.austrade.gov.au/news/economic-analysis/australia-has-the-third-freest-economy-in-the-world-says-us-think-tank

Tanniru, M., Xi, Y., & Sandhu, K. (2020). Leadership to Advance Innovation for Digital Healthcare Transformation. In *Leadership, Management, and Adoption Techniques for Digital Service Innovation.* IGI Global. Retrieved from: https://www.igi-global.com/book/leadership-management-adoption-techniques-digital/237849

Tareen, W. U. K., Dilbar, M. T., Farhan, M., Ali Nawaz, M., Durrani, A. W., Memon, K. A., Mekhilef, S., Seyedmahmoudian, M., Horan, B., Amir, M., & Aamir, M. (2019). Present status and potential of biomass energy in Pakistan based on existing and future renewable resources. *Sustainability, 12*(1), 249. doi:10.3390u12010249

Taylor, S., & Taylor, M. (2017). The aroma of opportunity: The potential of wine geographical indications in the Australia-India comprehensive economic cooperation agreement. *The Importance of Place: Geographical Indications as a Tool for Local and Regional Development*, 81-107.

Teasdale, S. (2011). What's in a name? Making sense of social enterprise discourses. *Public Policy and Administration, 27*(2), 99–119. doi:10.1177/0952076711401466

Techera, E. J., & Chandler, J. (2015). Offshore installations, decommissioning and artificial reefs: Do current legal frameworks best serve the marine environment? *Marine Policy, 59*, 53–60. doi:10.1016/j.marpol.2015.04.021

Thakur, R., & Sharma, A. (2018). India in Australia's strategic framing in the Indo-Pacific. *Strategic Analysis, 42*(2), 69–83. doi:10.1080/09700161.2018.1439328

Thakur, R., & Sharma, A. (2018). *India in Australia's Strategic Framing in the Indo–Pacific*. Strategic Analysis.

Thatcher, A., Zhang, M., Todoroski, H., Chau, A., Wang, J., & Liang, G. (2020). Predicting the impact of COVID-19 on Australian universities. *Journal of Risk and Financial Management, 13*(9), 188-208.

The Australian resources sector - significance and opportunities. (n.d.). https://www.industry.gov.au/data-and-publications/australias-national-resources-statement/the-australian-resources-sector-significance-and-opportunities

The Belt and Road Initiative. (2018, May 3). *HKTDC Research.* Retrieved January 26, 2021, from https://research.hktdc.com/en/

The BRI in Bangladesh. (2021). *"Win-Win" or a "Debt Trap"?* Retrieved from https://thediplomat.com/2021/11/the-bri-in-bangladesh-win-win-or-a-debt-trap/

The Business Standard. (2020, July 9). *Will China Deliver on its Rohingya Assurance?* https://tbsnews. net/opinion/will-china-deliver-its-rohingya-assurance

The Business Standard. (2021). https://www.tbsnews.net/economy/target-1-china-market-smooth-ldc-graduation-experts-329260

The Business Standard. (2021). *With China relationship on the rocks.* https://www.business-standard.com/article/international/with-china-relationship-on-the-rocks-australia-eyes-india-for-trade-120091600276_1.html

The Business Standard. (2021, Sept. 15). *Bangladesh, Australia ink first Tifa agreement.* Author.

The Daily Star. (2020, October 15). *Seven BAF training aircraft procured from China arrive.* https://www.thedailystar.net/seven-baf-training-aircraft-procured-from-china-arrive-1978617

The Economic Times. (2018). India to increase public health spending. Retrieved from India to increase public health spending to 2.5% of GDP: PM Modi. *The Economic Times.*

The Economic Times. (2021). *Australia eyes closer economic ties.* https://economictimes.indiatimes.com/news/international/world-news/australia-eyes-closer-economic-ties-with-india-after-trade-row-with-china/articleshow/81384874.cms?from=mdr

The Economic Times. (2021). *Covax says India's serum Institute bound to supply virus vaccines.* Retrieved from https://health.economictimes.indiatimes.com/news/industry/covax-says-indias-serum-institute-bound-to-supply-virus-vaccines/81985191

The Economist. (2010). Learning without frontiers: Globalisation and higher education. *The Economist, 397*(8706).

The Financial Express. (n.d.). *Harnessing benefits from OBOR initiative*. Retrieved from https://thefinancialexpress.com.bd/views/harnessing-benefits-from-obor-initiative-1553962144

The Guardian. (2021). *Australia vows to 'vigorously defend' itself.* https://www.theguardian.com/australia-news/2021/jun/24/australia-vows-to-vigorously-defend-itself-against-china-wto-complaint

The Herald-Sun. (2021). *China complains to WTO over Australia's trade measures.* https://www.heraldsun.com.au/news/world/china-complains-to-wto-over-australias-trade-measures/news

The Hindustan Times. (2021a). *India shares challenges that prompted us to join AUKUS: Australian envoy.* https://www.hindustantimes.com/india-news/india-shares-challenges-that-prompted-us-to-join-aukus-australian-envoy-101631859734070.html

The Hindustan Times. (2021b). *Australia looking to diversify trade ties.* https://www.hindustantimes.com/world-news/australia-looking-to-diversify-trade-ties-amid-difficulties-with-china-trade-minister-dan-tehan-101633107517025.html

The Offshore Petroleum and Greenhouse Gas Storage Act (2006).

The World Bank. (2021a). Retrieved from https://data.worldbank.org/indicator/SH.MED.NUMW.P3

The World Bank. (2021b). Retrieved from https://data.worldbank.org/indicator/SH.MED.BEDS.ZS

The World Bank. (2021c). *South Asia.* Retrieved from https://www.worldbank.org/en/region/sar

The World Bank. (2021d). *Current Health Expenditure (% of GDP).* Retrieved from https://data.worldbank.org/indicator/SH.XPD.CHEX.GD.ZS

The World Trade Organization. (2020a). *China — Anti-dumping and countervailing duty measures on barley from Australia.* https://www.wto.org/english/tratop_e/dispu_e/dispu_status_e.htm

The World Trade Organization. (2020b). *United States — Tariff Measures on Certain Goods from China.* https://www.wto.org/english/tratop_e/dispu_e/cases_e/ds543_e.htm

Theerthaana, P., & Hansa Lysander Manohar, L. H. (2021). How a doer persuade a donor? Investigating the moderating effects of behavioral biases in donor acceptance of donation crowdfunding. *Journal of Research in Interactive Marketing, 15*(2), 243–266. doi:10.1108/JRIM-06-2019-0097

Thu, H. (2021). *Australia should bet on digital engagement with Southeast Asia.* Retrieved from: https://www.aspistrategist.org.au/australia-should-bet-on-digital-engagement-with-southeast-asia/

Tilak, J. B. (2020, August 9). A policy with a right intention. *The Hindu.* https://www.thehindu.com/opinion/op-ed/a-policy-with-many-a-right-intention/article32254650.ece

Tillett, A., & Cranston, E. (2021). Going nuclear: PM to announce $90b French submarine deal is dead. *Financial Review.* https://www.afr.com/politics/federal/speculation-pm-will-announce-90b-french-submarine-deal-is-dead-20210915-p58rzo

TimesofIndia. (2021). Sri Lanka to end Covid-19 lockdown on October 1. *Times of India.* https://timesofindia.indiatimes.com/world/south-asia/sri-lanka-to-end-covid-19-lockdown-on-october-1/articleshow/86615691.cms

Timsina, K. P., & Culas, R. (2021). Australia's Free Trade Agreements (FTAs) and Potentiality of Wheat Exports: A Panel Gravity Model Approach. *Journal of East-West Business*, 1–28. doi:10.1080/10669868.2021.1974640

Timsina, K. P., & Culas, R. J. (2020). Do free trade agreements increase Australian trade: An application of Poisson pseudo maximum likelihood estimator? *Journal of East-West Business, 26*(1), 56–80. doi:10.1080/10669868.2019.1685056

Tingming, K. (2021). *Maintaining momentum: Australian supplements sector secures domestic and exports growth.* Retrieved from nutraingredients-asia.com: https://www.nutraingredients-asia.com/Article/2020/06/09/Maintaining-momentum-Australian-supplements-sector-secures-domestic-and-exports-growth#:~:text=Maintaining%20momentum%3A%20Australian%20supplements%20sector%20secures%20domestic%20and%20exports%20gr

Tithila, K. K. (2021, October 13). Higher studies in China: A new horizon for Bangladeshi students [Review of *Higher studies in China: A new horizon for Bangladeshi students*]. *Dhaka Tribune*. https://www.dhakatribune.com/bangladesh/education/2021/10/13/higher-studies-in-china-a-new-horizon-for-bangladeshi-students

Trade Map. (2021). *Trade statistics for international business development Monthly, quarterly and yearly trade data. Import & export values, volumes, growth rates, market shares, etc.* https://www.trademap.org/Index.aspx

Trading Economics. (2021a). *Australia Economic Indicators*. Retrieved from https://tradingeconomics.com/australia/gdp

Trading Economics. (2021a). *Mauritius Coronavirus COVID-19 Vaccination Rate*. Trading Economics. https://tradingeconomics.com/

Trading Economics. (2021b). *Afghanistan Economic Indicators*. Retrieved from https://tradingeconomics.com/afghanistan/gdp

Trading Economics. (2021b). *Mauritius Economy Remains in Recession*. Trading Economics. https://tradingeconomics.com/mauritius/gdp-growth-annual

Trading Economics. (2021c). *Bangladesh Economic Indicators*. Retrieved from https://tradingeconomics.com/bangladesh/indicators

Trading Economics. (2021c). *Tourism Revenues in Sri Lanka*. Trading Economics. https://tradingeconomics.com/sri-lanka/tourism-revenues

Trading Economics. (2021d). *Bhutan Economic Indicators*. Retrieved from https://tradingeconomics.com/bhutan/indicators

Trading Economics. (2021d). *Tourist Arrivals in Maldives*. Trading Economics. https://tradingeconomics.com/maldives/tourist-arrivals

Trading Economics. (2021e). *India Economic Indicators*. Retrieved from https://tradingeconomics.com/india/indicators

Trading Economics. (2021e). *Regulatory Quality*. Trading Economics. https://tradingeconomics.com/australia/regulatory-quality-percentile-rank-lower-bound-of-90percent-confidence-interval-wb-data.html

Trading Economics. (2021f). *Insurance and Financial Services (% of service exports)*. Trading Economics. https://tradingeconomics.com/sri-lanka/insurance-and-financial-services-percent-of-service-exports-bop-wb-data.html

Trading Economics. (2021f). *Maldives Economic Indicators*. Retrieved from https://tradingeconomics.com/maldives/gdp

Trading Economics. (2021g). *Nepal Economic Indicators*. Retrieved from https://tradingeconomics.com/nepal/gdp

Trading Economics. (2021h). *Pakistan Economic Indicators*. Retrieved from https://tradingeconomics.com/pakistan/indicators

Trading Economics. (2021i). *SriLanka Economic Indicators*. Retrieved from https://tradingeconomics.com/sri-lanka/indicators

Transparency International. (2020). *Corruption Perception Index (CPI) scores*. Transparency International. https://www.transparency.org/en/cpi/2020/index/mus

Transparency Mauritius. (2014). *Towards transparent and accountable political financing*. Transparency Mauritius. https://www.transparencymauritius.org/wp-content/uploads/2014/10/Transparency-Mauritius_Pledge_HD.pdf

Travel Weekly. (2021). *Australia's tourism sector bouncing back "Stronger than expected" says new government report*. Retrieved from https://www.travelweekly.com.au/article/australias-tourism-sector-bouncing-back-stronger-expected-says-new-government-report/

Trigwell, K., Prosser, M., & Waterhouse, F. (1999). Relations between teachers' approaches to teaching and students' approaches to learning. *Higher Education*, *37*(1), 57–70. doi:10.1023/A:1003548313194

TripAdvisor. (2021). *Explore Pakistan. Tripadvisor has 74086 reviews of Pakistan Hotels, Attractions, and Restaurants*. https://www.tripadvisor.in/Tourism-g293959-Pakistan-Vacations.html

Tripathi, S. (2021). *Bangladesh's Long Journey From "Basket Case" to Rising Star*. Foreign Policy. Retrieved from https://foreignpolicy.com/2021/04/10/bangladesh-independence-anniversary-basket-case-rising-star/

Trivedi, A. (2021, September 22). *Experts: September 2021 White House QUAD meeting*. https://www.atlanticcouncil.org/uncategorized/experts-react-the-september-2021-white-house-quad-meeting/

Tyushka, A. (2019). *Strategic partnerships, international politics, and IR theory*. doi:10.4337/9781788972284.00010

Uddin, M. J., & Bhuiyan, M. R. (2011). Sino-Bangladesh Relations: An Appraisal. *Strategic Analysis*, *32*(1), 1–24.

Uddin, M. N., Rahman, M. A., Mofijur, M., Taweekun, J., Techato, K., & Rasul, M. G. (2019). Renewable energy in Bangladesh: Status and Prospects. *Energy Procedia*, *160*, 655–661. doi:10.1016/j.egypro.2019.02.218

UIS. (2012). *Online database and glossary*. UNESCO Institute for Statistics. Retrieved from http:// www.uis.unesco.org

Ullah, Z., Khan, J., & Haq, Z. U. (2018). Coastal Tourism & CPEC: Opportunities and Challenges in Pakistan. *Journal of Political Studies*, *25*(2), 261–272.

Ullah, Z., Naveed, R. T., Rehman, A. U., Ahmad, N., Scholz, M., Adnan, M., & Han, H. (2021). Towards the Development of Sustainable Tourism in Pakistan: A Study of the Role of Tour Operators. *Sustainability*, *13*(9), 4902. doi:10.3390u13094902

UNCLOS. (1982). *United Nations Convention on the Law of the Sea*. United Nations. https://www.un.org/depts/los/convention_agreements/texts/unclos/unclos_e.pdf

UNEP. (2021). *Nairobi Convention*. United Nations Environment Programme. https://www.unep.org/nairobiconvention/

UNESCO. (2015). *Adult literacy rate, population 15+ years (both sexes, female, male)*. UIS Data Centre. Retrieved from http://data.uis.unesco.org/Index.aspx? DataSetCode=EDULIT_DS&popupcustomise=true&lang=en#

UNFCCC. (2018). *Health, Climate and Small Island States*. United National Framework Convention on Climate Change. https://unfccc.int/news/health-climate-and-small-island-state

UNFCCC. (2021). *Most Vulnerable Countries Leading Climate Response*. United National Framework Convention on Climate Change. https://unfccc.int/news/most-vulnerable-countries-leading-climate-response

United Nations Educational, Scientific and Cultural Organization. (2019). *Sustainable Development Goals: Bangladesh*. http://uis.unesco.org/en/country/bd

United Nations. (2017). *Resolution adopted by the General Assembly on 6 July 2017, Work of the Statistical Commission pertaining to the 2030 Agenda for Sustainable Development*. Retrieved from https://ggim.un.org/documents/a_res_71_313.pdf

United Nations. (2021). *Economic and Social Commission for Asia and the Pacific, Micro, Small and Medium sized Enterprises' Access to Finance of in Bangladesh*. MSME Financing Series No. 5. Available at https://www.unescap.org/kp/2021/micro-small-and-medium-sized-enterprises-access-finance-bangladesh

United Nations. (2021). *Sustainable Development Goals. 17 Goals to transform our world.* Retrieved from https://www.un.org/sustainabledevelopment/

United Nations. (2021e). *Sustainable Development Goals. 17 Goals to transform our world.* Retrieved from https://www.un.org/sustainabledevelopment/ https://sdgs.un.org/goals

United State Institute of Peach. (2021). *The Impact of COVID-19 on South Asian Economies*. United State Institute of Peach.

Universal College Bangladesh. (2021). Retrieved from https://ucbbd.org/

UNSGSA FinTech Working Group and CCAF. (2019). *Early Lessons on Regulatory Innovations to Enable Inclusive FinTech: Innovation Offices, Regulatory Sandboxes, and RegTech.* Office of the UNSGSA and CCAF.

UNSTATS. (2021). *The Sustainable Development Goals Report 2021*. Access dated 13 October 2021 from https://unstats.un.org/sdgs/report/2021/The-Sustainable-Development-Goals-Report-2021.pdf

Usman, M., Ali, Y., Riaz, A., Riaz, A., & Zubair, A. (2020). Economic perspective of coronavirus (COVID-19. *Journal of Public Affairs*.

Varghese, N. V. (2020). Internationalisation and cross-border mobility in Indian higher education. International Journal of African Higher Education.

Varghese, P. (2018). *Indian Economic Strategy 2035.* Department of Foreign Affairs and Trade. Retrieved from https://dfat.gov.au/geo/india/ies/index.html

Vlosky, R. P., & Wilson, D. T. (2020). Technology in the Classroom: Teaching Business Marketing in the Twenty-First Century. In Fundamentals of Business Marketing Education (pp. 159-170). Routledge.

Voinov Kohler, J. (2017). The Basel convention on the control of transboundary movements of hazardous wastes and their disposal 1989. In *Multilateral environmental treaties* (pp. 331–342). Edward Elgar Publishing. doi:10.4337/9781783477210.V.32

Volunteer, Go. (2021). *About Volunteering*. Accessed date 10 August 2021. https://govolunteer.com.au/about-volunteering/

Vučinić, M. (2020). Fintech and Financial Stability Potential Influence of FinTech on Financial Stability, Risks and Benefits. *Journal of Central Banking Theory and Practice*, *2*(2), 43–66. doi:10.2478/jcbtp-2020-0013

Walsh, D., & Cowley, R. (2016). Optimising beef business performance in northern Australia: What can 30 years of commercial innovation teach us? *The Rangeland Journal*, *38*(3), 291–305. doi:10.1071/RJ15064

Walters, C. (2012). *A Focus on Quality and a Long Term Strategy*. Australian Education International.

Weidenfeld, A. (2018). Tourism diversification and Its Implications for smart Specialisation. *Sustainability*, *10*(2), 319–331. doi:10.3390u10020319

Were, A. (2018). *Debt trap? Chinese loans and Africa's development options*. Academic Press.

Westerman, G., Bonnet, D., & McAfee, A. (2014). The Nine Elements of Digital Transformation. *MIT Sloan Management Review*. Retrieved from: https://sloanreview.mit.edu/article/the-nine-elements-of-digital-transformation/

WHO. (2017). *Country cooperation strategy*. WHO.

WHO. (2020a, Jan. 31). *Coronavirus declared global health emergency by WHO.* Retrieved from https://www.bbc.com/news/world-51318246 https://www.who.int/countries/bgd/

WHO. (2020b). *Working for global equitable access to COVID-19 vaccines.* Retrieved from https://www.who.int/initiatives/act-accelerator/covax

WHO. (2021). *Infection prevention and control guidance for long-term care facilities in the context of COVId-19 update.* Retrieved from https://www.who.int/publications/i/item/WHO-2019-nCoV-IPC_long_term_care-2021.1

Wignaraja, G. W., Panditaratne, D., Kannangara, P., & Hundlani, D. (2020). *Chinese Investment and BRI in Srilanka.* Chatham House. https://www.chathamhouse.org/2020/03/chinese-investment-and-bri-sri-lanka

WilburC. M. (2021). https://www.britannica.com/place/China

Wilby, D. (2016, February 1). *Douglas-Westwood: coming decommissioning boom to be driven by UK.* Oilfield Technology. https://www.oilfieldtechnology.com/offshore-and-subsea/01022016/douglas-westwood-coming-decommissioning-boom-to-be-driven-by-uk/

Wilder, A. (2009). The politics of civil service reform in Pakistan. *Journal of International Affairs, 63*(1), 19–37.

Wilkins, S., & Epps, A. (2011). Student evaluation web sites as potential sources of consumer information in the United Arab Emirates. *International Journal of Educational Management, 25*(5), 410–422. doi:10.1108/09513541111146341

Will, X. W. (2015). *A Story of Doomed Bulls: On the Cause of High Debt Rate Behind 2015 Chinese Stock Crash.* Academic Press.

Wirth, A. (2020). Cyberinsights: COVID-19 and What It Means for Cybersecurity. *Biomedical Instrumentation & Technology, 54*(3), 216–219. Advance online publication. doi:10.2345/0899-8205-54.3.216 PMID:32442003

Wojczewski, T. (2019). Identity and world order in India's post-Cold War foreign policy discourse. *Third World Quarterly, 40*(1), 180–198. doi:10.1080/01436597.2018.1552079

Wood Mackenzie. (2016). *Wood Mackenzie.* https://www.woodmac.com/web/woodmac/data

Workman, D. (2021, March 16). *Australia's Top 10 Imports.* https://www.worldstopexports.com/australias-top-10-imports/

World Bank & CCAF (2019). *Regulating Alternative Finance: Results from a Global Regulator Survey.* Author.

World Bank. (2018). *The World Bank.* Retrieved from http://www.worldbank.org

World Bank. (2018, March 29). *Belt and Road Initiative.* World Bank. https://www.worldbank.org/en/topic/regional-integration/brief/belt-and-road-initiative

World Bank. (2020). *Easy of Doing Business.* World Bank. https://data.worldbank.org/indicator/IC.BUS.EASE.XQ?locations=MU

World Bank. (2020, April). *South Asia Must Ramp Up COVID-19 Action to Protect People, Revive Economies.* Retrieved from Worldbank.org: https://www.worldbank.org/en/news/press-release/2020/04/12/south-asia-must-act-now-to-lessen-covid-19-health-impacts

World Bank. (2021a). *Data for Pakistan, India, Bangladesh, Sri Lanka, Nepal, Afghanistan.* https://data.worldbank.org/?locations=PK-IN-BD-LK-NP-AF

World Bank. (2021a). *Gross national income per capita 2019, Atlas method and PPP, World Development Indicators database.* Retrieved from https://databank.worldbank.org/data/download/GNIPC.pdf

World Bank. (2021b). *GDP growth (annual %).* https://data.worldbank.org/indicator/NY.GDP.MKTP.KD.ZG

World Bank. (2021b). *The World Bank in Bangladesh, Overview*. Retrieved from https://www.worldbank.org/en/country/bangladesh/overview#1

World Economic Forum. (2021). *Global Results*. https://reports.weforum.org/global-gender-gap-report-2020/the-global-gender-gap-index-2020/results-and-analysis/

World Health Organization Regional Office for South. (2021). *Sri Lanka Health System Review*. World Health Organization.

World Health Organization. (2017). *Nepal.* WHO.

World Health Organization. (2021, August 25). *Afghanistan*. Retrieved from http://www.emro.who.int/afg/programmes/health-system-strengthening.html

World Integrated Trade Solution. (2021). *Australia Product exports and imports to Bangladesh 2019.* Retrieved from https://wits.worldbank.org/CountryProfile/en/Country/AUS/Year/2019/TradeFlow/EXPIMP/Partner/BGD/Product/all-groups

World Trade Organisation. (2019). *World Trade Statistical Review 2019.* https://www.wto.org/english/res_e/statis_e/wts2019_e/wts2019_e.pdf

Worldmeter. (2021, September 1). *Australia*. Retrieved from Worldmeters.info: https://www.worldometers.info/coronavirus/country/australia/

Worldometers. (2021). *Sri Lanka*. Worldometers. Retrieved October 14, 2021, from https://www.worldometers.info/coronavirus/country/sri-lanka

Wring, D. (1997). Reconciling marketing with political science: Theories of political marketing. *Journal of Marketing Management*, *13*(7), 651–663. doi:10.1080/0267257X.1997.9964502

Wyeth, G. (2021). What We Can Learn from Australia's Sikh Community. *The Diplomat*. https://thediplomat.com/2021/06/what-we-can-learn-from-australias-sikh-community/

Wyman, O. (2020). *To Recovery & Beyond: The Future of Travel & Tourism in the Wake of COVID-19.* https://tcmih.ku.ac.ke/handle/123456789/243

XE. (2021). *Australian Dollar to US Dollar Exchange Rate Chart*. XE. Retrieved October 14, 2021, from https://www.xe.com/currencycharts/?from=AUD&to=USD&view=10Y

Xiang, H., Kuang, Y., & Li, C. (2017). Impact of the China–Australia FTA on global coal production and trade. *Journal of Policy Modeling*, *39*(1), 65–78. doi:10.1016/j.jpolmod.2017.01.001

Yhome, K. (2015). From "Look East" to "Act East": What it Means for India's Northeast? *Eastern Quarterly*, *11*(1-2), 18–29.

Yilmazkuday, H. (2019). Understanding the international elasticity puzzle. *Journal of Macroeconomics, 59*, 140-153. doi:10.1016/j.jmacro.2018.11.010

Yousaf, S. (2016). Political marketing in Pakistan: Exaggerated promises, delusive claims, marketable development projects and change advocacy. *Journal of Public Affairs*, *16*(2), 140–155. doi:10.1002/pa.1562

Yukun, L., Kun, L., & Lihua, Z. (2019, July 23). Chinese firm progressing with Padma Bridge project [Review of *Chinese firm progressing with Padma Bridge project*]. *China Daily*. http://www.chinadaily.com.cn/a/201907/23/WS5d366fa8a310d83056400807.html

Yunus, M. (2006). *Social Business Entrepreneurs Are the Solution, Skoll World Forum on Social Entrepreneurship*. Said Business School. Oxford University.

Yunus, M., Moingeon, B., & Lehmann-Ortega, L. (2010). Building social business models: Lessons from the Grameen experience. *Long Range Planning*, *43*(2), 308–325. doi:10.1016/j.lrp.2009.12.005

Zakaria, N., Ali, M., & Hossain, K. (2012). Underlying problems of ship recycling industries in Bangladesh and way forward. *Journal of Naval Architecture and Marine Engineering*, *9*(2), 91–102. doi:10.3329/jname.v9i2.10515

Zhang, F. (2019). In the Dark: How Much Do Power Sector Distortions Cost South Asia? South Asia Development Forum. Washington, DC: World Bank. doi:10.1596/978-1-4648-1154-8

Zhang, T. (2020). *Global and Asia Economic Outlook: Greater Bay Area Chief Economist Forum*. IMF. https://www.imf.org/en/News/Articles/2020/07/10/sp071020-speech-on-the-global-and-asia-economic-outlook

Zhou, Y., Jin, C. H., Huang, J. W., & Wang, R. M. (2021). Research on the impact of the Internet on the informatization teaching reform of marketing in universities. In *Computational Social Science* (pp. 576–583). CRC Press. doi:10.1201/9781003144977-87

Ziegler T., Shneor R. (2021). *The 2nd Global Alternative Finance Market Benchmarking Report*. Cambridge Centre for Alternative Finance. University of Cambridge.

Ziegler, T., & Shneor, R. (2020). *The Global Alternative Finance Market Benchmarking Report: Trends, Opportunities and Challenges for Lending, Equity, and Non-Investment Alternative Finance Models. Cambridge Centre for Alternative Finance*. University of Cambridge.

Zreik, M. (2021). The Regional Comprehensive Economic Partnership and Its Impact on the US-China Trade War. *Journal of Asia Pacific Studies*, *6*(3).

About the Contributors

Anita Medhekar is a senior lecturer in economics and holds a PhD from Deakin University, Australia. She has completed her double Masters in pure Economics as well as in Education. She has taught at undergraduate and post graduate levels in India, Indonesia, and Australia and has nearly 30 years of teaching experience. Currently, she is teaching at Central Queensland University, Rockhampton, Australia. Her research interests are in applied Micro and Macroeconomics, International Trade, Development Economics, Asia-Pacific Economies, Health Economics, Public Finance, Asia-Pacific Economies, South-Asia, Australian Economy, Tourism Economics, Bilateral Trade and Development for Peace, Public Policy, and Public-Private Partnerships. She has presented papers at numerous international conferences and received best research paper wards. She has numerous refereed publications in journals, conference proceedings, edited books, and book chapters to her credit.

Sreeparna Saha has a PhD from Deakin University Australia, in Applied Microeconomics, Development Economics and Policy. She has a decade of teaching experience in economics and statistics. She has research publications in Scopus listed journals, and conference presentations. Her research interest is in development economics, public policy, economics of education, sustainability, and political economy.

Farooq Haq holds a PhD in Marketing from Charles Darwin University, Australia and an MBA in Marketing from Central Queensland University, Australia. Dr Haq is among the primary researchers in the area of Marketing Spiritual Tourism and he is considered as an expert in Islamic Marketing. Since 2016, he has been a member of the Editorial Board for the Journal of Islamic Marketing that is published under Emerald (UK) and Scopus listed. The Journal of Islamic Marketing awarded him the Outstanding Reviewer for 2018. The research interests of Dr. Haq include special interest tourism marketing, Islamic marketing, Halal branding, medical and heritage tourism marketing.

* * *

Mohammad Ali is Academic Staff at Curtin Law School, Curtin University.

Susan Bandias has been employed at Charles Darwin university for more than 18 years. She has extensive experience in the education sector having taught across all levels of the education spectrum including primary, secondary vocational Undergraduate and post graduate levels. She has taken a leading role in community engagement and has successfully combined her professional interest in the social implications of information communication technology by actively engaging with the professions, the broader community.

Mamta B. Chowdhury completed her undergraduate in Economics and Mathematics and Masters in Economics from the University of Manitoba, Canada. She completed her Masters in Economics of Development and Ph.D. from the Australian National University. She has worked with several universities in Australia, Canada, and Bangladesh before joining Western Sydney University in 1999. Mamta has published a large number of refereed journal articles, books, and book chapters. Mamta has been acted as a Head of School, chief editor, joint editor, and on the editorial board of several journals and proceedings. Mamta has supervised several Ph.D. students and acting as one of the International Academic Leads of the School of Business of Western Sydney University. Mamta has been researching applied economics and finance of international trade and macroeconomic policy management predominantly, including the effect of workers' remittances, inward and outward foreign direct investment, foreign aid and trade, trade-in labour and education services, Australia's tourism and education sector. She has also done some studies in the area of teaching methods and their impacts on learning outcomes and the importance of quantitative skills in achieving better learning outcomes. Dr Chowdhury has done extensive research in the area of booming sector/s, competitiveness, the competitiveness of Australia's services exports. She has done some significant publications in the area of worker's remittances and their effects on economic and financial growth and development, stock markets of developing countries and extensive research in the area of economic and institutional determinants of foreign direct investment. She has developed a strong international research profile in Economics of Development. Dr. Chowdhury has been currently researching and done some recent studies in the area competitiveness of the tourism sector and its impact on the small and medium-sized business sector's employment and overall performance of the Australian economy.

Manisha Goswami, Area Chair-Business Communication, working in GLA University from the past 13 year in the capacity of Assistant Professor, recently received the opportunity by DTH Swayam Prabha for recording the lectures on government 34 DTH free online channel; has also been awarded with best teacher in the university and University Grant Commission of India has also awarded her with Junior Research Fellowship. She has published several research papers in national and international journal indexed in SCOPUS and Google Scholars. Her area of interest is Strategic Communication, International Business Management, Strategic Human Resource Management like Psychological Contract, Emotional Intelligence, Employer Branding, Employee Engagement.

Princi Gupta working as Assistant Professor in JECRC university, Jaipur. she has more than 5 years of Teaching & Research experience. she has ph.D in Marketing and her area of specialisation are International business & Marketing. she has published book on Digital Marketing "An Insight to fundamentals, Strategies & Implementations". She also holds Diploma in in German Language, Behavioural Science and Business communication, also actively participated and organised various departmental & university level workshops, conferences & events. To her credit there are Research paper publications in various National, Intentional, UGC, Scopus Indexed journals and Research paper presented in various regional, national seminars & International conferences.

Ikhlaas Gurrib holds a PhD in Finance and a Bachelor of Commerce (Economics and Finance) from Curtin University (Australia), a Master of Finance and a Master of Professional Accounting from Victoria State University, Australia. He is currently an Associate Professor (Finance) and the Head of the Accounting and Finance department at Canadian University Dubai. He previously taught at Curtin Business School in Australia and Saudi Arabia. Dr. Gurrib is also experienced in the finance industry, having worked as a Finance Manager with Westpac Bank, Australia. His research interests are in energy markets, macroeconomic analysis and financial markets, portfolio management, and cryptocurrencies markets.

Chureerat Haq is a PhD candidate with a scholarship from the Asia Pacific College of Business and Law at Charles Darwin University, Australia. Her research interests include social enterprise, business models, business partnerships, crowdfunding, financial inclusion, poverty alleviation, and women entrepreneurship. Chureerat Haq holds two master degrees, Master of Business Administration (MBA) in Management and Master by Research, both from Australia. During her Master by Research, Chureerat published two peer reviewed conference papers that she presented in Toronto, Canada, and Istanbul, Turkey. Chureerat has worked in a variety of organisations, including United Nations Children's Fund (UNICEF), universities, and private organisations in Thailand, Australia, and United Arab Emirates. Chureerat has been invited as a guest speaker at universities in Bangkok, Thailand and Dubai, the United Arab Emirates. Topics included business ethics, corporate social responsibility (CSR) and social enterprises.

Nahid Islam is an Assistant Lecturer at School of Economics and Finance in Curtin University.

Rahul Mehta is a final year student at the Canadian University Dubai who is majoring in International Business with an interest in Finance, Marketing, Tech, Mental Health and NGOs. Looking to learn and gain experience assisting a company to grow and develop to the best of my abilities through planning, organising, research and working as a team and learning from professionals in the industry.

Gayatri Nair is a recent marketing graduate from the Canadian University Dubai and a keen researcher. The author has previously successfully been able to submit a co-authored research paper to a prestigious conference paper for the 5th Canadian International Conference on Advances in Education, Teaching and Technology 2021. The same research paper has also been accepted in a Q2 Scopus journal which will be published next year in August. The author believes that marketing is not only about building awareness and promoting but also needs strong grounds for research. The changes being witnessed in the world today can have an effect on tomorrow.

Ahmad Okasha is an associate professor who holds a Doctorate degree in Health Services & Organization from Medical College of Virginia/Virginal Commonwealth University, Virginia, USA y Business Administration in Excellence Leadership and Innovation. Has MSc in Hospital Administration from Jordan University, Amman, Jordan. He has extensive experience in the healthcare industry. Ahmad is currently working at Canadian University Dubai as an associate professor in the School of Environmental Health Management.

Ataus Samad is an academic at the Western Sydney University School of Business. As an early career researcher, he published journal articles in Australian Business Deans Council (ABDC) ranked Personnel Review, Asia Pacific Journal of Human Resources (APJHR) and the Journal of Developing Areas (JDA) along with academics from the CQUniversity Australia, University of Melbourne, Bond University and RMIT University. Besides publishing in high quality peer reviewed journals, in December 2020 he published a research report on sustainable employment of migrants in the regional Queensland. He is currently involved in multiple research projects with academics from the Western Sydney University, RMIT University, Victoria University, and University of Queensland. He presented his research findings at several international conferences such as, the Australian Academy of Business and Social Sciences Conference 2014, Australasian Conference on Business and Social Sciences 2015, Tertiary Education Management Conference 2015, Australian and New Zealand Academy of Management (ANZAM) 2017, Developing Northern Australia Conference 2018, Australian Regional Development Conference 2019 which were appreciated by the participants. Furthermore, Dr Samad was a reviewer for Asia Pacific Journal of Human Resources (APJHR), The Journal of Developing Areas (JDA) and the Australian and New Zealand Academy of Management (ANZAM) conference 2019. He also presented his views on contemporary issues as a panel member at the ABC Television, ABC Radio, besides multiple newspapers in Australia. Dr Samad is a member of the recognised professional bodies such as the AACSB (Association to Advance Collegiate Schools of Business, Australian Human Resources Management Institute (AHRI), and the Association for Tertiary Education Management (ATEM). Furthermore, he is a member of the Western Sydney University Humanitarian and Development Research Initiative (HADRI). He was also a member of Centre for Tourism and Regional Opportunities and Centre for Regional Advancement of Learning, Equity, Access & Participation / Engaged Research at CQUniversity Australia. Dr Ataus Samad had been a member of the advisory panel for Queensland Government's Minister for Multicultural Affairs (2016-2018) and an advisory panel member (Acting Chair) of a not-for- profit organisation Regional Opportunities Australia (ROA, 2018-2020) based in Sydney, NSW.

Kamaljeet Sandhu is an active scholar, experienced & passionate about research in Digital Innovation & Strategy, Business Data Analytics, Digital Health, AI, IoT, Cryptocurrency, Blockchain, Cloud Computing, IT Startups, FinTech, Cybersecurity, Accounting, Corporate Governance & CSR, Supply Chain, ERP, SMEs, & Entrepreneurship. Editor of 4 Books & published internationally over 180 articles in peer-reviewed (refereed) journals, conferences, & book chapters. He earned his Ph.D. from Deakin University Melbourne campus, Australia. Having held multiple Leadership positions including Professor at the University of Northern British Columbia Canada, Senior Research Fellow at the University of South Australia, and other Senior Academic positions at: University of Wollongong, Charles Darwin University, Deakin University, & at the University of South Pacific, Fiji. As a Ph.D. Principal Supervisor (Advisor), has supervised & mentored several Ph.D. Research students to successful completion & students have successfully gained academic & research appointments at leading international universities & other organizations.

Md Sayfullah is a Commercial Counsellor Bangladesh High Commission, Canberra Australia Md Sayfullah did his Master of Business Administration (MBA) in 1999 from Dhaka University under the Department of Finance & Banking. He graduated in 1998 from the same educational institution. He is a career civil servant of the Bangladesh Civil Service. Sayfullah is currently on a diplomatic assignment in the Bangladesh High Commission in Canberra, Australia. He is officially involved in business, trade, and investment promotions between Bangladesh and Australia. He is concurrently accredited to New Zealand, the Republic of Fiji, Solomon Islands and Vanuatu to work for the above areas. He is responsible for working with Bangladeshi exporters and with investors & educational institutions in the region, emphasizing extensive industries, infrastructure, investment, and agri-food. In Canberra, he helped to negotiate and signed Trade and Investment Framework Arrangement (TIFA) between Bangladesh and Australia in September 2021. In addition, he assisted in organizing the first-ever Australia- Bangladesh Trade Conference (ABTC) in November 2019 in Sydney, Australia. In his long civil service career of 16 years, Sayfullah has worked under different official capacities in government ministries in Bangladesh. For example, in Bangladesh Parliament Secretariat, he played a role as a Private Secretary of the Chairman of the Standing Committee for the Ministry of Water Resources from 2014 to 2017. In the Ministry of Water Resources, he was primarily responsible for organizing press and media coverage from 2009 to 2013. In addition, he has the experience to arranges press conferences and press briefing sessions for the policymakers in Bangladesh. The Ministry of Information is also the major field where Sayfullah has worked before. Before joining the Bangladesh Civil Service in July 2005, he worked as a banker at BRAC Bank Ltd. and IFIC Bank Ltd in Bangladesh for three years. Thus, commencing his career in the banking sector in Bangladesh, Sayfullah has experience in both the private and public sectors. During his civil service career, Sayfullah received various professional training at home and abroad. He also attended several conferences/meetings at home and overseas. In addition, he has travelled to the USA, UK, UAE, Thailand, Singapore, New Zealand and Viet Nam for official purposes. Sayfullah is married to Rawshan Ara and blessed with two sons.

Faiz Shah is the Director of the Yunus Center at Asian Institute of Technology, and leads the Yunus Masters in Social Business & Entrepreneurship, the Professional Masters in CSR and the SDG Enterprise Lab. He is the Founding President of Yunus Thailand Foundation, and Managing Partner of Grameen Options advisory services. Over a four-decade international career, Dr. Shah has advised governments, UN agencies, and Fortune corporations, mentoring changemakers in 25 countries. He is an original contributor to the GRI standard, and author of "Responsible Business Framework: A Toolkit for Winning Companies". His latest publication is the Urdu edition of "A World of Three Zeros", by Professor Yunus.

Rajeev Sharma is a Marketing academic at the College of Business and Law of Charles Darwin University (CDU). Dr Sharma has more than 40 years of teaching experience. He has taught in many institutions and countries including Australia, India, Hong Kong, Malaysia, Nigeria and Papua New Guinea. He is a Fellow of the Australian Marketing Institute (AMI), Certified Practicing Marketer (CPM) and a life member. Dr Sharma has researched and published in many international journals. He has also presented research papers at International Conferences in London, Lyon, Rome, Freiburg, Cape Town, Bali, Amsterdam, Prague, New Delhi, and Las Vegas. His current area of research related to 'use of Social Media' in disaster management. Rajeev is currently supervising 4 doctoral students enrolled at CDU. He is on the editorial board of Indian Journal of Marketing.

Eman Zabalawi is an assistant professor who holds a Doctorate of Business Administration in Excellence Leadership and Innovation. Has MSc in Excellence Management from Leicester University, UK. Her experience varies between consultancy services, entrepreneurship and academia. Eman is currently working at Amity group as a consultant and corporate trainer in mapping corporation strategic directions, policy, and outcomes with excellence models followed by execution and internal audit. She is experienced in upskilling to meet national strategic directions and individuals KPI's for institutional innovation. She is a member of the Board of Directors of the Specialized Women – Arab League. Eman has a Higher Education Academy Fellowship and an Innovation Association of Innovation Professionals Fellowship. Her primary research interests cover strategic leadership, excellence models, the efficiency of performance, quality competition, standardization, improvement innovation, knowledge management, and employability. Her experience extends to over 20 years in the federal government of UAE.

Index

A

Academic Collaboration 146, 162, 165
Act East Policy 18, 21, 54-55, 281, 296, 299
affordable energy 23, 48
agreement 2-5, 9, 21-24, 26, 34, 56, 81, 84, 92, 101-104, 108, 118, 130, 136-137, 143-144, 152-153, 177, 184, 198, 219-220, 222, 226-230, 232, 235-237, 242, 260, 262, 264-265, 268, 272, 276, 278, 280-286, 294-296, 298-300, 314, 319, 329
Asia-Pacific region 80-81, 83, 90, 93, 260, 301-303, 310, 321, 323
Australia 1-19, 22-24, 26-27, 39, 41-44, 46-48, 50, 52, 55-61, 65-69, 71-73, 76-79, 81-84, 88-92, 94-102, 104-108, 110-111, 114-115, 117-124, 126, 128-129, 132-148, 150-156, 158, 160-168, 170-178, 185-187, 189-192, 194-197, 199-200, 207-217, 219-223, 225-230, 232-240, 243-264, 266-299, 301-330, 333-334, 336-339, 341-344, 346
Australia and Pakistan 57, 60-61, 66-67, 69, 71-72, 243-245, 247-249, 251-254, 256
Australian aid 124, 141, 173, 185, 197, 285
avenue 110, 219, 222

B

Bangladesh 1, 3-4, 8-10, 14, 16-17, 19, 24, 26-29, 31-32, 45, 47, 50, 52, 83, 117-143, 146, 148-149, 151, 155, 160, 166-187, 189-198, 200-202, 209-210, 213, 218-222, 225-237, 239-242, 255, 258, 301-306, 310-326, 334-338, 340, 347
Belt Road Initiative 192, 197
bilateral 1-6, 9-10, 14-15, 18, 21, 23-24, 26-27, 30, 45, 49-50, 59, 66, 77, 95, 101-103, 106, 111, 116-119, 121-122, 129, 137, 140, 142-144, 148, 152, 158, 160-161, 163, 165, 167, 173, 175, 178, 185, 189, 195, 197, 199-200, 208, 211-212, 217, 219-220, 222, 226-228, 235-237, 242, 244, 247-248, 251, 256, 259-264, 267-268, 272-273, 275-276, 279-285, 287, 289-290, 294-295, 301-302, 304-305, 308, 310-311, 315-316, 321-323, 328-329, 339, 342
bilateral agreement 219-220, 222, 226-227, 235-237, 242
bilateral collaboration 117, 144
Bilateral Programs 158, 165
bilateral relations 247, 259, 279-280, 282, 284
bilateral trade 3, 18, 21, 45, 50, 59, 95, 106, 116, 122, 129, 142-143, 161, 163, 175, 185, 189, 195, 197, 200, 208, 211-212, 217, 227, 256, 261-264, 272, 276, 280-282, 284, 287, 290, 295, 301-302, 304, 308, 310-311, 315-316, 321, 323
Bilateral trade agreement 21
blue economy 95-97, 102-109, 111, 113, 116-117, 121, 123, 136-137, 141, 143-144, 178, 187, 272
business model 135, 139, 157, 328-330, 336-338, 342

C

China 2, 4, 11, 16-17, 26-27, 52, 71, 76-79, 81, 98, 101-105, 142, 166-167, 169, 171-181, 183-185, 187, 189-198, 208-210, 216, 227, 235, 240, 245-246, 255, 257, 260-262, 264-265, 267, 275-276, 278, 280-282, 284-299, 301-302, 304-308, 310, 313, 315, 317-319, 321-323, 326, 332, 335
climate change 2, 4-5, 23-24, 26, 28, 50, 53, 56, 97, 105-108, 111, 115-117, 121, 124-125, 135, 142, 162, 168, 185, 189, 259, 261, 265, 273-274, 277, 279
clinical governance 212, 217
collaboration 1, 11, 22-23, 45, 50, 57-59, 66, 71, 75, 87, 89, 91, 93-94, 105, 110, 113, 117, 119, 123, 129, 136-137, 139, 144, 146-155, 159-163, 165, 175, 187, 211, 248-250, 252-255, 259-263, 267, 272-273, 276, 281, 283-284, 294, 302-303, 306, 317, 321, 332, 342
complementary medicine 199-200, 207-208, 210-213
Conducive Environment 157, 165
cooperation 1-6, 10-11, 14-15, 18, 21, 23-24, 26, 39,

45-46, 49-50, 53-54, 59, 66, 76, 82, 89, 91, 94, 101-103, 106, 113-114, 117-119, 121-122, 135, 137, 140-141, 147-149, 153-155, 158-160, 162, 164, 167-169, 171, 173, 177-178, 180, 182, 185-186, 189-190, 195, 198, 200, 207-208, 210-216, 218, 228, 247-252, 258, 260, 262, 264, 267-268, 272, 275-276, 280-286, 293-295, 297-298, 302, 308, 314, 322, 325, 328-329, 339
coronavirus 1-3, 6, 8, 10-15, 17-18, 20, 22, 95, 98, 114-116, 172, 199, 215-217, 346
Corporate Governance 84, 144, 297
COVID-19 1-5, 10-17, 19-20, 25, 27, 35, 42, 57-58, 60, 66-67, 71, 73-74, 77, 79-80, 89-90, 93, 95-99, 102-103, 107-111, 113-115, 117-125, 135, 138-141, 144, 155, 159, 165, 171, 173, 177, 185-186, 193, 199-201, 203-204, 209-210, 212-217, 228, 232, 243-244, 246, 251-254, 257-260, 265-267, 270, 272, 275, 280-282, 285-287, 289, 291-293, 301-302, 304-307, 312-313, 315, 321-322, 327-330, 332-333, 336-339, 342-346
crowdfunding 327-348
Cybersecurity Risk 21

D

debt trap 166-170, 182-183, 188, 190, 194-198, 227, 235
Debt Trap Diplomacy 167, 198
decommissioning 220-221, 223-225, 229, 233, 235-239, 241-242
deep learning 57-58, 60, 62, 67, 71, 160
digital enterprises 82-83, 91, 94, 186
digital health 1, 9, 11-12, 14, 16, 21, 82, 208, 211
Digital health technology 21
Digital Inclusion 90, 92, 195, 348
digital infrastructure 76-77, 79, 81-82, 90-91, 93-94, 186
Digital Strategic Partnership 76, 78-79, 84, 91, 94
digital technology 327, 331
diversity 5, 28, 50, 64, 73, 118, 121, 140, 144, 149-150, 158, 187, 190, 265, 345

E

economic development 4-6, 14, 22, 26, 28, 53, 100, 117-118, 121, 123, 136, 143, 146-147, 159, 165, 171, 173, 190, 195-197, 200, 205, 218, 220, 227, 246, 248, 261, 283, 322, 330
economic growth and development 301, 303, 305, 321, 323-324
education 1-3, 5, 10-12, 14-15, 18, 22, 24, 57-67, 69, 71-74, 76-78, 84, 92-93, 97-98, 117-123, 125-126, 129, 131, 134-137, 141, 144, 146-156, 158-165, 174-177, 185-186, 189, 196, 201, 205, 208, 211-213, 216, 218, 249, 262-264, 271, 281-286, 292, 302, 304, 306, 314-315, 317, 321-324, 328-329, 334-335, 346
Education Policy 67, 73, 146-147, 149, 152, 154-156, 160-162, 165
Education Policy in India 146
educational collaboration 58, 75, 152
Electricity Interconnection Power System 56
Embargo 299
Employability Skills 165
energy consumption 24, 28-29, 31, 33-35, 39, 51-52, 54, 56
energy security 23, 31, 47, 49-50, 121, 123, 135, 171, 261, 264, 273, 276-277
equity 113, 116, 118, 203-205, 214, 270, 277, 331-332, 334-335, 340, 343-344, 347

F

financial inclusion 76-77, 327, 329, 338, 342, 345, 348
focus groups 57, 59, 66-67, 69
free trade agreement 3-4, 26, 81, 101, 103, 136-137, 198, 260, 268, 272, 278, 280-284, 295-296, 299-300

G

geopolitical 27, 191, 260, 262, 274, 279-280, 282, 289-291, 301-302, 310, 322
global health crisis 22, 304
Global Trading Partnership 116
greenhouse gas 26, 54, 108, 111, 117, 135, 226, 241, 264-265, 270, 278-279

H

health 1-22, 25, 28, 31, 60, 67, 76, 82, 84, 91, 93, 95-96, 99, 101-103, 107-111, 115, 117-119, 121-122, 125, 129, 136-137, 151-152, 155, 157-158, 162, 177, 185, 193, 199-206, 208-209, 211-214, 216-218, 220, 233-234, 236-237, 241, 251, 271, 282, 285, 304-306, 312, 321, 328-330, 333
Health System 9, 13, 206, 216-217
healthcare services 3, 10-11, 110-111, 199-200, 202-203, 210, 217
healthcare systems 12, 14-15, 110, 199-201, 208-209, 213-214, 216-217
higher education 2, 15, 61, 64, 72-74, 77-78, 84, 117, 119, 134, 146-148, 150-155, 158-159, 161-165, 212, 315, 317

I

India 1-22, 24, 26-29, 32-34, 36, 39, 45, 47-50, 52-56, 59, 76-79, 81, 96, 98-99, 101-102, 104-105, 109, 113, 115, 118, 129, 136, 146-165, 168, 171, 173-174, 178, 180, 183-184, 187, 190, 193-195, 198, 200-201, 203-204, 207-215, 218, 226, 228-229, 238-240, 242, 247, 255, 258-288, 291-299, 302, 305, 307, 310-311, 313, 315, 317-319, 321, 323, 326, 334-335, 337, 340, 344, 347
Indo-Pacific 2, 4-6, 11, 16, 18-19, 26, 54, 56, 141, 191, 235, 260-261, 272, 275-277, 281-283, 285, 289, 293-295, 297, 299
infant mortality 155, 200, 204, 206, 215, 217
Interactive Learning Strategy 75
Island Economy 95

L

legal 39, 104, 106, 109, 139, 183, 219-222, 225-226, 229, 235-236, 238, 241, 290
liberalization 101, 168, 260, 267, 279
Look East Policy 21, 261, 299

M

marketing 57-75, 129, 142, 157, 212, 241, 243, 250, 252-258, 347
marketing mix 57, 59-60, 67, 69-70, 72, 75, 255
maternal mortality 200-201, 204, 217
Medical Standards 217
Medical Tourism 17-18, 203, 213, 217
microfinance 117, 124, 136-137, 144, 327, 329, 331-333, 338, 340, 343-344, 348
military 5-6, 166, 177-178, 186, 191, 198, 254, 261, 263, 275-276, 282, 293
Muhammad Yunus 327, 338, 346
Multilateral trade agreement 22
multi-sectoral 4, 21, 26, 118, 121-122, 140, 144

N

non-tariff barriers 3, 154, 299

O

offshore 103, 105, 186, 219-230, 232-242, 316, 319
offshore industries 220, 226, 228-230, 242
offshore structures 219-230, 232-237, 239, 242

P

Pakistan 2-3, 9-11, 13, 15-16, 20, 24, 26-29, 36-37, 45, 47, 52-55, 57-61, 65-69, 71-74, 79, 83, 101, 113, 144, 148-149, 155, 167, 169, 171-172, 187, 198, 200, 205-206, 208-210, 212, 214, 218, 226, 228-229, 235, 240, 243-249, 251-258, 310, 313, 323, 326, 334-338, 340, 343, 345
pandemic 1-2, 4, 6-7, 9-17, 22, 25, 35, 42, 58, 77-79, 90, 95-96, 109, 114, 118-120, 136-140, 148, 150, 155, 159, 165, 167, 177, 199-200, 209-212, 214-215, 230, 232, 235, 243-244, 246, 251-252, 258-259, 263, 267-269, 273, 275, 293, 301-302, 304-307, 312-313, 315, 321-322, 327-328, 333, 336-339, 342-343, 345
Paris Agreement 23-24, 34, 56, 108, 265
partnership 1-6, 15, 17-18, 22-23, 26, 39, 47, 50, 52, 54, 59-60, 66-67, 69, 71, 73-74, 76, 78-79, 81-82, 84, 90-91, 94, 97, 101-103, 109, 115-117, 125, 135, 138, 141, 144, 151, 153-155, 158, 160-162, 166-167, 170, 173, 185-186, 188-192, 198-199, 228, 243-245, 247-249, 251-258, 260-264, 266-267, 272-273, 277-278, 280-281, 283-286, 297, 299-301, 303, 305, 312, 314, 338, 342
partnerships 1, 3-4, 7, 10-11, 14-15, 20, 22-24, 26-27, 45, 48-50, 58-60, 66, 71, 82, 95-96, 101-102, 104-106, 109, 111, 115, 125, 146, 148, 150-156, 163, 186, 243-250, 252-255, 258, 263, 267, 273-274, 276, 290, 294, 307, 310-311, 327-330, 336-339, 341-342
Passive Learning Strategy 62, 75
personal health 12, 201, 217
pharmaceutical industry 11, 200, 207, 210, 214, 217
pharmaceuticals 10, 14, 119, 139, 199, 211, 217, 281, 306, 319-322
Political Economy 119, 144, 325
political marketing 58-59, 65-69, 72-75
politics 20, 49, 57-61, 64-67, 69-71, 73-74, 243, 249, 257, 261, 277, 279, 297, 326
post COVID-19 3, 15, 57-58, 66, 71, 95, 102, 140, 165, 243-244, 252-254, 258, 280, 328-329, 332

Q

Quad 2, 4, 6, 11, 16-19, 105, 118, 137, 178, 190, 194, 264, 267, 272, 278, 281, 284, 293, 295-299, 305

R

recycling 219-223, 225-237, 239-242, 319, 321, 323
recycling industry 219-222, 226-230, 232-234, 236-237, 239-240, 242, 319
Referral Centers 218
Regional Economic Comprehensive Partnership 300
regulatory framework 49, 98, 103, 149, 162, 336, 339, 341-342

renewable energy 24, 26-27, 32-35, 38, 44-45, 48, 51-55, 109, 112, 117-118, 121, 123-124, 135-137, 142-144, 158, 259, 264-266, 270, 272-273, 275-277, 279
resources sector 259, 263, 267-268, 270, 274, 278-279

S

SAARC 1-11, 13-15, 23-24, 26-40, 45-50, 53-54, 59-60, 71, 146-148, 150-151, 153-154, 160-162, 164-166, 168, 170, 185, 187-190, 194, 198-200, 208, 218, 249, 253-255, 258, 298, 302, 305, 308, 310-311, 314, 324
SAARC and Australia 23
SAARC nations 3, 5, 7, 9-11, 14-15, 23-24, 26-30, 36, 39, 47-50, 59-60, 71, 146-148, 150-151, 160, 165-166, 170, 189-190, 194, 198-199, 253-254, 310-311
scrap 219, 221, 228-229, 240, 242
SDGs 3, 15, 20, 22, 27, 95, 105, 108, 111, 115, 117-118, 121, 124-125, 137, 142, 243, 280, 327, 329, 342, 347
SDGs-14 116
SIDS 95, 105, 108, 116
skill development 146, 323
social enterprise 124, 296, 328-330, 332-333, 336-339, 341-348
Social Enterprise Ecosystem 339, 348
SOLO taxonomy 58, 61, 71-72, 75
sound management 221-222, 234-236
South Asia 1, 7-8, 10, 13, 16-17, 19, 21, 28, 53-55, 58, 71, 101, 120, 141, 147-149, 153, 157, 162-166, 171, 174, 178, 195, 198-201, 204, 208-213, 215-216, 218, 226, 228-229, 233, 235-236, 243-244, 249, 252, 255, 278, 283, 296, 301-302, 305, 310, 322, 324, 327-329, 332-337, 339-340, 342
Specialized Hospitals 202, 218
Stakeholder 74, 340, 343, 348
steel 119, 152, 220-223, 228-233, 236-238, 241-242, 291, 306, 319, 321, 324
strategic and diplomatic relationship 305
strategic partnerships 3, 7, 20, 22, 24, 48, 82
structures 154, 156, 213, 219-230, 232-237, 239, 242-243, 254, 319, 348
sustainability 5, 24, 49-50, 55, 95, 104, 116-117, 119, 123-124, 129, 135, 138, 140, 164, 169, 239, 252-253, 257, 260, 274
Sustainable Development 3, 15, 20, 22-25, 55, 93, 95, 105, 107, 111, 113, 116-117, 119, 121, 123-126, 129, 135-137, 143, 160, 185, 192, 196, 326, 329, 342, 345-347
Sustainable Development Goals (SDGs) 3, 15, 95, 105, 125, 329, 342

T

tariffs 50, 101, 198, 217, 267, 286, 290-291, 300
Teaching Hospitals 202, 218
TIFA 101, 103, 118, 121, 129-130, 137, 141, 143-144, 303, 305, 323, 325
tourism 2-5, 10, 12, 15, 17-18, 35, 66, 72, 78, 91, 98, 100, 102-104, 106-109, 111, 114-115, 117-119, 121, 124, 129, 136-137, 139, 141-143, 149, 180, 203, 213, 217, 243-258, 260, 281, 284, 292-293, 302, 306
tourism marketing 243, 250, 253-255, 258
tourism partnership 244-245, 248, 251-254, 256, 258
trade 2-6, 10-11, 14-15, 18, 20-24, 26-27, 30, 38-39, 42-47, 49-50, 52-55, 59, 71, 76-78, 81, 83, 91-92, 95, 97, 101-106, 111-113, 116-119, 121-122, 127, 129, 135-137, 140-147, 154, 161, 163, 166-169, 171, 173-175, 178-179, 184-192, 195, 197-200, 208, 210-215, 217, 219, 221-222, 227-228, 235-236, 238-239, 249, 256, 259-264, 267-268, 271-273, 276-278, 280-287, 289-326, 328, 337
trade and investment 3, 5, 15, 39, 42, 55, 101-103, 117-119, 121, 135, 137, 140, 144, 173, 185-186, 190, 192, 197, 217, 228, 239, 249, 259-260, 264, 272, 281, 285, 292, 301-306, 310-312, 314, 317, 319, 321-326
trade and investment partnership 303, 305, 312, 314
trade creation 280, 295, 300
trade diversion 280, 286, 295, 300
TRADE FRONTIERS 280, 292
trade war 227, 235, 281, 286-287, 290, 294-297, 299-300

V

vaccine 1-3, 9, 11-17, 99, 125, 139, 177, 204, 207, 211
value constellation 327-329, 337-338, 348
value proposition 328-329, 336-337

W

waste 24, 219, 234-237, 239-240, 242
Waste Dumping 242
win-win 196, 248, 262, 286, 320
women entrepreneurs 119, 327, 336, 338

www.ingramcontent.com/pod-product-compliance
Lightning Source LLC
LaVergne TN
LVHW062113300926
849161LV00010B/2450